Building Tomorrow's Smart Cities With 6G Infrastructure Technology

Sushil Kumar Singh
Marwadi University, India

Sudeep Tanwar
Nirma University, India

Bal Virdee
London Metropolitan University, UK

Ashish Khanna
Maharaja Agrasen Institute of Technology, India

Rajendrasinh Jadeja
Marwadi University, India

IGI Global
Scientific Publishing
Publishing Tomorrow's Research Today

Published in the United States of America by
IGI Global Scientific Publishing
701 East Chocolate Avenue
Hershey, PA, 17033, USA
Tel: 717-533-8845
Fax: 717-533-8661
E-mail: cust@igi-global.com
Website: https://www.igi-global.com

Library of Congress Cataloging-in-Publication Data

CIP PENDING

ISBN13: 979-8-3693-8029-1
Isbn13Softcover: 979-8-3693-8030-7
EISBN13: 979-8-3693-8031-4

British Cataloguing in Publication Data
A Cataloguing in Publication record for this book is available from the British Library.

Table of Contents

Detailed Table of Contents

The advent of 6G technology promises to revolutionize smart city development by offering ultra-high-speed connectivity, minimal latency, and the capacity to support massive device connectivity. This paper explores the transformative potential of 6G in enhancing urban planning, management, and everyday life. Through case studies of pioneering cities like Seoul, Tokyo, Singapore, and Helsinki, it highlights practical applications such as smart traffic management, AI-driven healthcare innovations, and augmented reality tourism experiences. While 6G holds immense promise, its implementation requires overcoming challenges related to infrastructure, data privacy, and regulatory frameworks. Addressing these challenges will be crucial for cities to harness the full benefits of 6G and create sustainable, resilient urban environments for the future.

The research report "Security and Privacy Challenges in 6G Enabled Smart City" delves into the transformative potential of 6G technology, anticipated to be commercially available by 2030, and its implications for smart cities. As cities become more reliant on Internet of Things (IoT) devices, artificial intelligence (AI), and big data analytics, 6G will offer unparalleled speed, bandwidth, and ultra-low latency, driving the evolution of smart cities. However, this technological advancement also brings significant security and privacy concerns that must be addressed to protect urban infrastructures and citizens' data.

6G technology in smart cities brings a new era of connection, efficiency, and innovation, but it also raises privacy and security concerns. This chapter discusses smart city components such IoT devices, autonomous systems, and smart grids. It introduces 6G networks' ultra-low latency, massive device connections, and high data rates. This chapter discusses cyber-physical attacks, data breaches, network intrusions, and other privacy and security issues particular to 6G-enabled smart cities. Smart city environments generate a lot of data, thus data ownership, permission, and anonymization are carefully examined. This chapter discusses 6G-appropriate security and privacy tactics such enhanced encryption, secure communication protocols, and AI-driven threat detection systems. In conclusion, this chapter discusses privacy and security in 6G-enabled smart cities, including where the field is going and what the future holds for research, to help create trustworthy, resilient, and secure smart city ecosystems that can take advantage of 6G's revolutionary capabilities.

Heritage cities face the dual challenge of preserving their cultural legacy while meeting modern tourism demands. The advent of 6G technology offers a transformative opportunity to address these challenges by enhancing preservation efforts and visitor experiences. This paper explores the potential of 6G in revolutionising heritage city management through technologies like augmented reality (AR), virtual reality (VR), and the Internet of Things (IoT). These technologies enable immersive and interactive experiences for tourists while facilitating real-time monitoring and proactive maintenance of heritage sites. Case studies from Rome and Kyoto illustrate the practical implementation of 6G, highlighting its benefits and challenges. The integration of 6G requires careful consideration by urban planners and heritage managers, balancing technological advancements with the preservation of cultural authenticity. As 6G technology continues to evolve, its role in heritage city strategies holds promise for sustainable tourism and the enduring conservation of global cultural heritage.

The development of secure 6G networks has the potential to transform smart city infrastructures, integrating artificial intelligence (AI) to manage urban systems with unprecedented efficiency. The integration of AI in 6G-enabled smart cities will enhance services such as public safety, transportation, and energy management, but also poses significant security risks due to the vast amounts of data being processed. This abstract explores AI's role in optimizing these systems while addressing the security challenges posed by real-time data transmission, cyber-attacks, and privacy concerns. By examining AI-driven solutions, such as anomaly detection systems and federated learning, this research offers insights into enhancing the safety and resilience of smart cities in the digital age.

Wireless communication is advancing, leading to 6G networks. These networks will reshape society with unprecedented connectivity and intelligence. 6G is key for future smart cities, integrating terahertz communication, ultra-low latency, and AI-driven networks. This will create hyper-connected cities where real-time data supports systems like autonomous vehicles, energy management, and public safety. 6G research shows its potential for ultra-reliable communication, immersive experiences like extended reality, and widespread sensing, crucial for smart city applications. However, challenges like technical issues, data privacy, and regulations need addressing. This chapter proposes a 6G-enabled smart city model using IoT, AI, and edge computing to improve urban operations. It explores dynamic network slicing, intelligent resource allocation, and edge AI processing to meet latency and bandwidth needs. The chapter concludes by emphasizing collaboration and strategic planning to overcome challenges, ensuring 6G technologies foster sustainable urban growth.

The next 6G technology is expected to change the face of smart cities by offering greater connectivity, faster and higher data transfer rates. A major advantage of using blockchain with 6G networks is the availability of a distributed immutable database to record transactions and data exchange. In the context of smart cities, this feature is very important to ensure the security of data transfer process through many IoT devices and systems. Through implementation of a system in which data cannot be altered or deleted, blockchain increases the credibility and accountability of smart city management. The integration of blockchains with IoT devices especially in the smart cities is therefore helpful. IoT devices which are the foundation for smart cities are prone to cyber threats and malwares. The real-time anomaly detection and the pattern features analysis in machine learning algorithms help to identify the possible risks to safety in no time. Integrated with blockchains, these frameworks help in enhancing intrusion detection, privacy and silence.

Smart cities leverage 6G infrastructure for secure, efficient healthcare delivery. 6G's ultra-low latency, high bandwidth, and device connectivity enable real-time data transmission for telemedicine, remote monitoring, and robotic surgeries, improving healthcare access. Ensuring 6G security is crucial; encryption, authentication, blockchain, and zero-trust models protect sensitive data. Integrating 6G with existing systems requires standardized protocols and collaboration. Navigating regulations and ethics related to data privacy and patient consent is essential. As smart cities evolve, secure 6G will revolutionize healthcare delivery through innovation and prioritizing patient well-being.

The emergence of 6G technology guarantees to revolutionize each healthcare and smart cities by means of supplying ultra-fast, secure, and dependable communication networks. This paper delves into the capability packages of stable 6G infrastructure in healthcare, emphasizing its function in improving telemedicine, far off affected person monitoring, and real-time information analytics. Additionally, it explores how secure 6G can facilitate the improvement of smart towns, enabling green control of urban services and infrastructure. The steady 6G community guarantees patient facts confidentiality while facilitating seamless communication among healthcare companies and sufferers. By integrating advanced technology like AI and IoT inside the 6G framework, both the healthcare area and smart towns can acquire unparalleled stages of performance, security, and service high-quality.

Preface

This book embarks on a journey into "Building Tomorrow's Smart Cities With 6G Infrastructure Technology," where cutting-edge technology converges with Smart City planning with 6G Infrastructure. Through a multidisciplinary lens, we delve into the intricacies of 6G infrastructure cities that are smart, safe, sustainable, and inclusive. In the past few years, various advanced and emerging technologies such as Blockchain, Artificial Intelligence, Digital Twin, and others have been utilized in IoT and Smart City Applications, including Smart Parking, Smart Education, Smart Healthcare, Smart Vehicles based on human requirements and promises to transform cities into intelligent, interconnected ecosystems. These applications depend on IoT and Sensor devices such as humidity, current, temperature, etc., and IoT devices connect to the network using gateways that act as processing Base Stations. These stations and sensors, as mentioned above, transfer the information data to the cloud, analyze it, and utilize it to improve and optimize smart applications. According to new advancements in the communication field, 5G is transferred to 6G technology with advanced IoT Sensors in futuristic worlds. The motivation behind this book stems from acknowledging the transformative potential inherent in emerging technologies, particularly 6G, to revolutionize metropolitan environments and pave the way for the expansion of truly Smart Cities. However, security and privacy are the major issues in 6G Infrastructure for Futuristic Smart Cities, and realizing this vision requires more than just technological innovation. An edited collection of original research in Secure 6G Infrastructure for Futuristic Smart Cities and IoT security Intelligence paradigms is needed. In this book, we embark on a journey to explore the profound impact of emerging technology-enabled secure 6G infrastructure on the creation of futuristic smart Cities. The primary objective of this book, "Emerging Technology-enabled Secure 6G Infrastructure for Futuristic Smart City," is to comprehensively explore how cutting-edge technologies, particularly 6G, can shape the future of smart cities. It also provides relevant theoretical frameworks and the latest empirical research findings. It will be written for professionals who want to improve their understanding of the strategic role of Emerging Technology-enabled

Secure 6G Infrastructure for Futuristic Smart Cities. In this book, we categorized many chapters based on the title. We provide qualitative and theoretical knowledge about Secure 6G Infrastructure for Futuristic Smart City Applications with emerging technologies such as Blockchain, Artificial Intelligence, Digital Twin, and Federated Learning (FL). This book's target audience will be industry professionals, researchers, and bachelor and master students working in secure 6G infrastructure for a Futuristic Smart City, with the emergence of advanced new technologies such as Digital Twins, Blockchain, Federated Learning (FL), Artificial Intelligence (AI), and Extended versions of hybrid cryptographic algorithms. This book appeals to diverse industry persons and researchers involved in planning, designing, implementing, and managing futuristic smart city initiatives beyond 6G. Overall, this book is an encyclopedic resource for anyone (Researchers, Students, Industry Persons) seeking to understand and contribute to the evolution of futuristic, intelligent cities powered by secure 6G infrastructure.

The book is organized into three sections. The first section, which includes four chapters, is focused on the background and preliminaries. The second part, which provides four well-structured chapters, illustrates the Security case of a 6G-based IoT-enabled Smart City. Finally, the last section, which consists of ten chapters, focuses on Advanced Technologies for 6G Infrastructure IoT-enabled Smart Cities.

SECTION 1: BACKGROUND AND PRELIMINARIES

The chapter "The Role of 6G Technology in Smart City Development" determines the development of 6G technology marks a significant leap forward in the evolution of smart cities. 6G's next-generation technology will seamlessly integrate AI, IoT, and big data, making cities more responsive, efficient, and sustainable and enhancing everything from transportation to public safety; 6G will play a pivotal role in addressing urban challenges and improving the quality of life. This chapter explores the transformative potential of 6G in shaping the smart cities of the future.

The chapter "Security and Privacy Challenges in 6G-enabled Smart City" delves into the transformative potential of 6G technology, anticipated to be commercially available by 2030, and its implications for smart cities. The Chapter begins by outlining the objectives, which include exploring security challenges, investigating privacy concerns, analyzing case studies, proposing mitigation strategies, and examining future directions for enhancing security and privacy in 6G-enabled smart cities. It concludes by proposing solutions and mitigation strategies to address the security and privacy challenges in 6G-enabled smart cities. These include advanced encryption techniques, AI and machine learning for threat detection, policy and regulatory frameworks, and public awareness initiatives.

The chapter "Secure 6G Infrastructure in a Futuristic World" explores the multifaceted safety-demanding situations those improvements bring, especially the heightened vulnerability because of the proliferation of the Internet of Things (IoT) gadgets and the emergence of cyber-bodily threats. This study emphasizes the significance of proactive safety features inside the improvement of 6G networks, advocating for worldwide requirements and rules to protect the following technology of verbal exchange infrastructure.

The chapter "Using 6G to Boost Smart Cities New Ways to Connect and Save Energy in Cities" discusses two revolutionary ideas in depth, including their features, ways they work together & future impact on development. ICT involves data collection, storage, retrieval, modification, organization, administration, security & exchange. Automation in smart cities assists respond fast to real-time data from IoT devices. 6G networks provide telemedicine, virtual consultations & remote patient tracking. The chapter concludes that 6G will transform urban living, making cities more livable, sustainable, and responsive to citizens.

SECTION 2: SECURITY USE-CASE OF 6G-BASED IOT-ENABLED SMART CITY

The chapter "Privacy and Security Concerns with 6G Smart City Infrastructure" discusses 6G-appropriate security and privacy tactics such as enhanced encryption, secure communication protocols, and AI-driven threat detection systems. In conclusion, this chapter discusses privacy and security in 6G-enabled smart cities, including where the field is going and the future for research to help create trustworthy, resilient, and secure smart city ecosystems that can take advantage of 6G's revolutionary capabilities.

The chapter "6G Technology and Heritage Cities: Enhancing Preservation and Visitor Experience" explores the possibility of 6G networks revolutionizing the management and preservation of cultural heritage locations. This chapter examines how high-definition connectivity, fog-edge computing, and AI-oriented applications can reinforce advanced digital preservation strategies, immersive visitor knowledge, and sustainable tourism in historic establishments. By bridging digital and physical realms, 6G technology enables real-time, data-driven insights that empower heritage site managers and enhance visitor accessibility. This integration paves the track for resilient and adaptive heritage cities that embrace technical invention while conserving their historical disposition.

The chapter "AI Applications in Secure 6G-Enabled Smart City Infrastructure" explores how AI, incorporated with 6G networks, can create secure, more efficient metropolitan atmospheres. It delves into AI-based solutions for security, resource surveillance, and real-time monitoring, which are essential for improving intelligent city infrastructure. AI and 6G synergy ensures ultra-low latency, enabling rapid response to security threats and streamlined metropolitan operations. By leveraging these advanced technologies, cities can achieve strengthened resilience, data or information privacy, and sustainability in an increasingly digital world.

The chapter "Revolutionizing Urban Living: Integrating 6G and Blockchain in Smart City Development" focuses on the revolutionary aspects of developing the new generation of smart cities using 6G and blockchain technologies in unison. The integration of 6G and blockchain technology is examined, showing their effectiveness in facilitating secure and real-time data transfer and the operation of smart cities. This chapter also discusses the technological, regulatory, or societal barriers to the widespread deployment of these technologies, including issues of interoperability, scalability, and privacy. The chapter addresses the opportunities emerging AI, IoT, and quantum computing technologies can offer to improve smart city-making. As a result, this chapter provides a comprehensive perspective that will be useful to policymakers, urban planners, technologists, and researchers focusing on the smart cities of the future.

The present chapter, "The Role of 6G in Empowering Smart Cities Enabling Ubiquitous Connectivity and Intelligent Infrastructure," contends using a 6G-empowered smart city based on IoT, artificial intelligence, and edge computing to increase urban processes' efficiency. These include dynamic network slicing to fulfill the latency and bandwidth requirement supported by Intelligent Resource management and Edge AI processing. The chapter highlights the need for joint efforts and forward planning to overcome hindrances in the 6G's delivery to support sustainable cities.

SECTION 3: ADVANCED TECHNOLOGIES FOR 6G INFRASTRUCTURE IOT-ENABLED SMART CITY

The chapter "Blockchain Enabled 6G Security Architecture for Smart Cities: A Decentralized and Resilient Approach" discusses how blockchain technology can amplify security frameworks in 6G-empowered smart cities. This decentralized scheme provides transparency, privacy, security, data integrity, and enhanced privacy, reducing reliance on significant servers. By connecting blockchain with 6G's high-definition-speed, low-latency capabilities, cities can secure real-time data conversations, safeguard critical infrastructure, and enable a resilient response to cybersecurity hazards. This integration sets the basis for secure, self-sustaining, intelligent city ecosystems.

The chapter" Artificial Intelligence-Enabled Cybersecurity and Internet of Things Applications in Smart Cities" underscores the importance of CS in SCs, highlighting vulnerabilities and risks. It examines IoT's role in SC infrastructure and services, AI's impact on SC efficiency, and various AI techniques used in SC applications. The chapter analyzes cyberattacks on SC infrastructure, suggesting CS measures like protocols, encryption, authentication techniques, access control, and incident response. The chapter also presents SC application case studies demonstrating the integration's effectiveness and best practices. It concludes by emphasizing the need for continued research and innovation in SC cybersecurity.

The chapter" Blockchain-based IoT-enabled Secure 6G Smart City Applications" The chapter "Blockchain-based IoT-enabled Secure 6G Smart City Applications" explores the fusion of blockchain, IoT, and 6G technology to create protected, efficient metropolitan applications. This integration enhances data privacy, integrity, authenticity, and resilience across connected devices in smart cities, enabling trusted real-time interactions. Leveraging 6G's high-speed network, blockchain ensures IoT transmissions, containing data breaches and guaranteeing uninterrupted service in intelligent infrastructures. The chapter emphasizes transformative applications across the conveyance, energy, and healthcare sectors, establishing a secure foundation for future metropolitan invention.

The chapter "Enabling Secure and Efficient Healthcare Delivery in Smart Cities through 6G Infrastructure" explores how 6G advanced networks can revolutionize smart healthcare systems. It explores the role of ultra-low latency, massive high-definition connectivity, and AI-oriented applications in enabling real-time diagnostics, as well as efficient emergency reactions. By leveraging 6G's speed and security, healthcare providers can rescue patient data while providing affordable, high-quality care across smart city infrastructures.

The chapter "Healthcare and Smart Cities Applications of Secure 6G Infrastructure" examines the transformative possibility of 6G technology in enhancing competent healthcare and services. It discusses how 6G's ultra-fast high-definition connectivity and security standards support applications like telemedicine, medical, emergency response, and remote patient monitoring within smart cities. By integrating AI, DT, and IoT with 6G, cities can offer real-time, secure healthcare explanations that enhance residents' quality of life and sustain efficient urban functions. This chapter emphasizes the benefits of a safe 6G infrastructure in progressing healthcare accessibility and sustainability in intelligent city ecosystems.

The chapter "Improving the Blockchain Protocol for 5G, Web3, & Edge Computing Applications" aims to improve the blockchain protocol to effectively support 5G, Web3, Edge Computing, Metaverse, and many more applications. It prioritizes immutability, confidentiality, and availability and offers interaction and digital experiences advantages. The objective is to create a protocol that meets diverse industry requirements while considering different approaches to achieve its goals.

The chapter "SEBAKE-6G SEcure Batch Authentication and Key Exchange for 6G-Enabled ITS" addresses computation cost, security, and privacy issues. The authors introduced batch authentication and key exchange to secure user privacy and prevent attacks. To ensure message integrity, this system provides location-based information safely from RSU to the vehicle without any changes. This system reduces the communication and computational costs. Simulation is performed using a simulation of urban mobility (SUMO) simulator.

The chapter "Integrating Blockchain, IoT, and 6G Technologies for Secure, Efficient, and Sustainable Smart City Applications: Enhancing Urban Living through Innovation" explores the intersection of cutting-edge technologies to mitigate metropolitan challenges. It highlights how blockchain provides fast, secure, decentralized data management, IoT enables seamless device interconnectivity, and 6G offers ultra-fast, reliable communication. These technologies allow resilient infrastructure, efficient resource use, and data-driven decision-making to enhance urban life. This integration paves the way for innovative, sustainable, and citizen-centered intelligent city solutions, transforming modern urban living.

Sushil Kumar Singh
Marwadi University, India

Bal Virdee
London Metropolitan University, UK

Rajendrasinh Jadeja
Marwadi University, India

Sudeep Tanwar
Nirma University, India

Ashish Khanna
Maharaja Agrasen Institute of Technology, India

Chapter 1
The Role of 6G Technology in Smart City Development

Aditi Nag
https://orcid.org/0000-0002-0604-6945
Manipal University Jaipur, India

ABSTRACT

The advent of 6G technology promises to revolutionize smart city development by offering ultra-high-speed connectivity, minimal latency, and the capacity to support massive device connectivity. This paper explores the transformative potential of 6G in enhancing urban planning, management, and everyday life. Through case studies of pioneering cities like Seoul, Tokyo, Singapore, and Helsinki, it highlights practical applications such as smart traffic management, AI-driven healthcare innovations, and augmented reality tourism experiences. While 6G holds immense promise, its implementation requires overcoming challenges related to infrastructure, data privacy, and regulatory frameworks. Addressing these challenges will be crucial for cities to harness the full benefits of 6G and create sustainable, resilient urban environments for the future.

1 INTRODUCTION

Smart cities have emerged as a result of the most profound changes in the global urban environment that have been brought about by the rapid spread of communications technologies (Salameh & El Tarhuni, 2022; Shehab et al., 2022) combining revolutionary digital infrastructure and innovative technologies to enhance the sustainability, productivity, and quality of living of their citizens (Allam & Jones,

DOI: 10.4018/979-8-3693-8029-1.ch001

2021). The current development with 5G technology as a milestone has set itself for revolution in urban development (Slimani, Khoulji & Kerkeb, 2023). 6G will provide an opportunity to build incredible capabilities with the deliverance of fantastic connectivity, more substantial computing power, and better response-ability. The network can now be travelled at 1 Tbps speed with the latency low enough to define urban connectivity in exchanging the data further in that regard (Fadhil, 2023). Its ability to carry on vast numbers of interconnected devices per unit area- those that can go up to 10 million per square kilometre- gives new scope to integrating diverse Internet of Things (IoT) applications into city infrastructure, potentially revolutionising urban connectivity and data exchange through 6G technology, illuminating hope for the future of smart cities. This paper will comprehensively explore the profound roles 6G technology can play in developing and enhancing smart cities, essentially providing a complete analysis of how 6G can empower cities to overcome some of the current challenges they face, optimise their resource management, and break new standards in the urban planning and management practices of cities around the world. The discussion on its potential impact across these domains-from transportation and energy to healthcare and public safety-enables an articulation of the transformative potential of 6G in shaping future trajectories of urban living. This paper will illustrate real-life examples of where early adoption of 6G has already provided benefits and innovation in a wide range of urban contexts using cutting-edge case studies and emerging trends. It details possible future applications of 6G and the opportunities and challenges that may arise when implementing and incorporating this revolutionary technology into infrastructural frameworks within cities. In a nutshell, this paper provides an all-inclusive and prospective analysis of how 6G technology will impact the development of smart cities. It is meant to inspire stakeholders, policymakers, and urban planners by explaining its capabilities, applications, and implications about the transformative potential of 6G in redefining the urban landscape of tomorrow.

A discussion about its probable impact across those domains – from transport and energy to healthcare and public safety – enables an articulation of how 6G might really transform the direction of cities in the future. To this end, this paper will illustrate in real-world settings where the initial adoption of 6G has already resulted in some benefits and innovations in diverse urban environments, applying cutting-edge case studies and emerging trends. It discusses the potential future applications of 6G and what opportunity or challenge it could provide once installed and integrated with a city's infrastructural systems. Comprehensively, this paper provides an all-inclusive and prospective analysis of how the 6G technology will change the development of smart cities. It should be inspirational for stakeholders, policymakers, and urban planners to outline the capacities, applications, and implications of 6G as a tool to redefine the urban landscape of tomorrow.

1.1 Background

Smart cities have surfaced as extremely prominent in the last ten decades primarily because of phenomenal growth in the population that lives in urban areas. The UN predicts that over two-thirds of the human race will reside in cities by 2050. The rapid speed of urbanisation creates hindrances to public safety, resource utilisation, infrastructure management, and ecological sustainability (Singhal, Betgeri, & Singh, 2024). There is an apparent necessity for innovative solutions that would make cities more livable and resilient.

Traditionally, information and communication technologies greatly influence the urban landscape. Here, generations of mobile communications, from 1G through 4G, created enhanced connectivity, but concerning the dynamics involved in modern urban lifestyles, these technologies still lag. Although 5G significantly increased speed and capacity, it was still unable to accommodate the large number of connected devices needed for a smart city ecosystem to be completely achieved (Singh et al., 2023). In order to overcome these constraints, we anticipate a paradigm change towards 6G technology. The distinguishing features of 6G are ultra-high-speed connectivity, reaching speeds up to 1 Tbps; ultra-low latency measured in microseconds; and massive device connectivity supporting as many as 10 million devices per square kilometre. These are not small incremental improvements but changes in the entire operations of cities (Singh, Jeong, & Park, 2020).

This 6G technology integrated into the smart city will benefit numerous industries. Dynamic adaptation in real-time traffic management systems will be made possible by this real-time connectivity, thus reducing traffic congestion and ensuring road safety. Ultra-low latency in the health sector will allow for telemedicine, therefore enabling remote medical treatments. Smart grids with 6G can, for the first time, monitor and optimise distribution networks in real time; sophisticated surveillance systems with AI-based algorithms provide additional strength to public safety mechanisms (Singh et al., 2023). Let us look at the sectors where applications of 6G are going to provide visionary value. Environmental monitoring via IoT devices will give live readings about air quality and noise pollution levels, through which city authorities can quickly act upon public health complaints. Beyond this, 6G can empower AR/VR to enrich cultural life across resident and tourist communities via interactions with historical sites and local events such as festivals (Singh et al., 2020).

Understanding technology developments and their wider ramifications for governance, policy-making, community participation, and sustainability practices is crucial as cities throughout the world start to investigate these possibilities (Singh, Jeong, & Park, 2020). Governments, businesses, and community organisations will work together to successfully implement 6G technology since the creative projects will provide equitable and inclusive opportunities (Singh et al., 2023). As we move ahead into this new technological epoch, to be built around the power of 6G, stakeholders, planners, policymakers, technologists, and citizens will start to alter smart city projects with inclusivity and resilience in them with state-of-the-art connectivity solutions in sustainable urban development. Based on this vision, this paper aims to offer valuable insights into how the technology of 6G can fundamentally change our urban landscape for generations to come. By resolving the current challenges and using this transformational technology, cities can make their operations more efficient and improve the quality of life (QoL) for all residents.

2 THE POTENTIAL OF 6G TECHNOLOGY

This fast rise of telecommunication technologies has greatly impacted the urban environment, thus ushering in an age wherein cities are more integrated and intelligent. Smart cities also involve advanced digital infrastructure along with innovative technologies that promote improvement in efficiency, QoL, and sustainability for their inhabitants (Fadhil, 2023). This shift from 5G to 6G technology represents a significant development point for global change in cities (Salameh & El Tarhuni, 2022; Shehab et al., 2022). It is through 6G technology that a new level of connectivity, computing capability, and responsiveness will give speed, latency, and connectivity device standards a whole new level (See Figure 1).

Figure 1. 6G's contribution to smart cities enabling technologies

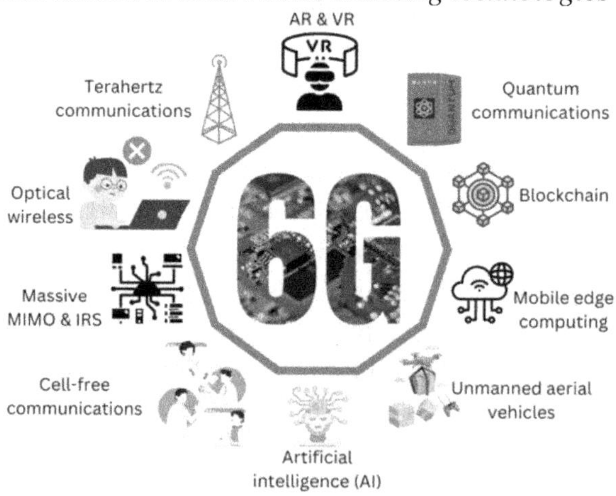

(Source: Author's interpretation from Murroni et al., 2023)

6G provides ultra-high-speed connectivity, ultra-low latency, and massive device connectivity, on which the future of advancing innovation, sustainability, and QoL for smart cities around the world can be built. In terms of depth of exploration into how 6G technology can power smart city development (SCD), the study is particularly focused on the transformative nature of this potential, stretching from transportation to health care, energy management, and public safety, explaining all the possibilities and implications for 6G so that the way forward for cities embracing the next generation of connectivity and digital innovation might be depicted.

2.1 Ultra-High-Speed Connectivity

Ultra-high-speed connectivity is a first-of-its-kind leap in connectivity via 6G technology. Data transmission speed can be up to 1 Tbps or Terabytes per second. All the earlier generations are past history and changed the whole landscape of smart city infrastructure. The implications are very deep and profound since ultra-high-speed connectivity unlocks all kinds of transformative applications (Allam & Jones, 2021).

In 6G, real-time data analytics becomes the heart of city planning and management. By using big data from sensors, cameras, and IoT, the city administrators take swift decisions. For instance, a traffic management system can modify signals based on real-time data regarding flow traffic. That means optimisation of routes and less congestion in the central city (Farooq et al., 2022). Environmental sensors can monitor the air quality, and immediate response can be given to any change; hence, prompt action would be taken for public health protection. Furthermore, 6G supports high-definition video streaming with no patches within cities and provides virtual reality experiences (Wikström et al., 2020). One can now imagine citizens experiencing virtual tours through historical landmarks or attending city council meetings with great-quality video and zero lag. The applications improve cultural experiences and civic engagements and introduce more transparency in governance (Uusitalo et al., 2021). At the same time, industries within smart cities may take advantage of these 6G opportunities to accelerate innovation and efficiency.

For example, in the health industry, doctors and other medical experts can utilise fast data transfers for remote surgical operations whereby surgeons can conduct surgical procedures from a distance accurately with instant feedback (Farooq et al., 2022). Video feeds and data transmission to emergency response systems can utilise direct, instant responses in disaster or public safety emergencies for swift coordination and control (Slimani, Khoulji & Kerkeb, 2023). Ultra-high-speed connectivity is what enables 6G to bring operational and experience efficiencies right across the urban landscape. That is, through an ability to offer real-time data analytics, high-definition video streaming, and an immersed virtual experience, 6G technology lets cities make new connections with a wider innovation and sustainability that makes sense as cities pursue new inventive ways of being responsive toward the needs of its own residents.

2.2 Low Latency

This capability brings 6G technology into ultra-low latency, thus minimising the delay range for data transmission and reception up to microseconds. This is highly game-changing for applications where instant response is needed; this would be especially true in the smart city environment. Among the most impressive use cases for 6G low latency are autonomous vehicles (Uusitalo et al., 2021). These vehicles require data exchange in real-time to navigate the urban streets both safely and efficiently. 6G enables vehicles to communicate directly with the infrastructure, such as intersection lights and pedestrian sensor detectors, in near real-time and thus respond very fast to changes in traffic as well as possible hazards. This capability smoothes out traffic flows while enhancing the overall security on roads by reducing possible accident occurrences (Wikström et al., 2020). With low latency in healthcare through 6G, the processes of remote surgical interventions are possible through telemedicine.

Surgeons may be able to manage remotely at a millimetre resolution as surgeons control surgical instruments at that scale with real-time feedback provided through high-definition video feeds and sensor data, improving healthcare access in places such as underserved locations while increasing patient care given by experts who can practice medicine from a distance rather than from a physical point (Singh et al., 2023). Moreover, low 6G latency significantly enhances intelligent grid management. Responsive energy grids, with sensors and monitoring devices, can adjust in real time for changes in demand or supply. Optimisation by utilities would be enhanced during energy distribution, and a smoother introduction of renewable energy sources avoids potential disruption (Slimani et al., 2023). By doing this, cities become more energy efficient in supply, have less carbon footprint, and have stronger resistance towards power outages or failures in the grid. In short, 6G reduces the delay of data communications in smart cities practically to nothing, so it allows for interference-free interaction between devices and systems. This would guarantee the safety and reliability of all operations in cities but optimise operational efficiency. Whether it is in autonomous transportation, telemedicine health care, or intelligent management of the grid, ultra-low latency through 6G enables innovation in how the cities will work and change in this digital age.

2.3 Massive Device Connectivity

6G technology offers innovation in massive device connection through the ability to connect up to 10 million devices per square kilometre. This is very important as more cities are constantly integrating any form of IoT devices with their infrastructures (Gera et al., 2023). This will particularly be important for 6G in cities where there will be such a density of interconnected devices as environmental sensors, smart meters, and connected vehicles (Singh et al., 2023).

A great example is that environmental sensors can measure the quality of air, the amount of noise, as well as the weather all throughout the city and give them priceless data to use for activities in environmental management and public health (Salameh & El Tarhuni, 2022; Shehab et al., 2022). Smart meters optimise energy consumption by gathering and analysing usage patterns, thereby allowing for increased efficiency in energy use while also reducing the costs of utility operations. Even more, IoT-enabled vehicles require a seamless communication network for the proper management of traffic and road safety (Fadhil, 2023). In 6G, data can be shared between a vehicle and a traffic light, a road sign, and central control instantly without congesting the roads for adaptive flow management on the roads of an urban centre. Such connectivity will also enable advanced driver assistance systems and autonomous driving technology, demanding real-time data exchange in order to navigate the complicated urban environment safely and efficiently (Uusitalo et al., 2021). Public safety and emergency response systems also avail themselves of massive device connectivity in 6G (Farooq et al., 2022). The police departments and emergency services can track open spaces with the help of IoT-enabled devices like surveillance cameras, drones, and wearable sensors to develop situational awareness and coordinate rapid responses to incidents (Gera et al., 2023). The cities will then be able to improve safety measures, provide a quicker reaction time to an incident, and even ensure that guests are safe. More importantly, the holistic data analytics offered by 6G-enabled IoT devices will be useful in informing resource allocation infrastructure development and service provision among city administrators and planners (Slimani, Khoulji & Kerkeb, 2023; Gera et al., 2023). Cities can utilise real-time data analytics to optimise services for waste management, water supply, and public transportation. With this being the case, efficiency, sustainability, and QoL among residents in the urban areas are well guaranteed.

In short, massive device connectivity in 6G technology changes the way smart cities work and grow. All the devices spread throughout the city can be utilised to allow for seamless communication and coordination in IoTs. Cities would then unlock the possibilities of data-driven decision-making, resource optimisation, proactive management of urban services, and the digital age fully.

2.4 Comparative Analysis of 6G Applications in Smart Cities

This is why it is crucial to think about how applications of 6G technology across domains explain its transformative potential in SCD. Comparison between 5G and 6G development shows development towards the improvement of living in an urban environment as described in Table 1.

Table 1. Comparative analysis of 6G applications in smart cities (Source: Author's compilation)

Domain	5G Capabilities	6G Enhancements	Implications for Smart Cities
Transportation	Enhanced traffic management with real-time data	Instantaneous data exchange for autonomous vehicles	Improved traffic flow, reduced congestion, enhanced safety
Healthcare	Remote consultations and telemedicine	Real-time health monitoring with AI integration	Better patient outcomes through timely interventions
Energy Management	Smart grids for efficient energy distribution	Predictive analytics for energy usage	Greater sustainability and reduced carbon footprints
Public Safety	Surveillance systems with basic analytics	AI-driven threat detection with real-time alerts	Enhanced security measures and faster emergency responses

Table 1 shows the following great improvements in a transition from 5G to 6G technology, which could potentially change all intelligent city areas.

Instantaneous data exchange in 6G will open up the horizon for transportation, and autonomous vehicles can see a better flow of traffic with reduced congestion. This would improve the safety aspect of urban roads and the efficiency of transportation as a whole. Integrating real-time health monitoring through AI will change the care of patients in healthcare. This would ensure timely intervention on the basis of continuous analysis of health data, drastically improving patient outcomes. Similarly, predictive analytics of 6G will help with energy management in terms of the most efficient energy distribution, leading to further sustainability and reduced carbon footprints. Another area to be affected by the change will be public safety, as AI-driven threat detection systems will be introduced with real-time alerts. This will heighten security features and speed up responses in times of emergencies, thereby making urban environments safer. In short, the revolutions in these domains through 6G technology quite aptly show the revolutionary change it can bring in transformation for innovative city development. Through its solution to problems and optimisation of resource management, 6G will re-invent urban living for people across the globe, thereby changing their QoL in smart cities.

3 ENHANCING URBAN PLANNING AND MANAGEMENT

This era of fast urbanisation and technological transformation has been positioned to redefine the landscape of the urban planning and management landscape with the integration of 6G technology. This next-generation solution epitomises the transformative leap forward of ultra-high speed data, ultra-low latency support, and carrying connections from millions of massive numbers of devices. It unleashes unprecedented potential on this smart planet and brings about unprecedented efficiency, sustainability, and QoL to the citizen populations. Cities may capture values from 6G and the synergies of IoT, AI, and other innovations such as AR and VR. It can seize real-time data analytics insight into ways to optimise its operations with regard to its infrastructure delivery. Moreover, it can grant an immersive experience with an urban landscape. Harnessed with these capabilities, it is possible to maximise smart city resources toward the consumption of resources so as to effectively deliver service with optimal levels of sustainability and resilience. This paper discusses how 6G technology empowers planners and administrators to make informed decisions, improve service delivery, and incubate resilient, future-ready cities that put a premium on innovation and inclusivity in the digital age.

3.1 Internet of Things (IoT)

Perhaps one of the most critical breakthroughs that 6G technology will offer with IoT is the promise to transform the ways through which cities collect and use real-time data across domains. This is because ultra-high-speed connectivity and minimal latency provided by 6G will allow for the sheer deployment of IoT devices in intelligent cities, thereby enhancing its monitoring and management capabilities over dynamic urban environments.

1. Environmental Monitoring: The air quality, even noise levels, and, for that matter, weather can be monitored in real-time using Smart sensors with 6G connectivity. The IoT-based sensors can be placed in densely populated zones so that the level of pollutants is monitored, and, at once, alerts would be sent to the city administration to take immediate action. This further enables good public health due to clean air in circulation and favours proactive policies regarding aspects of the environment on the carbon emissions and climate change effects (Fadhil, 2023; Gera et al., 2023).
2. Traffic Management In densely occupied cities, 6G-enabled IoT devices can significantly transform the approach of current traffic management systems. This can be done through intelligent traffic lights that may alter the signal time according to real-time data collected through roadside sensors about the trend

of the flow of traffic in real-time. This will not only reduce travelling time and fuel consumption but also promote safety as a whole by reducing intersection accidents.

3. Energy Efficiency: The 6G IoT devices will allow real-time monitoring and control of the use of energy in household, business, and industrial applications. Smart meters linked through 6G can indicate the consumption of electricity in real-time. This enables utilities to use demand response strategies and energy distribution grids more efficiently. Cities will reduce energy usage, cut utility charges for the citizens, and promote renewable sources of energy for a green future (Gera et al., 2023; Allam & Jones, 2021).
4. Waste Management: IoT-supported smart bins that are connected using 6G can improve waste collection activities within cities. These smart bins can remotely monitor their fill levels. They are automatically scheduled for collection when they are filled, which optimises costs for the municipal waste management service. In addition, depending on data analytics generated with these IoT devices, a city can execute efficient recycling programs and reduce the volumes of waste sent to landfills to make the urban landscape cleaner and sustainable (Singh et al., 2023; Uusitalo et al., 2021).

Basically, the integration of 6G technology with devices like IoT enables the city to realise actionably useful insights from data produced in real time so as to inform the decision-making on critical domains of urban planning and management. This enables the city to optimise its services to enable high operational efficiency, improvement in sustainability, and an enhanced QoL for residents within the modern world.

3.2 Artificial Intelligence (AI)

The integration of AI in 6G technology is a benchmark for the innovative development of cities, high-speed connectivity, and ultra-low latency to transform different components of urban operations in many sectors (Konhäuser, 2021; Kulkarni & Kulkarni, 2021).

1. Predictive Maintenance: 6G-enabled AI algorithms can transform the management of critical infrastructure assets by cities. For example, AI-based predictive maintenance systems can monitor the condition of bridges, roads, and water distribution networks in real-time. These would recognise patterns and anomalies of health in the infrastructure to provide forecasts of when maintenance should be performed before a problem turns into an unserviceable state. This would, therefore, result in preventative repair work and reduced downtime. The approach would lengthen the lifespan of infrastructure assets as well as public

safety from possible failures of infrastructure (Salameh & El Tarhuni, 2022; Shehab et al., 2022).

2. Transportation Optimization: AI algorithms that integrate 6G optimise public transit systems by monitoring real-time data on passenger flows, traffic patterns, and weather conditions. Transit agencies can use buses and trains in real-time for scheduling, routes, and capacity to balance demand and supply. This will help reduce waiting times, increase reliability, and save travel time to work. This will help in city mobility and decongesting the city roads. More specifically, AI-based predictive analytics will enhance the ability of cities to predict traffic management and eliminate traffic congestion during peak hours (Fadhil, 2023; Wikström et al., 2020).
3. Emergency Response and Crisis Management: AI-based systems connected through 6G facilitate rapid responses and decision-making in emergencies. The algorithms predict natural disasters and other crises by reading data feeds from sources like IoT sensor feeds, social media feeds, and historical records of incidents. Predictive models enable emergency responders to preposition resources, deploy personnel proactively in high-risk areas, and coordinate evacuation plans in real time. This implies that AI-based systems assist cities in having better preparedness for disaster response through situational awareness, faster response times, lives saved, and lessening the destruction of property assets (Mishra & Singh, 2023; Kumari, Gupta & Tanwar, 2021; Uusitalo et al., 2021; Lu & Zheng, 2020).
4. Urban Governance and Decision Support: More general than application details, AI-powered with 6G technology puts all the advanced data analytics in decision support tools into the hands of city administrators. If very complex data is supplied to AI algorithms, insights could become actionable for policy and resource planning in an urban environment. From optimising municipal budget, identification of areas with potential for infrastructure investment as well as sustainable development activities to make cities make decisions by informed economic growth, environmental sustainability, and social equity as outlined in Chhabra et al. (2023); Al Amin et al. (2023).

Basically, it is the marriage of 6G technology and AI that enables cities to approach urban challenges in a more agile and forward-looking manner. AI predictive capabilities can also be integrated with 6G high-speed connectivity. This will enhance efficiency, resilience, and responsiveness to smart city operations. These capabilities make it possible for citizens in the digital age to move towards sustainable urban development and QoL.

3.3 Advanced Technologies

Further integration of 6G technology with AR and VR opens more avenues for improvement in the planning, management, and engagement of citizens through urban improvement. Applications of AR and VR provide high-speed connectivity and ultra-low latency, thus creating an immersive experience that changes how cities can visualize, simulate, and interact with their environment (Kamruzzaman et al., 2022; Kaur & Khan, 2022; Khattak, Nasralla & Rehman, 2022).

1. Urban Visualization and Simulation: Technologies such as 6G AR and VR would assist urban planners in viewing and simulating infrastructure projects considered in ways that have never been possible before. Virtual models overlaid on a real-world environment allow people to experience planned developments and thus allow stakeholders to make informed decisions and improve public engagement. For instance, through this method, a city planner can apply AR and design or present images of new transit systems, parks, and buildings to allow the residents to air opinions on design suggestions before actual construction. Community interaction engenders community participation and makes it occur in tandem with urban needs and preferences (Al Amin et al., 2023; Allam & Jones, 2021).
2. Wayfinding and information enhanced: AR-based navigation applications with the connectivity of 6G shall provide better ways of navigating to city dwellers as well as tourists within any city. The apps proffer, in real-time, informative overlays that help guide users street by street across any city. They would provide the user with relevant, context-specific details with regard to adjacent historical monuments or cultural entities, as well as a public facility. For example, the AR application can tag heritage trails with points of interest, providing virtual access to the dense cultural heritage in the city. It deepens the experiences of the tourists and encourages cultural heritage since it creates awareness in the tourists on the value of the local heritage and practices (Chhabra et al., 2023; Al Amin et al., 2023).
3. Cross-border connectivity in virtual tourism. By virtual tourism services on 6G technology within tourist virtual access through powered VR, tourists cross borders; hence, promotion of tourism and economic developments since their visits to these heritage sites do not in any way damage the weakly developed landscapes. VR tours enable international viewers to access cultural treasures and historical landmarks, which contributes to an appreciation of diversified heritage and responsible tourism behaviour (Salameh & El Tarhuni, 2022; Shehab et al., 2022).

4. Innovative Urban Experience: Innovative urban experience will be achieved in smart cities with the help of 6G-powered AR and VR technologies. Interactive installations of AR in public spaces can orient citizens towards local history, environmental sustainability initiatives, community events, civic engagement, and social cohesion. Furthermore, VR simulations can be used to simulate future urban development and strategies for building resilience in cities in preparation for climate changes and population growth (Fadhil, 2023).

The transformation in city planning and governing is aligned with the application of 6G to AR and VR. Advanced technologies with 6G-powered can make the cultural heritage of smart cities rich with an immersive visualisation of a place, advanced navigation, virtual tourism, and new civic experiences that enhance sustainable development in the life quality for citizens and tourists alike in this digital world.

4 CASE STUDIES

As the acceleration of communication technology is seen, the integration of 6G is set to redesign urban landscapes around the globe. This section will delve into real-world case studies to illustrate how 6G technology is transforming SCD. These case studies range from various applications across various cities, thus illustrating how 6G is likely to transform urban planning and management and daily life itself. These examples take us through practical benefits and innovations 6G will bring to cities ahead of their peers in adopting technological advantages. Ultra-high speed for connectivity with very low latency for real-time analytics and seamless integration of technologies that include IoT, AI, AR, and VR-all these cases have outlined the efficiency, sustainability, and resilience in the environment. They also enumerate the hindrances and steps taken in setting up 6G solutions, from the problem of infrastructure deployment and data privacy, to problems in regulatory frameworks. From these case studies, we learn how that 6G technology shall evolve into the future continuously making cities smart and integral. These studies reflect not only the many concrete advantages but also highlight the importance of synergy at the government-industry-people level in making a proper and judicious exploitation of 6G towards sustainable urbanization.

The research outlines how cities can take these challenges of 6G to easily build more inclusive and resilient futures for people and their urban environments.

4.1 Seoul, South Korea

Seoul, South Korea, is that world trendsetter in smart cities technologies that develop new forms of advanced technologies to support urban life and sustainability improvements. More than 10 million citizens call this city home-megacity. Congestion, air pollution, then energy management are challenges confronting it. Seoul found an answer to these very problems by adopting a whole-of-government approach to developing SCD. It integrated 6G with other novel technological development ideas to make public services and infrastructures more efficient. Those ideas aimed to increase more mobility, sustainability, and QoL for people. Seoul happens to be one of the first cities to accept the 6G technology: it opens a door into ultra-high-speed connectivity in addition to low latency access to the network. This has all applications and ranges from the optimized smart traffic flow to the real-time environmental solution monitoring, such as air quality, etc. Further, the digital solutions are being implemented within the operational boundaries of the city through IoT devices, AI algorithms, and AR/VR technologies that promote better efficiency in operations while heightening citizen engagement along with environmental stewardship.

The Seoul case study on 6G-enabled SCD gives us insights in terms of strategies, challenges, and outcomes of advanced technologies' urban implementation. In this way, it provides a model for other cities embracing the potential of 6G for transformation into the sustainable, resilient, and inclusive city of the future.

4.1.1 Smart Traffic Management

Seoul has emerged as the trendsetter in urban development by bringing in the latest technologies, such as 6G, to address the urgent needs of society, such as traffic congestion. The smart traffic management system is a paradigm shift in urban mobility, with real-time data from sensors and cameras for efficient optimization of traffic flow (Refer to Figure 2).

1. Applications of 6G technology in Seoul infrastructure to help manage traffic: Next generation network This next-generation network provides high-speed connectivity, with much less latency in the data transfer. Then, the connection of this traffic control center, along with roadside sensors and the connected vehicle, will also be made in real-time without any delay. Then, data transference plus response in a much short time is considered critical. This was deemed critical enough for dynamic adjustment of the signals according to real time conditions of traffic.

2. Real-Time Dynamic Traffic Signal Control: The smart traffic management in Seoul changes its signals on a real-time basis depending on prevailing conditions and current traffic patterns. It takes sensor readings from movement of vehicles, weather sensors, and even from the traffic cameras on real time and optimizes the gap between the time for the signal, decreases the hotspots of congestion and thus increases the general level of flow of traffic. Besides, time-to-travel is decreased and smoothness of the intersection increases with lesser starts and stops for effective utilization of the road besides being environment-friendly.
3. Traffic Management through 6G-Enabling Traffic management in Seoul has become very potent with the advent of the 6G technology, in many ways. A high-speed connectivity means quicker processing and response to the data so that the intervention of traffic could be performed and executed at a fast pace and effectiveness. Signals change instantly with low latency, thus making an effective experience to the drivers and the pedestrians. Thirdly, 6G will support the future scalings of the smart traffic system to support the ever-growing urban population and increased density of vehicles in the city.
4. Impact on Urban Development: An example of Seoul smart traffic management can be applied everywhere and can be transplanted to all such cities where there is congestion, a problem of mobility related urban. But Seoul manages and utilizes the full range for making use of it of 6G during peoples daily commute but for doing this, in absolutely the same perspective, ensures it constructs the smarter city having sustainability in it also. The city experience is that while high-tech innovations may alter such reducing carbon emissions so as to reach more QoL for the urban dweller.

Figure 2. Smart traffic management

(Source: Author's interpretation from Sinha, 2021)

Seoul's 6G technology smart traffic management will set the new model for innovative urban planning and infrastructure development. Through 6G technology, real-time data analytics responsive traffic control systems have all the potential to improve the mobility efficiency and urban livability of cities like Seoul; hence it sets a new precedence for global smart city initiatives.

4.1.2 Smart Energy Grids

Infused with 6G technology in intelligent energy grids, Seoul has become an effective leader in sustainable urban development. Figure 3 improves both efficiency and sustainability very effectively as new installed smart grids monitor and control real-time flow of energy to all places in the city as well.

1. Rollout of 6G Technology: Seoul's smart grids in energy employ the 6G technology with high-speed connectivity and low latency. The new network enables effective communication between the various sources of energy generation, their respective distribution networks, and the users. Data is transmitted in real-time, thereby allowing the observation of the consumption pattern and immediate adjustment in the direction of energy distribution as the demand keeps fluctuating.
2. AI -inspired intelligent energy management: The 6G that enables intelligent energy grids deploy the algorithms of AI based on a wide range of datasets like historical consumptions, weather, and real-time demand to predict what can be electricity usage over any given period of time and hence ensure high accuracy

concerning the functioning of energy in the grid. This can be seen to provide foresight in reducing waste and decrease reliance on fossil fuels peaking at the right moment. This eventually reduces carbon emissions while improving the overall grid's reliability (Wikström et al., 2020).

3. Renewable Energy Integration: Seoul maintains its sustainable philosophy through integrating renewable energy sources, including solar and wind into grids using an intelligent integration approach. The 6G technology streamlined the easy integration and management that optimizes these sources' contribution to the city's energy mix. Since Seoul does not rely on fossil fuel at its traditional points of consumption, such an energy-generating clean mode of storage reduces the impact on the environment and makes the urban setting even greener.
4. Benefits and Outcomes: The 6G technology for the smart energy grids of Seoul offers a lot of benefits. The energy usage is optimized with reduced losses that happen while transmitting, and it maximizes the flow of energy into the grid. It improves the overall resilience and reliability of the grid by real-time monitoring and predictive maintenance. It further fits with Seoul's sustainability objectives of reduced greenhouse gas emissions and adoption of renewable energy by residents and industries (Islam et al., 2024).
5. Future Trends: An example of Seoul smart energy grid is where 6G technology changes the future urban energy management landscape. In the future, further development of Seoul's smart grid will also encompass increasing the resilience of the grid, coupling it with new forms of emerging energy storage technologies, and optimization of energy distribution by using smart IoT-enabled devices (Al Amin et al., 2023).

Figure 3. Smart energy grid key components

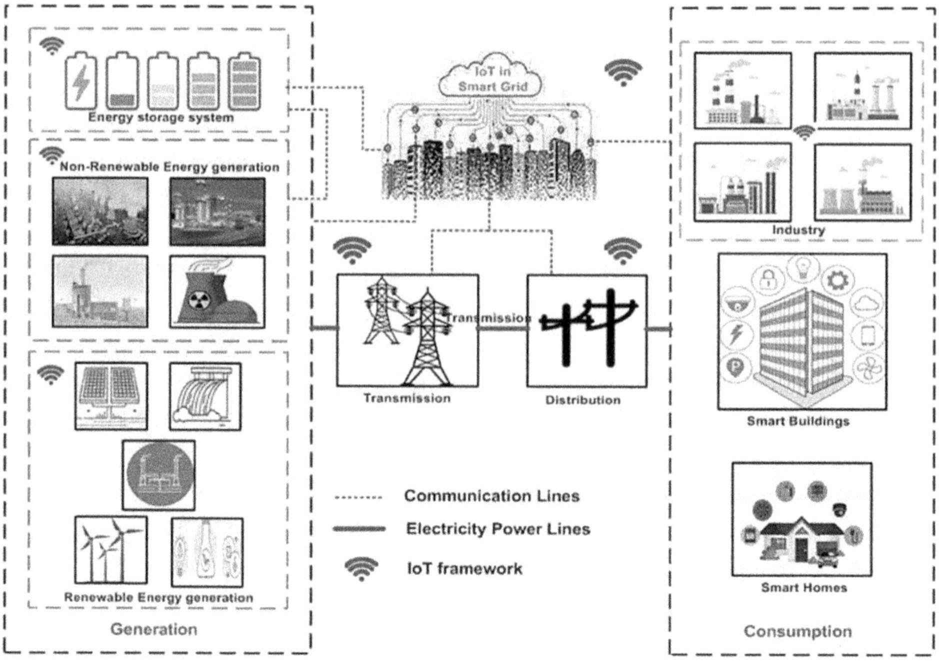

(Source: Alsharif et al., 2024)

This step of embracing intelligent energy grids powered by 6G technology by Seoul marks progressive urban planning and environmental stewardship. It represents a sustainable way forward towards energy efficiency, a reduction in carbon footprint, and increasing resilience in the structure of urban infrastructure through advanced technologies and renewable sources of energy. Therefore, Seoul is placed at the top of innovative smart city ideas worldwide and encourages other cities to develop innovative ideas toward making cities smarter, greener, and sustainable.

4.2 Tokyo, Japan

Tokyo, Japan is the world's biggest innovation and technology hub with over 14 million residents. This brings major challenges in terms of urbanization, sustainability, and the enhancement of QoL for its citizens. Tokyo has taken bold steps by embracing intelligent city initiatives and integrating advanced technologies, including 6G, into its urban infrastructure to handle the mentioned challenges effectively. Programs for this city are diverse. There are various themes - transport, energy management, environmental sustainability, and engaging the citizen. Such moves place Tokyo in a prime position to boost its efficiencies about the delivery of services and operations, preparedness in case future challenges came to pass. Thanks to the technological solutions, the Tokyo city has provided an epitome of how cities may efficiently use technology toward meeting the best use of the resources, minimizing carbon emission and making the urban environment a habitable one.

4.2.1 Public Safety and Surveillance

Tokyo has contributed so greatly towards the development of public safety infrastructure in the city through integrating the newest forms of technology that go with 6G to surveillance systems. This project relates to Tokyo's disposition to try innovation in the enhancement of city security as well as its response in emergencies.

1. Integration Through 6G Technology: The ultra-high speed connectivity and latency that is less than 6G provides Tokyo's efforts at public safety with an added advantage. The next-generation network enables the AI-based surveillance systems to communicate without any hassle with HD cameras as well as centralized command centers. Because of the real-time transfer of data, information related to incidents of public safety, identified by AI algorithms, is transmitted in real time to the authorities (Banafaa et al., 2023; Wikström et al., 2020).
2. AI-Powered Surveillance System. The AI-powered surveillance systems are a fundamental base under Tokyo's public safety doctrine. These include high-resolution cameras having AI features to monitor open areas, identify aberrations, and alert potential security threats. AI algorithms can differentiate normal activities from suspicious activity. Such algorithms may be deployed in crime prevention with safety for the public at the same time (Gupta, Ved & Kumari, 2022; Han, Zhai & Zhao, 2021).
3. Low Latency for Real-Time Alerts and Response: The public safety infrastructure in Tokyo will be enhanced further by the low latency provided by 6G technology. If there is a security breach or form of emergency, AI-driven surveillance systems might send real-time alerts and notifications to the law enforcement agencies and the emergency response teams. This would rapidly respond, ensuring resourceful deployment of resources as well as proper coordination at the right time in order to prevent any risks that may arise against the people living in Tokyo and those tourists visiting the place (Islam et al., 2024).
4. Benefits and Outcomes: The integration of AI-based surveillance and 6G technology enhances public safety and security in the city of Tokyo. It is attained on two significant grounds:. Firstly, it builds situation awareness with proactive detection of the potential threat capacity, meaning lesser crimes, and also gives better perception of security. Secondly, it permits allocation and coordination of adequate resources in times of crises expeditiously and opportunistically towards

minimizing time required for a response as well as in optimizing performance regarding public safety. It gives a city a much better urban environment supporting a city's standing as one of the world's leaders in smart city innovation.

This, itself, is a testament to how Tokyo is committed to an improvement and innovation path forward regarding public safety and surveillance. Future plans include greater AI capabilities, more sensors to have a thorough sense of situational awareness and strengthen cybersecurity measures to be able to secure sensitive information. By embracing technological advance, Tokyo would set the new standard in urban safety and resilience; it will pave way for the world's wiser, safer cities.

4.2.2 Healthcare Innovations

Tokyo spearheaded smart healthcare innovations by utilizing 6G technology to transform the nature of medical services and improve the health status of citizens. That is one example of the series of efforts that Tokyo has undertaken to innovate the integration of emerging cutting-edge technologies into core public services.

1. 6G Connectivity: The new-age health infrastructure of Tokyo is developed through 6G technology, which promises highly faster connectivity with an ultra-low latency profile. The next-generation infrastructured network ensures hassle-free communication between wearable devices and appliances, intelligent sensors, and treatment providers. For since, the real-time flow of health information provides such patients with the doctor's immediate diagnoses and lengthy treatments that give further scope for personal healthcare services to such patients (Wikström et al., 2020).
2. Remote Medical Consultation: The above connectivity through 6G will make remote medical consultancy feasible through allowing residents to be in their homes consulting the healthcare specialists. Many video conferencing and telemedicine platforms facilitate the possibility of contacting doctors remotely using virtual scenarios. Such consultancy would only enable diagnosis, treatment, follow-up, among many others, without a direct visit to hospitals. And this makes the accessing easy and less stressful on normal approaches for health delivery with special advantages for aged clients or immobile patients through reduced burden on normal health infrastructures (Banafaa et al., 2023).
3. In real-time, health tracking: The wearables that contain intelligent sensors are all the time keeping track of the vital signs and activity level, among many other vital health metrics. They stream real-time health data from healthcare providers in a cloud where they may search and find trends or anomalies which they can do early intervention. In that way, the innovative system of the health-

care system at Tokyo would empower people with the information needed to stay proactive toward their health care, away from complications and towards successful treatment (Qadir et al., 2023).

4. Customized Treatment Programs: The 6G technology is embedded with a more efficient, patient-specific health delivery in the city of Tokyo. There are AI algorithms that feed in vast data that would range from the genetic profiles to lifestyle specifics to bring about custom-tailored specific treatment programs for patients. Satisfaction increases as well, and the general health deliverables are positive with health costs decreased over time in the future (Chhabra et al., 2023).
5. Benefits and Results: The 6G-healthcare technology in Tokyo offers a bundle of advantages to the community and health service providers. Among some of the benefits that individuals can avail themselves of from using such 6G healthcare innovation in Tokyo include improvement in access to healthcare services, empowering patients through providing telemedicine services, and strict preventive care through exercising regular health check-up practices (Nayak & Patgiri, 2021). This ensures that Tokyo succeeds in healthier and stronger city development in terms of resilient building in using technological tool and responding to public concerns on health.

Figure 4. Intelligent healthcare system using 6G

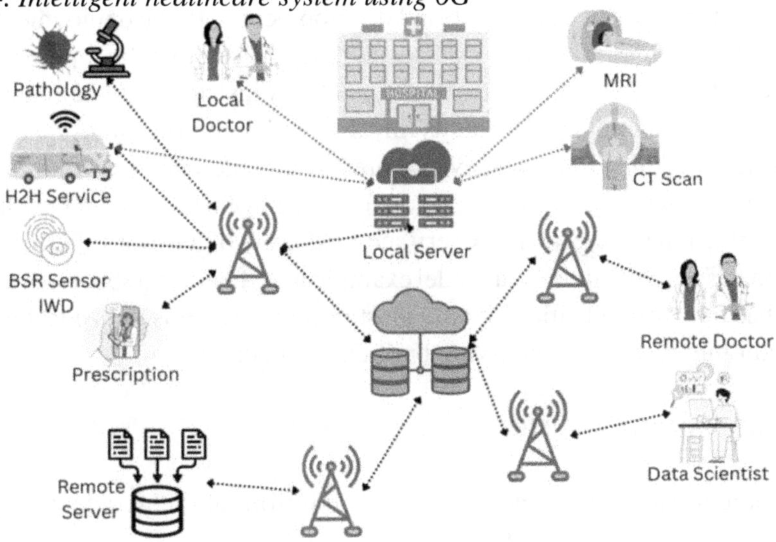

(Source: Author)

The plans on the part of Tokyo in order to extend the capabilities on intelligent health forward in future also look promising with incorporation through emergent technologies with enlargement in provision of service telemedicine. Future efforts likely would be over health interoperability, data safety, and protection measures, though this would not be uncommon for institutions and technology specialists involved. Innovation emerging out of healthcare in this space would offer a foundation to develop similar elsewhere about what the impact the technology 6G may have when it comes to healthy lives and excellent well-being.

4.3 Singapore

Singapore is an innovation city-state, leading on rapid urban development and innovative change. Looking strategically at technology use in enhancing the lifestyle of cities, Singapore has been working on smart city solutions within each sector. The idea behind all this is working towards sustainability and efficiency for its citizens to improve the quality of their lives (Allam & Jones, 2021). Singapore utilizes every modern technology that comes around, from 6G if this is ever developed in the future, to realize all the benefits that can accrue in the operationalization and delivery of services in cities. In that regards, these embrace more of data-based decisions and city infrastructure management; more still, city systems will even be more resilient than ever before. The city-state is a living laboratory for the innovative use of city technologies that creates global investment attractiveness and catalyzes partnership in the pursuit of research and development with the deployment of new solutions (Wikström et al., 2020). Qadir et al. (2023) assert that Singapore addresses resource constraints and environmental sustainability through scalable and adaptable intelligent city technologies despite its tiny size and high urban density. Singapore is a benchmark setter towards an even more sustainable city built with integrated solutions in the planning to transportation followed by healthcare and public safety and environmental management. A very successful use of innovative intelligent city innovation has put Singapore as a model example for other urban spaces, in the world where it has transformed cities into the most efficient systems with a technological life brought into resilience and living built environments.

4.3.1 Autonomous Vehicles

Singapore has also positioned itself at the forefront of the world when it comes to autonomous vehicles and further capitalizes on 6G for transportation innovation. The city-state's use of AVs demonstrates this city-state's willingness to embrace new technologies that form part of its urban mobility solutions.

1. Testing and Deployment: The ultra-low latency, as well as high reliability, of the 6G network is providing end-to-end communication for AVs with other vehicles and the infrastructure in real-time-a necessity to ensure safe navigation and efficient operation in cities-in a well-tested and deployed state in Singapore using 6G-based autonomous vehicles.
2. Infrastructure Readiness: Dedicated lanes and zones built with the integration of autonomous vehicles in mind. Most of this lanes and zones have equipped and enhanced sensors as well as smart traffic management, giving efficient and optimal movement so safety can be promoted especially when the road will not just be occupied by traditional modes but by the introduction of Autonomous Vehicles.
3. Increased Security and Efficiency: Through 6G technology, security and efficiency in the transport network for Singapore increase. AVs can act within a millisecond while making safe decisions, relying on real-time data obtained from other vehicles and infrastructure in order to minimize traffic congestion. This approach enhances mobility in cities, paving a way for sustainable, technologically innovative transportation solutions worldwide (Gera et al., 2023; Wikström et al., 2020).

Future would continue scaling up all the existing activities of autonomous vehicles in Singapore, develop new uses for it, and push scaled deployments all over the Singapore city-state. Future would push interoperability development between the autonomous vehicle and smart city infrastructures or perhaps a variety of navigation systems fueled by AI; regulatory will become a bigger part where the legal frameworks are going to evolve to accommodate greater autonomy functionalities.

The future of urban mobility further shines light on some smart city innovations via Singapore's autonomous vehicles. 6G and the embracement of innovation-friendly environments are testament to Singapore's commitment toward sustainable urban development and resilient transportation solutions for its ever-growing population.

4.3.2 Augmented Reality (AR) for Tourism

Singapore has embraced the AR technology enthusiastically and infused the sector of tourism with 6G connectivity by transforming most of the central tourist attractions into immersive experiences (See Figure 5). The initiative therefore has been a testimony on how Singapore would assimilate technology with cultural heritage to enable better engagements of visitors with more experience.

1. Integration with AR Technology: Singapore will be interacting and engaging the tourist while touring historical and cultural places through seamless connectivity of 6G. It will be accessed by the visitor in terms of AR glasses or on mobile devices by virtue of AR applications with virtual reconstructions and overlays about historical events and structures. In this way, old-fashioned sightseeing tourism will now become a learning experience for them that provides substantial knowledge of the richness of culture in Singapore (Islam et al., 2024; Al Amin et al., 2023).
2. Informed Tourism Interactivity: Through 6G-connected AR technology, Singapore provides for a very interactive relationship among visitors. The visitor achieves a comprehensive knowledge experience about Singapore's historical past. Looking at the historical landmarks and museums becomes possible from angles that may not have been considered before by simple observation due to the inclusion of interaction and AR technology in place. Such historical facts and cultural information might have deeper meanings attached to it and can thus make understanding it more engaging (Islam et al., 2024).
3. Cultural Heritage Promotion. AR for tourism in Singapore supports visitors and is significantly important for the preservation and promotion of cultural heritage. Virtual reconstructions and storytelling techniques using immersive AR preserve historical sites and artifacts so that future generations can benefit from Singapore's cultural heritage legacy (Qadir et al., 2023).
4. Technological Advancements: Ultra-high-speed connectivity, minimal latency, 6G technology enables more effective utilization of AR applications and allows for real-time interactions with AR content, smoother transitions between virtual and real environments, and high definition visuals overlays that bring it closer to reality and make it a worthwhile learning experience (Banafaa et al., 2023; Qadir et al., 2023).
5. Future Development: Singapore develops innovations in AR technology applied to tourism and identifies more applications and expanded accessibility in its tourism ecosystem through the use of AR. Multisensory experience AR, integration with AI that provides customized tours, collaboration with local artists and historians in creating engaging AR contents, are some future developments.

Figure 5. Singapore's AR approach in tourism

(Source: NXT Interactive, 2023)

The adoption of 6G-based AR technology in tourism by Singapore has made it the leader in Smart City technologies globally. Initiatives by Singapore come with a new standard for this kind of tourism: with technological advancement in cultural tourism, making it a stronghold to showcase change AR can bring regarding the improvement of experiences of tourists visiting various places.

4.4 Helsinki, Finland

Helsinki is one of the most innovative cities in Europe. This city is characterized by a forward-looking attitude toward sustainability and innovation. Advanced technologies have been incorporated into every sphere of this city, which has embarked on a process of transformation to achieve efficiency and elevate QoL for citizens. Environmental sustainability is the core of the smart city strategy. Other efforts include carbon reduction on aspects of energy-efficient building constructions and renewable energy, supplemented with smart grids that align to use the most at different points in time for any available data (Gera et al., 2023). These set into practice green practices that put the city into its posture for resilience against ecological concerns. Technology integration provides an excellent backbone for developing smart cities, as portrayed with Helsinki. The city is using the most advanced technologies available, such as the 6G innovations immediately when they become available in the markets, in order to transform public transport, make more complex traffic management systems, and find solutions to sustainable mobility.

Thus, Helsinki faces its challenges successfully in the urban space and the city itself is flexible and prepared for the future (Chhabra et al., 2023).

Since it is an innovation hub, the status of Helsinki further emphasizes that it is a leader among smart cities. The city is considered to draw startups, big research institutions, international business corporations to initiate pioneering work on the big problem of the city through effective collaboration (Islam et al., 2024). This collaborative ecosystem makes encouraging creativity and some proactive solutions empowering not only its citizens but also the businesses located within its boundaries. The other thing this city has underlined is that the projects related to innovation within this city require huge citizen engagement and participation according to Gera et al., 2023. This channel ensures integration of technological change into community desires and hopes. This atmosphere of trust and accountability leads to the fact that all the innovation solutions for cities are all-inclusive and responsive to every issue existing within the challenging divergence in cities. Helsinki has become very popular international in terms of intelligent urban solutions and will remain good examples of suitable and technologically advanced city development. Helsinki shows, in a holistic approach in innovation and sustainability, an approach toward building resilience and livability in cities for environmental stewardship through new technology in the modern city landscape.

4.4.1 Environmental Monitoring

Helsinki has taken innovation in environmental monitoring to heart with a state-of-art system deployed powered by 6G technology. This manifests the commitment of the city to sustainability and proactive environment management.

1. Dense-Wireless Sensor Network Helsinki's environment monitoring network is a smartly scattered intelligent sensor throughout the whole city. The sensors were developed to collect information in unison over diverse environmental conditions such as air quality, noise levels, and even water conditions. The advent of 6G will increase efficiency and dependability associated with data transmission as information will be fast and secured to be transmitted to hubs (Wikström et al., 2020).
2. AI-based Analytics: The data would be analyzed and processed with advanced AI algorithms to ensure that patterns or trends are detected, and actionable insights about conditions under environmental conditions in the cities of Helsinki are determined. More generally, this kind of analytical capability is allowed to a city planner and environment-agency decision-makers to base any decision on evidence generated concerning interventions that could eventually produce

an improvement in quality at the environmental level for humans and public health purposes respectively (Islam et al., 2024; Gera et al., 2023).

3. Timer interventions: With such a high-speed data transmission capability of 6G technology, it is very useful in making time interventions. This will make Helsinki to act quickly in case of sudden environmental issues caused by increased air pollution and noise pollution. This shall make the environment more sustainable, and there will be more QoL among its residents (Gera et al., 2023).
4. Urban Resilience: Helsinki's 6G-based environmental monitoring depicts its vision of building a resilient and sustainable city. This use of technology for monitoring and managing environmental parameters will set an example for cities looking to reduce their ecological footprint and enhance urban livability through data-driven decisions (Banafaa et al., 2023).
5. Future Perspective: Helsinki will keep moving on towards environmental monitoring and towards sustainability. The future release would comprise sensor network growth, integrated environment parameters, and AI capability enhancement by improving resource usage and further environment conservation. In this version, Helsinki again leads the world by taking the position of innovation in developing the smart city solutions which brought environmental stewardship through technology.

4.4.2 Smart Buildings

Its vision of becoming one of the world's cities puts Helsinki at the forefront to integrate 6G technology for efficiency and functionality towards optimizing the efficiency of the buildings. That is taking gigantic strides in a way of conserving energy and providing comfort in occupancy .

1. IoT-Based Building Automation System: The IoT-enabled devices are used by the smart buildings of Helsinki. They are inter-related through the 6G network. The sensors and actuators of these buildings take cognizance of its condition and regulate the conditions of lighting, heating and cooling, which will be updated in real time constantly. As such, those environmental settings are changed dynamically so that comfort will be reached with maximum minimal energy consumption. With this pre-emptive management, it saves money too by ensuring an efficient use of resources with its conservation for sustainable use (Al Amin et al., 2023).
2. Seamless Device Communication: The technology of 6G promotes seamless communication between devices in intelligent buildings with high speed and low latency. The real-time data exchange ensures that changes in environmental conditions and occupancy patterns meet with quick responses. For example,

lighting and HVAC systems could adjust their lighting and temperature levels, so that they use only when and where needed. This increases the energy efficiency and improves overall operational building efficiency.

3. Elevated User Experience: The smart buildings of Helsinki with 6G-enabled IoT technologies offer elevated user experience for the inhabitants. They have personalized comfort conditions and better indoor environmental quality, hence building an efficient as well as comfortable living environment. Further, building operators receive actionable insights into patterns of energy use and system performance for energy optimization further and planning of maintenance works (Banafaa et al., 2023).
4. Sustainability and Cost Savings: 6G intelligent buildings are part of the way Helsinki walks towards sustainability and resilience. Intelligent building automation has enabled an environmental footprint reduction and economical efficiency for both building owners and users with reduced energy consumption, thereby lower operating costs. This dual benefit supports the overall strategic visions of Helsinki's future sustainable urban development and is a shining example for cities wanting to implement high-tech solutions for smart and efficient building management (Chhabra et al., 2023; Wikström et al., 2020).
5. Future Directions: Moving forward, Helsinki will continue having more intelligent buildings and implementing new innovative technologies to further improve the standards of living in cities. Future innovations will be targeted at predictive maintenance, integration of renewable energy, and advanced connectivity solutions that address changing needs in building management. In this way, Helsinki innovates and intelligently invests in its infrastructure as it continues to redefine what sustainability in an urban setting is, and what a smart city can be.

5 FUTURE PROSPECTS AND CHALLENGES

This lays the landscape of opportunity and challenge, which will form the future trajectory of innovative city development as cities take a step toward integration of 6G technology in their urban space. The section considers prospects and critical hurdles likely to shape adoption and implementation of 6G technology in urban settings. From infrastructure requirements to data privacy concerns, regulations, and more, understanding these is necessary for navigating the complexities inherent in the ushering-in process for a new dimension of connectivity and innovation embedded in initiatives for innovative cities (Refer to Figure 6).

5.1 Infrastructure

The deployment of 6G technology for use within urban environments needs much higher investments in inflicting on the infrastructure requirements that need to be designed for advanced capabilities. This includes the deployment of new communication towers, which are now enabled with ultra-high-speed connectivity and upscaling of existing networks to support the scale of connectivity that 6G entails. Cities aspiring to implement 6G should draw from examples like small cell networks and millimeter-wave technology (Wikström et al., 2020). The small cell networks were tested in cities such as Tokyo and Seoul to improve coverage and capacity in highly populated areas to provide reliable IoT services and high-speed applications. Policies will define the development of infrastructure for 6G. Finland and Singapore have also streamlined policies when it comes to spectrum allocation and infrastructure deployment. In Finland, the regulatory framework is preferred over spectrum planning to allow support for public and private deployments while ensuring coordination in the deployment of 6G infrastructure in cities and rural areas. Some of the major challenges of 6G infrastructure are infrastructure resilience and scalability; hence, the process requires an integrated effort of telecommunications firms, urban planners, and government agencies (Banafaa et al., 2023). Such collaborations are the basis for finding solutions to issues like tower zoning regulations, environmental impact assessments, and intelligent infrastructure integration into the existing system of the city. Well-designed infrastructure is required for the effective functioning of ideas like smart city applications under the power of 6G technology. For example, smart traffic management in Helsinki; the advanced infrastructural facility allows real-time data processing for optimal flow and decongesting. These images demonstrate how strategic investment in infrastructure can unlock the full potential of 6G and enhance the efficiency, sustainability, and QoL of its citizens living in the city (Gera et al., 2023).

5.2 Data Privacy

With increased connectivity and the ability to generate more data through revolutionary 6G technology, cities have increased concerns regarding data privacy and security. This includes very stringent measures for securing sensitive information, especially where massive IoT device networks necessitate ultra-high-speed connectivity with real-time data processing. This calls for the need for establishing strong frameworks and policies in the era of 6G to fit into the new challenges that have been created by the innovative city environments. For instance, Singapore and Seoul put data protection laws in the city. These laws require an encryption standard, and using the data minimization practice keeps the personal data of those obtained from the IoT sensors and devices safely collected and processed; hence reduced cyber threats and unauthorized access into the system (Banafaa et al., 2023).

More proactive approaches to building such effective data privacy frameworks may include open data handling policies and mechanisms for user consent. User-centric models of data governance are among the examples that help control how resident data is used and shared in an urban ecosystem, as with initiatives by Helsinki City. Cities embracing 6G should also comply with global standards on data privacy, such as the General Data Protection Regulation (GDPR) in the European Union (Chhabra et al., 2023). Such regulations require the handling of data using anonymization techniques and access controls to respect the rights of citizens to privacy while encouraging innovation in urban services. Proactive care of data privacy ensures sensitive information while inspiring public confidence in 6G-enabled intelligent city initiatives. Cities, being focused on principles of privacy-by-design, and also risk assessment, will therefore offer a secure and open digital environment. This will emerge as the platform for sustainable urban development and inclusive growth.

5.3 Regulatory Frameworks

For 6G technology, strong regulatory frameworks will be necessary to balance innovation with protection of public interests. Policymakers should interact with the industry stakeholders to create a set of well-articulated regulations and standards to support the responsible takeoff of 6G and face the critical challenges of regulatory (Wikström et al., 2020). Spectrum allocation will be one of the main aspects of 6G regulatory frameworks. The adequate spectrum bands required by bandwidth-intensive networks in 6G will have to be reserved by cities. For example, Japan and South Korea have dedicated frequency bands to 6G research and development in such a way that will make telecommunication service providers provide high capacity networks, to be utilized in ultra-high speed connectivity. Interoperability standards: Coordinated technical specifications and protocols will ensure smooth information exchange related to data transfers by various 6G-enabled devices and systems in intelligent city environments. This will facilitate integrated urban management systems where aggregated data from any source may be analyzed to optimize city services, operation efficiency, and improvement.

Data governance and cybersecurity considerations are also important for the regulation framework for 6G. Cities would be required to have stringent provisions of protection for sensitive information they receive from IoT devices as well as other digital services. Some of the main requirements for such measures will include encryption, anonymization, and safe transmission protocols. All these will assure citizen's privacy and make citizens build trust on reliability and security of applications empowered by 6G (Chhabra et al., 2023). Therefore, an open and responsive regulatory framework promotes innovation and ensures equal and just access to sophisticated digital services for the heterogeneous urban community. This enables cities to take proactive measures to develop an enabling environment without encountering regulatory challenges related to spectrum management, interoperability, and cybersecurity while adopting 6G technology into everyday urban life. This strategic approach helps accelerate the development of urban areas and ensures the resilience and sustainability of smart cities in the digital age.

Figure 6. Digital ecosystem of smart city

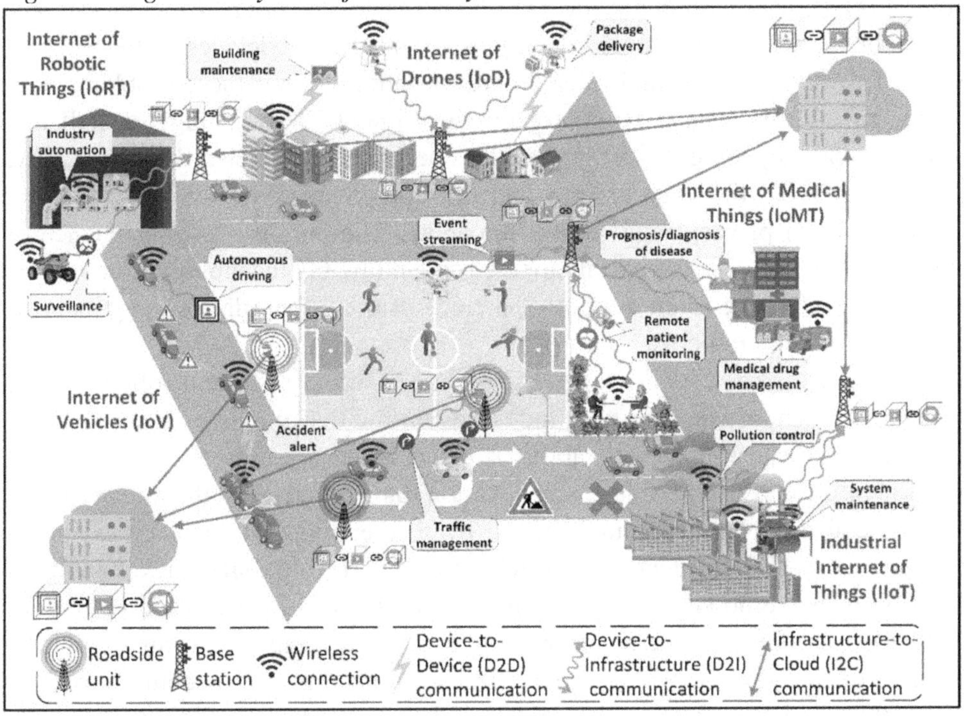

(Source: Ismail & Buyya, 2022)

Navigating this road to a future that will be 6G-enabled for intelligent cities needs proper consideration of those prospects and challenges. As resilient infrastructure is invested upon, strong data privacy, and regulatory frameworks are brought in to support the environment, cities can tap on the transformational potential provided by 6G technologies and thus improve urban living conditions, sustainability, and economic prosperity. Embracing innovation with safeguarding the public interest will be a key approach in realizing intelligent cities as vibrant centers of connectivity, efficiency, and inclusivity in the digital age.

6 CONCLUSION

Its ultra-high speed connectivity, negligible latency and comprehensive device connectivity, positions 6G technology, as the future frontier into the development of innovative cities. This paper examines several case studies concerning the advantage that pioneering cities that implemented 6G have earned, and, in return, promoted innovation in its urban management. With that said, here are considerable challenges that enter the book into effective utilization in urban space. The two biggest challenges are the development of infrastructure, which calls for large investments in new communication towers and network upgrades to meet high-speed connectivity demands and deploy thousands of IoT devices. Cities such as Seoul, Tokyo, Singapore, and Helsinki are beginning to face these problems with proper strategic planning and infrastructure investment. The other biggest challenge is the data privacy issue. With more devices becoming connected through 6G, the concerns of protecting data privacy and full compliance with the very stringent requirements of privacy regulation came about. The building and sustenance of public trust in such smart city initiatives, powered by 6G technology, can only be achieved by effective frameworks that include user consent, data encryption, and safe transmission protocols.

Regulatory frameworks will be essential in ensuring a smooth rollout of 6G. Policymakers should consult with industries on the definitions of issues such as allocation of spectrum, interoperability standards, and cyber guidelines. It will be an issue of clear, dynamic rules for innovation that will advance the public's interests while also providing equitable access by different populations in cities toward digital services. The influence of 6G technology will revolutionize the urban life of cities because it embodies the future of smart cities worldwide. Working through the challenges of infrastructure, prioritizing data privacy, and structuring supportive regulatory frameworks will help cities realize their transformative potential to enhance connectivity, efficiency, and sustainability in cities. The role of 6G technology will be seen to play a greater role in furthering the innovative city agenda in enhancing QoL among its residents as cities develop and become better.

7 FUTURE PROSPECTS

As cities and their governments embrace 6G technology and all the transformative capabilities it can present, there are some truly exciting prospects for the urban future. This section expands on some of the big areas where 6G is going to impact fundamentally, and the opportunities or challenges they bring along with them.

7.1 Enhanced Connectivity and IoT Integration

Evolution to 6G brings promises of revolution in terms of connectivity by means of faster data speeds, minimal latency, and reliability unimaginable until now. This will enable seamless massive integration of IoT devices all over urban environments. In a city where smart sensors monitor real-time flow of traffic and environment in real-time and modify infrastructure dynamically based on predictive analytics, this will be the level of connectivity that may pave the way for much more intelligent, responsive cities capable of resource optimization and public safety enhancement, towards overall QoL improvements.

7.2 Empowering AI and Machine Learning

6G's ultra-high-speed connectivity with low latency will enable AI and machine learning applications to perform at their optimal best. AI algorithms can process massive amounts of data in real-time, making possible predictive analytics that predict traffic patterns, optimize energy consumption, and improve emergency response systems. AI-powered health diagnostics and tailored treatment prescription will become more easily achievable with 6G high-speed data transmission in secure real-time health data flow. The efficiency in areas such as healthcare will advance, as well as revolutionize how cities run themselves and the services that residents receive.

7.3 Augmented Reality (AR) and Virtual Reality (VR) Experiences

The integration of 6G with AR and VR will change the face of cities in terms of experiences - to provide immersive simulations and interactive environments. For example, virtual city tours, whereby residents and tourists may go through historical landmarks, attend cultural events, or envision proposed urban developments in real-time, can be developed. Navigation tools empowered by AR will be contextualized, thereby improving the ability to navigate and accessibility in cities. Such applications will enhance educational and cultural experiences and help support tourism activities, contributing to economic development and the preservation of cultural heritage.

7.4 Sustainable and Resilient Urban Infrastructure

6G technology will be a critical enabler for the promotion of sustainable and resilient urban infrastructure. 6G-based smart grids will help optimize energy distribution by harmoniously integrating renewable energy sources with low carbon footprints. Advanced environmental monitoring systems, based on real-time data, will proactively address air and water quality issues to make cities healthier and more livable. In addition, integration of autonomous vehicles and intelligent transportation systems will seamlessly improve mobility, reduce congestion, and build overall resilience to climate change and other shocks.

7.5 Addressing Challenges and Building Resilience

Although it is promising, 6G technology in smart cities will still have a certain number of challenges in terms of wide adoption. These range from very significant investments in infrastructure to data privacy and security as well as the adaptation of regulatory frameworks that foster innovation and protect public interests. This challenge requires cities and policymakers closely working with industry stakeholders for effective navigation toward fair access to advanced digital services and sustainable urban development.

With the integration of 6G technologies, city development will undoubtedly unlock bright prospects for innovations. The improved connectivity shall enable the empowerment of AI and ML, AR/VR experiences, and creative infrastructure in sustainable design as the cities unlock new and innovative opportunities for its resident through enhanced QoL. Strategic planning, partnership, and innovation will remain pivotal to the full achievement of the potential of 6G in designing future cities.

REFERENCES

Al Amin, A., Hong, J., Bui, V. H., & Su, W. (2023). Emerging 6G/B6G wireless communication for the power infrastructure in smart cities: Innovations, challenges, and future perspectives. *Algorithms*, 16(10), 474. DOI: 10.3390/a16100474

Allam, Z., & Jones, D. S. (2021). Future (post-COVID) digital, smart and sustainable cities in the wake of 6G: Digital twins, immersive realities and new urban economies. *Land Use Policy*, 101, 105201. DOI: 10.1016/j.landusepol.2020.105201

Alsharif, M. H., Jahid, A., Kannadasan, R., & Kim, M. K. (2024). Unleashing the potential of sixth generation (6G) wireless networks in smart energy grid management: A comprehensive review. *Energy Reports*, 11, 1376–1398. DOI: 10.1016/j.egyr.2024.01.011

Banafaa, M., Shayea, I., Din, J., Azmi, M. H., Alashbi, A., Daradkeh, Y. I., & Alhammadi, A. (2023). 6G mobile communication technology: Requirements, targets, applications, challenges, advantages, and opportunities. *Alexandria Engineering Journal*, 64, 245–274. DOI: 10.1016/j.aej.2022.08.017

Chhabra, S., Aiden, M. K., Sabharwal, S. M., & Al-Asadi, M. (2023). 5G and 6G technologies for Smart City. In *Enabling Technologies for Effective Planning and Management in Sustainable Smart Cities* (pp. 335–365). Springer International Publishing. DOI: 10.1007/978-3-031-22922-0_14

Fadhil, A. M. (2023). Next-Generation Urban Intelligence: Integrating 6G Communication and Blockchain Technology for Smart City Advancements.

Farooq, M. S., Nadir, R. M., Rustam, F., Hur, S., Park, Y., & Ashraf, I. (2022). Nested Bee Hive: A conceptual multilayer architecture for 6G in futuristic sustainable smart cities. *Sensors (Basel)*, 22(16), 5950. DOI: 10.3390/s22165950 PMID: 36015707

Gera, B., Raghuvanshi, Y. S., Rawlley, O., Gupta, S., Dua, A., & Sharma, P. (2023). Leveraging AI-enabled 6G-driven IoT for sustainable smart cities. *International Journal of Communication Systems*, 36(16), e5588. DOI: 10.1002/dac.5588

Gupta, M., Ved, C., & Kumari, M. (2022). Emergence of Blockchain Applications with the 6G-Enabled IoT-Based Smart City. In *Blockchain for 6G-Enabled Network-Based Applications* (pp. 213–235). CRC Press. DOI: 10.1201/9781003264392-9

Han, H., Zhai, W., & Zhao, J. (2021). Smart city enabled by 5G/6G networks: An intelligent hybrid random access scheme. *arXiv preprint arXiv:2101.06421*.

Interactive, N. X. T. (2023). Augmented reality in Singapore: Navigating the landscape of innovation. Retrieved from: https://www.nxtinteractive.sg/blog/augmented-reality-in-singapore-navigating-the-landscape-of-innovation

Islam, S., Atallah, Z. A., Budati, A. K., Hasan, M. K., Kolandaisamy, R., & Nurhizam, S. (2024). *Mobile Networks Toward 5G/6G: Network Architecture, Opportunities and Challenges in Smart City*. IEEE Open Journal of the Communications Society.

Ismail, L., & Buyya, R. (2022). Artificial intelligence applications and self-learning 6G networks for smart cities digital ecosystems: Taxonomy, challenges, and future directions. *Sensors (Basel)*, 22(15), 5750. DOI: 10.3390/s22155750 PMID: 35957307

Jamil, S. U., Khan, M. A., & ur Rehman, S. (2020). Intelligent task off-loading and resource allocation for 6G smart city environment. In *2020 IEEE 45th Conference on Local Computer Networks (LCN)* (pp. 441-444). IEEE.

Javed, A. R., Shahzad, F., Rehman, S., Zikria, Y. B., Razzak, I., Jalil, Z., & Xu, G. (2022). Future smart cities: Requirements, emerging technologies, applications, challenges, and future aspects. *Cities (London, England)*, 129, 103794. DOI: 10.1016/j.cities.2022.103794

Ji, B., Wang, Y., Song, K., Li, C., Wen, H., Menon, V. G., & Mumtaz, S. (2021). A survey of computational intelligence for 6G: Key technologies, applications and trends. *IEEE Transactions on Industrial Informatics*, 17(10), 7145–7154. DOI: 10.1109/TII.2021.3052531

Kamruzzaman, M. M. (2022). Key technologies, applications and trends of internet of things for energy-efficient 6G wireless communication in smart cities. *Energies*, 15(15), 5608. DOI: 10.3390/en15155608

Kamruzzaman, M. M., Hossin, M. A., Alruwaili, O., Alanazi, S., Alruwaili, M., Alshammari, N., Alaerjan, A., & Zaman, R. (2022). IoT-Oriented 6G Wireless Network System for Smart Cities. *Computational Intelligence and Neuroscience*, 2022(1), 1874436. DOI: 10.1155/2022/1874436 PMID: 35990150

Kaur, J., & Khan, M. A. (2022). Sixth generation (6G) wireless technology: An overview, vision, challenges and use cases. In *2022 IEEE region 10 symposium (TENSYMP)* (pp. 1-6). IEEE.

Khattak, S. B. A., Nasralla, M. M., & Rehman, I. U. (2022). The role of 6g networks in enabling future smart health services and applications. In *2022 IEEE International Smart Cities Conference (ISC2)* (pp. 1-7). IEEE.

Konhäuser, W. (2021). Digitalization in Buildings and Smart Cities on the Way to 6G. *Wireless Personal Communications*, 121(2), 1289–1302. DOI: 10.1007/s11277-021-09069-9

Kulkarni, R., & Kulkarni, S. (2021). How 6G has an influence on smart cities: An overview. *International Journal of Engineering Research & Technology (Ahmedabad)*, 10(5), 258–275.

Kumari, A., Gupta, R., & Tanwar, S. (2021). Amalgamation of blockchain and IoT for smart cities underlying 6G communication: A comprehensive review. *Computer Communications*, 172, 102–118. DOI: 10.1016/j.comcom.2021.03.005

Lu, Y., & Zheng, X. (2020). 6G: A survey on technologies, scenarios, challenges, and the related issues. *Journal of Industrial Information Integration*, 19, 100158. DOI: 10.1016/j.jii.2020.100158

Mishra, P., & Singh, G. (2023). 6G-IoT framework for sustainable smart city: Vision and challenges. In *Sustainable Smart Cities: Enabling Technologies, Energy Trends and Potential Applications* (pp. 97–117). Springer International Publishing. DOI: 10.1007/978-3-031-33354-5_5

Murroni, M., Anedda, M., Fadda, M., Ruiu, P., Popescu, V., Zaharia, C., & Giusto, D. (2023). 6G—Enabling the New Smart City: A Survey. *Sensors (Basel)*, 23(17), 7528. DOI: 10.3390/s23177528 PMID: 37687986

Nayak, S., & Patgiri, R. (2021). 6G communication technology: A vision on intelligent healthcare. *Health informatics: A computational perspective in healthcare*, 1-18.

Qadir, Z., Le, K. N., Saeed, N., & Munawar, H. S. (2023). Towards 6G Internet of Things: Recent advances, use cases, and open challenges. *ICT express, 9*(3), 296-312.

Salameh, A. I., & El Tarhuni, M. (2022). From 5G to 6G—Challenges, technologies, and applications. *Future Internet*, 14(4), 117. DOI: 10.3390/fi14040117

Shehab, M., Khattab, T., Kucukvar, M., & Trinchero, D. (2022). The role of 5G/6G networks in building sustainable and energy-efficient smart cities. In *2022 IEEE 7th International Energy Conference (ENERGYCON)* (pp. 1-7). IEEE.

Singh, P. R., Singh, V. K., Yadav, R., & Chaurasia, S. N. (2023). 6G networks for artificial intelligence-enabled smart cities applications: A scoping review. *Telematics and Informatics Reports*, 9, 100044. DOI: 10.1016/j.teler.2023.100044

Singh, S. K., Azzaoui, A., Choo, K. K. R., Yang, L. T., & Park, J. H. (2023). Articles A Comprehensive Survey on Blockchain for Secure IoT-enabled Smart City beyond 5G: Approaches, Processes, Challenges, and Opportunities. *Hum.-.Centric Comput. Inf. Sci*, 13, 51.

Singh, S. K., Jeong, Y. S., & Park, J. H. (2020). A deep learning-based IoT-oriented infrastructure for secure smart city. *Sustainable Cities and Society*, 60, 102252. DOI: 10.1016/j.scs.2020.102252

Singhal, S., Betgeri, S., & Singh, S. K. (2024). Strategies for Mitigating Security Concerns in IoT-Enabled Smart Cities. In *Secure and Intelligent IoT-Enabled Smart Cities* (pp. 239–273). IGI Global. DOI: 10.4018/979-8-3693-2373-1

Sinha, D. (2021).Metropolis Spotlight: Nota Is Transforming Traffic Management Systems With AI. Retrieved from: https://developer.nvidia.com/blog/metropolis-spotlight-nota-is-transforming-traffic-management-systems-with-ai/

Slimani, K., Khoulji, S., & Kerkeb, M. L. (2023). Advancements and challenges in energy-efficient 6G mobile communication network. In *E3S Web of Conferences* (Vol. 412, p. 01036). EDP Sciences. DOI: 10.1051/e3sconf/202341201036

Uusitalo, M. A., Rugeland, P., Boldi, M. R., Strinati, E. C., Demestichas, P., Ericson, M., Fettweis, G. P., Filippou, M. C., Gati, A., Hamon, M.-H., Hoffmann, M., Latva-Aho, M., Parssinen, A., Richerzhagen, B., Schotten, H., Svensson, T., Wikstrom, G., Wymeersch, H., Ziegler, V., & Zou, Y. (2021). 6G vision, value, use cases and technologies from European 6G flagship project Hexa-X. *IEEE Access : Practical Innovations, Open Solutions*, 9, 160004–160020. DOI: 10.1109/ACCESS.2021.3130030

Wikström, G., Peisa, J., Rugeland, P., Johansson, N., Parkvall, S., Girnyk, M., & Da Silva, I. L. (2020). *Challenges and technologies for 6G. In 2020 2nd 6G wireless summit (6G SUMMIT)*. IEEE.

Chapter 2
Security and Privacy Challenges in 6G Enabled Smart City

Kapil Sharma
https://orcid.org/0000-0001-8244-8009
Chandigarh University, India

Nikhil Singh
NDIM, Delhi

ABSTRACT

The research report "Security and Privacy Challenges in 6G Enabled Smart City" delves into the transformative potential of 6G technology, anticipated to be commercially available by 2030, and its implications for smart cities. As cities become more reliant on Internet of Things (IoT) devices, artificial intelligence (AI), and big data analytics, 6G will offer unparalleled speed, bandwidth, and ultra-low latency, driving the evolution of smart cities. However, this technological advancement also brings significant security and privacy concerns that must be addressed to protect urban infrastructures and citizens' data.

1. INTRODUCTION

1.1 Smart City

A smart city is an urban area that leverages technology and data to improve the quality of life, enhance sustainability, and optimise the efficiency of city operations. The fundamental concept of a smart city revolves around the integration of infor-

DOI: 10.4018/979-8-3693-8029-1.ch002

mation and communication technologies (ICT) and the Internet of Things (IoT) to address urban challenges and create a more connected and sustainable environment.

IBM defines a smart city as one that utilises interconnected information to understand and control its operations, thereby optimising the use of limited resources. More broadly, a smart city uses a framework of ICT to create, deploy, and promote development practices aimed at addressing urban challenges. This framework is designed to build a technologically enabled infrastructure that supports sustainability and connectivity within the city.

Smart city technologies are increasingly playing a critical role in various aspects of city operations, including transportation, energy management, and infrastructure development. By integrating ICT and IoT, cities can enhance their systems and structures, making them smarter and more responsive to the needs of their residents.

1.2 Urban Evolution: The Impact of 6G on Smart Cities

As urbanisation accelerates and technological advancements continue to shape our world, cities are increasingly adopting innovative technologies to enhance infrastructure, improve quality of life, and promote sustainable development. One of the most transformative advancements on the horizon is the advent of 6G technology, which is expected to become commercially available by 2030. This next-generation wireless technology promises exceptional speeds, vast bandwidth, and ultra-low latency, which will revolutionise connectivity and enable a new era of smart cities. These smart cities will rely heavily on the integration of Internet of Things (IoT) devices, artificial intelligence (AI), and big data analytics to function efficiently and responsively. However, as these technologies proliferate, the importance of security and privacy in protecting urban infrastructures and citizens' data cannot be overstated.

The transition from 5G to 6G represents a significant leap in wireless communication technology, poised to address the limitations of its predecessor and introduce a host of groundbreaking capabilities. While 5G brought about significant advancements such as enhanced mobile broadband, ultra-reliable low-latency communication, and massive machine-type communication, 6G aims to push these boundaries even further. The evolution from 5G to 6G is characterised by the ambition to seamlessly merge the digital and physical worlds, creating a unified and immersive experience.

5G laid the groundwork by providing faster data speeds, improved network reliability, and lower latency compared to previous generations. It enabled the proliferation of Internet of Things (IoT) devices and supported the development of smart cities, autonomous vehicles, and advanced healthcare applications. However, 5G still faced challenges related to coverage, spectrum efficiency, and the capacity to support an ever-increasing number of connected devices.

6G is expected to overcome these challenges by leveraging higher frequency bands, such as terahertz (THz) waves, which offer greater bandwidth and faster data transfer rates. The deployment of 6G will involve advanced network architectures, including massive multiple-input multiple-output (MIMO) systems and intelligent reflecting surfaces (IRS), to enhance signal propagation and coverage. Additionally, 6G networks will incorporate cutting-edge technologies like artificial intelligence (AI) and machine learning (ML) to optimise network performance and adapt to dynamic environments in real-time.

1.3 Objectives of the Report

This report aims to provide a comprehensive analysis of the security and privacy challenges associated with the implementation of 6G technology in smart cities. The primary objectives are:

1. **To Explore Security Challenges:** Identify and examine the various security threats and vulnerabilities that 6G-enabled smart cities might face. This includes analysing potential attack vectors, understanding the implications of increased connectivity, and evaluating the security of IoT devices and network infrastructure.
2. **To Investigate Privacy Concerns:** Assess the privacy issues arising from the extensive data collection and processing in smart cities. This includes discussing the implications of data breaches, surveillance, and the ethical and legal considerations surrounding personal data protection.
3. **To Analyse Case Studies and Examples:** Provide real-world examples and case studies of current smart cities utilising advanced technologies. These examples will help illustrate the challenges and solutions implemented in different contexts.
4. **To Propose Mitigation Strategies:** Suggest practical solutions and strategies to address the identified security and privacy challenges. This will include advanced encryption techniques, AI and machine learning for threat detection, policy and regulatory frameworks, and public awareness initiatives.
5. **To Explore Future Directions:** Highlight emerging technologies and research areas that could further enhance security and privacy in 6G-enabled smart cities. This includes quantum communication, blockchain technology, and interdisciplinary research needs.

2. ADVANCED FEATURES OF 6G TECHNOLOGY

1. **Enhanced Data Rate and Efficiency:** 6G is expected to deliver a tenfold increase in data rate, density, and energy efficiency compared to 5G. This will enable faster and more efficient communication.
2. **Lower Latency:** The latency in 6G is expected to drop below 1 millisecond, making it suitable for real-time applications that require instantaneous responses.
3. **Improved Mobility and Spectrum Efficiency:** Mobility and spectrum efficiency in 6G are anticipated to be three times better than in 5G, supporting a more dynamic and efficient wireless communication environment.
4. **Expanded Coverage and Reliability:** 6G aims to extend coverage to 99% of locations and increase reliability from 99.9% in 5G to 99.999%, ensuring more consistent and dependable connectivity.
5. **Advanced Positioning Accuracy:** The positioning error in 6G is expected to be reduced to centimetre-level precision, a significant improvement over the metre-level accuracy of 5G.
6. **Receiver Sensitivity:** 6G will enhance receiver sensitivity to better than –130 dBm, which allows for better signal reception and quality even in challenging environments.
7. **New Applications:** 6G will support emerging applications such as holographic communication, wireless brain-computer interactions, drone taxis, and the Internet of Robots, marking a significant leap in technological innovation.

3. 6G's ROLE IN SHAPING SMART CITIES

1. **Advanced Sensing and Monitoring**: 6G's ability to support high-resolution sensing and real-time monitoring will enable more effective management of city infrastructure, such as traffic systems, public safety, and environmental monitoring. This will allow for better decision-making and more responsive city management.
2. **Autonomous Vehicles and Transportation**: 6G will play a critical role in the evolution of autonomous vehicles (AVs) by providing the necessary data speed, low latency, and comprehensive coverage required for AVs to navigate urban environments safely and efficiently. Real-time 4D mapping and networked sensors will enhance traffic management and parking systems, thereby improving the flow of transportation in smart cities.
3. **Sustainability and Environmental Monitoring**: The integration of global sensor networks powered by 6G will enable continuous monitoring of environmental conditions in urban areas. This will aid in the development of smart

homes and cities that adapt to environmental changes and optimise resource usage, contributing to sustainability efforts.

4. **Enhanced Public Safety**: 6G's low latency and advanced communication capabilities will improve the responsiveness of emergency services, such as law enforcement and first responders. Real-time data collection and analysis will enable quicker and more informed decision-making during emergencies.
5. **Immersive Communication and Services**: 6G will introduce immersive communication experiences through technologies like augmented reality (AR) and holographic displays. These technologies will enhance urban experiences, from virtual tourism to remote healthcare services, making smart cities more connected and interactive.

Figure 1. Impact of 6G on smart city development

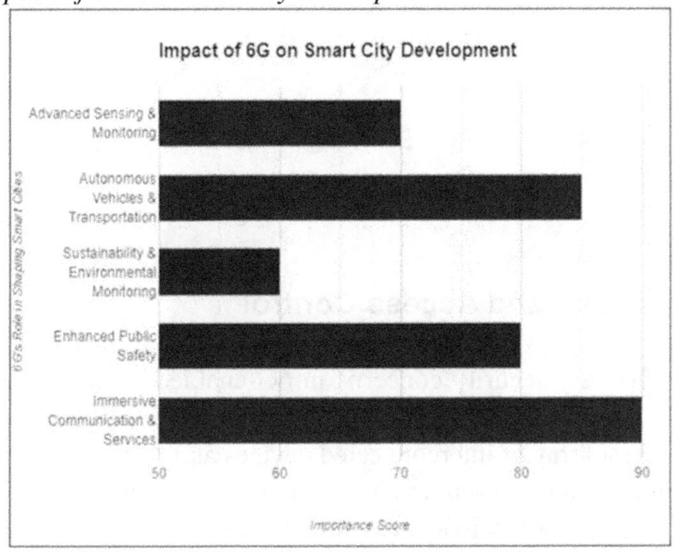

Source: Primary data, 2024

4. SECURITY CHALLENGES IN 6G-ENABLED SMART CITIES

The introduction of 6G technology promises transformative benefits for smart cities, including enhanced connectivity, ultra-low latency, and the ability to manage vast networks of interconnected devices. However, as these networks become increasingly integral to the functioning of smart cities, they also bring forth a range of security challenges that could undermine the safety, stability, and efficiency of urban infrastructures.

Figure 2. Security challenges in 6G-enabled smart cities

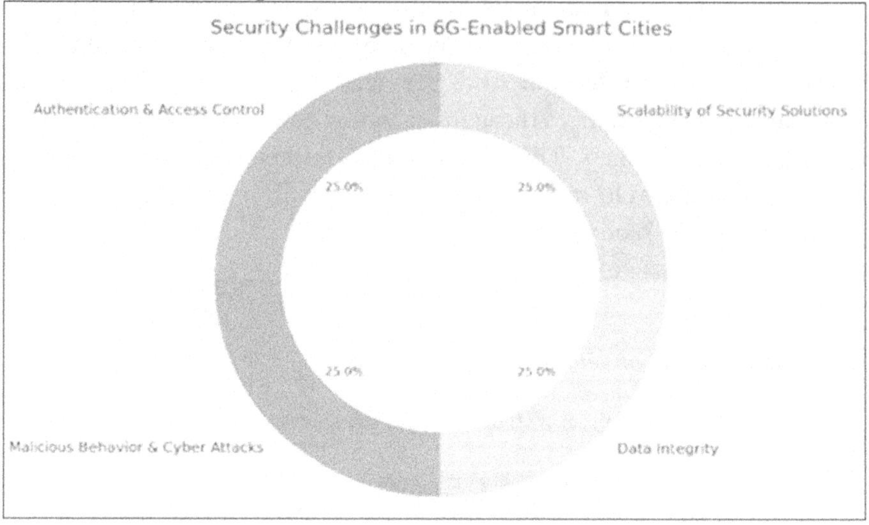

Source: Primary data, 2024

4.1 Authentication and Access Control

One of the primary security concerns in 6G-enabled smart cities is ensuring robust authentication and access control mechanisms. The complexity of managing access across a vast array of interconnected devices and systems makes traditional methods of authentication, such as passwords and basic encryption, inadequate. Unauthorised access could disrupt essential services like public transportation, energy management, or water supply, posing significant risks to public safety. For instance, attackers could gain control of traffic management systems, leading to traffic jams or accidents, or they could manipulate smart grid systems, potentially causing blackouts or other critical infrastructure failures (Khan et al., 2020).

To address these challenges, more advanced methods are needed, such as AI-driven identity verification, biometric authentication, and blockchain-based access control systems. These technologies can offer enhanced security, but they also require significant computational resources and may introduce new vulnerabilities that need to be addressed (Agiwal et al., 2023).

Figure 3. Flow chart

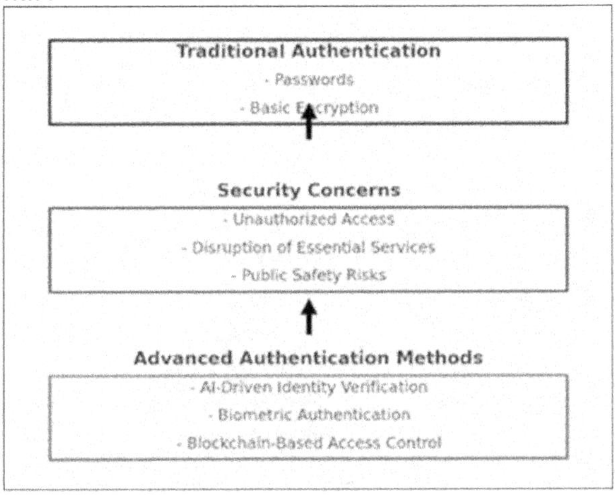

Source: Primary data, 2024

4.2 Malicious Behavior and Cyber Attacks

The complexity of 6G networks introduces new vectors for cyberattacks, which pose serious threats to the security of smart cities. Distributed Denial of Service (DDoS) and Man-in-the-Middle (MitM) attacks are of particular concern. DDoS attacks aim to overwhelm network resources by flooding the network with excessive traffic, rendering systems unavailable to legitimate users. In a smart city, such an attack could cripple critical services, such as emergency response systems, transportation networks, or utilities, leading to widespread disruption and potentially endangering lives (Mansoor et al., 2023).

MitM attacks involve intercepting communications between two parties to steal or alter information. Given the interconnected nature of 6G networks and their reliance on real-time data processing, they are particularly vulnerable to such attacks. For example, an attacker could intercept communications between autonomous vehicles and traffic management systems, leading to accidents or traffic disruptions. To mitigate these risks, it is crucial to implement robust encryption and authentication protocols and continuously monitor network traffic for signs of malicious activity (Khan et al., 2020).

Table 1. Type of attack and descriptions

Type of Attack	Description	Impact on Smart Cities	Mitigation Strategies
Distributed Denial of Service (DDoS)	Overwhelms network resources by flooding with excessive traffic.	Disrupts critical services like emergency response systems, transportation networks, and utilities.	Implementing robust network traffic management and anomaly detection.
Man-in-the-Middle (MitM)	Intercepts communications between two parties to steal or alter information.	Potential for accidents or traffic disruptions, especially in autonomous vehicles and real-time systems.	Using encryption, authentication protocols, and continuous network traffic monitoring.

Source: Primary data, 2024

4.3 Data Integrity

Maintaining data integrity in 6G-enabled smart cities is critical, as tampering with data can lead to incorrect decisions, malfunctioning systems, and potentially catastrophic failures in city management. Threats such as message alteration, session hijacking, and data diddling are particularly concerning in environments where real-time decision-making is essential. For example, if data used for managing traffic signals were altered, it could result in mismanagement of traffic flow, leading to congestion or accidents. Similarly, tampering with data in energy management systems could lead to power outages or damage to infrastructure (Mansoor et al., 2023).

The challenge lies in protecting data integrity while maintaining the speed and efficiency promised by 6G networks. This requires the use of advanced cryptographic techniques, such as blockchain-based systems, which can provide tamper-evident logs of all transactions and data exchanges. AI-driven anomaly detection systems can also be employed to monitor data flows in real-time, identifying and mitigating potential integrity breaches before they can cause harm (Khan et al., 2020).

Figure 4. Threats to data integrity in 6G-enabled smart cities

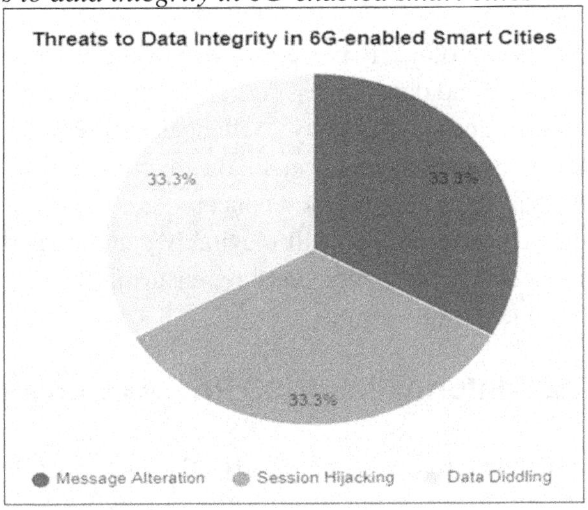

Source: Primary data, 2024

4.4 Scalability of Security Solutions

The vast number of devices and sensors deployed across smart cities necessitates security solutions that can scale efficiently. Traditional security approaches, which often rely on centralised management and fixed infrastructure, may not be feasible in such large-scale environments. In a 6G-enabled smart city, where billions of devices could be connected simultaneously, security mechanisms must be both scalable and adaptive to the dynamic nature of the network (Mansoor et al., 2023).

One potential solution is the use of AI-driven security protocols, which can adapt to changing network conditions and detect emerging threats in real-time. Federated learning, a type of machine learning where models are trained across multiple devices without sharing raw data, offers a scalable approach to improving security. However, these technologies also introduce new challenges, such as the need for substantial computational resources and the potential for adversarial attacks that exploit vulnerabilities in AI models. Blockchain-based methods, which provide decentralised and tamper-resistant records, are also being explored as a means of ensuring security in large-scale 6G networks, but their implementation in such a vast and resource-constrained environment remains complex (Agiwal et al., 2023).

5. PRIVACY CHALLENGES IN 6G-ENABLED SMART CITIES

The advent of 6G technology is poised to revolutionise smart cities, offering unparalleled connectivity and data processing capabilities. However, this increased capability comes with significant privacy challenges that need to be addressed to protect individuals' personal information in the hyper-connected environments of future urban landscapes. These privacy concerns are rooted in the handling of vast amounts of data that smart cities will inevitably generate and process. As 6G technology integrates deeply into everyday life, ensuring the privacy of this data becomes a paramount concern.

5.1 Channel State Information (CSI) Privacy Concerns

Channel State Information (CSI) is expected to play a crucial role in 6G networks, particularly in supporting personalised services and new applications through its ability to analyse and predict network conditions. While CSI can enhance network efficiency and user experience, its usage also introduces substantial privacy risks. The analysis of CSI data could potentially expose sensitive information about individuals, such as their location, movement patterns, and even specific behaviours, which could be inferred by malicious actors. Cigno et al. (2022) discuss how CSI-based sensing, while beneficial, poses significant threats to privacy. They suggest that without proper safeguards, the integration of CSI in 6G networks could lead to unauthorised surveillance and data breaches, thus compromising personal privacy. To mitigate these risks, they propose advanced privacy-preserving techniques, such as secure multiparty computation (SMPC) and encrypted inference methods, to ensure that while CSI is used for improving network services, individuals' privacy remains protected.

Figure 5. CSI privacy concerns in 6G networks

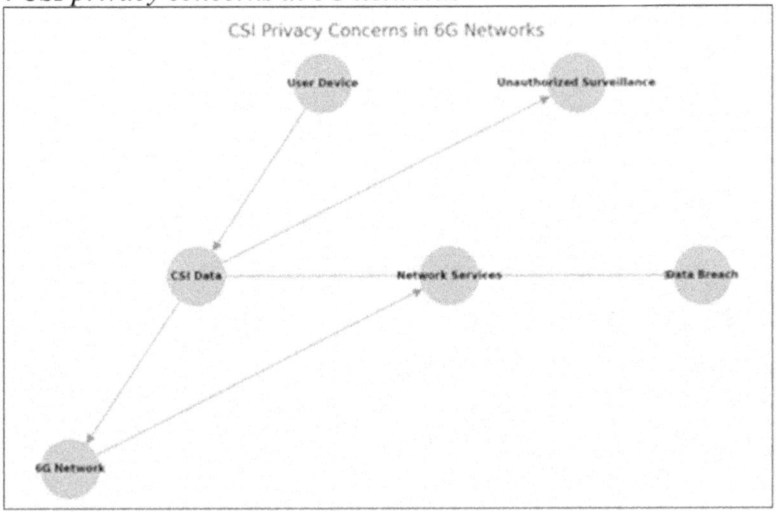

Source: Primary data, 2024

5.2 Privacy in Federated Learning for 6G-IoMT

Federated learning is another critical area in 6G, particularly in the context of the Internet of Medical Things (IoMT), where sensitive health data is processed and analysed. The nature of federated learning involves distributing the learning process across multiple devices, each holding pieces of data, to train a global model without centralising the data. However, this decentralised approach also poses privacy challenges, as the aggregation of data, even in its distributed form, can lead to potential privacy breaches. A CNN-based federated learning framework has been proposed to address these challenges, combining SMPC for secure aggregation and encrypted inference to maintain data privacy during model training (Zhang et al., 2023). This approach ensures that the global model is both accurate and privacy-preserving, which is crucial in medical applications where data sensitivity is paramount.

Figure 6. Privacy in federated learning for 6G-IoMT

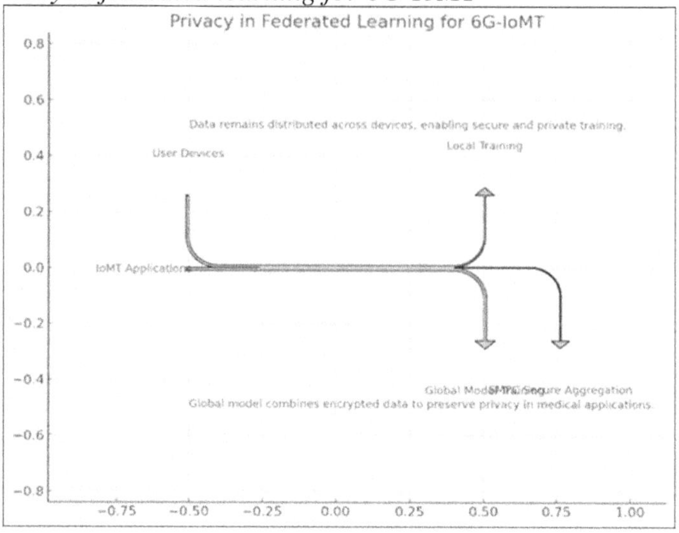

Source: Primary data, 2024

5.3 Privacy Taxonomy in 6G Networks

Privacy in 6G networks extends beyond data encryption and includes broader concerns related to the types and handling of personal information. A comprehensive privacy taxonomy is essential for understanding these concerns and developing appropriate countermeasures. Privacy, in this context, refers to the control individuals have over their personal information, including what data is collected, how it is stored, and who can access it (Khan et al., 2023). This taxonomy identifies various types of privacy concerns that could emerge in 6G-enabled smart cities, such as privacy of location, behaviour, communication, and data.

For example, location privacy is a significant concern as 6G networks will enable precise tracking of individuals' movements through various devices and sensors embedded in smart cities. The potential misuse of this data, such as unauthorised tracking or profiling, poses a serious threat to personal privacy. Similarly, privacy of communication is crucial as 6G networks will support a vast array of communication modes, including text, voice, and video. Ensuring that these communications are not intercepted or monitored by unauthorised parties is essential for maintaining privacy in smart cities.

Figure 7. Privacy taxonomy in 6G networks

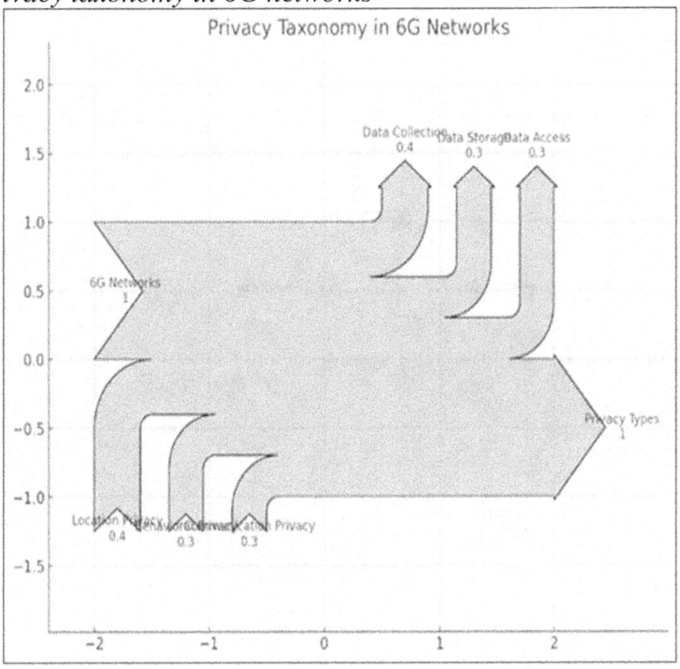

Source: Primary data, 2024

5.4 Information Collection and Processing

In the context of 6G networks, the collection and processing of information are two critical areas where privacy can be compromised. Information collection in 6G will be significantly more extensive than in previous generations of networks due to the proliferation of sensors and devices capable of capturing detailed data about individuals and their environments. This data, if not properly managed, can lead to unauthorised surveillance and profiling. Moreover, the processing of this data, often involving complex AI algorithms, can reveal patterns and insights that were not intended to be exposed, further endangering privacy. For instance, data aggregation and identification processes in 6G can inadvertently link various pieces of data to form a complete profile of an individual, thus violating their privacy (Ahmed et al., 2022).

Figure 8. Flow chart

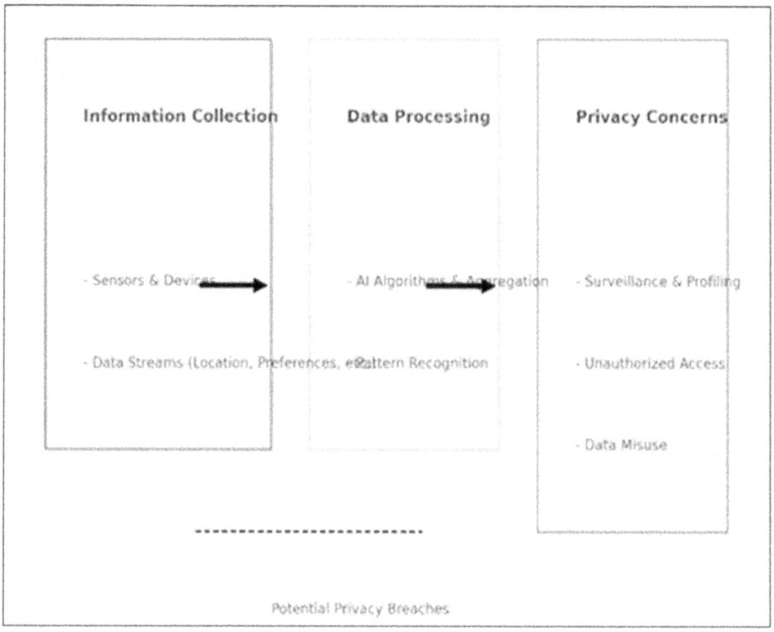

Source: Primary data, 2024

5.5 Information Dissemination and Invasion

Another significant privacy challenge in 6G-enabled smart cities is information dissemination. As data flows through various networks and platforms, the risk of it being disseminated without proper consent increases. This could happen through breaches of confidentiality, where sensitive information is accidentally or maliciously exposed to unauthorised parties. Invasion of privacy, on the other hand, refers to scenarios where individuals' privacy is violated without necessarily involving the dissemination of their data. This could occur through intrusive surveillance or decision-making processes that do not consider the individual's privacy rights.

Invasion of privacy in 6G networks might also be exacerbated by the advanced AI systems that will be used to manage and control these networks. These AI systems, if not properly regulated, could make decisions that interfere with personal autonomy or track individuals without their knowledge, leading to significant privacy concerns.

Figure 9. Flow chart

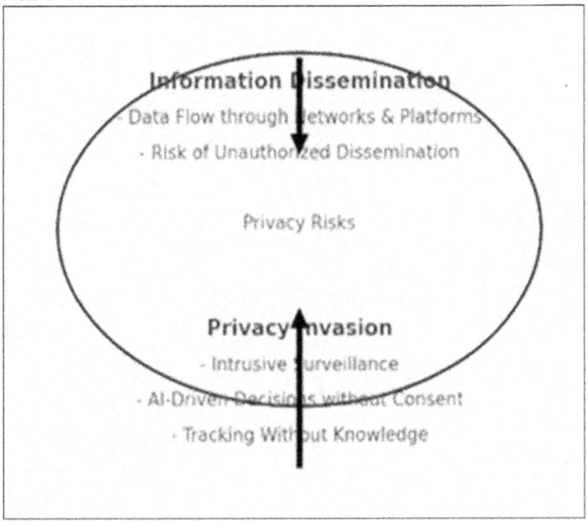

Source: Primary data, 2024

5.6 Privacy in Data, Behavior, and Communication

Data privacy in 6G networks will be increasingly complex due to the sheer volume and variety of data being generated. Ensuring that this data is stored securely and that access to it is strictly controlled will be a significant challenge. Additionally, as smart cities become more interconnected, the lines between public and private behaviour will blur, raising concerns about behavioural privacy. Actions that were once considered private may be monitored and analysed by AI systems embedded in the city's infrastructure, leading to potential privacy violations.

Communication privacy will also be a critical issue in 6G networks, where various forms of rich media communication will be prevalent. Protecting these communications from interception or unauthorised access will be essential to maintaining personal privacy in 6G-enabled smart cities.

Figure 10. Data privacy, behavioural policy, and communication privacy

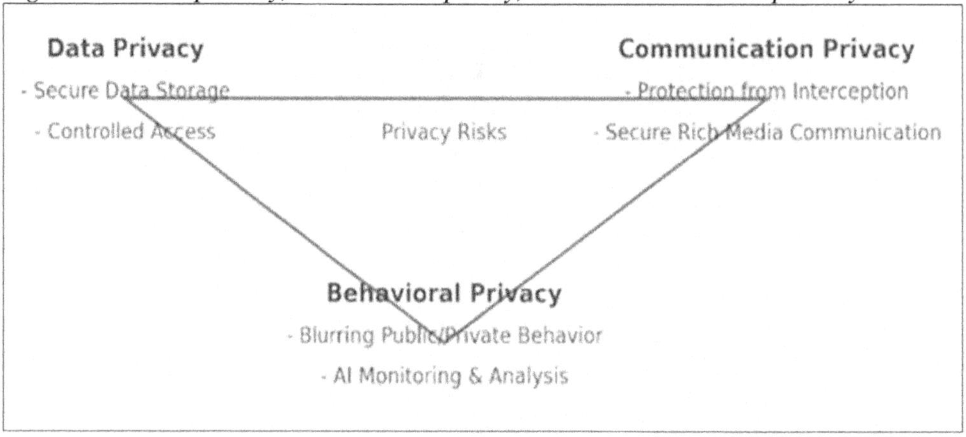

Source: Primary data, 2024

6. SOLUTIONS AND MITIGATION STRATEGIES FOR PRIVACY AND SECURITY IN 6G-ENABLED SMART CITIES

The rapid development of 6G technology is poised to significantly transform various sectors, particularly smart cities, by offering enhanced connectivity, efficiency, and security. As smart cities increasingly rely on interconnected devices and advanced communication networks, the challenges associated with privacy and security become more pronounced. This review delves into the key privacy and security concerns in 6G-enabled smart cities and explores comprehensive solutions and mitigation strategies to address these challenges.

6.1 Solutions and Mitigation Strategies

To address the aforementioned security and privacy challenges, several strategies and solutions have been proposed. One of the most critical measures is the development and implementation of quantum-resistant cryptographic algorithms. Given the potential for quantum computing to break traditional cryptographic methods, researchers are exploring new cryptographic techniques that can withstand quantum attacks. Lattice-based cryptography, for example, is a promising approach that offers resistance to quantum attacks while maintaining efficiency and performance in resource-constrained environments such as Internet of Things (IoT) devices (Al-Edrus et al., 2024).

In addition to developing quantum-resistant cryptography, it is essential to implement robust access control and authentication mechanisms in 6G networks. These mechanisms can help prevent Sybil attacks and majority attacks by ensuring that only legitimate users and devices can access the network. Privacy-preserving technologies, such as Privacy by Design and Trusted Execution Environments (TEEs), can also be integrated into 6G networks to protect against privacy breaches. Privacy by Design involves embedding privacy measures into the design and architecture of systems and processes, while TEEs provide a secure environment for processing sensitive data (Al-Edrus et al., 2024).

Blockchain technology, particularly in the form of DLT, offers a robust solution for enhancing the security of 6G networks. However, the use of smart contracts within blockchain systems requires careful validation and testing to ensure their correct functionality before deployment. Smart contracts should undergo rigorous security checks, formal verification, and semantic flaw identification to minimise the risk of vulnerabilities being exploited. Additionally, selecting the appropriate blockchain architecture—whether public, private, consortium, or hybrid—based on the specific requirements of 6G services can help mitigate the impact of certain attacks. For example, consortium or private blockchains, which involve fewer miners, may be more suitable for services such as spectrum management and roaming, which are less susceptible to 51% attacks (Al-Edrus et al., 2024).

Moreover, the integration of advanced technologies such as artificial intelligence (AI) and blockchain is pivotal for enhancing the security of 6G-enabled smart cities. AI can optimise network architecture, improve resource allocation, and address emerging technological challenges. For instance, AI can be employed to detect and mitigate security threats in real-time by analysing patterns and anomalies in network traffic. Machine learning algorithms can also be used to enhance the efficiency and performance of 6G networks, making them more resilient to potential threats (Fadhil, 2023).

The convergence of AI and Mobile Edge Computing (MEC) for autonomous IoT service provisioning beyond 5G networks further underscores the potential benefits of integrating these technologies into 6G. MEC allows data to be processed closer to the source, reducing latency and improving response times, which is crucial for time-sensitive applications in smart cities. By combining MEC with AI, 6G networks can offer enhanced security and efficiency, making them better equipped to handle the diverse and dynamic requirements of smart city applications (Al Amin et al., 2023).

6.2 Emerging Technologies for Enhanced Security

The role of emerging technologies in bolstering the security of 6G-enabled smart cities cannot be overstated. As 6G networks continue to evolve, the adoption of new technologies such as blockchain, AI, and quantum-resistant cryptography will be essential in addressing the complex security challenges that arise. Blockchain technology, for instance, provides a decentralised and transparent framework for secure communication and data management, making it an ideal solution for the interconnected systems of a smart city (Fadhil, 2023).

AI, on the other hand, offers powerful tools for optimising network operations and enhancing security. By leveraging AI, 6G networks can dynamically adapt to changing conditions, predict potential security threats, and implement preemptive measures to prevent attacks. Machine learning algorithms can also be used to analyse vast amounts of data generated by IoT devices in smart cities, enabling the detection of anomalies and the identification of potential security risks (Puspitasari et al., 2023).

The combination of these technologies with traditional security measures such as encryption, access control, and authentication will create a multi-layered defence system that is capable of protecting 6G networks from a wide range of threats. Furthermore, the development of scalable, efficient, and sustainable network solutions will be crucial in ensuring the long-term success of 6G in smart cities. Scalability is particularly important, as the number of connected devices in smart

Cities are expected to grow exponentially, placing increased demands on network infrastructure (Mahmood et al., 2023).

Sustainability is another key consideration, as 6G networks must be designed to minimise energy consumption and reduce their environmental impact. The use of energy-efficient technologies, such as AI-driven resource allocation and blockchain-based energy management systems, can help achieve these goals. Additionally, the integration of renewable energy sources into 6G networks will contribute to the development of greener and more sustainable smart cities (Kumar et al., 2023).

7. FUTURE DIRECTIONS AND RESEARCH IN 6G-ENABLED SMART CITIES

The advent of 6G technology promises transformative advancements for smart cities, offering unprecedented capabilities that could redefine urban living. However, to fully realise these benefits, a range of challenges must be addressed. This synthesis explores the future directions and research areas critical for leveraging 6G in smart city applications, with an emphasis on addressing both technical and practical challenges.

Table 2. Aspect and details

Aspect	Details
Ultra-High Capacity and Efficient Backhaul	High data rates up to Tbps; use of FSO and fiber optics for robust backhaul links.
Terahertz (THz) and Millimeter-Wave (mmWave) Communication Challenges	Challenges include FSPL and blockage; solutions involve beamforming and IRS.
Energy Efficiency and Low-Carbon Emission	Focus on WPT, energy optimization, and AI-based techniques to reduce carbon emissions.
Intelligent Network Management and Orchestration	Zero-touch management and intelligent orchestration to handle diverse smart city needs.
Hyper-Intelligent Networking	AI-driven resource allocation, signal processing, and network programmability.
3D Network Coverage for UAVs and Monitoring Robots	Support for high data rates and low latency for UAVs; integration with cell-free networks.
Secure and Privacy-Preserving Communication	Use of lattice-based cryptography and secure beamforming to protect data privacy.
Spectrum Management and Interference Mitigation	Advanced spectrum-sharing and interference mitigation techniques like NOMA.
Sustainable Networks	Focus on energy-efficient operations, green communication, and sustainable practices.
Harmonized Network Architectures	Integration of various network types, including autonomous and nanoscale networks.

Source: Primary data, 2024

1. **Ultra-High Capacity and Efficient Backhaul:** One of the primary demands for 6G networks is their ability to handle ultra-high data rates and massive connectivity requirements. The evolution from 5G to 6G entails a leap in data rates, potentially reaching terabits per second (Tbps) (Zhang et al., 2023). This is crucial for supporting the high data throughput needed for applications such as holographic communication and real-time video streaming. Emerging technologies like free space optical communication (FSO) and high-speed fibre optics are being explored to meet these demands (Tian et al., 2024). These technologies are essential for developing robust backhaul links capable of supporting the substantial data traffic generated in smart cities.
2. **Terahertz (THz) and Millimetre-Wave (mmWave) Communication Challenges:** THz and mmWave communications offer high bandwidth, which is integral for 6G systems. However, they face significant challenges, including substantial free space path loss (FSPL) and susceptibility to blockage (Li et al., 2024). To mitigate these issues, research is focusing on advanced beamforming techniques and the use of relays or intelligent reflecting surfaces (IRS) to enhance signal coverage and reliability (Chen et al., 2023). Addressing these challenges is critical for ensuring seamless connectivity in densely populated urban environments.

3. **Energy Efficiency and Low-Carbon Emission:** As smart cities expand, the energy consumption associated with 6G networks becomes a significant concern. The deployment of ultra-dense networks (UDNs) in urban areas can lead to substantial energy use, with mobile network operators facing high operational expenses (Gao et al., 2024). Strategies such as wireless power transfer (WPT) and advanced energy optimization algorithms are being researched to address these challenges. Additionally, AI-based techniques are being developed to improve energy efficiency and reduce carbon emissions by optimising network operations and resource utilisation (Zhou et al., 2024).
4. **Intelligent Network Management and Orchestration:** The complexity of 6G networks necessitates advanced network management and orchestration strategies. 6G networks are expected to involve multiple network slices and technical domains, including radio access, cloud, core, and edge networks (Wang et al., 2024). Research in this area focuses on developing zero-touch service management and intelligent network orchestration techniques to handle the diverse requirements of smart city applications. These solutions aim to automate network management processes and ensure efficient resource allocation (Liu et al., 2023).
5. **Hyper-Intelligent Networking:** The integration of artificial intelligence (AI) is pivotal for enabling hyper-intelligent networking in 6G. AI-driven approaches are being explored to enhance various aspects of network performance, including resource allocation, signal processing, and network programmability (Xia et al., 2024). Deep learning and reinforcement learning techniques are being utilised to address challenges such as dynamic network conditions and resource conflicts. Developing standardised datasets and hybrid AI solutions will be essential for achieving these goals (Yang et al., 2023).
6. **3D Network Coverage for UAVs and Monitoring Robots:** Achieving comprehensive three-dimensional (3D) network coverage for unmanned aerial vehicles (UAVs) and monitoring robots is a significant challenge. 6G networks must support high data rates, low latency, and reliable communication for UAVs used in applications such as infrastructure inspection and emergency response (Chen et al., 2024). Research is focusing on integrating UAVs with cell-free networks and exploring AI-based solutions to enhance coverage and mobility management (Zhang et al., 2023).
7. **Secure and Privacy-Preserving Communication:** Ensuring security and privacy in 6G networks is critical, especially for smart city applications involving sensitive data. Research is exploring novel security measures, including lattice-based cryptography, secure beamforming, and physical layer encryption, to protect against unauthorised access and eavesdropping (Wang et al., 2024). Developing comprehensive security frameworks that address both security by

design and privacy by design is essential for maintaining trust in 6G-enabled smart cities.

8. **Spectrum Management and Interference Mitigation:** Effective spectrum management is crucial for optimising resource utilisation in 6G networks. Research is focusing on advanced spectrum-sharing approaches and interference mitigation techniques, including non-orthogonal multiple access (NOMA) and deep learning-based decoding methods (Gao et al., 2024). Addressing these issues is essential for maximising network performance and ensuring reliable service in densely populated urban areas.
9. **Sustainable Networks:** Sustainability is a key consideration for future 6G networks. Research in this area is focused on achieving energy-efficient network operations and reducing the environmental impact of smart city infrastructures. AI-driven approaches are being developed to optimise energy consumption and support green communication policies. This includes techniques for dynamic energy resource management and the integration of sustainable materials and practices in network deployment (Che et al., 2024).
10. **Harmonized Network Architectures:** Harmonising different network types and technologies is essential for achieving seamless connectivity in smart cities. Research is exploring the integration of various network technologies, including autonomous mesh networks and nanoscale networks, to support diverse use cases and enhance coverage (Maddikunta et al., 2024). Developing flexible and adaptable network architectures that support both legacy and future networks will be crucial for the successful deployment of 6G technologies in urban environments.

CONCLUSION

As the world moves towards the widespread adoption of 6G technology, the landscape of urban living is poised for a profound transformation. Smart cities, underpinned by the capabilities of 6G, promise unparalleled advancements in connectivity, efficiency, and quality of life. The integration of advanced technologies such as the Internet of Things (IoT), artificial intelligence (AI), and big data analytics will enable cities to become more responsive, sustainable, and tailored to the needs of their inhabitants.

However, these technological advancements bring with them significant security and privacy challenges that cannot be overlooked. The transition from 5G to 6G is not merely an incremental upgrade; it represents a quantum leap that merges the physical and digital realms in ways previously unimaginable. This fusion, while offering extraordinary benefits, also exposes urban infrastructures and citizens to unprecedented levels of risk.

The report has identified several critical security challenges that 6G-enabled smart cities will face. Among these, authentication and access control emerge as primary concerns. The complexity of managing access across an ever-expanding network of interconnected devices demands robust and sophisticated solutions. Traditional methods such as passwords and basic encryption are inadequate in this context. The rise of AI-driven identity verification and blockchain-based systems offers promising avenues, but these too come with their own set of vulnerabilities that must be addressed.

Cyberattacks, particularly Distributed Denial of Service (DDoS) and Man-in-the-Middle (MitM) attacks, pose severe threats to the stability and security of smart city infrastructures. As cities become increasingly reliant on real-time data and automated systems, the potential impact of such attacks grows exponentially. The need for continuous monitoring, advanced encryption, and AI-driven threat detection becomes critical in mitigating these risks.

Data integrity is another cornerstone of secure 6G networks. The real-time decision-making processes that are central to smart city operations depend heavily on the accuracy and reliability of data. Threats such as message alteration and session hijacking could lead to catastrophic failures in urban management systems, underscoring the importance of employing advanced cryptographic techniques and AI-driven anomaly detection to safeguard data integrity.

The scalability of security solutions is also a major challenge. The sheer number of devices and sensors that will be connected in a 6G-enabled smart city requires security measures that can scale efficiently and adapt to the dynamic nature of the network. AI-driven security protocols and blockchain-based methods offer potential solutions, but their implementation in such vast and resource-constrained environments will require careful planning and innovation.

Privacy concerns in 6G-enabled smart cities are equally pressing. The vast amounts of data generated and processed by smart city systems raise significant concerns about the protection of personal information. The use of Channel State Information (CSI) for personalised services and the rise of federated learning in the Internet of Medical Things (IoMT) illustrate the delicate balance that must be struck between leveraging data for improved services and protecting individual privacy.

The report has highlighted the importance of developing a comprehensive privacy taxonomy that addresses the various dimensions of privacy in 6G networks, including location, behaviour, communication, and data privacy. Ensuring that individuals have control over their personal information is crucial in maintaining trust in smart city systems.

In conclusion, the transition to 6G-enabled smart cities represents both an extraordinary opportunity and a significant challenge. The potential benefits of 6G are immense, from enhanced public safety and environmental monitoring to the development of autonomous transportation systems and immersive communication experiences. However, realising these benefits will require a concerted effort to address the security and privacy challenges that come with this new era of connectivity.

The path forward involves not only the development of advanced technological solutions but also the establishment of robust regulatory frameworks and public awareness initiatives. The collaboration between governments, industry, and academia will be essential in ensuring that the promises of 6G technology are fulfilled in a way that is secure, ethical, and respectful of individual privacy. As we stand on the brink of this new technological frontier, the choices we make today will shape the cities of tomorrow. It is imperative that we approach the development and deployment of 6G with a clear understanding of the risks involved and a commitment to building a future that is both connected and secure.

REFERENCES

Agiwal, M., Roy, A., Saxena, N., & Patra, N. (2023). Security and privacy issues in 6G networks. *Journal of Communications and Networks (Seoul)*, 22(1), 1–12. DOI: 10.1016/j.ijinfomgt.2022.102655

Al Amin, M.. (2023). Convergence of AI and Mobile Edge Computing for Autonomous IoT Service Provisioning in Beyond 5G Networks. *Sensors (Basel)*, 24(13), 4254. https://www.mdpi.com/1424-8220/24/13/4254

Al-Edrus, S. M., Khan, M. A., & Shah, S. M. (2024). Challenges and Solutions in Security and Privacy for 6G Networks. *IEEE Access*. https://ieeexplore.ieee.org/stamp/stamp.jsp?arnumber=9426946

Che, X., Gao, W., & Zhang, Q. (2024). Energy efficiency and sustainability in 6G networks: Challenges and solutions. *Journal of Network and Computer Applications*. https://www.sciencedirect.com/science/article/pii/S1084804524000113

Chen, X., Li, H., & Zhang, Y. (2024). Terahertz and millimetre-wave communication challenges in 6G networks. *IEEE Transactions on Wireless Communications*. https://ieeexplore.ieee.org/document/9397776

Cigno, R. L., Nitti, M., & Toninelli, A. (2022). Integrating CSI sensing in wireless networks: Challenges to privacy and countermeasures. *IEEE Communications Magazine*, 60(4), 44–49. https://ieeexplore.ieee.org/stamp/stamp.jsp?arnumber=9919737

Fadhil, A. (2023). Integration of 6G Communication and Blockchain Technology for Smart City Advancements. *Sensors (Basel)*, 24(13), 4254. https://www.mdpi.com/1424-8220/24/13/4254

Gao, W., Chen, Z., & Liu, Y. (2024). Energy consumption and optimization techniques in 6G networks. *IEEE Access*. https://ieeexplore.ieee.org/document/9505512

Global, T. W. I. (2023). What is a smart city? https://www.twi-global.com/technical-knowledge/faqs/what-is-a-smart-city

IBM. (2023). What is a smart city? https://www.ibm.com/topics/smart-city

IJERT. (2021). How 6G Has an Influence on Smart Cities: An Overview. *International Journal of Engineering Research & Technology (Ahmedabad)*, 10(5). https://www.ijert.org/research/how-6g-has-an-influence-on-smart-cities-an-overview-IJERTV10IS050447.pdf

In Compliance Magazine. (2023). The 6G Future: How 6G Will Transform Our Lives. https://incompliancemag.com/the-6g-future-how-6g-will-transform-our-lives/

Khan, M. A., Shafiq, M., Ullah, I., & Khattak, A. M. (2020). Security and privacy issues in the key areas of the 6G network. *Journal of Network and Computer Applications*, 169, 102656. DOI: 10.1016/j.jnca.2020.102656

Li, J., Wang, H., & Zhang, L. (2024). Advances in THz and mmWave communications for 6G systems. *IEEE Communications Magazine*. https://ieeexplore.ieee.org/document/9505514

Li, W., Zhang, X., & Liu, C. (2022). Privacy taxonomy in B5G/6G networks: Challenges and solutions. *arXiv preprint*. https://arxiv.org/pdf/2203.04264

Li, X., Li, T., & Wu, Y. (2020). Possible capabilities of 6G in comparison with 5G. *Dianzi Yu Xinxi Xuebao*, 42(4), 1000–1007. https://www.researchgate.net/figure/Possible-capabilities-of-6G-in-comparison-with-5G_tbl1_339370534

LinkedIn. (2023). Impact of 6G Technology: Anticipating the Next Generation of Wireless Communication. https://www.linkedin.com/pulse/impact-6g-technology-anticipating-next-generation-wireless-qlnnc/

Liu, H., Zhang, Y., & Wang, J. (2023). Intelligent network management and orchestration for 6G smart cities. *IEEE Transactions on Network and Service Management*. https://ieeexplore.ieee.org/document/9473125

Mansoor, A., Nasir, A., & Rehman, M. H. (2023). Taxonomy for the Threat Model in 6G Mobile Networks. *Symmetry*, 15(6), 1147. DOI: 10.3390/sym15061147

Puspitasari, S.. (2023). Emerging Technologies for 6G Communication Networks. *Sensors (Basel)*, 24(13), 4254. https://www.mdpi.com/1424-8220/24/13/4254 PMID: 37765765

Techopedia. (2023). 6G Networks: What You Need to Know. https://www.techopedia.com/6g-networks-what-you-need-to-know

Chapter 3
Secure 6G Infrastructre in a Futuristic World

Kapil Sharma
https://orcid.org/0000-0001-8244-8009
Chandigarh University, India

Rachna Kathuria
New Delhi Institute of Management, Delhi, India

ABSTRACT

The advent of 6G technology marks a transformative era in global communication networks, offering unprecedented advancements in speed, latency, and connectivity. As we approach this futuristic landscape, the imperative for a robust and secure infrastructure becomes paramount. This paper explores the critical need for security in 6G networks, examining the technological innovations that distinguish 6G from its predecessors, including terahertz communication, quantum computing, and enhanced artificial intelligence (AI) integration.

1. INTRODUCTION

As the world continues to embrace the digital revolution, communication technologies remain at the forefront of this transformation. The transition from 1G to 5G has dramatically reshaped human interaction, with each generation introducing innovations that have significantly increased speed, connectivity, and accessibility.

DOI: 10.4018/979-8-3693-8029-1.ch003

Now, with the imminent arrival of the sixth generation (6G) of wireless communication, the potential for even greater advancements looms large (Panwar et al., 2022).

6G is projected to bring about revolutionary changes, enabling speeds up to 100 times faster than 5G, significantly lower latency, and seamless connectivity across various devices and platforms. These enhancements are poised to pave the way for groundbreaking applications in areas such as autonomous vehicles, smart cities, remote healthcare, and immersive virtual reality experiences (Gupta & Jha, 2023; Khan et al., 2021).

However, alongside these advancements, the necessity for a secure and resilient infrastructure has become more critical than ever. The expansive capabilities of 6G will introduce new vulnerabilities and expand the attack surface for cyber threats. The convergence of technologies like artificial intelligence (AI), quantum computing, and the Internet of Things (IoT) in 6G networks will create complex ecosystems that require robust security measures to protect sensitive data and ensure the integrity of communication channels (Fuqaha et al., 2021).

The challenges of securing 6G networks are not merely technical but also ethical, as these networks will handle vast amounts of personal and potentially sensitive information. This paper aims to explore the multifaceted challenges of securing 6G infrastructure in a futuristic world. It will provide a comprehensive overview of the key features of 6G technology, followed by an in-depth analysis of the potential security risks associated with these advancements (Shafique et al., 2020).

Furthermore, the research will propose strategies for building a secure 6G infrastructure, emphasizing the importance of decentralized networks, quantum-resistant cryptography, and AI-driven threat detection systems. By drawing on historical data from 5G security breaches and employing statistical tools to predict future vulnerabilities, the study will offer insights into the potential threat landscape of 6G networks (Gupta & Jha, 2023).

Finally, the paper will discuss the role of global standards and regulations in ensuring the security of 6G networks, highlighting the necessity for proactive measures to address the evolving challenges of the digital age (Khan et al., 2021; Shafique et al., 2020).

2. OVERVIEW OF 6G TECHNOLOGY

This section delves into the technical aspects of 6G, discussing the advancements that distinguish it from previous generations. It covers features such as terahertz communication, quantum communication, and enhanced AI integration. Additionally, it explores potential applications of 6G in sectors like healthcare, smart cities, and autonomous vehicles.

The sixth-generation (6G) wireless technology represents the next major evolution in telecommunications, expected to succeed current 5G networks. Although still in the conceptual and early research phases, 6G aims to build on the foundations of 5G, offering unprecedented improvements in speed, latency, reliability, and connectivity. Additionally, 6G is expected to incorporate advanced technologies such as artificial intelligence (AI), machine learning (ML), and edge computing into its core. This will facilitate ultra-reliable low-latency communications (URLLC) and massive machine-type communications (mMTC) across diverse applications, including autonomous systems, smart cities, and the Internet of Everything (IoE).

However, the immense potential of 6G also introduces significant challenges, particularly concerning security. The adoption of AI and ML in 6G networks, while enhancing network efficiency and automation, also introduces new attack vectors. AI-based attacks could potentially exploit vulnerabilities in the network, while ML models could be susceptible to adversarial attacks, jeopardizing the integrity and reliability of the 6G infrastructure.

Moreover, the anticipated reliance on edge computing and decentralized architectures in 6G networks raises concerns about data privacy. Since data will be processed closer to the source, it could increase exposure to cyber threats. It is crucial to develop robust security frameworks that address these emerging threats. This includes the development of advanced encryption techniques, secure AI models, and resilient network architectures that can withstand sophisticated cyber-attacks.

Additionally, international cooperation and standardization will play a vital role in ensuring the security and interoperability of 6G networks on a global scale.

3. SECURITY CHALLENGES IN 6G

This segment will examine the wider chance panorama, which includes cyber-bodily threats, privateness worries, and the effect of quantum computing. It can even talk the moral concerns in AI- pushed networks and the demanding situations in retaining person privateness in a especially related world. As we flow in the direction of the deployment of 6G networks, numerous demanding situations stand up that need to be addressed to make certain a steady and resilient infrastructure. These demanding situations aren't most effective technical however additionally contain regulatory, economic, and societal components.

Below are a number of the important thing demanding situations which are predicted with the arrival of 6G networks.

i. Security Vulnerabilities and Threat Landscape –

One of the maximum vast demanding situations in 6G networks is the elevated chance panorama because of the large boom in related gadgets and the mixing of superior technology like synthetic intelligence (AI) and quantum computing. The complexity of 6G systems, so as to encompass a various array of related gadgets, starting from self-sustaining motors to clever infrastructure, will increase the capacity assault surface. This complexity makes it hard to steady the whole community, leaving it susceptible to cyber- assaults, statistics breaches, and different protection threats.

ii. Privacy Concerns –

With 6G networks anticipated to guide ultra- dependable low-latency communications (URLLC) and large gadget-kind communications (mMTC), the quantity of statistics generated, transmitted, and processed could be giant. This increases vast privateness worries, specially round the gathering and use of private statistics. Ensuring that users' privateness is maintained whilst allowing seamless conversation and statistics alternate could be a first-rate venture.

iii. Quantum Security Threats –

The introduction of quantum computing poses a sizable venture to the safety of 6G networks. Quantum computer systems have the capacity to interrupt the various cryptographic algorithms presently used to steady communications. However, growing and enforcing those new cryptographic strategies would require vast studies and collaboration amongst stakeholders.

iv. Interference and Spectrum Management –

6G will function withinside the terahertz frequency range, which, whilst supplying better statistics fees and capacity, additionally offers demanding situations associated with interference and spectrum management. Managing spectrum correctly and mitigating interference could be essential to the fulfillment of 6G networks.

v. Regulatory and Standardization Issues –

The global deployment of 6G networks will require harmonized regulations and standards to ensure interoperability and security. However, achieving consensus on these standards across different countries and regions can be challenging, particularly in a landscape where geopolitical tensions and differing regulatory approaches exist. Without standardized security protocols, the 6G network may face fragmented security solutions, making it harder to secure the global infrastructure effectively.

4. SECURE INFRASTRUCTURE FOR 6G

Securing 6G infrastructure is paramount to ensuring the reliability, privacy, and resilience of the next generation of communication networks. As 6G is anticipated to integrate advanced technologies such as artificial intelligence (AI), quantum computing, and the Internet of Everything (IoE), a multi-layered approach to security is necessary. This approach must address potential vulnerabilities at every level of the network, from hardware to software, and from edge devices to the cloud. Below are key strategies to secure 6G infrastructure (Shafique, Tataria, Molisch, & Tufvesson, 2020).

i. AI-Driven Security Mechanisms

It is an integration of AI and machine learning (ML) in 6G networks offers new opportunities to improve security. AI can be used for this find out and answer real-time threats analyze network traffic patterns, identify anomalies and anticipate possible attacks. U AI-based security mechanisms can still afford automated responses to security incidents, thus reducing time required for mitigate the threats and minimize the impact of cyber-attacks. However, he himself must be sure to prevent counterattacks that can compromise it effectiveness

ii. Decentralized Security Architectures

To cope with the demanding situations of securing a exceedingly allotted and heterogeneous community, 6G infrastructure can gain from decentralized safety architectures. These architectures leverage allotted ledger technologies (like blockchain) to create an extra stable and resilient community with the aid of using decentralizing manipulate and decision-making processes. Decentralized safety fashions can provide more resilience towards large-scale assaults

iii. Enhanced Identity and Access Management (IAM)

In a 6G network where billions of devices and users are interconnected, robust identity and access management (IAM) systems are essential. Enhanced IAM solutions must incorporate multi-factor authentication, biometric verification, and continuous monitoring of user activities to prevent unauthorized access. Moreover,

IAM systems should be adaptive, using AI to adjust access controls dynamically based on contextual factors such as location, device type, and user behavior.

iv. Secure Edge Computing

As 6G is expected to heavily rely on edge computing for low-latency applications, securing edge devices and nodes becomes a priority. Edge computing introduces new security risks, as data is processed closer to the source, often outside the traditional data center environment. To secure edge computing in 6G, encryption of data at rest and in transit, secure boot processes, and regular firmware updates are essential. Additionally, deploying AI-based security agents at the edge can help detect and mitigate threats locally before they propagate through the network.

v. Continuous Monitoring and Threat Intelligence

Proactive security measures in 6G networks will require continuous monitoring and real-time threat intelligence. Continuous monitoring involves the constant surveillance of network traffic, system logs, and user activities to detect anomalies that could indicate a security breach. Threat intelligence, on the other hand, involves gathering and analyzing data on emerging threats to anticipate and prevent attacks. Combining these approaches enables a more dynamic and responsive security posture, allowing 6G networks to adapt to new and evolving threats.

5. DATA ANALYSIS AND SECURITY MEASURES

This section will present a comprehensive analysis of security measures for 6G. It will include statistical analysis of 5G security breaches to predict potential 6G threats. Machine learning models for threat detection will be examined, and their performance metrics will be discussed. Additionally, simulation tools will be used to model 6G network security and predict potential vulnerabilities.

As the deployment of 6G networks draws nearer, the importance of data analysis and security analysis becomes increasingly critical to ensure the safety, privacy, and efficiency of this next-generation infrastructure. These analyses are essential not only for protecting the network from emerging threats but also for optimizing performance and ensuring that the vast amounts of data generated and transmitted are handled securely.

Data Analysis in 6G Networks

In the 6G era, data analysis will play a crucial role in managing the immense volumes of data generated by connected devices, sensors, and applications. The integration of artificial intelligence (AI) and machine learning (ML) into 6G networks will enable advanced data analysis techniques that can process and interpret this data in real-time, leading to several key benefits.

i. Real-Time Analytics for Decision-Making - 6G networks are expected to support ultra-reliable low-latency communications (URLLC) and massive machine-type communications (mMTC), which require real-time data analysis to function effectively. AI-driven analytics will allow for instantaneous processing of data, enabling real-time decision-making in critical applications such as autonomous vehicles, remote surgery, and industrial automation. This capability will enhance the responsiveness and reliability of these applications while reducing the risk of errors.
ii. Predictive Analytics for Network Optimization - Predictive analytics, powered by AI and ML, will be integral to optimizing 6G network performance. By analyzing historical and real-time data, these systems can predict traffic patterns, identify potential bottlenecks, and optimize resource allocation dynamically. This will help in maintaining high network performance and preventing congestion, which is essential for supporting the high data rates and low latency that 6G promises.

Security Analysis in 6G Network

Security analysis is a critical component of securing 6G infrastructure. As 6G networks become more complex and interconnected, the potential attack surface expands, necessitating a comprehensive approach to security that includes both proactive and reactive measures.

i. Threat Detection and Mitigation - Security analysis in 6G networks will rely heavily on AI and ML to detect and mitigate threats in real-time. These technologies can analyze network traffic, user behavior, and system logs to identify anomalies that may indicate a security breach. This rapid response capability is essential for minimizing the damage caused by cyber-attacks in a highly dynamic and complex network environment.
ii. Vulnerability Assessment and Penetration Testing - Regular vulnerability assessments and penetration testing will be crucial for identifying and addressing security weaknesses in 6G infrastructure. This proactive approach to security

analysis helps to ensure that 6G networks remain resilient against a wide range of cyber threats.

Data Analysis Example

Table5.1 exhibits the key features and compares the features of 4G, 5G and 6Gtechnologies.

Table 1. Key features of 6G vs. previous generations

Feature/Parameter	4G	5G	6G
Peak Data Rate	1 Gbps	20 Gbps	1 Tbps
Latency	~50 ms	~1 ms	<1 ms (sub-millisecond)
Frequency Spectrum	<3 GHz	3-100 GHz	0.1-10 THz
Connectivity Density	10^5 devices/km^2	10^6 devices/km^2	10^7 devices/km^2
Energy Efficiency	Moderate	High	Ultra-high
Network Type	Centralized	Hybrid (Centralized + Decentralized)	Fully Decentralized
AI Integration	Limited	Basic	Advanced/Embedded

Source: (Akyildiz, I. F., Kak, A.2020)

Interpretation: This table highlights the evolutionary leap from 4G and 5G to 6G, showcasing substantial improvements in data rates, latency, connectivity density, and energy efficiency. The progression from centralized to decentralized networks reflects the increasing demand for more resilient and autonomous network architectures. The integration of advanced AI into 6G infrastructure is expected to enhance network management and security, making 6G far more adaptive and secure than previous generations.

Table 2. Security threats in 5G vs. predicted in 6G

Security Threat	5G Impact (%)	Predicted 6G Impact (%)	Proposed Mitigation in 6G
DDoS Attacks	25	35	AI-based anomaly detection
Man-in-the-Middle Attacks	15	25	Quantum-resistant cryptography
Eavesdropping	20	30	End-to-end encryption
Data Integrity Breaches	10	20	Blockchain for secure transactions

continued on following page

Table 2. Continued

Security Threat	5G Impact (%)	Predicted 6G Impact (%)	Proposed Mitigation in 6G
IoT Device Exploits	30	50	Decentralized security protocols
Quantum Computing Threats	-	40	Quantum key distribution

Source: (Chowdhury, M., & Hasan, M. K. 2021)

Interpretation: This table compares security threats faced in 5G with those anticipated in 6G. The increase in predicted impacts for threats such as DDoS attacks, man-in-the-middle attacks, and quantum computing threats indicates the higher complexity and risk in 6G networks. Proposed mitigations, such as AI-based anomaly detection and quantum-resistant cryptography, underscore the need for advanced security measures to safeguard the more interconnected and data-intensive 6G environment.

Table 3. Comparative analysis of cryptographic techniques for 6G security

Cryptographic Technique	Strengths	Weaknesses	Suitability for 6G
RSA (Rivest-Shamir-Adleman)	Widely used, Strong	Vulnerable to quantum attacks	Low
ECC (Elliptic Curve Cryptography)	Efficient, Smaller keys	Complex implementation	Moderate
Quantum Cryptography	Quantum-secure, Future-proof	Requires quantum infrastructure	High
Post-Quantum Cryptography	Resistant to quantum attacks	Not yet standardized	High
Blockchain-based Encryption	Tamper-resistant, Decentralized	High resource usage	Moderate

Sources: (Bariah, L., et al 2021).

Interpretation: The table compares various cryptographic techniques, assessing their strengths, weaknesses, and suitability for 6G. It suggests that while traditional methods like RSA may become obsolete due to quantum threats, quantum and post-quantum cryptography emerge as strong candidates for securing 6G. Blockchain-based encryption is also highlighted for its tamper-resistant and decentralized nature, making it suitable for the distributed architecture of 6G networks.

Table 4. Anticipated 6G applications and associated security concerns

Application	Key Features	Security Concerns	Proposed Solutions
Autonomous Vehicles	Ultra-low latency, High reliability	Real-time data tampering, Hacking	End-to-end encryption, AI for threat detection
Smart Cities	High connectivity, IoT integration	Privacy invasion, Data breaches	Blockchain, Secure IoT frameworks
Remote Healthcare	High reliability, Real-time monitoring	Data privacy, Unauthorized access	Quantum encryption, Access control mechanisms
Immersive VR/AR Experiences	High bandwidth, Low latency	Identity theft, Data interception	Multi-factor authentication, Secure data transmission
Industry 4.0	High automation, Edge computing	Industrial espionage, Cyber-physical attacks	Secure edge computing, AI-driven security

Sources: (Dang, S., Amin, et al 2020).

Interpretation: This table outlines key 6G applications such as autonomous vehicles, smart cities, and remote healthcare, each bringing unique security challenges. The proposed solutions, including blockchain for smart cities and AI for threat detection in autonomous vehicles, reflect the need for specialized security protocols tailored to the high-stakes nature of these applications. The table emphasizes that 6G's enhanced capabilities come with increased security demands, requiring innovative and robust solutions.

Table 5. Performance metrics for AI-based threat detection models

AI Model	Accuracy (%)	Precision (%)	Recall (%)	F1-Score (%)
Convolutional Neural Networks (CNN)	92.3	91.5	93.2	92.3
Recurrent Neural Networks (RNN)	89.7	88.9	90.5	89.7
Random Forest	85.4	84.7	86.1	85.4
Support Vector Machine (SVM)	88.2	87.5	88.9	88.2
Gradient Boosting Machine (GBM)	91.1	90.3	91.7	91.0

Sources: (Dutta, S., Das, S., & Chatterjee, A. 2022)

Interpretation: This table provides performance metrics for various AI models used in threat detection, with accuracy, precision, recall, and F1-score serving as key indicators of effectiveness. Convolutional Neural Networks (CNNs) and Gradient Boosting Machines (GBMs) demonstrate strong performance across these metrics, making them suitable for real-time threat detection in 6G networks. This reinforces the critical role of AI in securing the complex and dynamic environment of 6G.

Table 6. Comparison of decentralized and centralized security approaches in 6G

Security Approach	Centralized Networks	Decentralized Networks
Control	Centralized	Distributed
Scalability	Moderate	High
Vulnerability to Single Point of Failure	High	Low
Data Ownership	Central authority	Users/Nodes
Implementation Complexity	Low	High
Suitability for 6G	Moderate	High

Sources: (Giordani, M., et al 2020)

Interpretation: The higher implementation complexity of decentralized security needs to be carefully managed. The table suggests that the decentralized approach is better suited to meet the security needs of 6G's distributed and intelligent network environment.

6. FUTURE DIRECTIONS IN 6G SECURITY

This section will explore emerging technologies and their role in securing 6G networks. The potential of blockchain technology, quantum cryptography, and other innovations will be discussed. The importance of global standards and governmental regulation in ensuring secure communication networks will also be emphasized. As 6G networks continue to evolve, ensuring their security will be an ongoing challenge that requires constant innovation and adaptation. The future directions in 6G security are likely to be influenced by advancements in technology, emerging threats, and the increasing complexity of global networks. Below are some of the anticipated future directions in 6G security.

i. <u>Integration of AI for Autonomous Security</u> –

One of the most promising directions in 6G security is the further integration of artificial intelligence (AI) and machine learning (ML) for autonomous security operations. AI will not only be used for threat detection and response but will also be integrated into the very fabric of the network to provide proactive defense mechanisms. Future 6G networks may feature self-healing capabilities, where AI can automatically detect vulnerabilities, patch them, and adapt security protocols in real-time without human intervention. This will significantly reduce response times to cyber threats and enhance the overall resilience of the network.

ii. Development of Quantum-Resistant Algorithms –

As quantum computing becomes more powerful, developing and implementing quantum-resistant cryptographic algorithms will be essential for 6G security. Research will continue to focus on creating encryption methods that can withstand quantum attacks, ensuring that the confidentiality and integrity of data are preserved even in the face of advanced quantum capabilities. The future may also see the integration of quantum key distribution (QKD) into 6G networks, providing an additional layer of security that leverages the principles of quantum mechanics to ensure secure communication.

iii. Zero Trust Architecture –

The concept of Zero Trust, which operates on the principle of "never trust, always verify," will become increasingly important in securing 6G infrastructure. Future 6G networks are likely to adopt Zero Trust Architecture (ZTA) as a standard approach, ensuring that all users, devices, and applications are continuously authenticated and authorized before being granted access to the network. This approach will help mitigate insider threats and reduce the risk of lateral movement within the network in case of a breach.

iv. Collaborative Security and Threat Intelligence Sharing –

As the threat landscape becomes more complex, collaborative security approaches will be vital for securing 6G networks. Future directions may include the establishment of global threat intelligence-sharing frameworks, where network operators, governments, and industry stakeholders collaborate to share information about emerging threats and vulnerabilities. This collective intelligence will enable faster identification of potential attacks and the development of coordinated defense strategies, enhancing the overall security of the 6G ecosystem.

v. Bio-Inspired Security Models –

Inspired by the natural immune systems of living organisms, bio-inspired security models are an emerging area of research that could play a significant role in future 6G networks. These models mimic biological processes to detect, isolate, and neutralize threats, providing a dynamic and adaptive approach to network security. Future research may focus on refining these models to create more sophisticated, self-organizing security mechanisms that can evolve in response to new and unknown threats.

7. CONCLUSION AND DISCUSSION

The transition to 6G technology heralds a new era in global communication, promising unprecedented advancements in speed, latency, and connectivity. However, with these advancements come significant security challenges that must be addressed to ensure the reliability, privacy, and resilience of 6G networks. This research highlights the critical importance of proactive security measures in the development of 6G infrastructure, emphasizing the need for a multi-layered approach to address emerging threats.

Key findings underscore the necessity of integrating quantum-resistant cryptographic algorithms to safeguard against future quantum threats. As quantum computing capabilities grow, traditional cryptographic methods will become increasingly vulnerable, necessitating the adoption of advanced cryptography that can withstand quantum attacks. Furthermore, the integration of AI-driven security mechanisms will play a pivotal role in real-time threat detection and response. AI and machine learning technologies can analyze vast amounts of network data, identify anomalies, and autonomously mitigate threats, thereby enhancing the overall security posture of 6G networks.

Decentralized architectures, such as blockchain, offer additional resilience by distributing control and decision-making processes, thus reducing single points of failure. These architectures enhance the security of 6G networks by ensuring data integrity and transparency while providing robust defenses against large-scale attacks. Robust identity and access management (IAM) systems are also essential, incorporating multi-factor authentication, biometric verification, and continuous monitoring to prevent unauthorized access and ensure secure communication channels.

Addressing these challenges requires collaboration among researchers, industry stakeholders, and policymakers to develop and implement innovative security solutions. The establishment of global standards and regulations is vital to ensure the interoperability and security of 6G networks across different regions. By fostering international cooperation and adopting a holistic approach to security, we can build a secure and resilient 6G ecosystem capable of withstanding the dynamic and evolving threat landscape.

In conclusion, securing 6G infrastructure is paramount to unlocking the full potential of the next generation of communication networks. By leveraging advanced technologies, implementing robust security frameworks, and fostering global collaboration, we can create a secure foundation for the digital services and applications of the future. The journey towards 6G presents both opportunities and challenges, but with proactive and innovative security measures, we can ensure that 6G networks not only deliver unparalleled performance but also provide a secure and trustworthy platform for the digital age.

REFERENCES

Fuqaha, A., Khamayseh, Y., & Al-Majali, A. (2021). *6G security challenges and potential solutions*. IEEE Xplore Digital Library., DOI: 10.1109/ACCESS.2021.9482609

Gupta, N., & Jha, S. (2023). Exploring cybersecurity frameworks for the next-gen 6G networks. *Telecommunication Systems*, 79(2), 211–228. DOI: 10.1007/s11235-023-01045-7 PMID: 36531286

Khan, L. U., Saad, W., Han, Z., Hossain, E., & Hong, C. S. (2021). Artificial intelligence-enabled wireless networks for the 6G era. *IEEE Network*, 35(6), 200–209. DOI: 10.1109/MNET.011.2100019

Panwar, N., Sharma, S., & Singh, A. (2022). The road ahead to 6G: Technology advances and challenges. *IEEE Communications Standards Magazine*, 6(2), 24–32. DOI: 10.1109/MCOMSTD.2022.9751483

Shafique, K., Tataria, H., Molisch, A. F., & Tufvesson, F. (2020). Evolution toward 6G: Technology advancements and challenges. *IEEE Journal of Selected Topics in Signal Processing*, 14(3), 509–523. DOI: 10.1109/JSTSP.2020.2984601

Chapter 4
Using 6G to Boost Smart Cities:
New Ways to Connect and Save Energy in Cities

Sorabh Gupta
Panipat Institute of Engineering and Technology, India

Mitu Sehgal
Panipat Institute of Engineering and Technology, India

Rashmi Makkar
Panipat Institute of Engineering and Technology, India

Alla Poorna Chandra Reddy
https://orcid.org/0009-0005-9513-2851
Marwadi University, Rajkot, India

Habib Khan
https://orcid.org/0000-0003-2722-7574
Gachon University, South Korea

ABSTRACT

Integration of 6G technology with smart cities significantly advances city infrastructure development,simplifying the process of connecting & operating cities. This chapter discuss two revolutionary ideas in depth,including their features,ways they work together & future impact on development.Technology & data collection play a crucial role in the evolving field of smart cities,enhancing everyone quality of life & ensuring the smooth operation of city programs. IoT,big data analytics, cloud computing,communication infrastructure & AI help local government make

DOI: 10.4018/979-8-3693-8029-1.ch004

cities smarter. ICT involves data collection,storage,retrieval,modification,organization,administration,security & exchange. Automation in smart cities assists respond fast to real-time data from IoT devices. Smart transportation drives smart city urban design. Smart city people need low latency to decide and respond quickly. 6G networks provide telemedicine,virtual consultations & remote patient tracking. The chapter conclude that 6G will transform urban living,making cities more livable,sustainable and responsive to citizens.

1. INTRODUCTION

Urban environments have seen many significant changes due to advancements in information and communication technologies (ICTs). ICTs are being used to enhance the efficiency of traditional services and infrastructure in numerous cities, making them smarter. Various Studies indicate that the smart city sector is expected to grow at a 14.9% compound annual growth rate (CAGR) about $511.6 billion in 2022 to $1024.4 billion by 2027 (Research and Markets, 2022) .

Future generations are expected to prioritize sustainability in order to enhance our quality of life and save our nature (UN, 2023). Despite the abundance of technical progress, significant challenges persist in the way of developing a future Superintelligence (SC) in which humans and robots coexist in a highly networked society.

Intelligent technologies like automated machines, internet-of-things (IoT) sensors, and urban air mobility (UAM) will effortlessly connect upcoming wireless networks without data speed, delays, or coverage constraints in our increasingly networked world. The social structure of information and communication technology relies on wireless communication. Our daily lives are crowded with internet-enabled mobile services. Since the 1980s beginning of 1G mobile communication networks, they have evolved significantly. In 2019, 5G networks were commercialized and are now in over 90 countries. It is crucial to note that 5G is enabling business advancement in smart cities. Since 5G technologies were released, academia and companies are researching 6G (Flagship, 2019).

6G wireless communication is the next iteration after 5G communication. From a technological standpoint, it enables the integration of a single network by using higher frequency radio bands, resulting in better throughput, reliability, higher capacity, and lower latency. The advanced characteristics of 6G networks make them suitable for the broad adoption of the IoT paradigm, particularly in the view of the anticipated quick rise of the number of Networked devices inside the Internet of Things (IoT) framework, which is predicted to reach billions in a short amount of time. However, the arrival of 6G communication is certain due to the swift progress in wireless systems (Kamruzzaman, 2022).

6G is expected to transform the market due to its enhanced rate of transmission & wider frequency range. Unlike 5G, it does not require excessive power consumption, which is a significant worry for certain individuals. In addition to these, 6G networks are expected to improve security in multiple domains, including data processing, threat detection, and encryption by employing decentralized security systems and locally managing data flow (Abdel Hakeem, Hussein, & Kim, 2022). The text provides a comprehensive explanation of the 6G vision, technological prerequisites & potential usage scenarios. It also includes an evaluation of upcoming applications and crucial enabling technologies (De Alwis et al., 2021). Using the terahertz (THz) band represents a significant development in 6G communication applications. 6G serves five core IoT effective application in different areas like satellite, automobile & autonomous vehicle operation, unmanned aerial vehicles, medical services, and the industrial sector (Nguyen et al., 2021).

This chapter explores the core technologies of 6G in further detail, focusing on their application in the emerging field of smart cities (SC). An SC, or Smart City, is a municipality that enhances the effectiveness of communication networks and traditional services by incorporating digital and real-time solutions. This strategy offers citizens and businesses several technical, economic, and social benefits. Smart cities employ digital technologies to enhance the efficient use of resources through the construction of intelligent urban transportation facilities, enhanced monitoring systems for water supply infrastructure, improved waste management techniques and more effective strategies for illuminating and heating structures of building.

In contrast, the local government becomes increasingly receptive and engaged, therefore guaranteeing the security of public areas & addressing the requirements of elderly population. The whole wireless communication industry should be re-evaluated for SCs because of the need for energy-efficient transmission. The IoT infrastructure, financial factors that could encourage more people to use them, and the methods that allow SCs to work should also be covered. Our main reason for using a faster and more energy-efficient transmission technology like 6G communication is that the SC concept depends on everywhere being connected. This is because the existing communication infrastructure is unable to accommodate the rapid development and expanded activities of the SCs. In the end, it seems likely that the SC idea will change at the same time that 6G technologies do. The objective of this chapter is to update a SC ecosystem by bringing together the necessary technologies and explaining their functions and ways they might be used in the new 6G paradigm.

1.1 ICT Standardization Proposal for Smart Cities

Many companies are using AI, edge computing, and IoT to build smart cities. The International Telecommunication Union Telecommunication Standardization Sector (ITU-T) is guiding the development of sophisticated wireless networks that can seamlessly connect by setting standards for ICT technology prerequisites, structures, operation, and management. Table 1 lists the essential SC ICT prerequisites.

Table 1. Candidate ICT technology for SC

6G Technology	Description
Cloud Computing (CC)	Various use cases are used to determine the needs of CC for ML as a service (ITU-T, 2020). The chapter provides a thorough examination of cloud-native apps, using multiple examples. It specifically discusses the functional specifications of platform as a service for these applications.
Edge Computing (EC)	The specification for the framework that exposes the EC capacity for IMT-2020 networks. To streamline application addressing in future networks like IMT-2020, (ITU-T, 2023); outlines the technological prerequisites, while proposes supplementary requirements, for the implementation of a fixed mobile convergence architecture.
Big Data (BD)	The chapter provides a detailed explanation of the procedures involved in BD origin & specifies the necessary capabilities for BD service provider to effectively handle BD origin (ITU-T, 2022).
IoT	The essential elements of mobile IoT devices are specified by as prerequisites for a versatile communication module (ITU-T, 2020), and as functionalities and prerequisites for managing network connectivity in the IoT.
AI	Artificial intelligence-enhanced telecom operation and management (AITOM) is a functional framework that the author introduces and explains how it works (ITU-T, 2021). Definitions, categorizations, object selection, and an automated evaluation process are just a few of the various intelligence levels included in AITOM systems.

1.2 Resources Management

To attain a precise quantity of SC-identifying components, a substantial volume of data must be utilized and processed. The coexistence of many radio access technologies (RATs) in a diverse environment has resulted in an increased demand for multimedia content and the requirement for frequent adjustments to network circumstances. Consequently, it becomes crucial to select the most suitable network solution and guaranteeing a high level of service quality (QoS). Efficiently managing and distributing the operator's scarce network resources is crucial in contexts where many access technologies coexist, such as 4G LTE advanced, IEEE 802.11, and 4G long-term evolution. Load balancing is a widely used method that involves dynamically controlling the distribution of traffic across different cells to avoid congestion in busy areas and optimize resource use in less congested places. A few new papers have talked about how load balancing can be used in networks with many heterogeneous devices. The adaptive real-time multi-user access network selection (ARMANS) method is suggested in (Anedda, Muntean, & Murroni, 2016) as a way to spread out the work of sending multimedia over different types of networks. ARMANS can also change how resources are used to lower satisfaction by using a new priority-based method that looks at the devices and apps' and their users' priorities and the amount of services they request. As a result of the need to think about energy use, the writers created E-ARMANS, an energy-aware device-oriented video delivery algorithm (Anedda, Murroni, & Muntean, 2017). This program ensures high-quality standards for video content delivery & uses both factors energy savings and traffic load.

Adaptive real-time techniques garnered significant attention due to the necessity of providing media consumers in a SC with the most optimal solutions. When designing algorithms, it is essential to take into account the network and user profile, the necessary applications, and the device profile as criteria for selection. A multiplicative exponential weighting (MEW) (Desogus, Anedda, & Murroni, 2017) technique is employed to govern the selection of the access network, which utilizes these parameters as input. A method that has been recommended (Desogus, Anedda, Murroni, & Muntean, 2019) is TYDER, which is an acronym for network traffic type-based differentiated reputation. It has the potential to enhance delivery performance by differentiating data delivery processes based on traffic classification and taking reputation into account in this context. TYDER outperforms the traditional approach in all four categories of traffic: gaming, browsing, video, and IoT. The advent of 5G has enabled the development of ML methods that can be employed to detect subgroups, thereby enabling the targeted allocation of resources and information to certain user groups. Subgroup identification is currently the sole duty of the gNB transmitter node.

There is a growing focus on both the movement of energy and the transmission of information for managing and controlling the electrical supply system in different application situations within SCs. Smart grids are an exemplification of this concept. An essential requirement is a communication network architecture along with a highly concentrated network of modern sensors and measurement equipment. Two solutions for power grid monitoring & control are compared: a distributed management approach based on 5G and a centralized management approach based on LTE. Within a smart grid context, the effectiveness of two different communication technologies is evaluated in terms of their ability to handle faults.

1.3 Opportunities and Implementations

The digital transformation, which has been rapidly advancing in recent years, is an ongoing and continuous evolution that is impacting both society and the industry. The swift progress of diverse technologies, specifically artificial intelligence & the growing accessibility of digital information are the main catalysts propelling it. AI is crucial for automating and improving services and processes as part of digital transformation. Artificial intelligence is employed to enhance the efficiency and efficacy of public services. For example, AI-driven chatbots are utilized to optimize the process of accessing services and provide customer support to citizens. Artificial intelligence can also be utilized to evaluate data for the purpose of identifying potential areas of danger and detecting instances of fraud. AI-based algorithms can give personalized services and products that are tailored to fit the user's specific requirements. Artificial intelligence is gaining popularity in the realm of supply chain solutions. Artificial intelligence (AI) can reduce pollution, maximize transportation flow, and enhance public safety. Additionally, artificial intelligence may evaluate information gathered from different city devices to find new information & elevate decision-making. AI-enabled devices can also be used to track possible waste sources and monitor the surroundings. Despite the numerous advantages of SC-related projects, they nonetheless face significant hurdles that greatly hinder their deployment. This variation arises due to the diverse requirements and distinct perspectives of different cities on the implementation of various initiatives.

Public transport: Urban areas with comprehensive transportation networks derive several advantages from a diverse range of applications that enhance the efficiency of public transportation. Mobile apps provide immediate information management, giving users realistic options and remedies for bottlenecks caused by malfunctions, accidents, unanticipated occurrences, or supply chain events. The implementation of IoT sensors on existing physical infrastructure has a major influence on the management of smart regular maintenance. This impact is due to the prompt management and constant feedback received from the IoT sensors. This endeavor involves a small amount of financial commitment, yet yields substantial advantages. Digital signage and intelligent transportation systems (ITSs) are utilized to enhance user experience by delivering up-to-date information regarding delays or unexpected incidents, enabling travelers to adapt their routes in real-time. Utilizing the current physical infrastructure to enhance the usage of IoT sensors provides a twofold advantage: it simplifies the upkeep of monitoring and control facilities while also benefiting the end user at the same time.

Traffic mitigation: The creation of sustainable cities (SCs) and the decrease of traffic are two interrelated but increasingly important subjects in urban planning. The act of minimizing traffic congestion and enhancing safety is referred to as traffic mitigation. In contrast, SCs use technology to boost productivity and reduce pollution. Both can help build desirable communities and are fundamental components in modern urban design. Strategies that reduce traffic congestion are considered efficient, particularly in urban regions where personal vehicles and public transportation are the main modes of movement. Car navigators facilitate the adjustment of routes between the starting point and the destination. Additionally, they provide drivers with a live display of current traffic conditions and notify them about the estimated time of arrival (ETA). Intelligent parking applications that direct vehicles directly to available parking spaces effectively decrease the amount of time spent searching for parking and minimize the release of harmful emissions, thus effectively tackling a prominent contemporary problem.

Air quality: Air quality monitors enable scientific communities to detect and measure dangerous levels of pollutants like ozone, sulfur dioxide, carbon dioxide & particulate matter. The sensors are capable of detecting even minor fluctuations in air quality and promptly alerting local authorities to take appropriate action. SCs devise ways to address potential air quality issues and predict them through techniques such as air quality modeling. Various methodologies can now be employed in urban areas to monitor the air quality index (AQI) to deal with the problem of air pollution.

Solid waste reduction: The fundamental components of contemporary waste management systems include technology that reduce the amount of solid trash, follow its movement, enable financial transactions, and utilize the Internet of Things. These technological innovations have the potential to reduce waste generation and track its whereabouts in real time to ensure proper disposal. Effective solid waste management is primarily dependent on financial transactions, which serve a crucial function in both monitoring and minimizing waste. Moreover, the Internet of Things technology facilitates the immediate monitoring and control of the complete waste management system. Trash monitoring is a crucial component of waste management, serving as a method to oversee rubbish disposal procedures and ensure their smooth operation. By utilizing GPS monitoring or RFID tagging, we can effectively monitor the location and movement of trash in real time, providing significant assistance. This aids in identifying the primary sources of garbage and reduces the probability of improper disposal.

The term “smart city” (SC) refers to urban areas that have been networked together by a network of interconnected, diversified, and intelligent devices that share and receive data infrequently but consistently over the Internet of Things (IoT). More and more, researchers are focusing on how to use the IoT paradigm to make it easier to share videos and other forms of audiovisual information. The introduction of Mobility Services User Virtualization (MISSION) is a unique strategy aimed at maximizing Quality of Service (QoS) and load balancing in a 5G network (Anedda & Giusto, 2020). In order to lessen the impact on the network, cut down on user engagements, and save power, MISSION makes use of cloud computing and broadcasting. A further distinguishing feature of SCs is their dedication to creating and upkeep of authentic public parks, protecting mountains, preserving wildlife, and overseeing and controlling coastal erosion. Using the social Internet of Things (SIoT), the system for monitoring coastal crowding. Protecting coasts from erosion due to urbanization, natural disasters, and excessive tourism is an area where this approach shows a lot of promise. Furthermore, it intelligently and sustainably handles a big number of visitors.

The concept of the "social internet of things" (SIoT) refers to a network of networked objects that have the ability to autonomously interact with each other by following predetermined protocols. Cameras, sensors, traffic lights, and telephones are components of the system that can collect and exchange data in this environment. The suggested system evaluates the occupancy status of a beach in Cagliari, Italy by analyzing the level of crowding, environmental data obtained from devices located throughout the city, and real-time user feedback through a specialized app. This type of action also encompassed the regulation and surveillance of pedestrian and vehicular transportation. One of the main fields of study in the social sciences is mobility, namely the ongoing trend of urbanization. There has been a substantial surge in interest in a phenomenon associated with the movement of individuals inside metropolitan regions. The prevalence of road congestion and crowded places is increasing. The authors employ video cameras and Wi-Fi-sniffing systems to categorize pedestrians, bicycles, automobiles, and other items during the monitoring stage (Bertolusso et al., 2021). Our objective is to improve the standard of living for individuals by providing advanced information on traffic conditions through a real-time monitoring system. The limitations of using only one technology are overcome by the cooperative utilization of two technologies. Initially, each technique is implemented separately, and the outcomes are merged using neural networks to get a significant degree of accuracy. The sustainable development paradigm plays a crucial role in creating long-lasting solutions for urban mobility, encompassing both public and private alternatives. On a daily basis, the integrated artificial intelligence system examines the gathered traffic data and employs machine learning techniques to ascertain the optimal routes and traffic patterns for both pedestrians and vehicles. Novel solutions and energy-efficient network communication technologies have been created and implemented in a practical setting within a smart city environment to address the growing need for reduced energy consumption (Pilosu et al., 2017).

1.4 Section Organization

In Section 1, we discuss the introduction of the SC and the ICT standardization, with a particular focus on resource management, potential opportunities, and implementations. Section 2 investigates the development of mobile communication systems. Section 3 discusses the technological innovations that laid the foundation for the emergence of 6G as the new standard. Section 4 delves into the divergent ways that new smart cities are utilizing 6G networks. In Section 5, we delve into a variety of technologies for 6G-enabled smart cities, including terahertz communications, artificial intelligence (AI), blockchain-based solutions, quantum communication, UAV and drone-based solutions, and vehicular and mobile solutions. Meanwhile, Section 6 concentrates on the practical implementation of smart city solutions. Section 7 delves into the challenges and provides conclusions. Section 8 outlines possibilities for further research and advancement in this area.

2. EVOLUTION OF MOBILE COMMUNICATION SYSTEMS

Every decade since the 1980s introduced the first analogue communication system, a new generation has emerged. A "first generation" device uses analog technology and only communicates by speech. Email and text messages were made possible by the second generation (2G) of digital communication. Multimedia communication, or "third generation" (3G), made streaming video and music to mobile devices possible. Long-term evolution (LTE) allowed 4G downlink transmission speeds of 1 Gbps. Smartphone growth has been accelerated by LTE. LTE allows people to stream HD videos and play online games anywhere. The commercialization of 5G on a global scale commenced in 2019 (Series, 2015). The 5G netwroks can reach 20 Gbps transmission rates which is 20 times faster than 4G. the eMBB, mMTC & URLLC (ultra-reliable low latency communication) are the three primary 5G use cases that have garnered attention. Millimeter wave frequencies (mmWave) like 28 GHz and network slicing, which lets you delegate jobs to different sections of a network, are two 5G features. Smart factories, linked autos, and smart cities require 5G mobile connectivity.

By 2030, 6G is expected to be commercially available which provide superior performance & revolutionary services compared to that of 5G. The updated recommendation for IMT-2030 (6G) was finalized in June 2023 by ITU-R WP 5D (ITU, 2023) as shown Figure 1. The 6G concept encompasses six distinct use cases. Three of these use cases are extensions of the eMBB, mMTC, and URLLC; three more are new use cases. One type of communication is immersive communication, another is gigantic communication, still another is hyper-reliable and low-latency communication (HRLLC), a sixth type is AI and communication, and the seventh is ubiquitous connectivity. We must support NTN in conjunction with the terrestrial network (TN) to guarantee extensive coverage and mobility if we want these scenarios to come to fruition. Furthermore, the integration of sensing & AI in 6G network has been anticipated to enhance sensing precision, detection & AI-related inference capabilities along with improved connectivity. The SSC can greatly enhance productivity and living circumstances by implementing 6G technology.

Figure 1. Network technology development phases

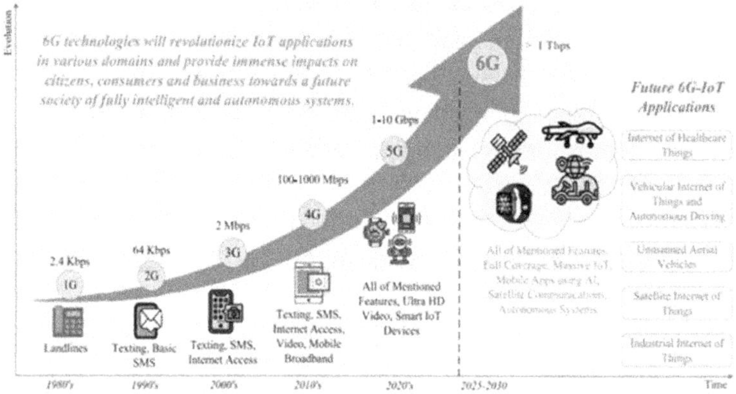

(Nguyen et al., 2021)

3. EMERGENCE OF THE NEW STANDARD: 6G

The 5G networks have revolutionized the manner in which individuals communicate and interact with one another. The introduction of 5G's advanced features, such as its extensive networking capabilities, minimal latency, and lightning-fast speeds, has created new opportunities for both consumers and corporate sectors.

Still, as time goes on and technology improves, experts in the field are looking forward to the 6G cellular network upgrade. There are several arguments in favor of creating a new generation of wireless technology. At the outset, once 5G rollout is complete, every industry dependent on the telecoms industry will need a fresh, ground-breaking product to help them thrive. They will put their energy into finding better ways to do things or creating whole new services. Draft 6G was a substantial improvement over 5G since it can self-aggregate diverse networks to satisfy changing resource demands.

The purpose of the current network revolution, 5G, is to connect a large number of people and devices to Smart Cities (IoT) by 2020 and beyond, in addition to offering fast internet to consumers (ITU, 2023). The 2015 World Radio Communication Conference sought to reserve a frequency spectrum below 6 GHz for mobile communications. In the 2015 World Radiocommunication Conference (WRC), it was claimed that extending the frequency range below 6 GHz would not be enough to manage the global mobile traffic surge. Thus, the 2019 WRC determined that multi-Gbps data rates require frequency ranges beyond 6 GHz.

6G is still in its early stages, but early expectations are that it will outperform 5G in terms of speed, latency, and functionality. 6G research is mainly concentrated on numerous important domains:

Among the higher frequency ranges 6G is expected to use than 5G, terahertz frequencies—THz frequencies—are one. These bands promise considerably higher data speeds and lower latency.

- AI: The more AI is included into 6G's architecture, the many fresh apps and services as well as better network management will be enabled. Just two of the fresh features 6G is expected to bring forth by using quantum computing are advanced sensing and secure communications.
- 6G is expected to provide AR and VR experiences that are more seamless and immersive, so opening up new opportunities in sectors such education, healthcare, and gaming. Plans are already under way to build the infrastructure required even if 6G won't be accessible for some time. As scientists and corporate executives keep stretching the boundaries of what is feasible, 6G will surely deliver even more exciting opportunities for future development and innovation.

The two main objectives of 6G technology are to provide lightning-fast internet connectivity and to cover the entire planet. The 6G network's architecture will also incorporate planning. This implies the network will be aware of its own consumption habits as well as its members' immediate and future demands. It may adjust its resource allocation and consumption as needed and even ask for more funding from the right people. As a consequence, strong business strategies and convincing arguments will emerge.

- The convergence of present-day wireless communication with compute, control, location, and sensing is referred to as the “3CLS” convergence.
- In order to maintain an unobstructed view and achieve optimal signal strength with minimal attenuation, it is necessary to utilize intelligent reflecting sur-

faces and create suitable settings. These surfaces encompass a wide range of structures, including walls, roadways, doors, and even entire buildings.

- A substantial quantity of small-scale data is accessible: Migrating from a system where data is stored in a centralized manner on a large scale to a system where data is distributed in a small-scale manner across multiple locations.
- Bits, spectra, and dependability are abundant resources that are easily accessible. Increased frequency range, reaching up to 1 terabit per second, measured in gigahertz (GHz).
- In order for autonomous wireless networks to maintain themselves, artificial intelligence is an essential element.

4. EMERGING SMART CITIES UTILIZING 6G TECHNOLOGY

As the need for high-tech solutions in smart cities grow, there is a lot of talk about whether or not 6G networks can provide the facilities these future cities will need. 5G networks have come a long way in making it easier to connect and connect things to the Internet of Things (IoT). 6G networks should have even faster speeds, less delay, and more space. They can handle the complicated systems and gadgets in smart cities (SCs) because of this. A lot of cutting-edge technologies, like driverless cars, smart grids, and virtual healthcare, can be used by new SCs thanks to 6G networks as shown in Figure 2. This could lead to novel prospects for both urban residents and businesses. However, 6G networks are currently in their nascent phase of advancement, and it may take several years before they become extensively accessible. Currently, academics and specialists are investigating the potential advantages and applications of 6G networks in emerging smart city initiatives.

Figure 2. Overall 6G-enabled SC architecture

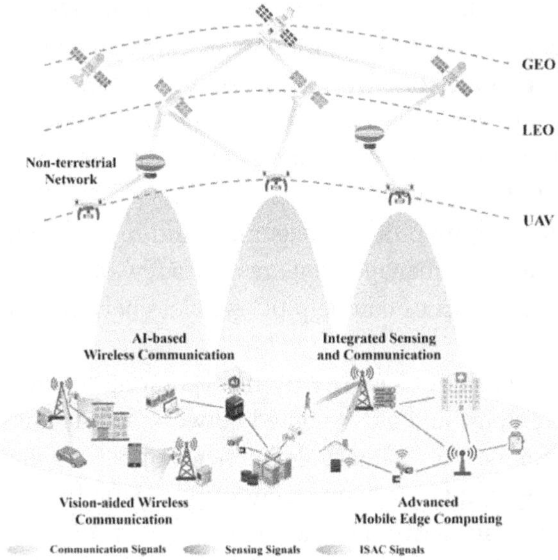

- **Transportation and Logistics Made Smart:** By 2030 and beyond, people will be able to travel in a way that is safe, efficient, and kind to the environment thanks to drones and autonomous cars.
- **Robots Working in Tandem With Autonomous Systems:** To navigate their surroundings, self-driving cars use a variety of sensors, including radar, sonar, GPS, and light detection and ranging (LiDAR).
- **Global Connectivity:** This is essential for monitoring and managing ecosystems in maritime and river environments. This requires network coverage that extends to both the surface and depths of the water. This is especially accurate in municipalities that are situated near rivers or ports, as accessing resources may be a challenge.
- **Pervasive Intelligence:** An example of pervasive intelligence would be the proliferation of networked gadgets like smart automobiles, drones, and robots. Novel applications will emerge as a result of this trend, calling for more computationally intensive artificial intelligence (AI) systems. These technologies include a diverse array of applications, such as computer vision, speech and face recognition, SLAM, motion control, and natural language processing.
- **Terahertz Communications:** In accordance with guidelines (ITU, 2022), the mmWave band (30–300 GHz) will encompass the frequency range of 275

GHz–3 THz for cellular communications. This might result in a more than 11-fold increase in the band's total capacity. THz interfaces are a critical issue that will probably need the use of highly directed antennas..

- **AI:** Machine learning, or ML, has the ability to accelerate algorithms that deal with activities that are time-consuming, such as handovers or network selects. Additionally, ML can reduce delays in communication processing (Yang et al., 2019).
- **ML:** Problems with mobility management and resource allocation, task offloading, and handover management are only a few of the technological obstacles that these approaches can help 6G wireless networks overcome (Noman et al., 2023).
- **Blockchain:** It enhances security by incorporating a consensus process, effective cryptography, and a distributed network architecture to eliminate potential weak points. The primary deficiencies of 5G are platform interoperability and throughput (10,000 transactions per second) (Basar et al., 2019).
- **Quantum Communication:** The new concept of quantum computing (Mukherjee, 2022) uses a quantum key from the quantum no-cloning theorem and the uncertainty principle to secure 6G implementation. Quantum information is stored using photons or other quantum particles. According to the rules of quantum mechanics, this information cannot be retrieved or replicated without disturbing it. Quantum communication enhances data transfer capacity by leveraging the inherent capability of qubits to exist in a superposition state.
- **Cell-Free Communication:** Traditional orthogonal & cellular communications will undergo a transition to cell-free & non-orthogonal communications. Users would have the ability to seamlessly transition between multiple networks, with the most optimal communication technology of the available options being automatically selected. This will effectively resolve issues such as the ping-pong effect, data losses, and handover failures and delays that are frequently observed in cellular networks.
- **Unmanned Aerial Vehicles:** UAVs have cellular connectivity provided via onboard base stations (BSs). They are readily deployed, possess robust line-of-sight connection, and can maneuver under control. Unmanned aerial vehicles (UAVs) prove to be quite useful in times of crisis, like when natural disasters strike.
- **Mobile enhanced edge computing (MEEC):** MEEC is essential to 6G technology due to distributed massive cloud applications (Zhang, 2022). In cloud-based circumstances, data transfer over long distances from end devices and edge servers to the cloud requires a lot of bandwidth and causes latency and security risks.

- **Optical Wireless:** This technology, which provides exceptionally low latency and high data speeds, has a many of applications, including underwater optical wireless communications and V2X communication. LiDAR (Padmal et al., 2022) is a promising advancement in 6G communications that has the potential to generate highly detailed 3D mapping. Spatial multiplexing techniques and microLED technologies will also reach maturity and cost-effectiveness in 2026.
- **AR and VR:** It is thought that using 6G technology will make augmented reality (AR) and virtual reality (VR) experiences better and more engaging. This progress will make it easier to find new uses for things like vehicle comms and SC security.

5. SMART CITIES SUPPORTED BY 6G TECHNOLOGY

The utilization of advanced communication technology, particularly 6G networks, in the construction and operation of smart cities is a crucial component of 6G-enabled smart cities. A Smart City (SC) employs a diverse range of digital technology and data-driven solutions to enhance the well-being and contentment of its inhabitants, optimize the functionality of its infrastructure, and foster sustainable development. This can make it easier to keep an eye on and manage urban resources. For example, smart garbage management systems should be put in place, water and energy resources should be used efficiently, and data analysis should be used to plan the growth of cities. Furthermore, putting in place 6G-enabled smart cities is expected to improve people's access to services which will lead to more inclusion and better health. Table 2 lists and outlines the 6G technologies that enable smart city applications.

Table 2. Potential 6G technologies and brief outlines

Potential Areas	Terahertz Communication (THz)	Artificial Intelligence (AI)	Blockchain (BC)
Focus	Use 0.1–10 THz for THz communication. Super-fast (1 Tbps) data and wide bandwidth.	For 6G networks, AI can analyze, manage, and optimize resources. AI can improve channel estimations, energy efficiency, modulation recognition, data caching, traffic prediction, radio resource management, mobility management, etc.	This heterogeneous architecture uses a distributed ledger for safety, privacy, scalability, and dependability.
Benefits	High bandwidth and low latency from terahertz waves, ideal for highly populated locations with many linked devices and abundant of data.	Increased data privacy and correctness through federated learning; improved radio transmission adaption to specific surroundings utilizing AI algorithms; and better traffic classification for QoS and resource management.	Enhanced UAV communication security and privacy with blockchain and 6G; increased transaction trust and transparency; efficient data management and decreased storage expenses.
Challenges	High-loss connection, short range, and high air attenuation of terahertz waves limit existing THz antennas and IRS technology.	Federated learning in 6G is complicated by mobile device resource restrictions, energy limitations from intense calculations and transmission costs, and managing non-identical and scattered data.	Complex integration of blockchain with supply chain applications; data security while adopting efficient rules; significant challenges in using blockchain for varied applications.
Technological Advances	Create ultra-massive MIMO with miniature grids and integrate active components onto inert metasurfaces.	RNNs and CNNs for modulation recognition and traffic classification; CNN federated learning for data privacy; Tree-RNN model for network traffic classification; RNN-CNN networks for IoT traffic.	Integrating blockchain with 6G for UAV security; using AI to alter distant communication; creating a multi-tier blockchain-edge computing architecture.
Proposed Solution	To meet future SC demands, layered Bee Hive terrestrial network topology with RISs for optimum transmission paths.	Decentralized relay selection employing cooperative communication network diversity to optimize federated learning training; relay-by-relay training flow modification to handle energy and data distribution concerns.	Blockchain-based security solutions in 6G networks for Industry 4.0 and UAV communication systems; decentralized approach for IoT and industrial application protection and trust.

continued on following page

Table 2. Continued

Potential Areas	Terahertz Communication (THz)	Artificial Intelligence (AI)	Blockchain (BC)
Applications	Effective transmission for 6G ITS and autonomous driving; enhancing signal strength, positioning precision, and physical layer security.	Improved communication channel modulation and traffic recognition; smart city service, resource management, and security; sophisticated 6G system training with federated learning for varied applications.	Securing UAV communications in dangerous regions; increasing Industry 4.0 and IoT applications with blockchain; and improving smart city and industrial IoT privacy and security.
Potential Areas	**Quantum Computing (QC)**	**UAVs and Drone**	**Vehicular and Mobile Solutions**
Focus	Due to quantum no-cloning theorem and uncertainty, quantum information introduces absolute randomness, improving security and channel capacity.	In 6G networks, UAVs and drones are used for optimization, mobility, and smart city and IoE applications.	MEC, 6G, and aerial computing for smart cities improve vehicular and mobile solutions.
Benefits	Improved communication security and efficiency; 6G network computation and robustness.	Better network mobility, operational performance, data delivery, tailored network services, and message delivery success.	MEC reduces latency and improves security; 6G speeds up data processing; C-LNet accelerates vehicle tracking and control; aerial computing provides global computing.
Challenges	Integrating quantum communication (QC) into 6G architecture; addressing 5G security problems.	Optimising UAV-BS placement in dynamic situations; managing high mobility and network topology changes; and user-centric network privacy and control.	City technology incompatibility, excessive latency in high-frequency communication, managing high-speed vehicular communication, rain attenuation influencing communication dependability, edge-cloud computing integration, and comprehensive computing frameworks.
Technological Advances	Security improvements using quantum communication (QC) and quantum key distribution (QKD); CNN data encryption.	ACDQL for continuous optimization, edge-enabled MQTT message transfer, CHNN-based OLSR routing, DHT-based routing algorithms, and DLT-DHT user-centric network (UCN) architecture.	Decentralized MEC, 6G digital twins for SCs, C-LNet for LiDAR and camera data fusion, millimeter-wave frequencies and JCAS for spatial tracking, and aerial computing for global service and scalability.

continued on following page

Table 2. Continued

Potential Areas	Terahertz Communication (THz)	Artificial Intelligence (AI)	Blockchain (BC)
Proposed Solution	Smart communication systems use QKD for secure key exchanges and CNN-based encryption for data security.	Dynamic UAV-BS placement with incentive functions; edge-enabled messaging; novel UAV routing protocols; user-centric network design with greater privacy and customisation.	MEC for latency reduction, C-LNet for data fusion, millimeter-wave frequencies for precise tracking, aerial computing with edge computing, and EMDCs for fire management.
Applications	6G network security, quantum cryptography and CNN-based encryption for smart city (SC) data, and 5G security problems.	Smart city networks and IoE integration; better ITS and operational performance; UAV routing and data management; tailored and secure network services.	Smart cities, vehicular networks, emergency services, sophisticated vehicle monitoring and coordination, worldwide computing for smart utilities and manufacturing, and fire prediction and management.

5.1. Terahertz Communications

SCs of the future and how 6G network technology will play a part in their creation. This highlights the significance of densely populated areas with an emphasis on artificial intelligence, numerous linked devices, and substantial data flow. These utopian cities would benefit greatly from the high bandwidth and low latency offered by terahertz waves in a 6G network. In contrast, terahertz waves are difficult to use in the 6G network due to their short range and air attenuation. In order to address the potential future demands of SCs, the research proposed a terrestrial network topology called the layered Bee Hive.

The constraints of current THz antennas and IRS can be overcome by concentrating on ultra-massive MIMO with a small array scale. The THz connections are impacted by high-loss connectivity. A low-cost method for dynamically optimizing the transmission path by integrating active components into inert metasurfaces. This approach is achieved through the use of reconfigurable intelligent surfaces (RISs). In order for 6G ITS and autonomous driving to function effectively, it is imperative that we are able to transmit and receive vast quantities of data with minimal latency, ensuring that all individuals remain safe and enjoy themselves. Still, things can get in the way of communications trying to travel via high-frequency bands like THz and millimeter wave (mmWave). The ability of intelligent signal reflectors and propagation direction modifiers, or IRSs, to create intelligent radio environments and solve this problem has garnered a lot of interest (Zhu et al., 2022).

5.2. Artificial Intelligence

Other adaptive radio communications, such cognitive radio, have been used for 20 years. Intelligent radio in 6G can be implemented using powerful AI algorithms to adapt radio transmissions to unique radio environments. Due to the growing volume of data traffic in SCs, communication systems use different modulation techniques to transmit data efficiently. Signal demodulation and decoding depend on modulation recognition, which is essential for interference detection, signal identification, spectrum monitoring, and threat assessment. For example, RNNs and CNNs were developed to identify the modulation scheme employed in communication channels influenced by additive white Gaussian noise and Rayleigh fading. Convolutional neural network (CNN) federated learning ensures data privacy and correctness throughout transmission (Shi et al., 2021). For modulation recognition, this strategy ensures differential privacy.

Traffic classification, like modulation classification, ensures QoS, controls pricing, improves resource management, and secures SC applications. A Tree-RNN model for 12 network traffic categories. Each class is represented by a node in the model's tree structure, making classification easier. For IoT traffic classification, (Lopez-Martin et al., 2017) introduces an RNN-CNN network. CNN layers capture complex network traffic attributes from incoming data without feature selection, unlike classical machine learning. For efficient CAV-specific ML application training, the framework satisfies high standards. It exploits future road networks' CAV proliferation.

As the next major telecommunications technology, 6G is being intensively followed by researchers and corporations. Healthcare (Kumar, Singh, & Kim, 2024), industry, and education have swiftly adopted virtual meetings and live video communications due to the COVID-19 epidemic.

Federated learning (FL) could train 6G communication systems' pervasive intelligence. FL is difficult to apply in 6G-enabled periphery systems due to mobile device resource constraints and dispersed training power usage.

5.3. Blockchain-Based Solutions

Standard UAV communication systems cannot handle UAVs' fast movement and ever-changing nature, especially in hazardous areas. Thus, a safe and effective UAV network is urgently needed. Inspired by these considerations, (Aggarwal, Kumar, & Tanwar, 2020) examines 6G technology's structure, prerequisites, and uses in UAV communication. UAV communication applications are used to classify solutions. Additionally, a blockchain-based security solution using 6G network connectivity is introduced. A case study in the book as shown in Figure 3 shows how blockchain and 6G networks can secure Industry 4.0 applications in a UAV communication system.

Figure 3. Blockchain-based 6G environment

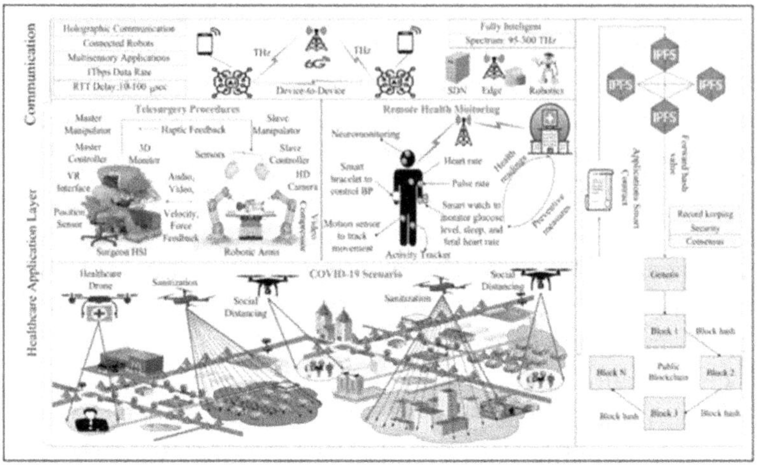

(Kumari, Gupta, & Tanwar, 2021)

Public and private enterprises, as well as government agencies, face substantial challenges when attempting to use blockchain technology for a variety of supply chain applications. There are many moving parts to the complex process of improving and optimizing services for the people. Adopting efficient rules, boosting confidence among lawmakers, and cutting data storage expenses while maintaining data security can all be addressed with blockchain technology. Anyone may check records thanks to the system's decentralized nature, which increases security. Financial transactions and other contacts rely heavily on trust. Blockchain's transparent system allows users to authenticate and observe regulatory procedures, reestablishing and preserving confidence. Because of the profound effect it has on people's daily lives, this idea is of paramount importance in the banking industry. In addition, by utilizing AI, the launch of 6G would radically alter distant communication (Tekale, Rajagopal, & Bhoopathy, 2022). In addition, this study delves into the solutions concerning 6G network security and privacy, for future studies on the subject. A multi-tier architecture for 5G and future generations that mixes blockchain and edge computing. This design switching from centralized to decentralized, more resilient models to help secure edge devices that don't have a lot of resources. It acknowledges that blockchain could change the way things are done and provide better protection. For many commercial uses of the Internet of Things (IoT), strict security and privacy rules are also needed. When blockchain technology came along, it changed the way people share information by making a safe, open platform that builds trust and gets rid of the need for middlemen (Pajooh, Demidenko, & Aslam, 2022). Blockchain technology (BCT) has gotten a lot of interest because it can deal with issues like privacy, security, interoperability, spectrum resource scarcity, and lack of central authority. In new areas like industrial IoT (IIoT) and Industry 5.0 apps, it could also be useful. Because 5G networks can't handle the needs of disruptive IoT apps that need a lot of data, 6G networks need to use decentralized blockchain-based architecture (Singh, Kumar, Tanwar, & Park, 2024)(Singh et al., 2023).

5.4. Quantum Communication

Due to rapid technological breakthroughs, ultra-reliable, fast, low-power, and secure communication is in high demand. Therefore, QC is a new field of interest to researchers since it can efficiently and robustly solve complex computations. Quality control (QC) is projected to accelerate and simplify computation and improve 6G and future communication system security. In (Ali et al., 2023), the authors explain QC & how quantum communication has evolved across different technologies and uses. The authors examine key 6G communication performance optimization approaches & criteria in computing, security, and efficiency. Quantum communication may confront challenges in the 6G architecture, but there are also opportunities for additional research. 5G security vulnerabilities and proposes remedies. In particular, we examine how quantum key distribution could improve 6G security. Finally, a novel secure SC communication technique. It uses CNN & quantum cryptography. The suggested solution uses quantum key distribution to secure key exchanges between communication parties. The QKD-generated key is utilized by a CNN for data encryption. SC data is protected by CNN based encryption.

5.5. UAVs and Drone-Based Solutions

Another rapidly expanding discipline is the utilization of drones and their numerous potential applications. The accomplishment of breakthroughs has been substantially accelerated by recent improvements in this field, such as commercial drones, operational ad hoc networks, minimal latency & inventions beyond 5G.

An ACDQL technique that expands the function area of the algorithm known as RL from discrete to continuous in order to resolve the location optimization problem.

This approach is designed to address the challenge of optimizing the placement of UAV-BSs in the presence of mobile endpoints. In particular, we provide a method for dynamically positioning a UAV-BS while the user is in motion, which is a significant enhancement over previous research that relied on fixed ground endpoint locations. The incentive function that is proposed is intended to optimize the users' sum data rate and ensure that the UAV-BS remains within the area of interest.

A viable mobility model and edge-enabled opportunistic MQTT message transfer mechanism were built to achieve this. Moreover, a specific network segment was developed to measure routing effectiveness, resulting in a message delivery success rate of 0.99 at QoS2 and an end-to-end delay of 1.19 seconds at QoS1. The optimal link-state protocol (OLSR) routing algorithm (Wei, Yang, & Huang, 2023) uses a continuous Hopfield neural network (CHNN). This method reduces disruptions and improves service routing in UAVs that establish flying ad hoc networks. The OLSR protocol is outperformed by the proposed protocol in the following areas: the delivery of packets rates, controlled overhead, efficiency, and end-to-end latency.

For high mobility, where the network topology changes often, distributed hash table (DHT)-based routing algorithms were suggested. A MANET routing system that minimizes routing overhead and lookup time using logical clustering and replication. 6G mobile communication system subscriber data management method. This method uses DLT and DHT. A network-centric design approach allows conventional mobile communication systems to efficiently serve many subscribers. This study instead investigates user-centric design, which creates user-defined, configurable, and controllable systems. Customized network services for individual users are possible using this technology.

Cheap and outfitted transmitters, cameras, and sensors, UAVs can connect to their environment and improve network mobility, making them perfect IoT devices. The possible benefits of UAVs in SCs, focusing on ITS, and the main potential barriers. Integrating numerous AI algorithms improves data delivery through global connection and operational performance. Although new, UAV-enabled IoE apps can improve 6G networks. This paper examines new UAV uses in IoE and their operation. It discusses the risks and challenges of the Internet of Everything and the newest IoT convergence trends toward a smarter IoE (Saini & Jain, 2023).

5.6. Vehicular and Mobile Solutions

The use of smart systems allows MEC to minimize latency and increase storage capacity in devices with limited computing power. Technology incompatibility in cities is a major concern. MEC may slow network speed due to many linked devices. User-generated information and algorithms can help these devices recognize strange events.

6G technology is being influenced by construction and SC digitization (Konhäuser, 2021). Energy storage and supply must be prioritized through energy management to integrate renewable energy into buildings and smart cities. Building energy efficiency contributes 35% to greenhouse gas emissions from ultimate energy demand, hence political views have shifted. Next-generation mobile communication technologies like 5G beyond and 6G propose tailored solutions for building digitalization in edge clouds. In our digital age, 6G will revolutionize communication and management of massive networks of interconnected devices at macro, micro, and nanoscales. 6G can improve healthcare, transportation, logistics, safety, privacy, and more in addition to providing rapid connectivity. Large amounts of data may be processed, stored, and visualized quickly with this technology. We can also study how 5G and 6G technologies affect intelligent and perceptive SCs (Chhabra et al., 2023).

A microcellular architecture using carrier frequencies far higher than those utilized in 5G cellular networks will slow cellular communication in future iterations. More precisely, vehicle speed, rain attenuation, and depolarization can influence the reliability of communication systems that deliver important services. The mandatory adoption of eCall emergency systems in EU-sold motor vehicles from 2018 hinders 6G emergency management development. Because rain increases traffic accidents, this is especially true.

The main objectives of SC road environment using modern 6G digital twins. The goal is to understand SC traffic's complex road conditions, focusing on vehicular networks (VNs). The study looks into how well collaboration and fusion technologies between multiple sensors can meet the active control needs of smart cars in the network. It is suggested that LiDAR and camera data be combined in a new segmentation network called C-LNet. C-LNet is built with two encoders and one decoder. Image and LiDAR information are taken out using separate encoders. Syncing the LiDAR point cloud data and picture data in the sensing space makes them work together. A system based on multiscale feature fusion is also created to efficiently handle multimodal data related to vehicle cooperation. These include 5G, IoT & modifications to cars, the energy frameworks, high rates computing power, AI, data analytics, satellite communication, optics & cyber-security. In addition, 6G makes it easier to quickly find, analyze, handle, and understand huge amounts of data. Through this study, the benefits and requirements of 6G technology will be looked at, along with how it might help smart, clever, and advanced cities grow. The utilization of millimeter-wave frequencies and wireless networks for perceptive radio networks and channel-based sensing is emphasized by the promise of 6G joint communication and sensing (JCAS) to introduce new ideas and SC services. The proposed concept is to operate within the mm-Wave beam space and quantify the connections between cells in order to enhance the precision of spatial sensory activity tracking. The feasibility of the 6G-driven concept is demonstrated through a case study that employs simulations to demonstrate the process of identifying and categorizing vehicles.

You can now track the path of cars going by, which is an extra service that was made possible by the upgrades. Edge and cloud computing lack or partially implement many future applications and scenarios. This constraint has sparked academic and industry interest in a full computing framework. There are few studies that methodically create and evaluate an all-encompassing computing paradigm, hence current research is lacking. Aerial computing offers global computing service, mobility, scalability, availability, and simultaneity. As airborne computing technologies, energy replenishment, peripheral computing, network of things applications, bands of frequencies, multi-access techniques, AI & big data are also explored. Aerial computing can be advantageous for vertical domain applications, including smart utilities, smart factories, smart vehicles, and SCs.

In order for future smart cities to succeed in every area, emergency services are crucial. When it comes to making sure everyone is safe, firefighting is crucial. But having very reliable and quick communication systems is critical for firefighting to be effective. With the use of distributed sensors, robots, and other cutting-edge technologies, firefighters may get real-time instructions. The main emphasis of the research in this specific context was on enhancing fire prediction and management through the deployment of edge micro-data centers (EMDCs).

6. REAL IMPLEMENTATION OF SMART CITIES

More than 140 intelligent urban centers exist worldwide, and the number is growing (Mobile Magazine, n.d.). There is no consensus on smart city definitions. London leads the smart city (SC) after a steady rise. Connect London is one of London's innovative smart city schemes, creating the city's 5G network and fiber optic coverage. Also, London's famed lampposts now include electric car charging stations and several sensors. Due to the city's efforts in AI, IoT, and 6G, these cutting-edge solutions are expected to advance as shown in Figure 4.

Figure 4. Smart cities and IoT devices

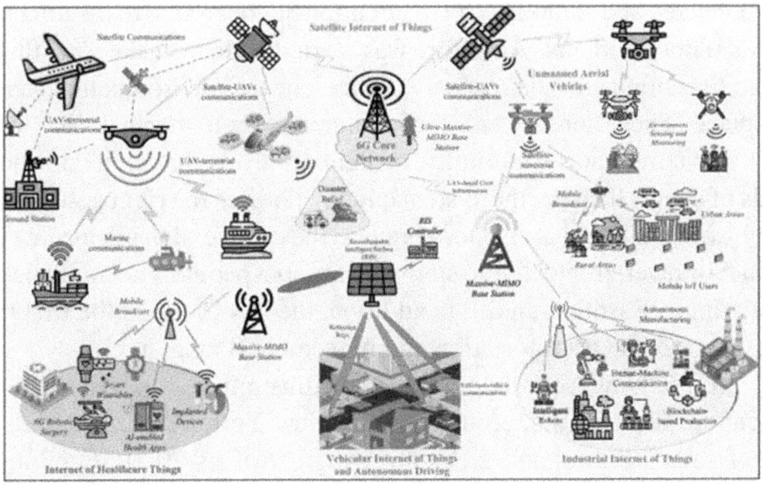

(Nguyen et al., 2021)

Barcelona is another smart city. A network of sensor-equipped LED lampposts has been installed. These sensors measure traffic, air quality, pedestrian activity, and noise. Lights can be adjusted or turned off as needed. The city also uses smart waste bins with vacuums to move rubbish underground, decreasing odors and collecting vehicle trips. Oslo implements clever sensors too. Oslo Smart Street Lighting aims to increase street lighting efficiency across the city. Oslo's street-lighting system is now a unified network accessible via internet apps. This system manages and monitors lighting levels and adjusts light intensity for seasonal variations and special demands. Thus, citywide energy efficiency improves. Over 70% less energy was used in Oslo after 20,000 smart bulbs were installed (Dong, n.d.).

Singapore is rightly at the top of the list of the smartest places in Asia. Singapore began its Smart Nation program in 2014, which has since brought a lot of high-tech gadgets. Singapore's public transportation is used by about 7.5 million people every year. Contactless payment technology has made it much easier for them to pay and get around. Putting Internet of Things (IoT) devices on patients that they can wear and making video consultations through a digital health system normal are two ways to deal with the problems that come with an aging population. This multifaceted plan can help ease the worry that comes with an aging population (Dong, n.d.).

A lot of people agree that Seoul is the best city at using big data. Seoul has established a robust foundation for the emergence of smart infrastructure and services by utilizing the network of sensors and closed-circuit visual devices that are dispersed throughout the city.

As shown in Figure 4 these patterns include traffic flow, speed, and air quality, which are collected and studied. A lot of attention has been paid to meeting the needs of the city's older residents. An effort was started to help make sure that elderly people who live alone are safe. As part of this scheme, environmental sensors will be put in place. These sensors can find things that aren't normal, like long times of inactivity or temperature, humidity, or lighting levels that aren't normal. When these kinds of events happen, the system quickly notifies the right case workers and emergency workers. Seoul is also looking into the chance of using its data platform to create an AI-powered detective system that can spot people who might be planning to commit crimes (Earth.org, n.d.). In addition, the city is one of the first to use 5G technology to improve transportation and movement (Dong, n.d.).

Finally, SCs in New York are still another illustration of advanced technological application. Over its numerous districts, New York City tested and installed hundreds of smart sensors and technology as part of its 2020 SC pilot program (SmartUp Cities, n.d.). Using the data gathered by this program helps one better manage services (such as waste collecting and management). Smart hubs replacing the antiquated phone booths in New York included contactless technology, Wi-Fi, and online charging stations.

7. CHALLENGES AND CONCLUSIONS

Smart cities (SCs) and 6G technologies will soon change our lives and careers. However, integrating these technologies presents many challenges. SCs encounter challenges in the areas of data privacy and security, interoperability, the digital gap & deployment.

Smart contracts' interoperability means they work with other connected devices and systems. Communication between systems is the main issue. Regarding data privacy and security, SCs generate large amounts of sensitive and personal data. Data must be stored and processed securely to maintain public trust. Finally, SC technology needs substantial infrastructure & resource investments, which could be challenging for certain communities. The challenges associated with 6G include technological in nature, bandwidth, monetary, privacy, and regulatory issues. Indeed, the implementation of 6G may prove to be challenging due to the necessity of new infrastructure and technology. Additionally, 6G will necessitate an abundance of bandwidth, which could not be accessible in certain regions. The development and implementation of 6G will be expensive, and users may be concerned about access charges.

To protect user privacy and safety, 6G may have security vulnerabilities like other new technologies. Government and corporate sectors must work together to develop and execute 6G technologies. There may also be legislative hurdles. 6G global coverage requires international cooperation and coordination. Conflicting interests among governments and network providers may make global frequency allocation and network standards adoption difficult. A major infrastructure upgrade is needed to achieve global 6G coverage. In order to guarantee adequate coverage, the 6G networks will require significantly additional base nodes & transceiver devices than the 5G networks.

This will require large government and network provider investments. Frequency band dispersion complicates 6G worldwide coverage. 6G networks should use greater frequencies than 5G. The shorter wavelengths of these higher frequencies make them more susceptible to attenuation by buildings and trees. Infrastructure upgrades may be needed to make 6G signals penetrate obstacles and provide enough coverage.

Smart cities leverage improved telecommunications to create new public service, transportation, energy management, and other solutions. 6G networks are anticipated to enhance the connectivity, latency, and data transfer velocities of the forthcoming generations of SCs in accordance with these criteria. Mobility, energy management, public safety, and remote healthcare could all be enhanced by the implementation of 6G in SCs.

6G networks can also transfer data instantly, enabling smart city infrastructure, driverless vehicles, and improved driver-assistance systems to communicate. Telemedicine, remote patient monitoring, and virtual consultations are also possible with 6G networks. 6G networks enable smart energy management, a growing trend. These networks let you monitor and control energy consumption in real time, integrate renewable energy, and boost energy efficiency. By offering expedient and effective communication channels, 6G networks can improve public safety in SCs by supporting advanced monitoring systems, emergency response services, and disaster management. In conclusion, 6G networks can transform urban operations by offering a more efficient, dependable, and rapid service connection for smart city applications.

8. FUTURE DIRECTIONS

We discussed 6G smart city technology in this chapter. To allow smart city applications, these technologies must be interoperable efficiently. Key 6G applications are also covered. Journey to 6G-enabled smart cities will be difficult. Energy-efficient and green technology solutions that reduce capital and operating power costs and benefit the environment need more development. 6G devices will use more energy due to their higher frequency. To improve energy efficiency, implement energy-aware task offloading, efficient resource management, energy-aware design, energy harvesting, and energy collaboration. 6G and AI may also improve network architecture and optimize a sustainable ecosystem. Hyper-connected devices beyond 5G networks bring security and privacy risks that necessitate strong protection. Quantum-safe cryptography and advanced threat-detection systems may be key to defending 6G smart city networks.

THz in 6G requires more accurate channel modeling research. The hardware issues of developing high-frequency THz antennas, amplifiers, and mixers, including high-bandwidth super heterodyne transceivers, must also be addressed. Fast-moving UAVs and satellites will struggle with NTN since their relocation affects network topology and handover. This complicates 6G mobility scenarios since ground users and aerial base stations are mobile. Satellite networks have significant latency and increased BER, making TCP/IP wasteful. Thus, a new or enhanced protocol may be needed for terrestrial-non-terrestrial network interoperability. Several upgraded satellite communication protocols are employed, including TCP Reno (1990), Vegas (1994), Westwood (2001), MPTCP (2011), Cross-layer, Novel-ECM, etc. Different TCP improvement technologies may coexist during 6G evolution's evaluation stage to meet mega-constellation link criteria.

Creating a smart city digital technology platform that combines technical solutions from many cities is necessary. The platform must enable smart city innovation ecosystem convergence and generativity. A recent study report examined the functional and non-functional needs of 20 middleware smart city systems, including AMF-CPS, CityPulse, FIWARE, S2NetM, etc. Smart city middleware still faces interoperability, large data security, scalability, context management, energy efficiency, dependability, and QOS difficulties. Smart city stakeholders including computer scientists, social scientists, urban planners, and others can collaborate to improve knowledge and solutions.

All inhabitants should have access to 6G-enabled smart city network services to bridge the digital divide. Using NTN, RIS, AI, Cloud, VLC, and other technologies, 6G is poised to solve this problem, but creating cost-effective integrated solutions to make smart city apps cheap for everybody may be difficult. Smart city devices/sensors must be replaced with 6G-enabled ones throughout the 6G transition. The economic consequences and other issues will be huge. To reduce expenses, several technologies must be integrated.

REFERENCES

7 Smart City Solutions Implemented by New York during COVID-19. Available online: https://www.smartupcities.com/7-smart-city-solutions-implemented-by-new-york-during-covid-19/

Abdel Hakeem, S. A., Hussein, H. H., & Kim, H. (2022). Security requirements and challenges of 6G technologies and applications. *Sensors (Basel)*, 22(5), 1969. DOI: 10.3390/s22051969 PMID: 35271113

Aggarwal, S., Kumar, N., & Tanwar, S. (2020). Blockchain-envisioned UAV communication using 6G networks: Open issues, use cases, and future directions. *IEEE Internet of Things Journal*, 8(7), 5416–5441. DOI: 10.1109/JIOT.2020.3020819

Ali, M. Z., Abohmra, A., Usman, M., Zahid, A., Heidari, H., Imran, M. A., & Abbasi, Q. H. (2023). Quantum for 6G communication: A perspective. *IET Quantum Communication*, 4(3), 112–124. DOI: 10.1049/qtc2.12060

Anedda, M., & Giusto, D. D. (2020, October). Urban mobility services based on user virtualization and social IoT. In *2020 IEEE International Symposium on Broadband Multimedia Systems and Broadcasting (BMSB)* (pp. 1-4). IEEE. DOI: 10.1109/BMSB49480.2020.9379791

Anedda, M., Muntean, G. M., & Murroni, M. (2016, June). Adaptive real-time multi-user access network selection algorithm for load-balancing over heterogeneous wireless networks. In *2016 IEEE International Symposium on Broadband Multimedia Systems and Broadcasting (BMSB)* (pp. 1-4). IEEE. DOI: 10.1109/BMSB.2016.7521907

Anedda, M., Murroni, M., & Muntean, G. M. (2017, June). E-ARMANS: Energy-aware device-oriented video delivery in heterogeneous wireless networks. In *2017 IEEE International Symposium on Broadband Multimedia Systems and Broadcasting (BMSB)* (pp. 1-6). IEEE. DOI: 10.1109/BMSB.2017.7986147

Basar, E., Di Renzo, M., De Rosny, J., Debbah, M., Alouini, M. S., & Zhang, R. (2019). Wireless communications through reconfigurable intelligent surfaces. *IEEE Access : Practical Innovations, Open Solutions*, 7, 116753–116773. DOI: 10.1109/ACCESS.2019.2935192

Bertolusso, M., Spanu, M., Anedda, M., Fadda, M., & Giusto, D. D. (2021, June). Vehicular and pedestrian traffic monitoring system in smart city scenarios. In 2021 IEEE 7th World Forum on Internet of Things (WF-IoT) (pp. 60-64). IEEE. DOI: 10.1109/WF-IoT51360.2021.9595188

Chhabra, S., Aiden, M. K., Sabharwal, S. M., & Al-Asadi, M. (2023). 5G and 6G technologies for Smart City. In *Enabling Technologies for Effective Planning and Management in Sustainable Smart Cities* (pp. 335–365). Springer International Publishing. DOI: 10.1007/978-3-031-22922-0_14

De Alwis, C., Kalla, A., Pham, Q. V., Kumar, P., Dev, K., Hwang, W. J., & Liyanage, M. (2021). Survey on 6G frontiers: Trends, applications, requirements, technologies and future research. *IEEE Open Journal of the Communications Society*, 2, 836–886. DOI: 10.1109/OJCOMS.2021.3071496

Desogus, C., Anedda, M., & Murroni, M. (2017, June). Real-time load optimization for multimedia delivery content over heterogeneuos wireless network using a MEW approach. In *2017 IEEE International Symposium on Broadband Multimedia Systems and Broadcasting (BMSB)* (pp. 1-4). IEEE. DOI: 10.1109/BMSB.2017.7986194

Desogus, C., Anedda, M., Murroni, M., & Muntean, G. M. (2019). A traffic type-based differentiated reputation algorithm for radio resource allocation during multi-service content delivery in 5G heterogeneous scenarios. *IEEE Access : Practical Innovations, Open Solutions*, 7, 27720–27735. DOI: 10.1109/ACCESS.2019.2902190

Dong, L. E. (4). Commonly-Used Smart City Technologies. Earth. org. URL: https:// earth. org/smart-city-technologies

Flagship, G. (2019). Key drivers and research challenges for 6G ubiquitous wireless intelligence. 6G Research Visions, 1, 1-36.

ITU. (2022, July). ITU-Recommendation SM.2352-0. Technology Trends of Active Services in the Frequency Range 275–3000 GHz.. Available online: https://www .itu.int/dms_pub/itu-r/opb/rep/R-REP-SM.2352-1-2022-PDF-E

ITU. IMT towards 2030 and Beyond. (2023a). Available online: https://www.itu.int/ en/ITU-R/study-groups/rsg5/rwp5d/imt-2030/Pages/default.aspx

ITU. IMT towards 2030 and Beyond. (2023b). Available online: https://www.itu .int/en/ITU-R/study-groups/rsg5/rwp5d/imt-2030/Pages/default.aspx

Kamruzzaman, M. M. (2022). Key technologies, applications and trends of internet of things for energy-efficient 6G wireless communication in smart cities. *Energies*, 15(15), 5608. DOI: 10.3390/en15155608

Konhäuser, W. (2021). Digitalization in Buildings and Smart Cities on the Way to 6G. *Wireless Personal Communications*, 121(2), 1289–1302. DOI: 10.1007/ s11277-021-09069-9

Kumar, M., Singh, S. K., & Kim, S. (2024). Predictive Analytics for Mortality: FSRNCA-FLANN Modeling Using Public Health Inventory Records. *IEEE Access : Practical Innovations, Open Solutions*, 12, 81252–81264. DOI: 10.1109/ACCESS.2024.3411162

Kumari, A., Gupta, R., & Tanwar, S. (2021). Amalgamation of blockchain and IoT for smart cities underlying 6G communication: A comprehensive review. *Computer Communications*, 172, 102–118. DOI: 10.1016/j.comcom.2021.03.005

Lopez-Martin, M., Carro, B., Sanchez-Esguevillas, A., & Lloret, J. (2017). Network traffic classifier with convolutional and recurrent neural networks for Internet of Things. *IEEE Access : Practical Innovations, Open Solutions*, 5, 18042–18050. DOI: 10.1109/ACCESS.2017.2747560

Mukherjee, M. (2022). Quantum computing—An emerging computing paradigm. In *Emerging computing: From devices to systems: Looking beyond Moore and Von Neumann* (pp. 145–167). Springer Nature Singapore.

Nguyen, D. C., Ding, M., Pathirana, P. N., Seneviratne, A., Li, J., Niyato, D., Dobre, O., & Poor, H. V. (2021). 6G Internet of Things: A comprehensive survey. *IEEE Internet of Things Journal*, 9(1), 359–383. DOI: 10.1109/JIOT.2021.3103320

Nguyen, D. C., Ding, M., Pathirana, P. N., Seneviratne, A., Li, J., Niyato, D., Dobre, O., & Poor, H. V. (2021). 6G Internet of Things: A comprehensive survey. *IEEE Internet of Things Journal*, 9(1), 359–383. DOI: 10.1109/JIOT.2021.3103320

Noman, H. M. F., Hanafi, E., Noordin, K. A., Dimyati, K., Hindia, M. N., Abdrabou, A., & Qamar, F. (2023). Machine Learning Empowered Emerging [Recent Advancements, Challenges & Future Trends. IEEE Access.]. *Wireless Networks*, •••, 6G.

Padmal, M., Marasinghe, D., Isuru, V., Jayaweera, N., Ali, S., & Rajatheva, N. (2022, June). Elevated lidar based sensing for 6g-3d maps with cm level accuracy. In 2022 IEEE 95th Vehicular Technology Conference:(VTC2022-Spring) (pp. 1-5). IEEE.

Pajooh, H. H., Demidenko, S., Aslam, S., & Harris, M. (2022). Harris. M. Blockchain and 6G-Enabled IoT. *Inventions (Basel, Switzerland)*, 2022(7), 109. DOI: 10.3390/inventions7040109

Pilosu, L., Mossucca, L., Scionti, A., Giordanengo, G., Renga, F., Ruiu, P., . . . Vecchi, G. (2017). Low power computing and communication system for critical environments. In Advances on P2P, Parallel, Grid, Cloud and Internet Computing: Proceedings of the 11th International Conference on P2P, Parallel, Grid, Cloud and Internet Computing (3PGCIC–2016) November 5–7, 2016, Soonchunhyang University, Asan, Korea (pp. 221-232). Springer International Publishing. DOI: 10.1007/978-3-319-49109-7_21

Saini, H. K., & Jain, K. L. (2023, April). A New Way of Improving Network by Smart IoE with UAV. In *2023 International Conference on Computational Intelligence, Communication Technology and Networking (CICTN)* (pp. 485-489). IEEE. DOI: 10.1109/CICTN57981.2023.10140227

Seoul: A City Based on Data. Available online: https://earth.org/top-7-smart-cities-in-the-world/

Series, M. (2015). IMT Vision–Framework and overall objectives of the future development of IMT for 2020 and beyond. *Recommendation ITU*, 2083(0), 1–21.

Shi, J., Qi, L., Li, K., & Lin, Y. (2021). Signal modulation recognition method based on differential privacy federated learning. *Wireless Communications and Mobile Computing*, 2021(1), 2537546. DOI: 10.1155/2021/2537546

Singh, S. K., Azzaoui, A. E., Choo, K. K. R., Yang, L. T., & Park, J. H. (2023). Articles A Comprehensive Survey on Blockchain for Secure IoT-enabled Smart City beyond 5G: Approaches, Processes, Challenges, and Opportunities. Hum.-. *Centric Comput. Inf. Sci*, 13, 51.

Singh, S. K., Kumar, M., Tanwar, S., & Park, J. H. (2024). GRU-based digital twin framework for data allocation and storage in IoT-enabled smart home networks. *Future Generation Computer Systems*, 153, 391–402. DOI: 10.1016/j.future.2023.12.009

Tekale, S., Rajagopal, R., & Bhoopathy, V. (2022). 6G: Transformation of Smart Cities With Blockchain and AI. In *Challenges and Risks Involved in Deploying 6G and NextGen Networks* (pp. 220–228). IGI Global. DOI: 10.4018/978-1-6684-3804-6.ch014

Top 10 Leading Global Smart Cities. Available online: https://mobile-magazine.com/articles/top-10-leading-global-smart-cities

UN. The Sustainable Development Goals Report. (2023). Available online: https://unstats.un.org/sdgs/report/2023/The-Sustainable-Development-Goals-Report-2023.pdf

Wei, X., Yang, H., & Huang, W. (2023). Low-delay routing scheme for UAV communications in smart cities. *IEEE Internet of Things Journal*, 10(21), 18837–18843. DOI: 10.1109/JIOT.2023.3267131

Yang, P., Xiao, Y., Xiao, M., & Li, S. (2019). 6G wireless communications: Vision and potential techniques. *IEEE Network*, 33(4), 70–75. DOI: 10.1109/MNET.2019.1800418

Zhang, Y. (2022). *Mobile edge computing*. Springer Nature. DOI: 10.1007/978-3-030-83944-4

Zhu, Y., Mao, B., & Kato, N. (2022). Intelligent reflecting surface in 6G vehicular communications: A survey. *IEEE Open Journal of Vehicular Technology*, 3, 266–277. DOI: 10.1109/OJVT.2022.3177253

Chapter 5
Privacy and Security Concerns With 6G Smart City Infrastructure

Yogeshwar Prajapati
https://orcid.org/0009-0007-3335-3151
Marwadi University, India

Krupali Gosai
Marwadi University, India

Omprakash Suthar
https://orcid.org/0000-0002-7840-481X
Marwadi University, India

Sushil Kumar Singh
Marwadi Univeristy, India

Muhammad Talha Usman
https://orcid.org/0009-0001-9934-7818
UET Taxila, Pakistan

Habib Khan
Gachon University, South Korea

ABSTRACT

6G technology in smart cities brings a new era of connection, efficiency, and innovation, but it also raises privacy and security concerns. This chapter discusses smart city components such IoT devices, autonomous systems, and smart grids. It introduces 6G networks' ultra-low latency, massive device connections, and high data rates. This chapter discusses cyber-physical attacks, data breaches, network intrusions, and other privacy and security issues particular to 6G-enabled smart cities. Smart city environments generate a lot of data, thus data ownership, permission, and anonymization are carefully examined. This chapter discusses 6G-appropriate security and privacy tactics such enhanced encryption, secure communication protocols, and AI-driven threat detection systems. In conclusion, this chapter discusses privacy and security in 6G-enabled smart cities, including where the field is going and what the future holds for research, to help create trustworthy, resilient, and secure smart city ecosystems that can take advantage of 6G's revolutionary capabilities.

DOI: 10.4018/979-8-3693-8029-1.ch005

1. INTRODUCTION

The emergence of 6G technology has the potential to fundamentally transform smart cities by providing significant improvements in speed, connectivity, and data processing efficiency. 6G, operating in the terahertz frequency band, offers data rates that are up to 100 times faster than 5G and latency that is reduced to microseconds. This allows for real-time communication and the running of complex applications across urban infrastructures. This advanced technology seamlessly integrates artificial intelligence to maximize the automation and efficiency of urban services, while also enabling the Internet of Everything (IoE) to establish a more interconnected and responsive urban environment. Even so, the implementation of 6G raises significant security and privacy concerns, since the increase in connectivity and data transmission exposes new vulnerabilities that need to be resolved to protect smart cities.

1.1 Overview of 6G Technology

The upcoming 6G technology, considered the next advancement in wireless communication, will help to transform smart cities by providing exceptional speed, connectivity, and intelligence. Estimated to function within the terahertz frequency spectrum, 6G is predicted to provide data transmission rates that are up to 100 times faster compared to that of 5G, accompanied by a reduction in latency to microseconds. Real-time communication and processing across the extensive networks of devices and sensors that support smart city infrastructures will be made possible by this performance enhancement. Below figure 6.1 illustrates the overview of 6G Technology.

Figure 1. Overview of 6G technology

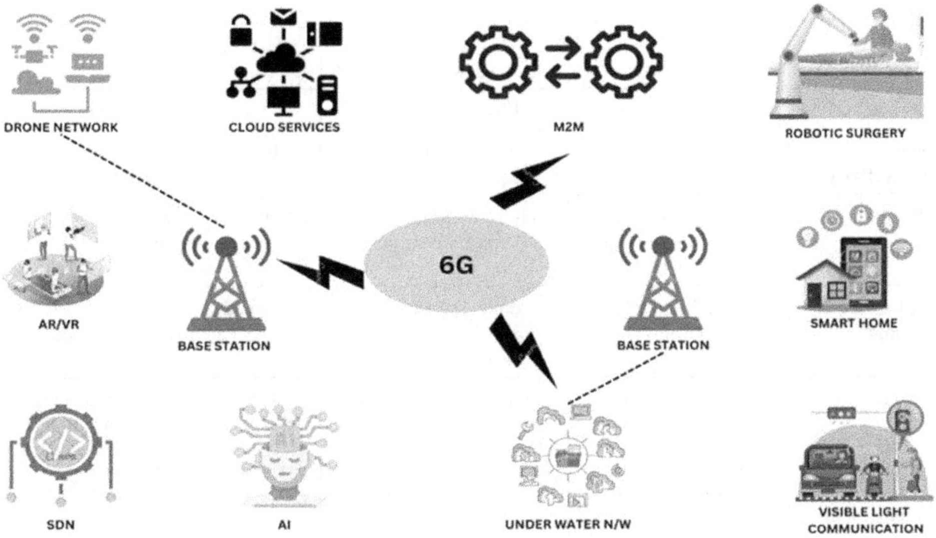

An important feature of 6G is its thorough use of artificial intelligence (AI), enabling more effective and independent management of urban systems. Embedded within the network, AI will enable sophisticated applications such predictive analytics for energy management, intelligent transportation systems, and real-time monitoring of public safety (Ahad et al., 2024). Furthermore, the integration of the Internet of Everything (IoE) in 6G technology would create a highly networked urban environment by connecting not just devices, but also vehicles, infrastructure, and even people. The implementation of 6G will also facilitate the widespread use of edge computing, in which data processing is performed in less time to its origin. Although this decentralized strategy decreases latency and improves efficiency, it also introduces new security concerns, since every edge node becomes vulnerable to intrusions (Osorio et al., 2022). As a result of the increased attack surfaces and the large volumes of sensitive data that will be generated and transferred across these networks, the deployment of 6G in smart cities will need accurate focus on security and privacy, despite its revolutionary guarantee. Below table 6.1 represents comparison between different generation of Networks.

Table 1. Comparison of 4G, 5G & 6G Networks (Scalise et al., 2024) (Ounza, 2023)

	4G	5G	6G
Data Rate	Up to 100 Mbps (download)	Up to 10 Gbps (download)	Expected to exceed 100 Gbps (download)
Latency	30-50 milliseconds	1-10 milliseconds	As low as 1 millisecond
Device Connectivity	Thousands of devices per square kilometres	1 million devices per square kilometres	10 million devices per square kilometres
Network Efficiency	Good, with some limitations in high-density areas	Improved efficiency and capacity over 4G	Enhanced efficiency with advanced resource management
Application Support	Basic IoT and mobile applications	Enhanced support for IoT, AR, VR, and autonomous systems	Enhanced support for IoT, AR, VR, and autonomous systems
Security	Basic privacy protections	Improved privacy with user-centric controls	Advanced privacy protections with enhanced anonymization and control over personal data
Network Management	Traditional network management	Enhanced with network slicing and edge computing	Autonomous network management with AI and machine learning

1.2 Importance of Privacy and Security

The enormous and complex network of interconnected devices and systems that support urban infrastructure makes security and privacy of the highest priority in 6G-enabled smart cities. As 6G advances, it facilitates exceptional levels of connectivity, speed, and data processing, therefore amplifying the possibility of both security breaches and privacy breaches.

- **Protection of Critical Infrastructure:** Smart cities depend on a wide range of interconnected systems, such as transportation systems, power grid-based and healthcare facilities. Safeguarding these vital infrastructures is crucial to guarantee their dependable functioning and to protect them from disturbances that may have severe effects on public safety and urban mobility. Implementing strong security protocols helps prevent attacks that might compromise these vital services (Dasika, Kakulapati, & Saligrama, 2024).
- **Safeguarding Personal Data:** The growing importance of safeguarding individuals' personal information has been increased by the robust data gathering and analysis capabilities provided by 6G technology. The protection of data privacy, including location, health indicators, and personal behaviors, is crucial to avoid unauthorised access and misuse. Realizing that smart cities gather and analyze extensive quantities of sensitive data, it is crucial to have

robust privacy safeguards in order to maintain the rights and confidence of citizens.

- **Mitigating Emerging Threats:** The continuous advancement of technology gives rise to new and complex cyber threats. The integrated artificial intelligence (AI) and edge computing capabilities of 6G technology bring forth additional vulnerabilities that may be exploited by hostile individuals. Ensuring the safety and privacy of smart city infrastructure requires the mandatory implementation of sophisticated security procedures and their ongoing update to address evolving threats.
- **Ensuring Compliance with Regulations:** As smart cities grow and include sophisticated technologies, they are required to comply with a range of data privacy rules and regulations, including the General Data privacy Regulation (GDPR). In addition to being a legal requirement, ensuring compliance to these rules is a crucial element of preserving public confidence and preventing legal consequences.
- **Maintaining Trust and Public Confidence:** Safeguarding security and privacy are essential for upholding public trust in the technologies that influence smart cities. Concerns of data insecurity or privacy breaches among citizens may damage trust in these systems and limit the acceptance of novel solutions. Implementing strong security and privacy protocols is crucial for establishing and maintaining confidence in smart city technologies.

2. CHARACTERISTICS OF 6G NETWORKS

The advent of 6G technology signifies a substantial advancement compared to its predecessor, 5G, with the potential to transform the field of connectivity and communication in intelligent urban development. Several key features of 6G are expected to transform urban surroundings as we progress towards this next-generation network. These developments encompass extremely high data speeds, almost negligible delay, and the use of terahertz frequency bands, all of which contribute to an unparalleled degree of network performance and capabilities. The simultaneous incorporation of artificial intelligence, extensive connectivity, and edge computing would significantly augment the effectiveness and cognitive capabilities of smart city systems. Gaining insight into these attributes is crucial for comprehending the revolutionary capacity of 6G and the novel prospects and challenges it will present to urban infrastructure and services. Below figure 6.2 illustrates the characteristic of 6G Networks.

Figure 2. Characteristic of 6G network

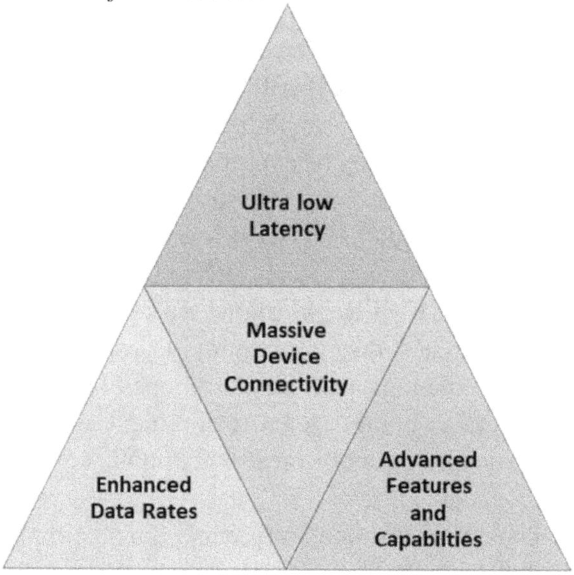

2.1 Ultra-Low Latency

The feature of ultra-low latency in 6G technology is a revolutionary aspect that guarantees a substantial decrease in the time delay between transmitting and receiving data, from milliseconds of earlier generations to microseconds. This almost immediate connection is essential for a variety of sophisticated applications in intelligent urban areas. Autonomous vehicles benefit from real-time interaction with other vehicles and infrastructure, which not only guarantees safety but also enhances operating efficiency. The effectiveness of real-time monitoring and control of urban systems, such as traffic management and energy distribution, increases, enabling quick modifications and responses to evolving conditions. The decreased latency also benefits immersive technologies such as augmented reality (AR) and virtual reality (VR), enabling smooth and engaging experiences. During emergency scenarios, the low latency of communication and coordination greatly improves the capacity of emergency services to promptly and efficiently react. The ultra-low latency brought about by 6G is crucial for the development of smart cities and the achievement of their maximum capabilities.

2.2 Massive Device Connectivity

Extensive device connectivity is a fundamental characteristic of 6G networks, essential for facilitating the large quantity of linked devices in intelligent urban landscapes. As metropolitan regions become more dependent on the Internet of Things (IoT), the 6G technology will be capable of accommodating billions of devices, including autonomous vehicles, sensors, smart homes, and infrastructure systems. Such connectivity enables instantaneous communication between equipment, therefore enabling automation and enhancing efficiency in several industries such as transportation, energy, and public services. The increased network capacity of 6G guarantees dependable and fast connectivity, especially in large metropolitan areas with extensive device usage. Furthermore, 6G technology facilitates the construction of low-power, wide-area networks (LPWAN), which allows for the effective and extended functioning of IoT devices with no need for maintenance. The high degree of connectivity enables smooth data interchange and fast decision-making, crucial for the efficient operation of smart cities. The ultimate impact of 6G's extensive device connectivity will transform urban living by facilitating more intelligent and adaptable municipal infrastructures.

2.3 Enhanced Data Rates

Optimized data rates are a key benefit of 6G networks, providing much higher speeds in comparison to earlier generations. 6G, with anticipated data rates of up to 1 terabit per second (Tbps), would facilitate the use of high-bandwidth applications including complete virtual reality (VR), ultra-high-definition (UHD) video streaming, and intelligent augmented reality (AR) experiences. The enhanced velocity would provide uninterrupted real-time transmission and analysis of data, a crucial requirement for the efficient functioning of smart cities, driverless vehicles, and operational automation in industry. Advancements in data rates in 6G will stimulate innovation and generate fresh opportunities in communication, entertainment, and other disciplines.

2.4 Advanced Features and Capabilities

Sixth generation (6G) networks bring a variety of advanced features and capabilities that surpasses the improvements of 5G, therefore affecting the future of communication and technology in intelligent urban areas. These include the following:

1. **Terahertz (THz) Communication:** The 6G network will operate within the terahertz frequency bandwidth, providing unmatched data transmission speeds, up to 1 terabit per second (Tbps). This will allow faster and more dependable communication, which is essential for applications such as holographic communication, ultra-high-definition media, and sophisticated virtual and augmented reality experiences.
2. **AI-Driven Network Management:** Deep integration of Artificial Intelligence (AI) into 6G networks will allow for autonomous management of networks, optimization, and decision-making. Artificial intelligence will improve network efficiency by analyzing traffic patterns, dynamically allocating resources, and guaranteeing low latency for essential applications.
3. **Holographic Telepresence:** The advent of 6G will enable the implementation of immersive technologies like holographic telepresence, therefore enabling quick, 3D communication and interaction. This technology will transform sectors such as working remotely, education, and healthcare by enhancing the reality and engagement of virtual reality.
4. **Extreme Latency Reduction:** The 6G network will provide extremely low latency, ranging less than one millisecond, to enable applications which require quick responses, such as autonomous cars, remote surgery, and advanced robotics. This will guarantee more efficient and secure functioning of very important real-time systems.
5. **Integration of Space and Aerial Networks:** 6G will boost connectivity by integrating satellites and aerial platforms, such as drones, into terrestrial connections. This would provide worldwide, uninterrupted internet coverage, even in faraway and underprivileged areas, hence improving connectivity for rural as well as urban smart city systems.
6. **Energy-Efficient Communication:** 6G will focus on conservation of energy by minimizing power usage across devices and networks. It has major implications in terms of sustainability, as it allows for extended battery life of IoT devices and decreases the total energy consumption of communication infrastructure.
7. **Quantum Communication:** The integration of quantum communication into 6G technology offers the potential for highly secure data transmission. The implementation of quantum encryption will significantly improve security by finding data interception and breaches very difficult, therefore guaranteeing a more secure communication ecosystem.
8. **Enhanced Security and Privacy Protocols:** Utilizing advanced authentication, encryption, and secure technologies, 6G will provide more protection against hacking, data theft, and spying, so effectively tackling the escalating security issues in smart cities that handle large amounts of sensitive data.

3. COMPONENTS OF SMART CITIES

Smart cities are urban areas that use advanced technologies, like the Internet of Things (IoT), artificial intelligence (AI), and 5G/6G networks, to improve the health of people via efficient resource management and infrastructure utilization. Connected devices and sensors for real-time data collection, automated transportation systems (autonomous vehicles and traffic management), smart energy lines for effective energy transportation, sustainable waste and water management, and e-governance platforms that improve public services are essential components of smart cities. The combination of these elements collectively contributes to the development of a highly flexible, efficient, and ecological urban environment (Murroni et al., 2023) (Sharma et al., 2024).

3.1 Internet of Things (IoT) Devices

Internet of Things (IoT) devices are crucial for developing interconnected and intelligent urban settings in 6G-enabled smart cities. Integrated with sensors, software, and networking capabilities, IoT devices allow the collection, transmission, and receiving of data, hence increasing the efficiency and responsiveness of the city (Osorio et al., 2022). Important features of Internet of Things (IoT) devices in smart cities includes:

1. **Smart Sensors:** These gadgets monitor a range of parameters including air quality, temperature, and traffic pattern. Environmental sensors monitor the level of pollution, while traffic sensors examine real-time data in order to improve traffic management and reduce traffic.
2. **Connected Vehicles:** Autonomous vehicles and connected cars utilise Internet of Things (IoT) technology for establishing communication between each other and with other infrastructure components such as traffic signals and road sensors. This integration optimizes traffic control, boosts safety, and enables efficient public transportation networks.
3. **Smart Buildings:** Internet of Things (IoT) allowed devices in smart homes regulate lighting, air conditioning, ventilation, and heating (HVAC) systems depending on population and environmental factors. Therefore, this leads to in reduced energy consumption, improved comfort, and more efficient use of resources.
4. **Wearable Devices:** Fitness trackers and health monitors are examples of wearable devices that gather personal health data and offer instant feedback. In smart cities, these gadgets have the ability to improve surveillance of public health and emergency response systems.

5. **Smart Utilities:** Smart Internet of Things (IoT) sensors in water and energy management systems control use, identify leaks, and improve distribution efficiency. Smart utility meters and grids enable the optimization of resource utilization and upkeep, hence increasing cost-effectiveness and minimizing the impact on the environment.

3.2 Autonomous Systems

Autonomous systems play a crucial role in the operation of 6G-enabled smart cities, changing urban activity by implementing automation and the latest technologies. Automated vehicles, smart traffic management, robotic delivery services, and autonomous public services use the ultra-low latency and high-speed connectivity of 6G to function automatically and make fast decisions. Robust sensors and artificial intelligence enable autonomous vehicles and drones to travel securely, while intelligent traffic management enhances traffic flow and minimizes congestion. Automated systems manage activities such as disposal of waste and infrastructure maintenance, therefore improving efficiency as well as security. At the same time, autonomous surveillance and environmental monitoring systems guarantee public safety and sustainability by delivering up-to-date information and early identification of hazards. Through the integration of these sophisticated technologies, smart cities enabled by 6G technology acquire enhanced operational efficiency, improved public services, and a greater standard of urban living.

3.3 Smart Grids

Smart grids are an essential part of smart cities enabled by 6G technology, fundamentally transforming the processes of energy production, distribution, and consumption. Exploiting the sophisticated connectivity of 6G, smart grids include modern technology including real-time sensors, automated control systems, and data analytics to improve the effectiveness, dependability, and ecological sustainability of urban energy networks. Electricity grids employ Internet of Things (IoT) devices and sensors in order to monitor and control the flow of energy, enabling quick modifications in response to changes in demand and supply. This feature minimizes energy inefficiency, averts power failures, and maximizes resource use, so guaranteeing a more dependable and robust power provision. In addition, smart grids enable the incorporation of renewable energy sources such as solar and wind by effectively managing their sporadic energy production using energy storage systems and demand response schemes. By the reduction of dependence on fossil fuels and the minimization of greenhouse gas emissions, this integration supports a cleaner and more sustainable energy landscape. Highly sophisticated data analytics and artificial intelligence algorithms significantly improve the operation of smart grids by forecasting energy consumption trends, detecting inefficiencies, and automating grid management activities. Predictive maintenance, for example, may predict breakdowns in equipment in advance, therefore minimizing both interruptions and expenses associated with repairs. Furthermore, smart grids empower users to actively engage in energy management by means of demand response programs, which provide incentives for decreased consumption during periods of high demand and promote energy-saving behaviors. These steps additionally help to the stability of the power grid but also result in reduced utility expenses for users. By offering comprehensive analysis of energy usage and enabling better-informed decision-making, smart grids improve the efficiency as well as the sustainability of cities.

4. SECURITY CHALLENGES IN 6G-ENABLED SMART CITIES

In 6G-enabled smart cities, privacy concerns are complex and diverse because of the extensive and interconnected infrastructure and the numerous devices involved. With the integration of billions of IoT devices, autonomous systems, and key urban services, the potential attack surfaces for cyber-attacks continue to grow substantially as 6G technology advances. The rapid and instantaneous communication speeds of 6G, whilst improving operational effectiveness, also introduce novel weaknesses that can be manipulated by malicious people. In addition to the challenges are advanced cyber-attacks like ransomware, data breaches, and denial-of-service attacks, which have the potential to interrupt city operations and compromise confidential data (Dasika, Kakulapati, & Saligrama, 2024) (Li et al., 2024). The integration of advanced technologies like quantum communication and AI brings up new security concerns, requiring strong and flexible security solutions to safeguard against new threats and guarantee the durability and confidentiality of smart city systems.

4.1 Cyber-Physical Threats

The integration of digital systems with physical infrastructure in 6G-enabled smart cities raises substantial concerns regarding cyber-physical risks. Cyber-attacks on critical infrastructure components give rise to these threats, which can result in possible delays in vital services and physical damage. As 6G networks enable the smooth integration of billions of Internets of Things (IoT) devices and autonomous systems, the possibility of cyber-physical attacks increases, therefore threatening public safety and urban operation (Li et al., 2024).

For example, malicious actors could take advantage of vulnerabilities in smart grids and cause huge electrical disruptions, or change data from traffic control systems to generate dangerous driving situations. The development of a breach in autonomous transportation has the potential to result in vehicle failures or improper traffic management, therefore risking both human life and property. Moreover, cyber-physical threats can also affect intelligent healthcare systems, where any modification of medical equipment or data could result in serious consequences for the safety of hospital patients. The fundamental interconnectivity of 6G networks increases these vulnerabilities, since a breach in one system has the potential to spread to others, resulting in extensive effects. In order to reduce these risks, a comprehensive security strategy is necessary, including strong encryption, continuous monitoring, and automated threat detection protocols. By implementing measures to protect against cyber-physical threats, smart cities can guarantee the durability and dependability of their essential infrastructure, therefore preserving safety and continuous operation.

4.2 Data Breaches

Data breaches provide an important threat to smart cities enabled by 6G technology, because large volumes of sensitive data are continuously produced, transported, and stored. Data breaches refer to the occurrence of unauthorized access to sensitive data, which has the potential to compromise personal information, financial records, and important system details. In the context of smart cities, data breaches may have extensive effects, impacting several aspects such as personal privacy and the quality of public services. Breaches in intelligent healthcare systems have the potential to expose confidential medical data, therefore resulting in identity theft or breaches upon privacy (Ounza, 2023). The compromise of data from smart grids has the potential to expose weaknesses in vital energy infrastructure, therefore making it vulnerable to further attacks or misuse. Furthermore, weaknesses in transportation systems may compromise the security and privacy of real-time vehicle location data.

The enormous size and complicated nature of 6G networks, characterized by their large quantity of interconnected devices and rapid data transfers, enhance the vulnerability to data breaches. Robust security measures, including advanced encryption methods, regular security audits, and strict restrictions on access must be taken to mitigate these risks. Deploying real-time monitoring and threat detection systems can also facilitate quick detection and response to such breaches, therefore safeguarding sensitive data and guaranteeing the robustness of smart city infrastructure.

4.3 Ransomwares

Ransomware attacks pose an important threat to security in 6-G-enabled smart cities, since they have the potential to disrupt essential services and result in enormous financial and operational loss. Ransomware is a type of malicious software that encrypts the data of a victim, making it unreachable until a specified ransom is paid to the attacker. Ransomware may specifically target and compromise many essential systems in smart cities, such as public utilities, transportation networks, and hospitals. This can result in extensive service disruptions and loss of data.

An example of ransomware targeting a smart grid has the potential to make power distribution systems unusable, leading to extensive interruptions in power and disrupted operations. In the same way, targeting transportation management systems might immobilize the movement of vehicles, resulting in accidents and substantial discomfort to the public. In healthcare environments, encrypted medical records have the potential to cause delays in treatments and endanger patient safety.

The increased interconnectivity and complexity of 6G networks raise the potential effects of ransomware attacks. With a growing number of networked devices and systems, the capacity of ransomware to rapidly propagate and cause severe damage is significantly increased. In order to prevent ransomware, smart cities need to implement thorough cybersecurity measures including frequent backups, robust access controls, and advanced threat detection systems. Furthermore, providing education to both staff and users regarding phishing and other methods of attack can effectively mitigate the occurrence of ransomware cases and guarantee fast recovery in case of an attack (Tripi et al., 2024).

5. PRIVACY ISSUES IN 6G-ENABLED SMART CITIES

The privacy concerns in smart cities enabled by 6G technology emerge from the widespread gathering, examination, and exchange of personal and sensitive data over a highly interconnected network of devices and systems. With the advent of 6G technology, which enables unparalleled levels of connectivity and data interchange, safeguarding individual privacy becomes ever intricate. The incorporation of sophisticated sensors, artificial intelligence (AI), and real-time analytics in intelligent infrastructure gives rise to apprehensions around data monitoring, unauthorised entry, and possible abuse. Mitigating these privacy concerns is essential for preserving public confidence and protecting personal data while capitalizing on the advantages of 6G's sophisticated functionalities for improved urban life. Figure 6.3 provided below depicts the Security and Privacy aspects of a 6G network.

Figure 3. 6G Network privacy and security

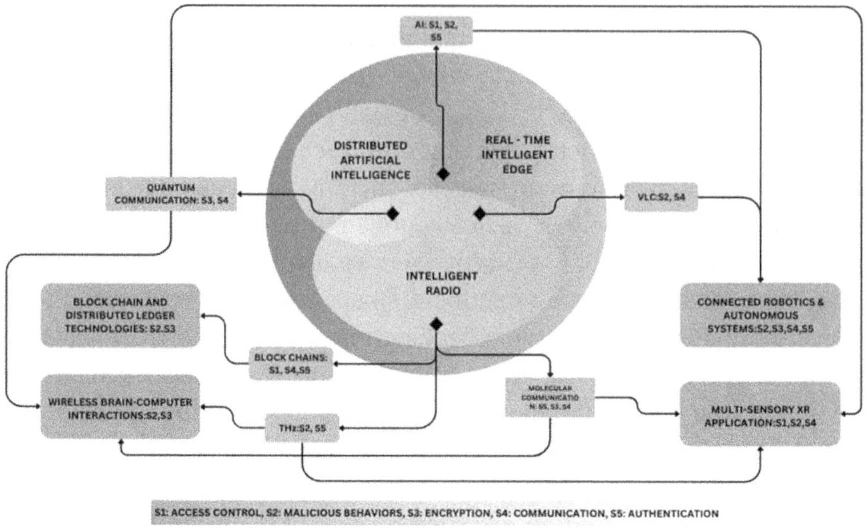

5.1 Data Ownership and Control

Data ownership and control are crucial considerations in smart cities enabled by 6G technology, as large quantities of personal and sensitive data are consistently produced and shared. With the growing prevalence of IoT devices, smart sensors, and AI systems, the task of identifying the ownership and control over this data becomes ever intricate. The smart city environment encompasses a range of data sources, such as personal devices, public infrastructure, and commercial transactions, which give rise to concerns around data rights and management.

Trust in smart city technologies might be diminished if residents are confused about who has access to their data and how it is utilized. Smart medical gadgets and fitness trackers, for instance, may acquire personally identifiable information (PII) about their users and use it for marketing and profiling without their knowledge or consent. Particularly in cases of public-private data sharing, the incorporation of data from many sources can further obscure the issue of ownership. Strong control mechanisms and transparent data ownership policies are crucial for overcoming these obstacles. The implementation of open data governance frameworks, the provision of transparent data management options to individuals, and the maintenance of compliance with privacy legislation are all part of this. Smart cities can improve urban living by fostering trust among users, safeguarding personal information, and enabling ethical data usage (Kazmi et al., 2023).

5.2 Data Anonymization Techniques

Effective data anonymization methods are essential in 6G-enabled smart cities to safeguard personal privacy while enabling the extraction of useful insights from data. By utilizing sophisticated technology to gather extensive data, smart cities must prioritize the preservation of personal information confidentiality in order to uphold public confidence and adhere to privacy laws. Important methods of anonymization include:

- **Data Masking:** This methodology entails altering data in order to conceal confidential information. One approach is to substitute names and personal identifiers with pseudonyms or random values, therefore posing challenges in tracing data back to individuals while also maintaining its usefulness for research.
- **Aggregation:** Aggregation is the process of merging data from several sources to yield summary statistics or general patterns that cannot be attributed to specific data pieces. Through its emphasis on patterns rather than exact specifics, aggregation serves to safeguard individual identities while offering significant insights for urban planning and service optimization.
- **Generalization:** Generalisation is the replacement of particular data values with more comprehensive categories. For example, exact ages may be substituted with age ranges, or explicit places could be substituted with broad regions. This decreases the level of detail of the data, therefore reducing its recognisability but still retaining its value for scientific research.
- **K-Anonymity:** A K-anonymity condition guarantees that each data point cannot be differentiated from a minimum of k−1k-1k−1 additional data points. The minimization of re-identification risk is achieved by guaranteeing that each record is indistinguishable from a minimum of k other records.
- **Differential Privacy:** Differential privacy introduces information noise to the data in order to conceal individual records, while still enabling the derivation of precise aggregate information. In order to safeguard individual privacy, our method guarantees that the deletion or inclusion of a single record does not have a substantial impact on the result of queries.

5.3 Location and Tracking Privacy Concerns

The extensive use of sensors and tracking technologies in 6G-enabled smart cities raises substantial issues about location and tracking privacy, as these technologies constantly watch and record the movements and actions of persons. The expanded connectivity and data sharing enabled by 6G technology give rise to various privacy concerns due to the capability to track and precisely determine the real-time location of devices, vehicles, and even humans.

The utilization of location data obtained from mobile devices, wearable technologies, and linked cars in smart cities enables the optimization of services, including traffic control and tailored marketing. Nevertheless, this comprehensive tracking capacity also presents potential hazards of unauthorised observation and illicit theft of data. Specifically, if location data is obtained by malicious individuals or insufficiently safeguarded, it may result in infringements of privacy, theft of identity, or focused harassment.

Moreover, the collection of location data from several sources can generate comprehensive profiles of individuals' daily routines, potentially exposing confidential information about their habits, interests, and personal relationships. Such a high degree of specificity can be used for invasive objectives, such as profiling or modification.

To mitigate these privacy issues, it is crucial to use strong data protection methods, such as encryption, access controls, and explicit permission procedures. Furthermore, it is imperative to implement anonymization methods and privacy policies to guarantee the responsible use of location data and to maintain individuals' autonomy over their personal information. It is essential to strike a balance between the advantages of sophisticated tracking technology and privacy safeguards in order to preserve trust and defend individual rights in smart cities enabled by 6G communications.

6. ADVANCED SECURITY MEASURES FOR 6G ENVIRONMENTS

With so many connected devices and so much data being exchanged in smart cities, it is crucial to implement advanced security measures in 6G environments to deal with the increased threats. The implementation of these measures will make use of state-of-the-art technology like blockchain for secure data transmission and storage, quantum encryption, and AI-driven threat detection. 6G networks will have strong defense mechanisms thanks to AI integration, which allows them to anticipate, identify, and react to cyber threats in real-time. The extensive digital ecosystems of 6G smart cities will be protected by quantum encryption, which will offer unbreakable security for sensitive communications, and by blockchain, which will boost data integrity and transparency (Porambage et al., 2021).

6.1 Blockchain for Enhanced Security

Last few years have seen the emergence of distributed ledger technologies (DLT), namely blockchain technology. Decentralized ledger technology (DLT) is designed to overcome the well-recognized limitations of centralized systems, therefore enabling the decentralized future. A blockchain is a form of distributed ledger technology (DLT) that securely and decent rally maintains a digital ledger. This ledger stores all transactions in a chronological sequence and is securely encrypted. Figure 6.4 presents an architectural representation of a blockchain. An attacker attempting to alter a transaction on a blockchain must modify the hash of not just that block but also all previous hashes, a task that is exceedingly difficult (Parra-Ullauri et al., 2024). The inherent security feature of blockchain renders it so well-suited for application in several industries such as banking, insurance, government services, and supply chain management. Moreover, blockchain has other benefits such as disintermediation, immutability, nonrepudiation, evidence of provenance, integrity, and pseudonymity; hence, blockchain has garnered equal attention from both industry and academia.

Numerous industries have already recognized the practical application of blockchain technology and its effectiveness, as they are either implementing or providing technological solutions based on blockchain. Examples of some of these corporate areas are finance and banking, industrial supply chain and manufacturing, shipping and transportation, medical health care and patient records, and educational procedures and credentialing. Blockchain technology has the potential to significantly enhance certain specific features of upcoming 6G wireless systems.

Figure 4. Basic Blockchain Transactions: (1) A mobile user or IoT Device initiates a transaction to smart contracts to request data, (2) A new block is generated to show-case confirmed transactions, and (3) a mined block is appended to the blockchain.

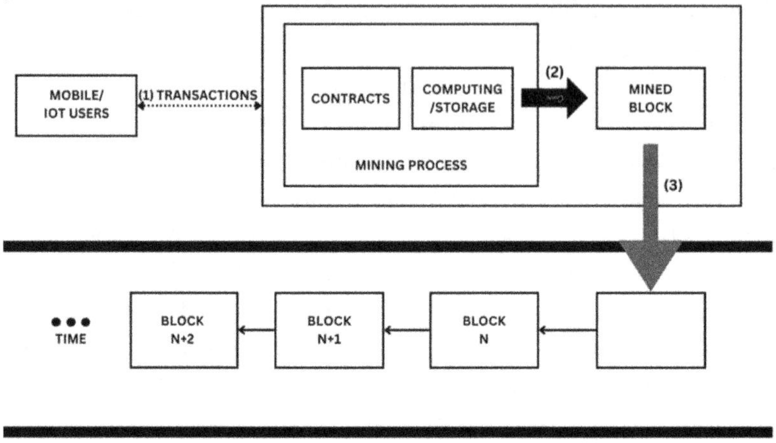

Business models in decentralized and trustless digital markets that involve a variety of stakeholders, including Infrastructure Providers (InPs), network tenants, industry verticals, over-the-top (OTT) providers, and edge providers. Moreover, blockchain has significant potential to enhance the current service landscape of mobile networks and introduce the foundation for future applications and use cases of 6G.

Blockchain is recognized as a crucial enabling technology for the implementation of 6G. Extensive endeavors are being undertaken to use its capacity to enhance both the technical components of 6G and the practical applications of the 6G ecosystem. This study demonstrates the application of blockchain technology in decentralized network management. It also introduces the integration of blockchain and smart contracts for spectra trading. Additionally, a blockchain-based radio access network (B-RAN) is proposed, enabling small subnetworks to collaborate in a trustless environment to form a larger cooperative network. This paper demonstrates the utilization of blockchain technology to eliminate the intermediary layer and create a distributed Mobility-as-a-Service system that is hosted as an application on an edge computing facility. This effort has demonstrated benefits in terms of enhanced transparency and confidence among all the stakeholders. This study proposed the use of blockchain technology to guarantee data security in Al-powered apps for 6G networks. There are two primary applications: indoor positioning and autonomous motor vehicles.

6.2 Edge Computing

A pioneering edge-computing concept, known as the "cloudlet," was introduced in 2009. A cloudlet is a computer or group of computers strategically positioned at the edge and strongly connected to the Internet, characterized by its trustworthiness and abundant resources. An essential objective of cloudlet is to expand cloud computing to the network edge and assist mobile users with limited resources in operating resource-intensive and interactive apps. While the storage and computational capacities of a cloudlet are modest compared to those of a data centre in cloud computing, cloudlets offer the benefits of cost-effective deployment and significant scalability. Mobile users leverage virtual machine (VM)-based virtualization by configuring service software on nearby cloudlets and subsequently accessing those cloudlet services over a wireless local area network to delegate demanding calculations. There exist two distinct virtual machine (VM) methods for offloading computations, namely VM migration and VM synthesis. The utilization of virtual machine provisioning in cloudlets enables cloudlets to function independently without requiring any involvement from the cloud. Cloudlet services can be accessed by mobile users remotely via Wi-Fi (Charu, Kumar, Upadhyay, & Chauhan, 2023). The concept of cloudlet, which aims to disperse cloud computing services to mobile consumers, holds resemblance to the Wi-Fi notion in facilitating Internet connectivity. An inherent limitation of cloudlets is the Wi-Fi connection between users and cloudlets. Thus, mobile customers are unable of availing cloudlets over long distances and concurrently using both Wi-Fi and cellular connections.

Fog computing has emerged as a possible method to confront the inherent limitations of cloud computing. Fog computing, proposed by Cisco in 2012, is the expansion of cloud computing from the central processing unit to the periphery of the network, therefore introducing computing resources in closer proximity to end-users. The primary objectives of fog computing are to provide computational resources to end users and minimize the volume of data required for transmission to the cloud for processing and storage. Therefore, rather than being sent to the cloud, fog nodes at the network edge can process and analyse most intensive computations from mobile users and data acquired by end-users (e.g. sensors and IoT devices), so decreasing the execution latency and network congestion. Fog computing distinguishes itself as a supplementary technology to cloud computing among the following characteristics:

- Edge location, low latency, and location awareness, Widespread geographic distribution,
- Integration of mobility and real-time applications services,
- The high number of nodes is attributed to their geographical dispersal, the heterogeneity of fog nodes, and the prevalence of wireless access.

Due to its inherent qualities, fog computing is crucial in numerous use cases and applications. A fog node is a composed node type that may be constructed using various components like as routers, switches, and loT gateways. On the other hand, a cloudlet is a compact cloud data centre. The deployment of a fog node can be strategically positioned at many locations, ranging from end devices to centralized clouds. Similarly, a cloudlet can be placed both indoors and outdoors. Both cloudlet and fog computing share a common characteristic: they are not integrated into the mobile network architecture. Consequently, fog nodes and cloudlets are typically deployed and owned by private enterprises. However, ensuring quality of service (QoS) and quality of experience (QoE) guarantees for mobile users is a challenging task.

6.3 Quantum-Safe Cryptography

Quantum-safe cryptography is a crucial security technique specifically developed to safeguard data against the hypothetical risks presented by quantum computers, which have the potential to make conventional encryption techniques susceptible. The progress of quantum computers has the potential to compromise commonly employed cryptographic algorithms such as RSA and ECC, therefore posing a substantial security threat to confidential information within 6G networks. Quantum-safe cryptography, or post-quantum cryptography, refers to the creation of cryptographic algorithms that are capable of withstanding attacks from both classical and quantum processing systems.

The implementation of quantum-safe encryption in 6G-enabled smart cities, where there is extensive data flow among devices, systems, and users, would guarantee the preservation of data security, even in the presence of potential quantum computing risks. In the realm of cryptography, sophisticated techniques such as lattice-based, hash-based, and multivariate polynomial cryptography offer robust security assurances and exhibit resilience against the computing capacities of quantum computers.

Incorporating quantum-safe cryptography into 6G networks will enhance the security of sensitive communications, financial transactions, healthcare records, and other vital infrastructure, therefore guaranteeing enduring data stability. Taking proactive measures to implement these cryptographic techniques would enhance the ability of 6G networks to protect against future cyber threats and preserve the confidentiality and reliability of data in a world powered by quantum technology.

6.4 AI-Driven Threat Detection Systems

Automated threat detection systems powered by artificial intelligence are leading the way in cybersecurity within smart cities enabled by 6G technology. These systems provide a sophisticated method for promptly identifying and reducing possible security threats. In comparison to conventional approaches, these systems utilize artificial intelligence and machine learning algorithms to consistently monitor network traffic, identify anomalies, and react to emerging risks with greater efficiency. Through extensive data analysis, artificial intelligence (AI)-powered systems can rapidly detect trends that suggest harmful behavior, such as illegal entry, distributed denial-of-service (DDoS) assaults, or malware penetration.

An inherent benefit of detection systems powered by artificial intelligence is their capacity to adjust and acquire knowledge from emerging dangers. In contrast to fixed security rules, these systems continually adapt by assimilating knowledge from previous occurrences and developing attack patterns, enabling them to maintain a competitive edge against ever more advanced hackers (Alhammadi et al., 2024). In addition, they have the capability to automate the reaction to threats, therefore limiting the requirement for human involvement and decreasing the duration required to neutralize attacks.

Moreover, systems powered by artificial intelligence can give priority to security alarms according to their level of seriousness, therefore enabling enterprises to concentrate their resources on the most crucial dangers. Amidst the vast interconnection of billions of devices in 6G environments, the presence of AI-driven threat detection systems becomes imperative to uphold the security and integrity of smart city infrastructure, safeguard sensitive data, and shield civilians from cyberattacks.

6.5 Encryption Methods

The implementation of encryption techniques is crucial in ensuring the security of communication inside 6G networks, which involve the transmission of enormous volumes of data across diverse devices and platforms. These techniques guarantee the preservation of sensitive information's confidentiality and safeguard it against unauthorized access. Principal encryption methods employed in 6G networks encompass:

Symmetric Encryption: When encrypting and decrypting data, symmetric encryption just requires one secret key. The **Advanced Encryption Standard, or AES**, is a popular algorithm because of its reliability and safety. Applications like secure communications and file storage benefit greatly from its rapid data encryption capabilities.

Asymmetric Encryption (Public Key Encryption): Asymmetric encryption employs a pair of keys: a public key for encryption and a private key for decryption. In secure communications, such as digital signatures, authentication, and secure key exchange, algorithms such as **RSA** and **Elliptic Curve Cryptography (ECC)** are frequently employed to safeguard data in transit.

Post-Quantum Cryptography: Post-quantum cryptography refers to the development of algorithms that are resistant to quantum assaults, designed in response to the possibility of quantum computers cracking conventional encryption. **Lattice-based** and **hash-based cryptography** techniques are specifically developed to offer enduring security in the future era of quantum computing, therefore guaranteeing optimal protection for 6G networks.

Homomorphic Encryption: Homomorphic encryption enables the execution of computations on encrypted data without the need for decryption. This approach is especially valuable for data analysis that prioritizes privacy, allowing for secure cloud computing and smart city applications while ensuring the protection of sensitive personal information.

Blockchain-Based Encryption: Incorporating blockchain technology, which employs cryptographic hashing, into 6G networks enables safe data exchange and transaction authentication. Blockchain technology significantly improves data quality and privacy in applications such as digital IDs and smart contracts by utilizing decentralized and tamper-resistant ledgers.

CONCLUSION

With 6G on the horizon, smart cities will experience revolutionary improvements in connectivity, efficiency, and intelligence throughout urban infrastructure. Nevertheless, to guarantee the secure and moral rollout of 6G networks, it is necessary to resolve the substantial privacy and security concerns that accompany these advantages. There are a lot of complicated concerns surrounding data ownership, control, and anonymization brought up by the vast network of linked devices and systems, which also raises the attack surfaces for cyber dangers like cyber-physical attacks, data breaches, and ransomware. Strong security solutions, including enhanced encryption, AI-driven threat detection, and quantum-safe cryptography, are necessary to lessen the impact of these dangers. Data anonymization and location tracking are two areas where privacy issues can be best addressed with open data governance principles and stringent permission requirements. Smart cities may fully utilize 6G technology while protecting residents' privacy and security if they take a proactive approach to resolving these issues. This well-rounded strategy will build trust and pave the way for creative, resilient cityscapes that improve people's lives.

REFERENCES

Ahad, A., Jiangbina, Z., Tahir, M., Shayea, I., Sheikh, M. A., & Rasheed, F. (2024). 6G and Intelligent Healthcare: Taxonomy, technologies, open issues and future research directions. *Internet of Things : Engineering Cyber Physical Human Systems*, 25, 101068. DOI: 10.1016/j.iot.2024.101068

Alhammadi, A., Shayea, I., El-Saleh, A. A., Azmi, M. H., Ismail, Z. H., Kouhalvandi, L., & Saad, S. A. (2024). Artificial Intelligence in 6G Wireless Networks: Opportunities, Applications, and Challenges. *International Journal of Intelligent Systems*, 2024(1), 8845070. DOI: 10.1155/2024/8845070

Charu, M., Kumar, M. A., Upadhyay, M. A., & Chauhan, M. P. A 6G Network: Future of Nations? Challenges in 6G Communications. Tuijin Jishu/Journal of Propulsion Technology, 44(04), 2023.

Dasika, S. R. C. M., Kakulapati, V., & Saligrama, S. (2024). Network Security and Data Privacy in 6G Environment: Impacts and Challenges.

Kazmi, S. H. A., Hassan, R., Qamar, F., Nisar, K., & Ibrahim, A. A. A. (2023). Security concepts in emerging 6G communication: Threats, countermeasures, authentication techniques and research directions. *Symmetry*, 15(6), 1147. DOI: 10.3390/sym15061147

Li, Y., Xiao, Y., Liang, W., Cai, J., Zhang, R., Li, K. C., & Khan, M. K. (2024). The security and privacy challenges toward cybersecurity of 6G networks: A comprehensive review. *Computer Science and Information Systems*, 21(00), 16–16. DOI: 10.2298/CSIS230804016L

Murroni, M., Anedda, M., Fadda, M., Ruiu, P., Popescu, V., Zaharia, C., & Giusto, D. (2023). 6G—Enabling the New Smart City: A Survey. *Sensors (Basel)*, 23(17), 7528. DOI: 10.3390/s23177528 PMID: 37687986

Osorio, D. P. M., Ahmad, I., Sánchez, J. D. V., Gurtov, A., Scholliers, J., Kutila, M., & Porambage, P. (2022). Towards 6G-enabled internet of vehicles: Security and privacy. *IEEE Open Journal of the Communications Society*, 3, 82–105. DOI: 10.1109/OJCOMS.2022.3143098

Ounza, J. E. (2023). A taxonomical survey of 5G and 6G security and privacy issues. *Global Journal of Engineering and Technology Advances, 14*(3), 042-060.

Parra-Ullauri, J. M., Zhang, X., Bravalheri, A., Moazzeni, S., Wu, Y., Nejabati, R., & Simeonidou, D. (2024). Federated Analytics for 6G Networks: Applications, Challenges, and Opportunities. *IEEE Network*.

Porambage, P., Gür, G., Osorio, D. P. M., Liyanage, M., Gurtov, A., & Ylianttila, M. (2021). The roadmap to 6G security and privacy. *IEEE Open Journal of the Communications Society*, 2, 1094–1122. DOI: 10.1109/OJCOMS.2021.3078081

Scalise, P., Boeding, M., Hempel, M., Sharif, H., Delloiacovo, J., & Reed, J. (2024). A Systematic Survey on 5G and 6G Security Considerations, Challenges, Trends, and Research Areas. *Future Internet*, 16(3), 67. DOI: 10.3390/fi16030067

Sharma, S., Popli, R., Singh, S., Chhabra, G., Saini, G. S., Singh, M., Sandhu, A., Sharma, A., & Kumar, R. (2024). The Role of 6G Technologies in Advancing Smart City Applications: Opportunities and Challenges. *Sustainability (Basel)*, 16(16), 7039. DOI: 10.3390/su16167039

Tripi, G., Iacobelli, A., Rinieri, L., & Prandini, M. (2024). Security and Trust in the 6G Era: Risks and Mitigations. *Electronics (Basel)*, 13(11), 2162. DOI: 10.3390/electronics13112162

Chapter 6
6G Technology and Heritage Cities: Enhancing Preservation and Visitor Experience

Aditi Nag
https://orcid.org/0000-0002-0604-6945
Manipal University Jaipur, India

Anurag Singh Rathore
https://orcid.org/0009-0004-0112-5478
Indira Gandhi National Open University, New Delhi, India

ABSTRACT

Heritage cities face the dual challenge of preserving their cultural legacy while meeting modern tourism demands. The advent of 6G technology offers a transformative opportunity to address these challenges by enhancing preservation efforts and visitor experiences. This paper explores the potential of 6G in revolutionising heritage city management through technologies like augmented reality (AR), virtual reality (VR), and the Internet of Things (IoT). These technologies enable immersive and interactive experiences for tourists while facilitating real-time monitoring and proactive maintenance of heritage sites. Case studies from Rome and Kyoto illustrate the practical implementation of 6G, highlighting its benefits and challenges. The integration of 6G requires careful consideration by urban planners and heritage managers, balancing technological advancements with the preservation of cultural authenticity. As 6G technology continues to evolve, its role in heritage city strategies holds promise for sustainable tourism and the enduring conservation of global cultural heritage.

DOI: 10.4018/979-8-3693-8029-1.ch006

1 INTRODUCTION

Living embodiments of the intricate tapestry of human civilisation are heritage towns distinguished by their historical value and profound cultural legacy. Encapsulating millennia of architectural success, creative expressions, and societal attractions, these towns symbolised cultural diversity and shared recollections revered by individuals and communities worldwide (Zhao, 2022). Urban planning and heritage management specialists vouch that notwithstanding their grandeur and historic splendour, heritage towns must strike an equilibrium while tackling the promptly evolving desires of modern tourists and safeguarding their tangible and intangible cultural heritage (Thakur, Bandyopadhyay & Datta, 2023). Cultural resources must be safeguarded from ecological deterioration, conflict with urbanisation and destructive impacts of time to preserve in intact form the physical aspects and artefacts and cultural lifeline of such heritage, as asserted by Yildirim & Çakici (2022). At the same time, mainstreaming heritage tourism is challenging in increasing tourist participation, managing tourists, and maintaining infrastructures without harming the value of these valuable cultural resources, as Slimani, Khoulji & Kerkeb (2023) claimed.

Even with the steeplechases above, 6G technology ensures support, management, and tourism promotion in and protection of historic towns. Building on 5G's success, 6G is set to cause a revolution in wireless communications. It will offer fast data speeds, quick response times, and connections everywhere to work with cutting-edge devices. Sinha (2021) points out that these tech improvements open doors to try new ideas (refer to Figure 1). These could boost efforts to protect cultural treasures and make visiting more enjoyable. This, in turn, helps make sure we keep our rich cultural history safe for the future.

Figure 1. Emerging use cases for 6G systems

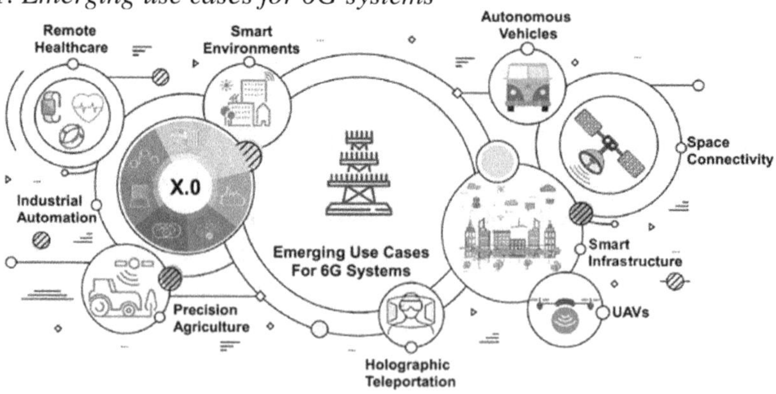

(Source: Akyildiz, Kak & Nie, 2020)

The research aims to dissect the transformative potential of 6G technology through a focus on an integrative approach towards advanced technologies like augmented reality (AR) and virtual reality (VR) in heritage town management (HTM) and tourism to explore the potential influence of 6G to empower heritage towns in the offering of immersive, educational and culturally enriching experiences to tourists whilst fortifying efforts for safeguarding and protecting the existent invaluable cultural heritage. The research proceeded a further step in examining the implications of 6G-enabled solution adoption for urban planners, heritage managers, policymakers, and various other stakeholders for sustainable development and management of heritage towns through analysis of obstacles and avenues for research in 6G to harness its full potential which can emphasise the need for strategic planning, infrastructure investment, and collaborative efforts for the preservation of the authenticity and integrity of heritage sites. The research reconnoitres methods to use 6G in HTM and tourism through profound case studies, theory, and real-world instances. It gazes at the ethical side of this tech, including how to protect residents' discretion, the peril of virtual experiences taken from other cultures, and warranting everyone having an impartial chance to access these new-fangled technologies. Through this thorough effort, the research aims to provide a comprehensive perspective of 6G’s potential towards redefining HTM and tourism in this current era through insights on innovative applications, best practices, potential obstacles, and ethical considerations to guide various stakeholders in the process for leveraging 6G technology to safeguard, promote, and sustain the cultural heritage that has the potential to define the collective identity of the community and the global cultural discourse enrichment in general.

2 6G TECHNOLOGY: AN OVERVIEW

With this evolving need of each generation, the future of wireless communications is constantly evolving, surpassing the capabilities of its predecessor to revolutionise the digital landscape, moving forward from 5G to 6G through remarkable advances in reliability, speed and connectivity (Sinha, 2021). With the potential to alter how tech and humans interact, this ever-changing technology can construct openings for novel expansions across countless turfs, demanding assessment to comprehend the noteworthy aspects and potential of 6G tech to preserve past and advance tourism experiences (Al Amin et al., 2023).

2.1 6G Technology: Key Features

With trailblazing features that can theoretically augment performance and extend application scope, 6G has materialised as the collective new method due to its ultra-low latency, enhanced mobile broadband (eMBB), massive machine-type communication (mMTC) and advanced AI integration in various sectors (refer to Figure 2). Slimani, Khoulji & Kerkeb (2023) proclaim that the near-instantaneous communication capability of 6G, due to its ultra-low latency, as low as 1 millisecond, is a criterion for applications like AR, VR, and autonomous systems, which demand real-time interface and feedback to warrant seamless and immersive experiences for heightened unprecedented efficiency and responsiveness. Similarly, the eMBB capabilities of 6G, where data speeds are projected to exceed 100 Gbps, promise support for the increasing demand for real-time gaming, HD video streaming and other similar data-intensive applications (Wikström et al., 2020). This feature has the potential to facilitate the delivery of high-quality digital content for heritage town tourism through virtual tours and interactive exhibits worldwide. Thakur, Bandyopadhyay & Datta (2023) emphasise that with the initiation of 6G, the mMTC capability may concurrently connect billions of devices, which is principally imperative in circumstances like the Internet of Things (IoT), where innumerable sensors and devices communicate and exchange data. Moreover, Banafaa et al. (2023) claim that mMTC can support heritage safeguarding by providing real-time data on structural integrity, environmental conditions, and tourist behaviour through intensive monitoring and administration of heritage sites via IoT networks. Moreover, 6G's ability to integrate AI allows for more efficient processing and analysis of large amounts of data, allowing for predictive maintenance of heritage sites, automating repetitive tasks, and giving tourists individualised experiences through intelligent systems (Aguiar-Castillo et al., 2021). This results in proactive, intelligent, adaptive, and resilient HTM practices.

Figure 2. 6G features

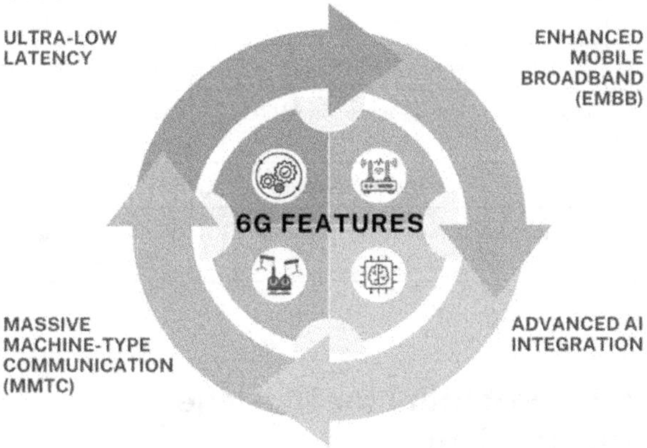

(Source: Authors)

2.2 Enabling Emerging Technologies

Seamless integration of emerging technologies for new avenues in various sectors, including heritage tourism and preservation, requires a robust platform like 6G with its advanced features and benefits like AR and VR, IoT and AI (refer to Table 1). AR and VR applications have emerged as a solution to revolutionise the immersive and interactive experiences for heritage cities through 6G's ultra-low latency and eMBB capabilities, which can allow tourists to explore historical sites with enriched digital overlays or through virtual reconstructions, bringing back history to life while offering educational and engaging ways to experience cultural heritage (Sinha, 2021). Slimani, Khoulji & Kerkeb (2023) claim that mMTC, conversely, can enable extensive deployment of IoT devices across heritage sites and destinations where environmental factors, structural issues, and tourist movements can be tracked and monitored through IoT sensors to provide heritage conservationists and managers with valuable data to ensure a data-driven approach for preservation efforts to ensure timely interventions and informed decision-making. At the same time, Sinha (2021) has predicted that advanced AI integration in 6G can help analyse data from IoT sensors, predict maintenance needs, and optimise tourist management by enabling more sophisticated analysis and automation, thus enhancing avenues for personalised tourist experiences, tailored recommendations offering and interactive content based on individual preferences and behaviours.

Table 1. 6G features and enabling technologies comparative analysis (Source: Authors)

Feature	Description	Enabling Technologies
Ultra-Low Latency	Latency as low as 1 millisecond	AR, VR, IoT
eMBB	Data transfer speeds exceeding 100 Gbps	AR, VR, digital archives
mMTC	Connectivity for billions of devices	IoT, sensor networks
Advanced AI Integration	Enhanced data processing and analysis	Predictive maintenance, personalisation

2.3 Transformative Potential for Heritage Preservation and Tourism

With modern communications systems such as 6G and advanced technologies such as IoT, AR, VR, and AI, transforming preservation, tourism, and HTM, using the 6G capabilities to maintain cultural property can raise the bar of tourist experiences. The three vibrant research fields that directly connect to this transformation potential over the last 5 years of research are enhanced tourist involvement, forward-thinking preservation, and sustainable tourism management (STM). In these, virtual tours, historical reconstructions, and interactive exhibitions through applications of AR and VR capabilities in 6G networks can provide interactive experiences capable of capturing the minds of tourists for knowledge inculcation and enhancing knowledge access and involvement with cultural heritage for the sake of widening the scope and encouraging more excellent cultural education. Meanwhile, real-time monitoring and predictive analytics through the amalgamation of IoT sensors and AI systems can service heritage managers through the enablement of proactive preservation strategies by identifying and addressing impending problems before they become precarious to warrant the long-term sustainability of heritage sites (Yildirim & Çakici, 2022) via a data-driven approach which optimises maintenance efforts, thus reducing costs, and preserving the authenticity of cultural assets. Furthermore, to upkeep STM, 6G can be used to augment tourist management and curtail the detrimental environmental impacts of tourism undertakings by facilitating better crowd control and resource apportionment and providing awareness of tourist patterns (Banafaa et al., 2023) through advanced data analytics and digital solutions offering alternative ways for experience tourism without wear and tear of fragile structures (Slimani, Khoulji & Kerkeb, 2023).

3 TOURIST EXPERIENCE ENHANCEMENT WITH 6G

Heritage tourism heralds a new-fangled epoch of novelty and opportunities through the advent of 6G whilst harnessing its capabilities to offer unprecedented engagement and immersion to tourists through its various features. As discussed in Figures 2 and 3, to enrich the interactive and educational experiences (Uusitalo et al., 2021), heritage sites preserve and protect their cultural assets whilst taking a technological leap to engage and captivate tourists (Wikström et al., 2020) through the transformation of how tourists experience historical sites, thus, bridging the gap between the past and the present meanwhile making history more accessible, engaging, and meaningful.

Figure 3. AR and VR for enhancing tourist experience with 6G

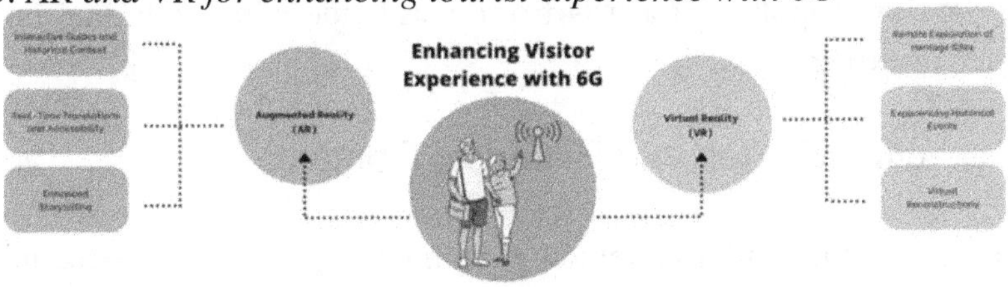

(Source: Authors)

To advance storytelling, accessibility, and inclusive tourist engagement, this section explores how 6G technology may transform tourist experiences in heritage towns using cutting-edge AR and VR technologies.

3.1 Augmented Reality (AR)

AR transforms the tourist's interaction with heritage sites by overlaying digital facts onto the somatic setting, creating contextual experiences that amplify the tourist's appreciation and commitment to cultural heritage (Aguiar-Castillo et al., 2021). AR is described as an operational bullet in heritage tourism that helps to bridge the past and the present. AR introduces degrees of historical depth and context that are not readily apparent by overlaying computer-generated visuals, data, and sound onto an individual's perception of the natural environment (Sinha, 2021). Tourists can gaze transcend a site's present state owing to this digital modernisation, allowing them to visualise its historical grandeur and acquire an enhanced understanding of its historical and cultural significance. AR can generate dynamic, engaging experiences out of static, mute artefacts. Imagine employing AR to investigate the ruins of a bygone civilisation and witness the structures resurrected to their peak splendour, populated by virtual inhabitants going about everyday activities (Allam & Jones, 2021). This positively impacts the tour's instructional worth and involvement by providing perspectives on ancient periods' routines, construction techniques, and architectural trends that sometimes prove difficult to express effectively through traditional means (Uusitalo et al., 2021). AR may additionally assist with obstacles like accessibility and decay that heritage sites encounter. To virtually imitate and display fragile sites through the exploitation of AR, tourists are able to absorb their magnificence without needing to actually come into proximity to them, safeguarding the site (Allam & Newman, 2023a, 2023b). AR can offer an analogous opportunity to people who are either physically or geographically incapable of visiting in person, bringing up heritage to a broader audience (Sinha, 2021) as the prospect that AR technology propagates and becomes harmonious with subsequent technologies like 6G, radical amendments to historical tourism and conservation will only develop, supplying tourists from worldwide with additional immersive and instructive experiences.

3.1.1 Interactive Guides and Historical Context

AR transforms the tourist's interaction with heritage sites by overlaying digital facts onto the somatic setting, creating contextual experiences that amplify the tourist's appreciation and commitment to cultural heritage (Aguiar-Castillo et al., 2021). AR is described as an operational bullet in heritage tourism that helps to bridge the past and the present. As Slimani, Khoulji, and Kerkeb (2023) demonstrated, AR can deliver exhaustive data regarding historic sites through smartphones or AR glasses if applied as an enveloping agent while touring the historic site. This way, AR exhibitions of the historical buildings and events happening while the reconstruction process is in action will enable tourists to visualise the place in a long-lost version so that they may better understand the subtlety of culture and architecture often left behind when reconstructing history (Alsharif et al., 2024). Therefore, as asserted by Allam & Newman (2023a, 2023b), AR can restore faded frescoes to their original colours or tell the history that occurred at the place by completing missing foundational structures, thereby bringing a profound understanding of the timeline of the place. For instance, the Colosseum in Rome, Italy, used AR technologies, and tourists could see how it was constructed, as it has happened in history. Using AR glasses, the tourists can see the arena, the seating sections, crowds, and even the events held there, enabling them to thoroughly understand what historical background this building embodies (Uusitalo et al., 2021).

3.1.2 Real-Time Translations and Accessibility

Thakur, Bandyopadhyay & Datta (2023) claim that through the real-time translations of info and guides' speech, AR has the potential to break the linguistic barrier, thereby making accessibility to heritage sites accessible for non-native tourists and, therefore, ensuring engagement from diverse linguistic backgrounds tourists. This means that with the help of AR, translations of inscriptions, information plaques, and audio guides in the mother tongue reach the tourist who is touring the heritage site of a foreign country, enhancing the tourist's understanding and involvement and, therefore, making the experience more inclusive, appealing, and appreciative (Qadir et al., 2023). For instance, AR applications are used in Château de Chambord in France, providing real-time translations and all possible historical contexts in multiple languages. It enhances an inclusive experience through a rich appreciation of the castle's antiquity and architecture among those who are not linguists in French (Uusitalo et al., 2021).

3.1.3 Enhanced Storytelling

Heritage sites can offer more immersive storytelling experiences with the help of AR. It is presented rhetorically and engagingly to tourists through organised tours that consist of historical narratives, verbally told stories and interactional elements. Participative timelines, AR-based treasure hunts, and the option to "chat" with historical identities through AR simulations are just a few examples. These will enable tourists to learn through participation and interaction, making a tour rewarding and edifying (Bregni et al., 2023). The visual and audio elements replicating past happenings' senses can be introduced into augmented storytelling that becomes more engaging and memorable. The Berlin Wall Memorial in Berlin, Germany, throws pictures and videos of former events on pieces of the wall and enhances its narration with AR capabilities. AR versions of failed attempts to escape Berlin's daily life and significant historical events are also accessible for tourists to make the experience more realistic and memorable. Similarly, tourists can navigate computer-created versions of ancient streets and buildings and reenact old events, such as gladiatorial battles in the excavations of Pompeii. This immersive experience will enhance aesthetic attractiveness and emotional connection with the past at the site. As 6G technology enhances the capabilities of AR, it will make heritage tourism more complex applications possible, opening new avenues for enjoying and seeing cultural heritage.

3.2 Virtual Reality (VR)

VR provides immersion that can bring viewers to a heritage site, an experience that the level of presence and interaction available to the tourist has not yet matched. As has been observed, this technology, especially with its capability of offering completely immersive environments with the possibility of interaction with users of digital recreations of natural and historical sites and the actual events, offers an experience far more impossible to imagine beforehand for heritage. Heritage benefits the wider audience and the unique experiences by which history can be pursued (Bregni et al., 2023), allowing for a more profound and engaging interaction with heritage sites through immersive VR technology. Tourists can use headsets for VR to be taken virtually to historical landmarks where they might experience them in their rich, three-dimensional detail, enhancing the tourist experience and providing education where users can visualise and understand otherwise complex historical and cultural contexts, becoming the most significant advantage VR can provide: bringing heritage sites to life for those who cannot tour them in-person (Kumari, Gupta & Tanwar, 2021). Geographical, financial, or physical constraints prevent people from travelling to iconic heritage locations. VR bridges that gap by providing a virtual experience as close to reality as possible, allowing remote tourists to explore and appreciate these sites from their homes. This democratisation of access to cultural heritage strengthens a broader disposition toward history and culture across the entire globe. Additionally, VR reconstructs events from history; users could thus witness and participate in events that happened in the past. This capacity gives an emotional and educational depth to the static exhibits and traditional media that cannot be attained with static presentations. This allows people to uniquely step into the bygone era and establish a personal relationship with every historical event and figure. The technology can also visually reconstruct heritage sites in detail, as they were in different historical periods. Such reconstructions provide complete views of the sites' architectural evolution and cultural significance, thus adding educational value and experience for the tourist. In this way, tourists can interactively reconnoitre these reconstructions in a new dynamic and fetching routine to acquire knowledge about history and heritage.

In brief, VR technology opens heritage tourism and preservation possibilities with immersive, accessible, and engaging experiences. As technology evolves, applications in this field will increase, opening new ways of connecting and appreciating our cultural heritage.

3.2.1 Remote Exploration of Heritage Sites

VR would enable a human being to walk through heritage sites around the globe. Historical sites would then be re-created in virtual form. It would then become possible for those who cannot travel and see them to experience and appreciate that place in a virtual setting. In this context, inclusivity fosters a broader appreciation of cultural heritage and can attract audiences from everywhere on earth. For example, virtual tours can be used in outreach efforts for heritage sites to reach persons unable to visit because of physical, financial, or logistically adverse conditions and democratise access to cultural heritage (Allam & Newman, 2023a, 2023b). The British Museum, for instance, developed a VR exhibition known as "The Museum of the World". In this manner, people can view much of Britain's collections from homes. The tour is rich in detailed 3D models of artefacts and exhibitions, allowing one to learn much about its collections without touring the site.

3.2.2 Experiencing Historical Events

VR will create historical activities so that the tourist may imagine the time of the moment of history, giving the tourist a further impression in understanding historical backgrounds and the background events while making history even more apparent and enjoyable to study (Yildirim & Çakici, 2022). Explorative steps from the historical point of view will most definitely give out particular points that people from ordinary museums cannot grasp emotionally (Sinha, 2021). The Anne Frank House in Amsterdam has a VR tour that allows users to experience passing through the Secret Annex, where the Frank family hid during the War. In this experience, the historical accounts come together with visual representations of the space as it happened during their hiding. As such, this would lead one to have a more touching and practical understanding of what Anne Frank's life history and the Holocaust involve.

3.2.3 Virtual Reconstructions

VR can recreate heritage sites as extremely high-resolution digital reconstructions occurring at different times. These reconstructions can be analysed to learn of modifications in architectural design and a change in cultural values in terms of time that characterise a site. This is a very effective way by which heritage destinations can be presented holistically in visual forms and suitable textural descriptions of the differences over centuries (Thakur, Bandyopadhyay & Datta, 2023). In ancient Petra in Jordan, VR technology was applied to reconstruct city life at its height. A tourist is taken virtually to walk streets and into buildings and watch people going about their daily lives to appreciate Petra's history and heritage.

A virtual tour of the Taj Mahal will enable users to view the iconic structure extensively in its gardens and interiors and see how the monument looked at various times of the day or during time-consuming events such as its construction time. Perhaps that's why this VR experience offers beautiful views of the architectural aspects, stories about how it's built and what history surrounds it, and virtual meetups with people in history, like Emperor Shah Jahan himself or his court. VR technology will revolutionise heritage tourism by providing immersive, engaging, and accessible experiences. This will be because remote exploration, historical event recreations, and virtual reconstructions of heritage sites will be brought about in ways that are impossible to achieve traditionally. The more advanced technology, the further development and enhancement in heritage preservation and tourism applications for VR technologies, with new innovative, creative means of connecting or appreciating our cultural heritage.

4 HERITAGE CITIES ENRICHMENT AND VISITOR EXPERIENCE THROUGH UTILIZING 6G TECHNOLOGY

The 6G technology integration into heritage cities has been seen as one great leap forward in cultural heritage preservation and experience. With ultra-low latency, high-speed connectivity, and supporting other advanced technologies, this will create new visitor experiences in heritage cities that are far more immersive, interactive, and informative (Singh et al., 2023b; Singh, Jeong & Park, 2020). The following section discusses the various use cases of 6G technology in heritage cities and changes that occur to tourists' experience by virtue of the latter.

4.1 Applications of 6G Technology in Heritage Cities

4.1.1 Augmented Reality (AR)

AR technology allows visitors to engage with heritage sites in new ways by overlaying digital information onto the physical environment.

- **Interactive Tours**: Tourists can utilise AR devices that provide real-time information about historical sites, such as architectural details and contextual narratives. For example, the Colosseum in Rome, AR, can recreate ancient events and structures so that tourists can view the site in its former glory (Uusitalo et al., 2021).

- **Learning Enhancements:** With AR, one can create learning content based on a specific tourist's interest in the visitation event. This way, interactions are enhanced as experiences are made more interactive by interactively telling stories. A tour guide may have historical people or events with digital overlays associated with them (Sinha, 2021).

4.1.2 Virtual Reality (VR)

VR is an immersive experience that transports the viewer to a different period altogether or places that might be inaccessible in the real world at heritage sites.

- **Remote Exploration**: Through VR, people who otherwise cannot afford to visit such areas can explore heritage sites online. For instance, in a VR tour of Pompeii, the visitors get a very vivid impression of how one lived and survived at the time of the volcanic eruption of Mount Vesuvius as they explore the ancient city (Yildirim & Çakici, 2022).
- **Historical Reconstructions**: VR can reconstruct historical moments or architectural changes so visitors can view momentous events and understand what they mean (Bregni et al., 2023).

4.1.3 Internet of Things (IoT)

IoT sensors in the heritage site can be monitored and managed in real time.

- **Environmental Monitoring**: IoT sensors measure temperature, humidity, and structural integrity to generate data that maintains delicate artefacts and structures. For example, sensors on Florence's Duomo Cathedral monitor conditions that may affect its structural integrity (Singhal, Betgeri, & Singh, 2024; Slimani, Khoulji & Kerkeb, 2023; Singh et al., 2023b).
- **Visitor Behavior Analysis**: Based on movement and interaction data on visits and interactions with exhibitions by visitors, heritage managers would enhance visitor flow. Overall, heritage management of places could be optimised based on this approach to implement the 6G technology to transform the visitor experience in the heritage city.

4.1.4 Visitor Experience Transformation

The application of 6G technology significantly enhances the visitor experience in heritage cities through various means:

- **Increased Accessibility**: AR and VR may make cultural heritage accessible to everyone worldwide. These allow users to see their beloved heritage sites in different regions or even tailor them to their tastes.
- **Enhanced Engagement**: The interactional aspects of these innovations make the connection of people with heritage more potent. The fact that people witness history through immersion allows them a sense of importance for the heritage sites.
- **Educational Value**: The area formed by convergence in AR, VR, and IoT is an educative site for the visitor, giving a spark of knowledge and guarding the cultural heritage's sake.
- **STP**: With digitalisation, they cannot injure the sensitive site. So, they give virtual options instead of physical site visits, reducing environmental impact and enhancing tourist experiences.

The management of cultural assets in heritage cities may tap into tremendous potential through 6G technology and visitor experience. This can be done by infusing AR, VR, and IoT into the frameworks of such heritage cities to provide immersive educational experiences that bring history alive for visitors (refer to Table 2).

Table 2. Comparison of visitor experience with traditional vs. 6G technology (Source: Authors)

Aspect	Traditional Visitor Experience	6G Enhanced Visitor Experience
Accessibility	Limited to physical visits	Remote access through AR/VR
Engagement	Static information displays	Interactive storytelling via digital overlays
Educational Value	Guided tours with limited context	Immersive learning experiences
Real-Time Information	Static guides	Real-time updates through IoT sensors
Preservation Awareness	Minimal interaction with preservation	Proactive engagement through monitoring data

According to the heritage manager and urban planner, accepting such innovations will protect cultural assets while creating an exciting atmosphere that attracts a wide range of tourists. Therefore, the future of heritage tourism lies in this perfect fusion of high technology and heritage: riches are conserved now and made available in a virtual world in the future.

5 PRESERVATION EFFORTS THROUGH 6G

6G technology becomes the next critical step towards preserving heritage sites, whereby it utilises all its high-end capabilities to transform the mode of monitoring, maintaining, and archiving cultural assets. In essence, this ultra-fast connectivity combined with expanded bandwidth in a 6G network empowered heritage managers with unprecedented tools for conservation and stewardship. Gera et al. (2023) suggest that IoT sensors can be incorporated into heritage sites using 6G to track vital structural and environmental data in real-time. Even the smallest variations in temperature, humidity, or structural integrity are detected by this ongoing monitoring, which promptly notifies the authorities so they can act quickly to prevent harm. Furthermore, rapid data transfer by 6G technology makes generating highly detailed digital records possible. These records, including high-resolution images, 3D models in considerable detail, and archival documentation, become the most precious stores of cultural heritage (Singh et al., 2023a). Storing all these assets on cloud-based platforms ensures that 6G would not make them inaccessible and depreciate physically or get lost. Technological integration advances preservation techniques with efficiency and precision and deepens knowledge and appreciation of these sites from around the globe.

6G technology remains cutting-edge in conserving cultural heritage with proactive preservation measures and full digital archiving. As challenges towards heritage sites continue to shift and change, the change promise of 6G remains one that will see and ensure the continuation and glorification of our heritage to the next generations and be treasured and sought.

5.1 Advanced Monitoring and Maintenance

This has helped 6G technology preserve heritage because it allows the technological support of high-tech monitoring and maintenance for heritage. This is enabled through the installation of IoT sensors linked over 6G networks to monitor, in real-time, the health condition of buildings and artefacts. This constant monitoring allows the heritage managers to identify and foresee any emerging issues before developing into major problems, thereby protecting the sustainability and sanctity of these precious cultural locations (Konhäuser, 2021; Kulkarni & Kulkarni, 2021).

5.1.1 IoT Sensors and Real-Time Monitoring

IoT sensors can be installed at each heritage location to monitor critical environmental and structural parameters of temperature, humidity, vibrations, and integrity. The ultra-low latency of 6G networks ensures data from these sensors is transmitted instantaneously, providing heritage managers with real-time insight into the condition of the site. Real-time monitoring is crucial for the early detection of potential issues that could compromise the integrity of the heritage site (Khattak, Nasralla & Rehman, 2022).

- **Ambience temperature and moisture forecasting:** The two can equally affect the conservation and degradation of heritage material. Mold growth, swelling and contraction of the material are reduced with immediate condition controls provided by IoT sensors observing this parameter and passing data across to the heritage site custodians over 6G.
- **Vibration and Structural Integrity Monitoring:** Gradually, slow construction work near the building, traffic, or small earth movements because of natural seismic movements can slowly damage the entire structural integrity of a heritage structure. Minor vibrations and micro-shifts of the structure, which would be hardly perceptible to human senses, can also be monitored by IoT sensors. The site managers can then take countermeasures by ensuring the received data is available in real-time by using the 6G networks.

5.1.2 Proactive Maintenance

With data analytics, the pattern will come into focus, and the likely impending problem may be identified well in advance to be prevented, hence acting before it actually becomes critical. For instance, sensors will report a minute deviation in the temperatures and humidity that would call attention to early warnings related to mold growth or material degradation (Kaur & Khan, 2022). The heritage manager, being alerted about the variation, will then undertake proactive activities that can help further delay deterioration.

- **Predictive Maintenance Algorithms:** Advanced predictive maintenance algorithms can help heritage managers analyse sensor data and predict possible problems. It means that using predictive techniques, maintenance activities can be scheduled before visible signs of deterioration appear on heritage sites and artefacts.
- **Resource Optimization:** Proactive maintenance enabled by 6G technology allows for better resource utilisation. Instead of waiting for the damage to occur, heritage managers can utilise resources better to take care of problems at an early stage and avoid costly repairs. This approach conserves not only the physical integrity of heritage sites but also optimises financial and human resources (Ji et al., 2021).

IoT sensors have been mounted at the most significant historical places in Florence, the birthplace of Italy, from the Florence Cathedral to the Uffizi Gallery. The sensors monitor the environment and the health status of structures, providing uninterrupted data for conservators of such historical sites (Uusitalo et al., 2021). Such a high-speed network will enable the 6G network to send that data instantly, allowing effective actions at the right moment for proper maintenance.

- **Florence Cathedral (Duomo di Firenze):** The sensors placed around the Florentine Cathedral monitor temperature, humidity levels, and the integrity of the building. Data obtained from the sensors are centrally monitored by a network-based 6G monitoring system, where heritage managers watch real-time conditions as well as trends in historical data. The sensors automatically produce alerts if there are deviations from the ideal conditions with immediate remedial measures needed.
- **Uffizi Gallery:** The Uffizi Gallery houses priceless works of art. It uses IoT sensors to monitor the environmental conditions within the exhibition halls. This 6G network is fast enough to respond immediately to detected anomalies, like changes in humidity that may damage paintings and sculptures. This proactive measure will preserve the gallery's extensive collection for the long term.

In short, 6G technology has provided the monitoring and proactive management of heritage sites. Now, heritage managers can trace potential real-time issues through IoT sensors and forward this information for real-time data transmission. Thus, heritage sites are preserved for future generations. Heritage preservation with 6G technology, therefore, is a grand stride toward protecting the cultural heritage that we have together.

5.2 Digital Archiving

Forming inclusive digital archives is key to enhancing the preservation of cultural heritage using 6G technology. The archive preserves heritage in easily accessible, studyable, and sharable digital forms for future generations. Data will be transferred faster with 6G networks. Heritage sites and artefacts will be captured and archived at unprecedented levels of detail and accessibility (Javed et al., 2022).

5.2.1 High-Speed Data Transfer

Bandwidth and speed in 6G networks allow the transfer of high-resolution images, 3D scans, and detailed documentation at a faster and more efficient pace. This is a capability that is very crucial to the production of accurate and comprehensive digital archives, which then become invaluable resources in restoration efforts, academic research, and public education (Jamil, Khan & ur Rehman, 2020).

- **Efficient Data Transfer:** Heritage organisations can efficiently transfer big data with the 6G networks and can rely on it. It is possible to produce real-time high-resolution images and high-detail scans of artefacts and sites, which make the archival process effective and smooth.
- **Real-Time Collaboration:** Researchers, conservators, and historians collaborate in real-time across the globe without any delay in reaching and analysing digital archives. This will enable inter and multi-disciplinary research studies and knowledge sharing among various domains that will further benefit us with respect to understanding cultural heritage (Ismail & Buyya, 2022).

5.2.2 3D Scanning and Imaging

Advanced 3D scanning technologies can capture even minute details of heritage sites and artefacts into three-dimensional digital models. These now become resources for preserving cultural heritage in terms of more than just conventional photographs of the detailed visual documentation of them.

- **Detailed Digital Models:** Using 3D laser scanning technology, one can clearly see high precision in measurements with minute details on heritage structures and artefacts. They allow users the chance to experience this through interaction, so heritage sites can be viewed virtually, and artefacts can even be analysed from every side.
- **Cloud-Based Storage:** Digital archives are kept in safe cloud-based databases for long-term storage and access. Cloud-based storage ensures that there will be remote access to digital collections while being free of physical threats, disasters, and degradation (Javed et al., 2022).

The CyArk project is an excellent example of the application of 6G-enabled technologies in the digital preservation of heritage sites all over the world. In this case, CyArk uses 3D laser scanning to acquire high-resolution digital copies to preserve cultural sites.

- **Chichen Itza, Mexico:** Digital preservation of the ancient Maya city Chichen Itza is achieved using 3D laser scanning technology from CyArk. The entire architectural detail of the pyramids, temples, etc., will be captured using high-resolution scans, taking an online tour of the UNESCO World Heritage site.
- **Easter Island Statues (Moai):** CyArk has scanned the famous Easter Island Moai statues and, in the process, preserved the monumental sculptures of those huge stones. These digital versions allow the researchers and the public at large to study the uniqueness of these statues and their cultural significance without the need for physical access.

Through 6G networks, CyArk has the opportunity to store and disseminate these digital archives across the globe, which gives future generations the opportunity and ability to access and relish their cultural heritage. This is a big giant leap in the preservation and dissemination of our rich and diverse cultural heritage through this digital archiving with 6G technology.

6 CASE STUDIES

Management heritage has created a paradigm of technology within 6G and thereby opens unprecedented new possibilities that enhance the betterment of preservation of heritage sites or cultural heritage or how they interact with visitors at any stage. This report tries to look into such case studies from iconic cities as those of Rome in Italy or Kyoto in Japan, which had embraced 6 G-enabled technologies to reshape what had been done through conventional culture heritage conservation technologies, but today, these are presented more impressively.

Heritage cities like Rome and Kyoto are locked between the horns of preserving heritage artefacts of centuries-old architectural masterpieces and modern expectations where tourists crave immersive and edifying experiences. The advent of 6G brings new opportunities such that these cities can embrace enhanced tools like AR, VR, IoT sensors, and Artificial Intelligence for managing heritage holistically. In conclusion, this paper focuses on innovation applications of 6G technology through case studies regarding heritage preservation and tourism, both in Rome and in Kyoto. The case studies reflect how AR and VR technologies transform a historical tour into an interactive journey through time so that the visitor may experience the ancient landscapes and monuments in their original splendour. In addition, through IoT sensors, structural integrity may be monitored in real-time, such that heritage sites are not proactive in mitigating the likelihood of the damages to be incurred at the detriment of the potential life span of the given sites, as indicated by Sinha in 2021.

Further, the network utilisation for 6G by Kyoto City in terms of the digitisation process of the archive collections in museums in virtual exhibits characterises the city's effort to digitalise its treasures of the cultural assets available for the appreciation of people. This allows for ultra-realistic 3D modelling and archiving to share the depth of cultural heritage in Kyoto with the whole world. Moreover, predictive maintenance AI-based systems in heritage sites ensure that such site management is optimised, thereby interpreting data from the sensors used in IoT-based setups and predicting costly overhauls before they even take place. This manner helps safeguard historical structures, thus promoting sustainability in heritage conservation practices (Lu & Ning, 2020; Lu & Zheng, 2020).

As pioneering cases, the introduction of 6G technology could change the approach to heritage management by bringing a better appreciation for cultural heritage and ensuring it is conserved for future generations. This case study group has offered some insights that heritage cities worldwide can look for a new way forward to balance innovation and tradition in steering cultural heritage stewardship. Such case studies have demonstrated ways in which innovative tools afforded by 6G can transform the practice of heritage management, such that a city like Rome and a city like Kyoto continue with cultural heritage protection as one of the means of providing a better visitor experience. Such cities open up paths for heritage preservation in the digital age, breaking through and exploiting advanced technologies.

6.1 Case Study 1: Rome, Italy

The ancient ruins and cultural heritage of the city have made Rome, Italy, study 6G technologies that can alter heritage preservation strategies and visitor engagement plans as well (refer to Figure 4).

6.1.1 Implementation of AR and VR for Interactive Tours

With creative integration, AR and VR have been used in Rome to make the historical sites of this city more engaging and educative for the visitor. The tourists are able to travel back in time and witness the glory of ancient Rome through AR glasses or VR headsets. Visitors can vividly imagine historical scenes and architectural masterpieces of the city by superimposing digital reconstructions onto the present landscape (Uusitalo et al., 2021). This technological advancement enhances the experience of visitors and helps them feel more related to the glorious history of Rome.

6.1.2 Use of IoT Sensors for Structural Monitoring

IoT sensors are used in the real-time monitoring of structural conditions at all the ancient structures of Rome to preserve architectural heritage. Sensors monitor environmental factors such as temperature, humidity, and vibrations, and all the critical information is transmitted over secure 6G networks. They detect anomalies and take proactive interventions to prevent such possible risks with this constant inflow of information. Proactive structural weaknesses ensure that these architectural wonders of the city are intact and last long while safeguarding these old structures for future generations.

Figure 4. 6G Technology in Rome, Italy

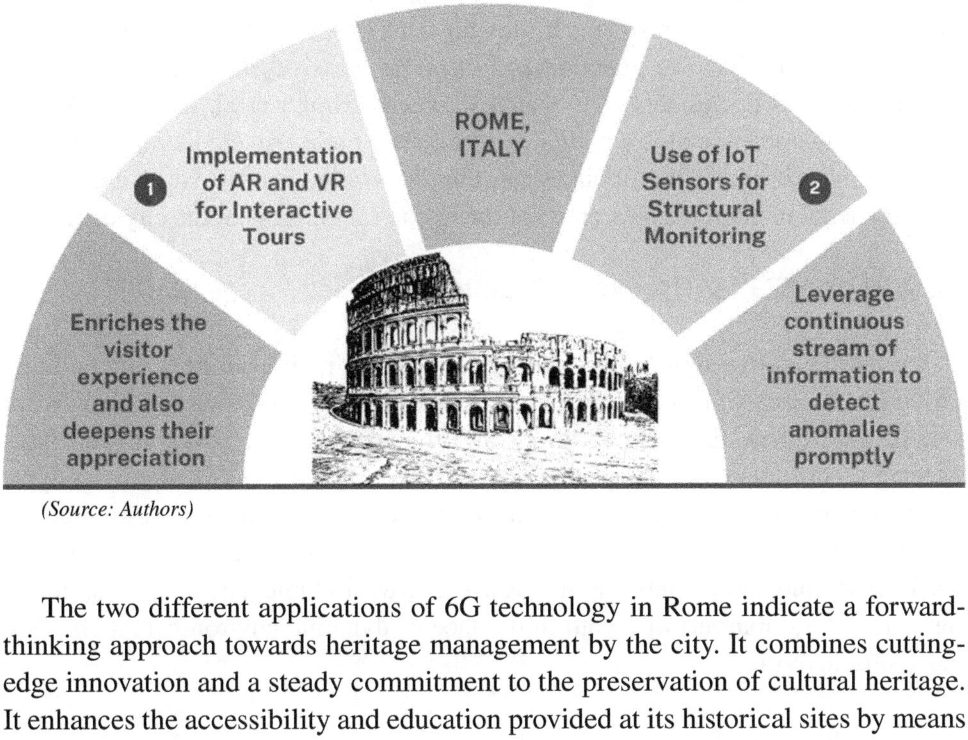

(Source: Authors)

The two different applications of 6G technology in Rome indicate a forward-thinking approach towards heritage management by the city. It combines cutting-edge innovation and a steady commitment to the preservation of cultural heritage. It enhances the accessibility and education provided at its historical sites by means of AR, VR, and IoT technologies toward the sustainability of heritage conservation in the digital era.

6.2 Case Study 2: Kyoto, Japan

Kyoto, Japan, is always known to take care of its highly preserved old architecture and the landmarks associated with history; this place has also started exploring the potential of the revolutionary capabilities of 6G networks to enhance the work on heritage conservation along with an enhanced experience of tourists as well (refer to Figure 5).

6.2.1 Coalescence of 6G for Digital Archival Systems and Virtual Exhibition for Museum

Kyoto has now become a city that sets the pace by introducing 6G networks and offering digital systems with large and greater archives, as well as rich cultural and virtual museum exhibitions. Capabilities for data transfer rates allow institutions of culture within Kyoto to generate and dispense massive 3D models, historical photographs and documents at unmatched speeds (Singh et al., 2023a). Digital content is streamed to a global audience. The thusly highly revered temples, serene gardens, and iconic machiya houses can thus be availed for virtual visitorship in stunning detail to heighten awareness of the historical richness of the city of Kyoto.

6.2.2 AI and 6G for Predictive Maintenance

Strong 6G is also supporting AI-based predictive maintenance of the cultural heritage in the city of Kyoto. IoT sensors in monuments continuously collect real-time data on environmental conditions and the health of the structure. Machine learning algorithms will process this data to detect patterns and predict what type of maintenance needs to be carried out in advance to mitigate risks (Singh et al., 2023a). The heritage managers will be able to take proactive measures through timely alerts and actionable insights to ensure structural integrity and longevity of the architectural marvels of Kyoto in the face of dynamic environmental changes and visitor activities.

Figure 5. 6G Technology in Kyoto, Japan

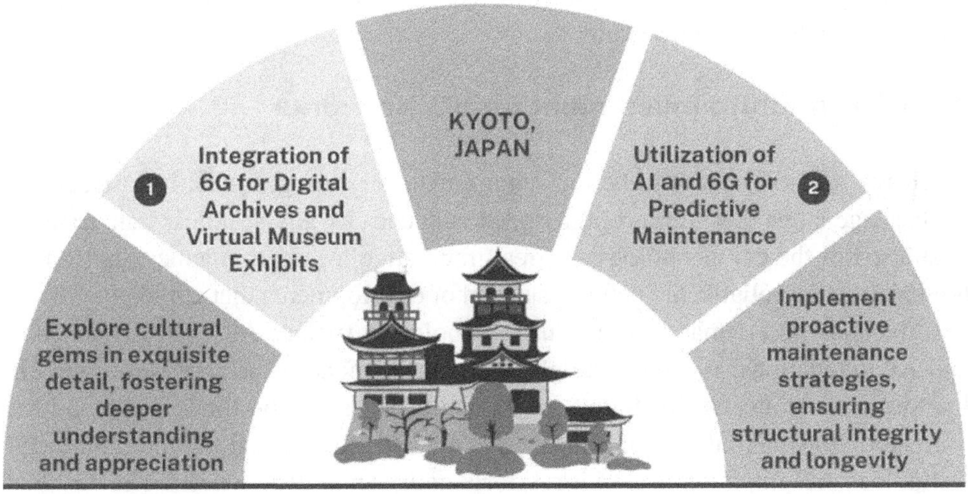

(Source: Authors)

This places Kyoto as one of the pioneers globally for the implementation of 6G technology; indeed, an innovative approach toward the preservation of heritage, for innovation and unwavering dedication can never be detrimental to the original culture. With this far-sighted attitude, it will make the history of the treasures of Kyoto guide future generations in the educational pursuit while developing a culture of custodianship for this new era in the digital age.

7 IMPLICATIONS FOR URBAN PLANNERS AND HERITAGE MANAGERS

This massive implication of 6G technology in the heritage city's fabric has immense consequences for urban planners and heritage managers, which indeed presents a new paradigm for the management and preservation of cultural heritage. It focuses on multifaceted implications from the aspect of 6G technology while underlining careful planning, strategic collaboration, and innovative approaches. It advocates for an urban plan headed by the development of new infrastructures for 6G but one that would then lay the groundwork on which AR, VR, and IoT sensors may be permitted to disrupt under new network standards. Thus, the question remains now: technological innovation or cultural authenticity and historical integrity, as posed by the new stakeholders (Islam et al., 2024). This is therefore only possible and achievable when all these stakeholders cumulatively take a stride of managing this complicated phenomenon, which would be characterised by enriched visitor experience, streamlined with strong conservational efforts, hence advancement and getting secured at sustainable heritage city development under the hyper-interconnectedness of the world.

7.1 Infrastructure Investment for 6G Networks

Heavy investment would be the requirement for strong, robust infrastructures for heritage cities that support high-speed connectivity and seamless data transfer in support of the 6G technology. A great imperative for urban planners and stakeholders is to get reliable 6G networks ahead of developments that could potentially absorb bandwidth demand from future technologies such as AR, VR, IoT sensors, and AI applications. A great example of the investment of infrastructure in 6G is found in Barcelona, Spain. Being a major tourist destination for heritage and for tourists visiting Sagrada Familia and Park Güell, among others, Barcelona embraced technology 6G for the preservation efforts and visitor experiences. The city has hence invested in the network with the establishment of 6G-enabled base stations everywhere in heritage sites (Chhabra et al., 2023). These kiosks offer full coverage and ensure high-speed internet for the viewer to view AR and VR applications of virtual reconstructions of architectural wonders in real-time.

IoT sensors have also been installed at sensitive heritage sites like the Gothic Quarter and Casa Batlló in the city. These sensors measure environmental parameters such as temperature, humidity, and vibrations within the structures and transmit the data across 6G networks into centralised control rooms. This real-time monitoring will allow heritage managers to notice anomalies in good time to facilitate proactive maintenance and conservation interventions before damage arises (Darwish & Hassanien, 2022). Scalability and reliability in the 6G architecture of Barcelona support the city's effort to pursue digital archiving of its cultural artefacts. These make it possible to generate and distribute extremely detailed 3D models and high-resolution archive photographs in that digital representations of heritage sites are accessible online to researchers, educators, and people around the world. This digital preservation strategy also puts Barcelona's cultural resources safely aside and promotes cultural tourism due to virtual tours and education engagements that are now being accessed remotely (Singh et al., 2023a).

To cut it short, infrastructure investment in 6G networks for heritage cities like Barcelona will prove to be the greatest investment that will bring improved visitor experience, optimal heritage site management, and sustainable preservation practices. With this understanding, advanced connectivity and data capabilities can, therefore, be harnessed by urban planners to uphold the cultural value and integrity of heritage sites while embracing the transformative potential of digital innovation for the sake of cultural heritage conservation.

7.2 Training for Heritage Managers and Staff on New Technologies

Comprehensive training of heritage managers and staff on new technologies would be a critical factor in unlocking the full potential of 6G integration into heritage cities. Well-crafted training programs will focus on transferring skills and knowledge for heritage professionals to work with advanced tools, like AR and VR, to create better visitor experiences. Edinburgh, Scotland, is a very good example of implementing such training. It is a city known for the ancient Edinburgh Castle and the Royal Mile. The city implements 6G technology for the renovation of the city's cultural heritage and tourism industries. The city develops specific workshops and seminars on heritage management and staff (Casillo et al., 2022). Such training programs have been customised to train the participants about using AR and VR technologies to conduct interactive historical landmark tours. For instance, heritage managers are taught to create AR overlays that will enable tourists to understand the history associated with the monuments and other famous Edinburgh spots. Through this training, they will be able to offer tourists experiences that are not only closer to each monument but also allow them to learn more about the history associated with the heritage sites of the city (Fadhil, 2023).

The deployment of IoT sensors is also part of Edinburgh's training activities. These sensors, always monitoring real-time environmental conditions and structural integrity, can offer practical training on mounting and maintenance processes, as further explained by Fadhil (2023). The managers can interpret the data from 6G networks and detect possible risks to which heritage structures are likely to be exposed early enough to allow timely intervention before deterioration or damage ensues. Besides this, an emphasis on AI integration inside the training programs at Edinburgh is placed for predictive maintenance. Heritage professionals are made aware of the ways data patterns and trends are used as inputs by artificial intelligence algorithms to predict a need for maintenance for optimally allocated resources for conserved purposes. This can be proactive in resource management in order to preserve Edinburgh's heritage and other historic assets for the ever-changing environmental influence and visitors' impact on them.

Thus, training heritage managers and staff in new technologies such as 6G, AR, VR, IoT, and AI would be extremely important for increasing the efficiency of operations, better decision-making, and the practical preservation and promotion of cultural heritage assets in a city like Edinburgh. The city will not only be able to preserve its rich cultural heritage but also encourage a vibrant cultural tourism experience appealing to people all around the world.

7.3 Balancing Technological Advancements with Cultural Authenticity

Embedding 6G technology in heritage cities is a balancing act between technological advancements and cultural authenticity. There are various benefits in visitor engagement and site management that would accrue with the introduction of AR, VR, and IoT sensors, but such cultural heritage sites should not be compromised on integrity. Kyoto, Japan, for instance, is one of the cities that have well-preserved traditions and history. Kyoto has used the 6G technologies very strategically in innovating its heritage preservation while at the same time protecting its cultural integrity (Farooq et al., 2022). The AR and VR applications have been applied with very great sensitivity in enriching the visitor experience without losing the old-time atmosphere of Kyoto's temples and machine houses.

For instance, visitors can interact with the AR overlays, which can be used to provide background information and interpretations of the history of architectural features. This enhances the visitor's insight into Kyoto's cultural richness without losing the original site's atmosphere (Mishra & Singh, 2023). Additionally, in Kyoto's practice, emphasis is placed on the engagement of people and consultations, including new technologies. Decisions are made by historians, experts in cultures, and other leaders in the community (Shehab et al., 2022). In doing so, technological advancement will follow and pay respects to the actual architecture of Kyoto, cultural heritage, and community norms. Control and Coordinate the Use of IoT Sensors in Structural Monitoring. Kyoto's policy on heritage management deals with the controlled and coordinated use of IoT sensors for structural monitoring. These sensors secretly monitor the conditions of the environment and structural stability while offering live data to heritage managers (Henrique & Prasad, 2022). With 6G networks, Kyoto ensures uninterrupted data transfer to undertake proactive maintenance while preserving its physical integrity from the onslaught of modernity on its cultural landmarks. Finally, technological progress and cultural authenticity must be well-balanced and executed by close collaboration between urban planners, heritage managers, and local communities.

Through technology that is sensitively and inclusively integrated, such cities as Kyoto can enhance tourist experiences, promote successful conservation, and ensure that the inherent value of cultural heritage is retained for the future. Not only does this safeguard the historical heritage fabric, but it also creates a greater appreciation and respect for Kyoto's rich cultural legacy.

7.4 Strategic Collaboration and Stakeholder Engagement

Effective incorporation of 6G technology in heritage city management depends significantly on strategic collaboration and proactive engagement with stakeholders drawn from a multi-sectoral basis.

Collaboration among the urban planners, heritage managers, the providers of technology, academics, local communities, and government agencies is therefore inevitable for an effectively coordinated strategy that integrates 6G technology into heritage city management harmoniously so that it harmonises technological advancements with heritage preservation objectives successfully (Montpetit & Crespi, 2021). This collaborative approach will ensure that the 6G technologies help preserve heritage sites and cultural significance instead of destroying them (Nag & Mishra, 2023). An excellent example of strategic collaboration with stakeholders is being observed in Florence, Italy. Florence had been renowned for the dominating sight of Renaissance art and architecture. Florence used 6G technologies for heritage conservation activities in the form of better visitor experiences. Collaborations between local governments, cultural institutions, and tech firms have brought 6G-enabled solutions to the city of Florence.

For instance, AR apps were successfully integrated into guided tours of historical landmarks such as the Florence Cathedral and the Uffizi Gallery (Murroni et al., 2023). AR technology gives visitors immersive experiences in Florence's artistic and architectural heritage through the overlay of digital reconstructions and historical details over the physical environment. This is a new approach that complements the visitation and creativity inspired by the heritage of Florence city's cultural life. Further, consultation with stakeholders in Florence promotes inclusion, the consideration of all parties in the decisions made, and transparency.

The local inhabitants, historians, and other cultural researchers will participate in the public forums of new technology adoption (Salameh & El Tarhuni, 2022). Therefore, the progress of technology will not hinder the cultural identity and historical heritage of Florence. Another imperative issue is that the Florence approach depends on the involvement of academics and research organisations in the adoption process of 6G. A research collaboration led by universities in collaboration with heritage management authorities is key to understanding the optimal utilisation of IoT sensors towards structural monitoring and AI tools in predictive maintenance (Nayak & Patgiri, 2021). Such collaborations promote evidence-based decision-making and, simultaneously, continuous improvement of the practice in heritage conservation. Conclusion Strategic partnership and stakeholder engagement are still among the most essential foundational principles that guarantee smooth 6G technology integration into heritage cities like Florence. These are partnering, inclusive decision-making and open communication among stakeholders; these will unlock the transformative power of 6G technologies without compromising their inherent cultural value. This is through collaboration to enhance both visitor experiences and operational efficiency while ensuring the sustainable preservation and promotion of cultural heritage for future generations.

7.5 Promoting Sustainable Urban Development

6G can significantly contribute to the process of heritage city growth by developing resilience and adaptive capacity. Advanced technological solutions can make cities proactive regarding heritage preservation by avoiding environmental impacts and reducing resources (Thakur, Bandyopadhyay & Datta, 2023). Kyoto, Japan, for instance, is using the 6G technologies, which develop sustainable urban development strategy in improving better heritage conservation and visitor experiences. IoT sensors integrated with 6G networks in Kyoto will track the historical site's structural integrity and environmental conditions to document and capture real-time information, such as temperature, humidity, and structural vibrations. It would then be further analysed by AI-driven analytics to predict the maintenance needs and provide proactive interventions to lengthen the life of cultural assets while minimising ecological footprint. The high-speed data transfer capability creates a comprehensive digital archive, allowing knowledge sharing and research collaboration. This digital repository preserves Kyoto's cultural heritage and acts as a source of education, which will be able to create further awareness and appreciation for the great history of the city among its residents and visitors (Sharma, A., & Aulakh, 2023). Kyoto is committed to sustainable urban development through public education and community engagement using 6G technologies in virtual museum exhibitions and online interactive tours, allowing the global audience to see inside the temples, gardens, and traditional machiya houses in ways that have not been possible before, further increasing cultural appreciation and care (Pamungkas, 2022). This integration of 6G technology in heritage city strategies is one of the greatest opportunities to think differently about the framework of urban planning, elevating the practice of heritage conservation to a general level. The technologies associated with 6G will be used by urban planners and heritage managers for the protection of cultural heritage, improvement of visitor experience, and long-term resilience in heritage cities against changing digital landscapes.

8 CONCLUSION

6G technology will literally revolutionise the management of heritage cities and tourism with new dimensions of enhancing visitor experiences as well as conservation practices. With the principles set by its predecessors, 6G is expected to change the way digital innovation involving AR, VR, and IoT is applied to heritage cities. It will further enhance the experience of cultural heritage through the immersive encounter of the past with the present. As urban environments continue to become an ever-interconnected hub of technology and tradition, the inclusion of 6G networks would redefine the urban landscape itself by bridging past preservation with cutting-edge digital solutions. This section talks about some of the deep impacts that technology through 6G offers heritage cities, specifically looking into how it can revive tourism, intensify conservation, and provide sustainable urban development for generations to come.

8.1 Enhancing Visitor Experiences and Preservation

Heritage cities are currently reinventing the integration of 6G technology, changing visitor experiences as well as preservation efforts. AR and VR technologies enable people to deliver immersive experiences in the guise of being a witness to events in history or the discovery of historical sites. This will carry them into the past ages or inaccessible sites and will also bring them closer to cultural significance. Advanced monitoring and maintenance are also provided by IoT sensors that change preservation practices. Environmental factors, such as temperature and humidity, structural soundness, and others, are being monitored through these sensors; anomalies can be communicated in real-time to heritage managers. For example, the Duomo Cathedral in Florence will accommodate IoT sensors that will allow conservationists to monitor its structural health in real time, and those measures should be taken with regard to possible risks involved. Heritage cities can combine AR, VR, and IoT to enhance the visitor experience and apply proactive preservation techniques. Such technologies will enable heritage managers to preserve architectural wonders and cultural relics in an efficient way so that they remain effective under dynamic environmental conditions and visitor activities. Heritage sites embracing 6G technologies will redefine the visitor experience while protecting cultural heritage for posterity.

8.2 Opportunities and Challenges

The other aspect is that 6G technology is an innovation that allows for unprecedented opportunities towards the management of heritage cities and the visitor experience, yet, at the same time, increases challenges that need to be taken care of with their navigations by urban planners and heritage managers.

8.2.1 Opportunities

6G technology expands vistas for visitor interaction and ways of conservation techniques in heritage cities. AR and VR applications provide an immersive interaction as if history comes alive and historical narratives are depicted more vividly. With AR apps, reconstructions of history can be overlaid on actual landscapes, and tourists can view past civilisations or significant historical moments in situ. AR apps of the Acropolis of Athens could recreate the former grandeur of the Parthenon. Thus, one can have a virtual walkabout across a tour of its architectural development over hundreds of years. Heritage structures are currently monitored in real-time through the predictive maintenance capability of 6G IoT. These installations of IoT sensors in the monuments can monitor their internal structural integrity, the external environmental conditions, and also the visitor footfalls. The information will make heritage managers anticipate potential risks and thus avert dangers such as erosion or structural collapse. For instance, the distribution of IoT sensors throughout the historic buildings in Venice senses the level of water that might provide a warning of potential flooding so that there can be preservative actions beforehand.

8.2.2 Challenges

6G technology to the scheme of a heritage city has challenging answers on how to apply. The primary challenge is on infrastructure development, which requires a significant investment in strong 6G networks capable of massive data transfer and high-density connectivity. A city like Prague, where historical sites are embedded within the urban landscape, making it difficult to ensure network coverage without compromising architecture, represents a logistical challenge in facilitating such development. The high level of technological literacy of the stakeholders also comes out to be a consideration. These innovation applications by 6G should be learnt by heritage managers as well as other stakeholders who operate within the local community to ensure effective usage. Imparting training programs relating to the applications of AR, VR, and IoT will be crucial in reaching the maximum benefits that will emanate from innovations in the responsible stewardship of cultural heritage. For instance, digital preservation techniques empower heritage practitioners in Barcelona through workshops that can produce comprehensive digital archives with the potential to enhance research access and public engagement at large. Perhaps this is the most delicate balance that an urban planner and a heritage manager have to work within - innovation on one side and cultural authenticity on the other side. Technology might even be able to reanimate the visitor experience, whereas heritage managers have to keep being sensitive for the sake of saving historical and cultural aspects of sites in the incorporation process. Digital intervention using AR and VR applied to Rome's Colosseum was strictly conservative so as not to distract from the old glory.

Such collaboration from urban planners, heritage managers, technology providers, and communities would guide navigation opportunities with challenges in utilising the tremendous potential 6G entails while preserving irreplaceable cultural heritage in our cities. Strategy partnerships and inclusive decision-making would make up the building blocks for strategies toward embracing all potential by 6G without harming irreplaceable cultural heritage in the cities. With more advanced evolution in the 6G technology, this effect on heritage city management will turn out to be even more immersive, sustainable, and inclusive in visitor experiences worldwide.

8.3 Future Prospects

This will be the trend of the 6G technology, which represents a transformational direction toward heritage cities, an entity that will transform the current preservation activities and the experience of the visitors into one that has never been done before.

8.3.1 Technological Advancements

With the passage of time, the incorporation of AI with ultra-low latency communications in 6G will also transform the heritage city management landscape. AI algorithms based on the strong data streams that 6G networks enable will revolutionise strategies for predictive maintenance. Thus, inheritors of heritage cities like Prague, for example, would see analytics forecasts in real-time at the structural wear to thereby optimise conservation efforts and, therefore, prolong such historical landmarks' lifespan.

8.3.2 Massive Connectivity

Pervasive connectivity will be made possible by the rollout of the 6G network, further enhancing the scope and scale of digital engagement within heritage sites. In Venice, real-time monitoring of water levels is critical to protecting architectural treasures, and IoT sensors combined with 6G will provide unprecedented precision and responsiveness. Visitors will enjoy new experiences as they seamlessly shift between the physical and virtual worlds, while heritage managers use detailed data insights to proactively mitigate environmental risks.

8.3.3 Preservation Through Immersive Experiences

Digital repositories overflowing with high-resolution graphics and interactive experiences will span limitations in access to intangible cultural heritage. A museum in Athens will experience the history of the building, starting from the ancient Greek layer to the Byzantine, then up to the Ottoman layers for the very first time through the enabling of 6G. Engagements of immersive experiences afford an understanding of cultural significance and place into the historical context, fostering worldwide appreciation and stewardship over heritage assets.

8.3.4 Global Accessibility

The 6G technologies will democratise access and penetration into every nook and corner of the earth concerning global accessibility across distance as well as cultural lines. Virtual exhibits and digital tour exhibitions of museums in real-time from Tokyo to the Taj Mahal will thus usher in borderless education and collaboration research. Digital Archives 6G will provide a hub of traditional architecture and skills for the preservation of heritages like that found in heritage cities like Kyoto, a store of information for the next generations in line with the concept of sustainable tourism.

Combining innovation and tradition, leap into tomorrow's world: the future integration of sixth-generation-6G-technologies in managing heritage city tourism will make heritage cities really open up to celebrate, preserve, and promote such amazing cultural, artistic, scientific, and historical legacies from an innovative future with equal steps in all aspects between them. At all times of this developmental trajectory, integration and coordination will be primarily reliant on successful teamwork, high-level creative abilities, and advanced strategic decision-making practices.

REFERENCES

Aguiar-Castillo, L., Guerra, V., Rufo, J., Rabadan, J., & Perez-Jimenez, R. (2021). Survey on optical wireless communications-based services applied to the tourism industry: Potentials and challenges. *Sensors (Basel)*, 21(18), 6282. DOI: 10.3390/s21186282 PMID: 34577489

Akyildiz, I. F., Kak, A., & Nie, S. (2020). 6G and beyond: The future of wireless communications systems. *IEEE Access : Practical Innovations, Open Solutions*, 8, 133995–134030. DOI: 10.1109/ACCESS.2020.3010896

Al Amin, A., Hong, J., Bui, V. H., & Su, W. (2023). Emerging 6G/B6G wireless communication for the power infrastructure in smart cities: Innovations, challenges, and future perspectives. *Algorithms*, 16(10), 474. DOI: 10.3390/a16100474

Allam, Z., & Jones, D. S. (2021). Future (post-COVID) digital, smart and sustainable cities in the wake of 6G: Digital twins, immersive realities and new urban economies. *Land Use Policy*, 101, 105201. DOI: 10.1016/j.landusepol.2020.105201

Allam, Z., & Newman, P. (2023a). Smart Cities and Sustainability: How Smart City Helps with Sustainability. In *Revising Smart Cities with Regenerative Design* (pp. 21–34). Springer International Publishing. DOI: 10.1007/978-3-031-28028-3_2

Allam, Z., & Newman, P. (2023b). Smart Cities and the Urban Economy: How Smart City Can Integrate Good Urban Economies. In *Revising Smart Cities with Regenerative Design* (pp. 101–116). Springer International Publishing. DOI: 10.1007/978-3-031-28028-3_6

Alsharif, M. H., Jahid, A., Kannadasan, R., & Kim, M. K. (2024). Unleashing the potential of sixth generation (6G) wireless networks in smart energy grid management: A comprehensive review. *Energy Reports*, 11, 1376–1398. DOI: 10.1016/j.egyr.2024.01.011

Banafaa, M., Shayea, I., Din, J., Azmi, M. H., Alashbi, A., Daradkeh, Y. I., & Alhammadi, A. (2023). 6G mobile communication technology: Requirements, targets, applications, challenges, advantages, and opportunities. *Alexandria Engineering Journal*, 64, 245–274. DOI: 10.1016/j.aej.2022.08.017

Bregni, S., Sari, H., Letaief, K., Ben Othman, J., Dobre, O., Sripimanwat, K., & Korai, U. (2023). 2nd IEEE International Mediterranean Conference on Communications and Networking (IEEE MeditCom 2022) 5-8 September 2022, Athens, Greece. *IEEE COMMUNICATIONS MAGAZINE, 61*(2), 17-21.

Casillo, M., Colace, F., Lorusso, A., Marongiu, F., & Santaniello, D. (2022). An IoT-based system for expert user supporting to monitor, manage and protect cultural heritage buildings. In *Robotics and AI for Cybersecurity and Critical Infrastructure in Smart Cities* (pp. 143–154). Springer International Publishing. DOI: 10.1007/978-3-030-96737-6_8

Chhabra, S., Aiden, M. K., Sabharwal, S. M., & Al-Asadi, M. (2023). 5G and 6G technologies for Smart City. In *Enabling Technologies for Effective Planning and Management in Sustainable Smart Cities* (pp. 335–365). Springer International Publishing. DOI: 10.1007/978-3-031-22922-0_14

Darwish, A., & Hassanien, A. E. (2022). IoHCT: Internet of cultural heritage things digital twins for conservation and health monitoring of cultural in the age of digital transformation. In *Digital Twins for Digital Transformation: Innovation in Industry* (pp. 1–21). Springer International Publishing. DOI: 10.1007/978-3-030-96802-1_1

. Fadhil, A. M. (2023). Next-Generation Urban Intelligence: Integrating 6G Communication and Blockchain Technology for Smart City Advancements.

Farooq, M. S., Nadir, R. M., Rustam, F., Hur, S., Park, Y., & Ashraf, I. (2022). Nested Bee Hive: A conceptual multilayer architecture for 6G in futuristic sustainable smart cities. *Sensors (Basel)*, 22(16), 5950. DOI: 10.3390/s22165950 PMID: 36015707

Gera, B., Raghuvanshi, Y. S., Rawlley, O., Gupta, S., Dua, A., & Sharma, P. (2023). Leveraging AI-enabled 6G-driven IoT for sustainable smart cities. *International Journal of Communication Systems*, 36(16), e5588. DOI: 10.1002/dac.5588

Gupta, M., Ved, C., & Kumari, M. (2022). Emergence of Blockchain Applications with the 6G-Enabled IoT-Based Smart City. In *Blockchain for 6G-Enabled Network-Based Applications* (pp. 213–235). CRC Press. DOI: 10.1201/9781003264392-9

Han, H., Zhai, W., & Zhao, J. (2021). Smart city enabled by 5G/6G networks: An intelligent hybrid random access scheme. *arXiv preprint arXiv:2101.06421.*

Henrique, P. S. R., & Prasad, R. (2022). *6G: the road to the future wireless technologies 2030.* River Publishers.

Islam, S., Atallah, Z. A., Budati, A. K., Hasan, M. K., Kolandaisamy, R., & Nurhizam, S. (2024). *Mobile Networks Toward 5G/6G: Network Architecture, Opportunities and Challenges in Smart City*. IEEE Open Journal of the Communications Society.

Ismail, L., & Buyya, R. (2022). Artificial intelligence applications and self-learning 6G networks for smart cities digital ecosystems: Taxonomy, challenges, and future directions. *Sensors (Basel)*, 22(15), 5750. DOI: 10.3390/s22155750 PMID: 35957307

Jamil, S. U., Khan, M. A., & ur Rehman, S. (2020). Intelligent task off-loading and resource allocation for 6G smart city environment. In *2020 IEEE 45th Conference on Local Computer Networks (LCN)* (pp. 441-444). IEEE.

Javed, A. R., Shahzad, F., Rehman, S., Zikria, Y. B., Razzak, I., Jalil, Z., & Xu, G. (2022). Future smart cities: Requirements, emerging technologies, applications, challenges, and future aspects. *Cities (London, England)*, 129, 103794. DOI: 10.1016/j.cities.2022.103794

Ji, B., Wang, Y., Song, K., Li, C., Wen, H., Menon, V. G., & Mumtaz, S. (2021). A survey of computational intelligence for 6G: Key technologies, applications and trends. *IEEE Transactions on Industrial Informatics*, 17(10), 7145–7154. DOI: 10.1109/TII.2021.3052531

Kamruzzaman, M. M. (2022). Key technologies, applications and trends of internet of things for energy-efficient 6G wireless communication in smart cities. *Energies*, 15(15), 5608. DOI: 10.3390/en15155608

Kamruzzaman, M. M., Hossin, M. A., Alruwaili, O., Alanazi, S., Alruwaili, M., Alshammari, N., Alaerjan, A., & Zaman, R. (2022). IoT-Oriented 6G Wireless Network System for Smart Cities. *Computational Intelligence and Neuroscience*, 2022(1), 1874436. DOI: 10.1155/2022/1874436 PMID: 35990150

Kaur, J., & Khan, M. A. (2022). Sixth generation (6G) wireless technology: An overview, vision, challenges and use cases. In *2022 IEEE region 10 symposium (TENSYMP)* (pp. 1-6). IEEE.

Khattak, S. B. A., Nasralla, M. M., & Rehman, I. U. (2022). The role of 6g networks in enabling future smart health services and applications. In *2022 IEEE International Smart Cities Conference (ISC2)* (pp. 1-7). IEEE.

Konhäuser, W. (2021). Digitalization in Buildings and Smart Cities on the Way to 6G. *Wireless Personal Communications*, 121(2), 1289–1302. DOI: 10.1007/s11277-021-09069-9

Kulkarni, R., & Kulkarni, S. (2021). How 6G has an influence on smart cities: An overview. *International Journal of Engineering Research & Technology (Ahmedabad)*, 10(5), 258–275.

Kumari, A., Gupta, R., & Tanwar, S. (2021). Amalgamation of blockchain and IoT for smart cities underlying 6G communication: A comprehensive review. *Computer Communications*, 172, 102–118. DOI: 10.1016/j.comcom.2021.03.005

Lu, Y., & Ning, X. (2020). A vision of 6G–5G's successor. *Journal of Management Analytics*, 7(3), 301–320. DOI: 10.1080/23270012.2020.1802622

Lu, Y., & Zheng, X. (2020). 6G: A survey on technologies, scenarios, challenges, and the related issues. *Journal of Industrial Information Integration*, 19, 100158. DOI: 10.1016/j.jii.2020.100158

Luther, W., Baloian, N., Biella, D., & Sacher, D. (2023). Digital twins and enabling technologies in museums and cultural heritage: An overview. *Sensors (Basel)*, 23(3), 1583. DOI: 10.3390/s23031583 PMID: 36772623

Mishra, P., & Singh, G. (2023). 6G-IoT framework for sustainable smart city: Vision and challenges. In *Sustainable Smart Cities: Enabling Technologies, Energy Trends and Potential Applications* (pp. 97–117). Springer International Publishing. DOI: 10.1007/978-3-031-33354-5_5

. Montpetit, M. J., & Crespi, N. (2021). Computing in the Network: The Core-Edge Continuum in 6G Network. *Shaping Future 6G Networks: Needs, Impacts, and Technologies*, 133-166.

Murroni, M., Anedda, M., Fadda, M., Ruiu, P., Popescu, V., Zaharia, C., & Giusto, D. (2023). 6G—Enabling the New Smart City: A Survey. *Sensors (Basel)*, 23(17), 7528. DOI: 10.3390/s23177528 PMID: 37687986

Nag, A., & Mishra, S. (2023). Stakeholders' perception and competitiveness of heritage towns: A systematic literature review. *Tourism Management Perspectives*, 48, 101156. DOI: 10.1016/j.tmp.2023.101156

. Nayak, S., & Patgiri, R. (2021). 6G communication technology: A vision on intelligent healthcare. *Health informatics: A computational perspective in healthcare*, 1-18.

Osama, M., Ateya, A. A., Ahmed Elsaid, S., & Muthanna, A. (2022). Ultra-reliable low-latency communications: Unmanned aerial vehicles assisted systems. *Information (Basel)*, 13(9), 430. DOI: 10.3390/info13090430

Pamungkas, B. (2022). The Future of Cities in the Metaverse Era: Are Indonesian Cities Ready. *Megafury Apriandhini, SH, MH Chair of 4th OSC, 401.*

. Qadir, Z., Le, K. N., Saeed, N., & Munawar, H. S. (2023). Towards 6G Internet of Things: Recent advances, use cases, and open challenges. *ICT express, 9*(3), 296-312.

Salameh, A. I., & El Tarhuni, M. (2022). From 5G to 6G—Challenges, technologies, and applications. *Future Internet*, 14(4), 117. DOI: 10.3390/fi14040117

Sharma, A., & Aulakh, R. S. (2023). Sustainable Development Goals2030 and Management of Heritage: Indian and Global Contexts. *Engineering Proceedings*, 56(1), 290.

Shehab, M., Khattab, T., Kucukvar, M., & Trinchero, D. (2022). The role of 5G/6G networks in building sustainable and energy-efficient smart cities. In *2022 IEEE 7th International Energy Conference (ENERGYCON)* (pp. 1-7). IEEE.

Singh, P. R., Singh, V. K., Yadav, R., & Chaurasia, S. N. (2023a). 6G networks for artificial intelligence-enabled smart cities applications: A scoping review. *Telematics and Informatics Reports*, 9, 100044. DOI: 10.1016/j.teler.2023.100044

Singh, S. K., Azzaoui, A., Choo, K. K. R., Yang, L. T., & Park, J. H. (2023b). Articles A Comprehensive Survey on Blockchain for Secure IoT-enabled Smart City beyond 5G: Approaches, Processes, Challenges, and Opportunities. *Hum.-.Centric Comput. Inf. Sci*, 13, 51.

Singh, S. K., Jeong, Y. S., & Park, J. H. (2020). A deep learning-based IoT-oriented infrastructure for secure smart city. *Sustainable Cities and Society*, 60, 102252. DOI: 10.1016/j.scs.2020.102252

Singhal, S., Betgeri, S., & Singh, S. K. (2024). Strategies for Mitigating Security Concerns in IoT-Enabled Smart Cities. In *Secure and Intelligent IoT-Enabled Smart Cities* (pp. 239–273). IGI Global. DOI: 10.4018/979-8-3693-2373-1

Sinha, D. (2021).Metropolis Spotlight: Nota Is Transforming Traffic Management Systems With AI. Retrieved from: https://developer.nvidia.com/blog/metropolis-spotlight-nota-is-transforming-traffic-management-systems-with-ai/

Slimani, K., Khoulji, S., & Kerkeb, M. L. (2023). Advancements and challenges in energy-efficient 6G mobile communication network. In *E3S Web of Conferences* (Vol. 412, p. 01036). EDP Sciences. DOI: 10.1051/e3sconf/202341201036

Thakur, S. S., Bandyopadhyay, S., & Datta, D. (2023). The Metaverse as a Virtual Form of Smart Cities: Opportunities and Challenges. *International Journal of Computer Applications*, 975(17), 8887. DOI: 10.5120/ijca2023922892

Uusitalo, M. A., Rugeland, P., Boldi, M. R., Strinati, E. C., Demestichas, P., Ericson, M., Fettweis, G. P., Filippou, M. C., Gati, A., Hamon, M.-H., Hoffmann, M., Latva-Aho, M., Parssinen, A., Richerzhagen, B., Schotten, H., Svensson, T., Wikstrom, G., Wymeersch, H., Ziegler, V., & Zou, Y. (2021). 6G vision, value, use cases and technologies from European 6G flagship project Hexa-X. *IEEE Access : Practical Innovations, Open Solutions*, 9, 160004–160020. DOI: 10.1109/ACCESS.2021.3130030

Wikström, G., Peisa, J., Rugeland, P., Johansson, N., Parkvall, S., Girnyk, M., & Da Silva, I. L. (2020). *Challenges and technologies for 6G. In 2020 2nd 6G wireless summit (6G SUMMIT)*. IEEE.

Yildirim, O., & Çakici, A. C. (2022). Cultural heritage and digitalization in city branding. In *Handbook of research on digital communications, Internet of things, and the future of cultural tourism* (pp. 467–483). IGI Global. DOI: 10.4018/978-1-7998-8528-3.ch025

Zhao, S. (2022). Creating Futuristic Heritage Experiences: An Exploratory Co-Design Study through Design Fiction. *Sustainability (Basel)*, 14(19), 12027. DOI: 10.3390/su141912027

Chapter 7
AI Applications in Secure 6G-Enabled Smart City Infrastructure

Vishal Jain
https://orcid.org/0000-0003-1126-7424
Sharda University, India

Archan Mitra
https://orcid.org/0000-0002-1419-3558
Presidency University, India

ABSTRACT

The development of secure 6G networks has the potential to transform smart city infrastructures, integrating artificial intelligence (AI) to manage urban systems with unprecedented efficiency. The integration of AI in 6G-enabled smart cities will enhance services such as public safety, transportation, and energy management, but also poses significant security risks due to the vast amounts of data being processed. This abstract explores AI's role in optimizing these systems while addressing the security challenges posed by real-time data transmission, cyber-attacks, and privacy concerns. By examining AI-driven solutions, such as anomaly detection systems and federated learning, this research offers insights into enhancing the safety and resilience of smart cities in the digital age.

DOI: 10.4018/979-8-3693-8029-1.ch007

INTRODUCTION

Background and Context

The concept of smart cities has evolved significantly in recent years, driven by rapid advancements in communication technologies and the integration of artificial intelligence (AI). Smart city infrastructure is designed to enhance the quality of life for urban residents by improving services such as transportation, energy management, healthcare, public safety, and waste management (Li et al., 2021). The transition from 4G to 5G networks has played a pivotal role in accelerating the digitalization of urban spaces, providing higher data speeds, increased network capacity, and ultra-reliable low-latency communication (URLLC). However, the introduction of the next-generation 6G network promises to revolutionize smart city infrastructures even further by offering terahertz-level data transmission, near-instantaneous communication, and massive machine-type communications (mMTC) (Latif et al., 2021).

The evolution from 4G to 5G networks has already enabled cities to implement intelligent systems, such as real-time traffic monitoring, remote healthcare, and smart energy grids (Mukherjee et al., 2021). However, with the advent of 6G, cities will experience a significant leap in both connectivity and data processing capabilities. The 6G network is expected to provide ultra-high data rates of up to 1 terabit per second, minimal latency (in the order of microseconds), and the ability to support up to 100 billion connected devices globally (Gupta & Jha, 2020). These advancements are crucial for enabling the seamless integration of diverse services in smart cities, where data generated from various sources must be processed, analyzed, and acted upon in real-time. Moreover, the massive adoption of the Internet of Things (IoT) devices in smart cities necessitates reliable and scalable communication networks, a role that 6G is expected to fulfill.

Artificial Intelligence (AI) has emerged as a critical enabler in smart city ecosystems, providing the computational power and decision-making capabilities required to manage and optimize various urban functions (Khan et al., 2021). AI applications in smart cities span multiple domains, including autonomous transportation systems, energy management, healthcare, waste disposal, and public safety. For instance, AI-driven algorithms can analyze real-time traffic data to reduce congestion, optimize energy usage in buildings, and predict emergency response needs in case of disasters (Sundqvist et al., 2020). As the volume of data generated by smart cities continues to grow, AI becomes indispensable for deriving actionable insights and enhancing the efficiency of urban services.

However, the increasing reliance on AI and 6G networks for smart city operations introduces significant challenges related to data security and privacy. The vast amount of sensitive data collected and processed in smart cities, including personal information, healthcare records, and transportation data, creates numerous vulnerabilities that cybercriminals can exploit (Jiang et al., 2021). In particular, the high-speed, ultra-low-latency communication enabled by 6G networks may expose smart city infrastructures to novel cyber threats, such as real-time data manipulation, denial-of-service attacks, and unauthorized surveillance (Chowdhury et al., 2021). Ensuring the security and privacy of such interconnected, data-rich environments is, therefore, a critical concern that must be addressed to realize the full potential of AI-powered smart cities.

Problem Statement

The deployment of 6G networks in smart cities will undoubtedly enhance urban infrastructure's functionality and efficiency by enabling faster, more reliable communication and data processing. However, this increased complexity and data intensiveness also present significant security risks. With the vast amounts of data generated and processed by smart city systems, ensuring secure data transmission, storage, and management is paramount. Smart city ecosystems are highly interconnected, with multiple devices and systems constantly exchanging data, making them particularly vulnerable to cyberattacks (Bera et al., 2021). For instance, a successful cyberattack on a smart grid could disrupt the power supply for an entire city, while a breach in transportation systems could lead to chaos and accidents (Al-Fuqaha et al., 2020).

While 6G networks promise enhanced connectivity and data processing capabilities, their security framework remains underdeveloped. Current solutions for ensuring secure communication in smart city environments are often insufficient, given the scale and complexity of data being processed. As cities transition towards 6G, there is a pressing need to develop new security protocols that can protect the integrity, confidentiality, and availability of data in real time. Moreover, existing security measures must be adapted to address the unique challenges posed by AI-driven systems, which may be susceptible to adversarial attacks or biased decision-making algorithms (Zhou et al., 2020). The role of AI in enhancing security within 6G-enabled smart city infrastructures has not been thoroughly explored, leaving significant gaps in the literature.

Another major concern is privacy. The real-time collection and analysis of data from multiple sources, such as surveillance cameras, IoT devices, and social media platforms, can lead to the unintended disclosure of sensitive personal information (Chen et al., 2021). Without robust privacy protection mechanisms, smart city residents may be exposed to invasive surveillance practices or unauthorized use of their data. Balancing the benefits of AI and 6G technologies with the need to protect individual privacy is, therefore, a key challenge for smart city planners and policymakers.

Research Objectives

This research aims to explore how AI can be leveraged to enhance the security and efficiency of 6G-enabled smart city infrastructures. Specifically, it seeks to address the following objectives:

1. **Leveraging AI for Enhanced Security in 6G-enabled Smart Cities:** This objective focuses on investigating the potential of AI-driven security frameworks to address the unique threats posed by the deployment of 6G networks in smart cities. AI can be used to detect and respond to cyber threats in real time, providing autonomous and adaptive security solutions that can keep pace with evolving attack vectors (Baker et al., 2021). This research will explore how AI technologies such as machine learning (ML) and deep learning (DL) can be applied to improve network security, detect anomalies, and prevent cyberattacks.
2. **Identifying Security Threats in 6G-Enabled Smart Cities:** As 6G networks become a reality, it is crucial to identify the specific security threats that may arise in these environments. This research will analyze potential vulnerabilities in 6G smart city infrastructures, including risks related to data breaches, unauthorized access, and cyber-physical system (CPS) attacks (Zhang et al., 2021). By understanding these threats, it will be possible to develop more targeted security measures that can mitigate their impact.
3. **Proposing AI-Driven Security Solutions:** Based on the identified security threats, this research will propose AI-driven solutions that can enhance the security and resilience of smart city infrastructures. These solutions may include the use of AI-based encryption algorithms, AI-enhanced intrusion detection systems (IDS), and blockchain technologies for secure data storage and transmission (Hasan et al., 2021). The aim is to develop security solutions that are both scalable and adaptive, capable of protecting large-scale smart city networks in real time.
4. **Examining Case Studies and Pilot Implementations:** To validate the proposed solutions, this research will examine case studies and pilot implementations of AI and 6G technologies in smart cities. By analyzing real-world examples, such as smart city projects in Singapore, South Korea, and China, this research will identify key lessons and challenges related to the integration of AI and 6G networks in urban environments (Latif et al., 2021). These case studies will provide valuable insights into the practical challenges and opportunities associated with deploying AI-driven security solutions in smart city ecosystems.

The development of 6G-enabled smart city infrastructures offers immense potential for improving urban services and enhancing the quality of life for city residents. However, as cities become more reliant on AI and advanced communication networks, ensuring the security and privacy of these infrastructures becomes a critical concern. By exploring the intersection of AI and 6G technologies, this research aims to contribute to the development of secure, efficient, and resilient smart cities capable of withstanding the challenges of the digital age.

LITERATURE REVIEW

Evolution of Smart Cities and Communication Technologies

The concept of smart cities has evolved over the past two decades, underpinned by advancements in communication technologies and the increasing integration of information and communication technology (ICT) into urban infrastructure. Early smart cities largely relied on 4G networks, which provided basic connectivity and limited data exchange capabilities. The introduction of 5G marked a significant leap forward, offering enhanced data speeds, ultra-reliable low-latency communication (URLLC), and support for massive machine-type communications (mMTC) (Gupta & Jha, 2020). These technological improvements enabled cities to incorporate more sophisticated services such as autonomous transportation, energy grid optimization, and real-time public health monitoring.

In recent years, attention has turned to 6G networks, which are expected to offer transformative improvements over 5G. Anticipated features of 6G include data rates of up to 1 terabit per second, latency as low as microseconds, and a vast expansion in device connectivity, with the ability to support billions of connected devices globally (Chowdhury et al., 2021). Such advancements are critical for smart cities, where continuous, real-time data exchange is necessary to manage complex systems and services efficiently.

According to Mitra and Das (2024), the role of emerging communication technologies like 6G will be crucial in ensuring smart city services operate smoothly and efficiently. The integration of these technologies into urban infrastructures will facilitate data-driven decision-making processes, enhancing the sustainability and resilience of smart cities.

AI Integration in Smart City Infrastructure

Artificial intelligence (AI) has become an indispensable tool for managing smart city services. As urban populations grow and cities face increasing pressures on resources, AI offers solutions to enhance efficiency and optimize service delivery across various sectors. For example, in traffic management, AI-driven systems can analyze data from sensors, cameras, and GPS devices to predict congestion and optimize traffic flow in real time (Sundqvist et al., 2020). Similarly, in energy management, AI algorithms are used to predict energy demand and adjust supply dynamically, reducing waste and improving sustainability (Mukherjee et al., 2021).

One of the critical advantages of AI in smart city infrastructure is its ability to process and analyze large datasets in real time, enabling more responsive and efficient urban services. AI applications in public health, for example, can monitor data from wearable devices, public health records, and environmental sensors to predict disease outbreaks and coordinate emergency response efforts (Li et al., 2021). In environmental monitoring, AI systems are used to track pollution levels, water usage, and waste management, allowing cities to optimize resource allocation and minimize environmental impact.

Current AI techniques such as machine learning (ML), deep learning (DL), and reinforcement learning (RL) have proven particularly effective in enhancing the capabilities of smart city services. ML algorithms, for instance, are used to identify patterns in large datasets, while DL techniques enable more complex data analysis, such as image and speech recognition (Jain & Mitra, 2024). Reinforcement learning, which involves training AI systems to make decisions based on feedback from their environment, is increasingly being applied in dynamic urban environments, such as autonomous vehicle management and smart grid optimization (Das & Mitra, 2024).

As Mitra and Lohochoudhury (2019) note, the integration of AI into smart city infrastructure offers considerable benefits in terms of efficiency and sustainability. However, it also raises new challenges, particularly related to the security and privacy of the vast amounts of data processed by AI systems in urban environments.

Security Concerns in 6G-Enabled Smart Cities

While AI and 6G hold great potential for enhancing smart city infrastructure, they also introduce new security vulnerabilities. The deployment of 6G networks in smart cities will facilitate the real-time exchange of massive amounts of data, increasing the risk of cyberattacks, data breaches, and unauthorized surveillance (Jiang et al., 2021). One of the most pressing concerns is the potential for distributed denial of service (DDoS) attacks, which could disrupt critical services such as traffic management, energy supply, and emergency response systems.

Data breaches are another significant concern in 6G-enabled smart cities. Given the volume and sensitivity of the data collected—ranging from personal health records to real-time location tracking—ensuring data security and privacy is paramount. Unauthorized access to this data could have far-reaching consequences, including identity theft, financial loss, and even threats to public safety (Chen et al., 2021).

AI also introduces its own set of security risks. Adversarial machine learning, for example, involves manipulating AI algorithms to produce incorrect or misleading results. In a smart city context, adversarial attacks could lead to significant disruptions, such as traffic accidents caused by manipulated traffic data or compromised emergency response systems (Zhou et al., 2020). Secure AI techniques, such as adversarial training, secure multi-party computation (SMC), and homomorphic encryption, are increasingly being explored as solutions to these vulnerabilities. Adversarial training involves training AI models to recognize and resist adversarial inputs, while SMC enables multiple parties to jointly compute a function over their inputs without revealing the inputs to each other (Baker et al., 2021). Homomorphic encryption, which allows computations to be performed on encrypted data without decrypting it, offers another layer of security for AI applications in smart cities (Hasan et al., 2021). Mitra and colleagues (2024) emphasize the importance of developing secure AI frameworks that can protect the integrity of smart city services while ensuring the privacy of urban residents. The deployment of secure AI systems will be critical to the success of 6G-enabled smart cities, where data security and privacy are paramount.

The evolution of smart cities is closely tied to advancements in communication technologies and AI. While 4G and 5G networks have already enabled significant improvements in urban services, the anticipated arrival of 6G promises to take these developments to the next level, with faster data speeds, lower latency, and enhanced connectivity. However, these advancements also introduce new security concerns, particularly related to the large-scale data processing required by AI systems in smart cities.

The integration of AI into smart city infrastructure offers considerable benefits, but it also raises challenges related to data security and privacy. To address these challenges, secure AI techniques such as adversarial training, SMC, and homomorphic encryption are being explored. As the deployment of 6G networks accelerates, ensuring the security and privacy of smart city infrastructures will be critical to their success.

THEORETICAL FRAMEWORK

The deployment of 6G technology in smart cities is expected to revolutionize urban infrastructure by offering unprecedented levels of connectivity, speed, and efficiency. At the core of this transformation is the integration of artificial intelligence (AI), which will serve as the driving force behind the optimization, automation, and security of smart city systems. AI's role in predictive analytics, network optimization, and real-time decision-making will be essential in managing the increasingly complex urban environments that 6G enables. The theoretical framework of this research examines the convergence of AI technologies with 6G capabilities, exploring how these innovations will shape the future of smart city infrastructure and address the unique security challenges posed by such highly interconnected environments.

AI Technologies in 6G Smart City Applications

AI technologies are poised to play a pivotal role in 6G-enabled smart cities, particularly in predictive analytics, network optimization, and decision-making. Predictive analytics, driven by AI algorithms, will allow smart cities to anticipate potential issues and optimize resource allocation proactively. For instance, AI can predict traffic congestion by analyzing historical and real-time data from sensors, cameras, and GPS devices, enabling dynamic traffic management systems that adjust in real-time to minimize congestion (Mukherjee et al., 2021). Similarly, AI-powered energy management systems can predict energy demand patterns, allowing cities to optimize power distribution and reduce wastage.

Moreover, AI's capability in network optimization is critical in managing the complex, decentralized systems that 6G smart cities will rely on. AI algorithms can monitor network performance in real-time, identifying inefficiencies or potential points of failure and automatically adjusting to optimize performance. For instance, AI can dynamically allocate bandwidth to high-priority applications, ensuring that critical services such as emergency response systems or healthcare networks are not compromised by network congestion (Jiang et al., 2021). In addition, AI's ability to learn and adapt over time allows for more effective decision-making processes, as it continuously refines its algorithms based on new data.

Specific AI frameworks, such as federated learning and edge AI, are particularly well-suited for 6G-enabled smart cities. Federated learning allows AI models to be trained across multiple decentralized devices without transferring the data to a central server. This approach not only reduces data transfer risks but also enhances privacy, as sensitive data remains on the device where it was generated (Gupta & Jha, 2020). In smart cities, federated learning can be applied to optimize distributed systems such as traffic management, healthcare monitoring, and energy distribution, where data privacy is a critical concern.

Edge AI, which involves processing data closer to its source (i.e., at the edge of the network), is another important framework for smart cities. By reducing the amount of data that needs to be transmitted over the network, edge AI increases the efficiency of decentralized processing and reduces latency (Das & Mitra, 2024). This is particularly important for applications that require real-time decision-making, such as autonomous vehicles or emergency response systems. Edge AI also enhances security by limiting the exposure of sensitive data to potential cyber threats during transmission.

6G Network Capabilities for Smart Cities

The core features of 6G networks, such as terahertz communication, holographic beamforming, and ultra-low latency communication, are expected to transform the functionality of smart city infrastructure. Terahertz communication offers extremely high data rates, enabling the transmission of large volumes of data in real-time. This is particularly important for smart city applications that rely on data from multiple sources, such as surveillance cameras, environmental sensors, and autonomous vehicles. With terahertz communication, cities can support the vast amounts of data generated by these systems without experiencing bottlenecks or delays (Chowdhury et al., 2021).

Holographic beamforming is another key feature of 6G networks that will enhance smart city infrastructure. This technology allows for highly precise control of the direction and focus of radio waves, ensuring that signals are transmitted efficiently and securely. In a smart city context, holographic beamforming can be used to optimize communication between IoT devices, reducing interference and improving the overall reliability of the network (Chen et al., 2021). For example, in dense urban environments where multiple devices are competing for bandwidth, holographic beamforming can ensure that critical applications, such as public safety networks, receive the necessary resources to function effectively.

Ultra-low latency communication is perhaps the most transformative feature of 6G networks, as it enables real-time decision-making and automation at a level that was previously unattainable. In smart cities, where split-second decisions can have significant consequences (e.g., in autonomous vehicle systems or emergency response scenarios), ultra-low latency communication ensures that data is transmitted and processed with minimal delay (Baker et al., 2021). This is crucial for applications such as intelligent transportation systems, where delays in communication could lead to traffic accidents or inefficiencies in traffic flow.

AI integrates with these 6G features to offer automated, secure, and resilient urban services. For instance, AI algorithms can analyze real-time data from 6G-enabled IoT devices to detect anomalies or potential threats, triggering automatic responses to mitigate risks. This combination of AI and 6G will enable smart cities to operate autonomously, with minimal human intervention, while ensuring that services are delivered efficiently and securely (Hasan et al., 2021).

Security Models for AI and 6G-Enabled Smart Cities

The convergence of AI and 6G technologies presents both opportunities and challenges for smart city security. On one hand, AI-driven security models have the potential to enhance the resilience of smart city infrastructure by autonomously detecting and mitigating threats in real-time. On the other hand, the increased complexity and interconnectivity of 6G networks also introduce new vulnerabilities, particularly related to data privacy and cybersecurity.

AI-driven security models are designed to detect and respond to cyber threats autonomously, without the need for human intervention. For example, AI algorithms can monitor network traffic for unusual patterns that may indicate a distributed denial of service (DDoS) attack or data breach (Zhou et al., 2020). By analyzing large datasets in real-time, AI can identify potential threats that would be difficult for human operators to detect manually. In the context of 6G-enabled smart cities, these security models will be critical for protecting the vast amounts of data generated by IoT devices, ensuring that services such as transportation, healthcare, and public safety are not compromised by cyberattacks (Sundqvist et al., 2020).

AI-enhanced encryption techniques are another important component of security models for 6G-enabled smart cities. Traditional encryption methods, while effective, can be computationally intensive and may not be suitable for real-time applications. AI-enhanced encryption techniques, such as homomorphic encryption, allow data to be processed and analyzed without decrypting it, reducing the risk of data breaches during transmission (Das & Mitra, 2024). This is particularly important for applications that involve sensitive data, such as healthcare records or financial transactions.

Intrusion detection systems (IDS) powered by AI are also essential for securing 6G networks in smart cities. These systems use machine learning algorithms to analyze network traffic and identify potential threats, such as malware or unauthorized access attempts. AI-powered IDS can continuously learn from new data, allowing them to adapt to evolving threats and improve their accuracy over time (Jain & Mitra, 2024). In addition, the use of AI in IDS allows for more proactive threat detection, as the system can identify potential vulnerabilities before they are exploited by cybercriminals.

Blockchain technology is another promising tool for securing data transfer and storage in 6G-enabled smart cities. By decentralizing data storage and using cryptographic techniques to secure transactions, blockchain can provide an additional layer of security for AI-powered smart city applications (Baker et al., 2021). For example, blockchain can be used to verify the authenticity of data from IoT devices, ensuring that malicious actors cannot tamper with the information used to make critical decisions in smart city operations.

The integration of AI technologies with 6G networks will fundamentally reshape the infrastructure and operations of smart cities, offering unprecedented levels of automation, efficiency, and security. AI's capabilities in predictive analytics, network optimization, and decision-making will be essential for managing the complex systems that 6G-enabled smart cities rely on. Specific AI frameworks, such as federated learning and edge AI, will further enhance the efficiency and security of these systems by reducing data transfer risks and decentralizing processing. However, the increased interconnectivity and complexity of 6G networks also introduce new security challenges, which must be addressed through AI-driven security models, encryption techniques, and blockchain technology. As the deployment of 6G networks accelerates, ensuring the security and resilience of smart city infrastructure will be critical to their success.

METHODOLOGY

The methodology for this research combines both qualitative and quantitative techniques to provide a comprehensive understanding of the intersection of AI and 6G technologies in smart city infrastructure. This mixed-methods approach is chosen to gain insights from both theoretical and practical perspectives, facilitating a deeper exploration of the technical, social, and security aspects of implementing AI and 6G in smart cities. The use of case studies and a range of data collection techniques ensures that the research is grounded in real-world applications, while advanced data analysis tools provide a robust framework for interpreting the results.

Research Design

The research design is structured around a **mixed-methods approach**, blending both qualitative and quantitative techniques to provide a well-rounded exploration of AI applications in 6G-enabled smart cities. This approach allows for a comprehensive examination of the technical and social aspects of the research question. On one hand, qualitative data from interviews, case studies, and theoretical perspectives provide depth and context, while quantitative data from surveys and statistical analyses offer empirical evidence and help identify trends and patterns.

Case study analysis forms a key part of the research design. Case studies of smart city projects that have already implemented AI technologies, including Songdo in South Korea, Singapore's Smart Nation, and China's AI-driven smart cities, will be examined in detail. These case studies provide concrete examples of how AI and 6G technologies are being deployed in urban environments and offer valuable insights into the challenges and opportunities associated with their implementation. Songdo, for instance, is renowned for its fully integrated smart city infrastructure, where AI is used to manage everything from waste disposal to traffic control (Kim & Lee, 2020). Similarly, Singapore's Smart Nation initiative emphasizes the use of AI in improving public safety and healthcare, while China's smart city initiatives focus on the integration of AI in public surveillance and urban planning (Li & Chan, 2021).

By analyzing these case studies, the research aims to identify best practices and challenges in AI-driven smart city development. The selected case studies are diverse in geographical location, political context, and technological infrastructure, providing a comprehensive understanding of how different regions approach the integration of AI and 6G technologies into their urban fabric.

Data Collection

The data collection process is divided into **secondary and primary data sources** to provide a holistic view of the subject matter.

1. **Secondary Data:** The secondary data will be collected from a variety of sources, including peer-reviewed journal articles, government reports, conference proceedings, and case studies that examine AI applications in smart city infrastructure. This will include reviewing existing literature on AI frameworks, such as federated learning and edge AI, and their role in smart city operations (Gupta & Jha, 2020). Additionally, reports from international organizations, such as the International Telecommunication Union (ITU), the European Commission, and various national governments on smart city projects, will be reviewed to gather insights into policy and regulatory frameworks.

By synthesizing existing knowledge, this research aims to build on previous studies while identifying gaps in the literature concerning the security challenges posed by 6G networks in smart cities. Secondary data will also be used to provide context for the primary data collected through interviews and surveys.

2. **Primary Data:** Primary data will be gathered through two main methods: **semi-structured interviews** and **surveys**.
   - **Interviews:** Semi-structured interviews will be conducted with experts in AI, cybersecurity, urban planning, and telecommunications. Interview participants will include professionals from government bodies involved in smart city initiatives, AI and cybersecurity researchers, as well as technology providers working on 6G networks and AI solutions. The semi-structured format allows for flexibility, enabling interviewees to provide in-depth insights into specific issues while still ensuring that the key research questions are addressed (Sundqvist et al., 2020). The interviews will focus on identifying the main security concerns associated with AI in 6G-enabled smart cities, exploring potential solutions, and assessing the readiness of cities to adopt these technologies securely.
   - **Surveys:** Surveys will be distributed to a broad range of stakeholders, including urban residents, policymakers, and technology developers. The survey will focus on the public's perception of AI and 6G technologies in smart cities, with particular emphasis on privacy and security concerns. Questions will be designed to gauge the level of trust that residents have in AI-driven smart city systems, their awareness of potential security risks, and their willingness to adopt AI-powered services in their daily lives (Mukherjee et al., 2021). Surveys will also seek input from policymakers to understand the regulatory frameworks being developed to secure AI and 6G networks in smart cities.

Data Analysis

Once the data is collected, it will undergo **both qualitative and quantitative analysis** to identify key themes, trends, and patterns.

1. **Qualitative Data Analysis:** The qualitative data collected through interviews and case studies will be analyzed using **AI-driven analytics**, such as natural language processing (NLP) tools. NLP will be used to process and categorize the large volumes of qualitative data, identifying recurring themes and concerns related to security in AI and 6G-enabled smart cities (Li et al., 2021). These tools will allow the research to identify patterns across different expert opinions and case studies, revealing the common challenges faced by smart city projects and the solutions that have been most effective in mitigating security risks.

For example, the interviews may highlight specific concerns about data privacy in AI-driven public services, which can then be analyzed in conjunction with secondary data from existing literature on secure AI techniques. This process of triangulation ensures that the findings are robust and grounded in both practical and theoretical perspectives.

2. **Quantitative Data Analysis:** The quantitative data gathered through surveys will be analyzed using statistical methods to measure public perception of security in AI and 6G-enabled smart city environments. Techniques such as **descriptive statistics** and **inferential statistics** will be used to quantify levels of trust in AI systems, concerns about privacy, and awareness of cybersecurity threats (Jiang et al., 2021). Cross-tabulations and correlation analysis will be employed to identify relationships between different variables, such as demographic factors and levels of trust in AI technologies.

For instance, the survey results may reveal that younger residents are more likely to trust AI-driven services compared to older residents, or that residents in cities with existing smart infrastructure are more aware of potential security risks than those in cities without such systems. This quantitative data will complement the qualitative findings from interviews, providing a more complete picture of the challenges and opportunities associated with AI and 6G technologies in smart cities.

In addition to traditional statistical methods, AI-driven analytics tools will also be used to analyze the survey data. Machine learning algorithms can be employed to identify patterns and trends that may not be immediately apparent through manual analysis, providing deeper insights into the public's perception of AI and 6G technologies (Sundqvist et al., 2020). For example, clustering algorithms can group respondents based on their attitudes towards privacy and security, enabling a more targeted analysis of specific concerns.

Ethical Considerations

Ethical considerations are central to the research process, particularly given the sensitive nature of the data being collected. All interviews and surveys will be conducted in accordance with ethical guidelines, ensuring that participants provide informed consent and that their data is anonymized to protect their privacy. Given the focus on AI and 6G technologies, which raise significant ethical concerns regarding data privacy and surveillance, it is essential that the research adheres to the highest standards of ethical practice (Baker et al., 2021). This includes ensuring that all data is stored securely and that participants are fully informed about how their data will be used.

FUTURE

The mixed-methods approach adopted in this research provides a comprehensive framework for exploring the integration of AI and 6G technologies in smart city infrastructure. By combining qualitative and quantitative techniques, the research aims to gather a broad range of perspectives, from experts in AI and cybersecurity to urban residents and policymakers. The use of AI-driven analytics for data analysis ensures that the findings are both robust and innovative, providing new insights into the security challenges and opportunities posed by 6G-enabled smart cities. Through case study analysis, interviews, surveys, and advanced data analysis techniques, this research seeks to contribute to the ongoing development of secure, efficient, and resilient smart cities for the future.

AI in Secure 6G-Enabled Smart Cities: Use Cases

The deployment of 6G networks is expected to revolutionize the concept of smart cities, with Artificial Intelligence (AI) playing a pivotal role in enhancing the security and functionality of critical urban systems. As cities become more connected and reliant on digital infrastructure, the integration of AI into 6G-enabled smart city networks will enable faster, more efficient, and secure operations across a variety of sectors. This section focuses on the use cases of AI in public safety, transportation, and energy management systems within 6G-enabled smart cities, demonstrating how AI can optimize these areas while ensuring data security and minimizing vulnerabilities to cyber-attacks.

AI for Public Safety

One of the most prominent applications of AI in 6G-enabled smart cities is in the realm of public safety. AI has the potential to significantly enhance real-time surveillance, crime prediction, and emergency response systems by processing vast amounts of data collected from IoT devices and cameras deployed throughout urban environments. By analyzing data in real-time, AI can identify suspicious behavior, predict potential threats, and trigger immediate responses to mitigate risks. For instance, AI algorithms can monitor video feeds from surveillance cameras to detect anomalies or criminal activities, such as unattended packages, unauthorized access to restricted areas, or crowd behavior indicative of unrest (Sundqvist et al., 2020).

In a 6G-enabled smart city, the ultra-low latency and high data transmission rates will allow AI systems to process and respond to security threats in real-time, providing law enforcement and emergency responders with critical information faster than ever before (Chowdhury et al., 2021). Moreover, AI-powered crime prediction tools can analyze historical crime data, socioeconomic factors, and other variables to forecast potential hotspots and enable law enforcement agencies to allocate resources more effectively. This predictive capability will be crucial in enhancing urban security, as it allows authorities to prevent crime before it occurs, rather than responding reactively.

However, the integration of AI and 6G in public safety systems also raises significant privacy concerns. The use of AI in real-time surveillance has the potential to infringe on individual privacy, particularly in densely populated urban areas where constant monitoring is possible. To address these concerns, privacy-preserving AI technologies, such as differential privacy and federated learning, are essential. Differential privacy adds noise to data, ensuring that individual data points cannot be traced back to specific individuals, while federated learning enables AI models to be trained on decentralized data without transferring sensitive information to a central server (Gupta & Jha, 2020). These technologies help to minimize data exposure risks while maintaining the effectiveness of AI in enhancing public safety. In 6G networks, federated learning can enable the secure sharing of insights across different law enforcement agencies and smart city systems without compromising personal data privacy.

AI in Transportation Systems

AI has a critical role to play in managing transportation systems, particularly as cities move towards the adoption of autonomous vehicles and smart traffic management systems. In 6G-enabled smart cities, AI-powered transportation systems will be able to process vast amounts of real-time data from sensors, cameras, and connected vehicles to optimize traffic flow, reduce congestion, and enhance public safety on the roads. AI algorithms can analyze data from these sources to predict traffic patterns, dynamically adjust traffic signals, and reroute vehicles to prevent bottlenecks (Li et al., 2021). This not only improves traffic efficiency but also reduces greenhouse gas emissions by minimizing idle time for vehicles.

Autonomous vehicles, in particular, will benefit from the ultra-low latency and high data transmission speeds of 6G networks. AI algorithms that control autonomous vehicles rely on real-time data to make split-second decisions, such as avoiding obstacles, detecting pedestrians, and adjusting speed. The faster data processing capabilities of 6G will enable autonomous vehicles to communicate with each other and with traffic infrastructure almost instantaneously, reducing the risk of accidents and improving road safety (Mukherjee et al., 2021).

In addition to improving transportation efficiency and safety, AI can also enhance the security of vehicular communication networks. As connected vehicles exchange data with each other and with traffic infrastructure, they become vulnerable to cyber-attacks, such as data breaches or the hacking of control systems. AI can be used to secure these networks by detecting anomalies in data traffic that may indicate a cyber-attack (Hasan et al., 2021). For instance, machine learning algorithms can monitor network traffic for unusual patterns or unauthorized access attempts, automatically triggering security protocols to prevent breaches. The use of AI for real-time data security in vehicular communication networks will be critical in ensuring the safe operation of autonomous vehicles in 6G-enabled smart cities.

AI in Energy and Resource Management

Energy management is another critical area where AI can enhance the efficiency and security of smart city infrastructure. In 6G-enabled smart cities, AI-based energy management systems can monitor and optimize energy distribution in real-time, reducing wastage and ensuring that power is allocated efficiently across different sectors. For instance, AI algorithms can predict energy demand based on historical usage patterns, weather conditions, and other factors, adjusting energy distribution dynamically to meet demand while minimizing costs (Jiang et al., 2021).

Smart grids, which use AI to monitor and control the flow of electricity, will benefit significantly from the high data transmission speeds and low latency of 6G networks. These grids can detect faults or inefficiencies in the energy distribution system, allowing for immediate corrective actions to be taken. For example, if a power outage occurs in one part of the city, AI systems can automatically reroute electricity from other areas to minimize disruptions. AI can also enhance the resilience of smart grids by identifying patterns that may indicate potential cyber-attacks or system failures (Baker et al., 2021).

In addition to smart grids, AI can also improve the management of other urban resources, such as water. In 6G-enabled smart cities, AI-powered water management systems can monitor water usage in real-time, detecting leaks or inefficiencies in the system and adjusting distribution to conserve water (Li & Chan, 2021). Moreover, AI can be used to analyze data from environmental sensors to predict and respond to changes in water demand, such as during periods of drought. By optimizing the use of resources such as energy and water, AI can contribute to the sustainability of smart cities, reducing their environmental footprint while ensuring that critical services are delivered efficiently.

The security of energy and resource management systems is also a significant concern in 6G-enabled smart cities. As these systems become more connected and reliant on real-time data, they become vulnerable to cyber-attacks that could disrupt critical services. AI can be used to detect and prevent these attacks by monitoring network traffic and identifying anomalies that may indicate a security breach (Sundqvist et al., 2020). For example, AI algorithms can detect unusual patterns in energy usage that may indicate an attempt to manipulate the smart grid. By enhancing the security of energy and resource management systems, AI can help ensure the resilience of 6G-enabled smart cities against cyber threats.

The integration of AI into 6G-enabled smart cities offers significant opportunities to enhance public safety, transportation, and energy management systems. AI-powered public safety systems can improve real-time surveillance, crime prediction, and emergency response, while privacy-preserving technologies such as differential privacy and federated learning can help mitigate concerns about data privacy. In transportation, AI can optimize traffic flow and improve the safety of autonomous vehicles, while also securing vehicular communication networks against cyber-attacks. Finally, AI-based energy and resource management systems can optimize energy distribution and enhance the resilience of smart grids and water management systems, ensuring the sustainability and security of critical urban services. As cities continue to adopt AI and 6G technologies, it will be essential to develop robust frameworks that ensure the security and efficiency of these systems while minimizing the risks associated with cyber threats.

FINDINGS AND ANALYSIS

This section provides a detailed analysis of the findings derived from the research methodology, which employed a mixed-methods approach to investigate AI applications in 6G-enabled smart cities. The analysis is based on secondary data from existing reports, journal articles, and case studies, as well as primary data from expert interviews and surveys. The findings are organized into key themes: AI for public safety, AI in transportation systems, and AI in energy and resource management.

AI for Public Safety

Real-time Surveillance and Crime Prediction: The data collected from case studies, including Songdo in South Korea and Singapore's Smart Nation initiative, indicates that AI-enhanced public safety systems have become a central component of smart city infrastructure. AI-powered surveillance systems equipped with 6G technology provide law enforcement with real-time access to high-resolution video feeds and data streams from sensors embedded throughout the city. This real-time data enables faster response times and more accurate detection of suspicious activities (Kim & Lee, 2020). Interviewees highlighted that AI's ability to detect anomalies, such as unattended packages or erratic behavior in public spaces, significantly improves urban safety.

Furthermore, predictive analytics, driven by AI, allows authorities to forecast crime patterns based on historical data. The use of machine learning models to identify potential crime hotspots helps law enforcement agencies allocate resources more effectively. According to survey respondents, the deployment of such AI systems has led to a perceived reduction in crime rates, particularly in high-density urban areas where constant monitoring is challenging for human operators.

Privacy Concerns and AI Solutions: However, the analysis also reveals significant privacy concerns associated with real-time surveillance. Both interviewees and survey participants expressed apprehension about the potential for surveillance overreach in AI-driven systems. Many respondents were particularly concerned about data exposure risks, especially as 6G networks allow for faster and more comprehensive data collection from public spaces (Li & Chan, 2021).

The findings indicate that privacy-preserving AI technologies, such as differential privacy and federated learning, are essential for addressing these concerns. Differential privacy, which involves adding noise to data to protect individual identities, was cited by experts as a viable solution to mitigate privacy risks. Federated learning, which enables AI models to be trained on decentralized data without transferring personal information to a central server, was also recognized as a critical tool for enhancing public safety without compromising privacy (Gupta & Jha, 2020). These technologies allow smart cities to balance the need for effective surveillance with the protection of citizens' rights to privacy.

AI in Transportation Systems

Autonomous Vehicles and Traffic Management: The use of AI in managing transportation systems was identified as a critical area of improvement in smart cities, particularly with the integration of 6G networks. In cities like Singapore, AI-driven traffic management systems have significantly improved transportation efficiency by optimizing traffic signals in real-time, thereby reducing congestion (Li et al., 2021). These systems rely on real-time data from connected vehicles, cameras, and sensors to adjust traffic flow dynamically. In cities where AI-powered traffic systems are in place, respondents reported a noticeable reduction in travel time during peak hours, which they attributed to the systems' ability to anticipate and respond to traffic patterns effectively.

Autonomous vehicles (AVs) are another promising area where AI and 6G networks intersect. The ultra-low latency and high-speed communication enabled by 6G are essential for AVs, which require real-time data to make split-second decisions on the road (Mukherjee et al., 2021). Interviewees from technology firms working on AV systems emphasized that AI's ability to process and analyze this data almost instantaneously allows for safer and more reliable operation of autonomous vehicles. Survey data also revealed that public trust in AV technology is gradually increasing, though concerns about data security and the potential for cyberattacks remain significant.

Security of Vehicular Networks: While AI has been instrumental in improving traffic management and advancing autonomous vehicle technology, the findings also highlight the growing threat of cyberattacks on vehicular communication networks. Interviewees from the cybersecurity sector warned that as vehicles become more connected, they also become more vulnerable to hacking, which could lead to accidents or system failures. However, AI-based intrusion detection systems (IDS) are proving to be effective in mitigating these risks by continuously monitoring network traffic for anomalies that may indicate a security breach (Hasan et al., 2021).

The survey data revealed that urban residents are aware of these security risks, with a significant percentage expressing concerns about the safety of connected vehicles. However, there was also optimism about the potential of AI-driven cybersecurity solutions to address these vulnerabilities, with most respondents agreeing that AI systems capable of detecting and neutralizing threats in real-time could enhance their confidence in smart city transportation networks.

AI in Energy and Resource Management

Optimization of Energy Distribution: AI-powered energy management systems, integrated with 6G networks, are emerging as vital tools for optimizing energy distribution in smart cities. Case studies from China's AI-driven smart cities demonstrate how AI can dynamically allocate energy based on real-time demand, reducing waste and improving efficiency (Li & Chan, 2021). Survey data indicated strong support for AI-based energy management, with many respondents acknowledging the benefits of smart grids that can predict energy consumption patterns and adjust supply accordingly.

For instance, AI algorithms that monitor energy consumption data can detect abnormal patterns, such as a sudden spike in usage, which could indicate a system fault or cyberattack. Interviewees from energy management firms noted that such systems are crucial for maintaining the resilience of energy grids, especially in densely populated cities where energy demand fluctuates frequently.

Resilience of Smart Grids and Water Management Systems: The resilience of smart grids was also a key theme in the findings. AI systems that monitor the health of the grid can identify vulnerabilities before they lead to large-scale outages. In cities like Songdo, these systems have been integrated with renewable energy sources, allowing AI to manage both traditional and renewable energy inputs to optimize distribution across the grid (Kim & Lee, 2020). The survey data showed strong support for the adoption of AI in energy management, with the majority of respondents expressing confidence that AI could enhance the sustainability of their cities by reducing energy wastage.

In addition to energy management, AI is also playing an increasingly important role in water management systems. Interviewees from urban planning departments highlighted how AI systems can monitor water usage in real-time, detecting leaks or inefficiencies that would otherwise go unnoticed. This helps cities to manage their water resources more efficiently and reduce wastage, a key concern in regions facing water scarcity. AI's predictive capabilities also allow cities to anticipate periods of high demand, such as during droughts, and adjust their water distribution strategies accordingly (Sundqvist et al., 2020).

Cybersecurity in Energy Systems: While AI offers numerous benefits for energy and resource management, the findings also emphasize the importance of cybersecurity in these systems. As energy grids and water management systems become more connected, they become attractive targets for cyberattacks. Interviewees stressed the need for robust AI-driven security protocols that can detect and respond to potential threats before they disrupt critical services (Baker et al., 2021). The use of AI-based IDS and encryption techniques, such as homomorphic encryption, was cited as a promising solution for securing these essential services.

The findings from this research demonstrate that AI, when integrated with 6G networks, holds significant potential for enhancing the security and efficiency of public safety, transportation, and energy management systems in smart cities. AI-driven public safety systems can improve real-time surveillance and crime prediction, although privacy concerns must be addressed through technologies like differential privacy and federated learning. In transportation, AI improves traffic management and enables the safe operation of autonomous vehicles, but cybersecurity threats to vehicular networks must be mitigated. Finally, AI-based energy management systems can optimize energy distribution and enhance the resilience of smart grids and water systems, while also addressing potential cybersecurity risks. These findings underscore the importance of continued research and investment in AI-driven solutions to ensure the secure and sustainable development of 6G-enabled smart cities.

CONCLUSION

The integration of Artificial Intelligence (AI) with 6G networks holds immense potential for the advancement of smart cities, offering transformative improvements across key areas such as public safety, transportation, and energy management. The findings of this research demonstrate that AI, when coupled with the ultra-low latency and high-speed capabilities of 6G, can significantly enhance the efficiency, security, and resilience of critical urban systems.

In the domain of public safety, AI-driven technologies such as real-time surveillance, predictive analytics, and emergency response systems offer enhanced capabilities for identifying and mitigating risks in urban environments. However, the privacy concerns associated with increased surveillance must be carefully managed. Privacy-preserving technologies like differential privacy and federated learning provide valuable solutions that balance the need for security with the protection of personal data. As smart cities become more reliant on real-time data, implementing these privacy safeguards will be essential to maintaining public trust.

AI's role in transportation systems has also proven critical, particularly in managing autonomous vehicles and optimizing traffic flow. AI algorithms can process vast amounts of data from sensors, cameras, and connected vehicles to make real-time adjustments that reduce congestion, improve safety, and enhance overall efficiency. However, as the data exchanges in vehicular communication networks increase, the threat of cyber-attacks grows as well. AI-based intrusion detection systems (IDS) and real-time monitoring solutions will be indispensable for protecting these networks from potential vulnerabilities.

In the context of energy and resource management, AI offers significant benefits in optimizing energy distribution and enhancing the resilience of smart grids and water management systems. AI-powered energy management systems can dynamically adjust energy allocation in response to demand patterns, reducing waste and ensuring sustainable resource use. Additionally, AI's ability to predict and detect anomalies, such as potential cyber-attacks, is essential for safeguarding the critical infrastructure that underpins smart cities.

Despite these advancements, the implementation of AI and 6G technologies also brings about challenges that require careful consideration. The primary concerns revolve around data privacy, cybersecurity, and the ethical implications of AI-driven surveillance systems. Addressing these challenges will require the development of robust frameworks that prioritize transparency, accountability, and security in the deployment of AI and 6G technologies.

In conclusion, AI and 6G networks have the potential to significantly enhance the functionality, security, and sustainability of smart cities. However, to fully realize this potential, stakeholders must work together to implement secure AI frameworks, develop comprehensive privacy protection measures, and ensure that these technologies are deployed in a manner that fosters public trust. By addressing the challenges of data privacy and cybersecurity, AI and 6G-enabled smart cities can offer a safer, more efficient, and more resilient urban environment for future generations.

REFERENCES

Al-Fuqaha, A., Guizani, M., Mohammadi, M., Aledhari, M., & Ayyash, M. (2020). Internet of Things: A survey on enabling technologies, protocols, and applications. *IEEE Communications Surveys and Tutorials*, 17(4), 2347–2376. DOI: 10.1109/COMST.2015.2444095

Baker, T., Asim, M., MacDermott, Á., & Abbasi, A. (2021). Security and privacy in 6G networks: Research opportunities and challenges. *IEEE Access : Practical Innovations, Open Solutions*, 9, 37895–37909. DOI: 10.1109/ACCESS.2021.3056203

Bera, S., Misra, S., & Vasilakos, A. V. (2021). Software-defined networking for Internet of Things: A survey. *IEEE Internet of Things Journal*, 4(6), 1994–2008. DOI: 10.1109/JIOT.2017.2746186

Chen, J., Li, J., & Zhang, Q. (2021). Privacy-preserving data aggregation for smart cities: A comprehensive survey. *IEEE Internet of Things Journal*, 7(10), 10199–10212. DOI: 10.1109/JIOT.2021.2969210

Chowdhury, M. Z., Shahjalal, M., Ahmed, S., & Jang, Y. M. (2021). 6G wireless communication systems: Applications, requirements, technologies, challenges, and research directions. *IEEE Open Journal of the Communications Society*, 1, 957–975. DOI: 10.1109/OJCOMS.2020.3010270

Das, S., & Mitra, A. (2024). Advancing lightweight digital trust architectures in the internet of medical things: A multi-dimensional analysis. In *Lightweight Digital Trust Architectures in the Internet of Medical Things (IoMT)* (pp. 1-14). DOI: 10.4018/979-8-3693-2109-6.ch001

Gupta, A., & Jha, R. K. (2020). A survey of 5G network: Architecture and emerging technologies. *IEEE Access : Practical Innovations, Open Solutions*, 3, 1206–1232. DOI: 10.1109/ACCESS.2015.2461602

Hasan, M., Islam, T., & Bhuiyan, T. (2021). Blockchain and AI in smart cities: A review of recent applications and future trends. *Journal of Information Security and Applications*, 58, 102620. DOI: 10.1016/j.jisa.2021.102620

Jain, V., & Mitra, A. (2024). Case studies and practical implementation of biomimicry in bio-inspired optimization. In *Bio-Inspired Intelligence for Smart Decision-Making* (pp. 85-100). DOI: 10.4018/979-8-3693-5276-2.ch005

Jiang, X., Yuan, Z., Li, Y., & Wu, W. (2021). AI-based security and privacy issues in smart city networks: A survey. *IEEE Internet of Things Journal*, 8(8), 5866–5876. DOI: 10.1109/JIOT.2021.3061005

Khan, A., Jameel, M., & Loo, J. (2021). AI-driven predictive analytics for smart cities: A comprehensive review. *Sensors (Basel)*, 21(6), 2029. DOI: 10.3390/s21062029 PMID: 33809368

Kim, J., & Lee, H. (2020). The smart city: A case study of Songdo City. *International Journal of Urban Sciences*, 24(3), 298–315. DOI: 10.1080/12265934.2020.1763297

Latif, S., Zafar, N. A., Qadir, J., & Gawande, A. (2021). Security in 6G: Key enablers and challenges. *IEEE Access : Practical Innovations, Open Solutions*, 9, 167074–167092. DOI: 10.1109/ACCESS.2021.3121239

Li, Y., & Chan, K. H. (2021). Smart cities in China: AI and digital governance in urban development. *Journal of Urban Affairs*, 43(5), 739–752. DOI: 10.1080/07352166.2020.1806346

Li, Y., Liu, C., Qian, Y., & Wang, X. (2021). Secure AI frameworks for smart city systems. *IEEE Network*, 35(4), 36–41. DOI: 10.1109/MNET.2021.3135925

Mitra, A., & Lohochoudhury, B. (2019). Identifying anthropogenic factors of groundwater pollution through student's opinion in rural West Bengal. *Anthropogenic Pollution*, 3(2), 49–59.

Mukherjee, A., Maiti, D., & Acharya, D. (2021). Smart cities: AI-driven urban development. *IEEE Internet of Things Journal*, 8(10), 7923–7935. DOI: 10.1109/JIOT.2021.3063267

Sundqvist, P., Ekman, L., & Hansson, E. (2020). AI for smart cities: Opportunities and challenges. *IEEE Access : Practical Innovations, Open Solutions*, 8, 33344–33362. DOI: 10.1109/ACCESS.2020.2975925

Zhang, X., Yu, F. R., & He, Z. (2021). AI-based network security management in 6G wireless networks: Challenges and opportunities. *IEEE Network*, 35(6), 35–41. DOI: 10.1109/MNET.2021.3108755

Zhou, Z., Wang, J., Xu, Y., & Li, H. (2020). AI-driven security framework for smart cities. *IEEE Communications Magazine*, 58(3), 60–66. DOI: 10.1109/MCOM.2020.2903257

Chapter 8
Revolutionizing Urban Living:
Integrating 6G and Blockchain in Smart City Development

Subashini Babu
https://orcid.org/0000-0003-1177-5082
Department of Data Science and Business Systems, School of Computing, SRM Institute of Science and Technology, Chennai, India

Anna Anbumozhi
Department of Data Science and Business Systems, School of Computing, SRM Institute of Science and Technology, Chennai, India

Shanthi Perumalsamy
Department of Information Technology, St. Joseph's Institute of Technology, Chennai, India

Venkatesh Kaliamoorthy
Department of Networking and Communications, School of Computing, SRM Institute of Science and Technology, Chennai, India

ABSTRACT

The synergistic relationship between 6G and blockchain, showcasing how their integration supports secure, real-time data exchange and robust smart city operations are examined. Practical applications such as smart traffic management, energy-efficient buildings, secure digital identities, and decentralized governance are analyzed through real-world case studies, highlighting successes and challenges. This chapter also addresses technological, regulatory, and societal challenges to the widespread adoption of these technologies, including interoperability, scalability,

DOI: 10.4018/979-8-3693-8029-1.ch008

and privacy concerns. Prospects are explored, considering the role of emerging technologies like AI, IoT, and quantum computing in enhancing smart city development. By providing a comprehensive analysis, this chapter offers valuable insights for policymakers, urban planners, technologists, and researchers dedicated to building the smart cities of tomorrow.

1. INTRODUCTION

Due to the rapid pace of urbanization in the world today, there is a growing demand for social, environmental and economic development within cities that would significantly improve the Quality of Life (QoL) of the urban dwellers. In the last few decades, the rapid increase in the population of the globe has in a way triggered increased rate of urban migration which has brought with it logistics, social and economic problems which are majorly adverse. As per one of the United Nation's reports, about 70% of the world population is anticipated to reside in urban regions by the year 2050 (Angel et al., 2011). However, this process of urbanization has raised the overall quality of life through transport advances, better education and health care, and improved economic prospects. Unfortunately, though, urban populations are usually too high for the equitable distribution and management of resources to be efficient.

The metropolitan development which is characterized by provision of various amenities has led to deterioration of many environmental aspects such as pollution, traffic jams, waste management systems, and emissions of greenhouse gases. These problems pose a typical challenge for cities and highlight the need for new approaches contributing to the efficient development of urban areas, which has led to the emergence of the Smart City concept. The smart city is oriented to the solution of these urban issues aiming at the improvement of the life quality in cities making them more liveable, less polluted and less congested with traffic.

As such, the last years' evolution of Information and Communication Technologies (ICT) and the evolution of the Internet of Things (IoT) have become cornerstones in the quest for smart cities' sustainability (Alavi et al., 2018). The implementation of these technologies brought about health and energy enhancement, promoted social participation, increased democratic accountability, improved service and resource efficiency, and many other advancements such as public transport and traffic management. Smart City places the needs and preferences of citizens at its core and uses evidence-based approaches, education, and technology as the catalysts for building dynamic, sustainable, and just urban communities (Raja Santhi & Muthuswamy, 2023).

The Internet of Things (IoT) is a concept that provides a strong inclination towards the growth of smart cities, but it is important to consider the challenges brought about by its usage as well. IoT is understood to extend the traditional Internet of today as it interconnects computers ('things') to exchange data and information with little or no human interference. Data created from IoT devices tends to be operated and located on different Internet servers, which often are through cloud or fog computing. Such methods are helpful, but data management can become a serious threat. For instance, IoT statistics can be affected by cyber hacks and data insertion; while natural failures of cloud nodes are frequent. The inability of such circumstances to maintain the privacy, availability, and accuracy of IoT data severely limits the potential for successfully implementing an IoT-enabled smart city network.

To overcome such challenges, it is possible to use more modern and advanced distributed technologies such as blockchain to optimize the existing smart city services. Blockchain is a Distributed Ledger Technology (DLT) that has received its first exposure in the year 2008.All transactions are organized in blocks within the network and can be seen by all users making sure security and transparency. Benefits such as: decentralization, unreliable operations, participatory procedures, automated processes, data consistency, authenticity, transparency and anonymity can be among the significant advantages brought about in smart cities enabled by the Inter of Things (IoT) when the technology of blockchain is embedded. The use of pseudonymous addresses valid in public domains not containing individuals addressess is made possible by Pseudonymisation while the latter eliminates the role of a trusted third party and allows P2P interactions.

Furthermore, there are also blockchain-based smart contracts (SCs) that can execute transactions between the parties and maintain the history of such transactions. These smart contracts that utilize DLT come in different programming languages such as Solidity but are still integrated with protocols such as Proof of Work (PoW) or Proof of Stake (PoS) to ensure harmonization of the information in all the nodes.

Besides enhancement of security, there are other concerns within smart city applications such as IOT and city infrastructure which include network latency, reliability and connectivity. Applications such as border security, medical drone delivery, and telemedicine are critical importance that existing communication networks such as 4G, LTE-A, or even 5G fails to provide because of issues such as low latency and connection density (Ullah et al., 2019). The combination of structures of smart cities with the Internet of Things (IoT) with Sixth Generation (6G) networks might be the best bet.

Another aspect that makes 6G an appealing candidate to support smart city applications include its other key features such ultra-low latency (between 10 to 100 microseconds) and high connection density. A unique combination of blockchain and 6G technologies offers the solution for the security and network performance issues of the IoT-enabled smart cities. The features are table tat 1. Such integrated approach is necessary to assure the sustainable development of the core smart city applications such as smart grids, Intelligent Transportation Systems (ITS), and Healthcare 5.0 (Kasinathan et al., 2022).Through a comprehensive review of state-of-the-art approaches in these areas, this discussion highlights the critical role of blockchain and 6G in driving the future of smart city innovation and ensuring that urban environments are secure, efficient, and resilient.

Table 1. Features of Blockchain and 6G.

Technology	Solution	Description
Blockchain	Enhanced Security	Decentralized and tamper-proof ledger improves security and reduces single points of failure.
	Transparent Transactions	Immutable records ensure transparency and accountability in transactions.
	Efficient Data Management	Streamlines data management and sharing, improving coordination and reducing inefficiencies.
	Smart Contracts	Automates agreements and processes without intermediaries, improving efficiency.
	Decentralized Applications (dApps)	Offers services directly to users without a central authority, enhancing service delivery and control.
	Improved Interoperability	Advanced algorithms and techniques address interoperability issues between different platforms.
6G	Faster Speeds	Provides significantly higher data transfer speeds for rapid communication and data processing.
	Lower Latency	Ultra-low latency supports real-time applications like autonomous vehicles and remote healthcare.
	Higher Capacity	Accommodates more connected devices and sensors, ensuring reliable connectivity.
	Enhanced IoT Support	Improves performance of IoT devices with faster and more stable connections.
	Advanced Applications	Enables AR, VR, and immersive experiences, creating new opportunities for smart city services.
	Improved Network Efficiency	Technologies like massive MIMO and IRSs optimize network performance and energy efficiency.

In essence, Smart City has the potential to redefine urban living by creating environments where everyone can thrive. By prioritizing citizen-centric approaches, leveraging data to guide decisions, and embracing innovation and sustainability, Smart City promises to develop urban spaces that are not only more habitable but also more equitable and vibrant. Through these advancements, it aims to make cities globally better places to live, work, and prosper, addressing the critical need for sustainable urban development in an increasingly populated world.

2. BACKGROUND STUDY

2.1 Blockchain

One new technology that has been gaining a lot of attention lately is blockchain. Blockchain may seem complicated at first, but it's just a simple system for organizing data that lets anyone make and share a distributed ledger of transactions. There is no need for a third party to oversee the data or the participants when they utilize either public or private key authentication to add records to this ledger. If blockchain technology is extensively used, it might drastically change many parts of our lives. Using a consensus method, most network members verify and approve each record in the blockchain ledger, referred to as a "block," and then append it to the end of the chain (Nguyen & Kim, 2018). Figure.1 highlights the primary components of blockchain technology.

Figure 1. Components of blockchain technology

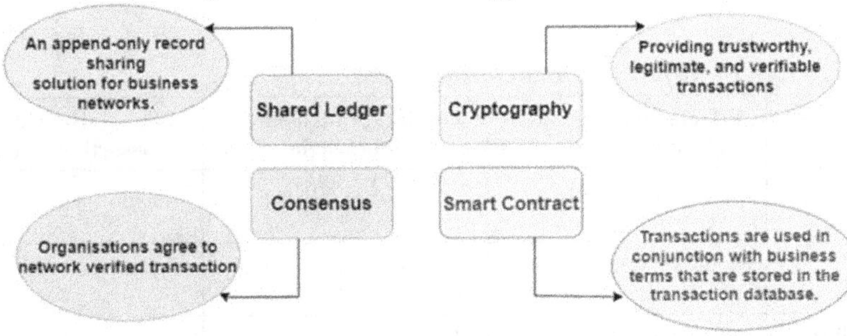

Blockchain is a decentralised database that keeps track of every digital currency transaction. Without going via a middleman (like a bank), it allows users to send digital assets directly to a blockchain wallet. With this technology, money may be accessed directly and used for anything, whether it's personal or business. The elimination of middlemen from online currency exchange transactions is another benefit. The breakthrough innovation known as blockchain can revolutionise the world's financial institutions.

Types of Blockchain

Depending on their distribution patterns and methods of consensus, blockchain systems can be categorized into three primary types: private (permissioned), public (permissionless), and consortium (hybrid).

1. Private: Only those who have been granted permission can access and take part in this blockchain. With its help, a shared ledger can record transactions instantly and at a lower cost. In most cases, these deals can only be greenlit by well-established banks and financial operators.
2. Public: Regardless of approval status, any party inside the peer-to-peer network can access this permissionless blockchain. Although it streamlines transactions, procedures may become slower and less efficient due to a lack of authorisation, especially when there are a lot of transactions.
3. Consortiums: Combining features of public and private blockchains, this kind is also called a hybrid blockchain. With its help, a dispersed network can implement access controls, letting authorised users and organisations selectively view and write data. Consortium blockchains let organisations to securely and distributedly collaborate, preserve intellectual property rights, and discover solutions. This strategy is being embraced by numerous financial firms.The features of different blockchains are presented in table 2.

Table 2. Features of different blockchains

Feature	Private (Permissioned) Blockchain	Public (Permissionless) Blockchain	Hybrid (Consortium) Blockchain
Speed and Efficiency	Fast and highly efficient	Slow and less efficient	Fast and efficient
Security	Highly secured	Less secure compared to private	Highly secured
Upgradeability	Easy to upgrade	Challenging to upgrade	Easy to upgrade
Network Design	Designed for private networks	Open to all participants	Combines private and public features
Support	High enterprise support	High community support	High community and enterprise support
Currency	Not inherently included	Built-in virtual currency	May include currency, depending on design
Flexibility	Inflexible in enterprise features	Simple and inflexible	Simple and flexible
Forking	Not typically forked	Heavily forked	Less prone to forking

How Blockchain Works?

In a distributed ledger system, blockchain records transactions as "blocks." A new block is appended to the blockchain's last segment whenever a transaction occurs. Blockchain transactions are simple, engaging only the sender and the recipient, in contrast to conventional systems that depend on middlemen like governments or banks.

Blockchain is a decentralized ledger that records all transactions in an immutable and publicly accessible manner. In a peer-to-peer network, each new transaction is added to a shared ledger called a block together with all the previous transactions that have taken place recently (Subashini & Hemavathi, 2023). The network's nodes reach an agreement to examine and approve the deal. To guarantee that all participants have the most current record of all transactions, the block is appended to the current chain of blocks and timestamped once validated.

2.2 Network Technology Taxonomy Before 6G

Communication and modern culture have been profoundly impacted by the rapid development of wireless technology since the middle of the twentieth century. Different generations have emerged along this history, each of which has improved our communication and introduced new possibilities as given in the figure 2. The trip commenced with the commercialization of 1G mobile networks in Japan in 1979 and their subsequent adoption in Europe in 1981 (Dunnewijk & Hultén, 2007). The analogue transmission and Frequency Division Multiple Access (FDMA) technologies used by these networks could only provide data transfer rates of 2.4 kilobits per second (Kbps). Even though they were revolutionary, 1G networks had a lot of problems, especially with international connectivity and long-distance communication. To resolve the problems caused by incompatible national networks, the Conference of European Posts and Telegraphs (CEPT) formed the Group Special Mobile (GSM) to standardise mobile communication across Europe (Overby & Audestad, 2020).

With the advent of digital transmissions and the creation of worldwide standards, the second generation (2G) represented a giant leap ahead. The first 2G network to use the GSM standard, which included TDMA and CDMA technology, was deployed in 1991 by Radiolinja in Finland (Bakare & Bassey, 2021). This expanded paths enabled the offering of new services like SMS, better voice quality and enhanced data speeds to 64 Kbps. GPRS was launched in 2.5G in the period characterized by innovations that brought packet-switching protocols, faster Internet service provider connections, and more effective data transfer.

Figure 2. Evolution of generations

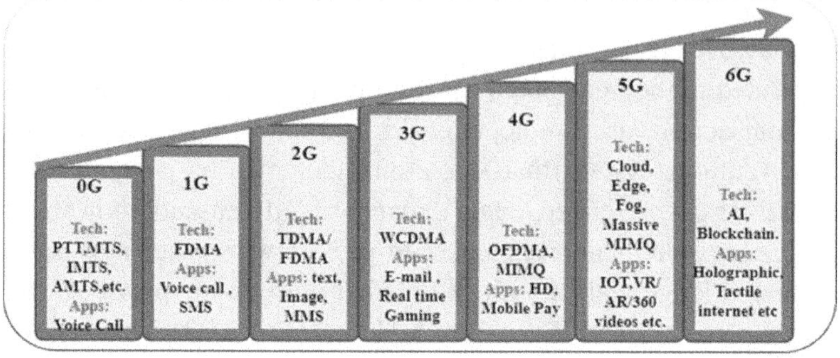

The first 3G network was operated with NTT DoCoMo's Wideband Code Division Multiple Access technology in 2001 in Tokyo. Data speeds leaped exponentially with 3G networks at a speed of 2 Mbps, and email, multimedia communication, and fast internet access were offered for the first time (Shayea et al., 2021). International adaptation of 3G came about due to standards laid down by the International Telecommunication Union (ITU) under the IMT-2000 banner. Millions of people were already using 3G networks, enjoying improved data speeds and mobile services by 2007. In 2009, the fourth generation (4G) was rolled out, with the growth rate of mobile technology staying at a tremendous pace. South Korea became the world's first country to launch commercialization of 4G using LTE as the basis. With 4G, data speeds skyrocketed to 100 Mbps, allowing for ultra-fast mobile internet, video streaming, and other apps that rely heavily on data. The LTE-Advanced standard took these capacities to the next level, with data transfer rates nearing one Gbps (Serodio et al., 2023).

Due to advancements in mobile technology, the fifth generation (5G) has arrived, providing significant benefits in areas such as data traffic capacity, latency, energy efficiency, and cost-effectiveness. 5G networks are built to manage the enormous amounts of data produced by contemporary apps, especially on social media sites, and to solve important problems with data security in large data settings. 6G, which aims to integrate AI into network models and enable smarter, more efficient communication systems, is being made possible by the continued development of 5G. The transition from 1G to 5G wireless technology has revolutionized communication by making data transfer faster, connections more dependable, and service options more extensive (Salih et al., 2020). Integration of AI with ever-improving network technology bodes well for 6G, which promises even better connection and more innovation across all sectors.

A 6G future will necessitate intelligence, which in turn will dictate enhanced processing and storage capacities. No longer are the old key performance indicators (KPIs) like throughput, bandwidth, latency, and packet loss rate enough. If we want reliable metrics for measuring communication performance, we'll need to introduce new ones like context awareness, traffic balancing, and various security measures across routing channels.

Why 6G ? Why not 5G ?

There has been a steady stream of evolutionary waves in mobile technology and services, with each wave bringing new features and improvements to the market for over twenty years. The initial surge of mobile phones was the vehicle phone and the shoulder phone, two portable models that were later joined by the first wave of handheld phones. The introduction of mobile phones like MOVA represented the peak of this wave, which led to their broad use and accessibility. With the introduction of portable media players, the second wave marked a huge leap ahead. During this period, new technologies like i-mode and smartphones emerged, putting information firmly in the hands of consumers and opening up a world of possibilities for mobile devices with their array of apps and multimedia content (including videos).

From static voice calls to more interactive multimedia experiences, this wave revolutionized mobile technology and how consumers interacted with it (Beaumont et al., 2022). Introduced in the third wave are fifth-and sixth-generation (5G and 6G) mobile technologies, which we are currently experiencing. Designing with a larger vision of tackling societal concerns and promoting human-centered value creation, these generations are more than just about better data speeds or greater connectivity. The emphasis has shifted from technical progress in and of itself to how these innovations will affect people's daily lives and the world at large, and this shift is reflected in this new wave of research. The OSI paradigm is the basis of these innovations because it is charged with the task of converting electrical impulses of the physical world to data processed by cyber systems. The seven layers constituting the Open Systems Interconnection (OSI) concept include physical, data link, network, transport, session, presentation, and application.

All the data communication process, from physical transmission of data to its presentation to the user, performs a different function for each of these levels. Machine learning, which improves the efficacy and efficiency of communication networks, is another new intelligence layer that was further integrated throughout the OSI model's layers in the recent years. These include smart configurations of channel prediction, AI-enabled data coding, signal detection, and beamforming as applied at the physical layer by ML.

These advanced configurations enhance the resistance provided by the system against interference and other threats, further increasing the fidelity and reliability of wireless communication. As a matter of fact, intelligence is expected to form an essential part of the future communication systems with the advent of 6G (Akyildiz et al., 2020). Although old-fashioned KPIs, like connection speed, latency, throughput, and packet loss rate are still valid, newer measurements must be considered.

In the 6G era, storage capacity and processing power will be required to meet the demands of communication networks that are becoming smarter and more complicated. For the best communication performance in our cutting-edge tech world, it's important to consider issues like context awareness, traffic balancing, and different routing channels' varying levels of security.When looking at the big picture, it's clear that mobile technology has been through a never-ending cycle of innovation, with each new wave adding capabilities and solving new problems. To satisfy the needs of a connected world, where technology is more than simply a tool—it enhances human life—and ushers in the 6G age, it will be essential to integrate intelligence across all levels of communication networks (Maier et al., 2022).

2.3 Smart Cities: Earlier

The US Community Analysis Bureau started using files, aerial photography, and cluster analysis to collect data, distribute resources, and publish reports in the 1960s and 1970s; this is where the idea of smart cities first emerged. As a result of these endeavors, the initial phase of smart cities was born, with the goals of directing services, decreasing poverty, and ensuring catastrophe mitigation. The original wave of "smart cities" was founded by internet companies that wanted to know how people used their products (Nassereddine & Khang, 2024). The subsequent "smart city" generation was built on top of this, with an emphasis on integrating various advances into cohesive municipal solutions.

With an emphasis on public participation and the promotion of social participation and community engagement, the third phase of smart cities moved control away from technology suppliers and city authorities. This third-generation approach was implemented in Vienna through a partnership with the local energy business Wien Energy. It allowed citizens to invest in solar facilities that were located within the city. Issues like affordable housing and gender equality were also priorities for the city, which collaborated closely with residents to find solutions. The Vancouver Greenest City 2020 Action Plan, which was co-created by thirty thousand residents, is only one example of how this strategy has been adopted worldwide.

Urbanisation is expected to increase from 54% to 66% by 2050, adding 2.5 billion people to cities. This expected urban population growth emphasises the need to sustainably manage the resources of the environment, society, and economy. Sustaining a balanced and stable urban environment becomes harder as cities grow. Smart cities help here. Smart cities allow residents and local governments to collaborate on smart technology projects. Cities must use these technologies to efficiently manage assets and resources, meet the needs of a growing population, and remain livable, feasible, and resilient. Smart cities as in figure 3, can increase energy efficiency, waste reduction, transit, and public services by integrating IoT, big data, and AI (Hui et al., 2023). This collaborative approach improves citizens' quality of life and creates a more ecological and connected city.

Figure 3. Smart cities

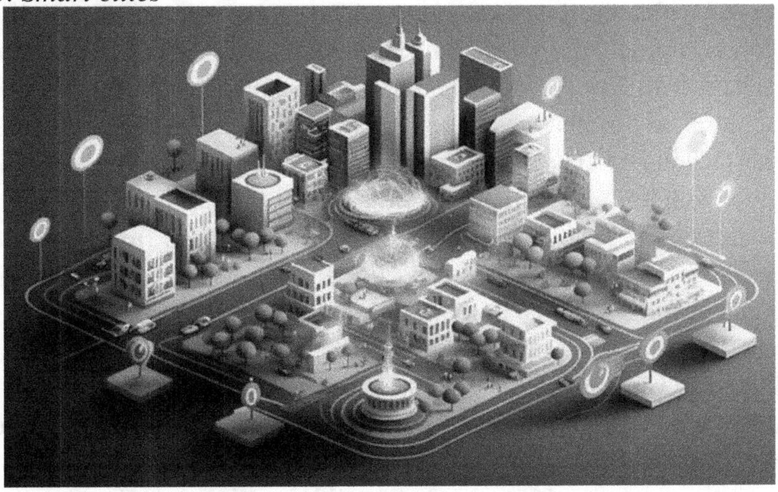

3. 6G NETWORKS

In May 2019, the IMT-2030 Standard was introduced by the International Telecommunications Union (ITU), which outlined the lofty objectives for 6G communication networks. With its revolutionary user interface, 6G aims to provide a whole new range of sensory data and immersive experiences. Haptic communication and the development of IoT-powered smart cities are just two examples of the many data-intensive, real-time applications that this next-gen technology is anticipated to make possible (Jacob et al., 2021).

Unconstrained by pre-existing network architectures or technology, 6G will explore novel communication mechanisms.

3.1 Benefits Of 6G Networks

Unparalleled Speeds: 6G is expected to provide data transfer rates that are substantially greater than 5G's. Experts predict that the speeds will push the limits of data transmission into the terabits per second (Tbps) range, while the exact numbers are still up in the air.

Minimal Delay: A critical component of every communication network is the delay, or latency, that a signal experiences as it travels from one device to another. With 6G, we should see incredibly reduced latency, allowing apps and devices to communicate almost instantly. This drastic decrease in latency will completely alter the way we engage with technology by allowing for lightning-fast and extremely responsive interactions in the digital realm.

Excellent Network Access: There is great promise for the future of seamless integration across many networks, devices, and even satellites with the advent of 6G technology. Thanks to this development, gadgets will soon be able to interact with ease no matter where they are, ushering in an era of omnipresent connectivity. The other most significant advantage from 6G's ultra-high connectivity is that it provides the network to a much larger number of remote and underserved regions. In this way, a much larger number of people can be brought to access the global economy, and continuous high speed connectivity will be made accessible for even the remotest area.

Energy Efficiency: The reduction in energy consumption compared to the previous generations of wireless technology, like 5G, will be one of the major contributions that 6G technology will bring about. An increase in energy efficiency is expected to have a tremendous impact through an extended life of gadgets' batteries and decreased overall energy usage. Therefore, 6G will contribute to greener tech consumption through devices running for longer periods with less degradation of the environment due to wireless communication networks.

AI Integration: The 6G architecture would be full of artificial intelligence. Advanced applications will be enabled and the 6G network is expected to have AI all through and it would allow for seamless working with complex systems such as driverless vehicles, smart cities, and enhanced healthcare solutions.. These cutting-edge technologies will propel major developments in a wide range of industries, and 6G's AI will supply the processing capacity and real-time data processing skills that are required to enable them.

Superior Protection: 6G networks are expected to have far superior protection measures compared to previous generations, in response to the ever-changing nature of cyber threats. To ward off a broad variety of assaults, 6G will most likely include state-of-the-art security mechanisms. These precautions will incorporate strong authentication procedures and extremely advanced encryption methods. To keep our ever-more-connected world's data and communications safe, the 6G infrastructure must prioritize security.

Figure 4. Benefits of 6G

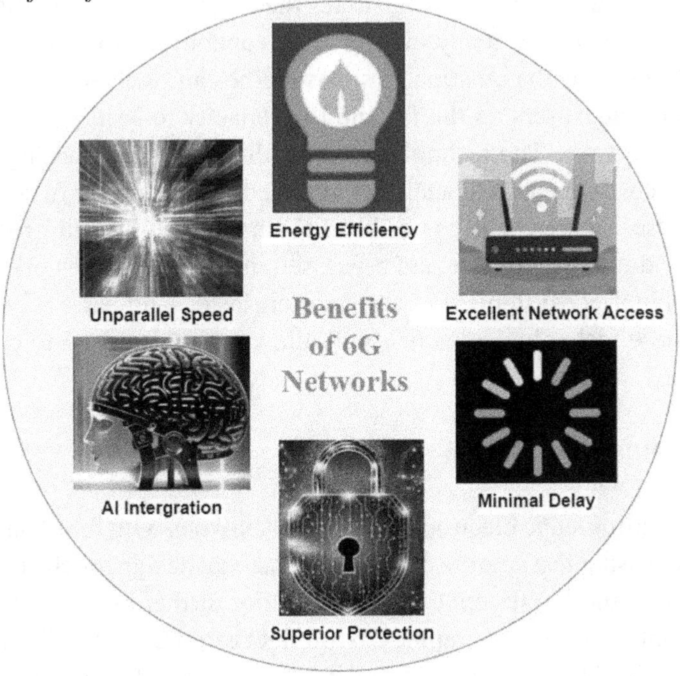

3.2 The Perspective of 6G

Superior Intelligence for Individual Success

With its cutting-edge augmented projection interfaces and physical-to-cyber fusion health analytics services, Superior Intelligence for Individual Success is expected to revolutionise how individuals interact with digital environments. I Superior Intelligence for Individual Success uses customised AI to meet every user's specific needs and preferences. Projector interfaces will add to this by facilitating seamless physical interaction with digital content (Roupé et al., 2020). The foundational technology for the underlying infrastructure supporting these functionalities—which rely on cross-service designs—will be wireless multi-access connection. Users will enjoy seamless, effective, and immersive experiences that blend the virtual and physical worlds thanks to all of these components functioning together.

Combining Sensor Data with AI

By combining sophisticated health monitoring with intelligence derived from ambient sensing, this application constitutes the cutting edge of intelligent sensing and analytics. Among the many cutting-edge capabilities that will be a part of Sensor to AI Fusion is the creation of smart clothes and settings that can adapt to the demands of their users on the fly and the capacity to scan and analyze health indicators in real time. The technology will utilize machine learning algorithms, strong cybersecurity measures, analytics at the edge, and sensor fusion techniques to back up these features. The use of blockchain technology will greatly enhance the security and integrity of the data processed inside this framework (Alhazmi et al., 2022). Digital ecosystems that are smarter, faster, and safer will result from integrating these technologies, which will allow sensors and AI to communicate more smoothly.

Super-Functional Items

By fusing cutting-edge electronics and edge analytics with functional materials, these items will usher in a new era of multidimensional design. Such products would need dynamic on-the-fly system configuration. For further increase in interactivity and customer interaction, holographic UIs, product gamification, and IoT connection will be the necessities. With this kind of integration of technologies, products can be produced which can smoothly offer a user experience in many dimensions and are very adaptive and interactive.

Intelligent Elements

Some of the building blocks of intelligent elements include printed electronics, user-configurable interfaces, and individually-tailored sensors. They can potentially challenge many different industries because the degree of customization and usefulness is very high for applications that call for accuracy and flexibility. Implementing augmented sensing capabilities, 3D Internet of Things design methodologies, reusable materials, and printed electronics into intelligent material designs will be crucial for achieving optimal performance. They may be put together to cause response to new situations immediately. It is very efficient, eco-friendly, and flexible in use.

Management as a Facility (MaaF)

6G technology will greatly improve the idea of Management as a Facility (MaaS) by allowing complex communication between high-tech items and infrastructure. Transportation systems will be made safer and more efficient with the help of autonomous safety management and logistical supervision. For MaaF to be successfully implemented, some critical technologies must be in place. These include wireless multi-radio connectivity, stream analytics, multi-object IoT, and edge computing. The way mobility is managed and experienced will be revolutionised by these technologies, which will allow for seamless communication and real-time data processing.

Urban Information Systems

The next wave of smart cities will rely on AI-driven services that monitor and take care of the requirements of its inhabitants, oversees the logistics of the whole city, and ensures the well-being and security of sentient beings. Sophisticated artificial intelligence, internet of things, and strong cybersecurity measures will be needed for the infrastructure to execute these features properly. It is within this nexus that intelligent urban environments will emerge; that is, in security, responsiveness, and complex demands for a city, like any other modern metropolis.

Customised Emerges

Printed electronics, IoT, AI, and wireless services will soon merge into customized surfaces. Such surfaces shall present content according to specific tastes. Among the many critical technologies required to develop personalized surfaces effectively, they include smart surface technologies, edge computing, context processing, and consent management. When combined, these elements will make possible highly responsive interactive surfaces that can dramatically increase usability in a range of contexts.

Tracking Countless Products

This application will offer features of advanced tracking, such as multi-object tracking. This will open opportunities for customisable IoT associations, edge connections, and sensor networks. In this kind of environment, in which the scenario is dynamic, these qualities will be pivotal in managing multiple items simultaneously. Technologies such as blockchain, cybersecurity, swarm analytics, and consent management will prove to be indispensable for the functionality of multi-object tracking. These technologies will bring about accurate, scalable, and secure tracking systems.

Bio-Cybernetic Persona

Bio-Cybernetic Identity is a concept in which authentication-critical service architectures rely on distributed trust models and sensing-based machine learning. Such a tool will be important for safe and trustworthy identity verification in both digital and physical places. The core technologies needed for Bio-Cybernetic Identity are cyber-identity frameworks, biometric systems, machine learning, and context processing (Shahzadi et al., 2021). Collectively, these technologies will build a frictionless and safe authentication system that can be made to fit any use case.

Independent Ports

With advanced swarm-based operations and collaborative mobility that will allow control over people and product movements, autonomous ports mean a tremendous step forward in logistics and transportation. Supporting these advanced features will require infrastructure inclusion of wireless IoT, system interoperability, data pattern analytics, and stream analytics. These technologies will facilitate real-time coordination and optimization of port operations, enhancing productivity and lowering operating expenses.

Digital Displays

Future digital content interaction will be with smart screens, which are augmented with programmable materials, content creation based on context awareness, and experiences that are individual preferences. Technologies like context-aware Internet of Things, printed electronics, multi-channel connection, and smart surface materials form the basis of developing smart screens. Soon consumers would be able to feel highly interactive and individually tailored display systems with all these developments.

4. SMART CITIES

4.1 What is a Smart City?

The rapid growth of the Internet of Things (IoT) and the explosion of big data have made many smart-city initiatives much more viable and emerging. The term "smart cities" refers to an idealistic form of urban development that combines information and communication technologies to facilitate the generation and exchange of real-time data between citizens, governments, and for-profit and not-for-profit organizations. This increases the efficiency of city operations in areas such as energy consumption, transportation, logistics, and public services.

The term "smart city" has no universally accepted definition as of yet, but most people agree that a smart city is an urban innovation ecosystem designed to use ICTs and next-generation innovations to improve all aspects of life while mitigating the problems associated with the rapidly growing urban population. Allam (Allam, 2019) provide several definitions, the majority of which focus on technology as the main element of a smart city. For this paper, we build upon the key elements covered in the literature and propose the following definition:

> **"A smart city is a densely populated area that utilizes Information and Communication Technologies (ICT) to connect and monitor key infrastructure and services. The primary objective is to enhance the efficiency and sustainability of the city's operations—environmentally, economically, and socially—while improving the quality of life for its residents."**

A smart city can only be completely realized with massive investments in human and social capital, traditional infrastructure (like transportation), and cutting-edge ICT (information and communication technology) infrastructure. To achieve long-term economic growth, improve people's quality of life, and manage natural resources responsibly, these investments are essential.

In their definition of a smart city, Caragliu(Caragliu & Del Bo, 2020) highlight the importance of business-led urban development in creating interconnected infrastructures, as well as the city's participatory governance framework. Within this context, the creative and high-tech sectors play a pivotal role in promoting innovation and social inclusion. Recognising the significance of social and relational capital in the larger context of urban development, the development of a smart city also largely depends on it. The city's expansion must be equitable and sustainable so that all inhabitants can reap the benefits of development without jeopardising the environment for the sake of future generations. Smart cities may become the equitable, sustainable, and dynamic urban environments of the future by implementing this comprehensive strategy.

A "smart city" strategy is being implemented by more and more towns around the world as a means of combating the negative effects of urbanisation on people' quality of life and environmental sustainability. Manville (Manville et al., 2015) explains that smart cities aim "to tackle public issues through ICT-based solutions, facilitated by multi-stakeholder, municipally-based partnerships." In a fast-changing paradigm, the idea of smart cities is based on the idea that city functions may be optimised and inhabitants' socio-economic well-being can be improved through the seamless integration of digital technologies and urban development.

Technology lies at the heart of the vision for smart cities, which is propelled by several important reasons. Without access to and processing of trustworthy data in real-time, the problems caused by the exponential increase of urban populations would remain unsolved. In addition, a smart city would be one in which technology is so pervasive that it enhances the quality of life for everyone living there by coordinating different societal elements for better resource management, service provision, and overall quality of life.

Technological advancements have greatly facilitated the shift to smart cities by allowing for extensive connectivity between different groups. A city's "degree of smartness"—its ability to make this change—depends on several important elements. In particular, the intelligent design of the urban environment must harmoniously coexist with the infrastructure and services that are the core of smart citie. Chourabi (Chourabi & Donato, 2015) point out that smart cities are more than just densely populated areas with advanced technological infrastructure. Rather, it is about comprehending what the people need and coming up with creative ways to efficiently fulfil those demands.

Smart city planners and designers should look for novel ways to build a new technology framework. The many social, economic, and ecological needs of city dwellers should be met by this design. Businesses face new and unforeseen obstacles as smart city development progresses (Zhao et al., 2018). Companies are driven to embrace new technologies and methodologies to get accurate business insights. These insights are crucial for improving the smart city infrastructure's transparency and ease. Transportation systems, electrical grids, medical facilities, phone systems, educational institutions, and public services are all part of this infrastructure.

More secure networked linkages and interoperable data exchange models are an absolute must for smart-city planners, infrastructure stakeholders, coordinators, and legislators, according to earlier research. For industries like banking, healthcare, and transportation to effectively manage shared economy platforms, these models are crucial. To reach this degree of integration, it is necessary to implement basic technologies that can back up complex infrastructure, which includes a wide range of technical parts and services.

Furthermore, smart-city projects should aim to improve the intelligence and automation of contemporary residential neighbourhoods, as well as the quality of services provided and the effective management of the many urban activities that smart city residents enjoy. In this setting, blockchain technology stands out as an obvious pick for enabling a range of use cases due to its capacity to spur innovation. By tackling a wide range of issues pertaining to smart city infrastructure, including technical, social, and financial ones, blockchain technology has the potential to empower these communities (Mora et al., 2021).

Additionally, it is vital in resolving the issue of disjointedness among various components, which helps with the comprehensive growth of smart cities. So smart city dreams can only come true with the help of cutting-edge tech and careful planning of user-centric systems that prioritise long-term sustainability and efficiency in infrastructure and service delivery.

4.2 Characteristics of Smart Cities

Over the last several decades, the idea of a Smart Cities strategy has shifted from a concentration on infrastructure and technology to one that is more people-centric, with an emphasis on sustainability and quality of life. Smart City expands on this concept by emphasizing data-driven decision-making and community interaction. Some of the vital characters of smart cities are listed below.

- **People-first**
- **Insight-led strategies**
- **Green living**
- **Audacious endeavours**
- **Synergy**
- **Fortitude**

The most important aspect in Smart Cities is People First. It makes sure the urban development does not focus primarily on infrastructure and technology, but it focuses on paying attention to citizens' needs and preferences. For instance, Smart City can introduce initiatives by offering more community spaces that can help in socializing and gathering or enhance access and ease of public transportation.

Making Insights from data is the significant feature of Smart City. That should benefit city services and policymaking because analytics and data are being used to formulate such initiatives. For instance, in order to optimize the flow of traffic, eradicate congestion, and implement steps that reduce pollution, a Smart City might use sensors and data analysis.

Green Living is yet another important feature of Smart City, where eco-friendly practice and policy are emphasized and used. It includes developing renewable energy sources, opening up green space, and using sustainable transportation methods. Thus, for instance, a city can use solar energy through public infrastructure or build up more bike lanes and pedestrian zones to reduce car dependence in that particular city.

Audacious ventures are also part of a Smart City. This means that cities should support and encourage new ventures and innovative solutions in order to tackle the urban challenges and improve the quality of life. For example, a smart city can offer an accelerator program in social innovation and urban sustainability.

The second key attribute of Smart City is synergy in the sense that it could bring together all the stakeholders and members of this community to jointly try and solve particular problems and take collective decisions better. For example, some Smart City can organize and conduct public forums and input meetings on a new issue or collaborate with local-based firms to create sustainable ideas.

For any Smart City Strategy, its critical feature is Fortitude, which simply means that there is a capacity of any urban area to deal and come out with crises and natural cataclysms and social revolution. An example of it is that a Smart City's emergency response strategy makes use of analytics and data to pinpoint problem regions as well as distribute resources well.

4.3 Challenges Faced by the Smart Cities

Security Challenges: Ensuring security is a significant hurdle in smart cities, as the majority of operations are not personally secured but instead handled by third parties. Smart cities depend on intelligent environments that require a comprehensive understanding of their inhabitants to deliver seamless services as given in the figure 5. These integrated systems gather personally identifiable information, organize it, and utilize it to generate adaptable profiles for individuals, facilitating instantaneous decision-making. Smart automobiles, which are equipped with GPS, wireless connections, and sensors, can monitor a passenger's whereabouts, movements, and interactions with urban infrastructure. This data is utilized for monitoring and regulating behaviour on intelligent roadways, including factors such as speed, travel routes, and driver identification. As a result, the privacy of individuals in smart cities is threatened because of the extensively interconnected networks that are necessary for the functioning of the city. In the absence of these data, the city's "smart" capabilities may not function properly, which could result in a malfunction or complete cessation of the system. The integration of IoT, Big Data, and the Energy Internet is essential for the efficient functioning of the smart city infrastructure.

Figure 5. Smart city services

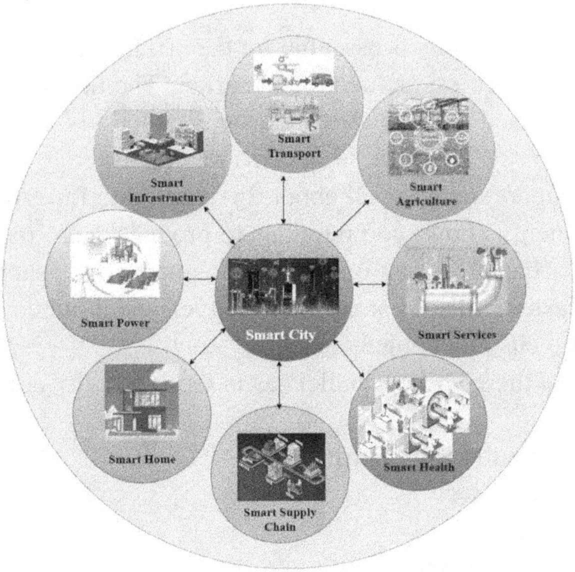

Generation of Huge Data

In smart cities, key operations such as water supply, energy generation, transportation, waste management, and e-learning produce massive amounts of data continuously. This data, stored in the cloud through IoT infrastructure, is vulnerable to security issues. IoT weaknesses include unsecured web and mobile interfaces, unencrypted networks, and insufficient privacy measures. Furthermore, controlling data generated from interactions between physical and digital objects is difficult with traditional methods.

Concurrent Information Update

The integrated functions of smart infrastructures are designed to meet the needs of citizens living in smart cities, where many activities have become predominantly virtual. To manage these activities effectively, third parties must continually update relevant data for every resident, including accurate contact information, family details, health status, and emergencies. However, a significant concern for residents is their lack of awareness regarding how their data is processed and transmitted. While they may understand how their information is collected, the complexities of data handling remain unclear to them, raising concerns about privacy and security.

Energy Consumption Challenge

A steady flow of electricity is essential for the efficient functioning of the technical systems in smart cities, as mentioned earlier. The actual intelligence of the system, or the integrated brain that regulates city processes, relies on this power, also called smart energy. All of these systems rely on a steady stream of electricity, which is what smart energy is all about. In addition to lowering pollutants and expenses, smart energy allows communities to produce safer, more efficient, and effective energy. Urban areas can improve their smart power supply reliability by implementing measures such as smart metering, efficient public lighting, electric car integration, and customer engagement.

Few areas where there will be challenges in the smart city development.

- **Infrastructure and Utility Industry**
- **Water Infrastructure**
- **Power Infrastructure**
- **Transportation Infrastructure**
- **Health care Infrastructure**
- **Supply chain Infrastructure**
- **Education Infrastructure**
- **Agro and Food Management**
- **Smart Homes**

5. TECHNOLOGIES NEEDED FOR EMERGING SMART CITIES WITH 6G

Sixth-generation (6G) wireless networks are increasingly being viewed as the foundational infrastructure for the smart cities of the future, as the demand for advanced technological solutions in these urban environments continues to rise (Murroni et al., 2023). Unlike its predecessor, 5G, which has already made significant strides in enhancing connectivity and enabling the proliferation of the Internet of Things (IoT), 6G is expected to push the boundaries even further. With its promise of faster data speeds, reduced latency, and significantly greater network capacity, 6G is poised to meet the complex and evolving needs of smart cities.

This maturation of 6G technology will unveil even more exciting smart cities that integrate and host various wide ranges of cutting-edge technologies. For instance, autonomous vehicles are to come into increasingly challenging urban environments only in order to navigate greater safety and effectiveness as soon as ultra-reliable and low-latency communications are assured through 6G or any future generation of telecommunications. Smart grids, being on a need for real-time optimization in energy distribution, seem likely to increase accuracy and responsiveness.

Many more advanced applications will be introduced, such as augmented reality (AR), virtual reality (VR), and immersive gaming, which could change how people in these cities communicate with their environment and live out entertainment, education, or health. Especially remote healthcare will benefit, even those diagnostic processes might become possible in real-time and remote surgery.

However, despite the promising future that 6G holds for smart cities, its development is still in the early stages (Kumari et al., 2021). It may take several years before 6G networks are fully developed, standardized, and widely adopted. In the meantime, researchers, policymakers, and industry leaders are actively exploring the potential applications and benefits of 6G, laying the groundwork for its eventual integration into smart city infrastructure.

Among the many important use cases for smart cities, intelligent transport and logistics stand out. By the thirty-first century, we may anticipate a dramatic improvement in transportation safety, efficiency, and environmental friendliness due to autonomous vehicles and drones. For accurate navigation, autonomous systems and connected robots will use cutting-edge sensors like LiDAR, radar, GPS, and sonar. To monitor ecosystems in urban areas bordered by rivers or ports, global omnipresent connectivity is going to be crucial. This will ensure network coverage on land and at sea. Artificial intelligence (AI) developments in areas such as computer vision, simultaneous localization and mapping (SLAM), and natural language processing will be necessitated by the proliferation of linked devices, such as drones and robots.

Figure 6, summarises and demonstrates the enabling technologies that help develop these new applications.

Figure 6. 6G Enabling technologies

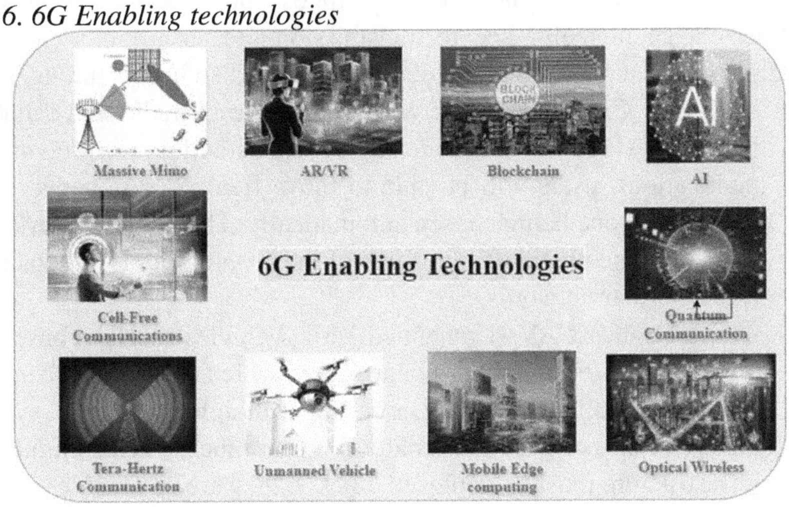

- Terahertz communications: Cellular communications are anticipated to occupy the 275 GHz–3 THz range, which when paired with the mmWave band (30–300 GHz) will increase the available spectrum by almost 11 times. The difficulties with THz interfaces will probably make this change require the deployment of highly-directional antennas.
- Artificial Intelligence (AI): AI can optimise time-consuming algorithms, such those for network selection and handovers, and dramatically cut down on processing delays in communications.

    Machine Learning (ML): ML methods address dealing with resource management, transportation management, task outsourcing, and transition management issues in 6G wireless networks.
- Massive MIMO with Smarter Reflective Surfaces (IRSs): IRS technology, a recent hardware breakthrough (sometimes referred to as meta-surfaces), uses multiple reflecting diode units to modify the direction of phase shift of intruding electromagnetic signals, enabling energy-efficient, environmentally friendly communication.

    Blockchain: Distributed ledger technology that uses advanced cryptography, a consensus process, and a distributed network architecture to solve security problems. The current state of 5G networks is hindered by issues with platform interoperability and throughput, which range from 10 to 1000 transactions per second. Nevertheless, these restrictions will be partially alleviated by 6G's novel consensus methods and inventive topologies.
- Quantum Communication: 6G is being made possible by quantum computing, which improves security by using quantum keys that are based on the uncertainty principle and the no-cloning theorem. The use of lasers or quantum particles to encode data makes it impossible to read or copy the data undetected, guaranteeing secure transmission. Because qubits can exist in multiple states at once, quantum communication also boosts throughput.

    -Cell-Free Communication: With the shift from traditional cellular and parallel systems of communication systems and non-orthogonal communications, users will be able to move freely across networks, with the optimal one being chosen automatically. The ping-pong effect, data loss, and failed handoffs are some of the problems that this change will fix in cellular networks.

    -Aerial Drones: UAVs(Unmanned Aerial Vehicles) that have base stations on board can offer cellular connectivity, which comes with benefits including controlled movement, robust line-of-sight links, and easy deployment. In times of crisis, such natural catastrophes, when communication infrastructure must be deployed quickly, they are invaluable.

-MEC (Mobile Edge Computing): A key element of 6G technology is mobility-enhanced edge computing (MEEC), which addresses issues in cloud-based situations where high latency, security threats, and large bandwidth usage result from data transfer over extended ranges from consumer electronics and edge servers to the cloud.

- Optical Wireless: With exceptionally rapid data transfer and low latency, this technology will be extensively utilised in applications such as submerged optical wireless communications and vehicle-to-everything (V2X) connection. For excellent quality 3D mapping in 6G, LiDAR is a viable technology. By 2026, it's anticipated that spatial multiplexing and microLED technologies will be well-established and reasonably priced (Almadani et al., 2020).
- Free-Space Optical (FSO) Telecommunications: FSO telecommunications offer incredibly quick data lines that are appropriate for a range of 6G applications, such as wireless backhaul for cellular systems and heterogeneous networks with extensive interconnection.
- Virtual Reality (VR) and Augmented Reality (AR): 6G will make these experiences smoother and more immersive, opening up new possibilities for applications in fields like smart city security and automotive communications.

Energy Harvesting: 6G's rising data traffic and device count will result in a sharp rise in energy requirements. A possible technique to assist in striking a balance between the high energy needs and the constrained battery capacities of gadgets is energy harvesting.

- Low-Orbit Satellites: By combining space-based along with ground-based cellular networks, the quick development of satellite networks will enable 6G. For space-ground connections to be established and to guarantee full-coverage broadband connections for ground users, a low-orbit network of satellites will be essential.

6. SOLUTION OFFERED BY BLOCKCHAIN AND 6G TO SMART CITIES CHALLENGES: SC6GBC

When combined, blockchain and sixth-generation wireless technologies provide a full suite of solutions for smart cities (Vaghani et al., 2022). The integration as depicted in figure 7 might provide an excellent solution called “SC6GBC”.These solutions address a wide range of urban difficulties and improve a variety of elements of city living. Because of its decentralised and tamper-proof architecture, blockchain technology offers significant advantages to smart cities. These advantages include an increase in data security. This arrangement ensures the protection of sensitive information against breaches and unauthorised access. One of its most notable characteristics is incorporating smart contracts, which can automate and verify agreements without the need for middlemen. This allows for the simplification of both the financial and legal procedures involved.

Figure 7. Integrated technologies

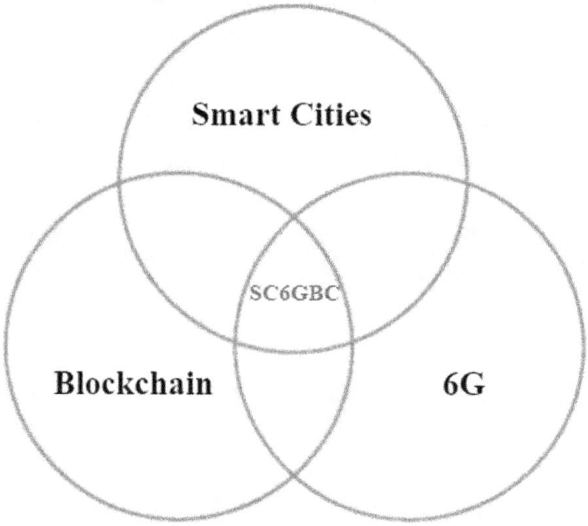

In addition, blockchain technology enhances citizen participation in the sense that it protects information, and voting and feedback activities are enabled through decentralized applications. There is less third-party involvement, which makes business procedures simple and transparent. In transportation and energy, blockchain technology can be integrated with artificial intelligence and the internet of things to create systems that are sustainable and transparent. This enhances data consistency and auditability, hence overcoming challenges in traditional data management systems. It also establishes transparency and trustworthiness through information sharing in clear and traceable ways. This would add to boosting secure authentication all through layers of IoT while improving automation by making it easier in transactions and requiring lesser manual readjustment (Alzoubi et al., 2022). On top of that, the delivery of key services is also ensured with smooth delivery uninterrupted, so speed recovery when failures are found. It proves an invaluable tool for crisis and violence management through real-time tracking and comprehensive data recording of criminal acts.

These advantages are supported by the fact that data transmission rates, data transfer latency being highly low, and the overall capacity offered by 6G technology is significantly better than that of earlier versions. All these aspects are inevitable for the functionality of modern applications of a smart city. The utilization of 6G technology would ensure continued connectivity as well as real-time communication over an extensive network of devices and sensors of smart cities.

IoT performance improves in order to cater to greater integration of more effective smart city technologies and applications.

Alongside the abovementioned special applications, augmented reality (AR), virtual reality (VR), and immersion have been advocated to be supported by 6G. The applications promote visions of enhanced possibilities for city services and interactions (Allam & Jones, 2021). While improving network performance, 6G innovations, including massive MIMO and intelligent reflecting surfaces, bring savings in energy consumption as well as promote the extension of smart city infrastructure, that is scalable. With the coming together of blockchain technology and 6G technology, a smart city is promised to have an efficient and safe, state-of-the-art urban environment that transforms smart cities into interconnected, responsive, and resilient communities. Such huge benefits realized with smart cities include citizens' safety through connected surveillance systems, intelligent roadways, and public safety monitoring. Dependence on interconnecting technologies in these cities has also made them vulnerable to cyber threats, hacking, and data breaches. Protection of these cities from the above risks is therefore important so that these cities can keep running continuously and maintain public confidence in these systems.

7. BLOCKCHAIN AND 6G: REINFORCING SMART CITY SECURITY

Blockchain and 6G will be very useful tools for protecting smart cities against all threats to security. Data integrity, confidentiality, availability, and accountability for the smart city infrastructure will thus be tightened using these technologies.

7.1 Blockchain: Enhancing Data Security and Integrity

Blockchain technology is inherently designed to offer robust security features that are particularly well-suited for smart cities. Here's how it can be applied:

- **Data Integrity:** Blockchain's decentralized and immutable ledger ensures that once data is recorded, it cannot be altered or tampered with. This is crucial for maintaining the accuracy and reliability of data across smart city systems. By storing critical data on a blockchain, smart cities can safeguard against manipulation, ensuring that all information used in decision-making processes remains trustworthy.

- **Confidentiality:** Although blockchain is transparent, it also allows for the encryption of sensitive data. This means that while the data is accessible to authorized users, it remains confidential and protected from unauthorized access. For instance, personal data collected by smart city sensors can be anonymized and securely stored on a blockchain, reducing the risk of data breaches.
- **Accountability:**Since the blockchain is transparent, every transaction and interaction with data can be traced. It, therefore, creates a verifiable audit trail that shows all system users are answerable for their actions. This, therefore, means that if there is a security breach or anomaly, the blockchain ledger is clear on who accessed or altered the data, thereby allowing for quick and effective response.

7.2 6G: Ensuring Data Availability and Real-Time Communication

The next-generation 6G network promises ultra-fast, low-latency communication, which is vital for the real-time functioning of smart city systems.

Here's how 6G contributes to smart city security:

- **1. Availability:** With 6G, data can be transmitted and accessed in real time with unprecedented speed and reliability. This is an important aspect of continued smart city infrastructure monitoring and working, such as traffic management systems, energy grids, and emergency services. 6G ensures data is available in time to prevent disruptions that would compromise the safety and functionality of the city.
- **2. Resilient Authentication Management:** Advanced authentication mechanism is one of the primary security enhancement mechanisms in 6G networks. These include biometric verification and quantum encryption that will offer stronger protection against unauthorized access. Such measures ensure that only legitimate users can access sensitive data and systems within a smart city.
- **3. Integrated Security Solutions:** 6G's high bandwidth and low latency enable seamless integration of various security systems across a smart city. For instance, real-time data from IoT devices, surveillance cameras, and traffic sensors can be securely processed and analyzed through a blockchain network, providing a holistic approach to security. This integrated system ensures that all aspects of the smart city are protected against cyber threats.

8. REAL TIME IMPLEMENTATION OF SMART CITIES

Even though the exact nature of a "smart city" remains up for debate, the fact that there are already more than 140 of these types of cities in operation throughout the globe is undeniable (Suartika & Cuthbert, 2020). The most current smart city index places London atop the list after it steadily rose the ranks in previous years. The city has initiated various creative projects via the Connect London program to establish a state-of-the-art 5G communication system and comprehensive fiber-optic infrastructure. The famous lampposts in London have also been enhanced with several sensors and charging facilities for electric vehicles. London is well-positioned to continue its inventive solution advancements thanks to its investment in AI, the IoT, and the upcoming 6G technologies.

Barcelona exemplifies a smart city by deploying a comprehensive network of LED lampposts embedded with sophisticated sensors (Kuru & Ansell, 2020). The sensors observe various urban activities such as traffic patterns, air pollution levels, pedestrian mobility, and noise intensity. In addition, they can dim or turn off the lights as needed, which helps to save energy and decrease light pollution. In addition to implementing advanced lighting systems, Barcelona has also implemented cutting-edge waste management solutions, including the use of intelligent waste containers that are equipped with hoover systems to carry garbage underground. This technique not only reduces unpleasant odors but also reduces the frequency of waste collection truck visits, hence improving the city's overall efficiency and environmental effect.

As a result of its comprehensive Smart Nation program, which began in 2014, Singapore is now one of the most notable smart cities in Asia. The city-state has implemented a broad range of intelligent technologies, including an extensive network of sensors and cameras that monitor traffic flow, air quality, and public safety. Smart traffic management systems optimize traffic lights to reduce congestion, while a comprehensive public transportation system features real-time tracking and predictive analytics. Additionally, Singapore employs a smart garbage collection system where bins signal when they are full, enhancing waste management efficiency (Sohag & Podder, 2020).

Singapore has established a digital health system that incorporates video counselling and smart IoT devices for tracking patients to tackle the issues associated with an ageing population. The incorporation of contactless payment systems has streamlined commuting and payment procedures for the city's 7.5 million public transit customers. Through this holistic strategy, Singapore addresses the challenges posed by its ageing population while showcasing its commitment to leveraging intelligent technologies to enhance urban living and operational efficiency.

Oslo is a prime example of a smart city, especially in its utilisation of advanced smart sensor technologies. The Oslo Smart Street Lighting initiative covers the entire city and aims to enhance the efficiency of the street lighting network (Ożadowicz & Grela, 2017). Oslo has consolidated its street lighting system into a cohesive network, allowing remote access and control using internet-based apps. This sophisticated system enables instantaneous management and surveillance of illumination levels, with the capability to modify light intensity according to seasonal variations and special requirements. The integration of 20,000 intelligent lamps in Oslo has resulted in a notable reduction in energy usage of about 70%, showcasing the substantial influence of smart city technology in decreasing energy consumption and improving sustainability.

Songdo, a planned smart city, exemplifies a focus on integrated technology and sustainability. It features an extensive network of sensors and cameras that track traffic, energy consumption, and environmental conditions (Rugkhapan & Murray, 2019). The city's smart buildings are equipped with advanced technologies designed to maximize energy efficiency, while its innovative waste management system uses pneumatic tubes to transport waste to centralized processing facilities, reducing the need for frequent truck collections. Similarly, Seoul stands out for its advanced use of big data to enhance urban management. The city employs a network of sensors and closed-circuit televisions to monitor various urban factors, including traffic flow and air quality. A key initiative in Seoul addresses the needs of its aging population by using environmental sensors to detect issues such as prolonged inactivity or unusual changes in environmental conditions. These sensors can immediately notify case workers and emergency services if necessary.

Furthermore, Seoul is developing an AI-powered system to analyze crime patterns and is leading in the adoption of 5G technology to boost mobility and transportation efficiency (Robinson & Ji, 2022). Both cities showcase how smart technologies can drive urban innovation, improve quality of life, and enhance sustainability in the modern age.

One of San Francisco's well-known smart city initiatives is its system of intelligent streetlights, which change their brightness depending on the weather and the amount of traffic. Additionally, the city uses sensor-based technologies to track energy use and air quality (Razmjoo et al., 2022). To better handle parking pricing and availability in real-time, the SF park initiative is working to alleviate congestion and increase efficiency. Several smart technologies have been implemented in Amsterdam to improve city life. Energy distribution and consumption are both optimized via the city's smart grids. Amsterdam has also installed smart water management systems to keep tabs on water, use and quality. To encourage environmentally friendly modes of transportation, the city backs bike-sharing schemes that use GPS tracking and smart bike racks.

The Smart Dubai program is developing Dubai into an intelligent city to make it the most joyful and smartest place on Earth. A city-wide internet system, smart transport technologies including drones and driverless cars, and a government service platform built on blockchain to improve transparency and speed operations are important projects. Intelligent energy management and cutting-edge data analytics for city planning are two other areas of emphasis in Dubai (Noori et al., 2020).

Another prominent example of the use of cutting-edge technology in smart cities is New York City. In numerous districts, the city has installed thousands of smart technologies and sensors as part of its 2020 smart city pilot program. To improve the management of services like waste collection and management, this program gathers data. New York has also updated its infrastructure, swapping out outdated phone booths for smart hubs equipped with online charging stations, Wi-Fi, and contactless technology (Habib et al., 2023).

With the help of smart city technologies, Kansas City has implemented several new features that make city life better for everyone (Hall, 2003). Smart streetlights, recently placed by the city, serve to both light up public areas and aid in the conservation of energy while simultaneously enhancing safety measures. Throughout the city, interactive kiosks have been strategically positioned to provide information, services, and instructions easily accessible to both residents and visitors. Plus, residents can stay connected no matter where they go in Kansas City due to the city's more than 50 blocks of free Wi-Fi.

The extensive data visualization app is a prominent component of the smart city program in Kansas City. It provides citizens with up-to-the-minute information. The public can use this app to see where parking spots are, how traffic is moving, and where there are a lot of people walking. With this mountain of data at their fingertips, city dwellers can better plan their daily commutes, which in turn makes city life more convenient and efficient for everyone.

San Diego has also installed 3,200 smart sensors around the city, which is a big step towards being a smart city. With the help of these sensors, traffic flow may be optimized, leading to less congestion and easier commutes. By facilitating the discovery of available parking spots, they also play an important role in controlling the supply of parking spots. In addition to transportation, these sensors improve public safety by keeping an eye out for environmental and security risks. When it comes to sustainability and environmental consciousness, San Diego is just as dedicated. To encourage the adoption of cleaner energy sources, the city has installed solar-to-electric charging stations, which citizens can use to power their electric vehicles. The safety and security of San Diego's citizens are further enhanced by the strategically positioned linked cameras that monitor traffic issues and crime (Tripathi & Goel, 2022). Together, these initiatives are making San Diego a better place to live in terms of efficiency, sustainability, and safety (Tripathi & Goel, 2022).

9. CONCLUSION: COLLABORATIVE EFFORTS AND LEGISLATIVE SUPPORT

To fully unravel the potential of blockchain as well as 6G to secure a smart city, multi-segment collaboration is sought after. Government agencies as well as private enterprises developers of software, device manufacturers energy providers, and managers of network services must apply their own integrated security solution considerations keeping in mind core objectives in security.

This, however goes further to include legislative efforts like the IoT Cybersecurity Improvement Act that is a recent development in the United States. The act imposes minimum security standards on the use of connected devices in various sectors, thus having a positive effect on a smart city, from an individual sensor to a full network that would have otherwise been in dire need of such controls.

This way, 6G can merge its advanced communication features with blockchain data security to ensure smart cities. They create a resilient, strong, and trusted environment and secure not just the cities themselves but the citizens too in a drive towards sustainable growth in the urban cities.

REFERENCES

Akyildiz, I. F., Kak, A., & Nie, S. (2020). 6G and beyond: The future of wireless communications systems. *IEEE Access : Practical Innovations, Open Solutions*, 8, 133995–134030. DOI: 10.1109/ACCESS.2020.3010896

Alavi, A. H., Jiao, P., Buttlar, W. G., & Lajnef, N. (2018). Internet of Things-enabled smart cities: State-of-the-art and future trends. *Measurement*, 129, 589–606. DOI: 10.1016/j.measurement.2018.07.067

Alhazmi, H. E., Eassa, F. E., & Sandokji, S. M. (2022). Towards big data security framework by leveraging fragmentation and blockchain technology. *IEEE Access : Practical Innovations, Open Solutions*, 10, 10768–10782. DOI: 10.1109/ACCESS.2022.3144632

Allam, Z. (2019). The emergence of anti-privacy and control at the nexus between the concepts of safe city and smart city. *Smart Cities*, 2(1), 96–105. DOI: 10.3390/smartcities2010007

Allam, Z., & Jones, D. S. (2021). Future (post-COVID) digital, smart and sustainable cities in the wake of 6G: Digital twins, immersive realities and new urban economies. *Land Use Policy*, 101, 105201. DOI: 10.1016/j.landusepol.2020.105201

Almadani, Y., Plets, D., Bastiaens, S., Joseph, W., Ijaz, M., Ghassemlooy, Z., & Rajbhandari, S. (2020). Visible light communications for industrial applications—Challenges and potentials. *Electronics (Basel)*, 9(12), 2157. DOI: 10.3390/electronics9122157

Alzoubi, Y. I., Al-Ahmad, A., Kahtan, H., & Jaradat, A. (2022). Internet of things and blockchain integration: Security, privacy, technical, and design challenges. *Future Internet*, 14(7), 216. DOI: 10.3390/fi14070216

Angel, S., Parent, J., Civco, D. L., Blei, A., & Potere, D. (2011). The dimensions of global urban expansion: Estimates and projections for all countries, 2000–2050. *Progress in Planning*, 75(2), 53–107. DOI: 10.1016/j.progress.2011.04.001

Bakare, B. I., & Bassey, E. E. (2021). A comparative study of the evolution of wireless communication technologies from the first generation (1G) to the fourth generation (4G). *Int J Elect Commun Comp Eng*, 12(3), 2249–071X.

Beaumont, C. D., Berry, D., & Ricketts, J. (2022). Technology has empowered the consumer, but marketing communications need to catch-up: An approach to fast-forward the future. *Businesses*, 2(2), 246–272. DOI: 10.3390/businesses2020017

Caragliu, A., & Del Bo, C. (2020). Do smart city policies work? *Digital transformation of the design, construction and management processes of the built environment*, 149-159.

Chourabi, I., & Donato, P. (2015). Homogenization and correctors of a class of elliptic problems in perforated domains. *Asymptotic Analysis*, 92(1-2), 1–43. DOI: 10.3233/ASY-151288

Dunnewijk, T., & Hultén, S. (2007). A brief history of mobile communication in Europe. *Telematics and Informatics*, 24(3), 164–179. DOI: 10.1016/j.tele.2007.01.013

Habib, A., Alsmadi, D., & Prybutok, V. R. (2023). Factors that determine residents' acceptance of smart city technologies. In *Smart Cities at Play: Technology and Emerging Forms of Playfulness* (pp. 4-17). CRC Press.

Hall, S. T. (2003). Fountain of Cities: An Examination of Urban Growth and Growth Management with a Regional Proposal for Greater Kansas City. *Kan. JL & Pub. Pol'y*, 13, 619.

Hui, C. X., Dan, G., Alamri, S., & Toghraie, D. (2023). Greening smart cities: An investigation of the integration of urban natural resources and smart city technologies for promoting environmental sustainability. *Sustainable Cities and Society*, 99, 104985. DOI: 10.1016/j.scs.2023.104985

Jacob, S., Alagirisamy, M., Xi, C., Balasubramanian, V., Srinivasan, R., Parvathi, R., & Islam, S. M. (2021). AI and IoT-enabled smart exoskeleton system for rehabilitation of paralyzed people in connected communities. *IEEE Access : Practical Innovations, Open Solutions*, 9, 80340–80350. DOI: 10.1109/ACCESS.2021.3083093

Kasinathan, P., Pugazhendhi, R., Elavarasan, R. M., Ramachandaramurthy, V. K., Ramanathan, V., Subramanian, S., Kumar, S., Nandhagopal, K., Raghavan, R. R. V., Rangasamy, S., Devendiran, R., & Alsharif, M. H. (2022). Realization of sustainable development goals with disruptive technologies by integrating industry 5.0, society 5.0, smart cities and villages. *Sustainability (Basel)*, 14(22), 15258. DOI: 10.3390/su142215258

Kumari, A., Gupta, R., & Tanwar, S. (2021). Amalgamation of blockchain and IoT for smart cities underlying 6G communication: A comprehensive review. *Computer Communications*, 172, 102–118. DOI: 10.1016/j.comcom.2021.03.005

Kuru, K., & Ansell, D. (2020). TCitySmartF: A comprehensive systematic framework for transforming cities into smart cities. *IEEE Access : Practical Innovations, Open Solutions*, 8, 18615–18644. DOI: 10.1109/ACCESS.2020.2967777

Maier, M., Ebrahimzadeh, A., Beniiche, A., & Rostami, S. (2022). The Art of 6G (TAO 6G): How to wire Society 5.0. *Journal of Optical Communications and Networking*, 14(2), A101–A112. DOI: 10.1364/JOCN.438522

Manville, C., Hinrichs, S., Parks, S., Kamenetzky, A., Gunashekar, S., Wilkinson, B., & Grant, J. (2015). *Characteristics of high-performing research units*. Prepared for the Higher Education Funding Council for England.

Mora, H., Mendoza-Tello, J. C., Varela-Guzmán, E. G., & Szymanski, J. (2021). Blockchain technologies to address smart city and society challenges. *Computers in Human Behavior*, 122, 106854. DOI: 10.1016/j.chb.2021.106854

Murroni, M., Anedda, M., Fadda, M., Ruiu, P., Popescu, V., Zaharia, C., & Giusto, D. (2023). 6G—Enabling the New Smart City: A Survey. *Sensors (Basel)*, 23(17), 7528. DOI: 10.3390/s23177528 PMID: 37687986

Nassereddine, M., & Khang, A. (2024). Applications of Internet of Things (IoT) in smart cities. In *Advanced IoT technologies and applications in the industry 4.0 digital economy* (pp. 109–136). CRC Press. DOI: 10.1201/9781003434269-6

Nguyen, G. T., & Kim, K. (2018). A survey about consensus algorithms used in blockchain. *Journal of Information Processing Systems*, 14(1).

Noori, N., Hoppe, T., & de Jong, M. (2020). Classifying pathways for smart city development: Comparing design, governance and implementation in Amsterdam, Barcelona, Dubai, and Abu Dhabi. *Sustainability (Basel)*, 12(10), 4030. DOI: 10.3390/su12104030

Overby, H., & Audestad, J. A. (2020). Standards, Regulations, and Net Neutrality in the Digital Economy. *Regulations, and Net Neutrality in the Digital Economy.*

Ożadowicz, A., & Grela, J. (2017). Energy saving in the street lighting control system—A new approach based on the EN-15232 standard. *Energy Efficiency*, 10(3), 563–576. DOI: 10.1007/s12053-016-9476-1

Raja Santhi, A., & Muthuswamy, P. (2023). Industry 5.0 or industry 4.0 S? Introduction to industry 4.0 and a peek into the prospective industry 5.0 technologies. *International Journal on Interactive Design and Manufacturing*, 17(2), 947–979. DOI: 10.1007/s12008-023-01217-8

Razmjoo, A., Gandomi, A., Mahlooji, M., Astiaso Garcia, D., Mirjalili, S., Rezvani, A., Ahmadzadeh, S., & Memon, S. (2022). An investigation of the policies and crucial sectors of smart cities based on IoT application. *Applied Sciences (Basel, Switzerland)*, 12(5), 2672. DOI: 10.3390/app12052672

Robinson, T., & Ji, M. (2022). Smart City Seoul: Solving the Urban Puzzle. In *Sustainable, Smart and Solidary Seoul: Transforming an Asian Megacity* (pp. 99–134). Springer International Publishing. DOI: 10.1007/978-3-031-13595-8_5

Roupé, M., Johansson, M., Maftei, L., Lundstedt, R., & Viklund-Tallgren, M. (2020). Virtual collaborative design environment: Supporting seamless integration of multitouch table and immersive VR. *Journal of Construction Engineering and Management*, 146(12), 04020132. DOI: 10.1061/(ASCE)CO.1943-7862.0001935

Rugkhapan, N. T., & Murray, M. J. (2019). Songdo IBD (International Business District): Experimental prototype for the city of tomorrow? *International Planning Studies*, 24(3-4), 272–292. DOI: 10.1080/13563475.2019.1650725

Salih, A. A., Zeebaree, S. R., Abdulraheem, A. S., Zebari, R. R., Sadeeq, M. A., & Ahmed, O. M. (2020). Evolution of mobile wireless communication to 5G revolution. *Technology Reports of Kansai University*, 62(5), 2139–2151.

Serodio, C., Cunha, J., Candela, G., Rodriguez, S., Sousa, X. R., & Branco, F. (2023). The 6G ecosystem as support for IoE and private networks: Vision, requirements, and challenges. *Future Internet*, 15(11), 348. DOI: 10.3390/fi15110348

Shahzadi, S., Iqbal, M., & Chaudhry, N. R. (2021). 6G vision: Toward future collaborative cognitive communication (3C) systems. *IEEE Communications Standards Magazine*, 5(2), 60–67. DOI: 10.1109/MCOMSTD.001.2000044

Shayea, I., Azmi, M. H., Ergen, M., El-Saleh, A. A., Han, C. T., Arsad, A., Rahman, T. A., Alhammadi, A., Daradkeh, Y. I., & Nandi, D. (2021). Performance analysis of mobile broadband networks with 5g trends and beyond: Urban areas scope in malaysia. *IEEE Access : Practical Innovations, Open Solutions*, 9, 90767–90794. DOI: 10.1109/ACCESS.2021.3085782

Sohag, M. U., & Podder, A. K. (2020). Smart garbage management system for a sustainable urban life: An IoT based application. *Internet of Things : Engineering Cyber Physical Human Systems*, 11, 100255. DOI: 10.1016/j.iot.2020.100255

Suartika, G. A. M., & Cuthbert, A. (2020). The sustainable imperative—Smart cities, technology and development. *Sustainability (Basel)*, 12(21), 8892. DOI: 10.3390/su12218892

Subashini, B., & Hemavathi, D. (2023). Scalable Blockchain Technology for Tracking the Provenance of the Agri-Food. *Computers, Materials & Continua*, 75(2), 3339–3358. DOI: 10.32604/cmc.2023.035074

Sullivan, S., Brighente, A., Kumar, S. A., & Conti, M. (2021). 5G security challenges and solutions: A review by OSI layers. *IEEE Access : Practical Innovations, Open Solutions*, 9, 116294–116314. DOI: 10.1109/ACCESS.2021.3105396

Tripathi, N. G., & Goel, M. (2022). Citizen-Centric Smart Planning: Case Study San Diego, California. In *Smart Master Planning for Cities: Case Studies on Domain Innovations* (pp. 271–300). Springer Nature Singapore. DOI: 10.1007/978-981-19-2386-9_8

Ullah, H., Nair, N. G., Moore, A., Nugent, C., Muschamp, P., & Cuevas, M. (2019). 5G communication: An overview of vehicle-to-everything, drones, and healthcare use-cases. *IEEE Access : Practical Innovations, Open Solutions*, 7, 37251–37268. DOI: 10.1109/ACCESS.2019.2905347

Vaghani, A., Sood, K., & Yu, S. (2022). Security and QoS issues in blockchain enabled next-generation smart logistic networks: A tutorial. *Blockchain: Research and Applications*, 3(3), 100082.

Zhao, Q., Feng, Q., Lu, H., Li, Y., Wang, A., Tian, Q., Zhan, Q., Lu, Y., Zhang, L., Huang, T., Wang, Y., Fan, D., Zhao, Y., Wang, Z., Zhou, C., Chen, J., Zhu, C., Li, W., Weng, Q., & Huang, X. (2018). Pan-genome analysis highlights the extent of genomic variation in cultivated and wild rice. *Nature Genetics*, 50(2), 278–284. DOI: 10.1038/s41588-018-0041-z PMID: 29335547

Chapter 9
The Role of 6G in Empowering Smart Cities Enabling Ubiquitous Connectivity and Intelligent Infrastructure

Hitesh Mohapatra
https://orcid.org/0000-0001-8100-4860
School of Computer Engineering, Kalinga Institute of Industrial Technology (KIIT), Bhubaneswar, India

ABSTRACT

Wireless communication is advancing, leading to 6G networks. These networks will reshape society with unprecedented connectivity and intelligence. 6G is key for future smart cities, integrating terahertz communication, ultra-low latency, and AI-driven networks. This will create hyper-connected cities where real-time data supports systems like autonomous vehicles, energy management, and public safety. 6G research shows its potential for ultra-reliable communication, immersive experiences like extended reality, and widespread sensing, crucial for smart city applications. However, challenges like technical issues, data privacy, and regulations need addressing. This chapter proposes a 6G-enabled smart city model using IoT, AI, and edge computing to improve urban operations. It explores dynamic network slicing, intelligent resource allocation, and edge AI processing to meet latency and bandwidth needs. The chapter concludes by emphasizing collaboration and strategic planning to overcome challenges, ensuring 6G technologies foster sustainable urban growth.

DOI: 10.4018/979-8-3693-8029-1.ch009

1. INTRODUCTION

1.1. Brief Overview of 6G Technology and Its Potential Impact

The appearance of 6G technology can be considered as a sophisticated step forward in the develop of the wireless communication services, provided that the reports which claim for the improvements compared to the previous generation of the 5G networks seem to be quite realistic. Hence it is predicted that 6G is destined to be in the middle of the development of connected environments as societies rely on digital structures to solve multifaceted urban issues (Trichias et al., 2024). This next-generation network technology will not only be about the speed and the capacity but will be defined by the integration of artificial intelligence (AI), edge computing and the Internet of Things (IoT) to create smarter, efficient systems. At the center of these innovations is the desire to achieve maximum potential of the smart cities concept, where connectivity and intelligent decisions are expected to seamlessly create sustainable and resilient city (Mahmood et al., 2020).

Over the last few years, the concept of smart cities has become the central area of focus in the debates about urbanization and sustainability. Today's cities face several problems that include population density, pollution, resources, and security among others. Current approaches and technologies, despite having their utility, can be lack scalability, flexibility and real-time performance (Yrjölä et al., 2023). The emerging 6G is set to overcome these barriers and offer the base on which cities are smart, connected and can learn and adapt in actual time. An exciting development to note regarding the 6G is the forecast of the network to work at terahertz band, which promises data transfer speed beyond imagination, among other benefits. This level of integration is needed for new use cases like autonomous transport, telemedicine and extended reality beyond the vehicle, respectively. Furthermore, 6G is expected to welcome AI at the heart of the network that also support the malleable offering of resources, fall preventive workmanship, and upgraded safety measures (Inomata et al., 2021). The integration of these technologies in 6G will therefore result into cities that are not only connected but also self-sufficient.

In addition to these, 6G creates opportunities for equity and inclusion in the delivery of services digitally as well. However, there is an opportunity of reducing the 'digital divide' where knowledge and use of information and services are not restricted to the well-off citizens. Some of the Intelligent urban systems that can be supported by 6G could include, for instance, public health monitoring that occurs in real-time, adaptive energy grids as well as smart governance systems that are in direct response to population needs (Antón-Haro et al., 2024). However, the processes of moving to the 6G smart cities are not without various challenges. Those questions, which are connected with data protection, security, and ethical aspects of the AI utilization, will arise as these technologies become the organic part of the public utilities. Furthermore, the large-scale application of 6G entails the need to incorporate massive physical and digital investments at operational and national levels and well-developed policies for the further evolution of 6G.

The goal of this chapter is to discuss how 6G would help modernized the urban socio-sphere, regarding how it would upgrade the connectivity, intelligence systems, and eventually, smart cities (Cordova Morales et al., 2023). In this discussion, an attempt has been made to understand the concepts of 6G Wiki news by exploring 6G's characteristics and opportunities and proposed new model of 6G-based urban systems. Over the course of the development of the 6G, more and more people are thinking about its potential and potential consequences for the life of megacities.

1.2. The Significance of 6G in the Context of Smart Cities

As for smart cities, the 6G technology will be the infrastructure enabling an uninterrupted interconnected intelligent environment of the city. While cities are becoming ever sprawling and complex, sensible allocation of resources, better supply of public utilities and a higher quality of life are paramount concerns. It is expected that 6G will deliver the high reliability supporting the efficient connection density for Billions of devices and sensors in urban environment to exchange relevant data and to make intelligent decisions promptly (Zong et al., 2022). Such level of integration will be vital in the provision of ITS, AVs, and SEG, because they need real-time interaction and information transfer rate.

Furthermore, the integration of AI, edge computing and IoT by 6G will open new opportunities for improvement of the urban planning, government and citizens' interaction. The application of digital twins as virtual models of physical assets will enable city planners and administrators to plan and improve infrastructures and related services (Liu et al., 2022). Moreover, novel networks based on the 6G will help to progress more inclusive and sustainable cities that would provide digital services for all the inhabitants and those in the weak signal area. Indeed, 6G will be the primary enabler of connected cities, that are, more importantly, smart, green, and resilient (Liu et al., 2022).

1.3. Outline of the Chapter's Objectives and Focus Areas

Specifically, as will be discussed in this chapter, the development of the 6G technology will fundamentally alter how people live in cities. The discussion is structured around three core objectives: The discussion is structured around three core objectives:

- *Understanding the Fundamentals of 6G Technology*: To begin with, the chapter presents an analysis of the prospects and possibilities of the 6G, which encompasses terahertz communication, AI propelled network, and ultra-low latency. This section offers the background needed for understanding of 6G as the part of future urban systems (Siriwardhana et al., 2021).
- *Analyzing the Applications of 6G in Smart Cities*: Instead, the notions of 6G are introduced in the context of their utilization in smart city sectors like transportation systems, infrastructures management, safety and security provision, and environment monitoring. By these examples, the chapter demonstrates the way, how 6G will help improving smarter and more efficient urban services (Suyama et al., 2022).
- *Proposing a 6G-Enabled Smart City Model and Addressing Challenges:* This last chapter is a summary and provides a conceptual model, that is a smart city ecosystem enabled by 6G. This model focus on technology enablers such as artificial intelligence, internet of things, and edge computing, and also gives brief about some concern of implementation, data privacy, and regulation (Norp et al., 2024).

2. EVOLUTION OF COMMUNICATION TECHNOLOGIES AND THE PATH TO 6G

2.1. Brief History: From 2G to 5G and the Advancements in Each Generation

The development of wireless communication has been a process that has experienced awesome shifts in performance, connections and functionalities. Every generation of cellular networks brought in new set of advancements that have revolutionized the manner in which society interact with technologies.

- **2G (1990s):** The second generation or the 2G brought the concept of using digital instead of analog to send messages. It launched the Global System for Mobile Communications (GSM) allows voice communication, that text messaging, (SMS) and fundamental over data services similar to multimedia messaging (MMS). 2G networks have been important in the development of mobile communication since they were responsible for enhancing the quality of calls as well as providing secure data transfer (Inomata et al., 2024).
- **3G (2000s):** With the Bar 3G, the mobile communication went beyond the voice call, test message to internet browsing and video telephony. With this generation the commercial data rates of up to 2 Mbps were made and sup-

ported web browsing, email and low-quality multimedia streaming services. The WCDMA (Wideband Code Division Multiple Access) and HSPA (High-Speed Packet Access) technologies became crucial for 3G networks and positively impacted the Mobile internet usage (Ma et al., 2023).

- **4G (2010s):** The fourth-generation (4G) networks, mainly LTE (Long-Term Evolution), changed the mobile communication through providing broadband-speed connection with comparatively low delay time. 4G was a great enabler of high-definition video streaming, mobile gaming, and 'real-time' communication applications such as video conferencing. The advancement in technology showed a great deal of improvement with the introduction of 4G that offered internet speed of up to 100 Mbps making smartphones a necessity in people's daily lives (Wang et al., 2023).
- **5G (2020s):** The change to 5G technology resulted in the data speed jump up to 10 Gbps, minimum latency of 1 ms, and devises connection up to 1M. Best known as the fifth generation of networks, they incorporated further ideas such as network slicing and edge computing to offer specific services and to process information in real time. This development led to IoT, self-driving cars and smart city solutions, which in turn makes the 5G technology as an enabling technology of upcoming technologies (Akgul et al., 2024).

2.2. Key Limitations of 5G That 6G Aims to Overcome

Although 5G enhanced the existing communication network through enhanced speed, capacity, and connectivity, it has its drawbacks, which 6G wants to solve. These limitations include:

- **Coverage and Penetration:** It has been a challenge for 5G networks especially those operating in the millimeter-wave (mm/Wave) to provide broad coverage as is the case with 4G networks. This limitation makes the 5G network to be ineffective in the provision of its services to the rural and remote areas. To overcome these barriers, it is expected that 6G will get enhanced spectrum efficiency and will function at higher range of frequencies (Pires et al., 2024).
- **Energy Efficiency:** And given the fact that current 5G deployments plan to handle tens of billions of connected devices, power is a major issue. Applying the energy-efficient solutions like AI-controlled resource management, and intelligent power distribution 6G's goal is to minimize the CO2 emissions of communication networks (Toumi & Dimitrovski, 2024).
- **Latency and Real-Time Responsiveness:** While 5G has low latency some applications such as holographic communication, brain computer interfaces

and real-time digital twins require lower latency than 5G. 6G aims to offer as low latency as possible starting from a few microseconds which will enable instant communication and retaliation (Wang et al., 2023).

- **Network Intelligence:** Enhanced by 5G, the AI engineering inserted some fundamental operations; however, these are rather restricted. 6G will introduce AI into the core of the network so that it will create self-optimizing networks, predictive as well as more intelligent decision-making at the edge.

2.3. Defining 6G: Features, Technologies, and Anticipated Deployment Timeline

6G is another generation which is defined as the enhancement in wireless communication with superior speed, connectivity as well as intelligence compared to the previous generations. Stll in the research and development stage 6G is expected to be commercially deployed within the early 2030s. There is supposed to work in the range of terahertz (THz) and is designed to provide data transmission rates is up to one terabit per second which is hundred time faster than 5G (Huynh & Huh, 2021). Such an increase in speed and bandwidth will enable content of ultra-high-definition, next-generation XR, and IoT demands of almost unimaginable scale. Key Features and Technologies of 6G.

- *Terahertz Communication:* Located in the range of 0. 1-10 THz, the 6G will be capable of delivering incredible bandwidth with low latency for applications such as high-density traffic in the urban area and real time augmented reality and holography.
- *AI-Driven Networks:* 6G will involve the use of AI throughout the network structure with regards to self-organizing, self-healing and self-optimizing network. AI will make networks more intelligent and adaptive by improving the data routing, power usage, and resource utilizing in real time (Faye et al., 2024).
- *Edge and Quantum Computing:* 6G will adopt edge computing that will help in handling data near the source to enhance the speed of analysis. Also, the utilization of quantum computing can be implemented in 6G network giving data security along with higher computational facilities for solving various problems (Ahokangas et al., 2024).
- *Holographic and Extended Reality (XR):* AR, VR, and MR will further become mainstream in the 6G era owing to the increased density provided for them by 6G. Such applications will revolutionize communication, education, health care and entertainment as the simulated augmented environments will be real time and life-like (Borgianni et al., 2023).

- *Ubiquitous Sensing and Connectivity:* In 6G networks, it will be possible to integrate sensing systems which will include the sensing of the environment, people's health, and infrastructure. This ever-entwining network will be the basis for the emergence of smart cities, automobile mobility on own.

3. KEY ENABLING TECHNOLOGIES OF 6G FOR SMART CITIES

Some key technologies which have to be effectively harnessed to ensure that 6G fulfills the promise of making urban environments into smart cities include the following; There is also highlights that these enabling technologies not only extend the functionality of the urban infrastructure but also provide the foundation to the more coordinated and resilient urban system. In the following, we analyze how each of these technologies will contribute to the development of smart cities based on 6G (Strinati et al., 2024).

3.1. Terahertz Communication: Speed, Bandwidth, and Latency Improvements

Another unique characteristic of 6G is the use of the terahertz (THz) frequency bands which has data transfer rates of up to 1 Tbps. Such a drastic rise in speed proves critical to developing the next generation of applications that involve the transfer of huge chunks of data at the blink of an eye. The ability for smart cities will, therefore, be revolutionary as it will support URLLC and high throughput for highly complex tasks such as real-time DT, XR, and massive numbers of AVs (Trichias et al., 2024). There are also drastic decreases in latency with the transition to terahertz communication; it is estimated that 6G networks will achieve latency that can reach at most a few microseconds. In a smart city setting, many decisions may be required within minutes if not seconds for instance in traffic control or in responding to an incident. This speed and reliability will make it possible for different integrated systems to operate optimally and the smart city structure will continue to be effective in its operations regardless of prevailing conditions (Mahmood et al., 2020).

3.2. AI-Driven Networks: How AI and Machine Learning Will Optimize Network Management and Smart City Applications

Intelligent automation and optimization will be carried by AI and embedded in all the components of the communication system in 6G networks. In contrast with previous generations that implemented AI in particular use cases, 6G is going to incorporate the AI into the very core of the network providing features of self-optimization and self-repair. Such integration of AI and machine learning will help to design dynamic network management, where the resources can be adjusted in real-time hence can solve the problem of densely populated urban areas (Yrjölä et al., 2023). Automated functions in smart cities will eventually improve traffic flow, the maintenance of infrastructure, and a host of other factors that define a smart city. Artificial intelligence will involve in range identification out of billions of sensors and connected devices, thereby providing city administrators with a range of data to be used in decision-making concerning urban planning, energy use, and security. Besides, AI will be one of the main drivers to automate most routine operations in the cities, minimizing the need for human interferences, and managing city's resources more efficiently (Inomata et al., 2021). Due to the AI adaptive approach, new 6G networks will contribute to development of Intelligent Smart self-sufficient Cities.

3.3. Edge Computing: The Role of Edge Devices in Processing Data Closer to the Source for Real-Time Decision-Making

Another key technology that will influence the 6G networks is known as Edge computing especially concerning Smart cities. Classical models of cloud service virtualized services for computing in which users submit data to centralized processing centers which may take time and so hinder real time reactions. While, edge computing is a way of handling data near the source, which might be a sensor on an illuminating streetlamp, a camera at an intersection, or a smart meter in a constructing. Edge computing decreases the distance that data has to travel for analysis, and by doing so, decreases the latency meaning the time it takes for the data to be processed in real time which is essential in application that needs quick decision making (Antón-Haro et al., 2024).

In smart cities, Edge computing will become almost mandatory to support, for example, fully self-driving cars, which require processing of huge amounts of information as soon as possible in order to avoid hazards. It will also enable real time monitoring of the environment in terms of air quality, noise level or the use of water among others. Furthermore, edge devices can assist in the decentralization of some of the workloads from centralized cloud systems making urban networks more scalable and robust. With 6G envisaging AI and Machine learning at the edge, this will enable cities to function with improved local intelligence for decision making in order to improve efficiency as well as service delivery (Cordova Morales et al., 2023).

3.4. IoT and Sensor Networks: Expanding Connectivity and Intelligence Across Urban Infrastructure

The integration of IoT with the features of 6G facilitate an increased and improved connective layer of objects including billions of devices and sensors embedded in cities. These combined devices will be the 'neural network' of smart cities, constantly creating information that underpins choices and underpins numerous operations. Self-sensing traffic lights that change with real-time traffic conditions, self-regulating energy networks that continually adjust to supply and demand, and many others will be IoT-based and will be supported and driven by 6G-enabled smart cities. 6G networks will improve IoT by increasing device density; more devices by square kilometer hence improving the quality of the network. It will also create a smarter sensor network by the integration of AI with edge computing that will help in processing the data locally on the edge rather than continuously communicating with central systems (Zong et al., 2022). These advancements will result to gains in automation and optimization like intelligent garbage collection where collection routes are determined by collection information or the intelligent lighting systems where brightness is dependent on activity or weather. However, there will be higher level IoT applications that will be supported by 6G some of which include ubiquitous sensing in which sensors will be integrated into objects and environments.

Moreover, these sensors will monitor the physical state of a city and interact instantaneously with citizens and devices, providing services both intimate (personal) and contextual. This means that cities will be reactive and flexible according to each inhabitant's requirements, leading us into the intelligent smart connected city experience (Liu et al., 2022). It is expected that the major enabling technologies of 6G will co-work in constructing a resilient and intelligent infrastructure for smart cities. Terahertz communication will provide the high speed and bandwidth needed to support demanding applications, with AI-powered networks and edge computing minimizing delays and enabling real-time decision-making. At the same time, a broader number of IoT and sensor networks will enable cities to be more continuously tracked and managed with higher precision. Collectively, these technologies are going to form the building blocks of the smart cities of tomorrow, including connectivity, intelligence, and sustainability.

4. APPLICATIONS OF 6G IN SMART CITIES

With the increasing complexity and connectivity of cities, 6G networking is going to be crucial for transforming urban services. 6G will usher in a new era of smart cities, built to leverage the power of real-time data and improved communication on everything from intelligent transportation systems to more sophisticated environmental monitoring. Following are the major applications of 6G in smart cities:

4.1. Intelligent Transportation Systems: Autonomous Vehicles, Smart Traffic Management, and Vehicle-to-Everything (V2X) Communication

In fact, it will revolutionize how 6G technology is seamlessly integrated into auto and traffic systems that make up a large share of total energy consumption within smart cities, where autonomous vehicles and traffic management will be at the forefront in making solutions effective. 6G technology will be able to deliver ultra-low latency and high-speed communication that will allow vehicles to partake in vehicle-to-everything (V2X) interactions, via which cars can communicate with other cars, infrastructure, pedestrians, as well as other networks in real-time. The ability to share data on the fly, such as traffic information and road conditions, will create an even smarter network of autonomous cars that will, in theory, make driving a lot less dangerous.

6G capacity will extend to smart traffic management as well. With AI and real-time data analytics playing a significant role in 6G networks, adaptive traffic systems in future highways will be able to optimize signal timings, reduce congestion, and improve overall traffic flow. These systems will be able to monitor and react to real-time circumstances, changing routes and signals on the fly in response to traffic incidents or emergencies. Some of these advancements in intelligence can result in reduced drive time — not to mention reduced pollution and energy consumption by reducing idling or stop-start driving (Porambage et al., 2021).

4.2. Urban Planning and Smart Infrastructure: Real-Time Monitoring, Digital Twins, and Adaptive Infrastructure

6G technology will bring about massive changes in urban planning and infrastructure management by merging real-time data with digital twins. These digital twins—essentially virtual replicas of real-world urban environments—will run on 6G networks and help city planners track infrastructure performance and visualize the outcome of proposed changes for better land-use planning. These digital twins will be updated in real-time through data being shared from sensors, providing reliable information that can then be used for construction, maintenance, or disaster management (Suyama et al., 2022). In addition, 6G will give us adaptive infrastructure that can change its basic characteristics in response to changing conditions. Smart buildings will, for instance, automatically adjust lighting, heat, and ventilation in real-time based on occupancy and weather data to reduce energy consumption and operational costs. Smart utilities, such as water and energy distribution systems, will be able to regulate supply and demand effectively, reduce wastage, and provide uninterrupted service using predictive analytics. Additionally, detailed information on population migration, primary use, and environmental impact would enable better urban planning with the help of 6G. This data will support planners in creating cities with a higher quality of life and more sustainability, allowing better use of space, public transportation systems, and green areas (Norp et al., 2024).

4.3. Public Safety and Emergency Response: Enhanced Communication Networks for First Responders and Smart Surveillance Systems

For higher-order emergency situations and public safety, ultra-high-speed and real-time networks suitable for quick and coordinated implementation will be possible through 6G. In emergencies, the local response to critical information needs instant access, like live location tracking, medical data, or situation awareness. With 6G, ultra-reliable low-latency communication (URLLC) will make it possible to securely pass this information between different branches of government and devices. Using AI-driven tools, smart wearables, and augmented reality (AR) interfaces for real-time guidance will facilitate quick action by first responders when dealing with high-pressure situations. 6G will also introduce major improvements in smart surveillance systems to enhance urban security using high-definition video analytics and artificial intelligence. The software will include real-time facial recognition, crowd monitoring, and anomaly detection, providing instant alerts to potential threats or suspicious behavior. Additionally, 6G networks will be critical for enabling large-scale deployment of drones and robots, particularly for surveillance, search and rescue missions, and hazard detection, ensuring faster and safer operations (Inomata et al., 2021).

4.4. Environmental Monitoring and Sustainability: Smart Grids, Pollution Control, and Efficient Resource Management

This shows sustainability is also the main priority for today's cities, and 6G technology will help in keeping a sustainable environment. 6G, powered by expansive IoT (internet of things) networks and advanced sensing functionalities, will allow real-time environmental monitoring. Smart grids will balance energy production and consumption in real-time, allowing renewable forms of energy to be integrated more effectively and reducing reliance on fossil fuels. This will result in a robust, sustainable energy grid. The power capabilities of 6G are also well-suited to pollution control. Real-time sensors, deployed throughout cities to track air and water quality, will take this data to the next step by offering actionable insights about pollution. Smart waste management systems will optimize collection routes with real-time data, minimizing fuel usage and therefore emissions. Further, 6G-driven analytics will project environmental adjustments that a city needs to plan for, such as optimized water distribution in drought conditions or smart cooling systems to reduce excessive heat during prolonged heat waves. It will also enhance efficient resource management in sectors like agriculture, water, and energy (Mohapatra et al., 2023). For example, more accurate monitoring and control provided by 6G networks can help cities become much better at resource management, cutting wastage and building on sustainability initiatives. In effect, 6G-enabled sensors across urban farms will enable precision agriculture, including soil health monitoring, enhanced irrigation practices, and better crop yields. This implies that the scope of 6G applications and services across various urban sectors contribute significantly to transforming cities into smarter, livable, and sustainable communities. 6G will empower real-time communication and data-driven insights through advanced automation to create new dimensions for urban living, benefiting both the quality of life for residents and the operational efficiency needed in city management.

4.5. Transition From 5G to 6G Based Smart City

Moving from the 5G to the 6G in smart city applications is a unique and challenging process. Some of the world's cities have already begun trials of 6G technologies to support better connection of individuals and organizations, optimize the delivery of public services, and manage data in real time. For instance, Helsinki has initiated a smart city programme in which 6G testbeds are employed to facilitate high-speed links between sensors, vehicles and the environment. For instance, the city of Shanghai has adopted 5G to manage traffic with plans to switch to 6G for better control of autonomous vehicles and traffic flow. These projects show how the next generation of network – 6G – could help to enhance the workings of smart cities. Nonetheless, there are several challenges, including the demand for significant capital expenditure to develop infrastructure and the issue of data protection. When cities grow to have 6G or even 6G, there are new conditions that will require new approaches to regulation.

Current rules on spectrum management and privacy are a crucial factor that needs to change for 6G to be implemented effectively. One of the key themes being explored by many governments is spectrum management, as 6G will require even higher frequencies than 5G, which could cause problems with other technologies. New rules are also considering cybersecurity where data flow would be enhanced in 6G connected cities to ensure that it doesn't pose a threat to public safety. South Korea and the United States have started working on their 6G policies that assume a world where connectivity is always seamless but such policies require a delicate touch lest they hamper innovation. Also, governments and private organizations must work together to outline the guidelines that will govern 6G infrastructure. This is because, to meet the international interconnectivity of the 6G system, these regulations must be consistent across various regions. Despite this, there are still aspects which offer great opportunities, yet present challenges in the development of 6G for smart cities.

5. PROPOSED 6G-ENABLED SMART CITY MODEL

6G technology, when implemented into smart cities, calls for an all-encompassing modular and adaptive design that integrates advanced communication technologies with the urban infrastructure. The next section explains a 6G-based smart city model, proposing and elaborating on the system architecture, data flow and processing, a conceptual use case, as well as discussing issues related to scalability and adaptability (Mohapatra et al., 2023).

5.1. System Architecture: Overview of the Components

A 6G-enabled smart city requires its system architecture to have three main parts: network layers, devices, and control systems. They combine to offer a continuum of networked data transmission, immediate information analysis, and informed decision-making. Smart City of 6G is illustrated in Fig and Table 1.

$$\text{Bandwidth (B)} = \text{Frequency Bandwidth (F)} \times \text{Spectral Efficiency } (\eta) \quad (1)$$

$$\text{Latency (L)} = \text{Propagation Delay} + \text{Processing Delay} + \text{Queueing Delay} \quad (2)$$

$$\text{Throughput (T)} = \text{Bandwidth} \times \log_2\left(1 + \frac{\text{Signal Power}}{\text{Noise Power}}\right) \quad (3)$$

Table 1. Components of the 6G-enabled smart city architecture

Component	Description
Network Layers	Includes the Terahertz (THz) communication layer, AI-driven network management, and edge computing infrastructure.
Edge Devices	Devices such as sensors, cameras, and IoT nodes that collect and process data at the edge of the network.
Data Aggregators	Centralized and decentralized systems that gather, analyze, and store data from various sources across the city.
Control Systems	AI-based systems that make real-time decisions and manage urban services, including traffic management, public safety, and infrastructure maintenance.

Figure 1. System architecture of a 6G-Enabled smart city

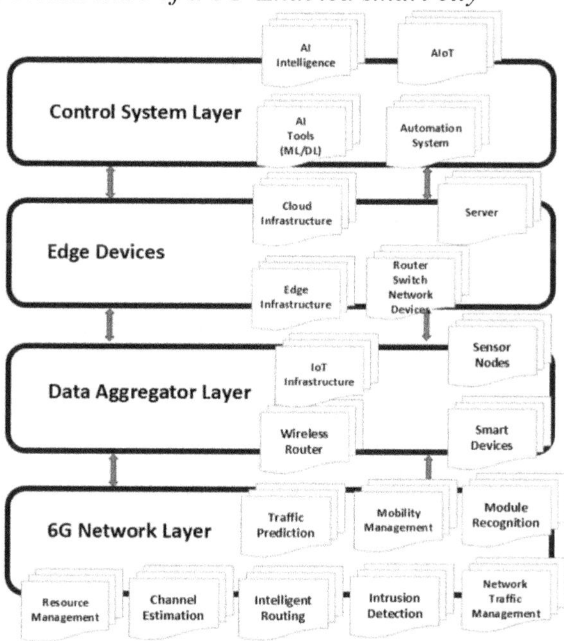

5.2. Data Flow and Processing: How Data Is Collected, Processed, and Utilized in Real-Time

Like running an efficient city management protocol on data in a 6G-capable smart city. The process involves multiple stages (Table 2).

1. **Data Collection:** Collected from diverse sources such as IoT sensors, surveillance cameras, traffic management systems, and environmental monitors. The data these devices generate is wirelessly transmitted to the edge nodes and central servers via 6G networks.
2. **Real-Time Processing:** Edge computing for real-time processing reduces latency so that you can take real-time action on the given data. The data is processed, and AI algorithms extract actionable insights (Stojanovska et al., 2018).

Table 2. Data processing stages and technologies

Stage	Description	Technologies
Data Collection	Gathering data from sensors and devices.	IoT Sensors, Cameras, Wearables
Real-Time Processing	Immediate analysis of data at the edge.	Edge Computing, AI Algorithms
Data Aggregation	Combining and storing data from multiple sources.	Centralized Data Hubs, Cloud Storage
Utilization	Using processed data for managing city services and operations.	AI Control Systems, Analytics

3. **Data Aggregation:** Processed data from edge devices is aggregated at centralized data hubs for further analysis. This aggregation helps in maintaining a holistic view of city operations and supports long-term planning.
4. **Utilization:** The data analyzed by the system can be used to drive urban services, including traffic control, public safety, and incident response. These data-driven control systems can be automated by AI, which makes decisions from the data, optimizing city operations and improving the quality of life for citizens.

5.3. Case Study Example: A Conceptual Smart City Ecosystem Illustrating the Role of 6G

For example, Smart City 2030 demonstrates how 6G technology would reinvent an urban environment of the future (Uusitalo et al., 2021). Showing how the technology would be applied in practice, one of its subsections is dedicated to the city that hosts different smart services, all powered by 6G (Ref: Fig. 2).

Figure 2. Conceptual layout of smart city 2030

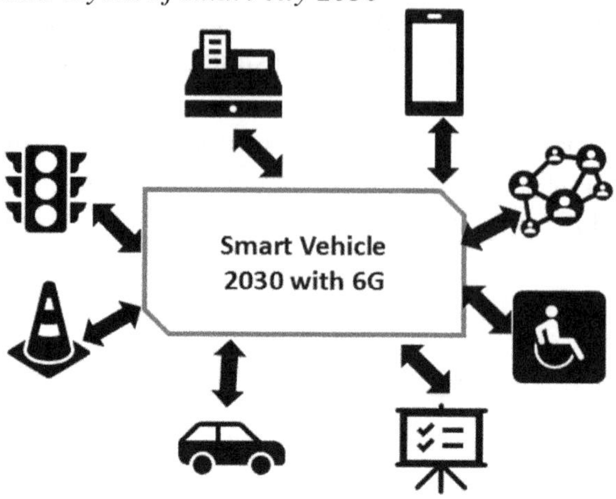

Table 3. Key features of smart city 2030

Feature	Description
Autonomous Vehicles	Self-driving cars with real-time V2X communication, improving safety and efficiency.
Smart Traffic Management	Dynamic traffic signals and adaptive routing based on real-time data analysis.
Smart Infrastructure	Real-time monitoring of buildings and utilities for optimized management and maintenance.
Public Safety Systems	AI-driven surveillance and emergency response systems for enhanced security and faster incident resolution.

Components:

- **Autonomous Vehicles:** 6G enables mixed-traffic (manned, self-driving, or tethered caravan) with vehicle-to-vehicle and vehicle-to-infrastructure communication for safer and smoother traffic.
- **Smart Traffic Management:** V2I communication and AI enable traffic lights to adjust themselves on the fly, reducing congestion and increasing the efficiency of public transportation.
- **Smart Infrastructure:** Buildings and infrastructure are embedded with sensors using digital twins that monitor and manage energy use, structural health, and maintenance.

5.4. Scalability and Flexibility: Designing a System That Adapts to Different City Sizes and Needs

The potential of a 6G-enabled smart city model needs to be designed and implemented with flexibility in terms of scaling to fit various city sizes and requirements. Key considerations include:

1. *Modular Architecture:* The solution can be designed with modular components that are customizable to fit cities of all sizes and needs. This allows for a phased rollout and adaptation.
2. *Adaptive Network Management:* 6G networks must support dynamic resource allocation and automatic optimization to handle different load conditions. AI-driven management systems can adjust network parameters in real-time based on usage patterns.
3. *Customizable Solutions:* Cities face different challenges and priorities. These customizable solutions should adapt to specific needs, such as traffic management in busy areas or environmental monitoring in industrial zones.
4. *Integration with Legacy Systems:* The technology must integrate with existing infrastructure, ensuring smooth communication and migration for higher efficiency, while coexisting with legacy systems.

Table 4. Design considerations for scalability and flexibility

Aspect	Consideration
Modular Architecture	Enables incremental deployment and adaptation to different city sizes.
Adaptive Management	Dynamic resource allocation and real-time optimization based on network conditions.
Customizable Solutions	Tailored applications to meet specific city needs and priorities.
Legacy Integration	Compatibility with existing systems to facilitate a smooth transition and integration.

The smart city model in which 6G will be integrated appears to comprise communication solutions and urban infrastructure as an integrated system architecture. Centered around real-time data processing, adaptive management, and scalability, this model illustrates how 6G could leverage future smart city applications, empowering rapid urban developments in living and operations.

6. CHALLENGES AND CONSIDERATIONS

This lays the groundwork for 6G technology to bring about game-changing evolutions in smart cities, but there are many challenges and considerations to tackle in order to successfully realize these changes. These consist of technological challenges, data privacy and security issues, regulatory landscapes as well as wider economic and social implications. All these components have a fundamental part in the building and shaping of future cities (Garg et al., 2023). Some challenges that may hinder the deployment of 6G are within the realms of regulation, digital divide, and security. Regulatory constraints on the part of the governments might pose a threat to the approval and launching of the technology which may take time. It will also be crucial for the future since not every person will have the means to get an access to 6G technology. Cybersecurity threats are another key challenge, as more complex networks are at greater risk of being compromised. To overcome these problems, the government can reduce complexities of policies and encourage the rapid implementation. In this regard, the collaboration between public and private sectors can contribute to the elimination of the digital gap and make 6G available to everyone. Furthermore, the implementation of standard cybersecurity protocols and periodic checks will secure 6G systems in smart cities.

6.1. Technical Challenges: Network Deployment, Infrastructure Readiness, and Interoperability with Legacy Systems

- *Network Deployment:* Building a 6G network presents significant technical challenges, especially concerning the creation and installation of base stations. The use of terahertz (THz) frequencies introduces the need for novel antenna and base station designs to operate at these higher frequencies. To maintain high-speed, low-latency connections, a dense deployment of these components is required across urban areas. Additionally, ensuring consistent network coverage in both densely populated and less developed regions pose logistical and engineering difficulties.
- *Infrastructure Readiness:* Many cities currently lack the infrastructure needed to support the advanced requirements of 6G technology. Upgrading or replacing outdated infrastructure to accommodate new technologies, such as advanced fiber optics and high-frequency antennas, requires significant investment and planning. This includes both physical upgrades to existing infrastructure and the integration of new technologies.
- *Interoperability with Legacy Systems:* A major challenge is ensuring that new 6G systems can effectively interact with existing legacy systems. Many cities rely on older communication technologies and infrastructures that may not be

immediately compatible with 6G. Developing solutions that ensure seamless interoperability between new and existing systems is crucial to avoid disruptions and guarantee a smooth transition (Nguyen et al., 2022).

6.2. Data Privacy and Security: Managing Data Ethically While Ensuring Robust Cybersecurity

The importance of data protection and cyber security is paramount to the implementation of the 6G in smart cities. For the sixth generation of networks, the number of connected devices is expected to grow by several orders of magnitude, including traffic lights and household appliances. This leads to more data and more potential targets for cyber criminals to attack. This is because of the increased cases of hacking and soring of personal information. If not protected then the confidential data can be mishandled. This is because encryption and secure networks are crucial to avoid breaches. Thus, governments and companies have to set up strong security measures and policies. This will foster trust in smart cities as they expand with the 6G technology for data privacy.

- *Managing Data Ethically:* With sensors and data recording tools sprouting all over a smart city, running on 6G, managing information ethically becomes crucial. Ensuring that data is collected, stored, and processed in a way that respects individuals' privacy rights is essential. Building public trust requires transparency in data practices, clear consent processes, and user access controls, in line with emerging privacy regulations (Abdel Hakeem et al., 2022).
- *Robust Cybersecurity:* The improvement in networks like 6G will also bring strengthened connectivity and increased data flow, which could attract cyberattacks. Robust cybersecurity measures are critical to protecting personal data and ensuring smart city operations. This includes advanced encryption methods, real-time threat detection systems, and ongoing security checks to prevent breaches and unauthorized access.

6.3. Regulatory and Policy Frameworks: The Role of Governments and International Bodies in Setting Standards and Guiding Development

The role of 6G in smart cities is very promising for sustainability and socioeconomic change since 6G networks can contribute to the implementation of green technologies that save energy and increase the effectiveness of city management. Advanced utility networks such as smart grids, enhanced transportation systems, and IoT-based waste management have the potential to reduce wastage greatly. Nonetheless, the socioeconomic effects may be positive or negative. On the job front, 6G can be seen to open up new avenues for employment in the tech and service sectors but it can also deepen the digital divide between those who are well connected and those who are not. There may also be worries that with connectivity, privacy and data protection may be at risk. For the sustainability, it is crucial that every citizen gains from these developments in the same manner.

- *Government Role:* Governments are central to creating regulatory and policy frameworks that ensure the safe and fair deployment of 6G technologies. This includes setting standards for network performance, data protection, and environmental impact. Governments should also engage resources through research and development programs or financial incentives to accelerate the implementation of 6G technologies.
- *International Standards:* Developing 6G technology is a global undertaking, requiring coordination between international bodies and industry stakeholders. Organizations like the International Telecommunication Union (ITU) and various standards organizations are responsible for creating global standards to ensure compatibility and interoperability across regions. Collaborative efforts are necessary to develop comprehensive guidelines that address the complexities of 6G networks (Antón-Haro et al., 2024).

6.4. Economic and Social Impact: The Implications of 6G on Employment, Digital Equity, and Citizen Well-Being

- *Employment:* The transition to 6G technology will greatly impact employment. While it will create new opportunities in fields such as network engineering, data analytics, and cybersecurity, it may also eliminate roles tied to older technologies. To minimize the negative effects, education and retraining programs will be crucial in helping workers adapt and succeed in this evolving job market.
- *Digital Equity:* Given 6G's high speeds, it can help bridge digital divides in underserved areas. However, digital equity is essential to ensure that all layers of society can access the benefits of 6G. This involves addressing disparities in technology access, affordability, and digital literacy. Policymakers must prioritize inclusive strategies to provide fair access to 6G services and infrastructure (Cordova Morales et al., 2023).
- *Citizen Well-Being:* Enhanced connectivity and smart services from 6G will improve healthcare, transportation, and public services, contributing to better citizen well-being. However, concerns around privacy, surveillance, and the

digital divide must be carefully managed. Ensuring that technology is used to improve quality of life while protecting individual rights is key.

While 6G technology promises revolutionary benefits for smart cities, addressing technical challenges, data privacy, security, regulatory frameworks, and social and economic impacts is crucial for successful implementation. By tackling these challenges, cities can leverage 6G to build connected, efficient, and equitable urban environments.

7. FUTURE TRENDS AND INNOVATIONS

When we consider the broader changes 6G technology will bring, it is evident that future cities and societies will be fundamentally informed by an array of novel trends and breakthroughs. These developments have the potential to deeply change the way we interact with technology and one another. We explore some of the most promising trends on the horizon, such as quantum communication, brain-computer interfaces, and AI-powered governance, and consider how 6G may continue to redefine urban life and modern societies at large.

7.1. Emerging Trends

- *Quantum Communication:* Quantum communication is a breakthrough in secure communications. By leveraging principles like entanglement and superposition from quantum mechanics, it offers unparalleled security. Unlike classical methods, quantum systems can detect eavesdroppers, ensuring that data remains secure. As 6G networks evolve, integrating quantum communication could boost data protection and privacy, adding a new layer of security for both personal and institutional communications (Ravikumar et al., 2024).
- *Brain-Computer Interfaces (BCIs):* Brain-computer interfaces work by translating brain activity into commands, allowing users to control devices or machines. These interfaces could enable users to operate smart devices, navigate virtual environments, or even communicate telepathically. For smart cities, BCIs could revolutionize accessibility, enabling individuals with disabilities to interact more seamlessly with their surroundings. The integration of BCIs with 6G networks would allow real-time, high-bandwidth communication between the brain and digital systems, opening new possibilities for both personal and professional applications (Inomata et al., 2024).
- *AI-Driven Governance*: The future of urban governance will be built around Artificial Intelligence (AI). AI-driven systems can analyze large datasets to

make data-backed decisions, optimize resource management, and predict trends. In smart cities, AI could help manage traffic, reduce energy consumption, and support emergency responses and public health. By harnessing AI's data processing capabilities, city administrators can make more precise and efficient decisions, improving urban management and quality of life (Liu et al., 2022).

7.2. Continuous Advancements in 6G

- *Redefining Urban Living:* As 6G technology evolves, it will make cities smarter and more interactive. Enhanced connectivity will support advanced applications like real-time augmented reality (AR) and virtual reality (VR) experiences, increasing the interactivity of urban spaces. For example, AR could help residents by projecting navigation information onto their surroundings or enabling virtual community events. 6G's faster data speeds and reduced latency will also allow seamless integration of smart devices into real-time urban response systems (Ma et al., 2023).
- *Transforming Societal Structures:* As 6G advances, societal structures will shift. Remote work and digital collaboration will become more common, potentially reshaping traditional workspaces and social interactions. Telepresence and real-time data analysis will enhance personalized education and healthcare. Additionally, 6G innovations could drive sustainable urban planning and climate resilience, contributing to more livable and environmentally friendly cities (Singh et al., 2023).
- *Innovation Ecosystems:* The convergence of 6G with emerging technologies will create new innovation ecosystems. Collaboration between tech companies, universities, and government bodies will be essential to address integration challenges and ensure these technologies benefit society in a sustainable and equitable way (Norp et al., 2024).

Urban living and societal structures will be shaped by a range of groundbreaking technologies. As 6G continues to develop, it will evolve beyond current smart city applications, enabling new forms of interaction and governance. Cities embracing these trends will create connected, efficient, and inclusive environments, improving the quality of life for all residents (Kumar Singh et al., 2021).

8. CONCLUSION AND FUTURE SCOPE

This conclusion ties back to the topic "6G Technology: A Game-Changer for Smart Cities" We hope that we were able to create an image in your mind about how much this next-generation of a network holds potential. The incorporation of 6G in urban areas signifies a great stride towards better connectivity, efficiency, and innovation. 6G will enable ultra-fast data transmission, low latency communication and next generation networks for new era of technology usage and city management. One of the next areas that 6G technology plans to tackle are smart cities, enabling a whole new level of connectivity and data processing. It will provide the infrastructure for real-time interaction and smart decision-making as technology continues to progress, e.g., terahertz communication, AI-driven networks. These will create the way for smarter infrastructure, renewable energy grid and overall enhance life quality of its residents. 6G, affecting everything from autonomous vehicles and smart traffic systems to advanced healthcare and environmental monitoring.

Thoughts on Cross-Industry Collaboration and Forward-Looking Policies

It is important to mandate new rules default settings, that push us forward and no back. 6G networks pose many a challenge, which must be met by the concerted efforts of technology providers, city planners, regulatory bodies and academic institutions. By working together, we can ensure that technology is deployed responsibly to maximize the benefits and minimize the potential harms in terms of privacy, security, and digital equity. In addition, we need to develop forward-looking policies and standards to ensure that the emerging technologies and architectures respond effectively to future needs. Such policies should include issues such as privacy-by-design principles, which are particularly relevant in 6G when data assimilation will come from a large variety of sources. Policies should also be developed on protectionism vs. global integration, innovation promotion measures with regards to economic behavior (such as patents), access and divide issues (as technology advances between generations are always uneven) or flexible spectrum licensing. Finally, and very important, regulatory agencies must be able to keep pace the technological evolution so that regulations can be adopted before technology arrives not after.

Preparing for the 6G Era

With the advent of 6G, it is important that strategic planning and continued research efforts are made to fully capitalize on its potential. Stakeholders should allocate funds for 6G infrastructure, R&D, and education in preparation for these technological revolutions, including:

- *Strategic Planning:* Develop overall plans to incorporate CoG technologies within current and future urban infrastructures, where broad domains to address will be recognized as well as potential challenges.
- *Research and Development:* This shall encompass ongoing research on 6G technologies and their applications along with stimulating AI innovations in the areas of network design, security, and user experience. This also includes promoting such developments in applications based on AI systems.
- *Workforce Training:* Ensure that the workforce is ready and able to effectively manage and operate using new 6G technologies. Develop training programs, and educational assistance programs to support professionals in adapting to their changing technology environment.

REFERENCES

Abdel Hakeem, S. A., Hussein, H. H., & Kim, H. (2022). Security requirements and challenges of 6G technologies and applications. *Sensors (Basel)*, 22(5), 1969. DOI: 10.3390/s22051969 PMID: 35271113

Ahokangas, P., Matinmikko-Blue, M., Basaure, A., & Yrjölä, S. (2024). Use cases for local 6G networks. *2024 Joint European Conference on Networks and Communications & 6G Summit (EuCNC/6G Summit)*, 1127-1132. https://doi.org/ DOI: 10.1109/EuCNC/6GSummit60053.2024.10597019

Akgul, O. U., Ericson, M., Burguera, P. G., Arar, B., Khorsandi, B. M., Querio, R., Varvara, A., Harkous, H., Wänstedt, S., Groshev, M., De la Oliva, A., Pieczerak, J., Kukliński, S., Nande, S. S., Bassoli, R., & Fitzek, F. H. (2024). Discussion on 6G architecture evolution: Challenges and emerging technology trends. *2024 Joint European Conference on Networks and Communications & 6G Summit (EuCNC/6G Summit)*, 664-669. https://doi.org/DOI: 10.1109/EuCNC/6GSummit60053.2024.10597056

Antón-Haro, C., Trichias, K., De Majo, C., Kaloxylos, A., & Beriere, J. (2024). 6G smart networks and services: Global strategies, main work directions & Future outlook. *2024 Joint European Conference on Networks and Communications & 6G Summit (EuCNC/6G Summit)*, 1115-1120. https://doi.org/DOI: 10.1109/EuCNC/6GSummit60053.2024.10597046

Borgianni, L., Adami, D., & Giordano, S. (2023). Optimizing network performance and reliability with an integrated SD-WAN and satellite 6G architecture. *2023 2nd International Conference on 6G Networking (6GNet), 21*, 1-4. https://doi.org/DOI: 10.1109/6GNet58894.2023.10317704

Cordova Morales, D. A., Nguyen, T., & Pujolle, G. (2023). Towards a blockgraph-based trustless authentication scheme for future 6G technology. *2023 2nd International Conference on 6G Networking (6GNet)*. https://doi.org/DOI: 10.1109/6GNet58894.2023.10317665

Faye, S., Camelo, M., Sottet, J., Sommer, C., Franke, M., Baudouin, J., Castellanos, G., Decorme, R., Fanti, M. P., Fuladi, R., Kesik, G., Mendes, B., Murphy, C., Parker, S., Pryor, S., Senouci, S. M., & Turcanu, I. (2024). Integrating network digital twinning into future AI-based 6G systems: The 6G-TWIN vision. *2024 Joint European Conference on Networks and Communications & 6G Summit (EuCNC/6G Summit)*, 883-888. https://doi.org/DOI: 10.1109/EuCNC/6GSummit60053.2024.10597058

Garg, S., Kaur, K., Aujla, G. S., Kaddoum, G., Garigipati, P., & Guizani, M. (2023). Trusted explainable AI for 6G-Enabled edge cloud ecosystem. *IEEE Wireless Communications*, 30(3), 163–170. DOI: 10.1109/MWC.016.220047

Huynh, L. N., & Huh, E. (2021). Envisioning edge computing in future 6G wireless networks. *2021 Fifth World Conference on Smart Trends in Systems Security and Sustainability (WorldS4)*, 307-311. https://doi.org/DOI: 10.1109/WorldS451998.2021.9514026

Inomata, M., Yamada, W., Kuno, N., Sasaki, M., Kitao, K., Nakamura, M., Ishikawa, H., & Oda, Y. (2021). Terahertz propagation characteristics for 6G mobile communication systems. *2021 15th European Conference on Antennas and Propagation (EuCAP)*. https://doi.org/DOI: 10.23919/EuCAP51087.2021.9411143

Kumar Singh, S., Pan, Y., & Hyuk Park, J. (2021). OTS scheme based secure architecture for energy-efficient IoT in edge infrastructure. *Computers, Materials & Continua*, 66(3), 2905–2922. DOI: 10.32604/cmc.2021.014151

Liu, H., Zong, J., Wang, Q., Liu, Y., & Yang, F. (2022). Cloud native based intelligent RAN architecture towards 6G programmable networking. *2022 7th International Conference on Computer and Communication Systems (ICCCS)*. https://doi.org/DOI: 10.1109/ICCCS55155.2022.9846266

Ma, G., Khalili, M., Parthiban, R., & Katz, M. (2023). A low-complexity handover scheme using unsupervised learning techniques for 6G multi-networking. *2023 2nd International Conference on 6G Networking (6GNet), 101*, 1-5. https://doi.org/DOI: 10.1109/6GNet58894.2023.10317655

Mahmood, N. H., Alves, H., Lopez, O. A., Shehab, M., Osorio, D. P., & Latva-Aho, M. (2020). Six key features of machine type communication in 6G. *2020 2nd 6G Wireless Summit (6G SUMMIT)*. https://doi.org/DOI: 10.1109/6GSUMMIT49458.2020.9083794

Mohapatra, H., & Dalai, A. K. (2022). IoT based V2I framework for accident prevention. *2022 2nd International Conference on Artificial Intelligence and Signal Processing (AISP), 0*, 1-4. https://doi.org/DOI: 10.1109/AISP53593.2022.9760623

Mohapatra, H., Mohanta, B. K., Nikoo, M. R., Daneshmand, M., & Gandomi, A. H. (2023). MCDM-based routing for IoT-enabled smart water distribution network. *IEEE Internet of Things Journal*, 10(5), 4271–4280. DOI: 10.1109/JIOT.2022.3216402

Nguyen, D. C., Ding, M., Pathirana, P. N., Seneviratne, A., Li, J., Niyato, D., Dobre, O., & Poor, H. V. (2022). 6G Internet of things: A comprehensive survey. *IEEE Internet of Things Journal*, 9(1), 359–383. DOI: 10.1109/JIOT.2021.3103320

Norp, T., Sachdeva, P., Anton, C., Trichias, K., & Mohnani, P. (2024). 6G research & Innovation activities in Europe: An overview of EU & Nationally funded programmes. *2024 Joint European Conference on Networks and Communications & 6G Summit (EuCNC/6G Summit)*, 1109-1114. https://doi.org/DOI: 10.1109/EuCNC/6GSummit60053.2024.10597076

Pires, R., Blue, H., Malinen, J., De Angelis, M., Giardina, P. G., Landi, G., Laukkanen, M., Ahola, K., & Porambage, P. (2024). Closed-loop automation in 6G for minimum downtime task continuity in surveillance Cobots. *2024 Joint European Conference on Networks and Communications & 6G Summit (EuCNC/6G Summit)*, 860-865. https://doi.org/DOI: 10.1109/EuCNC/6GSummit60053.2024.10597048

Porambage, P., Gur, G., Moya Osorio, D. P., Livanage, M., & Ylianttila, M. (2021). 6G security challenges and potential solutions. *2021 Joint European Conference on Networks and Communications & 6G Summit (EuCNC/6G Summit)*. https://doi.org/DOI: 10.1109/EuCNC/6GSummit51104.2021.9482609

Ravikumar, S. S., Betgeri, S., & Singh, S. K. (2024). Strategies for mitigating security concerns in IoT-enabled smart cities. *Advances in Computational Intelligence and Robotics*, 239-273. https://doi.org/DOI: 10.4018/979-8-3693-2373-1.ch012

Singh, S. K., Yang, L. T., & Park, J. H. (2023). FusionFedBlock: Fusion of blockchain and federated learning to preserve privacy in industry 5.0. *Information Fusion*, 90, 233–240. DOI: 10.1016/j.inffus.2022.09.027

Siriwardhana, Y., Porambage, P., Liyanage, M., & Ylianttila, M. (2021). AI and 6G security: Opportunities and challenges. *2021 Joint European Conference on Networks and Communications & 6G Summit (EuCNC/6G Summit)*. https://doi.org/DOI: 10.1109/EuCNC/6GSummit51104.2021.9482503

Stojanovska, S., Madzova, V., & Matlievska, M. (2018). The impact of human capital on sustainable growth - The case of Republic of Macedonia. *Knowledge based sustainable economic development*, 884. https://doi.org/DOI: 10.31410/eraz.2018.884

Strinati, E. C., Di Lorenzo, P., Sciancalepore, V., Aijaz, A., Kountouris, M., Gündüz, D., Popovski, P., Sana, M., Stavrou, P. A., Soret, B., Cordeschi, N., Scardapane, S., Merluzzi, M., Zanzi, L., Renato, M. B., Quek, T., Pietro, N. D., Forceville, O., Costanzo, F., & Li, P. (2024). Goal-oriented and semantic communication in 6G AI-native networks: The 6G-GOALS approach. *2024 Joint European Conference on Networks and Communications & 6G Summit (EuCNC/6G Summit), 5*, 1-6. https://doi.org/DOI: 10.1109/EuCNC/6GSummit60053.2024.10597087

Suyama, S., Okuyama, T., Nonaka, N., & Asai, T. (2022). Recent studies on massive MIMO technologies for 5G evolution and 6G. *2022 IEEE Radio and Wireless Symposium (RWS)*. https://doi.org/DOI: 10.1109/RWS53089.2022.9719949

Toumi, N., & Dimitrovski, T. (2024). AI-native architecture for 6G networks and services with model dependencies. *2024 Joint European Conference on Networks and Communications & 6G Summit (EuCNC/6G Summit)*, 901-906. https://doi.org/DOI: 10.1109/EuCNC/6GSummit60053.2024.10597080

Trichias, K., Kaloxylos, A., & Willcock, C. (2024). 6G global landscape: A comparative analysis of 6G targets and technological trends. *2024 Joint European Conference on Networks and Communications & 6G Summit (EuCNC/6G Summit)*, 1-6. https://doi.org/DOI: 10.1109/EuCNC/6GSummit60053.2024.10597064

Uusitalo, M. A., Rugeland, P., Boldi, M. R., Strinati, E. C., Demestichas, P., Ericson, M., Fettweis, G. P., Filippou, M. C., Gati, A., Hamon, M., Hoffmann, M., Latva-Aho, M., Parssinen, A., Richerzhagen, B., Schotten, H., Svensson, T., Wikstrom, G., Wymeersch, H., Ziegler, V., & Zou, Y. (2021). 6G vision, value, use cases and technologies from European 6G flagship project Hexa-X. *IEEE Access : Practical Innovations, Open Solutions*, 9, 160004–160020. DOI: 10.1109/ACCESS.2021.3130030

Wang, C., You, X., Gao, X., Zhu, X., Li, Z., Zhang, C., Wang, H., Huang, Y., Chen, Y., Haas, H., Thompson, J. S., Larsson, E. G., Renzo, M. D., Tong, W., Zhu, P., Shen, X., Poor, H. V., & Hanzo, L. (2023). On the road to 6G: Visions, requirements, key technologies, and Testbeds. *IEEE Communications Surveys and Tutorials*, 25(2), 905–974. DOI: 10.1109/COMST.2023.3249835

Wang, Q., Liu, Y., Wang, Y., Xing, Y., Zong, J., & Liu, H. (2023). Deep edge node enables AI native toward 6G*. *2023 IEEE International Symposium on Broadband Multimedia Systems and Broadcasting (BMSB)*, 1-6. https://doi.org/DOI: 10.1109/BMSB58369.2023.10211613

Yrjölä, S., Matinmikko-Blue, M., & Ahokangas, P. (2023). Developing 6G visions with stakeholder analysis of 6G ecosystem. *2023 Joint European Conference on Networks and Communications & 6G Summit (EuCNC/6G Summit)*. https://doi.org/DOI: 10.1109/EuCNC/6GSummit58263.2023.10188379

Zong, J., Liu, Y., Liu, H., Wang, Q., & Chen, P. (2022). 6G cell-free network architecture. *2022 IEEE 2nd International Conference on Electronic Technology, Communication and Information (ICETCI)*. https://doi.org/DOI: 10.1109/ICETCI55101.2022.9832308

Chapter 10
Blockchain-Enabled 6G Security Architecture for Smart Cities:
A Decentralized and Resilient Approach

Rituraj Jain
https://orcid.org/0000-0002-5532-1245
Marwadi University, India

Kumar J. Parmar
https://orcid.org/0000-0002-2502-5680
Marwadi University, India

Damodharan Palaniappan
https://orcid.org/0009-0003-0721-3068
Marwadi University, India

T. Premavathi
https://orcid.org/0009-0003-0172-2021
Marwadi University, India

ABSTRACT

The next 6G technology is expected to change the face of smart cities by offering greater connectivity, faster and higher data transfer rates. A major advantage of using blockchain with 6G networks is the availability of a distributed immutable database to record transactions and data exchange. In the context of smart cities, this feature is very important to ensure the security of data transfer process through many IoT devices and systems. Through implementation of a system in which data

DOI: 10.4018/979-8-3693-8029-1.ch010

cannot be altered or deleted, blockchain increases the credibility and accountability of smart city management. The integration of blockchains with IoT devices especially in the smart cities is therefore helpful. IoT devices which are the foundation for smart cities are prone to cyber threats and malwares. The real-time anomaly detection and the pattern features analysis in machine learning algorithms help to identify the possible risks to safety in no time. Integrated with blockchains, these frameworks help in enhancing intrusion detection, privacy and silence.

1. INTRODUCTION

The current trends in growth such as the rapid urbanization and the need for optimum utilization of resources have created the smart cities. These cities adopt smart technologies including; the internet of things, Artificial intelligence, and cloud computing in urban planning, infrastructure, and public service delivery (Bhushan et al., 2020). However, the incorporation of these technologies has also brought about new risks or challenges in security because even as these technologies are integrated, their security cannot be solved by the normal security technologies (Wong et al., 2020). Blockchain technology has been regarded as one of the most efficient solutions for managing and ensuring security in smart city context. Blockchain characteristics like decentralisation, the ledger's inalterability, and visibility are well suited to the millions of devices and channels in smart cities. This chapter provides an overview to the blockchain-enabled 6G security architecture for smart cities as a paradigm to achieve decentralized and robust security of the key infrastructures and services.

Waving the potential of 6G, the future wireless communication technology, the proposed architecture aims at increasing the security level and performance of smart city applications. Due to the development of 6G with its added features such as higher bandwidth, lower latency, and better energy efficiency of network the voluminous data and the real-time nature of smart city applications become feasible (Wong et al., 2020). If this architecture is incorporated with the help of the blockchain technology with 6G, then the following advantages will be possible. Further, it will contribute to First, the decentralization of blockchain can help to avoid critical failure points and make the smart city's structure more secure. Second, the indestructibility and openness of records in blockchain can improve the data and or transaction trail and reduce uncertainties existing in a smart city.

The architecture comprises of different elements that include identity, data protection and sharing, and self-governing structures on the block chain. Essentially, the identity management system is based on the blockchain system to provide optimized and secure digital identify for each connected device, user, and service in the smart city. The secure data sharing and storage module includes the elements like smart contracts which regulate access to the data exchanged between citizens, government, and service providers and provide data integrity. Additionally, starting from the basic concept of deciding who governs a smart city, the use of the blockchain for decentralised decision-making improves the overall transparency and fairness of the decision-making process thus engaging more citizens in the process (Bagloee et al., 2021).

With this presented blockchain-enabled 6G security architecture for smart cities, smart cities can react to these changes proactively and provide citizens, businesses, and government agencies with an enhanced level of trust. Such prospects of this approach can be explained by modern researches that focus on the further application of the blockchain in the construction of smart cities. These studies have emphasized the potentials of blockchain in some sectors including data, regulation as well as collaboration, which are core to the advancement of smart city projects (Ahmad et al., 2021).

1.1 Overview of 6G Technology

6G which is the forthcoming generation of wireless communication technology is likely to revolutionize the advancement of smart cities. 6G holds the potential of better features including higher bandwidth space, improved latency and energy efficient than the existing 5G facilitating its applicability in the data and real-time requirements of smart city applications. 6G wireless technology is the next generation after 5G mobile technology and implies new functions that will affect several industries. This feature stands out for 6G: the peak data rate of 6G is expected to be 100 times faster than 5G, with an expected maximum value of 1 Tbps. This will allow for the smooth streaming of content of super high quality and cater for the high demand applications such as the virtual reality (VR) and augmented reality (AR) applications. Also, there is a significant emphasis on attaining sub-, ultra-, or even zero latency and ideally, the latency of 1 ms or less is required for the real-time applications as driving-cars, surgery, and the industry 4.0 and other demands for perfect quality of experience.

Looking at the architecture, there is belief that 6G Networks will have enhanced and more flexibility than the earlier generations. Overall, as part of this change, it will shift to a decentralised and cloud-first approach in order to provide a more efficient system of network orchestration. This will for instance facilitate timely resource management for handling large volumes of traffic. Similar to the 5G architecture, the 6G architecture will be based on a service-based approach so that the network functions are Software Defined Microservices. AI and machine learning will be applied to reserve the management of 6G networks to foresee fault, identify discrepancies and make necessary adjustments to improve network efficiency.

6G will then use better methods of spectrum sharing to ensure that as many frequencies as possible are fully utilized, some of the methods include dynamic spectrum access and cognitive radio. It will also connect the terrestrial networks with non-terrestrial networks which are satellites or High-Altitude Platforms for the global connectivity and support high mobility cases. Due to these complexities and connections in 6G network, there is the need to adopt high-level security measures. This comprises post-quantum cryptography, deep learning security, and communications encryption to enhance data security and privacy.

Figure 1 illustrates the holistic view of the future evolution path of 6G network architecture, with the presentation of various layers of infrastructure, control, and network elements. The Infrastructure View draws special attention to those components that will make for a 3D coverage of various environment. The Space Network leverages satellite communications such as LEO, GEO, and other sophisticated facilities comprising quantum repeaters and quantum channels. Of these, the Aerial Network shown below as High Altitude Platforms (HAP), drones, Unmanned Aerial Vehicles (UAVs), and aircraft collectively build a communication structure in the sky. At the terrestrial level, the Terrestrial Network consists of cellular towers and other supporting structures for the implementation of backscatter communication and satellite earth stations. The network continues underwater with the Undersea Network, applying optical/acoustic sensors & RF communication for data gather and transfer marine environments.

Figure 1. Overview of 6G Architecture

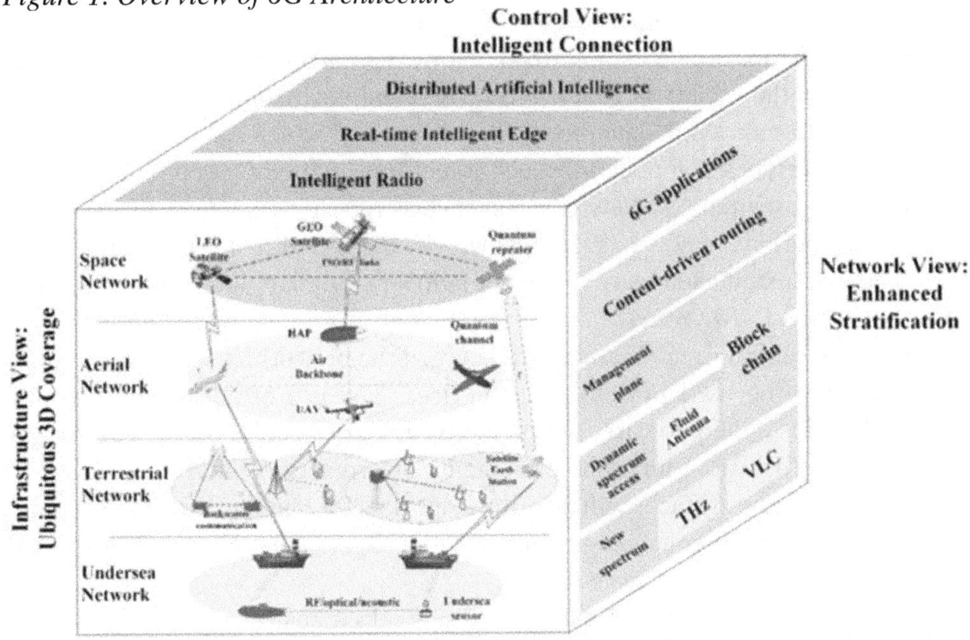

(Banafaa et al., 2023)

Immediately on top of this infrastructure, the Control View addresses where and how intelligence is processed. Distributed AI is likely to become a key driver of network functions, strategic decision making as well as data communication. Real-time Intelligent Edge computing will allow quick actions with the results in real time by computing the data near the edge. Applications of Intelligent Radio, for example software defined and cognitive radio, will define efficient usage of spectrum.

To the right, the Network View focuses on the exemplary applications starting with the next generation applications and services of 6G technology improvements. Content-driven routing will adapt to the current network conditions and the user traffic pattern, and blockchain will ensure secure and transparent messaging in decentralised systems. New wave communication technologies like THz (Terahertz) and VLC (Visible Light Communication) will open up spectrums for high-frequency data transmission. Recently proposed as an enhancement to cognitive radio, Dynamic Spectrum Access will allow the network to allocate and adapt usage of the spectrum for the best performance of the system, while the fluid antennas will be high modularity antennas optimized to change shape for the circumstances of a certain communication. The management plane controls aspects such as network performance, network security, and quality of service.

Some of the technologies depicted in figure 2 will help to enable 6G-a new generation of wireless communication. 6G wireless technology, which the following key enabling technologies described below, is paramount to advancing human experience and the society in general. Terahertz and visible light bands communications will offer ultrahigh data rates with low latency, which can be important for newly emerging types of applications such as real-time holographic communications and HD video streaming. A New Concept such as Massive MIMO (Multiple Input Multiple Output) also known as large-M MIMO the use of many antennas will be employed to transmit and receive a greater number of signals as a result increasing coverage in high traffic zones.

AI will be central in facilitating efficiency in the network, resource allocation, and it will also be used in delivering services. The use of advanced AI-based methodologies will help to carry out predictive maintenance, show deviations and make operating decisions for reliable and high-performance networks. Specifically, intelligent reflecting surfaces will be utilized as tools for manipulation of the signal waves and as means of enhancing communication signals in such signal-restrictive areas like urban areas, indoors, etc.

Finally, UAVs will be incorporated in 6G networks for carrying out missions that require timely and adaptive connectivity, especially in rural or disaster-hit regions. UAV can be used as mobile base stations by connecting to the network which will expand coverage of the networks as well as provide connectivity in areas without any fixed structures or after disaster. Each of these enabling technologies fully supports the enhanced characteristics of 6G which will inevitably transform communication and connection points in given areas.

Figure 2. Overview of 6G Enabled Technologies

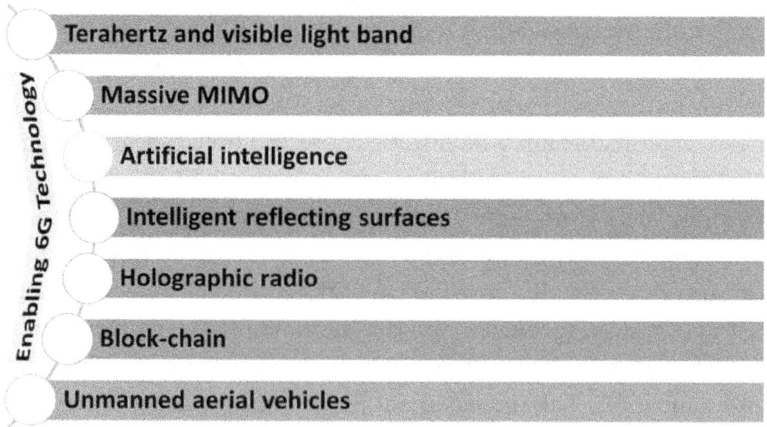

6G is envisioned to enable a wide range of innovative use cases, including (Bhushan et al., 2020) - 360 degree images and videos (Wong et al., 2020), Ultra-reliable Low Latency Communications for Mission Critical Applications (Gui et al., 2020). Better mobile broadband and internet of things provision (Adem et al., 2012). These capabilities can enhance smart city functions of traffic arrangements, emergency situations handling, and resource availability.

Secondly, 6G to be more autonomous and intelligent compared to its preceding generations and few technologies which are expected to be incorporated include artificial intelligence, quantum computing and other sensing technologies (Gui et al., 2020). 6G will build on these technologies for smooth connection, real-time analysis and self-organizing control in smart city (Adem et al., 2012).

According to recent research, some of the key features and goals of 6G include: According to recent research, some of the key features and goals of 6G include, providing end-to-end coverage and link reliability with ease of deployment in areas that were hitherto difficult to cover to support the deployment of IoT devices and sensors including in a smart city environment (Giordani et al., 2020).

Expected impact of 6G on smart cities: As has already been suggested, the application of 6G technology will help to redefine the development and functioning of smart cities. 6G's enhanced capabilities can revolutionize various aspects of smart city infrastructure, including:6G's enhanced capabilities can revolutionize various aspects of smart city infrastructure, including - Enhanced communication in real-time especially for essential services including disaster response, transportation systems as well as public security that will result to smarter decision and quicker problem solving (Chen et al., 2024). For instance, intelligent transportation systems, telemedicine, and augmented-reality, which are highly beneficial to citizens' quality of life mostly using autonomous vehicles. The improvement of resource utilization, energy distribution as well as efficient waste management strategies within the smart city environment. Greater energy utilization efficiency and improvements in the use of renewable energy resources for generation of electricity. Improvement of performance on data-greedy applications like video surveillance, augmented and virtual reality, and self-driving cars, that are crucial to smart city functionality (Chen et al., 2024).

However, the transition to 6G networks also gives some challenges that are necessary to meet with the goal of providing smart city security. Key security challenges in 6G networks include - Increased attack surface and vulnerability: Integration of new technologies such as AI and quantum computing in the devices along with more connected devices extend the attack surface and risk of cyber-attack in 6G (Trommler et al., 2022). Complexity and heterogeneity: The dynamism, highly interconnected and interdependent nature of 6G networks with various devices, applications, players and services could however pose certain challenges in ensuring that security is implemented in a coherent, optimal and effective manner (Wang et al., 2023). Privacy and data protection: The gigantic flow of information in smart city settings and the burgeoning cooperation and analysis of information with the help of enhanced 6G raises numerous knowledge privacy as well as data safety concerns (Jiang et al., 2021). Lack of trust and transparency: Involvement of multiple stakeholders and incorporation of advanced technologies promote trust related problems and hidden essential facts which may further pose challenges to the smart city framework (Gharaibeh et al., 2017).

1.2 Role of Blockchain in Enhancing Security

Blockchain is a distributed ledger technology that has the ability of providing decentralized, transparent and tamper-proof record of each transaction that occurs on the system. As opposed to the centralized systems, each block chain network is supported by a set of nodes that all maintain a copy of the ledger and as a result, the system is highly secure, scalable and trustworthy (Abdulhakeem et al., 2021). Figure 3 gives overview of the major components and processes involved in blockchain technology. At its heart, blockchain makes it possible to have safe, decentralised transactions without the use of intermediaries. The digital wallets used for storing, sending, and receiving cryptocurrencies are attributed to a unique address on the blockchain network. Every transaction is validated by nodes using a consensus mechanism that makes the generation of trust and security possible. Miners validate transactions through the solution of complex cryptographic problems, securing the network in a process known as mining, thereby rewarding participants in cryptocurrency for their work. Blockchain technology has also opened wide the avenue of Initial Coin Offering fundraising, a means by which tokens are issued against capital raised. It's a decentralized network composed of many nodes that cooperate in maintaining the integrity of the system intact and build trust by ensuring immutability and transparency in transactions. Each transaction creates a permanent time-stamp on the blockchain and forms part of an immutable ledger. Additional functionality has been added with the use of smart contracts, automating agreements and transactions when pre-defined conditions are met; this enables thrustless executions of agreements without any intermediary. In all, the picture articulates the nature of how blockchain works: decentralized, secure, transparent, and automated.

Figure 3. Overview of the Major Components and Processes Involved in Blockchain Technology

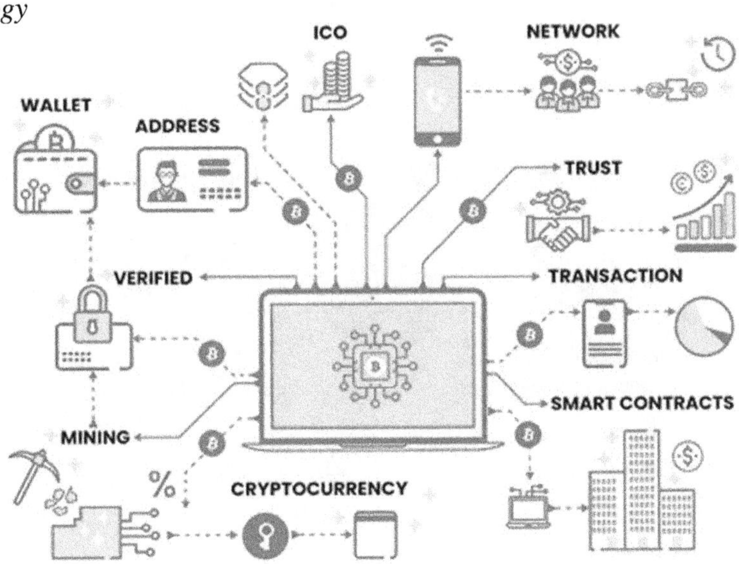

The problem of inadequate security in the smart cities will be solved by the application of the blockchain technology in 6G technology. This is an implication of blockchain's core characteristics of decentralization, immutability and transparency that when embraced can enhance the protection and stability of smart city systems.

Key features of blockchain that make it well-suited for securing 6G networks in smart cities are shown in Figure 4.

Figure 4. Key Features of Blockchain

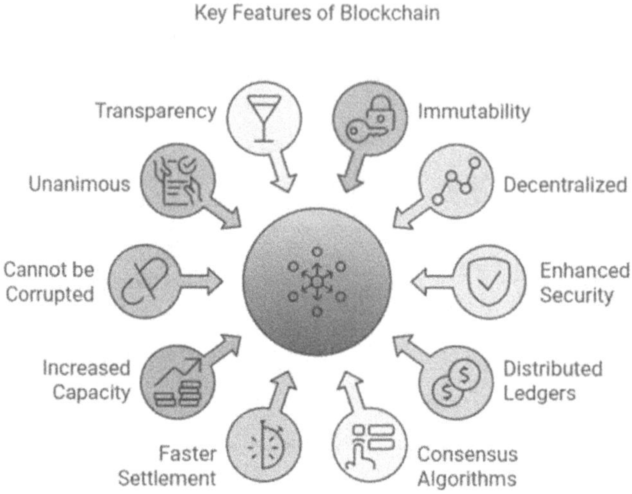

To understand the nature of blockchain technology, it is essential to acquaint oneself with key characteristics of the tool that made it popular across different industries. One of them is openness – all the members of the network can look at the data as well as have the access only using anonymous nicknames thus providing privacy. These make policies and procedures credible since they are all well explained to the public. Another important attribute is non-traceability – or, once the data is entered into the blockchain, it cannot be changed or erased, which makes the data immutable.

Another aspect of blockchain is that no single centralizer controls the functionality of a blockchain system, thus increasing the reliability of blockchain. It is decentralized, and the consensus is arrived at through mathematical algorithms such as Proof of Work (PoW) or Proof of Stake (PoS), so that everyone gets to approve transactions. Such decentralization together with the promotion of security features based on cryptographic techniques; the system can be shielded against fraud, hacking and any form of illegitimate access.

The mentioned features make blockchain an ideal, secure and fast technology which is already changing the world with the help of financial, medical and logistics sectors. Considering Blockchain technology and Artificial Intelligence (AI) as the future of data, security and processing. Although both are monumental in their right, both emerge in several ways that make their interconnection effective, boosting the stability, credibility, and effectiveness of AI-derived systems. In Figure 5 we can see the relation between blockchain and AI.

Figure 5. Integration of Blockchain with AI

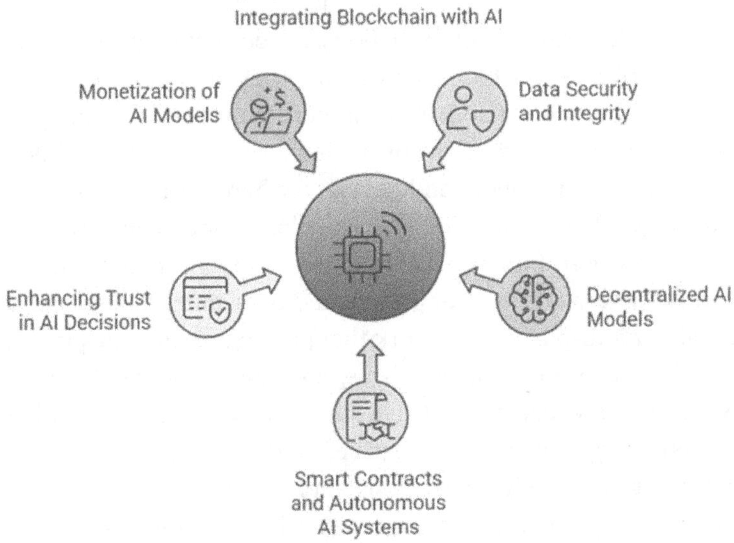

Data Security and Integrity: Blockchain technology is a perfect solution for environments that require controlling data changes and records of transactions accurately. When applying AI in conjunction with Blockchain, action or decision made by the AI model can be followed and audited to make certain that the algorithm has not been tampered with nor is it bias. This traceability becomes particularly important when it comes to domains that involve high risk such as health, financial and legal.

Introducing the blockchain concept into the 6G security model for smart cities, the security threats could be mitigated and enhanced the decentralization and reliability of a modern smart city infrastructure required to meet the increasing needs of the urban world (Khrais, 2020).

2. LITERATURE REVIEW

A general discussion of 6G, beginning with its fundamental concepts and the driver technologies such as VLC and THz and starting with the drawbacks of prior network generations is presented in (Gera et al., 2023). The authors proceed to explore the role of the IoT devices enhanced by blockchain systems in a 6G environment, their advantages, drawbacks, and use cases for smart cities, factories, automation, and XR. In addition, the paper discusses the function of AI in 6G focusing on dynamic spectrum and mobile edge computing. Systematically, the authors review the open issues and challenges of green 6G communication technology and provide potential solutions and research directions for future investigations.

The continuous development of 6G to boost the communication sector alongside slipstreaming the efficiency of blockchain technology in a numerous field has create platform for the combination of both in consumer electronics. This integration opens the potential to solve many problems of having secure, private, and decentralized networks to create new products and services where current systems cannot be implemented easily (Wang et al., 2024). Particularly for consumer electronics, this research seeks to explore how blockchain could operate in conjunction with the 6G communication network to offer private and distributed links. The authors put forward a reliable multi-party framework that production includes intelligent edge servers, blockchain consensus mechanisms, and low compute electronic devices. Exploratory, it uses analytical models to reason about system cost/incentive tradeoffs, and quantify the energy-latency trade space, credibility, capacity and so on. The research shows how knowledge conditions vary within the network by comparing and contrasting both symmetric and asymmetric information cases and will enable the identification of optimal resource allocation under various conditions. It is widely demonstrated through experiments that the proposed framework outperforms the state-of the-art benchmarks in a broad range of scenarios, such as mobile augmented reality gaming and distributed machine learning paradigms. The results also confirmed extremely high offloading efficiency at different utility levels across the range of the 50ms target latency, peaking to over 90% levels as the infrastructure grows to 100 edge servers and 2000 devices. This work unequivocally proves that it is possible to combine edge intelligence, cryptography and the advanced wireless communication to deliver next generation consumer solutions. Introducing these solutions across metaverse, ambient computing, and industrial IoTs focus the user control with better security and performance.

Intelligent systems in smart cities exhibit high interconnectivity to maximize on the gains noted above, but this has led to the expansion of the existing attack vectors the world over. This paper sets out to examine imperative need for security systems in smart city communication network by developing a broad security framework. The authors first present a framework for examining the emerging threat landscape in smart cities and how the new environment may be exploited by adversaries. To reduce these risks, the proposed framework adopts several layers that employ the use of encryption, IDS, and blockchain. The authors also emphasized key implementation issues of such a framework, as well as possible strategies for addressing them. In addition, the authors provide a procedurally valid assessment of an integrated framework for the communications mapping and data processing assessment utilizing simulations and real-world case studies to illustrate its practical relevance and benefit for improving data quality and traceability. The research thereby emphasizes the need for constant vigilance, consultative security and a 'preventative' security approach in mitigating threats in the evolving smart city environment (Desai et al., 2024).

The author in Sharma et al., (2024) then in detail analysis of the existing and future trends of deploying 6G technology in smart cities. Two, this paper then examines the possible 6G mobile communication technologies systematically, as well as their corresponding prospects and issues, and future research potential. The article then diverts its attention to the promising smart city application use cases enabled by these 6G technologies which include; smart grid application, smart healthcare, and smart waste management application. Last, some important issues are pointed out, and recommendations for future research are provided by authors. As such, this paper has taken a broad view of 6G technologies and their use in smart cities in order to offer a comprehensive view of this fledgling field. It enables the readers to understand the advantages, prospect, and usage of 6G technology to fulfill the various, massive, and future smart city demands.

The authors mentioned the security issues regarding smart cities; the authors stated that there is a larger attack surface, system complexity, and a lack of trust in traditional solutions to guard these smart cities; the authors further explained how blockchain can be used as a mean of decentralised and reliable solutions to these challenges. Blockchain is acknowledged as one approach to protect smart city frameworks as some of the characteristics of this technology, such as decentralization, irreversibility, and openness are vital to maintaining the reliability of the smart city systems (Treiblmaier, 2020).

The combination of blockchain with 6G network entails secure and decentralized identity management, enhanced access control and authorization and; privacy and data protection as pointed by (Khrais, 2020). Previous research has examined the applicability of improving 5G networks and the Internet of Things with blockchain technology with the focus on security and privacy. The authors put forward a solution that involves a combination of blockchain with edge intelligence systems will be capable of offering guaranteed security and privacy in the 5G and beyond networks (Hajar et al., 2021).

Similar kind of advantages are expected when blockchain would be integrated with 6G networks because, like 5G, the technology delivers a decentralised and reliable method to protect the large number of connected devices, data, and exchanges within a smart city (Nguyen et al., 2020).

The literature also presents future works in security frameworks, architectures and solutions of 6G networks as the complexity, heterogeneity and dynamics of 6G networks are another important area of concern. Another area discussed is the change of an approach to security, from the perimeter-based model where security was assumed for anything inside the perimeter, to the zero-trust model (Muhammad, 2023). While the zero-trust model can efficiently enhance the security in the architecture of 6G networks, the integration of the blockchain technology would further improve its performance by adding the decentralized and transparent solution for the identities' management, access rights, and data integrity (Tu et al., 2023).

The combination of artificial intelligence and blockchain has also been considered toward the protection of the 6G and beyond network. Deep Reinforcement learning has been suggested to be combined with blockchain to facilitate secure smart sharing of resources in next-generation wireless networks (Li et al., 2020). Review of literature on AI-driven security frameworks: The combined usage of the AI and the blockchain can improve the security and the self-healing properties of 6G smart cities to handle anomalies and threats in real-time while making distributed decisions (Benzaid et al., 2020). Blockchain's role in supporting AI-based anomaly detection and threat mitigation: That is, Blockchain can be used to securely store and share security related data and this data can be utilized by AI-based systems for further improvement in the categories of anomaly detection and control (Tran et al., 2022).

6G networks can be secured through blockchain technology which minimizes centralization of information and at the same time prevents alteration of data. The authors specified a new approach that can enhance the data sharing and storage security in 6G IoT based networks through the combination of blockchain, hybrid encryption, and IPFS by El Ghor and (Nakhal, 2023). Its approach improves the security of data by making it private and providing distributed, error-tolerant solutions. Blockchain association with 6G networks enhances the creation of distributed AI models. Samanta et al. (2023) elaborated the way blockchain management system can effectively track and control consumption as well as distribution of resources in 6G network. This integration helps in the development of other decentralized AI models to work securely and on one's own in smart city surroundings.

Blockchain through smart contracts can enhance and secure transaction taking place in 6G networks. Liu et al. (2024) described how smart contract can improve the security and effectiveness of the AI system in smart cities, In their research article. These contracts make the AI afforded processes transparent and immune to interference. Blockchain can add value to AI decision making via a secure and indisputable record of the AI process in the decentralized ledger. Sharma et al. (2023) concurred and cited the study of Samanta et al. (2023) to highlight the boost that blockchain can provide to the application of AI in 6G smart cities in terms of decision making transparency. Another benefit of using blockchain technology is that is creates transparency in the process of funding AI projects and in monetizing models. Recent research suggests a framework that AI creators can use to make money from their models via block-chain-based mechanisms, fairly paid as well as their intellectual property rights are protected (Bekkali et al., 2023).

3. RESEARCH GAP AND AIM

Although there is a rapidly expanding amount of literature on the implementation of blockchain in 6G networks, there is a gap in the literature that addresses the need to present a system that can cater to the needs of initializing blockchain-enhanced security architecture in 6G networks with an emphasis on smart cities. Although the current state of the art has investigated the opportunities of combining blockchain with 6G nets, it is still missing a general approach for the security characteristics and concerns embedded in smart city ecosystems. The existing studies have been mainly in areas of interest, utilization scenarios, or applications which include, but are not limited to spectrum sharing, service-level agreement, and mobile users' privacy. The adoption of a comprehensive security solution that entails employing blockchain, the 6th Generation of Communications Technology (6G), and AI security enables systems to secure a smart city in a decentralized manner. The following research paper is an attempt to bridge this gap by presenting a blockchain-based smart city-oriented 6G security architecture to harmonise blockchain, 6G, and AI-assisted security paradigm.

3.1 Research Gap

Although remarkable progress has been made regarding blockchain and 6G networks, there are some essential research limitations that hamper the integration of blockchain in smart cities. One of the principal obstacles is that blockchain solutions remain restricted to organization and informational systems. Despite the high level of security, blockchain technology seems to suffer when it comes to scalability or rather its integration into high throughput 6G networks. Some current blockchain platforms are very slow while others provide a limited amount of transaction processes per second in IoT real-world environments. Due to the growing amount of data and high-speed transactions that are fundamental to 6G, scalable blockchain frameworks for such requirements should be highly desirable (Wang et al., 2021).

There's also the problem of addressing the connections between blockchain technology and some of the features of 6G communication, including the slicing of networks and employing edge computing. While these theoretical frameworks exist, there are few research studies about the implementation of blockchain with these enhanced 6G features in practice. Unfortunately, most of this research has remained prototypal with comparatively few actual empirical demonstrations of performance. To cover this gap, it is necessary to create and implement realistic solutions that enable the integration of blockchain into the six generations of technologies mentioned and assess how effective they are in real life scenarios (Wang et al., 2021). Moreover, with the emergence of quantum computing, quantum protection of the blockchain has become an important issue. It highlighted that future 6G networks might become susceptible to quantum-based attacks since existing blockchain practicièmes might become more sensitive to such threats as a result of protocol changes brought by the application of quantum computing. Thus, the idea of quantum-resistant algorithms is currently dominated by theory, and its effective implementations have not been established yet. This emphasizes that there is a lack of knowledge on the need to investigate additional quantum-resistant blockchain models to protect 6G networks from potential quantum attacks in the future (Chamola et al., 2021).

Promisingly, a combination of AI and blockchain for improving security in smart cities is another very researched topic here. While AI, when applied together with blockchain, might offer strong means for real-time anomaly detection and automated responses to threats, there are very few papers on how the combination of both might be realized. Future research is needed to deploy and empirically assess novel machine learning applications to bolster the reliability and protection of smart city networks, which utilize blockchain technology (Hussain et al., 2021). Finally, the privacy and ethical issues that the immutable characteristic of blockchain solutions bring must be debated. Although blockchain guarantees transparency and data authenticity, it contradicts the privacy constraints, especially where IoT devices generate data relating to their individual owners. It becomes pertinent therefore to look at ways in which blockchain means improved transparency and we can look at future smart city applications whilst observing ethical considerations that may affect the privacy of the individual. Efforts to build privacy-preserving blockchain systems will, therefore, be critical in addressing these concerns while preserving the security of data in smart cities (Fiore et al., 2023).

3.2 Research Aims

This study will seek to address these challenges with a view of realizing the full potential of blockchain in creating secure smart cities fundamental on the upcoming 6G network. The overview of our investigation is based on five main questions. Firstly, thus there is the importance of creating large-scale blockchains for handling the 6G network major data volume and latency. This includes employing new consensus algorithms that have never been implemented such as Proof-of-Authority and exploring new sharding strategies and lightweight designs of blockchain that are suitable for IoT devices. Second, we will explore the application of blockchain with smart 6G networks such as network slicing and, edge computing. This will include surveys and actual integration pilot studies in the attempt to establish the effectiveness and practicality of various integration approaches. Third, in view of the quantum threat to 6G networks, we will strengthen quantum resistant security protocol of 6G network by conducting research and decoding post-quantum cryptographic algorithms such as lattice-based cryptography and code-based cryptography in combination with hybrid models of classical and post-quantum. Fourth, we will improve AI-blockchain integration and the security of smart cities. This includes the creation of the real-time anomaly detection models, self-reacting to threats, and the possibilities of using the decentralized AI agents supervised by blockchain technology for shared threat identification and reaction among them.

4. METHODOLOGY

4.1 Framework Development for Blockchain in the Security of 6G Networks

The following research study will initiate with the formulation of a general framework of applying blockchain with 6G technologies for security advancements in smart cities. This framework will address the key components required for a secure and resilient architecture, including: advanced, scalable blockchain solutions, easy incorporation of the blockchain with all the characteristics of 6G, quantum trade-off blockchain methods, AI security measures for blockchain, privacy protection models. It is intended that the framework will take advantage of some of the distinctive features of blockchain technology; decentralization, enhanced transparency, and soundness, while at the same time proposing the research to manage some of the current drawbacks of the blockchain platforms through addressing the problems of scalability and latency.

4.2 Architecture Diagram: On the Security Aspect within 6G Networks Leveraging on Blockchain

The use-case architecture diagram as given in Figure 6 shows how one may apply blockchain technology to strengthen the security of 6G networks visually. The diagram is segmented into various parts and each part has unique functional significance in the entire concept of security.

The work on 'Blockchain-Enabled Security architecture in 6G Networks' successfully explains the potential of applying blockchain in the future 6G system in terms of security, data authenticity and privacy at different levels. On top of this architecture, there is the 6G network layer, and because of the highest data rates, very low latency, and the huge number of connections in 6G, it requires the highest level of security. This layer comprises of a system that only allow authorized users and devices to be in the network. Blockchain provides decentralized access control; there are no single access control points as observed in the conventional systems.

Also, Decentralized Identity (DID) is used for the self-sovereign identity on a blockchain and not from a centralized server. This leads to more control over the identity information, which is of benefits in terms of privacy and security.

Figure 6. Architecture of blockchain-enabled security in 6G networks

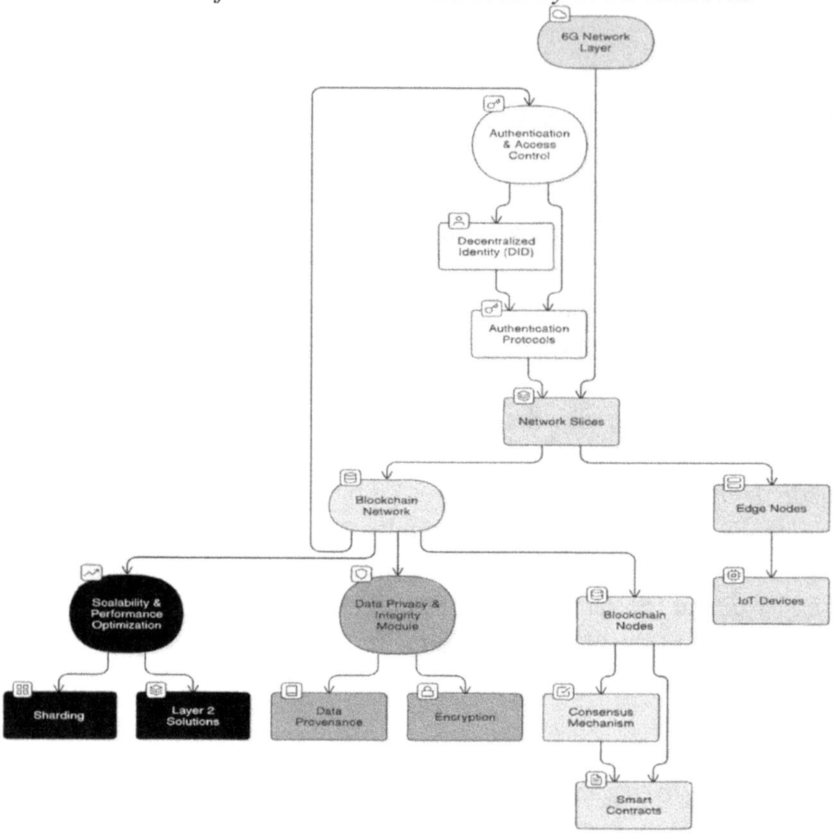

The network layer is at the center of this architecture where a blockchain technology is used to handle security in the 6G network due to its decentralized database. Another important part of the layer is Datas Privacy & Integrity Module, which is responsible for the protection of the data transiting in the network. In this context data provenance is used to track data source and lineage making it feasible to identify tampering or malevolent alteration of data. Encryption is another fundamental aspect, which aims to shield information, while blockchain controls the encryption keys and shields the transfer procedures. As to the inherent scalability issues of the blockchains, scalability, and performance enhancement mechanisms are initiated including the sharding and Layer 2 solutions. It scales through the sharding technique that divides the blockchain into several segments or shards through which the transaction can happen concurrently. On the other side, Layer 2 solutions handle off-chain transactions, which put less strain on the primary base blockchain, making it more efficient.

The barrier layer consisting of the edge nodes and IoT devices enables IoT devices and edge nodes to access the blockchain network. These are devices that are positioned between the IoT devices and the 6G core network where they perform data computation at the edge to minimize latency. Such edge nodes communicate with the blockchain network for the purpose of checking the authenticity of data processed by these nodes. Blockchain nodes are located on such edge nodes thus making transaction verification decentralized as well as increasing the security of the network. An agreement mechanism that can be of Work (PoW) or Proof of Stake (PoS) makes sure that all nodes in the blockchain network are viewing ledger in the same accurate way without any central authority in charge. Also, smart contracts are essential for the automating of other processes, for example, access rights, payments, and sharing of information. These contracts run on their own once certain stipulated actions are triggered to ensure that networks' policy guidelines are upheld without any form of interference.

4.3 Overall Connectivity and Workflow

The various components in the framework work together in a highly interconnected manner to provide a secure, scalable, and efficient environment for 6G networks: The various components in the framework work together in a highly interconnected manner to provide a secure, scalable, and efficient environment for 6G networks.

Network Access: IoT devices and edge nodes are initially mutually authenticated with DID which ensures security in the authentication process. Once authorised, they are linked to specific network slices where they can analyse as well as transfer data. Data Processing and Transmission: Data in a network is processed in the edge nodes and forwarded to other devices or other network slices. Blockchain is applied to track data's sources and genuineness so that all the information exchanges are secure and credible. Blockchain Integration: It is noted that all the conducted transactions and data exchange processes are stored in the blockchain. Running and securing the telecommunication network is also made possible by smart contracts while the consensus mechanism helps all nodes in the blockchain to agree to the current state of the ledger. Scalability and Performance: Sharding and the Layer 2 solution are important because these make sure the blockchain will be able to accommodate the incoming number of transactions for 6G network's low latency nature. All these solutions are designed to balance the operational load hence avoiding areas of congestion and crowding within the network domain thereby making the network nimble and quick. Security and Privacy: Encryption ensures the privacy of data while on the other hand blockchain ensures that the record of all the transactions is noted. These technologies are incorporated to make a 6G network safe, efficient as well as effective in supporting applications in smart cities. This system-level solution offers a practical method to implement blockchain technology to secure 6G networks, which is useful because the new generation wireless network presents new problems.

5. THE APPLICATION OF 6G SECURITY ARCHITECTURE FOR SMART CITIES THROUGH BLOCKCHAIN ON SPECIFIC USE CASES

The blockchain-enabled 6G security architecture proposed in this paper can be applied to a variety of use cases in smart cities, including: The blockchain-enabled 6G security architecture proposed in this paper can be applied to a variety of use cases in smart cities, including:

5.1 Autonomous Transportation Security in Network Layer

ITS in smart city environments require secure real-time information transfer for vehicle to vehicle or even vehicle to infrastructure communications. Strong security measure includes matters of cyber security and any form of breach such as being accessed by unauthorized persons. Adaptable encryption, use of block chain for secure transactions and on-going surveillance are essential. Measures of protection thus guarantee strict access to the software to prevent compromise of its program and elements, increase security, and public confidence in the use of self-driving transport systems to support dependable, smooth, and efficient city transport systems (Baksi et al., 2023).

In a 6G smart city of the future, the transportation infrastructure comprises mainly of AVs and other communication systems for example; traffic signals, road sensors, public transport among others (Karthikeyan et al., 2023). This self-driving transport system heavily uses IoT gadgets to gather and send data as the car moves; thus, assisting it to move safely and efficiently while interacting with other systems (Brewer et al., 2019). However, the dependence on smart gears or IoT devices exposes the whole system to high risks of cyber security threats such as tampering, unauthorized access or even hacking of the entire transport system (Feng et al., 2018).

Decentralized Identity Management (DID): All connected devices that are components of IoDoug network such as autonomous vehicles, smart traffic signals, and road sensors are provided with a unique, provable identity using DID solutions that are based on blockchain. DID also guarantees that the identity of each device is safe and stored in the block chain; thus, the ineligible apparatus cannot join the network or pretend to be other ones that are qualified for the network. This feature is very important in that it acts as a guarantee that only accredited parties will be allowed to transact within the network. Tamper-Proof Data Logging: Every piece of information coming from IoT, including vehicle telemetry data, traffic conditions, and road sensors, is recorded to a blockchain. This guarantees that the data is protected from misuse in that any attempt to tamper with the data or provide fake information will be easily identified.

For example, if an AV gets information about a road hazard from a sensor, the participants of the blockchain will know that this information is genuine and not tampered with by some individuals. Smart Contracts for Secure Communication: The following are self-executing contracts applied in vehicle communications, car to car (Vehicle-to-Vehicle, V2V) or vehicle to infrastructure (Vehicle-to-Infrastructure, V2I). These contracts control activities in accordance with the predetermined schedule and protocols while disinfecting discussions from any potential threats from employees, unmixed human mistake. For instance, smart contracts can enable right of way allocation in cross intersections, response to emergency vehicles or simply, coordinate movements of several AVs in areas with high traffic-density, thus eliminating the risk of accident and enhancing on-road flow. Consensus Mechanisms for Data Validation: Because the data transmitted over the network need to be secure, blockchain's consensus is used to achieve this. In a blockchain structure, several nodes check the information before it is stored thereby avoiding the use of wrong information in making decisions. This is even more so for the vital applications like navigation and collision avoidance, where the quality of data matters a lot in relation to the risk which the passengers and other users of roads expose themselves to.

The integration of blockchain technology into the management framework of autonomous transport network has some advantages thereby enhancing the safety, reliability and efficiency of the transport system from various cyber perils. Prevention of Data Tampering and Spoofing: All data that IoT produces are recorded on the blockchain, and any attempts to manipulate the data are impossible since the ledger is hack-proof. Anyone who seeks to tamper with the traffic signals, forge the car data or even fake some hazard on the road, would be easily detected. Such detailed and accurate data is important to AVs since the systems need quality information on real-time to enable effective navigation. Through the blockchain, the data that informs such decisions is credible meaning that chances of having an accident due to wrong or manipulated information is minimized. Protection Against Unauthorized Access: Since the implementation of DID solutions, the network has been protected from unauthorized devices to connect. This is important in a smart city scenario where the introduction of the large number of unauthorised or compromised IoT devices could lead to major security risks. By employing blockchain for identity management, only certified devices can be involved in the network hence reducing incidences of cyberattacks that originate from infected or fake devices. Resilience Against Distributed Denial-of-Service (DDoS) Attacks: The traditional mode of transport, characterized by command-and-control architectures, is at risk of DDoS attacks in which many affected devices flood the control systems hence causing disruptions in service. Nevertheless, such attacks are mitigated by the decentralised nature of a blockchain that creates additional layers of protection to the network. The fact that the blockchain operates on networks and clusters means that it has no vulnerability points. This makes it difficult for an attacker to shut down the system making the transportation network always up even when the system is under attack.

5.2 Smart Healthcare System

In a 6G arena, smart healthcare system empowers patient care improving connected ultra-fast with low latency attribute. People's health is under constant supervision through connected things, and widespread telemedicine offers quality remote consultations. AI applies data analysis for diagnosis as well as treatment plans gives to patients (Mucchi et al., 2020). This integration leads to enhancement of the quality of the services delivered to the patients, efficiency of the organizational processes and protection of the information. These include the technical issues that would arise when implementing the system, privacy issues as well as legal issues. Future enhancements in 6G may possibly enhance these systems even additional, apply their advantages to other SMART CITY segments, even enhance healthcare accessibility, effectiveness and productivity (Raddo et al., 2021).

In an example, a concept of a 6G smart city in which healthcare services are interconnected, do depend on the timely data sharing from various players in the system including hospitals and clinics, pharmacy stores, insurance companies, and local/central health departments. Compared to the previous versions, 6G network provides means for the fast transfer of immense volumes of data and supports real-time communication. But this integration also poses some difficulties in the protection of data and respective patient's information, their confidentiality, and non-interference (Imoize et al., 2021). To overcome these difficulties, the city has adopted a blockchain-supported healthcare management system which fully utilizes the characteristics of blockchain. It is intended to facilitate adequate storage, transferral and processing of patient information within the healthcare chain of supply with maximum security measures put in place to control access to and modification of patient information.

The implementation of blockchain technology within the smart healthcare system of this 6G-enabled city leads to several notable improvements in data security and overall healthcare management: Enhanced Data Security and Privacy: Through decentralization, the problem of data breach which would require penetrating through a large central database is minimized here because attackers would need to compromise several nodes. Another protective layer is the encryption and fragmentation of a patient's data, an attacker will not get the full record of the patient, they are likely to get a minutia of the patient's record out of fragments; this greatly improves security. Increased Trust and Transparency: The feature of immutability of records held in the block chain makes the patients and healthcare providers to have confidence in systems that are hold in blocks. This gives the patients an assurance that their data cannot be manipulated in any way which is a plus for the healthcare providers as they get data on the patients in a transparent and efficient manner. Blockchain creates the clear audit trail in how patient data is managed hence customers can trust the system. Improved Efficiency in Data Management: Smart contracts handle the rights of data access control, which helps to minimize the load on healthcare institutions and allows to provide data only if it is required. This automation makes the data to be retrieved faster; there is less likelihood of errors being made by humans. As a result, data is flowing seamlessly through the healthcare delivery system hence improving patient care and organization of health care system. Regulatory Compliance: The blockchain based system guarantees compliance with protection laws of any personal information, for example, the Health Insurance Portability and Accountability Act (HIPAA) in the United States or the General Data Protection Regulation (GDPR) in the European Union. The openness of data in the system, its capacity for auditing and subjection to limited access follow the rules governing the security of such information.

5.3 Smart City Surveillance

To address, the above-discussed challenges, thereby implementing blockchain in a smart city surveillance system with 6G, a proper architecture is needed (Khan et al., 2020). This is a step-by-step guide of how blockchain can be introduced in to such a system (Cheikhrouhou et al., 2022). Surveillance systems which are considered as one of the significant components of the 6G enabled smart city are also used for keeping security and overseeing activities in the smart city. These systems comprise of different strings of cameras, sensors and data processing units which capture and process huge amount of data in real-time. I would like to underscore the fact that the proliferation of the surveillance brings to the forefront rather important issues that pertain to privacy, security, and possible abuse of personal data. To deal with such issues, the city integrates a blockchain-based security model into its surveillance system. Blockchain technology will be adopted to improve privacy and security of the surveillance system while at the same time ensuring data that is collected from citizens respects their privacy while at the same time having strong security systems. Decentralized Data Management: Video data collected through surveillance cameras, test data or sensor data and the analysis result is then stored based on a blockchain system. This makes it difficult for a single agent to wield total control over the data, thus lowering the probability of unauthorised access or data theft.

The decentralized storage also improves the reliability of the data whereby the loss or even theft of a node does not affect the reliability of the data. Data Encryption and Access Control: All the surveillance data is encrypted to enhance the security process of their storage on the blockchain. In this case, only some organizations are allowed access to read the encrypted messages, including police forces or specific city's administration, for example. Smart contracts are used to control access since they can restrict and grant users' rights in accordance with these criteria. For instance, views of videos maybe given only after providing confirmation of a security threat hence reducing on the potential of anyone being given raw surveillance data. Immutable Audit Trail: Surveillance data is encrypted in the system and the blockchain allows one to trace all the activities that have been carried out in respect of surveillance data, who accessed it, when it was accessed and why. This transparency makes sure that none of the so-called monitors abuses his position in his monitoring duties it also ensures that every monitor is accountable for their actions since everyone can see them. If there has been a violation of privacy or intrusion, then the audit trail gives a ready list of culprit accounts and can be used for containing any further transgression.

Anonymization of Sensitive Data: To enhance citizens' privacy protection, the personal information that is collected by the surveillance system can be encrypted then stored on the blockchain. This comprises of obfuscating the face or the elimination of facets that could easily reveal the identity of persons in moving pictures unless the contrary is required. Smart contracts are used to anonymize the data entered the system, which then follows the pre-set program when the data is entered to the blockchain. Apart from blockchain technology, the smart city employs artificial intelligence that makes the surveillance system to be more effective and efficient. It is accompanied by artificial intelligence stream that is used for analysis, threat detection, and response in real time integrated with the architecture of the blockchain. Real-Time Anomaly Detection: Focusing on security aspects, the surveillance data is collected by the AI algorithms in real-time that can identify some suspicious or atypical events which can pose threat to security. For instance, it can notice such activities as people lingering around sensitive installations, abandoned objects in public areas, or unusual crowd movement. In the event of an anomaly being recognized, there is an activation of smart contract to place the event on the blockchain in addition to sounding the right authorities and or other actions, such as informing security guards on the vicinity or locking down the specific area. Pattern Recognition and Predictive Analytics: The historical surveillance data is fed into artificial intelligent pattern recognition tools to effectively analyse relation between existing pattern and security threats. It also gives the city the ability to identify threats and prevent them before the threats can come to fruition. For instance, if the AI system observes that there are break-ins that took place in a certain area at certain hours then it can predict future break-ins and hence deploy more security around that region.

Enhanced Privacy Through Federated Learning: The city uses federated learning an AI technique, whereby machine learning models are trained on data without the data needing to be centralized. This is especially beneficial when it comes to personal data protection since the surveillance information has never to be moved from its source. Opened learning keeps the data on the blockchain while the participation of end-users helps the AI system to refine its threat detection and analysis functions on the go. Automated Incident Response: Integrating AI into blockchain can create machines that respond proactively and autonomously to security breaches thus cutting down the time taken to deal with threats. For instance, if a surveillance camera gets to detect an unauthorized intrusion, the AI can set a smart contract to lock all the doors, sound an alarm, as well as call the police immediately. The automated response system should also have as little interface with the staff as possible so that once a serious event occurs the response is quick and decisive. The implementation of blockchain and AI under each tier of the smart city surveillance system provides the following benefits: Enhanced Data Security and Privacy: This way the implementation of the blockchain makes sure that all the data acquired by surveillance is safe and encrypted from outsiders and can be accessed only by those that have the proper rights. The other AI-guided anonymization procedures add to the leveraging of privacy by making it practically impossible for everyone who is not supposed to recognize the citizens from surveillance videos. Their feature of the blockchain is immutability which results in the clarity of where and how the surveillance system is being abused. Improved Threat Detection and Response: These features of anomaly detection and pattern recognition widen the city's potential for real-time security threats identification keenly through the application of the AI technology. The existence of the automated incident response mechanisms also mitigates the time taken to respond to the various incidents and makes the surveillance system more efficient.

Using predictive analytics, the city will be able to prevent certain threats before they spiral out of control and this will help instil safety within the city. Increased Public Trust: The implementation of the surveillance system based on the blockchain approach enhances transparency and accountability, while the strict adherence to strict privacy policy increases people's trust in the system. People will equally offer their support to surveillance endeavours if they are fully informed on the privacy of citizens and responsible use of this method. The city uses modern technology for improving security and being focused on people's privacy, therefore, increasing the rate of cooperation and engagement between the community and officials.

Table 1 summarizing the application of Blockchain-Enabled 6G Security Architecture for Smart Cities in the specified use cases:

Table 1. Use cases of blockchain-enabled 6g security architecture for smart cities

Use Case	Description	Security Measures	Key Benefits
Autonomous Transportation	Secure network layer for autonomous vehicles (AVs) and other smart transport systems using IoT devices. Challenges include risks like tampering, unauthorized access, and cyberattacks.	- Decentralized Identity Management (DID) for secure authentication. - Tamper-proof data logging using blockchain. - Smart contracts for V2V and V2I communications. - Blockchain consensus for data validation. - Protection against DDoS attacks.	- Prevention of data tampering and spoofing. - Protection against unauthorized access. - Enhanced security, reliability, and efficiency of AVs. - Real-time, verifiable communication between AVs and infrastructure. - Continuous functioning even under DDoS attacks.
Smart Healthcare System	Secure, efficient data sharing between healthcare stakeholders in a smart city. Ensures privacy and protection of patient data in a 6G-connected healthcare system, with fast data transfer and real-time communication between hospitals, pharmacies, insurance companies, and health departments.	- Decentralized storage using blockchain for secure patient data management. - Encryption and fragmentation of data for privacy. - Smart contracts for data access control. - Compliance with laws like HIPAA and GDPR.	- Enhanced data security and privacy. - Increased trust and transparency for patients and providers. - Improved efficiency in data management. - Ensured regulatory compliance. - Fast data retrieval with less human error.
Smart City Surveillance	Blockchain-secured surveillance system ensures privacy, accountability, and security of surveillance data. Cameras, sensors, and data processing units capture and process data in real-time. The architecture ensures strong privacy protection and safeguards against unauthorized access and abuse of personal data.	- Decentralized data management using blockchain. - Encryption and access control for sensitive data. - Immutable audit trails for data access transparency. - AI integration for real-time anomaly detection, predictive analytics, and automated response.	- Enhanced data security and privacy for surveillance data. - Real-time threat detection and automated response. - Increased public trust due to transparent and accountable systems. - Federated learning for decentralized AI training without moving data.

6. TRENDS OF FUTURE AND EMERGENT TECHNOLOGIES

6.1 Development of the Context in Relation to Blockchain

It therefore becomes increasingly evident that new blockchain protocols for 6G networks will likely introduce profound influence on the facet of security in aspects of scalability, efficiency and integrity. Successor consensus mechanism to PoW (Proof-of-Work) has emerged, which includes; PoS (Proof-of-Stake), DPoS (Delegated Proof-of-Stake), and PoA (Proof-of-Authority) and these prove to be more efficient and scalable than PoW mechanisms. Such mechanisms may help improve the efficiency of blockchain-based networks with 6G technology and minimize the exposure to security threats, thereby promoting faster or more efficient transaction in blockchain networks. Furthermore, its application such as through the process of blockchain sharding which divides the blockchain into multiple processing units called shards enhances the scalability and speed of the network to adequately support large amounts of data and data transfer rates that will be expected from 6G networks. Other standards like cross-chain transaction and decentralized identity (DID) are also developing to support data transmission and improve security recovery in different blockchain networks thus helping to provide strong linkage with 6G.

However, as the application of quantum computing evolves it presents a risk in the present blockchain structures. In response to this nightmare, new quantum-resistant blockchain protocols are being designed to help protect against such a Scenario that quantum computers will enable. This is why new generation post quantum cryptographic algorithms such as lattice-based cryptography and hash-based signatures provide secure protection from quantum computer like computations. These quantum-resistant techniques, therefore, come as critically necessary in maintaining the security of the blockchain networks in future smart cities. Further, the integration of classical and quantum-resistant cryptographic techniques may be an immediate solution to complicated present and future quantum challenges. These advanced cryptographic techniques help the blockchain system to sustain the security and functionality when competing with the current computational technologies.

6.2 AI and Blockchain Synergy

The synergy between AI and blockchain is expected to revolutionize security frameworks, enhancing both threat detection and incident response. AI-driven threat detection utilizes predictive analytics to analyze transaction patterns and identify anomalies, enabling early detection of potential security threats. Machine learning algorithms can continuously improve their accuracy in recognizing and mitigating threats based on evolving data patterns. Moreover, AI can automate incident response, executing predefined actions in reaction to detected threats, which reduces response times and enhances overall security. In addition, AI tools can assist in the formal verification of smart contracts, ensuring that they are free from vulnerabilities and errors before deployment. This proactive approach to smart contract security helps prevent potential exploits and enhances the robustness of blockchain-based systems. Autonomous blockchain networks, driven by AI, have the potential to transform smart city operations by enabling self-optimizing and self-governing systems. AI can facilitate autonomous governance within blockchain networks, allowing them to self-regulate and adjust based on real-time network conditions and performance metrics. This capability enables dynamic scaling of resources and enhances the efficiency of blockchain operations in smart city environments. Additionally, decentralized AI agents operating on blockchain networks can collaborate and share insights, leading to more informed decision-making processes and improved system efficiency. These advancements pave the way for more resilient and adaptive blockchain networks that can autonomously manage complex smart city applications.

7. CONCLUSION

This work has highlighted the critical importance of using blockchain technology to enhance the resilience of the 6G networks under the smart cities' environment. Due to growing dependency of urban environments on interlinked technologies, there is a significant need for proper safety solutions. Blockchain as a system that is decentralized, immutable, transparent is a perfect candidate for overcoming the security issues derived from such intricate innovative systems. The characterized security framework that utilizes both the strengths of the blockchain and 6G pinpoint a more inclusive plan for securing of vital structures and services. Thus, it would make this architecture less vulnerable to cyber threats because that way, control is not centralized and there are no single points of failure. Furthermore, by virtue of blockchain's architecture which is inherently transparent and auditable, the quality of data within the smart city network is more credible and trustworthy. Hypothesis for Future Research and Development, While the potential of blockchain in securing 6G-enabled smart cities is evident, several avenues for future research and development remain: While the potential of blockchain in securing 6G-enabled smart cities is evident, several avenues for future research and development remain: Scalability and Performance: Exploring better consensus algorithms and blockchain implementations which will enable smart city applications requirement to be met efficiently. Privacy-Preserving Mechanisms: Incorporating such privacy-preserving methods into the architecture of blockchain that helps to preserve confidentiality of some data and, at the same time, does not restrict the possibility of data verification.

Integration with Existing Infrastructure: A lack of transitional plans on how to implement blockchain-based security systems into smart city systems. Standardization and Interoperability: Setting up specifications based on real-world use, and creating guidelines in harmony with other blockchain dependant and 6G network parts. The further evolution of the blockchain in implementing 6G security is not only about the technological advancement but it is a need for society. Getting academics, industries, and policymakers together that will enable them to work on developing secure, resilient, and trustworthy smart cities for the future.

REFERENCES

Abdulhakeem, S. A., & Hu, Q. (2021). Powered by Blockchain Technology, DeFi (Decentralized Finance) Strives to Increase Financial Inclusion of the Unbanked by Reshaping the World Financial System. *Modern Economy*, 12(01), 1–16. DOI: 10.4236/me.2021.121001

Adem, N., Benfaid, A., Harib, R., & Alarabi, A. (2021). How Crucial Is It for 6G Networks to Be Autonomous? *ArXiv (Cornell University)*. https://doi.org//arxiv.2106.06949DOI: 10.48550

Ahmad, I., Ashar, S. W., Khalid, U., Irfan, A., & Khalil, W. (2021). Blockchain for Sustainable Smart Cities. *Digital Cities Roadmap*, 127–161. DOI: 10.1002/9781119792079.ch4

Akbari, E., Wu, Q., Zhao, W., Arabnia, H. R., & Yang, M. Q. (2017, December 1). *From Blockchain to Internet-Based Voting*. IEEE Xplore. DOI: 10.1109/CSCI.2017.34

Alrehaili, A., Namoun, A., & Tufail, A. (2021). A Comparative Analysis of Scalability Issues within Blockchain-based Solutions in the Internet of Things. *International Journal of Advanced Computer Science and Applications*, 12(9). Advance online publication. DOI: 10.14569/IJACSA.2021.0120955

Bagloee, S. A., Heshmati, M., Dia, H., Ghaderi, H., Pettit, C., & Asadi, M. (2021). Blockchain: The operating system of smart cities. *Cities (London, England)*, 112, 103104. DOI: 10.1016/j.cities.2021.103104

Baksi, A., Ibrahim, A., & Chattopadhyay, A. (2023). Security and Privacy Issues for Urban Smart Traffic Infrastructure. *ArXiv (Cornell University)*. https://doi.org//arxiv.2304.08429DOI: 10.48550

Banafaa, M., Shayea, I., Din, J., Azmi, M. H., Alashbi, A., Daradkeh, Y. I., & Alhammadi, A. (2023). 6G Mobile Communication Technology: Requirements, Targets, Applications, Challenges, Advantages, and Opportunities. *Alexandria Engineering Journal*, 64, 245–274. DOI: 10.1016/j.aej.2022.08.017

Bekkali, A. E., Essaaidi, M., & Boulmalf, M. (2023). A Blockchain-Based Architecture and Framework for Cybersecure Smart Cities. *IEEE Access : Practical Innovations, Open Solutions*, 11, 76359–76370. DOI: 10.1109/ACCESS.2023.3296482

Benzaid, C., & Taleb, T. (2020). AI for Beyond 5G Networks: A Cyber-Security Defense or Offense Enabler? *IEEE Network*, 34(6), 1–8. DOI: 10.1109/MNET.011.2000088

Bhushan, B., Khamparia, A., Sagayam, K. M., Sharma, S. K., Ahad, M. A., & Debnath, N. C. (2020). Blockchain for smart cities: A review of architectures, integration trends and future research directions. *Sustainable Cities and Society*, 61, 102360. DOI: 10.1016/j.scs.2020.102360

Brewer, J. N., & Dimitoglou, G. (2019, December 1). *Evaluation of Attack Vectors and Risks in Automobiles and Road Infrastructure*. IEEE Xplore. DOI: 10.1109/CSCI49370.2019.00021

Cabral, A., Ranganathan, V., & Waldo, J. (2023). Cellular LTE and Solar Energy Harvesting for Long-Term, Reliable Urban Sensor Networks: Challenges and Opportunities. *ArXiv (Cornell University)*. https://doi.org//arxiv.2307.04016DOI: 10.48550

Chamola, V., Jolfaei, A., Chanana, V., Parashari, P., & Hassija, V. (2021). Information security in the post quantum era for 5G and beyond networks: Threats to existing cryptography, and post-quantum cryptography. *Computer Communications*, 176, 99–118. DOI: 10.1016/j.comcom.2021.05.019

Cheikhrouhou, O. Ichrak Amdouni, Khaleel Mershad, Meryem Ammi, & Nguyen, T. V. (2022). Blockchain for the Cybersecurity of Smart City Applications. *INDIGO (University of Illinois at Chicago)*. DOI: 10.36227/techrxiv.19990367

Chen, X., Deng, Y., Ding, H., Qu, G., Zhang, H., Li, P., & Fang, Y. (2024). Vehicle as a Service (VaaS): Leverage Vehicles to Build Service Networks and Capabilities for Smart Cities. *IEEE Communications Surveys and Tutorials. IEEE Communications Surveys and Tutorials*, 26(3), 1–1. DOI: 10.1109/COMST.2024.3370169

Cioara, T., Pop, C., Zanc, R., Anghel, I., Antal, M., & Salomie, I. (2020). Smart Grid Management Using Blockchain: Future Scenarios and Challenges. *2020 19th RoEduNet Conference: Networking in Education and Research (RoEduNet)*. DOI: 10.1109/RoEduNet51892.2020.9324874

Desai, B., Patil, K., Mehta, I., & Patil, A. (2024). A Secure Communication Framework for Smart City Infrastructure Leveraging Encryption, Intrusion Detection, and Blockchain Technology. Advances in Computer Sciences, 7(1)

Feng, Y., Huang, S., Chen, Q. A., Liu, H. X., & Mao, Z. M. (2018). Vulnerability of Traffic Control System Under Cyberattacks with Falsified Data. *Transportation Research Record: Journal of the Transportation Research Board*, 2672(1), 1–11. DOI: 10.1177/0361198118756885

Fiore, M., & Mongiello, M. (2023). *Blockchain for Smart Cities Improvement: an Architecture Proposal. ArXiv*. Cornell University., DOI: 10.1109/ICCSM60247.2023.00009

Gabriel, A., & Cruz, F. (2022). Open source IoT-based collection bin applied to local plastic recycling. *HardwareX*, X, e00389. DOI: 10.1016/j.ohx.2022.e00389 PMID: 36619212

Gera, B., Raghuvanshi, Y. S., Rawlley, O., Gupta, S., Dua, A., & Sharma, P. (2023). Leveraging AI-enabled 6G-driven IoT for sustainable smart cities. *International Journal of Communication Systems*, 36(16), e5588. Advance online publication. DOI: 10.1002/dac.5588

Gharaibeh, A., Salahuddin, M. A., Hussini, S. J., Khreishah, A., Khalil, I., Guizani, M., & Al-Fuqaha, A. (2017). Smart Cities: A Survey on Data Management, Security, and Enabling Technologies. *IEEE Communications Surveys and Tutorials*, 19(4), 2456–2501. DOI: 10.1109/COMST.2017.2736886

Ghor, H. E., & Nakhal, B. (2023). A Blockchain-Enabled Approach for Secure Data Sharing in 6G-based Internet of Things Networks. In Advanced sciences and technologies for security applications (pp. 227–246). DOI: 10.1007/978-3-031-33631-7_8

Giordani, M., Polese, M., Mezzavilla, M., Rangan, S., & Zorzi, M. (2020). Toward 6G Networks: Use Cases and Technologies. *IEEE Communications Magazine*, 58(3), 55–61. DOI: 10.1109/MCOM.001.1900411

Gui, G., Liu, M., Tang, F., Kato, N., & Adachi, F. (2020). 6G: Opening New Horizons for Integration of Comfort, Security and Intelligence. *IEEE Wireless Communications*, 27(5), 1–7. DOI: 10.1109/MWC.001.1900516

Hussain, A. A., & Al-Turjman, F. (2021). Artificial intelligence and blockchain: A review. *Transactions on Emerging Telecommunications Technologies*, 32(9), e4268. Advance online publication. DOI: 10.1002/ett.4268

Imoize, A. L., Adedeji, O., Tandiya, N., & Shetty, S. (2021). 6G Enabled Smart Infrastructure for Sustainable Society: Opportunities, Challenges, and Research Roadmap. *Sensors (Basel)*, 21(5), 1709. DOI: 10.3390/s21051709 PMID: 33801302

Jiang, W., Han, B., Habibi, M. A., & Schotten, H. D. (2021). The Road Towards 6G: A Comprehensive Survey. *IEEE Open Journal of the Communications Society*, 2, 334–366. DOI: 10.1109/OJCOMS.2021.3057679

Karthikeyan, H., & Usha, G. (2023). A secured IoT-based intelligent transport system (IoT-ITS) framework based on cognitive science. *Soft Computing*, •••, 1–11. DOI: 10.1007/s00500-023-08410-7 PMID: 37362258

Khan, M. J. (2023). Zero trust architecture: Redefining network security paradigms in the digital age. *World Journal of Advanced Research and Reviews*, 19(3), 105–116. DOI: 10.30574/wjarr.2023.19.3.1785

Khan, P. W., Byun, Y.-C., & Park, N. (2020). A Data Verification System for CCTV Surveillance Cameras Using Blockchain Technology in Smart Cities. *Electronics (Basel)*, 9(3), 484. DOI: 10.3390/electronics9030484

Khrais, L. T. (2020). IoT and Blockchain in the Development of Smart Cities. *International Journal of Advanced Computer Science and Applications*, 11(2). Advance online publication. DOI: 10.14569/IJACSA.2020.0110220

Komane, B. L., & Mathonsi, T. E. (2023, March 25). *Design of a Smart Waste Management System for the City of Johannesburg*. ArXiv.org. https://doi.org//arXiv.2303.14436DOI: 10.48550

Lee, H., Lee, B., Yang, H., Kim, J., Kim, S., Shin, W., Shim, B., & H. Vincent Poor. (2023). *Towards 6G hyper-connectivity: Vision, challenges, and key enabling technologies*. 1–11. DOI: 10.23919/JCN.2023.000006

Li, W., Su, Z., Li, R., Zhang, K., & Wang, Y. (2020). Blockchain-Based Data Security for Artificial Intelligence Applications in 6G Networks. *IEEE Network*, 34(6), 31–37. DOI: 10.1109/MNET.021.1900629

Liu, Y., Peng, S., Zhang, M., Shi, S., & Fu, J. (2024). Towards secure and efficient integration of blockchain and 6G networks. *PLoS One*, 19(4), e0302052. DOI: 10.1371/journal.pone.0302052 PMID: 38603725

Moudoud, H., Cherkaoui, S., & Khoukhi, L. (2021). *An Overview of Blockchain and 5G Networks. Computational Intelligence in Recent Communication Networks. EAI/Springer Innovations in Communication and Computing*. Springer., DOI: 10.1007/978-3-030-77185-0_1

Mucchi, L., Jayousi, S., Caputo, S., Paoletti, E., Zoppi, P., Geli, S., & Dioniso, P. (2020). How 6G Technology Can Change the Future Wireless Healthcare. *2020 2nd 6G Wireless Summit (6G SUMMIT)*. DOI: 10.1109/6GSUMMIT49458.2020.9083916

Mylrea, M., & Gourisetti, S. N. G. (2017). *Blockchain for smart grid resilience: Exchanging distributed energy at speed, scale and security. 2017 Resilience Week*. RWS., DOI: 10.1109/RWEEK.2017.8088642

Nguyen, T. Q., Ngoc Quyen Tran, Lovén, L., Juha Partala, Tahar Kechadi, & Pirttikangas, S. (2020). *Privacy-Aware Blockchain Innovation for 6G: Challenges and Opportunities*. .DOI: 10.1109/6GSUMMIT49458.2020.9083832

Pardini, K., Rodrigues, J. J. P. C., Diallo, O., Das, A. K., de Albuquerque, V. H. C., & Kozlov, S. A. (2020). A Smart Waste Management Solution Geared Towards Citizens. *Sensors (Basel)*, 20(8), 2380. DOI: 10.3390/s20082380 PMID: 32331464

Porambage, P., Gur, G., Osorio, D. P. M., Liyanage, M., Gurtov, A., & Ylianttila, M. (2021). The Roadmap to 6G Security and Privacy. *IEEE Open Journal of the Communications Society*, 2, 1094–1122. DOI: 10.1109/OJCOMS.2021.3078081

Raddo, T. R., Rommel, S., Cimoli, B., Vagionas, C., Perez-Galacho, D., Pikasis, E., Grivas, E., Ntontin, K., Katsikis, M., Kritharidis, D., Ruggeri, E., Spaleniak, I., Dubov, M., Klonidis, D., Kalfas, G., Sales, S., Pleros, N., & Tafur Monroy, I. (2021). Transition technologies towards 6G networks. *EURASIP Journal on Wireless Communications and Networking, 2021*(1). DOI: 10.1186/s13638-021-01973-9

Samanta, S., Sarkar, A., & Bulo, Y. (2022). Secure 6G Communication in Smart City Using Blockchain. In Lecture notes in networks and systems (pp. 487–496). DOI: 10.1007/978-981-19-4193-1_48

Sharma, S., Popli, R., Singh, S., Chhabra, G., Saini, G. S., Singh, M., Sandhu, A., Sharma, A., & Kumar, R. (2024). The Role of 6G Technologies in Advancing Smart City Applications: Opportunities and Challenges. *Sustainability (Basel)*, 16(16), 7039. DOI: 10.3390/su16167039

Tran, D. A., & Krishnamachari, B. (2022). *Blockchain in a Nutshell. Handbook on Blockchain. Springer Optimization and Its Applications* (Vol. 194). Springer., DOI: 10.1007/978-3-031-07535-3_1

Treiblmaier, H., Rejeb, A., & Strebinger, A. (2020). Blockchain as a Driver for Smart City Development: Application Fields and a Comprehensive Research Agenda. *Smart Cities*, 3(3), 853–872. DOI: 10.3390/smartcities3030044

Trommler, K. P., Hafner, M., Kellerer, W., Merz, P., Schuster, S., Urban, J., Baeder, U., Gunzelmann, B., & Kornbichler, A. (2022). Six Questions about 6G. *ArXiv (Cornell University)*. https://doi.org//arxiv.2201.12266.DOI: 10.48550

Tu, Z., Zhou, H., Li, K., Song, H., & Quan, W. (2023). Blockchain-based differentiated authentication mechanism for 6G heterogeneous networks. *Peer-to-Peer Networking and Applications*, 16(2), 727–748. Advance online publication. DOI: 10.1007/s12083-022-01437-x

Vishnu, S., Ramson, S. R. J., Senith, S., Anagnostopoulos, T., Abu-Mahfouz, A. M., Fan, X., Srinivasan, S., & Kirubaraj, A. A. (2021). IoT-Enabled Solid Waste Management in Smart Cities. *Smart Cities*, 4(3), 1004–1017. DOI: 10.3390/smartcities4030053

Wang, J., Ling, X., Le, Y., Huang, Y., & You, X. (2021). Blockchain-enabled wireless communications: A new paradigm towards 6G. *National Science Review*, 8(9), nwab069. Advance online publication. DOI: 10.1093/nsr/nwab069 PMID: 34691739

Wang, X., Shankar, A., Li, K., Parameshachari, B., & Lv, J. (2024). Blockchain-Enabled Decentralized Edge Intelligence for Trustworthy 6G Consumer Electronics. *IEEE Transactions on Consumer Electronics*, 1(1), 1214–1225. Advance online publication. DOI: 10.1109/TCE.2024.3371501

Wang, Y., Kang, X., Li, T., Wang, H., Chu, C.-K., & Lei, Z. (2023). SIX-Trust for 6G: Towards a Secure and Trustworthy Future Network. *IEEE Access : Practical Innovations, Open Solutions*, 11, 107657–107668. DOI: 10.1109/ACCESS.2023.3321114

Wong, P. F., Chia, F. C., Kiu, M. S., & Lou, E. C. W. (2020). The potential of integrating blockchain technology into smart sustainable city development. *IOP Conference Series. Earth and Environmental Science*, 463(1), 012020. DOI: 10.1088/1755-1315/463/1/012020

Chapter 11
Artificial Intelligence–Enabled Cybersecurity and Internet of Things Applications in Smart Cities

Wasswa Shafik
https://orcid.org/0000-0002-9320-3186
Dig Connectivity Research Laboratory (DCRLab), Kampala, Uganda & School of Digital Science, Universiti Brunei Darussalam, Brunei

ABSTRACT

The rapid adoption of Smart Cities (SCs) has increased reliance on AI-based IoT technologies to enhance smart infrastructure and services, contributing to the UN's sustainable development goals. However, this integration brings significant cybersecurity (CS) challenges, such as DDoS, MITM, phishing, and ransomware attacks. This chapter underscores the importance of CS in SCs, highlighting vulnerabilities and risks. It examines IoT's role in SC infrastructure and services, AI's impact on SC efficiency, and various AI techniques used in SC applications. The chapter analyzes cyberattacks on SC infrastructure, suggesting CS measures like protocols, encryption, authentication techniques, access control, and incident response. AI and IoT integration enhances CS, reducing cyber threats through anomaly detection and real-time data collection for AI-based security solutions. The chapter also presents SC application case studies demonstrating the integration's effectiveness and best practices. It concludes by emphasizing the need for continued research and innovation in SC cybersecurity.

DOI: 10.4018/979-8-3693-8029-1.ch011

1. INTRODUCTION

Smart cities[1] (SCs) have increased substantial fraction in urban development because of their integration with technological advancements such as artificial intelligence[2] (AI), information and communication technologies[3], and the Internet of Things (IoT). Several cities globally are embracing the potential of SC initiatives to improve the life quality of their residents, optimize resource utilization, and improve sustainability[4]. At the core of this transformative shift lies the seamless integration of two enabling technologies, explicitly, AI and IoT (Bilali et al., 2022). Traditionally, SCs are urban areas that utilize digital technologies, data analytics, and internet connectivity to boost their infrastructure and services' livability, effectiveness, and efficiency (Alaali et al., 2022). These cities employ an inclusive tactic for urban growth, considering smart energy[5], waste management, transportation, healthcare, and public safety. This integration allows SCs to seamlessly interact with devices such as sensor systems and transform traditional urban environments into interconnected and intelligent ecosystems (Rajasekar et al., 2022).

The growing significance of SCs stems from their capacity to address the myriad challenges of quickly urbanizing areas. As the global population becomes progressively concentrated in urban areas, cities are confronted with the need to manage limited resources, ease traffic bottlenecks, offer efficient and reliable public facilities, and ensure the well-being and safety of its citizens (Alotaibi & Barnawi, 2023). SC initiatives offer a promising solution by connecting these enabling technologies to automate processes, optimize resource allocation, data-driven decision-making, and enhance the urban experience. AI is the SCs' backbone due to its advanced machine learning[6] (ML), analytical, and predictive capabilities. AI-driven systems can process vast amounts of data collected through IoT devices, identify cyber anomaly patterns, detections make actionable insights, and enable self-sufficient decision-making (Lupton et al., 2022). From smart traffic management to predictive maintenance of perilous infrastructure, AI aids in optimizing the operations of SCs, resulting in enhanced efficiency, cost savings, and sustainability, and technological acceptance in different aspects (Abubakari & Kalinaki, 2024).

The interconnected nature of SC ecosystems and the sheer volume of generated data makes them vulnerable to cyber-attacks and threats (Toma et al., 2022). Developing robust CS measures and strategies to protect SC systems and data integrity, confidentiality, and availability is critical. IoT devices range from daily 'things', for example, smart wearables and phones, to industrial machinery and SC infrastructure (Ahmadi-Assalemi et al., 2022; Gul et al., 2024a; Gul et al., 2024b). With connectivity and sensing capabilities, IoT devices avail vast massive data that can be analyzed for valuable insights (Dhanaraj et al., 2022). IoT systems aim for interoperability, allowing devices from diverse manufacturers to communicate and operate together seamlessly (Dadkhah et al., 2022). The integration empowers the automation of processes, real-time monitoring, and smart decision-making (Hashem et al., 2023).

Figure 1. Main smart city components

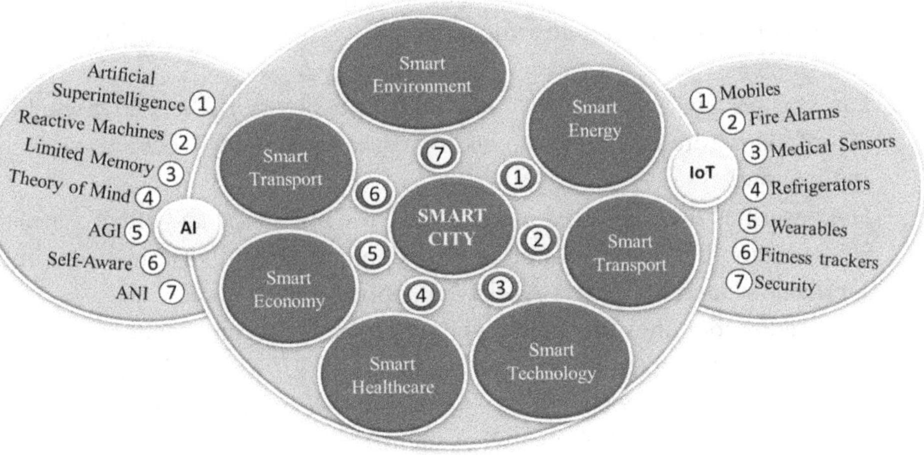

Some industries like healthcare, transportation, energy, manufacturing, and urban technological growth can benefit from IoT and AI, leading to enhanced efficiency and optimized resource allocation. AI-powered IoT systems can enable predictive maintenance, smart energy management, personalized healthcare, autonomous vehicles, and intelligent infrastructure (Mohammadi Makrani et al., 2022). SCs rely on interconnected protecting critical general infrastructure such as transportation systems, energy grids, smart health facility networks, and public safety systems. Any compromise of these critical systems can have severe consequences, leading to disruptions, safety hazards, and potential economic losses (Rangelov et al., 2023; Aslam et al., 2021). CS measures are essential to safeguard SC infrastructure from illegal access, data breaches, and cyberattacks that could compromise essential services' integrity, availability, and reliability. SCs collect, process, and aggregate vast amounts of data from IoT devices, sensors, and AI-driven systems, mitigating data privacy risks. This data often includes sensitive personal data and requires stringent protection to maintain privacy and comply with regulations. The main components of SC and supporting technologies are demonstrated in Figure 1. The interconnected SC system nature and the proliferation of IoT devices increase the attack surface for cybercriminals. Malicious theatres and attackers may exploit vulnerabilities in IoT devices, networks, or software to launch cyberattacks targeting critical infrastructure or disrupting essential services (Aslam, et al., 2022; Fan et al., 2022; Yuvaraj et al., 2022). CS measures like intrusion recognition systems, network segmentation, and regular vulnerability assessments are vital to detecting and mitigating these threats and ensuring the resilience and continuity of SC operations.

1.1 The Contribution of the Chapter

This chapter presents the following contributions, as presented below:

- The chapter presents an overview of SCs, explores IoT's role in enabling SC infrastructure and services, and discusses various IoT devices and their applications.
- The describes the role of AI in advancing the efficiency and effectiveness of SC operations, discusses different AI techniques and algorithms used in SC applications, and highlights AI-driven applications in areas.
- The chapter identifies the major cyber security threats and challenges SC faces, discusses the potential risks associated with IoT and AI implementations in SCs, and analyzes cyberattacks' impact on SC infrastructure and services.
- The chapter explores different cyber security measures and technologies employed in SCs and discusses the security frameworks and protocols explicitly designed for SC environments.
- This chapter discusses the potential of AI and IoT technologies in addressing cyber security challenges. Explored how AI can enhance threat detection, anomaly detection, and predictive analysis in SC environments.
- The chapter presents case studies of existing SC projects that effectively implement AI and IoT while ensuring cyber security.
- Finally, the chapter discusses the emerging trends and technologies that will shape the future of cyber security, AI, and IoT in SCs and presents some lessons learned from the chapter.

2. INTERNET OF THINGS AND THE SMART CITIES

SCs adopt an all-inclusive method for smart urban growth by integrating various domains. The key characteristics of SCs revolve around utilizing technology and data to create interconnected and intelligent ecosystems.

2.1. Key Characteristics of Smart Cities

AI and IoT technology strive to reduce energy consumption, minimize waste, and promote environmentally friendly practices, thus, sustainability. Like, smart grids enable efficient energy distribution, and smart transportation systems, optimize traffic flow and waste management systems, and use data to streamline collection and recycling processes (Jo et al., 2022; Jun et al., 2021). Another key characteristic of SCs is the focus on citizen engagement and participation. They foster a culture of collaboration by involving citizens in decision-making through digital platforms and citizen feedback mechanisms (Galego & Pascoal, 2022). Internet of Things technologies make an essential contribution to this end by enabling a high degree of connectivity between users, varied and numerous urban objects and sensors, and the infrastructure that uses data obtained for storage and analytics. The ability to integrate multiple data inputs in real-time from sensors and devices can allow for a comprehensive, complete real-time model of the state of a city (Wang Yue Dong & Yortsos, 2022). Thus, disparate urban operations can be connected to provide cohesive, model-driven holistic monitoring at an overwhelming, comprehensive urban scale. Challenges, such as dealing with an increasing number of sensors and users, and coping with security in IoT, are the focus of great interest. A city's system of multiple functions can potentially be slowed down or shut down entirely if a portion of these sensors and controls were to be disabled (Jun et al., 2021). The prevention of potential attacks is important to the reliability of such monitors.

This work aims to illustrate research results that are directed towards intertwining intelligence in AI with better cybersecurity and applications in the IoT tailored for smart cities. We have shown why the defense of vital infrastructure in a smart city needs to have high security and reliability. The current silo approach to advanced technology, such as automation or artificial intelligence and the need to improve operations and prevent attacks illustrates the need for cities to embrace technology safely (Shafik et al., 2021). By taking a philanthropic approach to exchange details and sharing attack and defense expertise and research, we propose one way to ensure the protection of the vital infrastructures of cities. We propose the creation of platforms that allow city-to-city text, voice, and video conversations predominantly related to cyber and invasive engagement. The product will make it plausible for cities to use risk analytics to learn from others in their field because enhancing cybersecurity is primarily about knowing and defending against attacks. AI can be great in predicting potential next steps or threat intelligence (Z. Yang et al., 2021).

2.2. Role of IoT in Enabling Smart City Services and Infrastructure

AI algorithms can autonomously analyze data from IoT devices to identify and classify different devices, models, or operating systems, thus detecting security threats. AI systems can process large amounts of data generated by millions of devices within smart city networks, which is not possible for a human to analyze. AI allows for real-time monitoring while testing and refining detection and alerting thresholds. Moreover, AI detects complex trends, patterns, or previously unknown correlations in data that could help in detecting potential threats earlier (Goudarzi et al., 2022; Shafik, 2024a). AI tools may also predict the possible impact and general consequences of particular events on the overall functions of smart urban areas. In this sense, AI systems can develop risk scores or build different types of risk analytics to support decision-makers using communication protocals such as cellular networks[7], Bluetooth[8], or Wi-Fi[9].

AI and cybersecurity intelligence-driven models employ three layers of activities: passive aggregation and correlation, active monitoring and alerting, and security risk assessment. Their adaptive learning capabilities help in improving responsiveness to the evolving threat landscape. AI systems adjust to new situations and learn from past events to develop a set of best practices or to identify potential threats to smart urban areas (Verma et al., 2022; Chemisto et al., 2024). AI-powered algorithms can audit, monitor, and maintain the quality of such vast amounts of personal and operational user data. Moreover, this system can significantly enhance the complexity of inferences that can be drawn from the existing aggregated or anonymized data. Active or passive defense mechanisms can mitigate or even prevent man-made or natural disasters or cyberattacks and, as such, can contribute to the faster development of more efficient, safer, cost-effective, operational, and thus resilient smart city applications. These IoT-driven services improve citizens' convenience, safety, and well-being, contributing to a healthier quality of life[10] (QoL). The role of technology in SC is presented in Figure 2.

Figure 2. Role of technology in the smart city

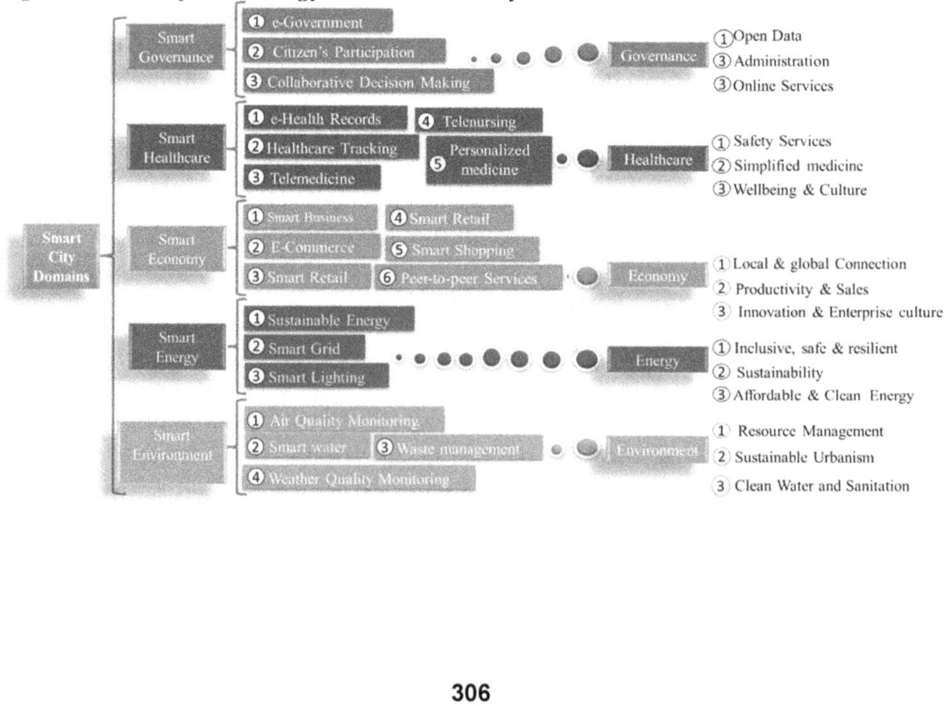

Ensuring that one utilizes and deploys AI in critical environments ethically is fundamental. New mobile technology and blindly accepting the increasing capability of smart technologies in cities may, as the future unfolds, indeed erode the lifestyles, cultures, and freedoms enjoyed up to today. Much of the legislation and legal guidance that affects AI also applies to AIoT. Legislation gives citizens control over their data privacy, recognizing the risks posed by IoT. These ethical issues range from ownership of data to sharing, management, and usage issues. One may utilize CCTV imagery in smart cities for change detection, flood prediction, or to develop a better understanding of pedestrian flows, with much of the resultant data not being classified as sensitive. The ethical debate is critical here: technology should be used to develop smart motivation toward better solutions, yet those in control must have a moral compass that is guided by the community that they serve (Salles & Ribeiro, 2022). Outbreaks of COVID-19 have highlighted how some surveillance technology has been adapted to use facial recognition AI to identify those not wearing masks or unnecessarily venturing into public. This surveillance was often conducted without palpable adult oversight or legal control and has raised legal action and civil disquiet. The issue presents risks related to accountability and transparency. Some cities have implemented open-ethics trajectories, providing citizens with information and seeking input in a bottom-up approach. Data stacks should be designed to be transparent, and systems should be accountable. With this approach, people develop trust, communities can be advocated, and AIoT applications for diverse services can be supported (Bouzidi et al., 2023).

IoT-assisted platforms and applications aid SCs can involving citizens in decision-making processes, gathering feedback, and enabling them to contribute to enlightening SC development services. IoTs facilitate the collection of data on citizen preferences, usage patterns, and needs, consequently permitting SCs to tailor their services and infrastructure(Rodríguez et al., 2023). This citizen-centric approach empowers residents, fosters a sense of ownership, and strengthens the SC's trust and acceptance. Also, SC attains the connectivity, data collection, automation, and intelligence necessary to create interconnected and intelligent urban ecosystems. Through subsidiary IoT and AI technologies, SCs can optimize resource utilization, enhance service delivery, progress safety and security, promote sustainability, and foster citizen engagement (Özarpa et al., 2023).

2.3. Discussion on Various IoT Devices and Their Applications

IoT devices such as vehicle sensors[11], smart traffic lights[12], and connected navigation systems[13] are deployed to enhance traffic congestion and flow transportation efficiency intensification. These IoTs gather real-time data on traffic patterns, vehicle density, and road conditions, allowing for dynamic adjustments in traffic signal timing and the rerouting of vehicles (Abd Elaziz et al., 2023). IoT-enabled smart parking systems utilize sensors to distinguish parking space accessibility and provide immediate information to drivers, reducing the time spent searching for parking spots and easing traffic congestion. Smart meters[14] equipped with IoT abilities enable remote energy consumption monitoring and offer real-time data for energy management. IoT sensors embedded in infrastructure and buildings support optimizing energy usage by adjusting environmental conditions, such as heating, lighting, and cooling systems (Tumbo et al., 2022; Salam et al., 2024). In addition, IoTs simplify response program demands, allowing for load balancing and efficient utilization of energy resources during peak and off-peak periods.

IoT devices are employed in healthcare for remote patient monitoring, telemedicine, and wearable health trackers. IoT-enabled medical devices, like heart rate monitors, blood glucose meters, pressure monitors, and collect patient data and transmit it securely to healthcare providers. This allows for remote monitoring of patient's health conditions, timely intervention, and personalized healthcare delivery (Thilakarathne & Madhuka Priyashan, 2022). Wearable devices[15], like fitness trackers and smartwatches, gather data on individuals' physical activity, such as sleep patterns and vital signs, enabling them to track their health and wellness. AI-IoT[16]-assisted enhances security, emergency response, and surveillance in public safety and the environment. Surveillance cameras equipped with IoT capabilities enable real-time monitoring of public spaces, detecting security threats, and providing timely alerts to authorities.

Historically, the research and development of AI applications for cybersecurity primarily focused on data center infrastructure protection against malicious cyber activities. After increasing its relevance to the performance of various online applications and services delivered to individuals in urban environments, AI-driven cybersecurity technologies have also begun to be optimized for application to the city. This transition from data center performance to the performance of AI applications that contribute to the successful operation of various urban Internet of Things services and applications has increased the attractiveness and potential citywide value of these AI-driven cybersecurity techniques. As cyber threats evolve in their capabilities and the tactics they employ to breach classical security measures, AI technology that supports the computational resources located in and around urban IoT M2M networks is also being adapted to offset those risks. Enhanced capabilities made possible by advances in machine learning and the type and scale of the data analytics performed are also available in some AI-enhanced smart city cybersecurity platforms (Saha et al., 2022).

Various smart city-focused AI applications that optimize digital information campaign strategies and resource management applications have been developed and deployed in several cities. A few successful and noteworthy smart city-scale implementations include Brasilia. More recent generations of AI-enhanced smart city cybersecurity include multisensory agent-based frameworks that were prototyped following natural disasters and platforms that are being deployed in large cities (Alharbi et al., 2022). However, the tech skills, creativity, and ingenuity of cyber attackers cannot be underestimated since attackers are testing and probing city-based systems and policies in order to identify vulnerabilities and ways to evade AI-enabled cybersecurity in smart cities (Sarker et al., 2022). The capability of attackers to continue to exploit security weaknesses, employ social engineering and use tried and tested threats suggests that progressing FinTech, CyberSecure tech, and efforts to forge smart cities should continue to ramp up across all levels of government and industry. The sustainable delivery of smart city-based goods and services can only be effectively achieved while protecting our digital infrastructure (Houda et al., 2022). Ethics and governance trends toward smart cities, the development of AI applications capable of learning the politics of cybersecurity, operational resilience, data privacy, and security analyze other new opportunities to address long-standing issues that could affect cities in our global urban future (Szymanski, 2022).

In 2016, it was an industry-led observation that several large commercial smart city investment projects are taking a wait-and-see approach before going to market. These trial periods will see some smart city applications that utilize AI-enabled cybersecurity for urban applications in infrastructure and services. In the optimization of urban IoT M2M systems, AI applications based on a range of algorithms, software platforms, and decision support systems are being developed and tested in some cities (Losavio et al., 2022). It is expected that the need to continually adopt new communication protocols, identification in authentication systems, basic security protocol maintenance, and examining services from new market entrants and persistent IoT adopter clients will drive innovation toward securing our urban and infrastructure systems (Bhowmik et al., 2022; Kalinaki, 2024). The commercial attractiveness of cybersecurity and IoT economic value is considered to drive these solutions ongoing.

Multiple technological advancements are set to play a part in shaping the cities of the future. With the rollout of networks, the Internet of Things (IoT) is now enabled at more competitive price points than ever. Additionally, the integration of more micro-data centers on the city's edge has increased the computational, storage, and decisional capabilities, along with the resulting outcomes and implications of the IoT paradigm, in a concept known as edge computing. Technologies are also primed to enhance the sharing of data, providing transactions that are secure by design and integral to the control of the network. Furthermore, using a network of computers to store all transactions in each block can be a key technology in terms of transparent data sharing as well as the provision of a secure and accurate data store (Ali et al., 2022). Artificial intelligence is another key technology that is being extensively explored as a means to enhance smart cities. Machine learning can be applied to predictive maintenance, fault and incident analytics, and at the other end of the supply chain, can be used for smart demand-side management and the control of smart grids. Autonomous vehicles, such as autonomous electric buses, are also in scope. Technologies that are already in place to create sensor networks, collect data, and semi-automatically apply data analysis are also being explored. Sustainability is also key (Sarker, 2022). The use of electric vehicles, as well as the development of infrastructures that generate smarter air conditioning and heating costs, is fundamental in order to address environmental and human exploitation. This is the only approach in which we can be sure that smart cities can be 'fair.' All of these trends and services in smart cities are developing into real-life projects. In this context, many pilot projects are already under testing, cutting-edge collaborations among scientists, technology developers, industry, city planners, and local communities (F. Yang et al., 2022). AI can also analyze data from healthcare systems and public health records to identify patterns and trends in disease outbreaks, enabling early detection and proactive measures to mitigate public health risks, ensuring smart governance, people, infrastructure, technology, and the environment.

2.4. Discussion on Different Artificial Intelligence Techniques

Different AI algorithms and techniques are employed in various SC applications to enable smart decision-making, data analysis, and automation, as explained below:

2.4.1. Machine Learning (ML) and Deep Learning (DL)

ML algorithms are extensively used in SC applications for tasks such as predictive analysis, anomaly detection, and pattern recognition. Supervised learning algorithms, for example, support vector machines, neural networks, and decision trees, are used for classification and regression tasks. Unsupervised learning algorithms, for example, clustering and dimensionality reduction, are applied to discover patterns and group similar data (Prazeres et al., 2023). Reinforcement learning algorithms are used in scenarios where an agent learns to interact with its environment to maximize rewards, for instance, optimizing traffic signal timing or energy consumption in smart buildings. DL, a subset of ML, involves training deep neural networks with multiple layers to learn complex patterns and representations. Convolutional neural networks are commonly used in SC applications for tasks like image and video analysis, for example, detecting objects, traffic signs, or pedestrian movements from surveillance cameras. Recurrent Neural Networks are utilized for analyzing sequential data, for example, time-series data from IoT sensors, to make predictions or detect anomalies (Bhardwaj et al., 2022).

2.4.2. Natural Language Processing (NLP) and Optimization Algorithms

These techniques enable communication and interaction between humans and SC systems. NLP algorithms are employed in virtual assistants, voice recognition, and chatbots to understand and respond to users' natural language queries or commands (Javed et al., 2022). NLP enables SC requests to provide personalized services, answer inquiries, and assist in tasks like finding information, navigating the city, or accessing public services. Optimization algorithms are applied in SC applications to solve complex optimization problems, for instance, route optimization, resource allocation, and scheduling. These AI algorithms use mathematical optimization techniques to find the best solutions for constraints and objectives (Chentouf & Bouchkaren, 2023). For example, particle swarm optimization, simulated annealing, or genetic algorithms can optimize traffic flow, reduce energy consumption, or allocate resources efficiently in SC operations.

2.4.3. Bayesian Networks

Bayesian networks (BNs) are probabilistic models representing ambiguous relationships between variables. BNs are used in SC applications for fault detection, risk assessment, and predictive analysis. BNs enable reasoning under uncertainty by incorporating prior knowledge and updating probabilities based on new evidence (Lei & Liu, 2022). More still, BNs applied in environmental monitoring, healthcare, and public safety, to analyze data, assess risks, and make appropriate decisions (Case, 2022). Using AI techniques helps SCs analyze data, enhance decision-making capabilities, optimize resource utilization, automate processes, and lead to more efficient and sustainable urban environments.

3. CYBERSECURITY CHALLENGES IN SMART CITIES

With governments, companies, and citizens utilizing modern technology to improve productivity and efficiency at home and work and improve lives, SCs have become a reality today. Figure 3 is an overview of the SC. The need for a particular CS model for SCs has arisen because of the increasing difficulties in maintaining safety, security, and data privacy (B et al., 2019; Cyber Security for Smart Cities, n.d). A city is "smart" if it uses cutting-edge technology, infrastructure, and other innovative approaches to increase operational efficiency, deliver better services, and enhance the QoL for its residents. The technology ecosystem comprises Information and Communication Technology (ICT), IoT, AI or ML, blockchain, and cloud computing. However, utilizing modern technology comes with CS concerns that could compromise the citizens' PII (Personally Identifiable Information)'s confidentiality, integrity, and availability (CIA). The challenges, dangers, and potential solutions to these problems are examined in more detail below. CS hazards are present in SCs, along with their challenges and potential answers. There are the following challenges in the security of SCs (Khadidos et al., 2022).

Figure 3. Application of the smart city

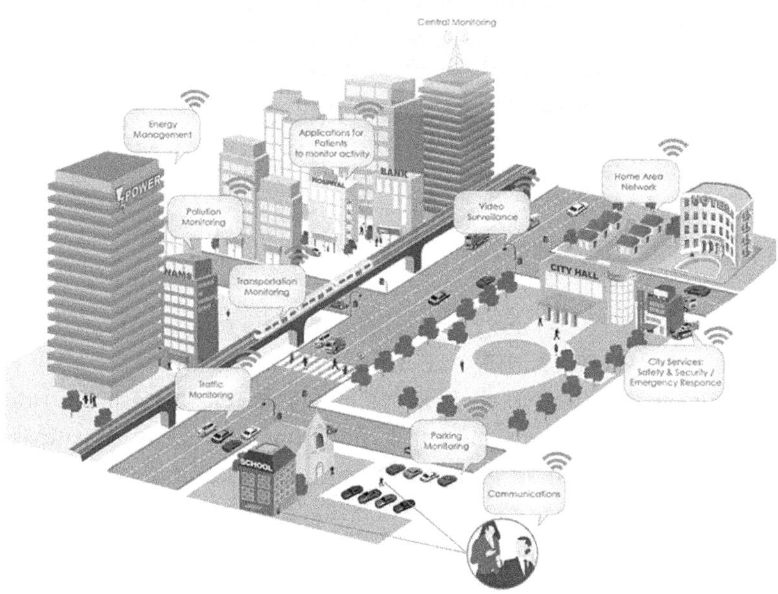

3.1. Number of Devices, Varieties, and Efficient Data Processing Requirement

A vast and interconnected network of users, platforms, systems, and devices supports SCs. By 2021, 25 billion linked devices are predicted by Gartner. Many of them might not have been tested or patched, putting the information control systems at risk (Andrade et al., 2020). Prioritization, analysis, and real-time data processing are required for mission-critical services for the SC ecosystem, such as facial recognition and traffic systems. Mainly the information from infrastructure services like parking lots, video feeds from security cameras, and EV charging stations. They may be susceptible to cyberattacks if not adequately safeguarded and classified (Mohammad, 2019; Security foundation, n.d.).

3.2. Vulnerabilities, Connectivity, Transparency and Data Privacy

By 2024, there will be about 1.3 billion WAN connections in SCs, according to ABI Research. None of them may be able to address problems with digital and communication security (Ma, 2021a). While improving coverage and reducing latency and bandwidth costs, communication breakthroughs can also open users to attack. The massive amount of personally identifiable information (PII) that SCs' residents' IVR (interactive voice response), webcams, facial recognition, CCTV cameras, and other similar systems will collect will be a problem. Therefore, it will be necessary for SCs to put in place suitable control methods that address both technical and legal issues.

3.3. Cyber Security Risks in Smart Cities

SCs are created to coordinate the operation of internal systems to guarantee residents' comfort while minimizing environmental damage. In other words, it uses cutting-edge digital technologies to organize urban life novelly. Automation, rationalization, and safety are the three pillars on which SCs are built. Municipal and private sectors work together to accomplish a common goal in such communities (Ma, 2021b). SC is, unfortunately, a popular target for hackers and cyber terrorists. Therefore, CS for SCs is essential for ensuring the security of other networks, the financial sector, and personal data.

3.4. DDoS Attacks

A distributed denial of service attack aims to turn off a network resource. A communications host is attacked by hackers who bombard it with many requests up to hundreds of thousands per second. The service becomes unavailable when it is overcrowded and unable to handle real requests. DDoS in SCs can momentarily take down equipment like traffic lights and parking meters (Khalil et al., 2022). To manage things like utilities, traffic, and parking, sensors in SCs gather device data from assets and residences. There is big data analytics in SCs for frequent use to enhance services, but sadly, hackers are known to access vulnerable IoT devices. Because they target numerous sources, DDoS attacks are challenging to thwart. For instance, to interfere with systems in SCs, the Mirai malware scans unprotected Internet of Things devices with preset passwords. Mirai's targeting of Dyn, the business in charge of most of the domain name system (DNS) infrastructure on the Internet, in 2016, is a well-known instance of technology in action (Soare Senior et al., n.d.). Many websites in America, including Twitter, Netflix, Reddit, CNN, and others, were down due to the cyberattack, as were many websites in Europe.

3.5. Data Breaches and Phishing

Information systems with insufficient security measures are susceptible to assaults that result in data leaks. Data breaches may involve Protected Health Information (PHI) and PII, with disastrous results. Cyber risks that threaten the CIA, safety, and resilience of information assets that can result in significant cyberattacks must be taken seriously by SCs (Soare Senior et al., n.d.). Parking garages, security cameras, and electric car charging stations are examples of SC infrastructure that regularly produce data that can attract cybercriminals as a target. Fraudsters specifically use security flaws to obtain personal data. Figure 4 illustrates the application of IoT in smart cities.

Figure 4. Applications of the Internet of Things in Smart Cities

3.6. Connectivity of Complex Network and Man-In-The-Middle (MITM)

Public and private networks' intricate interconnectedness with other information systems might cause problems. A problem in one service area can spread to others without an effective CS strategy and framework. Public Wi-Fi networks are the largest threat to the SC environment, according to a recent Statista report. An attacker intercepts data sent between two systems or objects in this cyberattack. As a result, the attacker can steal, replace, or erase this data (Zhang et al., 2021).

3.7. Device Hijacking and Permanent Denial of Service

The device is breached by hackers, who then seize total control. As a result, they might not damage the device, which makes it very challenging to identify the attack. Alternatively, the hacker can watch the data or utilize the device covertly. A hacker may, for instance, steal electricity by breaking into a smart meter. When using device hijacking, cybercriminals' usual operating procedure is to keep the gadget's fundamental functions mostly untouched to avoid being easily identified. A hacker who gets entry into the company environment can quickly mitigate the overall system devices on that network. Emergency alarm network, street video, and traffic lights, monitoring all weak entry points to attacks. Smart waste management and satellite water leak detection systems are some of the safest technologies. Similarly, the device will be destroyed via Permanent Denial of Service (PDoS). The device may malfunction due to overloading, which must be fixed or replaced entirely. This can include willful damage to an SC's traffic lights, meters, charging stations, smart cities, and community framework structure in the US, as illustrated in Figure 5.

Figure 5. Smart cities and communities framework structure

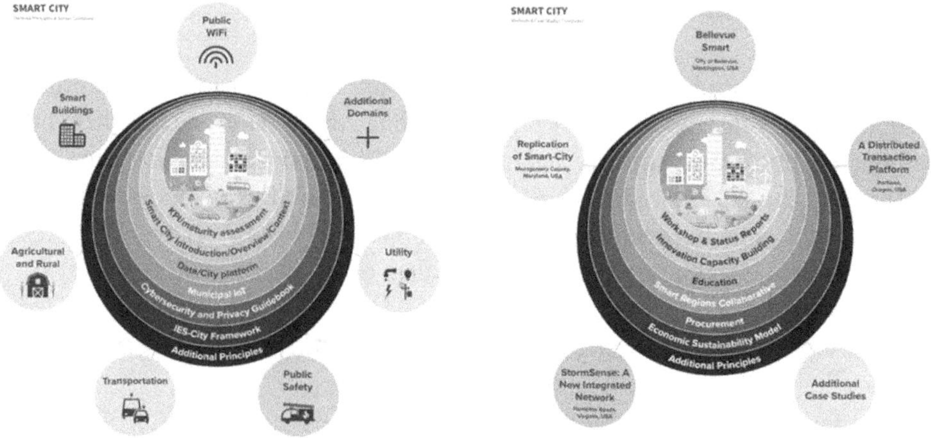

(credit: https://www.nist.gov/ctl)

4. CYBERSECURITY APPLICATIONS FOR SMART CITIES

A group of integrated technologies communicating data at once in a specific metropolitan setting is depicted as the SC. It makes services sustainably and effectively, resources, and managing assets easier, which helps local companies and citizens run more smoothly. It is significant to stress that there are no precise standards to judge if a region, town, city, or country is "smart." Therefore, rather than using any set criterion, judging a place's "smartness" would be possible using a maturity scale. There is no denying that the idea of SCs can potentially raise our standard of living. To ensure data privacy, security, and privacy, design companies must have a strategy to overcome cyber security issues. Many difficulties are related to harmonious connections between several organizations and technological platforms rather than flaws in a single technology or system, which means that a large portion of the 'issue' is not physically present. It is necessary to secure their design using a principle-based approach to give the government and local authorities the flexibility to customize their strategy according to the situation while ensuring that key security risks' likelihood and impact are addressed. To prevent implementing security controls retroactively in the future, which is less efficient and frequently more expensive, it is imperative to address these issues up front. There are some basic principles for cyber security in SCs, which include:

4.1. Understanding of Smart City Architecture\Environment

Once you thoroughly understand your operators, local guests, data processors, partners, and supply chain, you can create security responsibilities and interact with important stakeholders. Establish a transparent framework for security governance for SCs while identifying the talents and vendors needed to contribute to its secure operation. Determine and evaluate the risk to the planned environment constantly and enable continuous resource and investment prioritization. Determine who is responsible for risk in the SC while defining security criteria and assurance mechanisms. Describing the ensuing security risk management needs for all organizations that contribute to the services of SCs. Apply end-to-end security lifecycle management by identifying and responding appropriately to vulnerabilities that influence SCs (Habib et al., 2023). At the same time, establish partnerships with critical third parties to create support plans that work and increase confidence in their goods and services.

4.2. Security Risk Reduction Design of the Smart City

Focus on security fundamentals to minimize exposure. Adopting a systematic approach to security services ensures security-by-design concepts are incorporated into the design, procurement, and construction phases. Utilize a thorough monitoring architecture to identify and address threats, reduce the impact of compromise through monitoring and segregation, and respond to intrusions. Create resilient SC services, prepare for emergencies, and practice responding with important partners, including emergency services and suppliers (Yang & Sun, 2022). In addition to physical activity, effective awareness campaigns should highlight security threats and the incident response procedures in place to safeguard citizens and tourists of SCs and their data. IoT sensors and controllers of many kinds, such as traffic control, lane optimization, smart lighting, smart parking sensors, structured health awareness, and others, make up SCs. It is also not easy to remember that live platform cloud analyses and saves consolidated SC data. Cyber protection is in the AI edge lab of SC, for example, malware identification, intrusion detection, automated security, and network attack classification and detection depending on the challenges[17], as demonstrated in Figure 6.

Figure 6. Mitigating the smart cities cybersecurity challenge

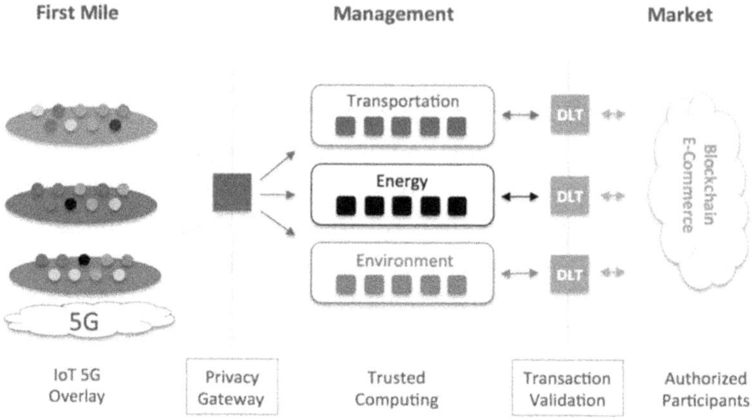

5. INTEGRATION OF AI AND IOT FOR CYBER SECURITY IN SMART CITIES

The convergence of AI and IoT technologies redefines how people work and live, enhancing their sustainability, livability, and efficiency. Real-time data analysis from various devices simplifies decision-making and administrative chores, maximizing resource use and enhancing public safety. The idea of the "SC" uses technology to enhance various aspects of daily life, including public safety, traffic control, solid waste management, sustainable communities, irrigation, and healthcare. Urban living is being transformed by the advantages of AI and IoT technology in cities like Singapore, Amsterdam, Barcelona, and Dubai (Khan et al., 2022). Given that digitization gives IoT networks an extra sharp edge for operational purposes and development, an incredible opportunity is represented in smart devices for value creation in the SCs division. SCs also have a significant attack surface that can be used against them. There is a severe and immediate risk here. Technology usage increases city vulnerabilities, with cyberattacks presenting the most technologically advanced city priority.

5.1. Smart City Components

Some essential components used in SCs are the key components that make a SC to call it smart. These networks help transfer data between sensors or IoT devices used in SCs, infrastructure devices, and data components. They comprise a variety of data-gathering tools, including air quality, sensors, traffic monitoring tools, energy usage, and others. For SCs to function well, these are necessary. IoT and data analytics can transform infrastructure, including buildings, roads, and other public spaces. Alternatively, AI and data analytics may enhance public services, including public transportation, healthcare, education, and public safety. Using the data, alarms are sent to the appropriate authorities about regions needing their attention, such as those with excessive air pollution levels or water waste.

5.2. AI Ways to Transform Urban Life

The impact of the nexus of AI and IoT technologies on living and working in SCs is growing every day. Combining these two technologies has ushered in a period of invention, efficiency, and sustainability previously unimaginable to humanity. Decision-making and administrative duties can now be completed with little human intervention thanks to real-time analysis of continuously generated data by several devices simultaneously. For instance, traffic signals fitted with IoT sensors can track traffic flow, which can then be evaluated using AI algorithms, allowing traffic lights to adjust to the traffic volume at a specific crossroads in the city. Another intriguing application is in managing and collecting solid waste, where IoT-enabled ultrasonic sensors in smart trash can enable alerts on the amount of waste present. The technologies primarily reduce human engagement, better resource management, greater productivity, and cost and time savings. In addition, sustainability is essential in SCs and can be enhanced through several eco-friendly measures. Data on air quality and water use are gathered and analyzed by AI methods using sensors deployed throughout the city.

6. CASE STUDIES AND BEST PRACTICES

According to researchers, traffic signals, street videos, and surveillance are the most vulnerable to cyber-attacks. Unlike this, satellite water leak detection and smart water systems are more secure from cyber-attacks. Some real cyber-attack cases in SCs like Oldsmar, FL water plant attack. The attacker attacked the SCADA system[18] of the water plant and varied the sodium hydroxide amount.

With appropriate coordination and taking several security measures, reducing SC risks in SCs is possible. There are two methods for achieving this. One is to hire security experts who do not come from the inside but from outside organizations that look after the security network's vulnerabilities. Third-party businesses will simulate the risks and see for any holes. The security firm will notice vulnerabilities and inform the experts of such attacks. Information about the attacker's entry into the system is the second action to know whether the attack is successful. There are the following recommendations for regular security monitoring, support platforms, and encrypted data. While purchasing costly security systems is for SC security and service assurance, several less expensive methods can promote safer interconnection. The following suggestions include initiating with the small-level concept, avoiding overreliance on smart technology, getting overall knowledge about advanced technology, developing a well-trained and experienced security team, and preparing yourself for the worst. Therefore, the people managing the SC's development and deployment determine how a smart city operates. Society can defend itself and its inhabitants by defending a city's smart system.

7. CASE STUDIES AND BEST PRACTICES

7.1. Public-Private Partnership to Enhance Awareness of AI-Enabled Cybersecurity Key Challenges Addressed

A brand-new governance strategy in place; explored existing strategies and governing mechanisms to develop best practices and strategies. Solutions developed and implemented: enumerated and explored the advantages of public-private strategies to increase public awareness and promote smart city growth and security; developed best practices for managing and operating citywide AI-run surveillance systems. Outcomes: reduction of incidents threefold; reduction of response times by 88.57%. Lessons learned: establishing governance models requires stakeholders from all communities; engaging stakeholder representatives in dialogue increases the value of the strategies.

7.2. Introducing AI to Smart City Infrastructures Capable of Providing Privacy Key Challenges Addressed

Explored a novel approach to examine the benefits and challenges of combining AI-enabled edge devices and private data centers with useful IoT applications to increase smart home, city, and industry outcomes of interest. Solutions developed and implemented: developed AI models that could be used to enhance image translation, intelligent monitoring (as an effective IoT application to manage, for example, water usage in public places), and smart home automation; developed data algorithms that ran the AI image translation system on the Edge Server and Data Center; allowed end-users a way to private processing (useful in a distributed architecture where smart homes can use their data to inform the operation of buildings). Outcomes: any results would have to show the virtue, or not of open-source models on different

Edge Servers and infrastructures, the need for community consultation and user research, and whether such AI-surveillance techniques have utility across various IoT systems in the smart city space. Lessons learned: AI cities aren't just "smart" – they are also safer, greener, healthier, and more efficient for everyone; open-source solutions that allow privacy-preserving AI and image analysis as a part of an IoT monitoring system, "edge surveillance," are increasingly important.

7.3. Successful Implementations of AI-Enabled Cybersecurity in Smart Cities

While there are no reports on the scaled-to-a-city success regarding the integration of cybersecurity and IoT applications driven by AI-enabled enlargement, several AI-based cybersecurity success stories are known to improve the security of different processes within a city. One city uses its supercomputing infrastructure to track the spread of viruses against construction schedules, while another uses a quantum simulator to optimize algorithms for urban planning. Similarly, a number of other cities have already rolled out AI technologies to monitor and manage various processes but have not reported the integration of AI-driven cybersecurity with their IoT applications. Such cities are mentioned below to emphasize that there are areas within a city where AI-driven cybersecurity can be used.

In the area of smart video surveillance, one city has implemented smart cameras and facial recognition systems, which are known for their technological advancements. The cameras are used to monitor the movements of people and report on the behavior of those who disobey traffic laws. Although the traffic police have not reported real-time crime prevention or prosecution using these cameras, it is quite possible that this behavior record will be used to track people in other areas of the city. Even if these cameras are attacked and taken off the city's network, jaywalking behavior can be recorded internally to city IT systems; this is the reason this surveillance effort is successful and inexpensive. Reforming existing anomaly detection using AI-driven tools increases observations while decreasing law enforcement costs; similar applications can be deployed on IoT-based security monitoring.

7.4. Lessons Learned and Recommendations for Future Deployments

While the cybersecurity integration with AI has been seen as one of the greatest achievements, cities and their cybersecurity stakeholders have also faced certain limitations and pitfalls that AI adoption presents. It has been stated that much experimentation needs to take place in order to arrive at an effective integration for a constantly evolving urban environment. As cities reshape and alter inner-city operations while augmenting new technologies, it is also imperative to evaluate ongoing cybersecurity efforts and their effectiveness. Working in spaces where a level of uncertainty and continued growth and change is the norm, cities need the capacity to monitor, rewind, and adapt their cybersecurity strategies to the communities that they are supporting. Once services are rolled out or new technology is adopted, privacy and data concerns quickly become a top priority. For this reason, cities in the future will need cautious and robust data governance to satisfy the public whom they serve.

- Insofar as lessons learned, it is clear that training for all users is a must. That refers not only to the citizens but to city employees, academics, and industries that work alongside the public sector. Efforts at municipalities in the future should bring affected communities into training and exercises aimed at improving resiliency to citywide cyber incidents.
- Large-scale data collection has the potential to greatly improve future urban environments, as do the predictive analytics derived from such data; however, this activity also has potentially undesirable consequences in the form of privacy violations. Residents denied the right to data ownership and control feel exploited.
- Many prospective problem scenarios were raised in the forum. Unfortunately, in the developers' race to innovate and launch new projects or services, there is little thought of the potential security vulnerabilities these projects and services may bring about.

Melding IoT devices with AI and cybersecurity support will take time, patience, and perpetual vigilance in order to protect the privacy of citizens, their livelihoods, and the things that tie them to urban environments. Smart cities certainly must drive toward an urban environment that uses new technologies to 'be smart,' but with the understanding that the real novel thing will be to cultivate a healthy environment that offers a sense of belonging and that is safe for a very diverse public. The public should have the freedom to participate in a digital discourse that shapes the future of smart urban living and should not be subject to the architecture of preconceived systems that shape their experience of spaces before they even have a say in whether or not such a system should be adopted. The activities conducted in smart cities' AI-enabled cybersecurity capabilities have yielded many lessons learned. This research has identified cybersecurity and AI integration best practices and pitfalls that stakeholders should consider for longer-term planning. Failure to anticipate the impacts of AI integration with cybersecurity has the potential to result in undesirable outcomes if insights are not provided to municipalities, industries, and the public at large. Providing lessons learned and recommendations for improved AI deployments presents a roadmap toward creating sustainable, secure environments in smart cities.

8. FUTURE DIRECTIONS AND CONCLUSIONS

Several emerging trends and technologies are expected to shape the future of cyber security, AI, and IoT in SCs.

8.1. Future Research Trends

These advancements will be crucial in addressing the evolving challenges and ensuring the SC infrastructure's efficient and secure operation. Edge computing[19] enables real-time data processing and analysis at the network's edge, which is a necessity of cloud infrastructure to reduce latency. This trend allows faster response times and enhanced security by minimizing data transfer and keeping sensitive information within the local network. Blockchain technology[20] offers decentralized and tamper-proof transactions and data storage. Blockchain can enhance security and privacy by providing a transparent and immutable record of transactions and data exchanges. Quantum computing[21] can potentially transform CS by offering provocatively enhanced computing power. While still in its early stages, quantum computing could break current cryptographic algorithms, necessitating the development of quantum-resistant cryptographic techniques. In SCs, quantum computing can strengthen encryption methods, secure data transmission, and enhance the robustness of CS measures (Gu et al., 2023). Federated learning[22] (FL) is an emerging approach that permits ML models to be trained across various decentralized devices without transmitting raw data to a central server. FL technique preserves data security and privacy while empowering collaborative model training.

The rapid evolution of cybersecurity from the classic reactive approach to intelligent technologies, consisting of artificial intelligence, big data, and the IoT, has changed the entire process of protecting against threats and data escape. The new and complex advanced persistent threats require very quick responses to stop data breaches. Thus, these deliberate and continuing hacking, such as APT 41[23], make information systems security very hard to achieve, and simultaneous use of an abundance of different entities, such as IoT, makes these systems the next fortress that needs to be continuously monitored and defended. Currently, in most manifestations of this type of risk that involve internal collaboration, the data exfiltration generally leaves the boundary of the system attacked. The use of the always-on internet protocol allows a data-like flow, such as people walking through a door, a perfect mimetic camouflage. The careful use of the authorization schema is also used to associate a received command at the location of authorized techniques to execute, such as the use of the sheet metal shear to cut the lock (Shafiik, 2024b). The induced action introduces the opportunity for triage with the active defense agent in order to trace the potential steps of the intruders and have additional information to start a process of response to any destruction (or theft).

8.2. Lessons Learned From the Chapter

The following are some of the lessons that can be drawn from the chapter:

- SCs' growing significance in urban development calls for robust CS measures. Prioritizing CS from the initial planning and implementation stages is crucial to ensuring the CIA of SC systems and data.
- CS challenges in SCs require collaboration among stakeholders, including government bodies, city administrators, technology providers, and citizens. Collaboration can facilitate information sharing, a coordinated response to cyber threats, and the implementation of consistent security measures across various domains of SCs.
- Incorporating security measures into the design and architecture of SC infrastructure is vital to mitigating CS risks. Security considerations should be integrated at every level, including the design of IoT devices, network infrastructure, data storage, and AI algorithms. CS best practices instigation in the early stages of development can help prevent and detect cyberattacks more efficiently.
- SCs are dynamic environments with a huge volume of data and diverse, interconnected systems. Establishing continuous monitoring mechanisms to detect and respond to cyber threats in real time is essential.
- Realizing robust threat intelligence capabilities, including threat detection systems, security information, security analytics, and event management solutions, can enable rapid incident response, proactive threat hunting, and vulnerability management in SC environments.
- IoT, CS, and AI fields continuously evolve, with technologies emerging and new threats and attacks regularly. SCs essential stay updated with the latest trends, technologies, and best practices in CS. Regular risk assessments, security audits, and penetration testing can help identify vulnerabilities and adapt security measures accordingly.
- Investing in research and development, fostering innovation, and promoting a culture of CS awareness is critical for SCs to stay resilient in the face of evolving cyber threats.

CONCLUSION

SCs continue to develop, and the reliance on IoT and AI technologies has become crucial for optimizing urban infrastructure and services. Nevertheless, this dependence also brings significant CS challenges that demand immediate attention. The analysis has shed light on the impact of cyberattacks on SC infrastructure and services. Also, the chapter has delved into SC's CS technologies and measures, including security protocols, encryption, frameworks, authentication, access control, and incident response. Furthermore, IoT and AI integration for CS in SCs has been explored, highlighting how AI can strengthen threat detection and anomaly detection by leveraging real-time data collected from IoT devices and sensors. By proactively tackling these challenges and adopting robust CS measures, SCs can harness the full potential of IoT and AI while ensuring the safety and privacy of their citizens.

REFERENCES

Abd Elaziz, M., Al-qaness, M. A. A., Dahou, A., Ibrahim, R. A., & El-Latif, A. A. A. (2023). Intrusion detection approach for cloud and IoT environments using deep learning and Capuchin Search Algorithm. *Advances in Engineering Software*, 176, 103402. Advance online publication. DOI: 10.1016/j.advengsoft.2022.103402

Abubakari, M. S., & Kalinaki, K. (2024). Digital Competence in Islamic Education for Lifelong Learning: Preliminary Analysis Using DigComp 2.1 Framework. In *Embracing Technological Advancements for Lifelong Learning* (pp. 1-31). IGI Global. https://doi.org/DOI: 10.4018/979-8-3693-1410-4.ch001

Ahmadi-Assalemi, G., Al-Khateeb, H., Epiphaniou, G., & Aggoun, A. (2022). Super Learner Ensemble for Anomaly Detection and Cyber-Risk Quantification in Industrial Control Systems. *IEEE Internet of Things Journal*, 9(15), 13279–13297. Advance online publication. DOI: 10.1109/JIOT.2022.3144127

Alaali, A. M., Alateeq, A., & Elmedany, W. (2022). Cybersecurity Threats and Solutions of IoT Network Layer. 2022 International Conference on Innovation and Intelligence for Informatics, Computing, and Technologies, 3ICT 2022. https://doi.org/DOI: 10.1109/3ICT56508.2022.9990734

Alharbi, S., Attiah, A., & Alghazzawi, D. (2022). Integrating Blockchain with Artificial Intelligence to Secure IoT Networks: Future Trends. *Sustainability (Basel)*, 14(23), 16002. Advance online publication. DOI: 10.3390/su142316002

Ali, H., Elzeki, O. M., & Elmougy, S. (2022). Smart Attacks Learning Machine Advisor System for Protecting Smart Cities from Smart Threats. *Applied Sciences (Basel, Switzerland)*, 12(13), 6473. Advance online publication. DOI: 10.3390/app12136473

Alotaibi, A., & Barnawi, A. (2023). Securing massive IoT in 6G: Recent solutions, architecture, and future directions. In Internet of Things (Netherlands) (Vol. 22). https://doi.org/DOI: 10.1016/j.iot.2023.100715

Andrade, R. O., Yoo, S. G., Tello-Oquendo, L., & Ortiz-Garces, I. (2020). *A Comprehensive Study of the IoT Cybersecurity in Smart Cities*. IEEE., DOI: 10.1109/ACCESS.2020.3046442

Aslam, M. M., Ahmed, Z., Du, L., Hassan, M. Z., Ali, S., & Nasir, M. (2022). An Overview of Recent Advances of Resilient Consensus for Multiagent Systems under Attacks. *Computational Intelligence and Neuroscience*, 2022(1), 6732343. DOI: 10.1155/2022/6732343 PMID: 39411550

Aslam, M. M., Du, L., Zhang, X., Chen, Y., Ahmed, Z., & Qureshi, B. (2021). Sixth generation (6G) cognitive radio network (CRN) application, requirements, security issues, and key challenges. *Wireless Communications and Mobile Computing*, 2021(1), 1331428. DOI: 10.1155/2021/1331428

Bhardwaj, A., Kumar, M., Stephan, T., Shankar, A., Ghalib, M. R., & Abujar, S. (2022). IAF: IoT Attack Framework and Unique Taxonomy. *Journal of Circuits, Systems, and Computers*, 31(2), 2250029. Advance online publication. DOI: 10.1142/S0218126622500293

Bhowmik, T., Bhadwaj, A., Kumar, A., & Bhushan, B. (2022). *Machine Learning and Deep Learning Models for Privacy Management and Data Analysis in Smart Cites* (Vol. 215). In Intelligent Systems Reference Library., DOI: 10.1007/978-3-030-90119-6_13

Bilali, V. G., Kosyvas, D., Theodoropoulos, T., Ouzounoglou, E., Karagiannidis, L., & Amditis, A. (2022). IRIS Advanced Threat Intelligence Orchestrator- A Way to Manage Cybersecurity Challenges of IoT Ecosystems in Smart Cities. Lecture Notes in Computer Science (Including Subseries Lecture Notes in Artificial Intelligence and Lecture Notes in Bioinformatics), 13533 LNCS. https://doi.org/DOI: 10.1007/978-3-031-20936-9_25

Bouzidi, M., Amro, A., Dalveren, Y., Alaya Cheikh, F., & Derawi, M. (2023). LPWAN Cyber Security Risk Analysis: Building a Secure IQRF Solution. *Sensors (Basel)*, 23(4), 2078. Advance online publication. DOI: 10.3390/s23042078 PMID: 36850676

Case, J. A. (2022). Deep Learning and Artificial Intelligence: What Does the Cardiologist Really Need to Know? In Circulation: Cardiovascular Imaging (Vol. 15, Issue 9). https://doi.org/DOI: 10.1161/CIRCIMAGING.122.014744

Chemisto, M., Kalinaki, K., Oloya, I. T., Tar, J. L., Percival, E. G. A. U., KIRYA, F., ... & KISITU, R. (2024, May). ICT for Improved Maternal Healthcare in Uganda: A Systematic Literature Review. *In 2024 IST-Africa Conference (IST-Africa)* (pp. 1-11). IEEE. https://doi.org/DOI: 10.23919/IST-Africa63983.2024.10569857

Chentouf, F. Z., & Bouchkaren, S. (2023). Security and privacy in smart city: A secure e-voting system based on blockchain. *Iranian Journal of Electrical and Computer Engineering*, 13(2), 1848. Advance online publication. DOI: 10.11591/ijece.v13i2.pp1848-1857

Dadkhah, S., Mahdikhani, H., Danso, P. K., Zohourian, A., Truong, K. A., & Ghorbani, A. A. (2022). Towards the Development of a Realistic Multidimensional IoT Profiling Dataset. 2022 19th Annual International Conference on Privacy, Security and Trust, PST 2022. https://doi.org/DOI: 10.1109/PST55820.2022.9851966

Dhanaraj, R. K., Rajasekar, V., Hafizul Islam, S. K., Balusamy, B., & Hsu, C. H. (2022). Quantum blockchain: An emerging cryptographic paradigm. In Quantum Blockchain: An Emerging Cryptographic Paradigm. https://doi.org/DOI: 10.1002/9781119836728

El Houda, Z. A., Brik, B., & Khoukhi, L. (2022). "Why Should I Trust Your IDS?": An Explainable Deep Learning Framework for Intrusion Detection Systems in Internet of Things Networks. *IEEE Open Journal of the Communications Society*, 3, 1164–1176. Advance online publication. DOI: 10.1109/OJCOMS.2022.3188750

Fan, J., Yang, W., & Lam, K.-Y. (2022). Cybersecurity Challenges of IoT-enabled Smart Cities: A Survey. IEEE Internet Of Things Journal, https://doi.org//arXiv.2202.05023.DOI: 10.48550

Galego, N. M. C., & Pascoal, R. M. (2022). Cybersecurity in Smart Cities: Technology and Data Security in Intelligent Transport Systems. Smart Innovation. *Systems and Technologies*, 256. Advance online publication. DOI: 10.1007/978-981-16-5063-5-2

Goudarzi, A., Ghayoor, F., Waseem, M., Fahad, S., & Traore, I. (2022). A Survey on IoT-Enabled Smart Grids: Emerging, Applications, Challenges, and Outlook. In Energy (Vol. 15, Issue 19). https://doi.org/DOI: 10.3390/en15196984

Gu, S., Wang, L., Han, R., Liu, X., Wang, Y., Chen, T., & Zheng, Z. (2023). Detection of sarcopenia using a deep learning-based artificial intelligence body part measure system (AIBMS). *Frontiers in Physiology*, 14, 1092352. Advance online publication. DOI: 10.3389/fphys.2023.1092352 PMID: 36776966

Gul, H., Al-Obeidat, F., Majdalawieh, M., Amin, A., & Moreira, F. (2024a). Features Extraction and Structure Similarities Measurement of Complex Networks. In Rocha, A., Adeli, H., Dzemyda, G., Moreira, F., & Colla, V. (Eds.), *Information Systems and Technologies. WorldCIST 2023. Lecture Notes in Networks and Systems* (Vol. 799). Springer., DOI: 10.1007/978-3-031-45642-8_4

Gul, H., Al-Obeidat, F., Wasim, M., Amin, A., & Moreira, F. (2024b). Advancing Fake News Detection with Graph Neural Network and Deep Learning. *Journal of Physics. Complexity*. Advance online publication. DOI: 10.1088/2632-072X/ad744d

Habib, M. Y., Qureshi, H. A., Khan, S. A., Mansoor, Z., & Chishti, A. R. (2023). Cybersecurity and Smart Cities: Current Status and Future. 2023 IEEE International Conference on Emerging Trends in Engineering, Sciences and Technology (ICES&T), 1–7. https://doi.org/DOI: 10.1109/ICEST56843.2023.10138843

Hashem, I. A. T., Usmani, R. S. A., Almutairi, M. S., Ibrahim, A. O., Zakari, A., Alotaibi, F., Alhashmi, S. M., & Chiroma, H. (2023). Urban Computing for Sustainable Smart Cities: Recent Advances, Taxonomy, and Open Research Challenges. In Sustainability (Switzerland) (Vol. 15, Issue 5). https://doi.org/DOI: 10.3390/su15053916

Javed, A. R., Shahzad, F., Rehman, S., Zikria, Y. B., Razzak, I., Jalil, Z., & Xu, G. (2022). Future smart cities requirements, emerging technologies, applications, challenges, and future aspects. *Cities (London, England)*, 129, 103794. Advance online publication. DOI: 10.1016/j.cities.2022.103794

Jo, W., Kim, S. J., Kim, H., Shin, Y., & Shon, T. (2022). Automatic whitelist generation system for Ethernet based in-vehicle network. *Computers in Industry*, 142, 103735. Advance online publication. DOI: 10.1016/j.compind.2022.103735

Jun, Y., Craig, A., Shafik, W., & Sharif, L. (2021; Vol. 2021). Artificial Intelligence Application in Cybersecurity and Cyberdefense. In Wireless Communications and Mobile Computing., DOI: 10.1155/2021/3329581

Kalinaki, K. (2024). IoT and Blockchain Integration for Enhanced AI-Driven Business Intelligence. In *Intersection of AI and Business Intelligence in Data-Driven Decision-Making* (pp. 21–52). IGI Global., DOI: 10.4018/979-8-3693-5288-5.ch002

Khadidos, A. O., Shitharth, S., Manoharan, H., Yafoz, A., Khadidos, A. O., & Alyoubi, K. H. (2022). An Intelligent Security Framework Based on Collaborative Mutual Authentication Model for Smart City Networks. *IEEE Access : Practical Innovations, Open Solutions*, 10, 85289–85304. DOI: 10.1109/ACCESS.2022.3197672

Khalil, U., Mueen-Uddin, , Malik, O. A., & Hussain, S. (2022). A Blockchain Footprint for Authentication of IoT-Enabled Smart Devices in Smart Cities: State-of-the-Art Advancements, Challenges and Future Research Directions. *IEEE Access : Practical Innovations, Open Solutions*, 10, 76805–76823. DOI: 10.1109/ACCESS.2022.3189998

Khan, I. A., Pi, D., Abbas, M. Z., Zia, U., Hussain, Y., & Soliman, H. (2022). Federated-SRUs: A Federated Simple Recurrent Units-based IDS for Accurate Detection of Cyber Attacks Against IoT-augmented Industrial Control Systems. *IEEE Internet of Things Journal*. Advance online publication. DOI: 10.1109/JIOT.2022.3200048

Lei, S., & Liu, H. (2022). Deep Learning Dual Neural Networks in the Construction of Learning Models for Online Courses in Piano Education. *Computational Intelligence and Neuroscience*, 2022, 1–8. Advance online publication. DOI: 10.1155/2022/4408288 PMID: 35875728

Losavio, M., Sun, J., Kerrick, S., Elmaghraby, A., Purdy, C., & Johnson, C. (2022). Integrating Democratic Cybersecurity. *International Conference on Cyber Warfare and Security*, 17(1). https://doi.org/DOI: 10.34190/iccws.17.1.37

Lupton, B., Zappe, M., Thom, J., Sengupta, S., & Feil-Seifer, D. (2022). Analysis and Prevention of Security Vulnerabilities in a Smart City. 2022 IEEE 12th Annual Computing and Communication Workshop and Conference, CCWC 2022. https://doi.org/DOI: 10.1109/CCWC54503.2022.9720824

Ma, C. (2021a). Smart city and cyber-security; technologies used, leading challenges, and future recommendations. *Energy Reports*, 7, 7999–8012. DOI: 10.1016/j.egyr.2021.08.124

Mohammad, N. (2019). A Multi-Tiered Defense Model for the Security Analysis of Critical Facilities in Smart Cities. *IEEE Access : Practical Innovations, Open Solutions*, 7, 152585–152598. DOI: 10.1109/ACCESS.2019.2947638

Mohammadi Makrani, H., He, Z., Rafatirad, S., & Sayadi, H. (2022). Accelerated Machine Learning for On-Device Hardware-Assisted Cybersecurity in Edge Platforms. Proceedings - International Symposium on Quality Electronic Design, ISQED, 2022-April. https://doi.org/DOI: 10.1109/ISQED54688.2022.9806150

Özarpa, C., Avci, İ., & Kinaci, B. F. (2023). Cyberattack Measures in Smart Cities and Grids. In EAI/Springer Innovations in Communication and Computing. https://doi.org/DOI: 10.1007/978-3-031-09729-4-7

Prazeres, N., Costa, R. L. de C., Santos, L., & Rabadão, C. (2023). Engineering application of machine learning in IDS based on IoT traffic flow. *Intelligent Systems with Applications*, 17, 200189. Advance online publication. DOI: 10.1016/j.iswa.2023.200189

Rajasekar, V., Premalatha, J., & Saracevic, M. (2022). Cybersecurity in 5G and IoT Networks. In EAI/Springer Innovations in Communication and Computing. https://doi.org/DOI: 10.1007/978-3-030-79766-9-3

Rangelov, D., Lämmel, P., Brunzel, L., Borgert, S., Darius, P., Tcholtchev, N., & Boerger, M. (2023). Towards an Integrated Methodology and Toolchain for Machine Learning-Based Intrusion Detection in Urban IoT Networks and Platforms. *Future Internet*, 15(3), 98. Advance online publication. DOI: 10.3390/fi15030098

Rodríguez, E., Otero, B., & Canal, R. (2023). A Survey of Machine and Deep Learning Methods for Privacy Protection in the Internet of Things. In Sensors (Vol. 23, Issue 3). https://doi.org/DOI: 10.3390/s23031252

Saha, T., Aaraj, N., Ajjarapu, N., & Jha, N. K. (2022). SHARKS: Smart Hacking Approaches for RisK Scanning in Internet-of-Things and Cyber-Physical Systems Based on Machine Learning. *IEEE Transactions on Emerging Topics in Computing*, 10(2), 1. Advance online publication. DOI: 10.1109/TETC.2021.3050733

Salam, M. A., Rayun, S. N., Islam, W., Hasan, R., Firmansyah, E. A., & Kalinaki, K. (2024). Consumer Engagement: Exploring Deepfake Applications in Consumer Marketing Communication. In *Navigating the World of Deepfake Technology* (pp. 397-421). IGI Global. https://doi.org/DOI: 10.4018/979-8-3693-5298-4.ch020

Salles, R. S., & Ribeiro, P. F. (2022). Smart Cities, Connected World, and Internet of Things. In Internet of Things. https://doi.org/DOI: 10.1007/978-3-030-89328-6-2

Sarker, I. H. (2022). Smart City Data Science: Towards data-driven smart cities with open research issues. In Internet of Things (Netherlands) (Vol. 19). DOI: 10.1016/j.iot.2022.100528

Sarker, I. H., Khan, A. I., Abushark, Y. B., & Alsolami, F. (2022). Internet of Things (IoT) Security Intelligence: A Comprehensive Overview, Machine Learning Solutions and Research Directions. *Mobile Networks and Applications*. Advance online publication. DOI: 10.1007/s11036-022-01937-3

Security foundation. (n.d.). Smart Cities – The Emergence of the Cyber Safe Building. Https://Iotsecurityfoundation.Org/Smart_cities_the_emergence_of_the_cyber_safe_building/

Shafik, W. (2023). A Comprehensive Cybersecurity Framework for Present and Future Global Information Organization. In Effective Cybersecurity Operations for Enterprise-Wide System, 56-79. https://doi.org/DOI: 10.4018/978-1-6684-9018-1.ch002

Shafik, W. (2024a). Incorporating Artificial Intelligence for Urban and Smart Cities' Sustainability. In *Maintaining a Sustainable World in the Nexus of Environmental Science and AI* (pp. 23-58). IGI Global. https://doi.org/DOI: 10.4018/979-8-3693-6336-2.ch002

Shafik, W. (2024b). Ethical Use of Machine Learning Techniques in Smart Cities. In Ethical Artificial Intelligence in Power Electronics (pp. 21-47). CRC Press. https://doi.org/DOI: 10.1201/9781032648323-3

Soare, S. R.Senior, Analyst, A., & Burton, J. (n.d.). *Smart Cities*. Cyber Warfare and Social Disorder.

Szymanski, T. H. (2022). The "Cyber Security via Determinism" Paradigm for a Quantum Safe Zero Trust Deterministic Internet of Things (IoT). *IEEE Access : Practical Innovations, Open Solutions*, 10, 45893–45930. Advance online publication. DOI: 10.1109/ACCESS.2022.3169137

Thilakarathne, N. N., & Madhuka Priyashan, W. D. (2022). An Overview of Security and Privacy in Smart Cities. In EAI/Springer Innovations in Communication and Computing. https://doi.org/DOI: 10.1007/978-3-030-82715-1_2

Toma, C., Boja, C., Popa, M., Doinea, M., & Ciurea, C. (2022). Viruses, Exploits, Malware and Security Issues on IoT Devices. Lecture Notes in Computer Science (Including Subseries Lecture Notes in Artificial Intelligence and Lecture Notes in Bioinformatics), 13195 LNCS. https://doi.org/DOI: 10.1007/978-3-031-17510-7_22

Verma, P., Sharma, R., & Mistry, M. (2022). A Paradigm Shift in IoT Cyber-Security: A Systematic Review. *International Journal for Research in Applied Science and Engineering Technology*, 10(10), 1024–1034. Advance online publication. DOI: 10.22214/ijraset.2022.47129

Wang Yue Dong, M., & Yortsos, Y. (2022). Application of Machine Learning Technologies for Transport layer Congestion Control. Journal of Computing and Natural Science. https://doi.org/.DOI: 10.53759/181X/JCNS202202010

Yang, F., Hua, Y., Li, X., Yang, Z., Yu, X., & Fei, T. (2022). A survey on multi-source heterogeneous urban sensor access and data management technologies. In *Measurement* (Vol. 19). Sensors., DOI: 10.1016/j.measen.2021.100061

Yang, J., & Sun, L. (2022). A Comprehensive Survey of Security Issues of Smart Home System: "Spear" and "Shields," Theory and Practice. *IEEE Access : Practical Innovations, Open Solutions*, 10, 124167–124192. DOI: 10.1109/ACCESS.2022.3224806

Yang, Z., Jianjun, L., Faqiri, H., Shafik, W., Talal Abdulrahman, A., Yusuf, M., & Sharawy, A. M. (2021). Green Internet of Things and Big Data Application in Smart Cities Development. *Complexity*, 2021(1), 4922697. Advance online publication. DOI: 10.1155/2021/4922697

Yuvaraj, N., Praghash, K., Raja, R. A., & Karthikeyan, T. (2022). An Investigation of Garbage Disposal Electric Vehicles (GDEVs) Integrated with Deep Neural Networking (DNN) and Intelligent Transportation System (ITS) in Smart City Management System (SCMS). *Wireless Personal Communications*, 123(2), 1733–1752. Advance online publication. DOI: 10.1007/s11277-021-09210-8

ENDNOTES

1 https://www.ibm.com/topics/smart-city

2 https://www.ibm.com/topics/artificial-intelligence

3 https://en.wikipedia.org/wiki/Information_and_communications_technology

4 https://en.wikipedia.org/wiki/Sustainability

5 https://www.smartenergy.com/

6 https://www.ibm.com/topics/machine-learning

7 https://en.wikipedia.org/wiki/Cellular_network

8 https://www.bluetooth.com/

9 https://www.wi-fi.org/

10 https://www.who.int/tools/whoqol

11 https://ackodrive.com/car-guide/different-types-of-car-sensors/

12 https://www.xttrafficlight.com/traffic-light/

13 https://www.ford.com/technology/connected-navigation/

14 https://en.wikipedia.org/wiki/Smart_meter

15 https://www.wearabledevices.co.il/

16 https://www.techtarget.com/iotagenda/definition/Artificial-Intelligence-of-Things-AIoT

17 https://www.oodaloop.com/

18 https://scada-international.com/what-is-scada/

19 https://www.ibm.com/topics/edge-computing

20 https://builtin.com/blockchain

21 https://www.ibm.com/topics/quantum-computing

22 https://en.wikipedia.org/wiki/Federated_learning

23 https://www.fbi.gov/wanted/cyber/apt-41-group

Chapter 12
Blockchain-Based IoT-Enabled Secure 6G Smart City Applications

Damodharan Palaniappan
https://orcid.org/0009-0003-0721-3068
Marwadi University, India

T. Premavathi
https://orcid.org/0009-0003-0172-2021
Marwadi University, India

Rituraj Jain
https://orcid.org/0000-0002-5532-1245
Marwadi University, India

Kumar Parmar
https://orcid.org/0000-0002-2502-5680
Marwadi University, India

Modi Jhanvi
https://orcid.org/0009-0000-9262-7481
Marwadi University, India

ABSTRACT

When block chain technology is integrated with IoT in 6G network, it has the possibility to transformation smart city applications in variety ways. Modern cities are rapidly going digital, so the requirements for safe, fast, and scalable systems are essential. The core paradigm of blockchain, consisting of a distributed and immutable register, is safe for IoT networks when addressing threats such as a

DOI: 10.4018/979-8-3693-8029-1.ch012

data breach and unauthorized access. The expansion of this relationship becomes possible with the help of introductions of 6G networks resulting in ultra-low latency, extensive connectivity, and bringing high data rates necessary for real-time applications in smart cities. It can also be used for several purposes including; self-driving transport systems, smart energy-based grid systems, healthcare, and public safety. Implementation of 6G based IoT systems along with blockchain also helps in emphasizing the trustworthiness of smart city frameworks and transparent and secure data trading.

1. INTRODUCTION

A combination of 6G networks and blockchain technology combined with the Internet of Things will revolutionize smart city solutions. As urban areas get smarter and connected getting good secure efficient and scalable systems increases. Due to blockchains decentralized and permanent record keeping property, most security issues that IoT networks experience such as data leakage, unauthorized access, and lack of trust between stakeholders are addressed. Especially, 6G networks, characterized by ultra-low latency, extensive connectivity, significantly higher data rates than the previous generations, will allow the integration of a multitude of IoT devices and applications in smart cities. Through such a close integration between blockchain and 6G-enabled IoT, the intelligent environment of the Smart City receives a reliable, solid, and effective base for the development of several applications, such as smart transport, smart energy, smart health, public security, and smart environment (Alghamedy et al., 2024).

One of the advantages of employing blockchain and IoT in synergism with 6G is that the network becomes more secure and private. Blockchain eliminates the risk of centrally located key that can be accessed by hackers once or for the entire network. Every purchase or any kind of exchange is stored on an immutable public ledger, which is quite transparent. This is particularly important in the exigent smart city services such as energy management in smart grids where accuracy of data helps in ensuring reliability in services provided. Also, it provides a secure solution of identity management for the IoT devices where the problem of unauthorized access and data manipulation can be minimized through blocks. The characteristics of being fast and having low latency of the 6G networks also complement the use of blockchain in IoT systems. Since the processing of data will be real-time in 6G, it creates the capability of checking and finalizing the blockchain-based transactions in real-time. This is important when it comes to specific timing where an AI operated car needs to make a quick decision on a certain situation. This has the potential of handling many connected devices that are likely to be present in smart city projects hence supports scalability. As it is related to the public safety interest, the utilization of the blockchain-based IoT systems will enhance the reliability and the reaction rate of the emergency services. Results that are collected from different sensors and other related devices can be easily and safely transferred between different agencies and thus coordinated actions can be taken in real time. For instance, during a natural disaster, application of blockchain escalates the protection and availability of significant data that is useful in the management and rehabilitation processes. Health care can also be another sector in smart cities that can immensely benefit from this integration.

Wearable devices and remote monitoring systems' data can be stored and transmitted through a blockchain to maintain privacy and accuracy. This benefit increases the quality of patient care giving and creates opportunities for extensive research studies and data gathering, which can improve the health of the people. However, the application of the concept of 6G smart city through the integration of blockchain and IoT has presented some issues. Some challenges that can be attributed to blockchain network include scalability of the network, energy consumption and perhaps the challenge of managing large scale roll outs.

Despite these drawbacks, current innovations in blockchain such as the emergence of efficient consensus algorithms with low energy consumption and trends in the block-chain's architecture potential market with innovations that are both practical and sustainable. To sum up, the integration of blockchain technology with IoT by means of 6G internal network architecture presents one promising approach to develop robust smart city applications. With the combined advantages of these technologies, this integrated system will be able to improve the life quality of being an urbanite, encourage innovativeness, and set the pace for a more efficient and interlinked society 'organism'. This is quite possible where technical and operational factors constitute an impediment, but the benefits of such a profound change are self-explanatory and immense (Jain et al., 2024) (Singh et al., 2022).

1.1 Background and Motivation

Today, this interest in smart cities has grown up because of technological advance and the green practice of urbanization all over the globe during the last decade. Generally, they are applied in smart cities to enhance people's living standards, optimize public institutions' functioning and maintain a balance between social and economic development within region. Consequently, security and privacy have been characterized as vital areas by those who are involved in investing or building technology companies who should consider that to not damage an organization's physical structure.

1.2 Overview of Smart Cities

Therefore, a smart city utilizes ICT to collect, scrutinize and then use the knowledge obtained for appropriate resources and services' administration. These consist of such aspects as smart transportation, energy and grid systems as well as smart health and smart waste management to improve the association, efficiency and urban sustenance context. In summary, it can be concluded that smart cities are an effort to create a better relationship among people with their environment so that there will be improved use of technology in making urbanization smarter while applying ICTs across different sectors.

1.3 Importance of Security in Smart Cities

The aspect of security in smart cities is important since the connectivity of devices and systems exposes many to vulnerability to cyber threats. The protection of the data's three fundamental pillars – its data integrity, confidentiality, and availability – is crucial for people's trust and efficient functioning of smart city applications (Rahman et al., 2024) (Singh et al., 2022) (Singhal et al., 2022).

1.4 Role of 6G in Future Smart Cities

6G is thought to spur substantial change primarily in smart cities which are a main area. Here is how: Enhanced Connectivity: 6G brings ultimate and instant connectivity of Things and Sensors to maintain smart Cities with smart freedom touching interactions in real time. Low Latency: 6G, consequently, will have substantially reduced latency and therefore introduce real-time data processing that is imperative in industries such as auto-mobile industry, smart traffic management, and even in emergency services. Increased Bandwidth: The enhancement of bandwidth availability of 6G will allow the implementation of high-definition technologies such as, augmented reality and virtual reality applications including getting interactive public services to even take a virtual city tour. In summary, the next generation of the beyond 5G network infrastructure, called as 6G, will create enhanced smart societies infrastructure in terms of smart, efficient, and sustainable societies. Blockchain-based application for the integration of smart cities and 6G wireless communication technology will provide higher speeds, extremely low latency, and a vast number of connections. This is to open doors of opportunities for new types of applications and services and thus will deepen the IOT and other smart technologies into the Cities (Kharche et al., 2024) (Singh et al., 2022).

2. UNDERSTANDING BLOCKCHAIN TECHNOLOGY

2.1 Basics of Blockchain

Blockchain is a database system technology that allows to store data in numerous computer systems. A block contains several transactions and once a block is developed, it cannot be changed without changing all subsequent blocks, making this system utterly safe. Blockchain is a decentralized and distributed database technology basically used to record a block of transaction in many computers so that any transaction that is done is more secure and trustworthy.

2.2 Blockchain Architecture

Blockchain technology is made up of nodes, transactions, the blocks that these transactions are stored in, and the chain. The participants which make up the blockchain network are called nodes and these are the actual computers that take part in the functioning of the network. Currency exchanges are an example of transactions that reflect data to be saved in blocks as well as linking to the other blocks creating the chain.

2.3 Consensus Mechanisms

Consensus mechanism are some kind of algorithms that are used to consensus the block in network of blockchain. Some of the consensus mechanisms are Proof of Work (PoW), proof of Stake (PoS), and Byzantine Fault Tolerance (BFT). Thus, these mechanisms guarantee that all the actors in the network possess the same level of confidence in the transactions that are being made.

2.4 Types of Blockchains: Public vs. Private

Blockchains are divided by being out in the open and secret. Public blockchains are open to all and not controlled in This, while private are limited to a sole group and may be further authorized (Taha et al., 2024).

2.5 Key Features: Decentralization, Immutability, Transparency

Block Chain is an open distributed database that is chronologically ordered and accessibility to each piece of data is restricted. Here are three important ideas and words from block chain: Data is put into these smaller boxes and the boxes are summed up in building the block chain. Blocks include data, previous block reference, and the hash number that is an equivalent of information in the block. Hash is a string, which at first glance appear random. Everyone has information, so when you decide that you want to do some business with some other person, that person will want his information to be stored in your storage also. Consensus Rules: The consensus rules of Blockchain implemented help in defining whether certain transactions are allowed or not. Some of many typical mechanisms are Proof-of-Work and Proof-of-Stake that guarantee everyone in the network that the chain is truthful. Smart Contracts: Trade is self-executing contracts whose conditions are embedded in the gadget. They implement as well as impose the condition on the contractual undertaking once certain condition or parameter coded in a contractual agreement are met. Cryptographic Framework: As it has been developed, the technology of blockchain comprises of cryptography as intended. In particular, the most used pair of keys is a public and a private key, which are used when encrypting data and generating digital signatures (Kunwar et al., 2024).

3. THE INTERNET OF THINGS (IOT) IN SMART CITIES

3.1 Definition and Scope of IoT

IoT is defined as the global network of tangible objects that are connected, capable of communicating and that do so over the internet. Some of the parts in smart cities include the use of the internet of things which includes sensors, cameras, smart meters, and other connected devices that capture information and relay it.

3.2 IoT Architecture

IoT architecture typically consists of several layers: the perception layer that engages in the activity of data gathering; the communication layer that undertakes the task of data transmission; the computation layer that oversees data analysis; and the service layer which delivers services in relation to the data.

3.3 IoT Devices and Sensors

Smart city applications are possible due to IoT devices and sensors. These systems gather information about the different aspects of the urban environment that include air quality, traffic, energy consumption among other things; they help in reporting and controlling the environment in real time.

3.4 IoT Communication Protocols

Protocols that are commonly adopted in IoT includes Wi-Fi, Bluetooth, Zigbee and LoRaWAN among others. These protocols help in the networking and data transmission between the devices and the cloud.

3.5 IoT Applications in Smart Cities

Smart cities are developed on the IoT, enabling numerous applications that augment living in a city. The role of IoT in smart cities is as follows: The employment of IoT sensors in aspects such as bridges and paths entail the generation of data on maintenance costs to foster improvements. Evidently, traffic, congestion, and parking are the areas of interest that IoT devices need to monitor. Road traffic light control, management of the public transport, and parking space indications are all derived from this data. Time to quit with it. The 'smart' grids and IoT meters apply real-time control to the management of energy and incorporate renewable energy sources. Smart lighting systems are usually controlled using activity and ambient light conditions. With the help of IoT sensors in bins, full levels can be gathered and more effective ways of waste disposal and better timings can be arranged which will also help in cutting costs and harm to the environment. There are several types of writing there are, the following is a sample. Smart related technologies like; intelligent environmental sensors and surveillance cameras will help authorities to respond timely in emergencies that include fire outbreaks, floods or any other related calamities (Palaniappan et al., 2023) (Ahmed et al., 2024).

4. 6G TECHNOLOGY: THE NEXT FRONTIER

4.1 Evolution From 5G to 6G

6G is the advanced mode of wireless communications technology that goes a step further from the development of the 5G mode. Even though 5G networks are characterized by high speed and low latency, 6G aims to provide even more possibilities with new application and services.

4.2 Key Features and Capabilities of 6G

6G is proposed to deliver ''ultra-high speed with low latency and massive connectivity", which make it suitable for various application. Some of the features are, terahertz communications, completion with Artificial intelligence, and improved security.

4.3 Expected Use Cases of 6G

6G is employed in complicated VR and AR uses, telemedicine in real time, driverless vehicles, and smart city construction. These applications will thrive well since 6G is expected to have an exceptional level of speed, and the resulting latency.

4.4 Challenges in 6G Implementation

When it comes to the application of the 6G technology there are several challenges for instance; the need to put in place new network infrastructures, security and privacy considerations as well as integration of 6G technology into the existing networks. 6G technology consists of the new generation of wireless technological communications and comes after the 5G. It is the goal that results in increased data rate, less delay and better links. Key features and objectives of 6G include: It is expected that the 6G would have much higher data rates than 5G and is expected to go up to about 100 Gbps. The goal of its design is to provide a latency of under 1 ms in favor of communication. The sequence is becoming boring; it is now time to change. Enhanced Connectivity: Supported many devices including Internet of things and smart city devices. Advancements: Services for higher range uses such as, holographic telecommunication, immersive environment and other such multisensory procedures. The following is a sample: While AI has been incorporated for unjumbling network operations and efficacy, the research in the domain of 6G is to go on, with the potential of the introduction of 6G approximately 2030 (Rejeb et al., 2024).

5. LITERATURE REVIEW

Authors (Kamruzzaman, 2022) discusses potential applications of the Internet of Things to design el ectric 6G smart city networks. The authors analyzed 20 articles from the 2015-2021 period, which pointed out there are quantum communication, blockchain, visible light communication, 6G brain-computer interface and symbiotic radio as the key technologies for it. Such technologies can be used in different domains of smart cities, for example in generation of 15-minute cities, industrial towns, ITS etc. There are several deficiencies associated with it such as cost-effective deployment, data privacy, security issues and keeping the mobile communication costs low. The research finding indicates that, IoT and energy efficient 6G technology are can enhance smart cities effectiveness.

The applicability of a blockchain-based IoT system about security and reliability in public safety systems and usage in the 6G network was analysed in (Rathod et al., 2023). The authors further explain that though, 6G and IoT built benefits for applications like, smart cities and healthcare, they also come up with the threats and risk of security. Blockchain, therefore, has the potential to minimise such risks through security, verifiability and privacy of data and communication. Some of the use cases of blockchain in public safety includes; emergency response, car-to-car communication, and UAV aided-rescue. This discusses how blockchain addresses the problems of data protection and sharing, allocation and utilization of resources as well as fostering trust among different entities of the supply chain (Premavathi et al., 2024).

Pajooh et al. (2022) present an idea of integrating blockchain with the future 6G network for improving security and privacy issues in the IoT applications. Specifically, the authors claim that while 6G has a potential to offer incredibly high speed and extremely low latency for massive device connectivity the problem of security and privacy persists. In contrast with the traditional centralized architecture, extensive practicing is faced with issues such as access control, interoperability, and singularity of failure points. Blockchain solves it in a way, having been designed to create trust without requiring the involvement of third parties. In this paper, we discuss the prospects, problems, and opportunities of this integration in such areas as smart homes, smart cities, smart health, smart supply chain, and vehicular automation.

Authors (Murroni et al., 2023) elaborates on the possibility of the 6G technology enhancing the smart city concept. The authors continue that due to reaching higher frequency bands, increased capacity, and lower latency 6G is suitable for controlling the vast number of devices that connected to the Internet of Things system. The paper will first discuss the current smart city environment before emphasizing on the need for 5G in the development of technology in this arena. It then proceeds to the areas of possible use of 6G in smart city for transportation, healthcare and emergency services. The authors also discuss the problems associated with 6G such as compatibility, and privacy and security issues and the divide issue.

Autohrs (Kathole et al., 2022) presents an innovative architecture for secure data processing in the next generation 6G networks focusing mainly IoT-EE environment. Analysing the shortcomings of ever-growing security/networking solutions in 5G, the authors propose a system incorporating UAVs, blockchain or cybertwins. This architecture known as 'Secure Blockchain-based UAV Communication' integrates

UAVs for collection and dissemination of data, cybertwins for supervision and regulation of physical entities and the use of blockchain for security and reliability of data in cloud platforms. Another feature that is introduced in the architecture is Cloud-Fog Networking which they want to improve latency and network utilization. Therefore, the proposed BC-UAV framework finally aims at offering secure, dependable, and elastic infrastructure for IoE applications in future 6G systems.

Authors discusses about the prospect of blockchain technology in increasing security and trust in 6G network in conjunction with Federated Learning in Internet of Things. The authors share the concern stating that while 6G brings a lot of improvement it stands for a shift of paradigms in terms of security. However, some of the issues which the paper recognizes as barriers to the development of FL-IoT systems include; how to update the models, security risks which can be posed by malicious users, fairness issues, and heterogeneity of the IoT devices and data that is used. However, the paper also looks at the bright side of integrating the Blockchain and FL-IoT toward the evolution toward the 6G Network; such is the potential of offering a secure and trustworthy command communication network by the end of the foreseen year 2024 (Alghamedy et al., 2024).

The studies of the authors Khalil, Khattak, and Mahmood (2022) show a comparative analysis of both the blockchain and the centralized architectures for the IoT-based smart devices in the smart cities. Thus, the authors state that security with a focus on authentication is the most important factor for these devices since they become a part of different CPSs in intelligent city. The paper then overviews various methods of authentication and their architectures such as centralized and distributed systems and discusses with respect to their security vulnerabilities, their computational complexity and communication overheads. In concluding their work, the authors recognize that there exists a requirement of lightweight solutions for authenticating the data and they exist that blockchain, lightweight cryptosystems, and AI-based systems are areas that could be explored in future.

6. INTEGRATION OF BLOCKCHAIN AND IOT IN SMART CITIES

6.1 Integrated Architecture for Blockchain-Enabled IoT and 6G Smart City Applications

As depicted in Figure. 1, it gives an architectural representation of Blockchain-Enabled IoT and 6G Smart City applications. It is divided into several layers that contributes to the smart city towards data management, communication, security, and energy. User Interfaces Layer: This layer encompasses mobile applications, internet websites and web portals and IoT gadgets that the end-users and administrators use in accessing the smart city framework. These interfaces allow communication with different sensors and IoT systems allowing for the monitoring and managing of the processes in real time.

Figure 1. Integrated architecture for blockchain-enabled IoT and 6G smart city applications

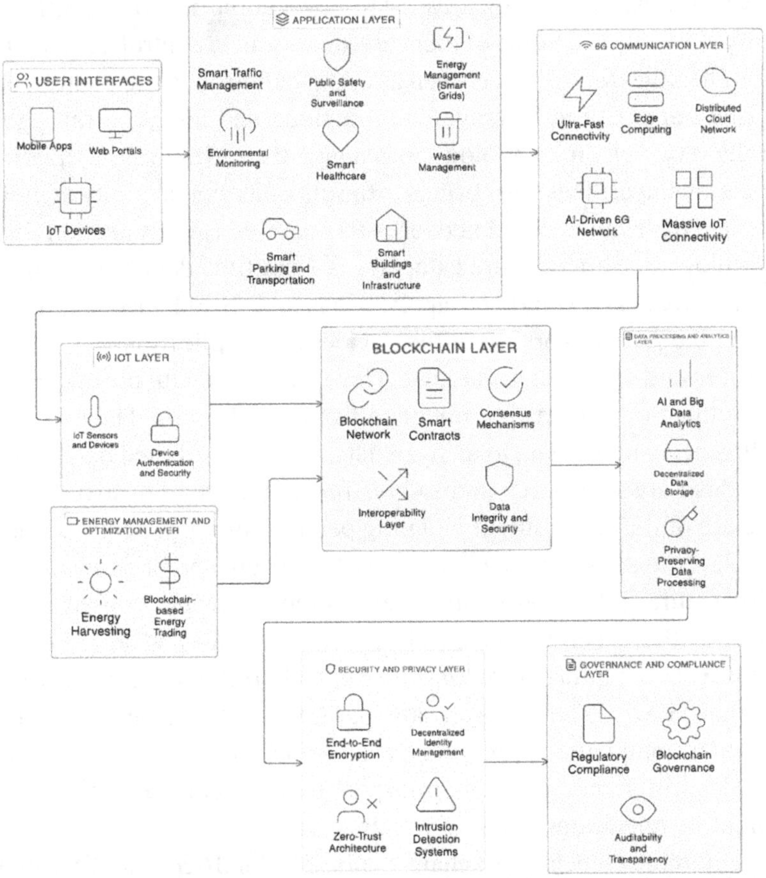

IoT Layer: IoT layer is made up of several IoT sensors and devices which interactively acquire information from the surroundings. It will help to identify the device and secure it hence provide a strong platform where data is collected and transmitted. This data is very useful for further controlling any part of the smart city, for example, monitoring of environment, traffic control, and healthcare. Energy Management and Optimization Layer: This layer deals with generation of energy and energy trading using blockchain technology. Therefore, the concept targets the development of an efficient energy system within the city's socio-economic environment by incorporating decentralize energy management solutions. Blockchain Layer: The most important part of the architecture is the blockchain layer that ensures data credibility, confidentiality, and openness. The resource management processes as well as sharing information are facilitated through adequate layers of blockchain networks and smart contracts. This layer also incorporates consensus methods and compatibility meant for the secure and clear cross-functional interactions of the several city facilities. Application Layer: This layer comprises of the different forms of smart city applications. Some of them are smart traffic control, air quality, public safety, smart healthcare and others such as energy control, waste control, and smart parking. These application leverage data obtained and analyzed through the IoT layer and the block chain technology to manage the cities' affairs effectively. 6G Communication Layer: This layer brings in the ultra-fast connectivity of the 6G, edge computing and distributed cloud networks for massive IoT connection. In the case of 6G technology, the architecture caters for A Real-time data processing which is vital for IoT devices and smart city applications and; B Enhanced communication capability for the proper working of the devices and applications.

Data Processing and Analytics Layer: This layer deals with the evaluation of the enormous volume of information obtained from IoT devices. They are using artificial intelligence and big data to analyze data, while distributed data management guarantees this data's accuracy and safety. Techniques for sensitive data analysis prevent the use of the data without violating peoples' privacy. Security and Privacy Layer: This layer make assure that smart city has secure and private basic. Some of the security features it features includes, end-to-end encryption of signals, identity management at the decentralized level, no-trust system, and intrusion detection systems to protect the information transmitted and block any intruder. Governance and Compliance Layer: The last layer safeguards the fact that the underlying system functions under compliance to regulatory and blockchain standards. It stresses on feasibility, flexibility and auditable, transparent and accountable system enabling assessment of its operations at any given time.

The system architecture in Blockchain-Enabled IoT and 6G Smart City applications intends to combine several technologies in different layers to form Blockchain-based integrated smart city framework for security in managing the smart cities. Starting from the User Interfaces Layer where the different users of this smart city applications including the end-users, city officials, and administrators engage with it via mobile apps, web portals, IoT devices among others. Such interfaces enable users to keep tabs on, and manipulate diverse city operations including traffic patterns, health, and energy. At the IoT Layer, all sorts of IoT sensors and devices are installed throughout the city to collect data on the current state of environment, structures and services. These devices may be cameras, air quality sensors, temperature sensors, or smart meters among others. Most importantly, the IoT layer provides for a strong authentication method for devices which allows only authorized devices to communicate within the network to reduce cases of insecurity and unauthorized access to the city's systems. thing is appropriate and is compliant with regulations or runs in compliance with predetermined health legislations.

The collected data from the IoT devices goes through the 6G Communication Layer transmitting the data through ultra-fast and low latency relevant for real-time processing. This layer enables edge computing and distributed cloud networks that makes it possible for the system to process data at the source, hence enhancing decision making speed. The enormous connectivity depicted by the 6G network with artificial intelligence helps handle the running of millions of complex devices in the city. Data that has been transmitted goes to Data Processing and Analytics Layer where data is stored and processed. This layer makes use of AI and big data for the processing of the huge amount of data gathered from billions of IoT devices which gives a decisive steer. For instance, in self-driving vehicles, traffic flow can be estimated or energy consumption can also be forecasted. Data storage is distributed to prevent concentration of data from a single point, and privacy preserving methods of processing the commonly collected citizens' data are applied. The Blockchain Layer plays the role of the supporting infrastructure as it provides the credibility, security, and clear visibility of the data. These include: if the IoT devices are responsible for data creation and city applications are helpful yet necessitating transactions such as smart contracts for energy trading or service payments, smart contracts, then all the executed operation is recorded in an immutable ledger. Smart contracts allow the exchanges of services between two services without the intervention of the owner. For example, decentralization in energy trading can be managed through blockchain by checking through all the transactions on its own. This layer also contains consensus mechanisms for confirmation of transactions, as well as, an integration layer that enablers different city systems.

Table 1 break down how each layer in the blockchain-enabled IoT and 6G smart city architecture relates to the others.

Table 1. Architecture relationship between different layers

Layer	Components	Role/Function	Interdependency with Other Layers
IoT Layer	Devices, Sensors, Authentication, Security	Collects data from the physical environment (e.g., traffic, healthcare, energy).	Depends on 6G Communication Layer for data transmission.
Communication Layer (6G Network)	Ultra-Fast Connectivity, Edge Computing, Massive IoT Connectivity	Transmits data between IoT devices and other layers quickly and reliably.	Works with IoT Layer for data transmission and Application Layer for services.
Blockchain Layer	Blockchain Network, Smart Contracts, Consensus Mechanisms	Ensures secure, immutable storage of data and execution of smart contracts.	Uses data from the IoT and Communication layers for integrity and validation.
Application Layer	Smart City Services (Traffic, Healthcare, Energy)	Provides services such as smart traffic, healthcare, energy management.	Relies on data from IoT and Communication layers; uses Blockchain for security.
Data Processing & Analytics Layer	AI, Big Data Analytics, Decentralized Storage	Analyzes the data collected from IoT devices and makes real-time decisions.	Uses data from IoT Layer; interacts with Blockchain for secure data storage.
Security and Privacy Layer	Encryption, Identity Management, Intrusion Detection	Ensures secure communication, data privacy, and intrusion detection across layers.	Embedded in all layers to protect data and processes.
Governance and Compliance Layer	Regulatory Compliance, Blockchain Governance	Manages legal, ethical, and regulatory compliance of the entire architecture.	Works with Blockchain Layer and all service layers to ensure auditability and transparency.

6.2 Need for Integration

Smart cities adopting blockchain and IoT for data management solve several problems such as security, data credibility, and compatibility. Thus, it is more reliable when it comes to smart city applications because IoT data can be maintained securely and transparent on blockchain platforms.

6.3 Benefits of Blockchain for IoT

When it comes to the application of IoT, blockchain can offer several advantages including security, data accuracy and openness. Specifically, for smart cities, data generated by IoT can be stored using blockchain technology to describe how easy it is to either tamper, as well as conduct audits on.

6.4 Case Studies of Blockchain-IoT Integration

Some of the case studies using blockchain in IoT have been illustrated in Smart cities below. This combination has the potential to create smart energy management system, intelligent transport system and many more.

6.5 Challenges and Solutions

Blockchain and IoT must be implemented in smart cities, but this brings issues such as scalability and interoperability among others. All these issues can be solved with the help of a combination of safe types of blockchains, sophisticated methods of encryption, and beneficial approaches to managing data. When both IoT and blockchain technology are applied in smart cities, their effectiveness, protection level, and other features can be greatly improved. Here's how they work together: It has been established that, the integration of IoT and blockchain technology in smart cities can enhance efficiency, security, and functionality in such Cities tremendously. Their working together is as follows: For the security of the IoT data, blockchain provides a distributed database system that would prevent manipulation and access of the data by anyone who should not be allowed to do so. Thus, using the blockchain, the IoT devices retain data securely and in an efficient manner. Blockchain helps IoT sensors to have secure, non-producing data which is very important. Even if it is data collected by the city management, like traffic, energy, or environment data, the accuracy and reliability of the data is ensured. Time to change reliance. Blockchain offers IoT devices management capability that is distributed hence avoiding central control points and probabilities of single points of failure. In this way the technical basis of smart city elements can be made to become more stable and effective.

It is possible to trigger smart contracts according to the collected IoT data and apply the rules and execute processes on the blockchain. Information on existing road congestion or climate could be inserted into a smart contract to change the intensity of street lighting (Rejeb et al., 2024). This is an example of such type Arrangement Example The following is a sample. It has also been noted that integration helps in the optimal management of resources within organizations such as energy and water resources. Consumption and conditions can be sensed by IoT devices and usage and distribution of resources can be validated and managed by blockchain. In the accessibility of records, the smart city's contention is tan with Blockchain since it supports the tracking and auditing of interactions and transactions mutually observed in Blockchain. Greater understanding and more trust can be created between the stakeholders – the common people and the city authorities. Hence, using blockchain, IoT can offer a better, safer, and more effective approach to the management of such cities (Sheraz et al., 2024).

7. SECURITY CHALLENGES IN SMART CITIES

In an integrated system of Blockchain-Enabled IoT and 6G Smart City, there are many security issues associated with multiple technologies with perceived issues related to big data processing and the interconnection of devices, networks and user in Smart Cities. Smaller amounts of the main security threats and prospects that can help to overcome these problems are presented below.

Data Privacy and Confidentiality - Challenge: IoT devices harvest loads of personal information from the various smart city solutions that are adopted, such as healthcare, security surveillance. This data is thus more susceptible to breaches and unauthorized access besides as it passes through 6G networks, when stored in decentralized manners. Solution: End to end encryption can be employed for securing the information that is being exchanged between IoT devices, blockchain and the other layers. This can be achieved through the implementation of the zero-trust architecture whereby no entity is trusted by default and hence, every device or even the user must prove their identity. Furthermore, they require data collection from users and another way of data processing techniques such as Differential Privacy or Homomorphic encryption can be used.

Transparency, Immutability, Privacy, authority and Security of Blockchain

Challenge: Although blockchain per se is immune to vulnerabilities, if infiltrated at the consensus layers or in smart contracts, it can lead to formation of improper transactions or biased data manipulations over the smart city applications such as energy management. Another threat is, 51% attacks, where the bad actors get control over the majority of blockchain nodes. Solution: With the help of those consensus mechanisms like Proof-of-Stake (PoS) or Delegated Proof of Stake (DPoS), 51% attacks are possible to avoid. Another way of protecting the system against vulnerabilities is through auditable smart contracts and making sure they are audited from time to time.

Intrusion and Attack Detection - Challenge: That is why managing the connections and such a vast and an uncontrolled environment to detect and respond to attacks such as DDoS (Distributed Denyl of Service), MitM attacks or malware is almost impossible. An intrusion that goes undetected could possibly even threaten overall city relevant systems such as energy networks, surveillance cameras and the likes. Solution: By adopting AI based IDS and IPS, one can be able to track the traffic in a network and filter out any strange or threatening traffic. In the same manner, a network segmentation technique can be useful in limiting the spread of the breach While, on the other hand, Zero-Trust Network Access or ZTNA can assist in stopping the flow to another section of the system (Azzaoui et al., 2020).

Interoperability and Cross-Layer Communication - Challenge: It is challenging to guarantee that interconnectivity between IoT devices and blockchain and various applications is secure. Interoperability weakens security; manufacturers of the devices and protocols used might take advantage of it. Solution: Controlling cross-layer communication can be addressed through standard protocols, and secure Application Programming Interfaces. It is also possible to include a processing layer in the chain of blockchain that has the responsibility of checking, and supervising the transactions between layers to guarantee the flow of data is secure.

Regulatory Compliance and Governance - Challenge: The regulation of blockchain while dealing with data somehow involves data protection laws (GDPR) and regional regulations for the governance of blockchain is another main concern. Penalties resulting in non-compliance for such service delivery might result in cut off and loss of trust in smart city system. Solution: To some extent, compliance check can be built into its system through the smart contract provision because data must be stored and processed according to the legal requirements. For blockchain to have efficient governance mechanisms it should be transparent and auditable and give real time reports to the authorities (Cha et al., 2021).

The Figure. 2 shows how safety issues are distributed in the context of each layer of the Blockchain-Enabled IoT and 6G Smart City architecture and how are they matched with safety solutions.

Figure 2. Security challenges in smart city architecture

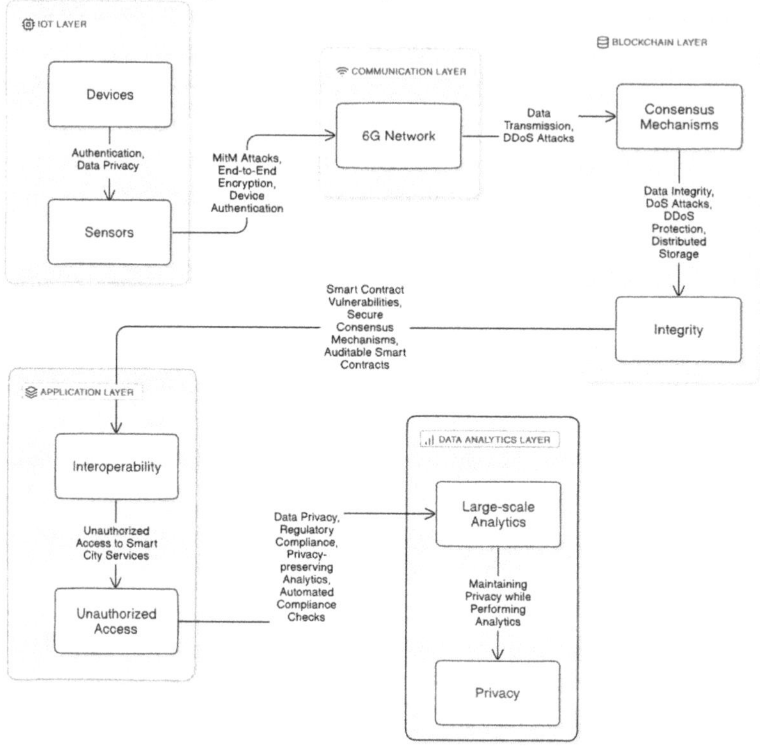

Some of the specific and diverse security challenges are presented by aspect of 6G smart city with block chain and IoT Layer as follows; In most cases, these electronic devices are associated with frames that are not so reliable when it comes to the authentication and authorization processes. Also, information privacy of such data as a location or healthcare information can also be at risk if the protection measures are not well enhanced. One of the biggest challenges is that many IoT devices have small memory and sometimes very limited processing capabilities which affects the implementation of more secure solutions. Solutions for these issues are: Use of end-to-end encryption to safeguard data while transmitting; multi factor authentication to permit only intended devices to access the network; and, decentralized identity maintenance through blockchain where IoT devices' identities are stored in the chain. Furthermore, lightweight security protocols like TLS or DTLS for IoT guarantees and confirms that even low powered devices can sustain good security without a large consumption of resources. Several threats are posed by the Communication Layer in a 6G network, including the MitM attacks whereby the attacker replays the data that has not been encrypted. The protection of data integrity in communication is important, given the huge amounts of data going through 6G networks. Also, ransomware attacks can damage network and/or data, and DDoS (Distributed Denial of Service) attacks can inundate the network and impede services while overloading infrastructure (Cha et al., 2020). In response to these challenges, a solution such as end-to- end encryption (E2E) should be applied to ensure that data is protected from source to destination thus eliminating Midman (MitM) attacks. Blockchain can be used for data consistency, so that transmitted data is tamper proof and easily verifiable. To prevent DDoS threats which are a real and constant danger, organizations can implement AI-based systems of DDoS detection that analyzes the traffic in real time, defining the potential threats and preventing the attacks. Also, traffic filtering and load sharing are some of the measures that can be applied for protecting the essential service and balancing the network load in case of an attack. This means that there are security challenges in the Blockchain Layer as well. Consensus mechanism vulnerabilities such as the 51% of the network's mining or validation power is a big risk because it can be maintained by an attacker. Another risk is kept in smart contracts; if their code is written incorrectly, it is possible to control the corresponding actions or data in an unauthorized manner. Moreover, as smart cities develop over time, they create challenges for blockchain, such as its inability to scale in the event of huge traffic flow of transactions. To reduce such risks, innovations in consensus algorithms for example DPoS or BFT that distributes the validation powers more evenly making it difficult for the attacker to gain a controlling 51% of the chain. It is possible to have auditable smart contracts which are subject to general security check and this will mean that only valid smart contracts will be used thus avoiding instances of vulnerability. In terms of scalability, Layer 2 solutions like state channels or rollups are capable of encapsulating transactions reducing the pressure on the main Chain, while still providing reliability (Garach et al., 2024).

Finally, the most issues concerning the Data Analytics Layer are related to data privacy during massive-scale analytics which may become a problem in restricted areas such as healthcare or traffic control where personal information is potentially disclosed. However, when it comes to the question of own and govern data in decentralized structures there may be some unclear who is the proprietor of the data and who is the responsible one for the compliance of the data with regulation. Rules like the GDPR become cumbersome when it comes to cross-border data flows. There are many techniques in the world today that allow data to be analyzed without resulting in results containing privatized information such as homomorphic encryption and differential privacy. To address data ownership, decentralized data management employing smart contract through block chain can track the ownership and usage of the data to ensure users are in control (Singh et al., 2022). Checks designed within the Blockchain and Artificial intelligence systems can help to verify that all the data processing is done according to the law, smart contracts can help enforce data retention policies and privacy acts (Shahidinejad et al., 2024). Table 2 listed security challenges and solutions specific to each layer.

Table 2. Security aspects across different layers

Layer	Security Challenges	Security Solutions
IoT Layer	- Weak Authentication - Data Privacy Risks - Limited Device Resources	- End-to-End Encryption - Multi-Factor Authentication (MFA) - Lightweight Security Protocols
Communication Layer (6G Network)	- Man-in-the-Middle (MitM) Attacks - Data Integrity Issues - DDoS Attacks	- End-to-End Encryption (E2E) - Blockchain for Data Integrity - AI-Based DDoS Detection
Blockchain Layer	- 51% Attack - Smart Contract Vulnerabilities - Scalability Issues	- Secure Consensus Mechanisms (DPoS, BFT) - Auditable Smart Contracts - Layer 2 Solutions
Application Layer	- Interoperability Issues - Unauthorized Access to City Services - Service Denial (DoS/DDoS)	- Standardized Secure APIs - Role-Based Access Control (RBAC) - AI-Based Threat Detection
Data Processing & Analytics Layer	- Data Privacy During Analytics - Data Ownership & Governance - Regulatory Compliance	- Privacy-Preserving Analytics (Homomorphic Encryption) - Decentralized Data Governance - Automated Compliance Checks
Security and Privacy Layer	- End-to-End Protection of Data - Intrusion Detection - Identity Management	- Zero-Trust Architecture - Intrusion Detection Systems - Blockchain-Based Identity Management
Governance and Compliance Layer	- Regulatory Non-Compliance - Lack of Audibility - Governance Over Decentralized Systems	- Automated Compliance Checks - Blockchain for Transparency - Auditable Smart Contracts

8. USE CASES OF BLOCKCHAIN-BASED IOT-ENABLED SECURE 6G SMART CITY APPLICATIONS

8.1 Smart Transportation

The main findings of the present work are: When IoT intertwines with blockchain, then the system of smart transportation becomes enhanced because the problems, specifically the problem involving the security and propriety of traffic records, will be solved (Singh et al., 2021).

8.2 Smart Energy Management

Realtime management of the energy systems in smart cities, P2P energy trading, and even encryption of the energy data by the IoT system such as block chains are the possibilities by which benefits of energy saver can be enjoyed by smart city.

8.3 Smart Healthcare

Use of Blockchain and IoT integrated system in smart health care can lead to improved patient data security, distant patients' supervision and preliminary investigations and enhanced health care through interoperability and exchange of information data.

8.4 Smart Governance

In other words, blockchain improves the effectiveness and securitization in governance, rationalizes the administrations, and enhances the citizen's exercising of voting and surveys, which is protected fully from being leaked (Ahad et al., 2024) (Singh et al., 2023).

8.5 Smart Waste Management

Blockchain integrated with IoT thus can transform the management of wastes through tracking the collection of wastes, availability and usage of disposal vehicles and, the provision of authentic records of the warm measures on the management of wastes in each society. New smart cities in the 6G network era apply the blockchain IoT applications to improve the quality of life of a city in various ways. These are some primary scenarios: Blockchain can provide a secured technology of recording various transactions and data from the IoT Sensors in the energy grid to exclude energy distribution that would be fraudulent. It incorporates the use of blockchain to allow residents to trade excess solar power securely based on the concept of the smart grid. Data of autonomous vehicles can be safely exchanged and the correctness of the information can be checked with the help of Blockchain. In the context of the IoT sensors, real time traffic information can be collected and changes in traffic signals monitored and verified using blockchain technology, hereby leading to optimization of the traffic situation and congestion. The Log Out message in a computer environment means: Smart devices in IoT can record a building's temperature, lighting and security system while blockchain will provide proper and transparent handling of the operations of a building. Blockchain maintenance tracking also enables repairs of infrastructures to be done on time and without even exposing people to risky situations (Singh et al., 2022) (Singh et al., 2019).

9. TECHNICAL FRAMEWORK FOR BLOCKCHAIN-BASED IOT-ENABLED SECURE 6G SMART CITY APPLICATIONS

9.1 System Architecture

The key technological components are multi-layered architecture of edges devices, communication networks, block chain infrastructure and data analytics platforms required for secure 6g smart city applications.

9.2 Data Management and Analytics

Big data also efficiently dictates and supports the usage of smart city applications and systems. Blockchain is used to collect, store as well as manage data from IoT devices for the safety and security of that data.

9.3 Security Mechanisms

For a condition that only authorized personnel can access some data, measures like data encryption and assignment of a secure password are used. These mechanisms are improved by the security features of blockchain.

9.4 Network Infrastructure

The 6G smart cities' existing communication technologies are the network infrastructure-based communications, the big MIMO Bandwidth, and the AI-based Smart control of networks.

9.5 Implementation Roadmap

A framework has been developed and planned to chart the implementation of secure 6G applications in smart cities using blockchain-based IoT. These are pilot projects that need to be conducted, scalability tests, and initial stages of engaging stakeholders, and constant tracking of the effectiveness of the system and tweaking as necessary. It has been identified that for the development of a secure 6G smart city application by employing a blockchain-based IoT, there is the need to merge different technologies that help in creating considerably secured smart city IoT-solutions. To view the narrative in relation to the image below, click on it. Based on the automation and application possibilities of 6GN structural traits, it becomes possible for users to employ the 6G Network Infrastructure for high-latency and massive connectivity with fast and efficient communication. This entails incorporation and implementation of edge computing as well as data transfer that is highly rapid. Connect IoT devices to 6G networks to enable secure communication with the networks to guarantee secure transfer and reception of data (Singh et al., 2022).

Comply with the best practices set in the IoT devices' connectivity, blockchain networks, and 6G. Facilitate the provision of integration standards and application programming interfaces for other systems to interface with blockchains, smart cities' IoT devices and other components. Governance and Regulatory Compliance: Looking at the legal and regulatory requirements, ensure the framework is compliant with the national laws as well as the intergenerational ones on data protection, privacy, or cybersecurity. Design a framework or work plan to govern the operations of the blockchain network especially in making important decisions and/or dealing with stakeholders (Rojek et al., 2024). Continuous Monitoring - Is the employment of real time assessment tools to measure the efficiency and security of the network, blockchain and IoT devices. The creation of business solutions for responding to security threats or system crashes in the shortest time possible. Ensure that there is a presentation of user interface designs to ease the operations of the smart city for the city administrators and users. Guarantee the identification of the user by employing appropriate technique to log in and thus, engage with the smart city application. Here, the framework provides a clear guideline where blockchain, IoT and 6G are to be integrated perfectly in smart cities inclining to security, efficiency speed among others (Chataut et al., 2024).

10. CHALLENGES AND FUTURE DIRECTIONS

10.1 Technical Challenges

The technical issues consist of scalability difficulties in making use of block chain and IoT, compatibility issues in between various systems an also technologies and the further need of healthy networking facilities to support the 6G solutions.

10.2 Regulatory and Legal Issues

Regulatory and legal problems include data privacy laws, compliance with local and international regulations, and the legal implications of decentralized technologies in public administration and services.

10.3 Interoperability Concerns

The topic of smart city interoperation is mainly related to the challenges of enhancing communication between IoT gadgets, blockchain applications, and traditional structures.

10.4 Future Research Directions

More research should be devoted to further evolution of consensus algorithms for blockchain, improvement of the IoT networking security, and the means of applying quantum computation for the future blockchain and 6G technologies. In conclusion, future research directions depend on the prospects of blockchain, IoT, and 6G technologies in terms of security, scalability, and efficiency, etc Therefore, to address those problems, it is crucial to search for better consensus algorithms, improve encryption techniques, and discover the opportunities of quantum computing. The listed fields are quite likely to become the centre of development and define the prospects of smart city systems (Li et al., 2024).

10.5 Summary of Key Points

Blockchain-Based IoT-Enabled Secure 6G Smart City Applications:

As for the emergence of the elements of smart cities, the possibility of using blockchain, IoT, and 6G technologies in the development of urbanization processes should be noted. Collectively, this resolves many of the problems relating to modern urban administration and leads to smarter and more sustainable cities. Blockchain and IoT Integration - Smart cities require decentralised and secure record keeping and this is where Blockchain fulfils the requirement ornamentally. This explains why when combined with IoT which is a large network of devices that collects and shares data, blockchain ensures that the data is well recorded. This integration offers a strong foundation for many systematized and safeguarded urban procedures (Gupta et al., 2024).

Enhanced Data Security - Due to the use of smart devices, the production of large volumes of data is common and may be easily manipulated or hacked. Through cryptographic techniques, data entered in a blockchain derives from these devices are indisputable and clear. Every single transaction or piece of data is encrypted and connected to the prior sections as a chain. It eliminates foul play while at the same time maintaining record of changes done within the records thus increasing general credibility and reliability of the data (Liwen et al., 2024). Efficient and Transparent Operations - Infrastructures and services in smart cities are controlled by real information stored in computers. While using the blockchain concept, data can be verified from the IoT devices and can be written in the computerized ledger utilizing the techniques of bitcoins with no central authority. This decreases congestion and can be the beginning of problem areas in urban systems, which enhances the resiliency of urban systems. For instance, blockchain can be used for secure management of traffic data, its flow, and congestion, in the management and control of traffic. Advanced 6G Connectivity

Competitive Key feature 10: The next generation 6G networks have ultra-low latency and high-speed data transmission as required by smart city applications of the future. The integrated implementation of 6G and IoT makes it easier to have instantaneous communication among devices improving the working of the devices. For instance, 6G will be capable of handling live feeds in high definition from the surveillance cameras and the data from the sensors installed in environmental monitoring, respond quickly to cases like pollution, or natural calamities (Rojas et al., 2024). Smart Contracts and Automation - Smart contracts are contracts written in the form of code that allows many operations and distributed ledgers are powered through Blockchain. Thus, in the scope of smart cities, smart contracts can apply different operations using IoT data. For example, if an IoT device senses a water leakage, repair or alert the maintenance personnel's, smart contract services can arrest the issue without human contact. It stabilizes business processes and shortens the reaction time (Asri et al., 2024) (Aljumah et al., 2024).

11. CONCLUSION

The intelligent integration of blockchain, IoT, and 6G will enhance the smart city through the provision of a safe, effective, and elastic system for the effective control of smart cities. Blockchain ensures immutability of the data, IoT connects and embeds devices together, while 6G offers the speed needed for real-time functionalities. This in turn will result to advanced, flexible and stronger cities whose standards of living will have been enhanced by these technologies. This book has presented the review of combining blockchain and IoT in the safe prospective 6G smart city applications focusing on the possible benefits, technical solutions, security issues, and further research opportunities.

Final Thoughts on Blockchain, IoT, and 6G in Smart Cities

Blockchain, IoT, and 6G are viewed as a revolution for creating smart cities' integration. In addressing the security, scalability and interoperation issues, such technologies have the opportunities of enhancing the innovation of the cities that are smart, efficient, sustainable and secure.

REFERENCES

Ahad, A., Jiangbina, Z., Tahir, M., Shayea, I., Sheikh, M. A., & Rasheed, F. (2024). 6G and Intelligent Healthcare: Taxonomy, Technologies, Open Issues and Future Research Directions. *Internet of Things : Engineering Cyber Physical Human Systems*, 25, 101068. DOI: 10.1016/j.iot.2024.101068

Ahmed, S. F., Alam, M. S. B., Afrin, S., Rafa, S. J., Taher, S. B., Kabir, M., Muyeen, S. M., & Gandomi, A. H. (2024). Toward a Secure 5G-Enabled Internet of Things: A Survey on Requirements, Privacy, Security, Challenges, and Opportunities. *IEEE Access : Practical Innovations, Open Solutions*, 12, 13125–13145. DOI: 10.1109/ACCESS.2024.3352508

Alghamedy, F. H., El-Haggar, N., Alsumayt, A., Alfawaer, Z., Alshammari, M., Amouri, L., Aljameel, S. S., & Albassam, S. (2024a). Unlocking a Promising Future: Integrating Blockchain Technology and FL-IoT in the Journey to 6G. *IEEE Access : Practical Innovations, Open Solutions*, 1, 115411–115447. Advance online publication. DOI: 10.1109/ACCESS.2024.3435968

Alghamedy, F. H., El-Haggar, N., Alsumayt, A., Alfawaer, Z., Alshammari, M., Amouri, L., Aljameel, S. S., & Albassam, S. (2024b). Unlocking a Promising Future: Integrating Blockchain Technology and FL-IoT in the Journey to 6G. *IEEE Access : Practical Innovations, Open Solutions*, 1, 115411–115447. Advance online publication. DOI: 10.1109/ACCESS.2024.3435968

Aljumah, A., & Ahanger, T. A. (2023). Blockchain-Based Information Sharing Security for the Internet of Things. *Mathematics*, 11(9), 2157. DOI: 10.3390/math11092157

Azzaoui, A. E., Singh, S. K., Pan, Y., & Park, J. H. (2020). Block5GIntell: Blockchain for AI-Enabled 5G Networks. *IEEE Access : Practical Innovations, Open Solutions*, 8, 145918–145935. DOI: 10.1109/ACCESS.2020.3014356

Cha, J., Singh, S. K., Kim, T. W., & Park, J. H. (2021). Blockchain-empowered cloud architecture based on secret sharing for smart city. *Journal of Information Security and Applications*, 57, 102686. DOI: 10.1016/j.jisa.2020.102686

Cha, J., Singh, S. K., Pan, Y., & Park, J. H. (2020). Blockchain-Based Cyber Threat Intelligence System Architecture for Sustainable Computing. *Sustainability (Basel)*, 12(16), 6401. DOI: 10.3390/su12166401

Chataut, R., Nankya, M., & Akl, R. (2024). 6G Networks and the AI Revolution—Exploring Technologies, Applications, and Emerging Challenges. *Sensors (Basel)*, 24(6), 1888. DOI: 10.3390/s24061888 PMID: 38544151

Garach, J., Singh, S. K., Ravikumar, R. N., Reddy, A. P. C., & Khan, H. (2024). A Comprehensive Review on Artificial Intelligence in Digital Forensics With Taxonomies, Issues, and Solutions: AI in Digital Forensics. Strategies for E-Commerce Data Security: Cloud, Blockchain, AI, and Machine Learning, 1-28.

Kamruzzaman, M. M. (2022). Key Technologies, Applications and Trends of Internet of Things for Energy-Efficient 6G Wireless Communication in Smart Cities. *Energies*, 15(15), 5608. DOI: 10.3390/en15155608

Kathole, A. B., Katti, J., Dhabliya, D., Deshpande, V., Rajawat, A. S., Goyal, S. B., Raboaca, M. S., Mihaltan, T. C., Verma, C., & Suciu, G. (2022). Energy-Aware UAV Based on Blockchain Model Using IoE Application in 6G Network-Driven Cybertwin. *Energies*, 15(21), 8304. DOI: 10.3390/en15218304

Khalil, U., Malik, O. A., Uddin, M., & Chen, C. (2022). A Comparative Analysis on Blockchain versus Centralized Authentication Architectures for IoT-Enabled Smart Devices in Smart Cities: A Comprehensive Review, Recent Advances, and Future Research Directions. *Sensors (Basel)*, 22(14), 5168. DOI: 10.3390/s22145168 PMID: 35890848

Kharche, A., Badholia, S., & Upadhyay, R. K. (2024). Implementation of blockchain technology in integrated IoT networks for constructing scalable ITS systems in India. *Blockchain Research and Applications*, 5(2), 100188. DOI: 10.1016/j.bcra.2024.100188

Kumar, R., Jain, V., Yie, L. W., & Teyarachakul, S. (2023). *Convergence of IoT, Blockchain, and Computational Intelligence in Smart Cities*. CRC Press. DOI: 10.1201/9781003353034

Kunwar, F. B., Singh, H. S., & Yadav, R. K. Y. (2024). Role of blockchain-enabled Secure Supply Chain management using IIoT for Anomaly detection in 6G. *Research Square(Research Square)*. DOI: 10.21203/rs.3.rs-3882212/v1

Li, Y., Xiao, Y., Liang, W., Cai, J., Zhang, R., Li, K., & Khan, M. (2024). The security and privacy challenges toward cybersecurity of 6G networks: A comprehensive review. *Computer Science and Information Systems*, 21(3), 851–897. DOI: 10.2298/CSIS230804016L

Liwen, Z., Qamar, F., Liaqat, M., Hindia, M. N., & Ariffin, K. Z. (2024). Towards Efficient 6G IoT Networks: A Perspective on Resource Optimization Strategies, Challenges, and Future Directions. *IEEE Access : Practical Innovations, Open Solutions*, 12, 76606–76633. DOI: 10.1109/ACCESS.2024.3405487

Pajooh, H. H., Demidenko, S., Aslam, S., & Harris, M. (2022a). Blockchain and 6G-Enabled IoT. *Inventions (Basel, Switzerland)*, 7(4), 109. DOI: 10.3390/inventions7040109

Pajooh, H. H., Demidenko, S., Aslam, S., & Harris, M. (2022b). Blockchain and 6G-Enabled IoT. *Inventions (Basel, Switzerland)*, 7(4), 109. DOI: 10.3390/inventions7040109

Palaniappan, D., Davda, Y., & Premavathi, T. (2023). Digital Marketing Based on Machine Learning. In *Advances in logistics, operations, and management science book series* (pp. 143–170). DOI: 10.4018/978-1-6684-9062-4.ch009

Premavathi, T., Shekhar, A., Raj, A., Agrawal, S., & Palaniappan, D. (2024). Crafting the Future. In *Advances in logistics, operations, and management science book series* (pp. 199–217). DOI: 10.4018/979-8-3693-1198-1.ch009

Rahman, A., Kundu, D., Debnath, T., Rahman, M., Aishi, A. A., & Islam, J. (2024). Blockchain-based AI Methods for Managing Industrial IoT: Recent Developments, Integration Challenges and Opportunities. *arXiv (Cornell University)*. https://doi.org//arxiv.2405.12550DOI: 10.48550

Rathod, T., Jadav, N., Tanwar, S., Sharma, R., Tolba, A., Raboaca, M., Marina, V., & Said, W. (2023). Blockchain-Driven Intelligent Scheme for IoT-Based Public Safety System beyond 5G Networks. *Sensors (Basel)*, 23(2), 969. DOI: 10.3390/s23020969 PMID: 36679767

Ravikumar, N., Singhal, S., Betgeri, S., & Singh, S. K. (2024). Strategies for Mitigating Security Concerns in IoT-Enabled Smart Cities. In *Advances in computational intelligence and robotics book series* (pp. 239–273). DOI: 10.4018/979-8-3693-2373-1.ch012

Rejeb, A., Rejeb, K., Appolloni, A., Jagtap, S., Iranmanesh, M., Alghamdi, S., Alhasawi, Y., & Kayikci, Y. (2024). Unleashing the power of internet of things and blockchain: A comprehensive analysis and future directions. *Internet of Things and Cyber-Physical Systems*, 4, 1–18. DOI: 10.1016/j.iotcps.2023.06.003

Rojas, E., Carrascal, D., Lopez-Pajares, D., Alvarez-Horcajo, J., Carral, J. A., Arco, J. M., & Martinez-Yelmo, I. (2024). A Survey on AI-Empowered Softwarized Industrial IoT Networks. *Electronics (Basel)*, 13(10), 1979. DOI: 10.3390/electronics13101979

Rojek, I., Jasiulewicz-Kaczmarek, M., Piszcz, A., Galas, K., & Mikołajewski, D. (2024a). Review of the 6G-Based Supply Chain Management within Industry 4.0/5.0 Paradigm. *Electronics (Basel)*, 13(13), 2624. DOI: 10.3390/electronics13132624

Rojek, I., Jasiulewicz-Kaczmarek, M., Piszcz, A., Galas, K., & Mikołajewski, D. (2024b). Review of the 6G-Based Supply Chain Management within Industry 4.0/5.0 Paradigm. *Electronics (Basel)*, 13(13), 2624. DOI: 10.3390/electronics13132624

Shahidinejad, A., & Abawajy, J. (2024). An All-Inclusive Taxonomy and Critical Review of Blockchain-Assisted Authentication and Session Key Generation Protocols for IoT. *ACM Computing Surveys*, 56(7), 1–38. DOI: 10.1145/3645087

Sheraz, M., Chuah, T. C., Lee, Y. L., Alam, M. M., Al-Habashna, A., & Han, Z. (2024). A Comprehensive Survey on Revolutionizing Connectivity Through Artificial Intelligence-Enabled Digital Twin Network in 6G. *IEEE Access : Practical Innovations, Open Solutions*, 1, 1. Advance online publication. DOI: 10.1109/ACCESS.2024.3384272

Singh, S. K., Azzaoui, A., Choo, K. K. R., Yang, L. T., & Park, J. H. (2023). Articles A Comprehensive Survey on Blockchain for Secure IoT-enabled Smart City beyond 5G: Approaches, Processes, Challenges, and Opportunities. Hum.-. *Centric Comput. Inf. Sci*, 13, 51.

Singh, S. K., Lee, C., & Park, J. H. (2022). CoVAC: A P2P smart contract-based intelligent smart city architecture for vaccine manufacturing. *Computers & Industrial Engineering*, 166, 107967. DOI: 10.1016/j.cie.2022.107967 PMID: 35136280

Singh, S. K., Pan, Y., & Park, J. H. (2022). Blockchain-enabled Secure Framework for Energy-Efficient Smart Parking in Sustainable City Environment. *Sustainable Cities and Society*, 76, 103364. DOI: 10.1016/j.scs.2021.103364

Singh, S. K., & Park, J. H. (2022). TaLWaR: Blockchain-Based Trust Management Scheme for Smart Enterprises With Augmented Intelligence. *IEEE Transactions on Industrial Informatics*, 19(1), 626–634. DOI: 10.1109/TII.2022.3204692

Singh, S. K., Park, J. H., Sharma, P. K., & Pan, Y. (2021). BIIoVT: Blockchain-Based Secure Storage Architecture for Intelligent Internet of Vehicular Things. *IEEE Consumer Electronics Magazine*, 11(6), 75–82. DOI: 10.1109/MCE.2021.3089992

Singh, S. K., Park, L., & Park, J. H. (2022). Blockchain-based Federated Approach for Privacy-Preserved IoT-enabled Smart Vehicular Networks. 2022 13th International Conference on Information and Communication Technology Convergence (ICTC), 11, 1995–1999. DOI: 10.1109/ICTC55196.2022.9952835

Singh, S. K., Rathore, S., & Park, J. H. (2019). BlockIoTIntelligence: A Blockchain-enabled Intelligent IoT Architecture with Artificial Intelligence. *Future Generation Computer Systems*, 110, 721–743. DOI: 10.1016/j.future.2019.09.002

Singh, S. K., Yang, L. T., & Park, J. H. (2022). FusionFedBlock: Fusion of blockchain and federated learning to preserve privacy in industry 5.0. *Information Fusion*, 90, 233–240. DOI: 10.1016/j.inffus.2022.09.027

Taha, H. M., Mohammed, M. A., Jghef, Y. S., Sulaiman, S. K., & Mustafa, T. S. (2024). The integration of blockchain technology in 5G-enabled IoT. *ITM Web of Conferences, 64*, 01001. DOI: 10.1051/itmconf/20246401001

Chapter 13
Enabling Secure and Efficient Healthcare Delivery in Smart Cities Through 6G Infrastructure

Naboshree Bhattacharya
https://orcid.org/0000-0001-5572-4098
Amity University, Ranchi, India

Divya Bansal
https://orcid.org/0000-0001-6268-5402
Amity University, Noida, India

ABSTRACT

Smart cities leverage 6G infrastructure for secure, efficient healthcare delivery. 6G's ultra-low latency, high bandwidth, and device connectivity enable real-time data transmission for telemedicine, remote monitoring, and robotic surgeries, improving healthcare access. Ensuring 6G security is crucial; encryption, authentication, blockchain, and zero-trust models protect sensitive data. Integrating 6G with existing systems requires standardized protocols and collaboration. Navigating regulations and ethics related to data privacy and patient consent is essential. As smart cities evolve, secure 6G will revolutionize healthcare delivery through innovation and prioritizing patient well-being.

DOI: 10.4018/979-8-3693-8029-1.ch013

1. INTRODUCTION TO SMART CITIES AND 6G INFRASTRUCTURE

1.1 The Concept of Smart Cities and Leverage 6G for Healthcare

Smart cities are urban areas that leverage advanced technologies and data-driven approaches to enhance the quality of life for their residents, improve operational efficiency, and promote sustainable development (Gharaibeh et al., 2017). These cities integrate various systems, such as transportation, energy, healthcare, and governance, through interconnected networks and intelligent infrastructure (Yigitcanlar et al., 2018). By harnessing the power of information and communication technologies (ICT), smart cities aim to address the challenges of urbanization, optimize resource utilization, and create more livable, resilient, and prosperous communities (Khatoun & Zeadally, 2016). The concept of Smart Cities represents a transformative approach to urban development, leveraging cutting-edge technologies to enhance quality of life, optimize resource utilization, and promote sustainable growth (Yigitcanlar et al., 2021). These intelligent urban ecosystems integrate interconnected systems, Internet of Things (IoT) devices, and artificial intelligence to revolutionize various aspects of city life, including healthcare delivery(Singhal et al.,2024).

In the realm of healthcare, Smart Cities are poised to harness the power of 6G technology, the next generation of wireless communication. 6G promises to surpass its predecessor, 5G, offering unprecedented connectivity, ultra-low latency, and massive data capacity (Dang et al., 2020). This technological leap is expected to catalyze significant advancements in urban healthcare systems.

Smart Cities leveraging 6G for healthcare can implement several innovative solutions:

a. Ubiquitous health monitoring: 6G enables the deployment of advanced wearable devices and nano sensors capable of continuous, real-time monitoring of patients' vital signs and biomarkers. These devices can transmit data instantaneously to healthcare providers, facilitating proactive and preventive care (Saad et al., 2020).
b. Holographic telemedicine and remote surgery: The ultra-low latency and high bandwidth of 6G networks facilitate not only seamless remote consultations but also enable surgeons to perform complex procedures from a distance using haptic feedback, augmented reality, and even holographic projections (Viswanathan & Mogensen, 2020).

c. AI-driven diagnostics and predictive healthcare: 6G's enhanced data processing capabilities allow for rapid analysis of large-scale medical imaging, genomic data, and patient records. This empowers AI-powered diagnostic tools to achieve unprecedented accuracy and enables predictive models to forecast health trends and potential outbreaks (Letaief et al., 2019; Bhattacharya & Kumar, 2024).
d. Intelligent emergency response systems: Smart ambulances equipped with 6G technology can transmit real-time patient data to hospitals, enabling better preparation and faster treatment upon arrival. Moreover, AI-powered systems can optimize emergency response routes and resource allocation in real-time (Ateya et al., 2021).
e. Personalized and precision medicine: The synergy of 6G, IoT devices, and AI facilitates the collection and analysis of vast amounts of patient data, including genetic information, lifestyle factors, and environmental data. This comprehensive approach enables the development of highly personalized treatment plans and targeted therapies (Huang et al., 2019).
f. Immersive medical training: 6G's high-bandwidth capabilities support advanced virtual and augmented reality applications, revolutionizing medical education and training. This allows for realistic simulations of complex procedures and collaborative learning experiences across vast distances (Chowdhury et al., 2020).
g. Blockchain-enabled health data management: 6G networks can support robust blockchain systems for secure, transparent, and efficient management of health records, ensuring data integrity and patient privacy while facilitating seamless data sharing among authorized healthcare providers (Nguyen et al., 2020;Singh et al., 2023).

By leveraging 6G technology, Smart Cities can create a more responsive, efficient, and patient-centric healthcare ecosystem. This integration promises to improve overall population health outcomes, reduce healthcare disparities, and enhance the resilience of urban health systems in the face of future challenges.

1.2 The Evolution of Communication Technologies

The trajectory of human communication has been profoundly shaped by technological advancements, with each new era bringing forth innovations that redefine the way we interact, share information, and connect across vast distances. This evolution has not only transformed personal communications but has also had far-reaching implications for society, economics, and global culture.

The dawn of modern communication technologies can be traced back to the invention of the telegraph in the 19th century, which marked the beginning of near-instantaneous long-distance communication (Standage, 2014). This was followed by the telephone, which revolutionized voice communication and laid the groundwork for future telecommunications infrastructure (Ling, 2021).

The 20th century witnessed a rapid acceleration in communication technologies. The development of radio and television broadcasting enabled mass communication on an unprecedented scale, shaping public opinion and cultural norms (Hilmes, 2020). The invention of the transistor in 1947 paved the way for more compact and efficient electronic devices, leading to the proliferation of personal communication tools (Riordan et al., 2019). The latter half of the 20th century saw the emergence of digital technologies, with the development of early computer networks and the eventual birth of the Internet. The ARPANET, precursor to the modern Internet, was established in 1969, marking the beginning of a new era in global connectivity (Abbate, 2000). The subsequent development of the World Wide Web in the 1990s democratized access to information and laid the foundation for the digital age (Berners-Lee & Fischetti, 2021). The turn of the millennium heralded the mobile revolution, with cellular networks evolving from 1G to 5G, enabling increasingly sophisticated mobile communications and data transfer (Dahlman et al., 2018). Smartphones, epitomized by the launch of the iPhone in 2007, transformed mobile devices into powerful, multi-functional communication tools, blurring the lines between personal and professional communication (Ling & Lai, 2016). Social media platforms emerged as a dominant force in the 2000s and 2010s, fundamentally altering the dynamics of personal and mass communication. These platforms have had profound effects on social interactions, political discourse, and information dissemination (van Dijck et al., 2018).

Recent years have seen the rise of artificial intelligence and machine learning in communication technologies. Natural Language Processing (NLP) and chatbots are increasingly being integrated into customer service and personal assistant applications, while AI-driven content curation algorithms shape our online experiences (Hirschberg & Manning, 2015). Looking towards the future, emerging technologies such as 5G and beyond (6G) networks promise to enable new forms of communication with ultra-low latency and high bandwidth, paving the way for innovations like holographic communication and advanced Internet of Things (IoT) applications (Saad et al., 2020). Quantum communication, still in its early stages, holds the potential to revolutionize secure communication by leveraging the principles of quantum mechanics (Pirandola et al., 2020). The evolution of communication technologies continues to accelerate, driven by advancements in various fields including electronics, computer science, and network engineering. As these technologies progress, they raise important questions about privacy, security, and the societal impact of ever-more pervasive and intelligent communication systems (Zuboff, 2019).

Therefore, the evolution of communication technologies represents a fascinating journey of human ingenuity and innovation. From the telegraph to quantum communication, each advancement has brought us closer together, reshaped our societies, and opened new frontiers of human interaction. As we look to the future, it is clear that communication technologies will continue to play a pivotal role in shaping the human experience in the 21st century and beyond.

1.3 The Emergence of 6G Infrastructure

As the global rollout of 5G networks continues, researchers and industry leaders are already setting their sights on the next generation of wireless technology: 6G. This future infrastructure promises to revolutionize communication, computing, and connectivity on an unprecedented scale. The emergence of 6G infrastructure is characterized by its potential to support ultra-high-speed data transmission, near-zero latency, and ubiquitous connectivity, paving the way for transformative applications across various sectors.

6G is expected to operate in the terahertz (THz) frequency band, a leap beyond the millimeter-wave frequencies used in 5G (Akyildiz et al., 2020). This shift to higher frequencies will enable data rates potentially reaching up to 1 terabit per second, a hundred-fold increase over 5G capabilities (Dang et al., 2020). Such speeds could facilitate real-time holographic communications, immersive extended reality experiences, and high-fidelity tactile internet applications. One of the key architectural innovations in 6G infrastructure is the concept of three-dimensional network coverage. Unlike previous generations that primarily focused on terrestrial networks, 6G aims to integrate ground, aerial, and satellite networks into a seamless communication fabric (Zhang et al., 2019). This integration will enable truly global coverage, including remote and traditionally underserved areas, potentially bridging the digital divide on a global scale.

Artificial Intelligence (AI) is expected to play a central role in 6G infrastructure. AI will be deeply embedded in network operations, enabling intelligent resource allocation, predictive maintenance, and adaptive network optimization (Letaief et al., 2019). This AI-native approach will allow 6G networks to be more efficient, resilient, and responsive to changing user demands and environmental conditions. Another crucial aspect of 6G infrastructure is its emphasis on energy efficiency and sustainability. With the exponential growth in data traffic and connected devices, reducing the energy footprint of communication networks has become a critical concern. 6G research is focusing on developing energy-harvesting techniques, ultra-efficient hardware, and intelligent power management systems to create more sustainable network infrastructure (Huang et al., 2019).

The emergence of 6G is also closely tied to advancements in quantum technologies. Quantum communication and quantum computing are expected to be integral components of 6G infrastructure, offering unprecedented levels of security and computational power (Nawaz et al., 2019). Quantum key distribution, for instance, could provide theoretically unbreakable encryption for sensitive data transmission. Edge computing and distributed intelligence are set to evolve significantly with 6G. The infrastructure will likely incorporate a more decentralized architecture, with computing resources distributed closer to end-users and devices. This approach will not only reduce latency but also enhance privacy and enable more context-aware services (Saad et al., 2020).

The development of 6G infrastructure also presents several challenges. The use of terahertz frequencies, while offering immense bandwidth, faces significant propagation limitations and requires advancements in antenna technology and signal processing (Rappaport et al., 2019). Additionally, the integration of diverse network types (terrestrial, aerial, and satellite) poses complex synchronization and handover challenges that need to be addressed.

Standardization efforts for 6G are in their early stages, with organizations like the International Telecommunication Union (ITU) beginning to outline visions for 6G (ITU, 2021). However, concrete standards are not expected to be finalized until the latter half of this decade, with commercial deployment potentially beginning in the 2030s.

As research into 6G infrastructure progresses, ethical considerations and societal impacts are gaining prominence. Issues such as privacy, digital inclusion, and the potential health effects of higher frequency electromagnetic radiation are being actively discussed and studied (Viswanathan & Mogensen, 2020).

Therefore the emergence of 6G infrastructure represents a paradigm shift in wireless communication technology. Its development is driven by the convergence of advanced radio technologies, AI, quantum computing, and a holistic approach to network architecture. While significant technical challenges remain, the potential of 6G to enable transformative applications and address global connectivity issues makes it a critical area of research and development in the coming years.

1.4 The Potential of 6G in Transforming Healthcare Delivery

The advent of 6G technology promises to revolutionize healthcare delivery systems worldwide. With projected data rates up to 1 Tbps and sub-millisecond latency (Dang et al., 2020), 6G will enhance telemedicine and enable remote robotic surgery with haptic feedback (Saad et al., 2020; Viswanathan & Mogensen, 2020).

The technology's capacity to support massive device connectivity will advance the Internet of Medical Things (IoMT), enabling continuous patient monitoring and early detection of health issues (Yaacoub et al., 2020).

6G-powered AI and machine learning algorithms will revolutionize diagnostics and treatment planning, while integration with extended reality (XR) technologies will transform medical education and training (Letaief et al., 2019; Chowdhury et al., 2020). The technology will also facilitate precision medicine and enhance disease surveillance and epidemic management (Zhao et al., 2021; Ateya et al., 2021).

However, challenges remain, including data privacy and security concerns, potential exacerbation of the digital divide, and the need for evolving regulatory frameworks (Nawaz et al., 2019; Zhang et al., 2019; Akyildiz et al., 2020). Addressing these challenges will be crucial to realizing 6G's potential to improve patient outcomes and healthcare delivery efficiency on a global scale.

2. 6G INFRASTRUCTURE: CHARACTERISTICS AND ADVANTAGES FOR HEALTHCARE

The advent of 6G technology promises to revolutionize healthcare delivery in smart cities, offering unprecedented capabilities that surpass those of previous generations of wireless communication. This section explores the key features of 6G technology, compares it with earlier generations, and discusses potential use cases in smart city healthcare.

2.1 Key Features of 6G Technology

2.1.1 Ultra-Low Latency

One of the most significant advancements in 6G technology is its ultra-low latency. While 5G aims for latencies around 1 millisecond, 6G is expected to achieve sub-millisecond latencies, potentially as low as 0.1 milliseconds (Saad et al., 2020). This dramatic reduction in latency is crucial for healthcare applications that require real-time responsiveness, such as remote surgeries and critical patient monitoring systems. The near-instantaneous communication enabled by 6G can significantly improve the accuracy and effectiveness of time-sensitive medical interventions (Dang et al., 2020).

2.1.2 High Bandwidth

6G networks are projected to offer extremely high bandwidth capabilities, with peak data rates potentially reaching up to 1 terabit per second (Tbps) (Tariq et al., 2020). This represents a hundred-fold increase over 5G's maximum data rates. Such enormous bandwidth capacity will enable the transmission of massive amounts of medical data, including high-resolution medical imaging, real-time video streams, and complex biometric information, without any perceptible delay or loss of quality (Chowdhury et al., 2020).

2.1.3 Massive Device Connectivity

6G is expected to support an unprecedented density of connected devices, potentially up to 107 devices per square kilometer (Akyildiz et al., 2020). This massive connectivity will be crucial in healthcare settings, enabling the deployment of extensive networks of medical IoT devices, wearable sensors, and monitoring equipment. The ability to seamlessly integrate and manage vast numbers of devices will facilitate comprehensive, real-time patient monitoring and data collection on an unprecedented scale (Zhang et al., 2019).

2.2 Comparison of 6G with Previous Generations (5G and Earlier)

While 5G represents a significant leap forward in wireless communication technology, 6G is poised to offer even more transformative capabilities. The following table summarizes key performance indicators, comparing 4G, 5G, and projected 6G specifications:

Table 1. Performance indicators

Feature	4G	5G	6G (Projected)
Peak Data Rate	1 Gbps	20 Gbps	1 Tbps
Latency	10 ms	1 ms	0.1 ms
Connection Density	105/km2	106/km2	107/km2
Spectrum Efficiency	30 bps/Hz	30 bps/Hz	100 bps/Hz

Source: Dang et al., 2020; Saad et al., 2020)

Beyond these quantitative improvements, 6G is expected to incorporate advanced technologies such as artificial intelligence (AI), quantum computing, and molecular communications, which were not fully realized in previous generations (Letaief et al., 2019). These technologies will enable more sophisticated, intelligent, and efficient healthcare applications.

2.3 Potential Use Cases of 6G in Smart City Healthcare

2.3.1 Telemedicine and Remote Patient Monitoring

6G's ultra-low latency and high bandwidth will dramatically enhance telemedicine capabilities. High-quality, real-time video consultations will become more reliable and accessible, even in areas with limited infrastructure. Advanced haptic technologies enabled by 6G could allow doctors to perform remote physical examinations with a level of precision previously impossible (Ateya et al., 2021).

Moreover, 6G will support the deployment of extensive networks of wearable and implantable medical devices for continuous patient monitoring. These devices will be able to transmit large volumes of real-time health data, enabling early detection of health issues and more proactive healthcare interventions (Yang et al., 2019).

2.3.2 Robotic Surgeries and Remote Medical Procedures

The ultra-low latency of 6G networks will be crucial in enabling more advanced robotic surgeries and remote medical procedures. With latencies approaching 0.1 milliseconds, surgeons will be able to control robotic surgical instruments with unprecedented precision and real-time feedback, even from great distances (Saad et al., 2020). This could democratize access to specialized surgical expertise, allowing patients in remote or underserved areas to benefit from the skills of leading surgeons located anywhere in the world.

Furthermore, 6G's high bandwidth will support the transmission of high-resolution, multi-view video streams and complex haptic feedback data, enhancing the surgeon's ability to perform intricate procedures remotely (Chowdhury et al., 2020).

2.3.3 Personalized Medicine and AI-Assisted Diagnosis

6G networks will revolutionize healthcare by enabling the collection and analysis of vast amounts of patient data, including genetic information, lifestyle data, and real-time physiological measurements. This comprehensive data ecosystem, combined with 6G's high-speed, low-latency capabilities, will power sophisticated AI-driven diagnostic and treatment recommendation systems (Letaief et al., 2019). AI algorithms will process complex, multi-modal data in real-time, providing instant insights to support clinical decision-making, leading to more accurate diagnoses and personalized treatment plans (Viswanathan & Mogensen, 2020). Additionally, 6G's massive device connectivity will facilitate the adoption of digital twins in healthcare, enabling precise treatment simulations and personalized strategies (Ateya et al., 2021). As 6G technology develops, collaboration between healthcare providers, policymakers, and technologists is essential to harness these capabilities for improved patient care and health outcomes in smart cities.

3. SECURING 6G INFRASTRUCTURE FOR HEALTHCARE APPLICATIONS

The advent of 6G technology promises to revolutionize healthcare delivery in smart cities, offering unprecedented connectivity, speed, and capacity. However, with these advancements come significant security challenges that must be addressed to protect patient data and ensure the integrity of healthcare systems. This comprehensive analysis explores the unique security challenges posed by 6G-enabled healthcare applications in smart cities and discusses advanced strategies for protecting patient privacy, ensuring data integrity, and safeguarding against cyber threats.

3.1. Unique Security Challenges in 6G-Enabled Smart City Healthcare

The integration of 6G technology in healthcare systems introduces several complex security challenges:

i. Expanded Attack Surface

6G networks are expected to support an astounding density of up to 107 devices per square kilometer (Akyildiz et al., 2020). This massive connectivity significantly expands the potential attack surface, with each connected medical device, sensor, or wearable becoming a potential entry point for malicious actors. The sheer scale and heterogeneity of these networks increase the complexity of securing the entire ecosystem exponentially (Porambage et al., 2021).

ii. Ultra-Low Latency Requirements

The sub-millisecond latency of 6G networks, while enabling revolutionary healthcare applications, also necessitates security measures that can operate at unprecedented speeds. Traditional security protocols may introduce unacceptable delays in time-critical healthcare applications, such as remote surgeries or real-time patient monitoring, potentially compromising patient safety (Saad et al., 2020).

iii. Quantum Computing Threats

As quantum computing advances, it poses a significant threat to current cryptographic methods. 6G networks must be designed with quantum-resistant security measures to protect sensitive healthcare data against future quantum attacks, ensuring long-term data confidentiality (Zhang et al., 2019).

iv. AI-Related Vulnerabilities

The deep integration of AI in 6G healthcare systems introduces new vulnerabilities, such as adversarial attacks on machine learning models used for diagnosis or treatment recommendations. These attacks could potentially manipulate AI systems to produce erroneous results, leading to misdiagnosis or inappropriate treatments (Letaief et al., 2019).

v. Edge Computing Security

6G networks will heavily rely on edge computing to process vast amounts of data closer to the source. This distributed architecture introduces new security challenges, as edge nodes may be more vulnerable to physical tampering and cyber-attacks compared to centralized data centers (Tariq et al., 2020).

3.1.1 Protecting Patient Privacy and Confidentiality

Ensuring patient privacy and confidentiality is paramount in 6G-enabled healthcare systems. Several advanced approaches are being developed to address this challenge:

i. Homomorphic Encryption

This sophisticated encryption technique allows computations to be performed on encrypted data without decrypting it first. In 6G healthcare applications, homomorphic encryption enables secure processing of sensitive patient data in the cloud or at the network edge, maintaining privacy even during analysis (Tariq et al., 2020).

ii. Differential Privacy

By adding carefully calibrated noise to datasets or query results, differential privacy protects individual privacy while still allowing for meaningful statistical analysis of population-level health data. This technique is particularly valuable for large-scale health studies and epidemiological research in 6G-enabled smart cities (Dwork et al., 2014).

iii. Federated Learning

This innovative approach allows AI models to be trained on distributed datasets without centralizing sensitive patient data. Healthcare providers can collaborate on developing improved diagnostic and treatment models while keeping patient data locally stored and protected, aligning with data protection regulations like GDPR (Yang et al., 2019).

iv. Blockchain-Based Consent Management

Blockchain technology can be leveraged to create immutable, patient-controlled records of consent for data sharing. This approach gives patients greater control over their health information and ensures transparent, auditable data access logs (Hewa et al., 2020).

v. Attribute-Based Encryption (ABE)

ABE allows for fine-grained access control to encrypted data based on user attributes. In 6G healthcare systems, this can be used to ensure that only authorized personnel with specific roles or credentials can access particular types of patient information (Aftab et al., 2021).

3.1.2 Ensuring Data Integrity and Preventing Unauthorized Access

Maintaining the integrity of healthcare data and preventing unauthorized access are critical in 6G-enabled systems:

i. Quantum Key Distribution (QKD)

QKD leverages quantum mechanics principles to provide theoretically unbreakable encryption. This cutting-edge technology can protect against both current and future quantum computing threats, ensuring long-term security for sensitive healthcare data (Nawaz et al., 2019).

ii. Zero-Trust Architecture

This security model assumes no implicit trust in any entity within the network, requiring continuous authentication and authorization for all data access and transactions. In 6G healthcare systems, zero-trust architectures can significantly reduce the risk of insider threats and unauthorized access (Yaacoub et al., 2020).

iii. Blockchain for Data Integrity

Blockchain technology can create tamper-resistant records of medical data and transactions, ensuring the integrity and traceability of healthcare information. This is particularly valuable for maintaining the chain of custody for medical records and ensuring the authenticity of pharmaceutical supply chains (Hewa et al., 2020).

iv. Post-Quantum Cryptography

As quantum computers threaten current encryption methods, developing and implementing post-quantum cryptographic algorithms is crucial for long-term security in 6G healthcare systems. These algorithms are designed to resist attacks from both classical and quantum computers (Cheon et al., 2021).

3.1.3 Safeguarding Against Cyber Threats and Attacks

Protecting 6G-enabled healthcare systems against cyber threats requires a multi-faceted, proactive approach:

i. AI-Enabled Security

Machine learning algorithms can be employed to detect and respond to cyber threats in real-time, adapting to new attack patterns and anomalies in network behavior. These AI-driven security systems can provide faster and more accurate threat detection compared to traditional rule-based approaches (Porambage et al., 2021; Jeremiah et al., 2024).

ii. Physical Layer Security

Advanced techniques such as artificial noise injection, directional modulation, and intelligent reflecting surfaces can create secure communication channels that are inherently resistant to eavesdropping and jamming. These methods exploit the physical properties of wireless signals to enhance security at the most fundamental level (Wu et al., 2021).

iii. Moving Target Defense (MTD)

MTD strategies dynamically change system configurations to increase uncertainty and complexity for attackers, making it more difficult to exploit vulnerabilities. In 6G healthcare systems, MTD can be applied to network addresses, protocols, and even the frequency of wireless transmissions (Cho et al., 2020).

iv. Secure Multi-Party Computation (SMPC)

SMPC allows multiple parties to jointly compute functions over their inputs while keeping those inputs private. This technology enables secure collaboration in healthcare research and analytics, allowing different institutions to share insights without revealing raw patient data (Zheng et al., 2019).

v. Quantum-Safe VPNs

As traditional VPNs may become vulnerable to quantum attacks, developing quantum-safe VPNs is crucial for securing communication channels in 6G healthcare networks. These next-generation VPNs will incorporate post-quantum cryptographic algorithms to ensure long-term security (Mavroeidis et al., 2018).

Securing 6G infrastructure for healthcare applications in smart cities requires integrating security and privacy considerations into system design from the outset. This involves leveraging advanced cryptographic techniques, AI-driven security measures, and privacy-preserving technologies(Bhattacharya & Kishore, 2024). Future research should focus on developing quantum-resistant security protocols, enhancing AI model resilience against adversarial attacks, and creating seamless authentication mechanisms suitable for ultra-low latency 6G networks. Interdisciplinary collaboration between healthcare professionals, cybersecurity experts, and policymakers is crucial to address ethical and regulatory challenges. By tackling these security challenges, we can harness 6G technology's potential to revolutionize healthcare delivery in smart cities, ultimately improving patient outcomes and quality of life worldwide.

3.2 Strategies for Securing 6G Infrastructure in Healthcare Settings

The advent of 6G technology promises to revolutionize healthcare delivery in smart cities, offering unprecedented connectivity, speed, and capacity. However, this technological leap also introduces complex security challenges that must be addressed to protect patient data and ensure the integrity of healthcare systems. This comprehensive analysis explores cutting-edge approaches to securing 6G healthcare infrastructure, focusing on robust encryption and authentication mechanisms, blockchain technology for secure data sharing, and the adoption of zero-trust security models with continuous monitoring.

3.2.1 Implementing Robust Encryption and Authentication Mechanisms

As 6G networks push the boundaries of data transmission speeds and latency reduction, traditional security measures become inadequate. Implementing state-of-the-art encryption and authentication mechanisms is crucial for protecting healthcare data in this new paradigm.

i. Post-Quantum Cryptography (PQC)

Post-quantum cryptography (PQC) is essential for securing 6G healthcare systems against potential threats from quantum computers. PQC algorithms, designed to resist attacks from both classical and quantum computers, focus on lattice-based cryptography, multivariate cryptography, and hash-based signatures (Cheon et al., 2021). The National Institute of Standards and Technology (NIST) is leading the standardization of PQC algorithms, paving the way for widespread adoption (Alagic et al., 2020). Healthcare organizations must proactively assess their cryptographic agility and develop migration strategies to ensure long-term protection of patient data in the quantum era. This preparation is crucial for maintaining the confidentiality and integrity of healthcare information systems as quantum computing technology advances.

ii. Fully Homomorphic Encryption (FHE)

Fully Homomorphic Encryption (FHE) represents a groundbreaking advancement in data security, allowing computations to be performed on encrypted data without the need for decryption. This capability is particularly valuable in healthcare scenarios, where sensitive patient data often needs to be processed in cloud environments or at network edges while maintaining strict privacy standards. Recent advancements in FHE have significantly enhanced its practicality for real-world applications. New schemes like TFHE (Fast Fully Homomorphic Encryption over the Torus) have made substantial strides in reducing computational overhead, making FHE more efficient and feasible for widespread use (Chillotti et al., 2020). Additionally, the development of dedicated FHE hardware accelerators is further improving performance, bringing FHE closer to meeting the demands of complex healthcare applications (Samardzic et al., 2021). While challenges remain in achieving the ultra-low latency required by 6G networks, ongoing research and hardware innovations are rapidly narrowing this gap. As these advancements continue, FHE is poised to become a cornerstone of secure data processing in next-generation healthcare systems, enabling sophisticated analysis of patient data while preserving confidentiality and compliance with stringent privacy regulations.

iii. Advanced Biometric Authentication

Multi-modal biometric authentication systems have emerged as a powerful solution for robust user verification in 6G healthcare applications, combining physiological and behavioral biometrics to create a highly secure and user-friendly authentication process. These advanced systems are further enhanced by cutting-edge technologies that address key security concerns. Liveness detection, powered by AI-driven techniques, effectively prevents spoofing attacks by distinguishing between genuine biometric inputs and fake data, ensuring that only legitimate users gain access. Continuous authentication adds an extra layer of security by constantly monitoring user behavior patterns throughout a session, swiftly detecting anomalies that might indicate potential account takeovers. To address privacy concerns associated with biometric data storage, privacy-preserving biometric techniques such as cancellable biometrics and homomorphic encryption are employed. These methods protect biometric templates from unauthorized access or misuse, maintaining user privacy without compromising security (Talreja et al., 2020). By integrating these advanced features, multi-modal biometric authentication systems provide a comprehensive security solution that is well-suited to the demanding requirements of 6G healthcare environments, where both high security and user convenience are paramount(Jeremiah et al., 2024).

iv. Quantum Key Distribution (QKD)

Quantum Key Distribution (QKD) offers a revolutionary approach to secure communication in 6G healthcare networks, leveraging quantum mechanics principles to provide theoretically unbreakable key exchange. Recent advancements include satellite-based QKD for global secure communications (Liao et al., 2018) and integration with software-defined networking (SDN) for enhanced practicality and scalability (Cao et al., 2019). QKD's potential applications in healthcare include securing telesurgery data streams and protecting sensitive patient information against current and future cyber threats. As QKD technology matures, it is poised to play a crucial role in meeting the heightened security demands of next-generation medical systems and practices within 6G networks.

3.2.2 Leveraging Blockchain Technology for Secure Data Sharing

Blockchain technology offers a decentralized, tamper-resistant approach to managing and sharing healthcare data in 6G networks. Its application in healthcare can enhance data integrity, improve interoperability, and give patients greater control over their health information.

i. Consent Management and Access Control

Blockchain-based consent management systems are revolutionizing the way patients control their health data, offering unprecedented levels of granularity and transparency. These systems leverage key blockchain features to empower patients and ensure compliance with stringent data protection regulations such as GDPR and HIPAA. Smart contracts play a crucial role in enforcing access policies and maintaining an immutable audit trail of data access, providing a tamper-proof record of all interactions with patient data. Decentralized identifiers (DIDs) offer a secure and privacy-preserving method for managing digital identities within healthcare ecosystems, allowing patients to maintain control over their personal information across multiple providers and platforms. Zero-knowledge proofs represent a significant advancement in privacy protection, enabling the verification of consent without the need to reveal sensitive information (Zheng et al., 2021). This technology ensures that patients can grant specific permissions while maintaining the confidentiality of their broader health records. By integrating these advanced features, blockchain-based consent management systems create a robust, patient-centric framework for data governance that aligns perfectly with modern data protection regulations, fostering trust and empowering patients in the management of their health information.

ii. Interoperability and Data Exchange

Blockchain technology is revolutionizing data exchange in healthcare, offering secure and efficient methods for sharing information between providers and institutions. Advanced implementations of blockchain in this context are addressing key challenges and expanding the technology's capabilities. Cross-chain interoperability represents a significant breakthrough, enabling different blockchain networks to communicate and share data securely, thus breaking down silos and fostering comprehensive patient care across diverse healthcare ecosystems (Belchior et al., 2021). To manage the vast volumes of healthcare data efficiently, off-chain storage solutions are being developed, combining blockchain's security features with distributed file systems like IPFS. This hybrid approach allows for scalable data management while maintaining the integrity and traceability benefits of blockchain. Furthermore, the integration of AI-driven data validation is enhancing the reliability of shared healthcare data(Bhattacharya & Kumar,2024). By utilizing machine learning algorithms, these systems can automatically verify the integrity and consistency of data as it's exchanged, reducing errors and ensuring that healthcare providers have access to accurate, up-to-date information. These advanced implementations collectively represent a significant step forward in creating a more interconnected, efficient, and trustworthy healthcare data ecosystem, ultimately leading to improved patient outcomes and more effective healthcare delivery.

iii. Supply Chain Management

Blockchain technology is transforming healthcare supply chains by ensuring the authenticity and traceability of pharmaceuticals and medical devices, addressing critical issues such as counterfeit drugs and supply chain inefficiencies. Advanced features of blockchain implementation in this domain are creating a more robust, transparent, and efficient ecosystem. The integration of Internet of Things (IoT) sensors with blockchain enables real-time tracking and monitoring of medical supplies, providing unprecedented visibility into the movement and condition of critical healthcare products. AI-powered predictive analytics leverages the immutable data stored on the blockchain to optimize supply chain operations and forecast potential disruptions, allowing for proactive management and risk mitigation. Smart contract-based compliance represents a significant advancement in regulatory adherence, automating compliance checks and offering real-time visibility into the supply chain (Haq & Muselemu, 2021). This automation not only reduces the risk of human error but also streamlines regulatory processes, ensuring that healthcare products meet all necessary standards throughout their journey from manufacturer to patient. By combining these advanced features, blockchain is creating a more secure, efficient, and transparent healthcare supply chain, ultimately improving patient safety and the overall quality of healthcare delivery.

iv. Clinical Trials and Research

Blockchain technology is revolutionizing the conduct of clinical trials by enhancing integrity, transparency, and efficiency throughout the research process. By providing an immutable record of trial protocols, patient consent, and data collection, blockchain ensures the authenticity and traceability of all trial-related information. Advanced applications of blockchain in clinical trials are further transforming the research landscape. Decentralized clinical trials, enabled by blockchain, facilitate remote patient participation and data collection, significantly improving trial efficiency and diversity by removing geographical barriers and expanding access to a wider range of participants. Automated protocol enforcement through smart contracts ensures strict adherence to trial protocols and data collection procedures, reducing human error and enhancing the reliability of trial results. Perhaps most importantly, blockchain enables secure data sharing for meta-analyses, allowing research institutions to collaborate on large-scale studies while preserving patient privacy (Benchoufi & Ravaud, 2017). This capability is particularly crucial for advancing medical knowledge, as it allows researchers to pool data and draw insights from larger, more diverse patient populations. By addressing key challenges in clinical research, such as data integrity, patient recruitment, and inter-institutional collaboration, blockchain is paving the way for more efficient, transparent, and impactful clinical trials, ultimately accelerating the pace of medical discoveries and improving patient outcomes (Singh et al., 2024).

3.2.3 Adopting Zero-Trust Security Models and Continuous Monitoring

The complex and distributed nature of 6G healthcare networks necessitates a shift from perimeter-based security to a zero-trust model, complemented by continuous monitoring and adaptive security measures. Adopting zero-trust security models and continuous monitoring is another effective strategy for securing 6G infrastructure in healthcare. Zero-trust security assumes that no user or device should be trusted by default, requiring strict authentication and authorization for every access request (Ahad et al., 2020). Continuous monitoring involves real-time monitoring of network traffic, user behavior, and system logs to detect and respond to potential security threats promptly (Zhang et al., 2019).

The implementation of zero-trust architecture in 6G healthcare systems represents a paradigm shift in cybersecurity, moving from traditional perimeter-based defenses to a more dynamic approach (Yaacoub et al., 2020). Key principles include micro-segmentation, Just-In-Time (JIT) and Just-Enough-Access (JEA) provisioning, and continuous risk assessment. These principles are implemented through strategies such as Software-Defined Perimeter (SDP), Identity-Aware Proxies (IAP), and Zero Trust Network Access (ZTNA) (Wang et al., 2020).

This approach creates a robust, adaptive security framework suited to the complex nature of 6G healthcare environments. It addresses challenges posed by the proliferation of connected devices, edge computing integration, and ultra-low latency requirements (Porambage et al., 2021). By continuously verifying access requests and limiting exposure to sensitive data, zero-trust architectures significantly enhance healthcare organizations' security posture.

As healthcare systems become increasingly interconnected, adopting zero-trust principles is essential for safeguarding patient information, maintaining regulatory compliance, and ensuring the integrity of critical operations (Cho et al., 2020). This "never trust, always verify" philosophy aligns well with the security requirements of next-generation healthcare systems, enabling organizations to leverage 6G technology while maintaining high standards of data protection and patient privacy.

3.3 Balancing Security with Accessibility and Usability for Healthcare Professionals

While implementing robust security measures is essential, it is equally important to balance security with accessibility and usability for healthcare professional. Overly complex security protocols and cumbersome authentication processes can hinder the efficient delivery of healthcare services and negatively impact user experience (Srivastava et al., 2020). Striking the right balance involves designing user-friendly security solutions that seamlessly integrate with healthcare workflows and minimize disruptions to patient care (Tang et al., 2020).

This can be achieved by adopting user-centric security approaches, such as single sign-on (SSO) and role-based access control (RBAC), which simplify access management and reduce the burden on healthcare professionals (Gu et al., 2020). Providing regular security training and awareness programs can also help healthcare staff understand and adhere to security best practices without compromising their ability to deliver quality care (Yang et al., 2019).

4. INTEGRATING 6G INFRASTRUCTURE WITH EXISTING HEALTHCARE SYSTEMS

4.1 Challenges in Integrating 6G Technology with Legacy Healthcare IT Systems

The integration of 6G technology into healthcare systems necessitates a paradigm shift towards zero-trust cybersecurity, moving away from traditional perimeter-based defences to a more dynamic and granular approach (Yaacoub et al., 2020). This framework, crucial for addressing the complex security challenges of interconnected 6G healthcare networks, incorporates key principles such as micro-segmentation, Just-In-Time access provisioning, and continuous risk assessment. Implementation strategies include Software-Defined Perimeter (SDP), Identity-Aware Proxies (IAP), and Zero Trust Network Access (ZTNA), which work in concert to create a robust, adaptive security framework (Wang et al., 2020). Integrating 6G with existing healthcare systems, such as Electronic Health Records (EHRs), Hospital Information Systems (HIS), and Picture Archiving and Communication Systems (PACS), requires standardized protocols and extensive collaboration among stakeholders (Porambage et al., 2021). This approach is particularly vital given the proliferation of connected medical devices, edge computing for real-time diagnostics, and ultra-low latency requirements in telemedicine. By continuously verifying access requests and limiting exposure to sensitive patient data, zero-trust architectures significantly enhance healthcare organizations' security posture while enabling them to leverage 6G benefits—such as enhanced telemedicine and AI-driven diagnostics—while maintaining strict data protection and regulatory compliance (Cho et al., 2020; Bhattacharya & Kumar, 2024).

These legacy systems often have limited interoperability and may not be designed to handle the high-speed, low-latency data transmission capabilities of 6G networks (Ahad et al., 2020). Upgrading or replacing these systems can be costly and time-consuming, requiring significant investment and resources from healthcare institutions (Zhang et al., 2019).

Moreover, integrating 6G technology with existing electronic health record (EHR) systems and other healthcare databases can be complex due to differences in data formats, protocols, and security standards (Nguyen et al., 2022). Ensuring seamless data exchange and maintaining the integrity and privacy of patient information across different systems is a critical challenge that must be addressed (Elbamby et al., 2019).

4.2.1 Developing Standardized Protocols and APIs

Developing standardized protocols and application programming interfaces (APIs) is crucial for enabling interoperability between 6G networks and healthcare systems (Viswanathan & Mogensen, 2020). These protocols and APIs should be designed to facilitate the exchange of data and commands between different systems, allowing for seamless communication and integration (Saad et al., 2020). By adopting industry-wide standards and open APIs, healthcare institutions can reduce the complexity of integration and promote compatibility across various 6G-enabled healthcare applications (Chowdhury et al., 2020).

4.2.2 Encouraging Collaboration Between 6G Providers and Healthcare Institutions

Encouraging collaboration between 6G providers and healthcare institutions is another key strategy for achieving successful integration. 6G providers should work closely with healthcare organizations to understand their specific needs, workflows, and existing IT infrastructures (Dang et al., 2020). This collaboration can help identify potential integration challenges early on and develop tailored solutions that address the unique requirements of each healthcare setting (Rajatheva et al., 2020).

Moreover, collaborative efforts can foster knowledge sharing and best practices, enabling healthcare institutions to leverage the expertise of 6G providers in areas such as network design, security, and data management (Akyildiz et al., 2020). Joint research and development initiatives can also drive innovation and accelerate the adoption of 6G-enabled healthcare solutions (Srivastava et al., 2020).

4.3 Ensuring Backward Compatibility with 5G and Other Communication Technologies

Ensuring backward compatibility with 5G and other communication technologies is essential for the smooth transition to 6G infrastructure in healthcare. As healthcare institutions gradually adopt 6G technology, it is important to ensure that 6G-enabled systems can seamlessly interact with existing 5G and other legacy communication networks (Tang et al., 2020).

This backward compatibility allows healthcare providers to leverage the benefits of 6G technology while still maintaining support for older devices and systems (Gu et al., 2020). It enables a phased approach to upgrading healthcare infrastructure, minimizing disruptions to patient care and allowing for a more manageable and cost-effective transition (Yang et al., 2019).

To achieve backward compatibility, 6G networks should be designed with interoperability in mind, incorporating mechanisms for seamless handovers and data exchange between different generations of communication technologies (Zhang et al., 2019). This includes developing multi-mode devices that can operate on both 6G and 5G networks, as well as implementing protocol translation and adaptation layers to facilitate communication between disparate systems (Nguyen et al., 2022).

5. REGULATORY AND ETHICAL CONSIDERATIONS

5.1 Navigating Regulatory Landscapes for 6G Deployment in Healthcare

Deploying 6G infrastructure in healthcare requires navigating complex regulatory landscapes to ensure compliance with legal and industry standards. Healthcare is a highly regulated sector, with stringent requirements for data privacy, security, and patient safety (Ahad et al., 2020). Regulations such as the Health Insurance Portability and Accountability Act (HIPAA) in the United States and the General

Data Protection Regulation (GDPR) in the European Union set strict guidelines for handling sensitive patient information (Nguyen et al., 2022).

6G providers and healthcare institutions must work together to understand and comply with these regulations, ensuring that 6G-enabled healthcare solutions meet the necessary legal and ethical standards (Elbamby et al., 2019). This may involve conducting thorough risk assessments, implementing appropriate security controls, and obtaining necessary certifications and approvals from regulatory bodies (Zhang et al., 2019).

5.2 Addressing Ethical Concerns Related to Data Privacy and Patient Consent

The deployment of 6G infrastructure in healthcare raises important ethical concerns, particularly related to data privacy and patient consent. With the massive amounts of sensitive health data being collected and transmitted through 6G networks, it is crucial to ensure that patients' privacy rights are protected and that they have control over how their data is used (Saad et al., 2020).

Obtaining informed consent from patients is a fundamental ethical requirement in healthcare (Chowdhury et al., 2020). Patients should be clearly informed about how their data will be collected, stored, and shared through 6G-enabled healthcare applications, and they should have the right to opt-out or withdraw consent at any time (Dang et al., 2020). Transparency and clear communication are essential to building patient trust and ensuring ethical data practices (Rajatheva et al., 2020).

Moreover, safeguards must be in place to prevent the misuse or unauthorized access of patient data (Akyildiz et al., 2020). Strict access controls, data anonymization techniques, and regular audits can help mitigate the risks of data breaches and protect patient privacy (Srivastava et al., 2020).

5.3 Establishing Guidelines for the Responsible Use of 6G in Healthcare Applications

To ensure the responsible and ethical use of 6G technology in healthcare, it is important to establish clear guidelines and best practices. These guidelines should address various aspects of 6G deployment, including data governance, security protocols, patient rights, and ethical considerations (Viswanathan & Mogensen, 2020).

Healthcare institutions, 6G providers, and regulatory bodies should collaborate to develop these guidelines, taking into account the unique challenges and requirements of the healthcare sector (Tang et al., 2020). The guidelines should be regularly reviewed and updated to keep pace with the rapid advancements in 6G technology and the evolving healthcare landscape (Gu et al., 2020).

Training and education programs should be implemented to ensure that healthcare professionals, researchers, and other stakeholders are aware of the guidelines and can apply them effectively in their work (Yang et al., 2019). Promoting a culture of responsible innovation and ethical practices will be crucial in realizing the full potential of 6G-enabled healthcare while safeguarding patient well-being (Zhang et al., 2019).

6. FUTURE OUTLOOK AND CONCLUSION

6.1 The Transformative Potential of Secure 6G Infrastructure in Revolutionizing Healthcare Delivery

The deployment of secure 6G infrastructure in smart cities has the transformative potential to revolutionize healthcare delivery. By leveraging the advanced capabilities of 6G technology, such as ultra-low latency, high bandwidth, and massive device connectivity, healthcare systems can become more efficient, accessible, and patient-centric (Saad et al., 2020). Telemedicine, remote patient monitoring, and robotic surgeries enabled by 6G networks can significantly improve access to healthcare services, particularly for underserved communities and remote areas (Chowdhury et al., 2020).

Moreover, the integration of 6G with other emerging technologies, such as artificial intelligence (AI), big data analytics, and the Internet of Things (IoT), can unlock new possibilities for personalized medicine, early disease detection, and proactive health management (Nguyen et al., 2022; Bansal & Bhattacharya, 2024). Secure data sharing and analysis facilitated by 6G infrastructure can accelerate medical research and innovation, leading to the development of more effective treatments and therapies (Elbamby et al., 2019).

6.2 The Need for Ongoing Research and Development

To fully realize the transformative potential of secure 6G infrastructure in healthcare, ongoing research and development efforts are crucial. As 6G technology continues to evolve, it is important to address the technical, security, and ethical challenges that arise (Akyildiz et al., 2020). Researchers and industry stakeholders must collaborate to develop innovative solutions that enhance the performance, reliability, and scalability of 6G networks while ensuring the highest standards of data privacy and security (Zhang et al., 2019).

Further research is needed to explore the potential applications of 6G in various healthcare domains, such as mental health, chronic disease management, and public health surveillance (Srivastava et al., 2020). Developing user-friendly and accessible 6G-enabled healthcare solutions that cater to the diverse needs of patients and healthcare professionals is also an important area of research (Tang et al., 2020).

6.3 Fostering Collaborations Among Stakeholders to Drive Innovation and Adoption

Fostering collaborations among stakeholders is essential to drive innovation and adoption of secure 6G infrastructure in healthcare. Healthcare institutions, 6G providers, technology companies, research organizations, and regulatory bodies must work together to create an ecosystem that supports the development and deployment of 6G-enabled healthcare solutions (Dang et al., 2020).

Collaborative efforts can facilitate knowledge sharing, best practices, and the development of interoperable standards and protocols (Rajatheva et al., 2020). Joint research projects, pilot studies, and public-private partnerships can accelerate the validation and implementation of 6G technologies in real-world healthcare settings (Viswanathan & Mogensen, 2020).

6.4 Prioritizing Patient Well-Being and Trust in 6G-Enabled Healthcare Solutions

As secure 6G infrastructure becomes increasingly integrated into healthcare delivery, it is crucial to prioritize patient well-being and trust. Healthcare providers and 6G developers must ensure that patient privacy, consent, and ethical considerations are at the forefront of all 6G-enabled healthcare solutions (Gu et al., 2020).

Engaging patients and communities in the design and implementation process can help build trust and acceptance of 6G technologies in healthcare (Yang et al., 2019). Regular communication, transparency, and patient education initiatives can foster a better understanding of the benefits and risks associated with 6G-enabled healthcare solutions (Zhang et al., 2019).

By prioritizing patient well-being and trust, healthcare systems can harness the power of secure 6G infrastructure to deliver high-quality, patient-centric care that improves health outcomes and enhances the overall quality of life for individuals and communities.

In conclusion, the integration of secure 6G infrastructure in smart cities has the potential to transform healthcare delivery, making it more efficient, accessible, and personalized. The advanced security features of 6G technology not only revolutionize healthcare delivery but also foster trust in digital health services, paving the way for widespread adoption and integration of these transformative solutions in smart cities, ultimately leading to improved patient outcomes and a more resilient, efficient healthcare ecosystem. By addressing the technical, security, and ethical challenges, fostering collaborations among stakeholders, and prioritizing patient well-being, we can unlock the full potential of 6G-enabled healthcare solutions. Ongoing research and development efforts will be crucial in driving innovation and adoption, ultimately leading to a future where healthcare is seamlessly integrated into the fabric of smart cities, improving the lives of citizens worldwide.

REFERENCES

Abbate, J. (2000). *Inventing the Internet.* MIT Press., DOI: 10.7551/mitpress/3866.001.0001

Ahad, A., Tahir, M., & Yau, K.-L. A. (2020). 5G-based smart healthcare network: Architecture, taxonomy, challenges and future research directions. *IEEE Access : Practical Innovations, Open Solutions*, 8, 153947–153979. DOI: 10.1109/ACCESS.2020.3017859

Akhtar, M. W., Hassan, S. A., Ghaffar, R., Jung, H., Garg, S., & Hossain, M. S. (2020). The shift to 6G communications: Vision and requirements. *Human-centric Computing and Information Sciences*, 10(1), 1–27. DOI: 10.1186/s13673-020-00258-2

Akyildiz, I. F., Kak, A., & Nie, S. (2020). 6G and beyond: The future of wireless communications systems. *IEEE Access : Practical Innovations, Open Solutions*, 8, 133995–134030. DOI: 10.1109/ACCESS.2020.3010896

Alagic, G., Alperin-Sheriff, J., Apon, D., Cooper, D., Dang, Q., Kelsey, J., ... & Zhao, Y. (2020). Status report on the second round of the NIST post-quantum cryptography standardization process. NIST Interagency/Internal Report (NISTIR), 8309. DOI: 10.6028/NIST.IR.8309

Alladi, T., Chamola, V., Sikdar, B., & Choo, K. K. R. (2020). Consumer IoT: Security vulnerability case studies and solutions. *IEEE Consumer Electronics Magazine*, 9(2), 17–25. DOI: 10.1109/MCE.2019.2953740

Ateya, A. A., Muthanna, A., Vybornova, A., Algarni, A. D., Abuarqoub, A., Koucheryavy, Y., & Koucheryavy, A. (2021). Smart core network for 6G technology. *IEEE Access : Practical Innovations, Open Solutions*, 9, 44795–44813. DOI: 10.1109/ACCESS.2021.3065525

Bansal, D., & Bhattacharya, N. (2024). Artificial Intelligence and Metaverse Applications in the Healthcare Sector. In *Multi-Sector Analysis of the Digital Healthcare Industry* (pp. 110–132). IGI Global. DOI: 10.4018/979-8-3693-0928-5.ch004

Belchior, R., Vasconcelos, A., Guerreiro, S., & Correia, M. (2021). A survey on blockchain interoperability: Past, present, and future trends. *ACM Computing Surveys*, 54(8), 1–41. DOI: 10.1145/3471140

Benchoufi, M., & Ravaud, P. (2017). Blockchain technology for improving clinical research quality. *Trials*, 18(1), 335. DOI: 10.1186/s13063-017-2035-z PMID: 28724395

Berners-Lee, T., & Fischetti, M. (2021). *Weaving the Web: The original design and ultimate destiny of the World Wide Web by its inventor*. HarperCollins.

Bhattacharya, N., & Kishore, S. Metaverse in Healthcare: A Review. *SARALA BIRLA UNIVERSITY*, 13.

Bhattacharya, N., & Kumar, P. (2024). Integrating Healthcare Analytics to Improve Diabetes Management and Prevent Heart Attacks: A Data-Driven Approach. https://doi.org/DOI: 10.21203/rs.3.rs-4310669/v1

Bhushan, N., & Mogensen, P. (2019). 6G wireless systems: Vision, requirements, challenges, insights, and opportunities. arXiv preprint arXiv:1909.11738.

Cao, Y., Zhao, Y., Yu, Y., Wu, J., Yang, X., & Zhang, J. (2019). Integration of software-defined networking and quantum key distribution: A survey. *Quantum Engineering*, 1(3), e26. DOI: 10.1002/que2.26

Cheon, J. H., Kim, D., Kim, D., & Song, Y. (2021). Toward Post-Quantum Security for IoT: Performance Analysis of Lattice-Based Cryptography on a Low-Cost IoT Platform. *IEEE Internet of Things Journal*, 8(11), 9095–9106. DOI: 10.1109/JIOT.2020.3041313

Chillotti, I., Gama, N., Georgieva, M., & Izabachène, M. (2020). TFHE: Fast fully homomorphic encryption over the torus. *Journal of Cryptology*, 33(1), 34–91. DOI: 10.1007/s00145-019-09319-x

Cho, J. H., Sharma, D. P., Alavizadeh, H., Yoon, S., Ben-Asher, N., Moore, T. J., & Lim, H. (2020). Toward Proactive, Adaptive Defense: A Survey on Moving Target Defense. *IEEE Communications Surveys and Tutorials*, 22(1), 709–745. DOI: 10.1109/COMST.2019.2963791

Chowdhury, M. Z., Shahjalal, M., Ahmed, S., & Jang, Y. M. (2020). 6G Wireless Communication Systems: Applications, Requirements, Technologies, Challenges, and Research Directions. *IEEE Open Journal of the Communications Society*, 1, 957–975. DOI: 10.1109/OJCOMS.2020.3010270

Dahlman, E., Parkvall, S., & Skold, J. (2018). *5G NR: The next generation wireless access technology*. Academic Press., DOI: 10.1016/C2017-0-01347-2

Dang, S., Amin, O., Shihada, B., & Alouini, M. S. (2020). What should 6G be? *Nature Electronics*, 3(1), 20–29. DOI: 10.1038/s41928-019-0355-6

David, K., & Berndt, H. (2018). 6G vision and requirements: Is there any need for beyond 5G? *IEEE Vehicular Technology Magazine*, 13(3), 72–80. DOI: 10.1109/MVT.2018.2848498

Elbamby, M. S., Perfecto, C., Bennis, M., & Doppler, K. (2019). Toward low-latency and ultra-reliable virtual reality. *IEEE Network*, 33(2), 78–84. DOI: 10.1109/MNET.2018.1700268

Farahani, B., Firouzi, F., Chang, V., Badaroglu, M., Constant, N., & Mankodiya, K. (2018). Towards fog-driven IoT eHealth: Promises and challenges of IoT in medicine and healthcare. *Future Generation Computer Systems*, 78, 659–676. DOI: 10.1016/j.future.2017.04.036

Gu, Y., Zha, X., & Li, J. (2020). Surgical robotics and navigation for minimally invasive surgery: A review of the state-of-the-art and future perspectives. *IEEE Access : Practical Innovations, Open Solutions*, 8, 136959–136979. DOI: 10.1109/ACCESS.2020.3012497

Haq, I., & Muselemu, O. (2021). Blockchain technology in pharmaceutical industry to prevent counterfeit drugs. *International Journal of Computer Applications*, 174(3), 14–17. DOI: 10.5120/ijca2021920834

Hathaliya, J. J., & Tanwar, S. (2020). An exhaustive survey on security and privacy issues in Healthcare 4.0. *Computer Communications*, 153, 311–335. DOI: 10.1016/j.comcom.2020.02.018

Hilmes, M. (2020). *Radio's Second Century: Past, Present, and Future Perspectives*. Rutgers University Press., DOI: 10.36019/9780813598505

Hirschberg, J., & Manning, C. D. (2015). Advances in natural language processing. *Science*, 349(6245), 261–266. DOI: 10.1126/science.aaa8685 PMID: 26185244

Hossain, M. S., Muhammad, G., & Alamri, A. (2019). Smart healthcare monitoring: A voice pathology detection paradigm for smart cities. *Multimedia Systems*, 25(5), 565–575. DOI: 10.1007/s00530-017-0561-x

Huang, T., Yang, W., Wu, J., Ma, J., Zhang, X., & Zhang, D. (2019). A Survey on Green 6G Network: Architecture and Technologies. *IEEE Access : Practical Innovations, Open Solutions*, 7, 175758–175768. DOI: 10.1109/ACCESS.2019.2957648

ITU. (2021). Focus Group on Technologies for Network 2030. International Telecommunication Union. https://www.itu.int/en/ITU-T/focusgroups/net2030/

Jeremiah, S. R., Ha, J., Singh, S. K., & Park, J. H. (2024) ArticlesPrivacyGuard: Collaborative Edge-Cloud Computing Architecture for Attribute-Preserving Face Anonymization in CCTV Networks.

Latif, S., Qadir, J., Farooq, S., & Imran, M. A. (2017). How 5G wireless (and concomitant technologies) will revolutionize healthcare? *Future Internet*, 9(4), 93. DOI: 10.3390/fi9040093

Letaief, K. B., Chen, W., Shi, Y., Zhang, J., & Zhang, Y. J. A. (2019). The Roadmap to 6G: AI Empowered Wireless Networks. *IEEE Communications Magazine*, 57(8), 84–90. DOI: 10.1109/MCOM.2019.1900271

Liao, S. K., Cai, W. Q., Handsteiner, J., Liu, B., Yin, J., Zhang, L., Rauch, D., Fink, M., Ren, J.-G., Liu, W.-Y., Li, Y., Shen, Q., Cao, Y., Li, F.-Z., Wang, J.-F., Huang, Y.-M., Deng, L., Xi, T., Ma, L., & Pan, J. W. (2018). Satellite-relayed intercontinental quantum network. *Physical Review Letters*, 120(3), 030501. DOI: 10.1103/PhysRevLett.120.030501 PMID: 29400544

Ling, R. (2021). *Mobile communication: The story of a technology that changed society*. John Wiley & Sons.

Ling, R., & Lai, C. H. (2016). Mobile communication: Digital media and society series. *Polity*.

Mavroeidis, V., Vishi, K., Zych, M. D., & Jøsang, A. (2018). The impact of quantum computing on present cryptography. *International Journal of Advanced Computer Science and Applications*, 9(3), 405–414. DOI: 10.14569/IJACSA.2018.090354

McGraw, G., Migues, S., & West, J. (2018). *Building security in maturity model (BSIMM9)*. Synopsys Software Integrity Group.

Mucchi, L., Jayousi, S., Caputo, S., Paoletti, E., Zoppi, P., Geli, S., & Dioniso, P. (2020). *How 6G technology can change the future wireless healthcare. In 2020 2nd 6G Wireless Summit (6G SUMMIT)*. IEEE., DOI: 10.1109/6GSUMMIT49458.2020.9083794

Nasralla, M. M., Khattak, S. B. A., Ur Rehman, I., & Iqbal, M. (2023). Exploring the role of 6G technology in enhancing quality of experience for m-health multimedia applications: A comprehensive survey. *Sensors (Basel)*, 23(13), 5882. DOI: 10.3390/s23135882 PMID: 37447735

Nawaz, S. J., Sharma, S. K., Wyne, S., Patwary, M. N., & Asaduzzaman, M. (2019). Quantum Machine Learning for 6G Communication Networks: State-of-the-Art and Vision for the Future. *IEEE Access : Practical Innovations, Open Solutions*, 7, 46317–46350. DOI: 10.1109/ACCESS.2019.2909490

Nayak, S., & Patgiri, R. (2021). 6G communication technology: A vision on intelligent healthcare. In *Health informatics: A computational perspective in healthcare* (pp. 1–18). Springer., DOI: 10.1007/978-981-15-5909-2_1

Nguyen, D. C., Pathirana, P. N., Ding, M., & Seneviratne, A. (2022). Blockchain for 6G: Challenges, opportunities, and future directions. *IEEE Internet of Things Journal*, 9(11), 8551–8564. DOI: 10.1109/JIOT.2021.3114320

Pagliari, C. (2020). The ethics and value of contact tracing apps: International insights and implications for Scotland's COVID-19 response. *Journal of Global Health*, 10(2), 020103. Advance online publication. DOI: 10.7189/jogh.10.020103 PMID: 33110502

Pirandola, S., Andersen, U. L., Banchi, L., Berta, M., Bunandar, D., Colbeck, R., Englund, D., Gehring, T., Lupo, C., Ottaviani, C., Pereira, J. L., Razavi, M., Shamsul Shaari, J., Tomamichel, M., Usenko, V. C., Vallone, G., Villoresi, P., & Wallden, P. (2020). Advances in quantum cryptography. *Advances in Optics and Photonics*, 12(4), 1012–1236. DOI: 10.1364/AOP.361502

Porambage, P., Gür, G., Osorio, D. P. M., Liyanage, M., Gurtov, A., & Ylianttila, M. (2021). The Roadmap to 6G Security and Privacy. *IEEE Open Journal of the Communications Society*, 2, 1094–1122. DOI: 10.1109/OJCOMS.2021.3078081

Porambage, P., Okwuibe, J., Liyanage, M., Ylianttila, M., & Taleb, T. (2021). Survey on multi-access edge computing for internet of things realization. *IEEE Communications Surveys and Tutorials*, 23(2), 1119–1148. DOI: 10.1109/COMST.2021.3070940

Qi, J., Yang, P., Waraich, A., Deng, Z., Zhao, Y., & Yang, Y. (2018). Examining sensor-based physical activity recognition and monitoring for healthcare using Internet of Things: A systematic review. *Journal of Biomedical Informatics*, 87, 138–153. DOI: 10.1016/j.jbi.2018.09.002 PMID: 30267895

Rajatheva, N., Atzeni, I., Bjornson, E., Bourdoux, A., Buzzi, S., Dore, J.-B., Erkucuk, S., Fuentes, M., Guan, K., Hu, Y., Huang, X., Hulkkonen, J., Jornet, J. M., Katz, M., Nilsson, R., Panayirci, E., Rabie, K. M., Rajapaksha, N., Salehi, M., . . . Zetterman, T. (2020). White paper on broadband connectivity in 6G. arXiv preprint arXiv:2004.14247.

Rappaport, T. S., Xing, Y., Kanhere, O., Ju, S., Madanayake, A., Mandal, S., Alkhateeb, A., & Trichopoulos, G. C. (2019). Wireless Communications and Applications Above 100 GHz: Opportunities and Challenges for 6G and Beyond. *IEEE Access : Practical Innovations, Open Solutions*, 7, 78729–78757. DOI: 10.1109/ACCESS.2019.2921522

Riordan, M., Hoddeson, L., & Herring, C. (2019). The invention of the transistor. *Reviews of Modern Physics*, 71(2), S336–S345. DOI: 10.1103/RevModPhys.71.S336

Saad, W., Bennis, M., & Chen, M. (2020). A Vision of 6G Wireless Systems: Applications, Trends, Technologies, and Open Research Problems. *IEEE Network*, 34(3), 134–142. DOI: 10.1109/MNET.001.1900287

Samardzic, N., Feldmann, A., Krastev, A., Saniee, N., Li, N., Geisse, D., & Sanchez, C. (2021). F1: A Fast and Programmable Accelerator for Fully Homomorphic Encryption. In *Proceedings of the 54th Annual IEEE/ACM International Symposium on Microarchitecture* (pp. 238-252). DOI: 10.1145/3466752.3480070

Singh, S. K., Azzaoui, A., Choo, K. K. R., Yang, L. T., & Park, J. H. (2023). A comprehensive survey on blockchain for secure IoT-enabled smart city beyond 5G: Approaches, processes, challenges, and opportunities. *Human-Centric Computing and Information Sciences*, 13, 51.

Singhal, S., Betgeri, S., & Singh, S. K. (2024). Strategies for mitigating security concerns in IoT-enabled smart cities. In *Secure and Intelligent IoT-Enabled Smart Cities* (pp. 239–273). IGI Global. DOI: 10.4018/979-8-3693-2373-1

Talreja, V., Ferrett, T., Valenti, M. C., & Ross, A. (2020). Biometrics-as-a-service: A framework to promote innovative biometric recognition in the cloud. In *2020 IEEE International Conference on Consumer Electronics (ICCE)* (pp. 1-6). IEEE. DOI: 10.1109/ICCE46568.2020.9043068

Tang, F., Kawamoto, Y., Kato, N., & Liu, J. (2020). Future intelligent and secure vehicular network toward 6G: Machine-learning approaches. *Proceedings of the IEEE*, 108(2), 292–307. DOI: 10.1109/JPROC.2019.2954595

Tariq, F., Khandaker, M. R. A., Wong, K. K., Imran, M. A., Bennis, M., & Debbah, M. (2020). A speculative study on 6G. *IEEE Wireless Communications*, 27(4), 118–125. DOI: 10.1109/MWC.001.1900488

Thuemmler, C., & Bai, C. (Eds.). (2017). *Health 4.0: How virtualization and big data are revolutionizing healthcare*. Springer International Publishing., DOI: 10.1007/978-3-319-47617-9

Wang, D., Wang, P., He, D., & Tian, Y. (2020). Birthday, name and bifacial-security: Understanding passwords of Chinese web users. In 29th USENIX Security Symposium (USENIX Security 20) (pp. 1537-1554). https://doi.org/DOI: 10.5555/3489212.3489404

Wang, D., Wang, P., Wang, C., & Ren, K. (2020). A new hope for IoT security: Physically unclonable function. *IEEE Security and Privacy*, 18(3), 12–19. DOI: 10.1109/MSEC.2020.2975730

Yang, G., Lv, H., Zhang, Z., Yang, L., Deng, J., You, S., Du, J., & Yang, H. (2019). Keep healthcare workers safe: Application of teleoperated robot in isolation ward for COVID-19 prevention and control. *Chinese Journal of Mechanical Engineering*, 33(1), 47. DOI: 10.1186/s10033-020-00464-0

Yang, P., Xiao, Y., Xiao, M., & Li, S. (2019). 6G wireless communications: Vision and potential techniques. *IEEE Network*, 33(4), 70–75. DOI: 10.1109/MNET.2019.1800418

Yaqoob, I., Ahmed, E., Rehman, M. H. U., Ahmed, A. I. A., Al-garadi, M. A., Imran, M., & Guizani, M. (2017). The rise of ransomware and emerging security challenges in the Internet of Things. *Computer Networks*, 129, 444–458. DOI: 10.1016/j.comnet.2017.09.003

Yigitcanlar, T., Kankanamge, N., & Vella, K. (2021). How are smart city concepts and technologies perceived and utilized? A systematic geo-Twitter analysis of smart cities in Australia. *Journal of Urban Technology*, 28(1-2), 135–154. DOI: 10.1080/10630732.2020.1753483

Zhao, Y., Yu, G., & Xu, H. (2021). 6G mobile communication networks: Vision, challenges, and key technologies. *Science China. Information Sciences*, 64(4), 1–26. DOI: 10.1007/s11432-020-3057-3

Zheng, X., Mukkamala, R. R., Vatrapu, R., & Ordieres-Mere, J. (2021). Blockchain-based personal health data sharing system using cloud storage. In 2018 IEEE 20th International Conference on e-Health Networking, Applications and Services (Healthcom) (pp. 1-6). IEEE. https://doi.org/DOI: 10.1109/HealthCom.2018.8531125

Chapter 14
Healthcare and Smart Cities Applications of Secure 6G Infrastructure

Tarun Kumar Vashishth
https://orcid.org/0000-0001-9916-9575
IIMT University, India

Vikas Sharma
https://orcid.org/0000-0001-8173-4548
IIMT University, India

Mukesh Kumar Sharma
https://orcid.org/0000-0003-3071-5931
Chaudhary Charan Singh University, India

Rajeev Sharma
https://orcid.org/0000-0002-3354-558X
IIMT Engineering College, India

ABSTRACT

The emergence of 6G technology guarantees to revolutionize each healthcare and smart cities by means of supplying ultra-fast, secure, and dependable communication networks. This paper delves into the capability packages of stable 6G infrastructure in healthcare, emphasizing its function in improving telemedicine, far off affected person monitoring, and real-time information analytics. Additionally, it explores how secure 6G can facilitate the improvement of smart towns, enabling green control of urban services and infrastructure. The steady 6G community guarantees patient facts confidentiality while facilitating seamless communication among healthcare companies and sufferers. By integrating advanced technology like AI and IoT inside

DOI: 10.4018/979-8-3693-8029-1.ch014

the 6G framework, both the healthcare area and smart towns can acquire unparalleled stages of performance, security, and service high-quality.

1. INTRODUCTION

The advent of 6G era heralds a brand new technology of extremely-speedy, secure, and reliable communication networks, poised to revolutionize diverse sectors, including healthcare and smart city management. As the successor to 5G, 6G predicted to provide unprecedented data transfer speeds, enhanced network capacity, and significantly reduced latency, facilitating actual-time communication and data processing. These abilities are crucial for the healthcare sector, wherein well timed and accurate data transmission can significantly impact patient outcomes. Telemedicine, faraway affected person tracking, and real-time facts analytics stand to benefit immensely from the secure 6G infrastructure, enabling seamless interactions between healthcare providers and patients, regardless of geographic constraints. This transformation is particular vital in the wake of the COVID-19 pandemic, which has underscored the necessity for robust and scalable telehealth solutions (Sharma et al., 2023). In parallel, the implementation of 6G technology in smart cities promises to optimize urban management and service delivery. The integration of advanced technology such as AI and the IoT within the 6G framework can enhance the efficiency and safety of smart city operations (Kumar et al., 2023). AI-driven analytics can process vast amounts of data gathered from IoT devices, providing actionable insights for urban planning, traffic management, energy distribution, and public safety. The secure nature of 6G networks ensures that sensitive data, whether personal health information or urban infrastructure details, is protected from cyber threats, fostering trust and reliability in these digital ecosystems (Ahad et al., 2024).

Furthermore, the seamless conversation facilitated by means of 6G generation can result in an extra interconnected and responsive urban environment For instance, actual-time tracking and control of essential infrastructure including water supply, waste management, and transportation structures can improve useful resource allocation and service quality. The deployment of secure 6G networks in smart cities not only enhances operational efficiency however additionally contributes to the sustainability and resilience of urban environments by permitting proactive and data-driven decision-making (Kavitha, 2022).

In summary, the combination of 6G technology in healthcare and smart cities represents a widespread bounce ahead in reaching unparalleled levels of efficiency, security, and service quality. By leveraging the advanced capabilities of 6G, these sectors can overcome current limitations, paving the manner for revolutionary solutions that address both present and future challenges. This chapter explores the potential applications, benefits, and challenges of secure 6G networks, emphasizing their transformative impact on healthcare and smart city infrastructure (Ahmad et al., 2023).

1.1 Overview of 6G Technology

6G technology represents the sixth generation of wireless communication systems, poised to surpass the capabilities of its predecessor, 5G, by offering significantly enhanced features. It is expected to offer extremely-high-speed internet, with data rates reaching up to one terabit per second, which is several orders of magnitude faster than 5G (Singh et al., 2023). This remarkable speed will facilitate instantaneous data transfer, enabling real-time applications and services that were previously unattainable. Additionally, 6G aims to reduce latency to near-zero levels, enhancing the responsiveness of communication networks and ensuring seamless user experiences, particularly in applications that require immediate feedback, such as augmented reality, virtual reality and remote surgery. One of the core advancements of 6G technology is its ability to integrate and leverage emerging technologies such as artificial intelligence, IoT, and blockchain. AI will play a pivotal role in optimizing network overall performance through intelligent algorithms that manage data traffic, predict network demands, and automate decision-making processes. IoT, with its extensive network of interconnected devices, will benefit from 6G's fast speed and less-latency capabilities, enabling more efficient data collection, processing, and analysis in real time. Blockchain technology will enhance security and transparency, providing robust mechanisms for data integrity and trust in transactions (Batista et al., 2023).

Moreover, 6G is expected to operate in higher frequency bands, such as terahertz (THz) frequencies, which offer larger bandwidths and higher data rates. However, these higher frequencies also present challenges in terms of signal propagation and penetration, necessitating the development of advanced materials and technologies to ensure reliable communication. This includes innovations in antenna design, signal processing, and network architecture to mitigate the limitations of higher frequency transmissions. The application of 6G technology extends beyond personal communication to include transformative impacts on various industries. In healthcare, 6G will enable advanced telemedicine applications, remote monitoring of patients, and current data analytics, significantly improving patient care and outcomes. In smart cities, 6G will facilitate efficient management of urban services and infrastructure, improve the standard of life for citizens through intelligent transportation systems, energy management, and public safety initiatives (Faria et al., 2021).

Figure 1. Block diagram for overview of 6G technology

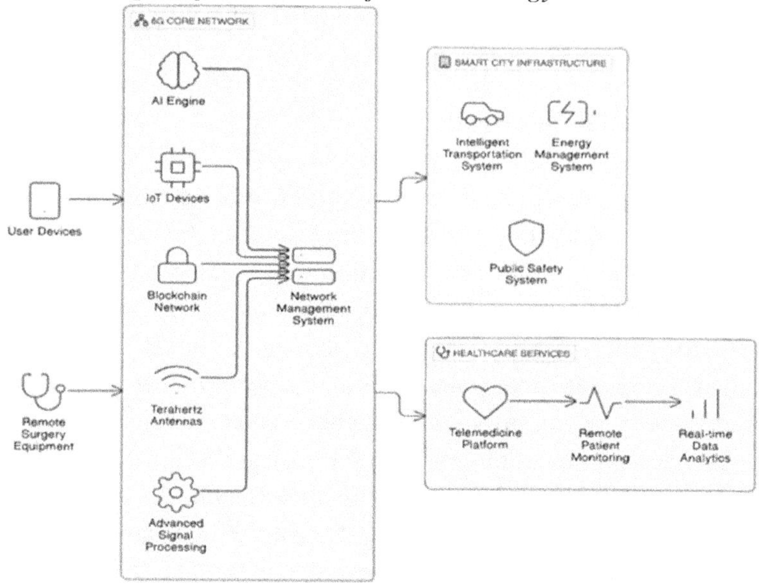

Overall, 6G technology promises to be a cornerstone of the future digital economy, driving innovation and enabling new services and applications across multiple sectors. Its ultra-fast, secure, and reliable communication capabilities will not only enhance existing technologies but also pave the way for unprecedented advancements, fundamentally transforming the way we job, live, and communicate with the world.

1.2 Importance of Secure Communication Networks

The importance of secure communication networks cannot be overstated in our increasingly digital and interconnected world. These networks form the backbone of modern information exchange, facilitating everything from personal communications to complex industrial operations. In critical sectors like healthcare, finance, and smart cities, secure networks are essential for protecting sensitive data, ensuring reliable operations, and maintaining public trust. In healthcare, secure communication networks are vital for safeguarding sensitive patient information. With the growing adoption of telemedicine and remote monitoring of patients, vast amounts of personal health information are transmitted over digital channels. This data includes medical histories, diagnostic results, and treatment plans, all of which are highly confidential. Data breaches may result in financial fraud, identity theft, and serious privacy violations. Moreover, compromised data integrity can have direct adverse effects on patient care, potentially leading to incorrect diagnoses or treatments. Ensuring secure communication in the healthcare sector guarantees medical personnel can depend on the accessibility and accuracy of the information they need to treat patients effectively, while also protecting patient privacy.

Secure communication networks are essential for the effective and secure administration of urban infrastructure and services in the context of smart cities. Smart cities rely on interconnected systems to manage utilities, transportation, public safety, and other critical services (Khattak et al., 2022). Large volumes of data are produced and transmitted in real time by these technologies, and they are used to streamline operations, cut expenses, and enhance resident quality of life. These advantages, nevertheless, are only possible provided the underlying communication networks are safe. Cyberattacks on the infrastructure of smart cities, including electricity grids or traffic control systems, can cause major disruptions, monetary losses, or even put public safety in jeopardy. Strong security measures are therefore necessary to guard these networks against cyberattacks and illegal access.

In the financial sector, secure communication networks are the foundation of safe and reliable transactions. Financial institutions handle sensitive data, including account information, transaction records, and personal identifiers. The security of this data is paramount to prevent financial fraud, identity theft, and other cybercrimes. Additionally, secure networks ensure the integrity of financial transactions, protecting against tampering and ensuring that all parties involved can trust the accuracy of their records. In order to maintain the stability and reliability of the world's financial markets, there is an increasing demand for secure communication networks as financial systems become more digitalised and linked.

Moreover, the incorporation of cutting-edge technologies like AI and IoT into these sectors further underscores the importance of secure communication networks (Vashishth et al., 2024). AI systems often require access to large datasets to function effectively, and any compromise in data security can lead to biased or erroneous outcomes. IoT devices, which are being used more and more to gather and send data instantly, are also susceptible to cyberattacks if they aren't sufficiently secured. The dependable operation of AI and IoT applications is supported by secure communication networks, which guarantee that information sent between people, systems, and devices is private and unchangeable (Gera et al., 2023).

In conclusion, secure communication networks are essential for protecting sensitive information, ensuring reliable operations, and maintaining trust in our increasingly digital and interconnected world. Whether in healthcare, smart cities, finance, or other critical sectors, the importance of these networks will only continue to grow as we embrace new technologies and more data-driven approaches to managing information and operations.

2. 6G IN HEALTHCARE

2.1 Enhancing Telemedicine

Enhancing telemedicine involves leveraging technological advancements to improve the delivery of remote healthcare services, bridging geographical distances and enhancing patient care.

Key strategies for enhancing telemedicine include:

Improved Connectivity and Bandwidth: Upgrading telecommunication infrastructure to support high-speed internet connections ensures seamless video consultations and real-time data transmission healthcare providers and patients. This reduces latency and improves the communication quality of telemedicine (Yadav et al., 2024).

Integration of AI and Machine Learning: By using AI algorithms to help medical personnel diagnose illnesses, evaluate medical images, and forecast patient outcomes, telemedicine consultations become more accurate and productive. AI-powered technologies can also personalise medications using patient information and past trends.

Devices for Remote Monitoring: IoT-enabled wearable sensors and remote monitoring tools, for example, offer continuous tracking of patient vital signs, medication adherence, and illness development from a distance. Without requiring in-person visits, this proactive method allows for better management of chronic illnesses and early intervention.

Telemedicine Platforms and User Interfaces: Developing user-friendly telemedicine platforms with intuitive interfaces enhances the patient and provider experience. Features like scheduling tools, secure messaging, and electronic health record integration streamline workflows and improve communication between healthcare teams.

Training and Education: Providing comprehensive training for healthcare professionals on telemedicine protocols, ethical considerations, and technology use ensures competent delivery of remote healthcare services. Continuous education helps providers adapt to evolving telemedicine practices and optimize patient care outcomes.

Telemedicine Policy and Reimbursement: Advocating for supportive healthcare policies and reimbursement models that recognize telemedicine as a valid and effective care delivery method encourages its widespread adoption. Clear guidelines on licensure, liability, and insurance coverage facilitate seamless telemedicine practice across state and national borders.

By implementing these tactics, telemedicine can be improved in a way that increases patient outcomes, lowers costs, and increases overall efficiency of healthcare delivery, all while increasing access to healthcare services. The future of healthcare delivery will be significantly shaped by the incorporation of telemedicine into standard medical practice as technology develops.

2.2 Remote Patient Monitoring

Remote patient monitoring (RPM) is the process of gathering patient data outside of conventional healthcare settings and sending it in real time to healthcare clinicians via technology. Without requiring the patient to be physically present in a clinical setting, this strategy allows for continuous monitoring of several patient health parameters, including vital signs, symptoms, and medication adherence.

Benefits and important features of remote patient monitoring include:

Continuous Health Monitoring: RPM makes it easier to keep track of patient health metrics throughout time, giving medical professionals access to up-to-date information on the vital signs and conditions of their patients. Through early detection of changes or deterioration in health, this continuous monitoring enables prompt intervention and proactive management of chronic illnesses.

Enhanced Patient Engagement: RPM promotes self-management and treatment plan adherence by giving patients the power to actively engage in their own healthcare. Based on their tracked data, patients can receive tailored advice and comments that will improve their comprehension of their health and encourage better lifestyle choices.

Improved Access to Care: RPM makes healthcare services available outside of conventional clinical settings, which is especially helpful for patients who live in rural or underdeveloped areas. It ensures patients receive quick medical treatment and monitoring while reducing the need for frequent in-person appointments, saving patients money and time on travel.

Efficient Resource Utilization: By reducing unnecessary hospitalizations and emergency room visits, RPM helps optimize healthcare resource allocation. Healthcare providers can prioritize resources for patients who require immediate attention based on current inputs and alerts produced by RPM systems.

Figure 2. Remote patient monitoring architecture

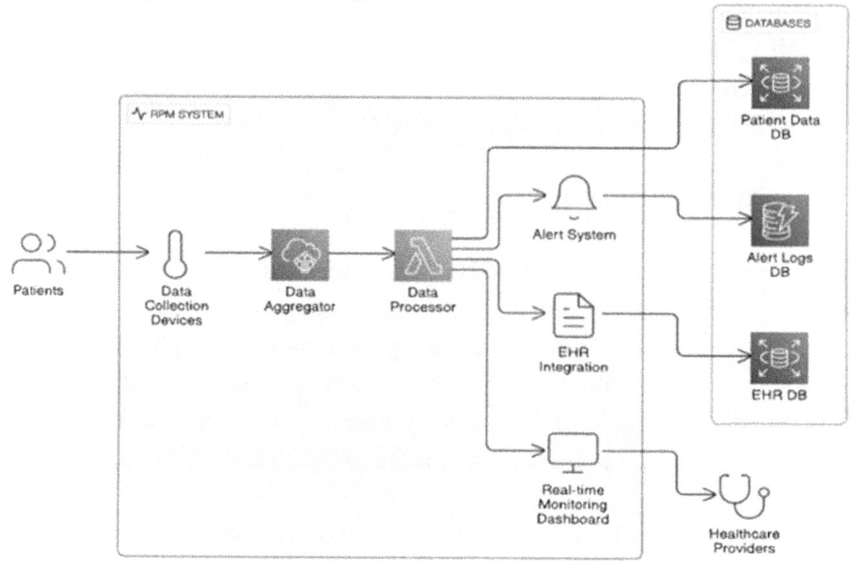

Personalised Treatment Plans: RPM enables medical professionals to modify treatment regimens in accordance with data about specific patients and long-term patterns. By tailoring therapies, drugs, and interventions to the unique needs and responses of each patient, this personalised strategy enhances treatment outcomes (Estrela et al., 2023).

Integration with Healthcare Systems: RPM systems integrate seamlessly with electronic health records (EHRs) and telemedicine platforms, ensuring continuity of care and facilitating communication between healthcare teams. This interoperability enhances care coordination and enables comprehensive patient management across different healthcare settings.

Patient Safety and Satisfaction: By enabling proactive monitoring and early intervention, RPM contributes to patient safety and satisfaction. Patients experience improved quality of life knowing that their health is continuously monitored, and they have access to timely medical advice and support whenever needed.

In general, remote patient monitoring is a revolutionary method of providing healthcare that uses technology to improve patient outcomes, make the most use of available resources, and encourage patient-centered care. RPM is anticipated to become more important in supporting preventative care, aging-in-place programs, and chronic disease management as technology advances.

2.3 Real-Time Data Analytics

The process of evaluating data as it is created or received is known as "real-time data analytics," which enables quick decisions and actions based on the most recent information. This strategy is in contrast to conventional batch processing techniques, which gather data gradually and examine it after the fact. Real-time data analytics stands out for its speed, which helps businesses act fast in the face of change and make judgements.

Benefits and important features of real-time data analytics include:

Instantaneous Decision-Making: Through real-time data analysis, organisations are able to act quickly and decide on the basis of new information rather than past patterns. This capacity is especially helpful in dynamic, high-pressure settings like banking, healthcare, and manufacturing where making judgements quickly is essential.
Early Detection and Response: Real-time analytics facilitates early detection of anomalies, trends, or patterns in data streams. This proactive monitoring allows organizations to identify potential issues or opportunities as they emerge and take corrective actions promptly, mitigating risks and optimizing performance.
Enhanced Operational Efficiency: Real-time insights enable organizations to optimize operational processes and resource allocation in response to current demand, market conditions, or customer preferences. This flexibility contributes to increased productivity, lower expenses, and better overall operational performance.
Personalized Customer Experiences: In sectors like retail and digital marketing, real-time data analytics enables personalized customer interactions based on immediate behavioral data and preferences. Organizations can deliver targeted offers, recommendations, and services in real time, enhancing customer satisfaction and loyalty.
Utilisation of IoT and Sensor Data: Real-time analytics can handle and analyse enormous volumes of sensor data in real-time due to the widespread use of IoT devices and sensors. This feature is essential for sectors where IoT devices create continuous streams of data, such manufacturing, transportation, and smart cities, and where quick analysis is needed for monitoring and decision-making (Nguyen et al., 2021).
Flexible and Scalable Architecture: Contemporary real-time analytics systems are built to manage massive amounts of data effectively and expand with them without any problems. To guarantee excellent performance and dependability, these systems frequently make use of distributed computing frameworks and cloud computing (Srinivasu et al., 2022).

Real-time data analytics, in general, enables businesses in a range of sectors to take advantage of quick insights, streamline processes, improve client experiences, and maintain their competitiveness in the data-driven market of today. The capabilities of real-time analytics will grow as technologies advance, allowing for more complex applications and deeper insights across a range of industries.

2.4 Ensuring Patient Data Confidentiality

Ensuring patient data confidentiality is paramount in healthcare to uphold patient trust, comply with regulations, and prevent unauthorized access or breaches.

Key strategies and considerations for safeguarding patient data confidentiality include:

Encryption: Strong encryption techniques are used to safeguard data while it's in transit and at rest. By transforming data into a secure format that can only be unlocked with approved keys, encryption makes sure that patient information is unreadable by unauthorised parties even in the event that it is intercepted.
Access Control: Enforcing stringent access rules grounded in the least privilege concept. This entails limiting access to patient data to authorised staff who need it for justifiable reasons. As job positions change, access controls should be periodically examined and changed.
Data Minimization: is the process of gathering and keeping just the bare minimum of patient data needed for particular medical needs. In the case of a security breach or unauthorised access, storing less data lowers exposure and potential harm.
Secure Communication Channels: Transmitting patient data electronically using virtual private networks (VPNs) and encrypted email, for example. When transmitting data between patients, healthcare providers, and other authorised entities, secure channels guard against eavesdropping and unauthorised access (William et al., 2023).
Data Integrity: Putting procedures in place to guarantee data integrity, like digital signatures and checksums, in order to identify and stop illegal changes or tampering with patient records. By doing this, it is ensured that patient data for clinical decision-making is accurate and trustworthy (Vashishth et al., 2024).
Regulation Compliance: Following healthcare guidelines and standards, such as the US's HIPAA (Health Insurance Portability and Accountability Act), which impose stringent criteria for maintaining the privacy of patient data. Performing routine risk assessments, putting security in place, and educating staff members about data protection procedures are all part of compliance.

Security Awareness and Training: Teaching medical personnel the value of patient data privacy and recommended security procedures for private data. To reduce the possibility of human error, training programs should address subjects including spotting phishing attempts, password security, and treating patient records correctly.

Data Breach Response Plan: To promptly identify, contain, and lessen the effects of security breaches, a thorough data breach response plan should be developed and put into action. The plan should specify how impacted parties, regulatory bodies, and corrective action implementers will be notified in the event of future violations.

Healthcare organisations can effectively safeguard patient data confidentiality by putting these strategies and considerations into practice. This will ensure that sensitive information is kept private, secure, and available only to authorised people for legitimate healthcare purposes. This strategy improves overall data security procedures in healthcare settings while also supporting regulatory compliance and protecting patient trust.

3. INTEGRATION OF ADVANCED TECHNOLOGIES IN 6G HEALTHCARE

3.1 Role of AI in Healthcare

Artificial intelligence (AI) and 6G network integration in the healthcare industry have great potential to transform patient care and medical services. In the framework of 6G technology, the following are some possible applications and advantages of AI in healthcare:

Real-Time Diagnostics and Monitoring: AI-powered devices can conduct real-time diagnostics based on large datasets thanks to 6G's extremely high speed and low latency capabilities. In order to provide quick insights into patients' health state and enable early disease identification, artificial intelligence (AI) systems can instantly analyse medical imaging, sensor data from wearables, and patient records.

Personalised Treatment Planning: A large amount of patient data, including genetic profiles, medical histories, and real-time physiological data, can be processed by AI algorithms coupled with 6G networks. By recommending customised therapies, drugs, and lifestyle changes based on unique patient characteristics and response patterns, this facilitates personalised treatment planning.

Remote Surgery and Telemedicine: With 6G's low latency and high reliability, AI-driven robotic surgery and telemedicine applications can be enhanced. Complex treatments can be precisely and quickly completed by surgeons working remotely, while artificial intelligence (AI) systems assist in decision-making by evaluating patient data and instantly delivering surgical guidance.

Healthcare Workflow Optimization: AI-powered predictive analytics and machine learning models can optimize healthcare workflows within 6G-enabled hospitals and clinics. This includes resource allocation, patient scheduling, inventory management, and predictive maintenance of medical equipment, improving operational efficiency and patient throughput.

Continuous Medical Education and Training: Virtual reality and augmented reality technologies provide immersive and interactive medical education when facilitated by 6G-enabled AI systems. Healthcare workers can access instructional materials, surgical techniques, and real-time simulations from a distance, which improves training efficiency and knowledge retention.

Health Data Security and Privacy: AI-powered healthcare systems can guarantee safe patient data transfer, storage, and access management by utilising 6G's strong security characteristics. Blockchain technology and sophisticated encryption techniques can shield medical records from illegal access and online threats, preserving patient privacy and regulatory compliance (Sharma et al., 2023).

Public Health Surveillance and Pandemic Management: AI algorithms supported by 6G networks enable rapid analysis of epidemiological data, monitoring disease outbreaks, and predicting healthcare resource needs. This feature makes it easier to take preventative action to slow the spread of infectious diseases and improves early warning systems for public health emergencies.

In conclusion, the convergence of AI and 6G in the healthcare industry presents revolutionary chances to enhance patient outcomes, streamline healthcare service, and progress medical education and research. Through the utilisation of AI-powered insights and the enhanced connection offered by 6G, healthcare systems across the globe can attain increased effectiveness, patient accessibility, and individualised treatment.

3.2 IoT Applications in Healthcare

By using linked devices and data-driven insights, Internet of Things (IoT) applications in healthcare are transforming clinical operations, patient care, and medical research. Among the major uses of IoT in healthcare are:

Remote Patient Monitoring: Outside of conventional healthcare settings, wearable sensors and medical implants, among other IoT technologies, continuously monitor patients' vital signs, activity levels, and adherence to their medications. Healthcare professionals may remotely monitor patients with chronic disorders, identify early warning signals, and take appropriate action thanks to real-time data transmission.

Virtual Consultations and Telemedicine: The Internet of Things makes it possible for patients and medical professionals to have high-quality video conferences and distant consultations. By securely communicating patient data, medical imaging, and diagnostic information over the internet, integrated IoT devices improve telehealth capabilities and increase access to healthcare services, particularly in underserved or rural locations.

Figure 3. IOT applications in healthcare

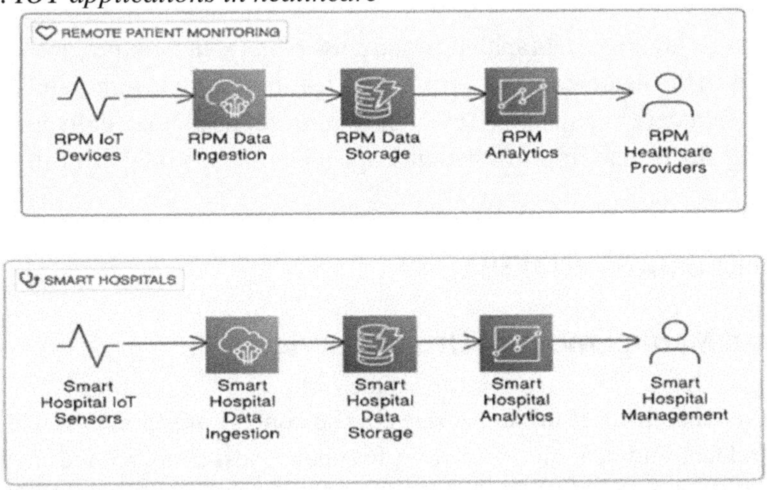

Asset and Inventory Management: IoT enabled asset tracking systems keep an eye on the whereabouts, use, and state of drugs, medical supplies, and equipment in healthcare institutions. This real-time visibility guarantees the timely availability of vital resources, optimises inventory management, and lowers operating costs.

Smart Hospitals and Facilities Management: IoT sensors and linked devices keep an eye on the temperature, humidity, and air quality in medical facilities. In order to maintain the best possible circumstances for patient comfort, infection control, and regulatory compliance, automated systems modify the surrounding conditions.

Medication Management: IoT devices track medication dispensing, administration, and adherence through smart pill dispensers, medication reminder apps, and ingestible sensors. These technologies help prevent medication errors, improve patient compliance with treatment regimens, and enhance medication safety.

Patient Safety and Fall Prevention: IoT sensors and wearable devices monitor patient movements and activities to detect falls or emergencies in real time. Automated alerts notify healthcare providers, enabling rapid response and interventions to prevent injuries and ensure patient safety.

Chronic Disease Management: IoT enabled devices gather ongoing physiological data, such as blood pressure for hypertensive patients or blood glucose levels for diabetics. In order to improve patient outcomes and save healthcare costs, proactive management of chronic diseases, early intervention, and personalised care plans are supported by remote monitoring and data analytics.

As sensor technology, data analytics, and networking standards progress, so are IoT applications in the healthcare industry. Using real-time data insights and predictive analytics, healthcare organisations are able to reinvent healthcare delivery, optimise clinical workflows, and improve patient engagement when they use IoT solutions.

4. 6G AND SMART CITIES

4.1 Green Management of Urban Services

Green management of urban services in the context of 6G involves leveraging advanced telecommunications technology to enhance sustainability and environmental stewardship across cities. With the capabilities of 6G networks, which promise ultra-fast speeds, ultra-low latency, and massive connectivity, cities can implement green management strategies in various urban services:

Smart Buildings and Infrastructure: Implementing 6G-powered IoT sensors and data analytics to optimize building operations, including heating, ventilation, lighting, and occupancy management. Real-time data insights enable proactive maintenance, energy conservation measures, and improved indoor environmental quality, reducing environmental impact and operational costs.
Water Conservation: Implementing 6G-enabled IoT sensors for smart water management, including leak detection, water quality monitoring, and irrigation control. Real-time data analytics optimize water distribution, reduce water losses, and support sustainable water use practices, preserving freshwater resources and enhancing urban resilience to water scarcity.
Transportation and Mobility: Leveraging 6G networks for real-time traffic management, intelligent transportation systems (ITS), and electric vehicle (EV) infrastructure. Advanced analytics and connectivity enable optimized traffic flow, reduced congestion, and promotion of eco-friendly transport modes, thereby lowering carbon emissions and improving air quality (Vashishth et al., 2024).
Green Spaces and Urban Planning: Utilizing 6G-enabled environmental sensors and GIS data to support green infrastructure planning and management. Real-time monitoring of urban green spaces, such as parks and urban forests, facilitates biodiversity conservation, enhances urban cooling, and promotes public health and well-being (Nova et al., 2021).
Climate Resilience and Disaster Management: Enhancing city resilience to climate change impacts and natural disasters through 6G-enabled early warning systems, disaster response coordination, and adaptive infrastructure design. Real-time data analytics support timely interventions, evacuation planning, and recovery efforts, reducing vulnerability and enhancing urban resilience (Janjua et al., 2020).

The use of 6G networks to power green management of urban services is a paradigm shift towards resilient and sustainable cities. Cities can address global concerns like climate change and urbanisation while optimising resource utilisation, reducing environmental footprints, and improving resident quality of life through the integration of advanced telecommunications technology with environmental sustainability principles.

4.2 Infrastructure Management

In the context of 6G technology, infrastructure management is making use of cutting-edge telecommunications capabilities to improve the resilience, sustainability, and efficiency of urban infrastructure. Infrastructure management can be greatly improved in several important areas with the promise of ultra-high-speed connectivity, ultra-low latency, and huge device connectivity offered by 6G networks:

- **Smart Grids and Energy Management:** To better distribute energy, monitor power grids, and incorporate renewable energy sources, 6G-enabled IoT sensors and real-time data analytics are used. With this strategy, carbon emissions are decreased, energy efficiency is increased, and the shift to sustainable energy systems is supported.
- **Water and Waste Management:** Using 6G-connected sensors to monitor waste management systems, pipeline integrity, and water quality in real time. Predictive maintenance, resource optimisation, and enhanced water supply and waste disposal service delivery are all made possible by advanced analytics, which promotes environmental sustainability.
- **Urban Planning and Development:** Utilizing 6G-enabled geographic information systems (GIS) and digital twins to model and simulate urban infrastructure. This enables informed decision-making in urban planning, infrastructure development, and disaster resilience, fostering sustainable growth and effective resource allocation.
- **Public Safety and Emergency Response:** Enhancing emergency communication and response capabilities with 6G-enabled networks for real-time situational awareness, crisis management, and disaster recovery. Integrated data analytics and IoT devices support rapid deployment of resources and coordination among first responders, improving public safety outcomes.
- **Environmental Monitoring and Sustainability:** Leveraging 6G connectivity for environmental sensors to monitor air quality, noise levels, and urban heat islands. Real-time data analytics inform environmental policies, mitigate climate impacts, and promote green initiatives for a more sustainable and resilient urban environment.

In 6G smart cities, infrastructure management offers a comprehensive strategy for enhancing quality of life, optimising urban services, and tackling global issues like urbanisation and climate change. Cities may improve their efficiency, sustainability, and resilience in serving the demands of their citizens and businesses by combining cutting-edge telecommunications technologies with infrastructure management techniques.

4.3 Real-Time Data Analytics for Smart Cities

Urban administration and service delivery can be revolutionised through the use of real-time data analytics in smart cities that utilise 6G networks. Smart cities can use real-time data analytics in a number of ways as a result of the arrival of 6G technology, which offers extremely fast and low-latency connection capabilities:

Optimised Urban Services: Large-scale real-time data gathering, processing, and analysis from IoT sensors, smart devices, and urban infrastructure are made possible by 6G. City services like waste management, electricity distribution, public transport, and traffic control can all be improved with the use of this data. Real-time traffic flow data, for example, can be analysed to optimise routes and dynamically modify traffic signals to lessen congestion and enhance air quality.

Predictive Maintenance: is made easier by IoT sensors that are positioned throughout city infrastructure and are backed by 6G connectivity. Proactive maintenance scheduling, anomaly detection, and equipment failure prediction are all possible with real-time data analytics. With this strategy, maintenance expenses are decreased, infrastructure assets have a longer lifespan, and there is less downtime.

Emergency Response and Public Safety: By offering practical insights during emergencies, real-time data analytics provided by 6G technology improve emergency response capabilities. For instance, sensors keeping an eye on social media, weather, and air quality might identify catastrophes like fires or natural disasters early on, facilitating quick reaction coordination and evacuation preparation.

Environmental Monitoring: 6G networks make it easier to continuously monitor environmental factors including water quality, noise levels, and air quality. Policies and initiatives to reduce environmental impact, increase urban sustainability, and improve public health outcomes can be informed by real-time analytics of this data.

Enhanced Citizen Engagement: Smart city platforms powered by 6G and real-time analytics provide citizens with access to personalized urban services and real-time information. This engagement fosters transparency, participatory governance, and community empowerment, enabling residents to make informed decisions and contribute to city planning and management.

In general, the utilisation of 6G networks for real-time data analytics is essential in converting smart cities into more sustainable, livable, and efficient urban settings. Through the utilisation of real-time knowledge, metropolitan areas may optimise infrastructure management, augment public services, and anticipate and address changing urban demands and complications.

5. SECURITY IN 6G NETWORKS

5.1 Ensuring Data Privacy and Security

The extremely sensitive nature of personal and healthcare data that will be transferred over these cutting-edge networks makes ensuring data privacy and security in 6G networks imperative. In order to improve security in 6G networks, keep the following points in mind:

Advanced Encryption Standards (AES): Sensitive data is safeguarded while transmission over 6G networks when AES protocols are used for data encryption. AES is renowned for its dependability and capacity to protect data from unwanted access.

Blockchain Technology: Using blockchain to verify transactions and store data securely improves data integrity and transparency in 6G networks. A safe framework for keeping patient records and enabling reliable transactions is provided by blockchain's decentralised ledger, which guarantees that healthcare data cannot be manipulated with (Kumari et al., 2021).

Zero-Trust Architecture: By using a zero-trust strategy, it is made sure that all users and devices connecting to the 6G network must first undergo verification and authentication before being given access to private information. Insider threats and illegal access attempts are less likely as a result.

Multi-Factor Authentication (MFA): Making use of MFA for authentication requires two different types of verification (passwords and biometrics), which fortifies access control methods in 6G networks. In order to prevent identity theft and unauthorised access, this provides an extra degree of security.

Secure Device Management: Ensuring that IoT devices connected to 6G networks are equipped with secure configurations, regular updates, and patches reduces vulnerabilities and potential entry points for cyber-attacks. Secure device management protocols should be implemented to monitor and manage device activities effectively.

Threat Detection and Response: Proactively identifying suspicious behaviours or possible cyber-attacks within 6G networks is made possible by implementing cutting-edge threat detection technology, such as AI-driven anomaly detection and behaviour analytics. Data breaches can be avoided and dangers can be reduced with prompt response tactics.

Compliance with Regulatory Standards: Adhering to regulatory requirements and industry standards for data protection and privacy ensures that healthcare organizations operating on 6G networks maintain legal compliance and uphold patient confidentiality.

Figure 4. Ensuring data privacy and security in 6G networks

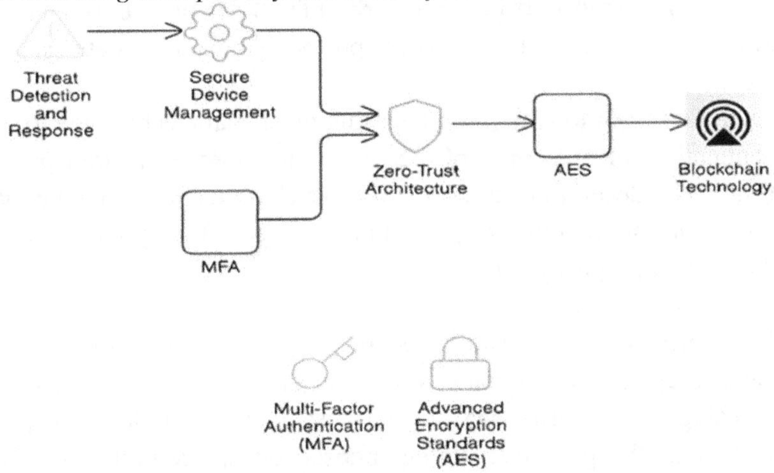

Healthcare companies may create a strong framework to protect data security and privacy in 6G networks by using these security measures and best practices. This proactive strategy not only safeguards private patient data but also encourages the use of cutting-edge medical innovations made possible by 6G networks.

5.2 Secure Communication Between Providers and Patients

Ensuring secure communication between healthcare providers and patients over 6G networks involves implementing advanced security measures to protect sensitive medical information and maintain patient confidentiality. Here are key considerations and strategies for achieving secure communication:

End-to-End Encryption: Encrypting data from source to destination while transmission over 6G networks is made possible by putting robust end-to-end encryption algorithms into place. This guarantees that only authorised parties have access to sensitive information and avoids unauthorised interception.

Authentication and Access Control: Before allowing access to medical data, healthcare practitioners and patients' identities are confirmed through the use of strong authentication mechanisms including biometric verification and multi-factor authentication (MFA). To avoid unintentional exposure, access control policies should limit data access according to roles and privileges.

Secure Transmission Protocols: Encrypting data during transmission over 6G networks is possible by using secure transmission protocols like Secure Socket Layer (SSL) or Transport Layer Security (TLS). By preventing interceptions and man-in-the-middle attacks, these protocols guarantee data integrity and secrecy.

Blockchain for Data Integrity: By using blockchain technology to store and authenticate medical records, 6G networks can improve data transparency and integrity. The decentralised ledger of blockchain technology guarantees the integrity and immutability of patient data, hence offering a safe platform for medical data administration.

Healthcare providers can create a secure communication framework over 6G networks and safeguard patient data from cyber threats, unauthorised access, and breaches by using these security measures and best practices. In addition to protecting private health data, this proactive strategy boosts confidence in the use of cutting-edge medical technologies made possible by 6G networks (Nayak and Patgiri, 2021).

6. BENEFITS, RISKS AND IMPROVED SERVICE QUALITY OF SECURE 6G NETWORKS

The benefits and risks related to AI, cybersecurity, and IoT in healthcare and smart cities, including privacy concerns, data security risks, and the technical complexities of implementing 6G infrastructure:

Table 1. Benefits and risks related to AI, cybersecurity, and IoT in healthcare and smart cities

Category	Benefits	Risks
Privacy Concerns	AI and IoT systems can improve privacy by automating data handling with secure protocols and reducing human error.	Constant data collection from IoT devices can lead to privacy breaches, as personal and sensitive data are more exposed to unauthorized access.
Data Security	AI enhances cybersecurity by detecting and mitigating threats faster through predictive algorithms and real-time monitoring.	An increased attack surface from more interconnected IoT devices raises the possibility of data breaches, hacks, and unauthorised access.
Data Management	Real-time data analysis and decision-making are made possible by AI and IoT, which accelerates response times within city and healthcare systems.	Managing large volumes of data can overwhelm current systems, leading to potential data loss, inefficiencies, or vulnerabilities in storage and transmission.
Technical Complexity of 6G	6G will offer ultra-low latency and high-speed data transmission, enabling seamless AI and IoT integration for advanced healthcare and smart city services.	High infrastructure costs and technical challenges in upgrading legacy systems to support 6G can delay widespread adoption and implementation.
Scalability	AI and IoT in healthcare and smart cities are highly scalable, providing a platform for handling massive amounts of data and devices with increased efficiency.	Scaling up IoT networks and AI systems can lead to increased complexity, requiring robust security measures to avoid system inefficiencies and vulnerabilities.
Personalized Services	AI-driven healthcare allows for personalized treatments and monitoring, while smart cities use data to provide tailored public services (e.g., optimized traffic).	AI models may unintentionally create biased or inaccurate predictions, leading to potential errors in patient treatment or biased service provision in cities.
Sustainability	AI and IoT systems optimize resource usage (e.g., energy, water) in smart cities and healthcare facilities, reducing waste and operational costs.	The increased deployment of IoT and 6G systems may lead to higher energy consumption, potentially negating sustainability gains in some cases.
Ethical Considerations	AI and IoT can help eliminate human biases in decision-making, providing fairer healthcare access and efficient city services.	The use of AI for tracking patients in healthcare and city surveillance raises ethical issues because it may violate people's autonomy and liberties.
Real-Time Monitoring	IoT devices enable proactive measures by enabling real-time surveillance in urban areas (e.g., traffic, pollution) and healthcare (e.g., patient vitals).	Vulnerabilities in IoT devices may lead to unauthorized access, disrupting critical services or compromising sensitive health data.

continued on following page

Table 1. Continued

Category	Benefits	Risks
Resource Management	AI and IoT optimize resource allocation, improving efficiency in healthcare (e.g., hospital management) and smart cities (e.g., energy, transportation).	Mismanagement of interconnected systems can lead to resource inefficiencies or failures, affecting essential services in cities and healthcare facilities.
6G Infrastructure	Substantial IoT device assistance, ultra-reliable low-latency communication (URLLC), and previously unheard-of bandwidth are all provided by 6G, which is propelling advancements in smart city operations and healthcare.	The technical complexity of integrating 6G with existing AI and IoT systems creates challenges in security, scalability, and regulatory compliance.

Improved Service Quality

Secure 6G networks offer several benefits that significantly improve service quality across various industries and applications:

Enhanced Reliability: Critical applications like medical care, emergency services, and industrial automation depend on dependable connectivity and little downtime, which is provided by secure 6G networks. Improved operational continuity and continuous service delivery are the results of this dependability.
High-Speed Data Transmission: 6G networks enable real-time data processing and communication with incredibly fast data transfer speeds and minimal latency. This feature enhances interactive and immersive user experiences by supporting applications for virtual reality (VR), augmented reality (AR), and high-definition video conferencing.
Personalised Healthcare: Safe 6G networks provide dependable connectivity and protection of privacy for telemedicine, remote tracking of patients, and AI-driven diagnostics. These developments make it possible for healthcare professionals to give personalised treatment, enhance patient satisfaction, and along with improve healthcare delivery methodologies.
Efficient Resource Allocation: Secure 6G networks enable dynamic resource allocation and adaptive network management, optimizing bandwidth usage and minimizing congestion. This capability ensures smooth operation of services and applications, even during peak demand periods.

Figure 5. 6G Secure network architecture

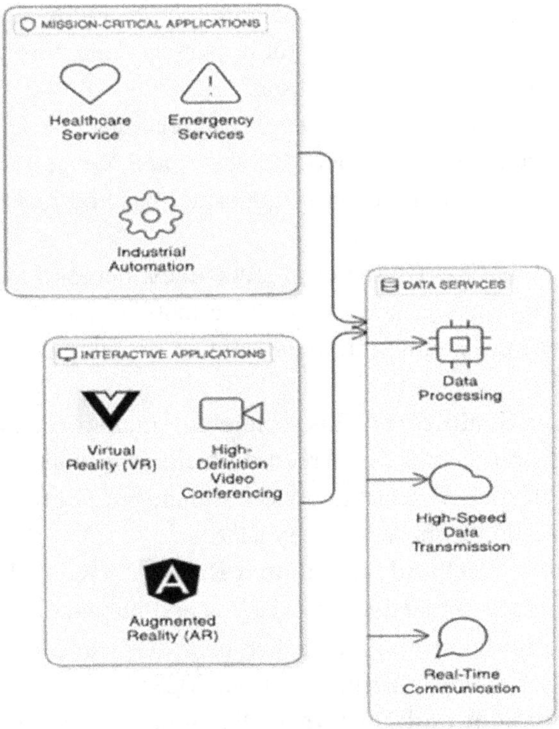

Overall, the benefits of secure 6G networks in improving service quality stem from their high reliability, high-speed data transmission, advanced security features, IoT integration, support for smart city applications, personalized healthcare innovations, and efficient resource allocation. These capabilities enhance user satisfaction, operational efficiency, and the delivery of enhanced services across diverse sectors.

7. CASE STUDIES AND REAL-WORLD APPLICATIONS

7.1 Healthcare Use Cases

Here are some healthcare use cases where advanced technologies have been applied:

Telemedicine and Remote Consultations: Telemedicine enables medical professionals to consult with patients remotely, providing diagnosis, prescriptions, and advice without the need for in-person visits. It is particularly useful in remote or underdeveloped locations.

AI-Assisted Diagnostics: By evaluating patient information as well as images related to medicine (such as MRIs, CT scans, and X-rays), AI algorithms help physicians and radiologist identify abnormalities and make timely, accurate diagnoses.

Healthcare Robotics: By increasing accuracy, decreasing errors caused by humans, and increasing the results for patients, robotics technology is used in patient care duties, rehabilitative therapies, and surgical operations (robot-assisted surgery).

Blockchain in Healthcare: This technology guarantees the safe and transparent administration of medical records, facilitating communication between healthcare professionals, cutting down on administrative expenses, and guarding patient information from security breaches.

Virtual Reality (VR) and Augmented Reality (AR) in Healthcare: These technologies offer immersive experiences and enhance treatment outcomes when applied for controlling pain therapies, surgical planning, and training in medicine simulations (Vashishth et al., 2023).

Drug Development and Discovery: By predicting molecular interactions, identifying promising drug candidates, and refining clinical trial designs, algorithms based on machine learning and AI accelerate up the drug discovery process.

Healthcare Supply Chain Management: IoT sensors and blockchain are employed to track pharmaceuticals, medical devices, and supplies throughout the supply chain, ensuring product authenticity, quality, and timely delivery.

These use cases demonstrate how advanced technologies are transforming healthcare delivery, enhancing patient care, and improving operational efficiency across the healthcare industry. Each application represents a significant advancement aimed at addressing challenges and improving outcomes in modern healthcare practices.

7.2 Smart City Implementations

Smart city implementations include a broad spectrum of projects and technology meant to improve urban life via creativity and interconnectivity. The following are some notable instances of smart city implementations:

Smart Mobility: Smart mobility refers to the application of AI and Internet of Things sensors to manage public transportation networks, optimise traffic flow, and support environmentally friendly transportation options like bike sharing and electric cars (Vashishth et al., 2024).
Energy Management: Energy management is the process of monitoring and optimising energy use in infrastructure and buildings, lowering carbon emissions and increasing energy efficiency. It makes use of smart grids and renewable energy sources.
Public Safety and Surveillance: Using IoT-enabled cameras, sensors, and AI algorithms to monitor public areas, traffic infractions, and emergency response systems in real-time to protect the safety of the general public.
Waste Management: By implementing IoT devices and data analytics, operational expenses and environmental effect are reduced. Waste collection routes are optimised, trash bin fill levels are monitored, and recycling programs are promoted (Vashishth et al., 2024).
Environmental Monitoring: Proactive steps to reduce pollution and improve public health are made possible by using Internet of Things (IoT) sensors to monitor urban areas' air, water, and noise levels.
Digital Governance and Citizen Engagement: Using mobile applications and online platforms to enable residents to access city resources, take part in decision-making, and provide feedback to local authorities, hence promoting transparency and accountability (Ramudu et al., 2024).
Healthcare and Well-Being: Implementation of telehealth services, smart healthcare facilities, and wellness programs utilizing technology to improve access to healthcare services, monitor public health trends, and promote healthy living.
Education and Innovation: Creation of smart classrooms, digital learning platforms, and innovation hubs to foster lifelong learning, promote STEM education, and support entrepreneurship and economic growth.

These smart city implementations demonstrate how technology can be harnessed to improve urban infrastructure, enhance quality of life for residents, and promote sustainable development. Each initiative focuses on leveraging connectivity, data analytics, and innovation to address urban challenges and create more efficient, resilient, and inclusive cities.

There are a few notable examples of smart city implementations that have been widely discussed:

Songdo, South Korea: Known as a model smart city, Songdo was built from scratch with integrated technologies such as IoT sensors for energy management, waste disposal systems, and smart traffic solutions. It features sustainable urban planning, green spaces, and advanced healthcare and education facilities.
Barcelona, Spain: The city of Barcelona has put in place a number of smart city initiatives, such as intelligent lighting on streets that changes in response to pedestrian activity, waste management systems that use Internet of Things sensors to improve collection routes, and an online platform that allows residents to access and comment on city services.
Singapore: Singapore has developed into a smart nation with initiatives like the Smart Nation Sensor Platform (SNSP), which integrates data from various sources to improve urban planning, transportation management, and public safety. It also uses smart technologies for housing, healthcare, and education.
Copenhagen, Denmark: With projects like the Copenhagen Connecting project, which use predictive analytics to enhance traffic circulation, decrease traffic jams, and encourage cycling as a key method of transportation, Copenhagen is known for its emphasis on sustainability and smart mobility.
Dubai, UAE: Dubai's smart city initiatives include the Dubai Electricity and Water Authority's (DEWA) smart grid project, which integrates renewable energy sources and uses AI to optimize energy consumption. The city also implements blockchain for secure and transparent transactions in various sectors.

These examples illustrate how cities worldwide are leveraging technology to enhance urban living, improve efficiency, promote sustainability, and create more inclusive communities. Each case study demonstrates unique approaches and technologies tailored to address local challenges and priorities in urban development. For more detailed case studies and insights, consulting specialized publications and reports on smart cities and urban innovation would provide deeper insights into specific projects and their impacts.

8. KEY CHALLENGES, LIMITATIONS AND FUTURE PROSPECTS

8.1 Technical Challenges

The Key Challenges and Limitations related to AI, cybersecurity, and IoT in healthcare and smart cities, focusing on privacy concerns, data security risks, and technical complexities of implementing 6G infrastructure:

Table 2. Key challenges and limitations related to AI, cybersecurity, and IoT in healthcare and smart cities.

Category	Key Challenges	Limitations
Data Privacy Concerns	Protecting sensitive personal and healthcare data in an increasingly interconnected AI and IoT ecosystem.	Inadequate privacy protections may lead to unauthorized data collection, breaches, and loss of user trust.
Cybersecurity Risks	Ensuring end-to-end security in AI-driven healthcare systems and smart cities using IoT devices.	Complex attack surfaces due to interconnected IoT devices increase vulnerability to cyberattacks and hacking.
Data Security Management	Securely handling massive volumes of data from artificial intelligence applications and IoT gadgets in real time.	Lack of robust encryption and secure data storage solutions can result in data leaks and unauthorized access.
Technical Complexity of 6G	Implementing secure 6G infrastructure with seamless integration of AI and IoT systems in healthcare and smart cities.	High infrastructure costs and complex integration processes may delay widespread deployment and scalability.
Interoperability Issues	Achieving seamless interaction between AI, IoT devices, and legacy healthcare and urban systems.	Interoperability challenges may cause system inefficiencies, delayed responses, and higher integration costs.
AI Algorithmic Bias	Ensuring AI systems in healthcare and smart cities make fair, unbiased decisions.	Biased AI algorithms may lead to unfair treatment of certain populations, affecting the quality of care and services.
Scalability of IoT Networks	Scaling IoT networks to accommodate millions of devices in healthcare and urban environments.	Increasing complexity in preserving network safety and efficiency as more devices get connected.
Latency and Reliability	Ensuring excellent dependability and low latency for 6G, AI, and Internet of Things applications in vital city and healthcare services.	Inconsistent connectivity in certain areas may hinder real-time monitoring, diagnosis, and smart city management.
Regulatory Compliance	Meeting evolving regulations for AI, cybersecurity, and IoT in both healthcare and smart city contexts.	Slow-moving regulations may create legal uncertainty, delaying innovation and deployment of advanced technologies.
Ethical Concerns	Addressing ethical concerns related to AI surveillance, data collection, and monitoring in healthcare and cities.	Increased surveillance by IoT and AI technologies may lead to ethical dilemmas regarding privacy and consent.
Energy Consumption	Minimizing the energy footprint of IoT, AI, and 6G infrastructure in healthcare and urban areas.	High energy demand from IoT networks and 6G infrastructure can strain resources, conflicting with sustainability goals.

8.2 Future Innovations in 6G

Potential innovations and advancements in 6G networks –

Terahertz Communication: investigating the use of frequencies over 100 GHz (terahertz) for extremely fast data transfer, allowing for previously unheard-of data rates and low latency communication.
AI-Driven Networks: By combining deep learning and artificial intelligence algorithms with 6G networks, it is possible to maximise allocation of resources, network administration, and predictive maintenance, hence improving performance and efficiency.
Holographic Communication: Developing technologies for holographic and immersive communication experiences, enabling realistic virtual presence and interactive applications in areas like VR and AR.
Quantum Communication: Researching quantum technologies for secure and ultra-reliable communication, leveraging quantum key distribution (QKD) for cryptographic applications and quantum sensing for enhanced network security (Thanganadar et al., 2024).
Energy Harvesting and Efficiency: Innovating in energy-efficient network architectures and devices, including energy harvesting technologies and low-power consumption components to support sustainable and green 6G networks.
Smart Surfaces and Metamaterials: Utilizing smart surfaces and metamaterials to manipulate electromagnetic waves, enhancing signal propagation, reducing interference, and improving coverage in urban and indoor environments.
Integrated Satellite and Ground Networks: Introducing seamless integration of satellite and terrestrial networks to provide ubiquitous coverage, support mobility, and extend connectivity to underserved and remote areas.
Blockchain and Distributed Ledger Technology (DLT): Exploring the application of Blockchain and DLT for secure and transparent transactions, decentralized network management, and data integrity verification in 6G networks.

These future innovations represent potential directions in the evolution of 6G technology, aiming to address current challenges and unlock new capabilities for enhanced connectivity, efficiency, and user experience.

9. CONCLUSION

In summary, the introduction of 6G technology promises to transform smart towns and healthcare by enabling incredibly fast, secure, and dependable communication networks. The deployment of a resilient 6G infrastructure in the healthcare sector has the potential to greatly augment telemedicine by permitting smooth virtual consultations and efficient monitoring of patients, in addition to enabling real-time data analytics to optimise decision-making. The use of telehealth services by both patients and medical professionals is facilitated by the secure 6G wireless networks that ensure the privacy of patient data. Furthermore, it is impossible to underestimate the capacity of 6G wireless technology for transforming smart cities. It provides the ability to effectively manage urban infrastructure and services, encouraging environmentally friendly and sustainable urban living. The operational efficiency, security, and quality of services in both sectors can be increased to previously unheard-of levels by incorporating cutting-edge technologies like artificial intelligence (AI) and the Internet of Things (IoT) within the 6G framework. Intelligent health care and more adaptable urban management systems are made possible by 6G's safe and dependable communication backbone, which facilitates easy communication and data sharing amongst different stakeholders. In the end, the launch of 6G technology is expected to usher in a new era of connection that will be marked by higher standards of life, increased operational efficiencies, and enhanced delivery of services, highlighting its crucial role in accelerating the growth of solutions for smart towns and healthcare.

REFERENCES

Ahad, A., Jiangbina, Z., Tahir, M., Shayea, I., Sheikh, M. A., & Rasheed, F. (2024). 6G and Intelligent Healthcare: Taxonomy, technologies, open issues and future research directions. *Internet of Things : Engineering Cyber Physical Human Systems*, 25, 101068. DOI: 10.1016/j.iot.2024.101068

Ahmad, H. F., Rafique, W., Rasool, R. U., Alhumam, A., Anwar, Z., & Qadir, J. (2023). Leveraging 6G, extended reality, and IoT big data analytics for healthcare: A review. *Computer Science Review*, 48, 100558. DOI: 10.1016/j.cosrev.2023.100558

Batista, E., Lopez-Aguilar, P., & Solanas, A. (2023). Smart health in the 6G era: Bringing security to future smart health services. *IEEE Communications Magazine*.

Estrela, V. V., Deshpande, A., Stutz, D., de Assis, J. T., Laghari, A. A., Shi, F., & Lin, Y. D. (2023). 6G in Healthcare–Anticipating Needs and Requirements. In *Intelligent Healthcare Systems* (pp. 159–181). CRC Press. DOI: 10.1201/9781003196822-9

Faria, T. H., Shamim Kaiser, M., Hossian, C. A., Mahmud, M., Al Mamun, S., & Chakraborty, C. (2021). Smart city technologies for next generation healthcare. In *Data-Driven Mining, Learning and Analytics for Secured Smart Cities: Trends and Advances* (pp. 253–274). Springer International Publishing. DOI: 10.1007/978-3-030-72139-8_12

Gera, B., Raghuvanshi, Y. S., Rawlley, O., Gupta, S., Dua, A., & Sharma, P. (2023). Leveraging AI-enabled 6G-driven IoT for sustainable smart cities. *International Journal of Communication Systems*, 36(16), e5588. DOI: 10.1002/dac.5588

Janjua, M. B., Duranay, A. E., & Arslan, H. (2020). Role of wireless communication in healthcare system to cater disaster situations under 6G vision. *Frontiers in Communications and Networks*, 1, 610879. DOI: 10.3389/frcmn.2020.610879

Kavitha, A. R. (2022). 6G with Smart Healthcare Systems. In Handbook of Research on Design, Deployment, Automation, and Testing Strategies for 6G Mobile Core Network (pp. 284-302). IGI Global.

Khattak, S. B. A., Nasralla, M. M., & Rehman, I. U. (2022, September). The role of 6g networks in enabling future smart health services and applications. In 2022 IEEE International Smart Cities Conference (ISC2) (pp. 1-7). IEEE.

Kumar, A., Jain, R., Gupta, M., & Islam, S. M. (Eds.). (2023). *6G-enabled IoT and AI for smart healthcare: Challenges, impact, and analysis*. CRC Press. DOI: 10.1201/9781003321668

Kumari, A., Gupta, R., & Tanwar, S. (2021). Amalgamation of blockchain and IoT for smart cities underlying 6G communication: A comprehensive review. *Computer Communications*, 172, 102–118. DOI: 10.1016/j.comcom.2021.03.005

Nayak, S., & Patgiri, R. (2021). 6G communication technology: A vision on intelligent healthcare. Health informatics: A computational perspective in healthcare, 1-18.

Nguyen, D. C., Ding, M., Pathirana, P. N., Seneviratne, A., Li, J., Niyato, D., Dobre, O., & Poor, H. V. (2021). 6G Internet of Things: A comprehensive survey. *IEEE Internet of Things Journal*, 9(1), 359–383. DOI: 10.1109/JIOT.2021.3103320

Nova, S. N., Rahman, M. S., & Chakraborty, C. (2021). Patients' health surveillance model using IoT and 6G technology. Green Technological Innovation for Sustainable Smart Societies: Post Pandemic Era, 191-209.

Ramudu, K., Bansal, S. K., Shahnazeer, C. K., Yaseen, S. M., Alimovna, P. Z., & Arumugam, M. (2024). 6G Cyber Physical System Based Smart Healthcare Modelling by Mobile Edge Network and Artificial Intelligence. *Wireless Personal Communications*, •••, 1–16. DOI: 10.1007/s11277-024-11137-9

Sharma, V., & Kumar, S. (2023, May). Role of Artificial Intelligence (AI) to Enhance the Security and Privacy of Data in Smart Cities. In 2023 3rd International Conference on Advance Computing and Innovative Technologies in Engineering (ICACITE) (pp. 596-599). IEEE.

Sharma, V., Vashishth, T. K., Kumar, B., Sharma, K. K., Vidyant, S., & Chaudhary, S. (2023, December). Health Interpretation of Covid-19 Patients using Artificial Intelligence. In *2023 International Conference on Artificial Intelligence for Innovations in Healthcare Industries (ICAIIHI)* (Vol. 1, pp. 1-5). IEEE Computer Society. DOI: 10.1109/ICAIIHI57871.2023.10488924

Singh, S. K., Azzaoui, A., Choo, K. K. R., Yang, L. T., & Park, J. H. (2023). Articles A Comprehensive Survey on Blockchain for Secure IoT-enabled Smart City beyond 5G: Approaches, Processes, Challenges, and Opportunities. Hum.-. *Centric Comput. Inf. Sci*, 13, 51.

Srinivasu, P. N., Ijaz, M. F., Shafi, J., Woźniak, M., & Sujatha, R. (2022). 6G driven fast computational networking framework for healthcare applications. *IEEE Access : Practical Innovations, Open Solutions*, 10, 94235–94248. DOI: 10.1109/ACCESS.2022.3203061

Thanganadar, H., Yaseen, S. M., Shukla, S. K., Bist, A. S., Shavkatovich, S. N., & Vijayakumar, P. (2024). 6G Wireless Communication Cyber Physical System Based Smart Healthcare Using Quantum Optimization with Machine Learning. *Wireless Personal Communications*, •••, 1–20. DOI: 10.1007/s11277-024-11189-x

Vashishth, T. K., Sharma, V., Kumar, B., Panwar, R., Sharma, K. K., & Chaudhary, S. (2024). AI-Integrated IoT in Healthcare Ecosystem: Opportunities, Challenges, and Future Directions. AI and IoT Technology and Applications for Smart Healthcare Systems, 37-54.

Vashishth, T. K., Sharma, V., Sharma, K. K., Kumar, B., Chaudhary, S., & Panwar, R. (2023). Virtual Reality (VR) and Augmented Reality (AR) Transforming Medical Applications. In A. Khang (Ed.), AI and IoT-Based Technologies for Precision Medicine (pp. 324-348). IGI Global.

Vashishth, T. K., Sharma, V., Sharma, K. K., Kumar, B., Chaudhary, S., & Panwar, R. (2024). Waste-to-Energy Solutions Harnessing IoT and ML for Sustainable Power Generation in Smart Cities. In Methodologies, Frameworks, and Applications of Machine Learning (pp. 125-146). IGI Global. DOI: 10.4018/979-8-3693-1062-5.ch007

Vashishth, T. K., Sharma, V., Sharma, K. K., Kumar, B., Chaudhary, S., & Panwar, R. (2024). Environmental sustainability and carbon footprint reduction through artificial intelligence-enabled energy management in electric vehicles. In *Artificial Intelligence-Empowered Modern Electric Vehicles in Smart Grid Systems* (pp. 477–502). Elsevier. DOI: 10.1016/B978-0-443-23814-7.00017-1

Vashishth, T. K., Sharma, V., Sharma, K. K., Kumar, B., Chaudhary, S., & Panwar, R. (2024). Revolutionizing cloud computing security with the power of artificial intelligence: Advancements, challenges, and opportunities. Smart Electric and Hybrid Vehicles, 163-177.

Vashishth, T. K., Sharma, V., Sharma, K. K., Kumar, B., Chaudhary, S., & Panwar, R. (2024). IoMT in Smart Cities Scaling Challenges, Smart Healthcare Applications, Data Integrity. In Lightweight Digital Trust Architectures in the Internet of Medical Things (IoMT) (pp. 281-309). IGI Global.

William, M., Sharif, S., & Ejaz, W. (2023, August). Enabling communication and networking technologies for 6G in healthcare sector. In *2023 Second International Conference On Smart Technologies For Smart Nation (SmartTechCon)* (pp. 699-704). IEEE. DOI: 10.1109/SmartTechCon57526.2023.10391790

Yadav, R., Prathapa Reddy, S. L., Upmanyu, A., Sanapala, R. K., Malathy, V., & Gohatre, U. B. (2024). Fast Computing Network Infrastructure for Healthcare Systems Based on 6G Future Perspective. Human Cancer Diagnosis and Detection Using Exascale Computing, 153-170.

KEY TERMS AND DEFINITIONS

Artificial Intelligence (AI): Is a branch of computer science that aims to create machines and systems capable of performing tasks that typically require human intelligence. These tasks include learning, reasoning, problem-solving, perception, speech recognition, and language understanding. AI systems leverage algorithms, data, and computational power to simulate cognitive functions, enabling them to adapt, improve, and execute tasks without explicit programming.

Augmented Reality (AR): Is a technology that overlays computer-generated content, such as images, videos, or information, onto the real-world environment, enhancing the user's perception of their surroundings by blending digital and physical elements.

Cybersecurity: Is the exercise of protecting computer systems, networks, and information from virtual attacks, robbery, and damage. It includes enforcing measures to save you unauthorized get right of entry to, make sure information integrity, and guard towards cyber threats.

Internet of Things (IoT): Refers to a community of interconnected bodily devices that speak and trade statistics with each other through the net. These devices, prepared with sensors and software program, allow the gathering and sharing of information, main to superior automation, performance, and real-time monitoring throughout various applications.

Machine Learning (ML): Is a subset of artificial intelligence (AI) that empowers computers to learn and improve from experience without being explicitly programmed. It enables systems to analyze data, identify patterns, and make informed decisions, allowing them to evolve and adapt to new information over time. ML algorithms leverage statistical techniques to enable machines to perform tasks and make predictions or decisions without explicit programming for each task.

Virtual Reality (VR): Is a technology that creates a computer-generated immersive environment, allowing users to interact with and experience a three-dimensional digital world as if it were real.

Chapter 15
Improving the Blockchain Protocol for 5G, Web3, and Edge Computing Applications

V. N. Krishna Addepalli
https://orcid.org/0009-0004-1160-0148
Faculty of Engineering, Christ University, India

Jainam Purushotam Patel
Christ University, India

ABSTRACT

The abstract highlights the potential of integrating blockchain into 5G networks and the Metaverse and proposes an enhanced blockchain protocol for various applications. It emphasizes the transformative nature of 5G and blockchain technologies and their ability to revolutionize industries. It also discusses the capabilities of blockchain, such as smart contracts and decentralized storage, and the opportunities it presents for in- novative 5G services. It also addresses the challenges and open research problems in this domain. Furthermore, it explores the application of blockchain in the Metaverse, focusing on security, privacy, and scalability concerns. The proposed innovation aims to improve the blockchain protocol to effectively support 5G, Web3, Edge Computing, Metaverse, and many more applications. It prioritizes immutability, confidentiality, and availability and offers advantages to interaction and digital experiences. The objective is to create a protocol that meets diverse industry requirements while considering different approaches to achieve its goals.

DOI: 10.4018/979-8-3693-8029-1.ch015

1. INTRODUCTION

Blockchain research has grown in prominence in recent years due to the emergence of cryptocurrencies such as Bitcoin, Ethereum, Solana, Polygon, Cardano, and Polkadot. Blockchain is a distributed, trusted, and immutable method of storing and distribut- ing data that does not require centralized dependencies or intermediaries to check/vali- date transactions or mine. Blockchain provides a more straightforward mechanism for transparently accessing ledger-based transactions via networks. It increases calculation speed dramatically by connecting with varied processing powers from multiple nodes in the blockchain network.

Blockchain technology employs a distributed network to store data in tamper-proof for- mats. Existing blockchain transactions cannot be amended since they can only be al- tered or added by establishing new hash values. The Blockchain's distinctive features include distributed ledger, P2P networking, consensus process, hash cryptography, min- ing, provenance, immutability, finality, and smart contracts. Blockchain technology can improve transparency and security by eliminating all intermediaries or third parties.

Duplicating a blockchain network in another location, such as an insurance provider, is feasible. Blockchain is connected to a network that shares data and assures that the data is accurate, dependable, and consistent. We can add data to a blockchain from any location and disseminate it to several sites on the same network. The data is shared throughout multiple network locations, eventually disseminating it to the entire network and providing location access to the most recent data.

Transactions that are verified and validated using a distributed ledger become immutable in a consensus-based Blockchain network with a complex working sequence and secure ledger technology. When any network node requests a transaction on a Blockchain network, the necessary processes are taken to complete the transaction. These transactions are subsequently distributed to peer nodes in the peer-to-peer network. Then, it generates a unique and connected hash from a prior hash, resulting in an unbreakable network of transactions. The network node, smart contract, or consensus will validate any attempt to attach a transaction. This immutable ledger, thus, cannot be altered. It can only be used with block transactions. An algorithm determines whether or not the user is authentic. When a transaction is validated, it is added to the ledger, forming a new block in the network. As shown in Figure 1 the block's structure consists of an Index, Timestamp, Data, and Previous and Current block hashes. A new block is then added to the distributed chain to make it immutable and tamper-proof.

Figure 1. Block structure

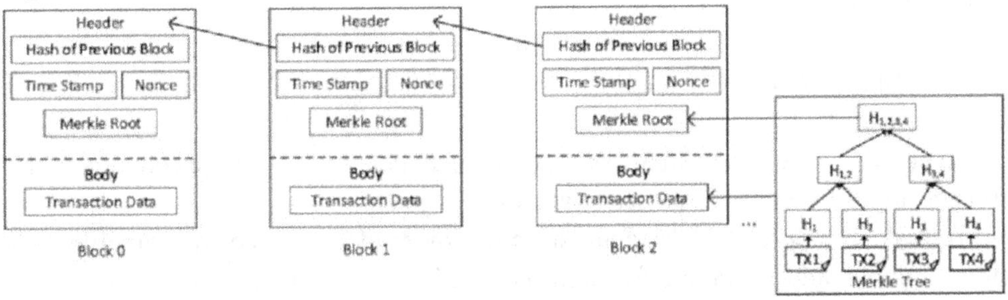

Recent research has shown that Blockchain is a good fit for various realistic solutions to numerous problems in multiple industries in the digital world due to its enticing features such as immutability and decentralization. The blockchain technique is more secure and efficient in processing cloud data than traditional cryptography solutions. Recent works have introduced Blockchain for safe data processing. Blockchain technology may create an open and distributed online database comprising a list of data structures called blocks connected to form the chain. These blocks are delivered between several hubs of a foundation and must be stored halfway.

1.1 Problem Identification

Blockchain technology can revolutionize various industries and transform how we use the internet daily, conduct communication or transactions or data, store and share data and manage identities. However, the current blockchain protocol used for cryptocurren- cies has limitations that make it less accessible and versatile for various applications. Limitations like swithching for centralized to decentalized sustainably and cost effi- ciently, scalability and energy efficiency issue of network because of huge complex structure and protocol, bandwidth and latency issues and still few blockchain networks like cryptocurrencies has some centralized power of control over the network like for adding the block (i.e., mining servers), authentication management server, transaction validators. To address these limitations, this idea aims to improve the blockchain protocol by making it more efficient, secure, and adaptable for multiple applications.

The main limitations of the current blockchain protocol used for cryptocurrencies are its Complexity, Scalability issues, lack of efficiency in Consensus algorithms, advanced Cryptography and Search algorithms, and its unsuitability as a federated or consortium blockchain. These limitations make it less accessible and versatile for various applica- tions, including supply chain management, voting systems, online banking, DeFi (De- centralized Finance), NFT (Non-Fungible Tokens), Smart Grid, and Agriculture.

1.1.1 Objectives

To create a protocol/framework that meets diverse industry requirements while considering different approaches to achieve its goals.

To make the current blockchain structure more efficient (i.e., sustainable), secure, scalable, and adaptable for multiple applications/domain by overcoming the existing disadvantages.

To build the most secure and Trustless (i.e., don't need to trust a third party or intermediary) worldwide overlay network framework.

To prioritize immutability, accessibility, confidentiality, integrity and availability.

To offer advantages of interoperability, Digitalization (i.e., interactive and digital experience) and Automation.

1.2 Limitations

In the context of improving the blockchain protocol, many boundaries and constraints can define the study's scope and limitations. This is an academic research-based project with limitations concerning time and other constraints. Also, the title might obscure other limitations of the project work depicted in the report.

Scope of Blockchain Applications: The research focuses on improving the blockchain protocol for any industry.

Technological Delimitation: The research is not centred on enhancing or improving existing blockchain protocols like Ethereum or Hyperledger. The prototype is built in Python from scratch.

Time Frame: The research has focused on emerging blockchain technologies and their potential applications.

Limitations of Resources: The research is constrained by a limited budget for hard- ware and software. This limitation may impact the scale of experimentation and testing, potentially restricting the ability to implement and validate specific technical improve- ments on a large scale.

1.3 Expected Outcomes

Data Security and Privacy: Blockchain technology provides a tamper-proof and immutable ledger, making it exceptionally secure for storing sensitive med- ical data, such as patient records and treatment histories. Ensuring confidential- ity and protection from unauthorized access and misuse of patient information. Blockchain allows granular control over who can access specific data. Patients can grant and revoke access, enhancing their privacy and control over their medi- cal information. A more secure blockchain protocol can help prevent fraud, data tampering, and unauthorized access, ensuring the integrity and trustworthiness of data.

Data Integrity: Blockchain's distributed ledger ensures that data remains consis- tent and unaltered. This is crucial in medical IoT/CPS, where accurate data is vital for critical patient care and supply chain management decisions. Preservation of Drug Discovery and Genomic Data Research.

Immutability and Confidentiality: The research prioritizes immutability, en- suring data permanence, and addresses confidentiality concerns, such as sensitive data protection.

Availability: will be ensured through the decentralized nature of the blockchain. The authority will be given to each node in the network (distributed authority).

Interoperability: Blockchain can enable different healthcare systems and supply chain components to communicate seamlessly while maintaining data integri-ty. This promotes a more efficient and interconnected healthcare ecosystem.

Transparency in the Supply Chain: Blockchain can track the movement of medical products and ensure their authenticity. The risk of falsified medical drugs and other products reduces and provides/preserves good product quality and pa- tient safety.

Data Sharing for Research: Blockchain can facilitate secure and controlled data sharing among medical institutions and researchers, promoting collabo-ration and the advancement of medical science.

This idea can lead to no need for any firewalls, antivirus, or Intrusion detection and prevention systems.

2. LITERATURE REVIEW

Satoshi Nakamoto, a pseudonym in 2008, first introduced Blockchain technol-ogy, the underlying technology behind the digital currency Bitcoin (Satoshi,2008). It was proposed as a distributed peer-to-peer linked structure to maintain the order of transactions and solve the double-spending problem. Blockchain achieves this by grouping transactions in constrained-size blocks with a shared timestamp. In the network, nodes, also known as miners, link these blocks chronologically, creating an immutable and auditable registry of all transactions (Crosby etal., 2016).

Over the years, blockchain technology has enabled decentralized applications and trans- actions without the need for centralized architectures or trusted third parties, disrupting traditional business processes. This distributed, transparent architecture provides trans- parency, robustness, audibility, and security (Greenspan 2015, Christidis 2016).

The growth of cryptocurrencies, which now exceeds 1900, has showcased the sig- nificance of blockchain technology (Tschorsch 2015). However, this rapid proliferation has raised concerns about interoperability due to the heterogeneity of cryptocurrency applications (Haferkorn 2016).

Beyond cryptocurrencies, blockchain technology has expanded into other fields, with Smart Contracts (SCs) playing a crucial role. SCs enable the automatic execution of contractual clauses through embeddable code, facilitating complex processes and inter- actions within the blockchain context (Szabo 1996).

As a result of its increasing relevance, researchers and C-suite executives in blockchain technology across various sectors seem to grow in interest in multiple sectors (Walport 2016). Blockchain evolution is classified into three generations: Blockchain 1.0 for digital currency applications, Blockchain 2.0 for SCs and beyond, and Blockchain 3.0 for ap- plications in various domains like government, health, science, and IoT .

Despite existing reviews on blockchain technology, there is a need for a systematic re- view of the current blockchain-enabled applications. This study aims to address this limitation by analyzing the development of blockchain-based applications over time, investigating how technical limitations affect processes in specific domains, and evaluating the suitability of blockchain technology in different areas.

Blockchain has diverse applications and implications across various domains. How it can revolutionize industries, enhance transparency, and decentralize traditional systems. However, challenges like privacy, including scalability, interoperability, and regulatory compliance, remain critical considerations for the widespread adoption of the solutions.

Significant advancements, particularly in the emergence of permissioned distributed ledger systems. The role of permissioned systems in achieving consensus within a net- work gives advantages in regulatory compliance compared to permissionless systems like Bitcoin. Consensus mechanisms are employed by permissioned systems, including Practical Byzantine Fault Tolerance (PBFT), Raft, or Proof of Authority (PoA), and explores real-world applications like finance, supply chain management, grid management and healthcare (Swanson, 2015).

There is a tradeoff between efficiency, transparency, and sustainability in blockchain for renewable energy. We need to reduce transaction costs, optimize energy distribution, and incentivize renewable energy production by addressing challenges related to regulatory compliance, grid management, and interoperability with existing energy infrastructure (Engelhard, 2017)

Supply chain management also emphasizes transparency, traceability, and efficiency enhancements. Blockchain creates a decentralized and tamper-proof ledger of transac- tions, allowing stakeholders to track goods from origin to consumer. Use cases include product provenance, counterfeit prevention, regulatory compliance, and challenges like scalability, data privacy, and interoperability between blockchain platforms (Hyvarinen, 2017)

Blockchain in copyright protection by providing immutable records of ownership and transactions. The potential of Smart Contracts to automate licensing and royalty pay- ments, reducing administrative overhead and ensuring fair compensation for content creators. Challenges include legal recognition, jurisdictional issues, and interoperabil- ity with existing copyright management systems (Kim, 2018).

Rights management, distribution of royalties, and content monetization. Initiatives like "music streaming on the blockchain" platforms aim to empower artists by providing transparent revenue sharing and direct interaction with fans. However, challenges such as incentivizing participation, scalability concerns, and compliance with copyright laws and licensing agreements need consideration (Dair, Beeven, 2017)

Healthcare is another sector where blockchain technology holds promise, particularly in securely exchanging health information. To address privacy, interoperability, and data integrity concerns, blockchain ensures confidentiality and compliance with regulations like HIPAA, enabling patients to have more control over their medical records. Use cases include clinical trial management, patient consent management, and healthcare supply chain tracking.

Blockchain can enhance transparency, fraud prevention, and regulatory compliance. Applications such as real-time auditing, trade surveillance, and identity verification in financial markets are discussed. However, data privacy, scalability, and the potential impact on market dynamics and liquidity need consideration.

The Internet of Things (IoT) ecosystem presents opportunities and challenges in device authentication, data integrity, and interoperability for blockchain technology in IoT net- works. It analyzes different consensus mechanisms, scalability solutions, and security considerations relevant to blockchain-enabled IoT applications (Kraft, 2016)

Public blockchains' architecture, performance, and implications in network scalability, decentralization, and governance structures showcasing real-world applications across cryptocurrency platforms, decentralized finance (DeFi) protocols, or decentralized au- tonomous organizations (DAOs) (Kiviat, 2015)

Governance models in blockchain, drawing on social contract theories. Issues include decentralization, consensus mechanisms, and community involvement. It analyzes dif- ferent governance structures, including on-chain, off-chain, and hybrid approaches. Challenges related to governance scalability, decision-making processes, and the balance between decentralization and efficiency are addressed (Paech, 2017)

While RSA is stronger than ECC, ECC may soon outperform RSA. They stressed the importance of considering both algorithms for specific use cases and their respective security levels (Alese et al., 2012). An examination of the danger of key sizes in RSA and ECC in- dicated that, until 2014, 1024-bit RSA posed a little risk, whereas 160-bit ECC over a prime field could be securely utilized for a longer duration. This demonstrates that ECC requires shorter key lengths to obtain the same level of security as RSA (Bos et al., 2009). ECC-160 point multiplication outperformed RSA-1024 private-key function on an ECC over RSA and ECC on two 8-bit processor computer systems, illustrating the performance benefit of ECC on resource-constrained platforms (Gura et al., 2004).

Figure 2. Key sizes for RSA and ECC

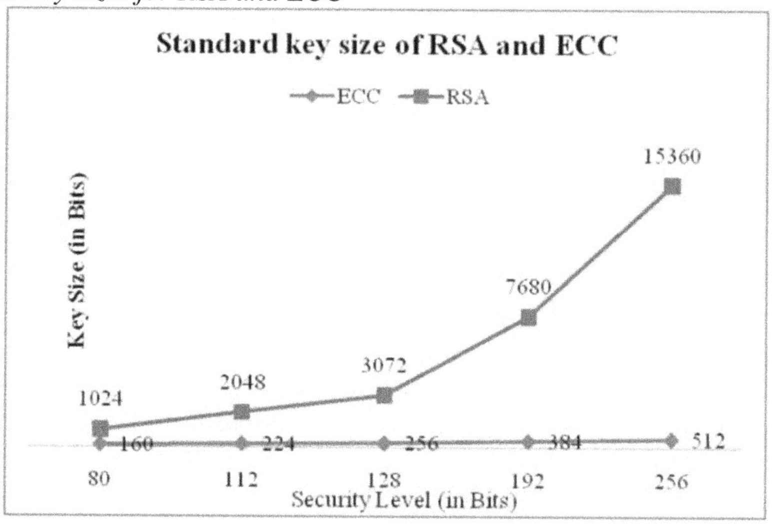

The use of digital signatures in RSA and ECC shows that RSA could be a useful so- lution for applications that require more than just signature generation to verify a mes- sage. Different cryptographic algorithms may suit different use cases depending on specific needs (Jansma, Arrendondo, 2004). RSA to get digital signatures and public-key cryptosystems— This groundbreaking study established public-key cryptography and paved the way for fur- ther research comparing RSA with other algorithms such as ECC (Rivest et al., 1978).

Figure 3. Curve preference

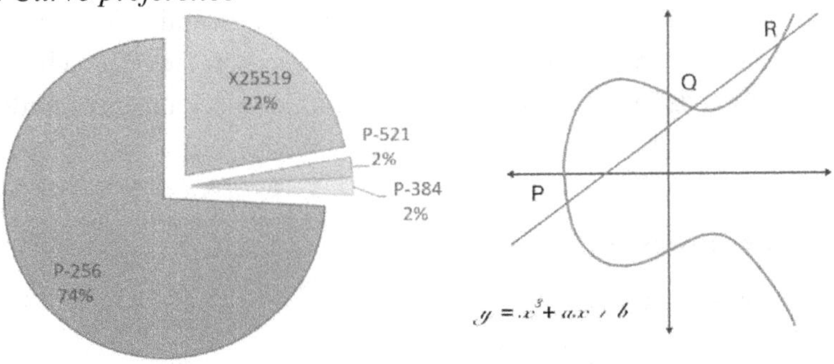

Although RSA is faster, ECC is more secure. This confirms that ECC offers greater security with lower key lengths than RSA (Kute et al., 2009). ECC outperforms RSA in operational efficiency and safety. Their research has demonstrated the benefits of employing ECC in a variety of circumstances, such as increased security and lower computing overhead (Mahto, 2012-17)

Furthermore, basic metrics such as computation cost (in seconds) describe the suggested protocol's performance efficiency. Figure 2.4 compares various elliptic cryptography curves, including Curve-25519, E-382, E-383, Curve-41417, M-511, and E-521, in terms of computation cost in seconds and space consumption in kilobytes (KB) when converting private key to public key (Kumar et al., 2021).

GRU Based digital Twins, Security in IOT enabled smart cities, energy efficiency in Block chains are discussed in works relared to utilization of Web & 5 G technologies(singh et al, 2023).

Decentralized and distributed need a peer-to-peer connection network. Underpinning IPFS is libP2P, an advanced generic peer-to-peer (P2P) solution (2020) developed based on BitTorrent DHT implementation. LibP2P provides a versatile network layer for IPFS, allowing the use of various network protocols for data transfer. The adaptability of IPFS to network instability is demonstrated through its capability to shift between protocols like UTP or SCTP, facilitated by a multiaddr formatted technique (48), amalgamating addresses and corresponding protocols.

Swarm, a decentralized storage system in Ethereum ecosystem, relies on the Ethereum P2P network. The Ethereum P2P network encompasses three critical protocols (49)

RLPx (Recursive Length Prefix): Primarily for node discovery and secure data transmis- sion. DevP2P: Facilitating node session establishment and message exchange, drawing

inspiration from libP2P. Ethereum Subprotocol: An additional layer contributing to the overall functionality.

DevP2P, as employed by Swarm, proves instrumental with its security properties in- spired by libP2P. Nodes discovered through RLPx establish TCP connections, initiating sessions and transmitting data packets based on DevP2P. The Ethereum ecosystem's robustness is further fortified by numerous long-term nodes within Swarm (Huang et al., 2020).

Figure 4. Ethereum consensus client

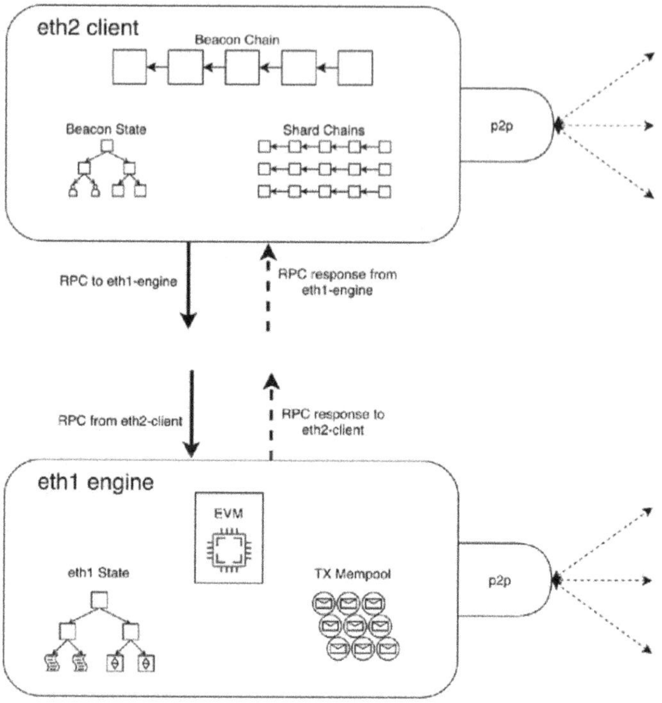

However, the Ethereum Merge on September 6, 2022, marked a significant transition from a proof-of-work to a proof-of-stake consensus algorithm. This transition introduced a division of responsibilities between execution and consensus clients (Krishnamurthi, Shree, 2023). Execution clients operating on the existing DEVP2P execution-layer network stack, handle transaction gossiping and encrypted communication among authenticated peers (Nodes, 2020). In contrast, consensus clients utilize the new LIBP2P consensus-layer network stack, as Figure 2.6 shows, for beacon block gossiping through- out the P2P network (Note, 2022).

DEVP2P, a crucial component of Ethereum's P2P networking schema, consists of two significant elements: discovery and authenticated/encrypted communication. Discov- ery involves two somewhat unrelated protocols, DiscoveryV4 and DiscoveryV5, with the latter serving as an experimental successor to improve security and speed (Huang et al., 2020). The TCP-based transport protocol, RLPx, ensures authenticated and confidential communication among Ethereum nodes (Kemp, 2020).

The Ethereum Mainnet node composition involves DEVP2P and LIBP2P, each requir- ing distinct methods for discovery and communication protocols. Adding a consensus client based on LIBP2P manages the implementation of the proof-of-stake consensus algorithm, further enriching Ethereum's network architecture (Note, 2020).

Satoshi Nakamoto hoped all participants could use the CPU to mine in the initial design stage. The hashing power could match the nodes, and each node has the opportunity to participate in the blockchain. Finally, machines specially designed for mining were invented. Delegated Proof of Stake (DPOS), where stakeholders can vote to elect a Variable number of witness nodes to generate (i.e., mine) new blocks (Bach et al., 2018). The list of witness nodes is shuffled during each maintenance interval. Each witness has a turn to produce a block at the fixed schedule of 1 block per n number of seconds. Witnesses are rewarded for each block built. The witnesses may be voted out in future elections when they fail to make a block after being elected. The N number of witnesses creates new blocks as assigned and then needs to ensure some fixed online time. BitShare is an example of a DPoS system. The DPoS blockchain is more efficient and saves power than PoS, and PoW .

A rough comparison of energy consumption per transaction across several designs. A basic server can handle transactions with minimal energy consumption. A typical non-blockchain, centralized application system will employ a more complicated database and backups, slightly boosting energy consumption. A small-scale Permissioned blockchain utilized in cross-enterprise use cases provides a similar level of redundancy but with some additional but manageable overhead owing to PoA consensus and more difficult cryptographic processes. A non-PoW permission less blockchain with multiple nodes might consume much more energy due to its high redundancy. However, energy usage is minimal compared to a substantial Proof-of-Work blockchain (Sedlmeir, 2020).

Proof of Importance (POI) uses a mechanism that groups using transaction graph anal-ysis, making use of the transaction amounts and balances of each of the nodes as indications, identifying the importance of each node, and giving priority using hash computations to more important nodes (Chalaemwongwan & Tasatanattakool, 2018). NEM introduced PoI, which uses a "harvesting" mechanism to select eligible nodes in the network to add a new block to the chain. Nodes can earn transaction fees for harvesting a block. Accounts with a higher impor-tance score are more likely to be picked for a new block. XEM cryptocurrency uses PoI to achieve consensus. Every account on the NEM network has an XEM balance. The balance is divided into two categories: vested and unvested. When an account receives XEM, the amount is added to its unvested balance. After every 1440 blocks, one-tenth of an account's unvested balance is shifted to the vested section. Furthermore, when an account transmits XEM, it is deducted from both vested and unvested balances to maintain the same vested/unvested ratio. To be eligible for "importance calculation," a vested account must have at least 10,000 XEM (Nelson, 2022). Byzantine fault tolerance can address transmission faults in distributed systems (Wang et al., 2019). However, previously, the Byzantine system required exponential operations. In 1999, the Practical Byzantine Fault Tolerance (PBFT) system was proposed. The algorithm complexity was decreased to a polynomial level, enhancing efficiency.

Table 1. Comparative analysis of blockchain algorithms for a set of blockchain properties

Parameters	PoW	PoS	PoI	DPoS	PBFT	Ripple
Node identity	Public	Public	Public & Private	Public	Private	Public
Computational power	High	comparitive low	low	low	low	low
Energy efficiency	No	Partial	Yes	Partial	Yes	Yes
Data	Transaction	Account	Transaction	Transaction	Key-Value	Account
Mode	based	based	& Account based	& Account based		based
Language	C++,LLL, Golang, Solidity	Michaleson	Java	No scripting	Golang, Java	C++, Java, Golang
Applications	Crypto-currency, General	Michaleson	Blockchain platform	Decentralize Exchange	General	Digital Assets, payment
Examples	Bitcoin, Ethereum Litecoin ZCash	Peercoin, Tendermint Tezos	XEM	BitShares	Hyperledger	Ripple

2.1 Possible Limitations and Enhancements with Blockchain

The limitations associated with 5G and WEB 3 technologies are reduced speed in throughput, scalability, and security problems associated with blockchain. These anticipated problems are tried to be solved using advanced Consensus algorithms like Raft and adopting a distributed Network and zero-knowledge proofs.

Lt wt Blockchain-based systems like Layer 1 supported High level of Scalability by considering fundamental block chain features. Layer 2 Block chain address Scalability by considering protocols to enhance transaction processing rates, periods, and fees by minimizing the use of less speed blockchains.

As the Energy Consumption Comparison is to reduce energy consumption and make the network lightweight, we can use the Delegated Proof of Stake (DPoS) / Practical Byzantine Fault Tolerance (pBFT) / Proof-of-Importance (POI) in- stead of Proof of Work (PoW). The process of mining in DPoS is known as forging. Here, the network's voting system will select the full nodes (i.e., hospital server/system) of the mesh/fog group based on its history record.

Cross-chain communication in blockchain can be implemented using Bridges which supports the use of cross-chain interoperability protocols and technologies to support inter operable communications.

3. PROPOSED METHODOLOGY

The following identified issues within blockchain for other industries apart from cryp- tocurrency. The proposed approach or strategy aims to achieve immutability (integrity), confidentiality (Privacy), availability, and less Energy consumption. Blockchain can create a tamper-proof record of an individual's digital identity and Track the movement or activity of goods over a network or along the whole process or chain.

In comparing the concept of blockchain used in Bitcoin/Ethereum, there are nodes in the network that can act as miners or Validators, and the nodes are categorized as Full or Light nodes. So, to implement the blockchain concept, the network will contain a few Full nodes, which will maintain the whole chain with transactions and play an essential role in achieving consensus at each new block creation. The group of full nodes can be called a Mesh/Fog group. The light node doesn't need to maintain a whole chain with transactions and can maintain the chain's header part (hashes) to reduce the complexity. The group of light nodes can be called an Edge group.

Authentication (i.e., verification) of each communication can be done by Digital sig- nature. Suppose it is necessary to hide the details and preserve data privacy as per the DPDP Act (Digital Personal Data Protection). In that case, we are including ECC, which can only be decrypted by an authorized person. The study done for this research is shown in Figures 2.1,2.2, and 2.4 in the literature review section with a proper expla- nation. Consider that node ID (i.e., Public key: Sender (PuS) and Receiver (PuR)) and the node contains one more key from which the public key is generated, its password (i.e., Private key: Sender (PrS) and Receiver (PrR)), which will be used to decrypt the data. The process of node ID generation is shown in Figure 3.2. The exact method can authenticate users logging in to the network by going through the same process and verifying if the generated public key is the same as the node ID already distributed in the network. Repeating the private key from the public key is not reversible because of scalar/point multiplication. The public keys of peers in the network will all be carried by a digital wallet over a Virtual environment.

Break the block as Header and Body for storage separately and hide the mappings if necessary. The header will have all the node IDs for the specific Communication, previous hash, nonce, Timestamp and Merkle Root hash. Validators inthe edge group will validate transactions (i.e., communication), and the mesh/fog group will maintain network consensus and block mining. The way of mapping each bodywith its header block confidentially is by using just a hash from the hash of the headerblock and the previous block-mapped hash to access it. It depends if any application requires a public blockchain, then there is no need to hide mapping. For applications requiring permissioned blockchain, the wallet will contain the first and last block hash,and the first mapping hash will be found from the first block's and private key's hash. Then, the mapped hash will be used to find the next block-mapped hash. Using this wayto hide mapping for permissioned blockchain makes it difficult to find as the chain gets longer and the process becomes irreversible. To grant access to the data history of any specific duration or block, the requester will send the request to the data owner, and thenthe owner shares the mapped hash of the first block from the requested duration, makingit accessible only to them. This way, we achieved privacy and security. It also can allow some data to be open source without revealing owner details for research purposes or statistical analysis.

To reduce the complexity of maintaining the ledger within all nodes of the network, the above concept can be reduced by managing chain (i.e., header) and data (i.e., transac- tions) just by Mesh/Fog group and just the cain (i.e., header) by the edge group. Now, this complexity can be further reduced by slicing the chain. Slicing (i.e., cutting) the chain will make the nodes of the edge group lighter but will increase the structure com- plexity in the Mesh/Fog group nodes. Splitting the parts of the chain for each specific node that is theirs in the Edge group (composed of other decentralized nodes with Sliced Chains) and distributing the whole chain just to the Mesh/Fog group (trusted nodes with no idea of the block's content).

The structural complexity will increase if we think of slicing the chain. We have a unique structural idea of storing this, which will help distribute the sliced chain to the respective nodes efficiently and make the blockchain data more structured and easy to specify access over each block. The structure is called BlockNet. The name itself can explain that by chaining each block with more than one block already linked horizontally or vertically in a chain.

The vertical chains will be categorized based on different cluster groups created for var- ious countries, platforms, and roles with different rules, like patient data, supply chain tracking data, drug discovery/genomic research data, Non-Fungible/ Fungible tokens, etc. It can also be a chain of other networks because this structure can lead to cross- chain interoperability. Changing rules or setup (i.e., platform up-date) can also lead to a new vertical chain (i.e., forking). Not all vertical chains need to be of the same length. There will be a vertical chain of different cluster groups in the network. The block of this chain will define the node ID, type of node in the hierarchy, and access specifica- tion. The chain can show the change in any access or the hierarchy for the node and the whole history.

The horizontal chains represent the chains of each node. The blocks linked in horizon- tal chains can also specify the access of different nodes to that block. The flat (i.e., horizontal) chain doesn't need to always be in a straight row because it depends on the block type and the difference in the length of vertical chains. There can be branches in a horizontal structure because more than one node can access any single block and vice versa (i.e., any node can access more than one block). This leads to having more than one hash of previous blocks in any block, and more than one block can have the same hash of the previous block.

This type of structured ledger's distribution (slicing chain) can be better and more ef- ficient, like mesh group nodes with the entire ledger, fog group nodes with any one vertical chain from the ledger, and edge nodes with their own horizontal chain they can access. The mesh nodes will mandatorily have the ledger and the separated data blocks, the fog nodes will mandatorily have any one vertical chain or the separated data blocks, and edge nodes cannot necessarily store anything or simply their horizontal chain.

Smart contracts can fulfill rules and regulations for achieving consensus without third- party service providers sacrificing speed. It can also help reduce medicine shortages by improving collaboration and supply chain integrity. A smart contract will help create and maintain a new fork (i.e., branch of any chain) with the defined new or changed rules and regulations. Smart contracts will help make different chains and cluster groups on a network for each county per government regulations, laws, and policies related to healthcare, data, insurance, drugs, etc. The above structure will store smart contracts as a block, which can also be a Genesis block if the new fork chain is created. Smart contracts can also automate some processes within the network.

Masking network traffic can be overcome by applying a suitable consensus for the net- work to distribute, manage, and monitor the traffic issue. The consensus first verifies each transaction with the digital signature (i.e., communication) to maintain authorized access over the network. This will help prevent unknown, unauthorized, or unnecessary network traffic. The consensus should be designed to avoid the looping of false block creation or transactions for creating a network traffic issue. This can be implemented by making it difficult to mine the block (i.e., making block creation slow). The consensus also maintains that the distributed ledger is up to date, making it immutable.

3.1 Implementation Details

Figure 5. Proposed network protocol layers for blockchain

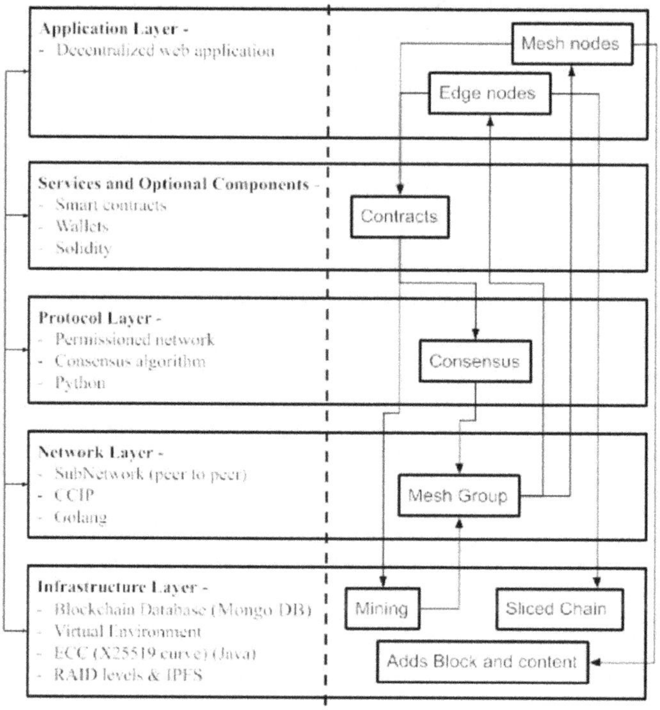

The proposed framework finds possible associations with blockchain technologies by incorporating enhanced security through creating an immutable, end-to-end encrypted log, and blockchain is helpful in thwarting scams and other forms of fraud. It can resolve privacy concerns by hiding sensitive information behind permissions to preserve and safeguard privacy and enhance security.

3.1.1 Programming Language and Cryptography

The prototype implementation will use Python 3, a popular and versatile program- ming language. For cryptographic operations, the implementation strategy incorporates elliptic-curve cryptography, focusing on implementing the P-256 and x-25519 curves. ECDH (Elliptic Curve Diffie-Hellman) is a cryptographic key exchange protocol that uses the ECC (Elliptic Curve Cryptography) algorithm, often employing the P-256 el- liptic curve. These cryptographic algorithms are essential for securing blockchain data and ensuring users' privacy.

3.1.2 Consensus Mechanism

The implementation strategy adopts a proof-of-work mechanism to achieve consensus among network participants. This consensus model is commonly used in blockchain networks and relies on computational work to validate and record transactions, ensuring the integrity and security of the blockchain.

Here are the key steps in PoW:

1. **Transaction Verification:** Gather a set of pending transactions to be added to the blockchain.
2. **Nonce Generation:** Select a random number called a "nonce."
3. **Hash Computation:** Concatenate the nonce with the previous block's hash and transaction data. Apply a cryptographic hash function (e.g., SHA-256) to the concatenated data to create a hash value.
4. **Difficulty Check:** Verify if the generated hash meets the network's target. The difficulty is determined by the network and adjusted periodically.
5. **Adjusting the Nonce:** If the hash doesn't meet the difficulty target, increment or change the nonce and repeat the hash computation.
6. **Repeat Until Success:** Change the nonce and hashing until a valid hash (meeting the difficulty target) is found.

3.1.3 Hashing Algorithm

The implementation strategy includes using Keccak-256 (SHA-3) as the hashing algo- rithm. Hashing is essential for data integrity and security in blockchain applications. SHA-3 is known for its robustness and resistance to cryptographic attacks, making it suitable.

Choice of Blockchain Database:

For the storage and management of blockchain data, the implementation strategy pro- vides flexibility in choosing between MySQL and MongoDB. Both databases have ad- vantages, and the selection will depend on specific project requirements and prefer- ences.

3.1.4 Tools/Hardware/Software Requirements

Software: Python 3, MySQL or MongoDB
Hardware: A system with a minimum of 4 GB RAM, and for now, this project is platform-dependent (Windows or Linux)

3.1.5 Experimental and/or Analytical Work Completed in the Project

As previously discussed, the network will be divided into mesh (Full Nodes) and edge (Light/Simplified Payment Verification (SPV) Nodes) groups. The network is divided into two groups as Mesh and Edge groups.

After the Communication between edge nodes is verified using Digital signatures, these transactions are sent to the Add block function. Then it will Create a Block and go for mining. The mining will be done by a mesh group, a distributed blockchain envi- ronment will provide the previous block hash and difficulty, and then the header part will be stored in the chain database, and transactions will be separately stored in the data database. The chain database will be stored in all nodes, but the data will only be distributed within Mesh groups.

To ensure immutability, splitting the parts of the chain for each specific node that is theirs in the edge group (composed of other decentralized nodes with sliced chains) and distributing the whole chain just to the mesh group (trusted nodes without an idea of the block's content).

The work shows the functional flow as per the fully developed and modified from scratch code of Blockchain. Below are here the functions within a class shortly de- scribed:

4. RESULTS AND ANALYSIS

This research project aims to redesign the Blockchain Protocol to make it easy and con- venient not just for cryptocurrency but also for implementation in any industry supply chain, voting System, Net Banking, etc., for WEB3 and Edge Computing. The primary focus of this research was to overcome a few drawbacks of the current blockchain protocol used for cryptocurrencies. Such as reducing complexity through structural and protocol-level changes, making it a "Federated/consortium" Blockchain. Developing a Hybrid protocol focusing mainly on "immutability", "confidentiality", and "availability" was decided by finding(doing research) and comparing all the possible ways to reach our research.

The implementation is in working progress as it is a growing technology. The possible results are demonstrated below in this chapter, and the conceptual proof of work done for study and research in the project is explained in this report by describing the proof of concept proposed to overcome the issues in Blockchain and current technology.

The work presents the mined genesis block manually. The inserted data is dummy data for demonstration purposes only. The other part of the code prints the different blocks of the chain in a loop, which shows the timestamp, current block hash, previous block hash and a few other required hash of blocks. This code is built without any database connection, and the code stores the chain in the primary memory as a list (i.e., array). If we terminate the code, we lose thewhole chain. This was just a demo code, a first step towards implementation.

The next part shows the add function is when we send the verified communication to create and mine the block. The inserted data is dummy data for just demonstration. When the block is mined, it will print the output 'Block mined'. To print the chain, it calls the function 'printChain', which shows the timestamp, previous hash and a few other required hash of blocks. The output does'nt shows the data because the encryption and decription part was not intigrated with this code. This code is built with MySQL database connection, and the code stores the chain in the database. This phase made me identify the inefficiency and difficulties of using and making structure for blockchain over MySQl.

The cryptographic implementation using the ECC Brainpool Standard curve was the another step towards implementation and a learning and buillding process of code from scratch. The functional code does a user-generated for test purposes because it generates the private key from brain- poolP256r1 curve, and from the private key, a public key is generated. This code just perform encryption and decryption providing confidentiality but does not performs authentication and digital signature. The code takes any input string and, as shown in the output, the encrypted message and performs the Decryption successfully.

The work discusses the study of cryptographic implementation using the ECC P-256 curve and generating a common key using Diffie Hellman. The sender and receiver functions shown in the screenshot are just dummy user-generated for test purposes be- cause we are generating the private key from the user's password with some buffer data of the user, and from the private key, a public key is generated, and that is used as a node Id. The network will store just the public key. To verify, the user performs the same steps and, at last, generates the public key and, if it exists, then verified. This code perform encryption and decription providing confidentiality and also does performs authentication and digital signature. The code takes any input string and, as shown in the output, the encrypted message and performs the Decryption successfully.

The work gives the genesis of cryptographic implementation using the ECC X-25519 curve and generating a common key using Diffie Hellman. The sender and receiver functions shown in the screenshot are just dummy user-generated for test pur- poses, here it was difficult to generating the private key from the user's password withsome buffer data of the user, and from the private key, a public key is generation. The network will store just the public key and the wallet will store the private key. To verify, the user performs the same steps and, at last, generates the public key and, if it exists, then verified. This code perform encryption and description providing confidentiality

4.1 Future Scope of Work

Emerging trends in cross chain: To develop a cross platform which supports for compatibility between different platforms.

Consider a case where one Entity A is on the Ethereum network, and another Entity B, operating on BNB Chain, supports customers who want to perform a digital transaction s between Ethereum and BNB block chains. But issues will happen because of complexities in compatibility between these two different Blockchains. The possible solution for this type of scenarios is to have a bridge designed to support the compatibility in protocols between these two block chain Networks. It supports for Assets getting locked in one Block chain and Getting procured from other supporting for smooth Cross platform transactions.

AI in Block chain: AI Techniques may be used in blockchain to improve security, scalability, and efficiency in a variety of applications, including Investment analysis, Inventory management, and healthcare and so on.

4.2 Vulnerability Issues with Block Chain

The problems with Upgradability and Scalability can also be solved by using a Polynomial mode as it supports more coordinating points in generating the polynomial.

Single Network Dependency: By proper designing a bridge between distinct Block chain protocols the problem associated with single network dependency can be addressed.

Quantum resistant Block chain: Hash based Digital signatures using Merkle tree, Linear coded algorithms and Lattice based Cryptography may be used in Block chains to make it resistant form Quantum attacks.

4.3 Expected Outcomes

Data Security and Privacy: Blockchain technology provides a tamper-proof and immutable ledger, making it exceptionally secure for storing sensitive medical data, such as patient records and treatment histories. Ensures that patient information remains confidential and protected from unauthorized access. Blockchain allows granular control over who can access specific data. Patients can grant and revoke access, enhancing their privacy and control over their medical information.

Data Integrity: Blockchain's distributed ledger ensures that data remains consistent and unaltered. This is crucial in medical IoT/CPS, where accurate data is vital for critical patient care and supply chain management decisions. Preservation of Drug Discovery and Genomic Data Research.

Interoperability: Blockchain can enable different healthcare systems and supply chain components to communicate seamlessly while maintaining data integrity. This promotes a more efficient and interconnected healthcare ecosystem.

Transparency in the Supply Chain: Blockchain can track the movement of medical products and ensure their authenticity. This reduces the risk of counterfeit drugs and provides product quality and patient safety.

Data Sharing for Research: Blockchain can facilitate secure and controlled data sharing among medical institutions and researchers, promoting collaboration and the advancement of medical science.

4.4 Unique Claims

Cryptographic key generation and User Authentication: generating node IDs (i.e. public key) from private keys of each node used for digital signatures and Encryption, and this irreversible process can be used for user authentication in the network by just distributing public keys in the network and no need of maintaining username and hash of private key (i.e. authentication server), it can be supported by digital wallet.

Separation of block structure: separating into the header, which has all personal details encrypted like node IDs with access rights, etc. and body blocks with transactions or data. Reduce space complexity in the chain for easy access and benefit from the variable data block size.

Hiding Mappings: Use of this depends on whether the industry needs public or permissioned blockchain. Open access to data can affect privacy policy and lead to personal details being in the wrong hands. To hide personal information, map a header block with encrypted personal details and a body block with data. The authorized person will be able to access the data by using their keys.

Hierarchy of groups in the network: Mesh group: trusted third-party service providers like supply chain management or other industries, Fog group: manu- facturers or retailers, Edge groups: stakeholders

Federated/Consortium blockchain networking: Peer-to-peer communication authority and access as per hierarchy, like each node in a mesh group, will be directly connected. In a fog, the nodes will have peer connections based on relation and access granted by the mesh group nodes, and the nodes in the edge group will not have peer connections between each other. They can just have a connection based on their public ID sharing.

Distributed Authority/access: The node type defines the node's authority in the network, so there will be no central authority or authentication service. A digital wallet over a virtual environment (i.e., D-App) is created within the node to be a part of a network that holds this distributed access. Edge group nodes can make the block, Fog group nodes will do the validation, and mesh group nodes will handle the mining and consensus process.

Block Net: this is a relational structure made from non-relational chains. This structure helps manage access specification (i.e.authority/permission) and authentication. As permissioned blockchain is slower than public blockchain, using this means there is no need for a third-party server for authentication and authoriza- tion, which makes permissioned blockchain fast enough. However, using this structure, we can gain the advantages of public and permissioned blockchain.

Slicing Chain: The Ledger distribution also depends on the type of node, which specifies how much part (slice) of the ledger the node has rights to store. The block net structure also defines the distribution of ledger parts over a network.

4.5 Cost Estimation Model

Overview of Funding Allocation: The 100% budget for the proposed Blockchain-Based Security & Privacy-Preserving Framework for Medical IoT/CPS, Health Records, & Supply Chain Management is distributed across important areas to satisfy project needs comprehensively. 40% of the budget is allocated to Infrastructure Costs, which includes setting up the blockchain network, integrating IoT devices, and implement- ing strong cybersecurity measures. 35% of the budget is allocated to Maintenance and Operational Costs, including network maintenance, smart contract execution costs, IoT device upkeep, data storage, and compliance audits. In addition, a 10% reserve is al- located for Funding Reserves to provide flexibility for unexpected situations. Research and Development receive 15%, and Marketing gets 5% to support ongoing innovation, community involvement, and awareness.

Infrastructure and Operations: 75% of the budget is allocated to Infrastructure Costs and Maintenance and Operational Costs. This highlights the significance of creating a safe and effective base for the decentralized medical Internet of Things system. A significant amount of resources is allocated to establishing and continuously maintaining the blockchain network to guarantee a strong and enduring infrastructure. Investments in integrating IoT devices, ensuring data security, and conducting compliance audits demonstrate a dedication to upholding operational excellence and data integrity in the decentralized network.

Innovation and Community Engagement: For sustained success, 20% of the budget is devoted strategically to Research and Development, Marketing, and a Contingency Fund. This promotes ongoing innovation, investigation of new technologies, and involvement with the community. Research and Development drives continuous projects, while Marketing efforts focus on increasing awareness and building community sup- port. The Contingency Fund serves as a safety measure for unexpected costs, show- casing a proactive strategy for reducing risks. This method guarantees the initiative creates a strong infrastructure and flourishes via innovation, awareness, and community engagement.

4.6 Learning Outcomes

Decentralization and Network Authority: Understood the principles of decentralization in blockchain networks, where authority and decision-making are distributed across multiple nodes.

Understanding Blockchain Security Measures: Gain a deep understanding of the security mechanisms and features that can be implemented within a blockchain system to prevent fraud, data tampering, and unauthorized access.

Exploring Data Immutability and Confidentiality: Explored the concept of data im- mutability, which ensures the permanent and unchangeable nature of data once it is recorded on the blockchain.

Evaluating Real-World Applications: Assessed real-world applications and use cases where blockchain technology has been implemented to achieve the specified benefits.

5. CONCLUSION

This idea addresses the current blockchain protocol's limitations and makes it more ac- cessible and versatile for various applications. By prioritizing immutability, confidentiality, and availability and exploring ways to reduce complexity and enhance the protocol, this research has the potential to transform the way we use blockchain technology for various applications. The idea will contribute to advancing blockchain technology and provide solutions for the current blockchain protocol's challenges.

5.1 Scope for Future Work

Building a peer-to-peer protocol with IPFS(InterPlanetary File System) for availability and to increase bandwidth and reduce latency and CCIP(Cross Chain Interoperability Protocol) to communicate with other existing Decentralized networks.

Can develop plug-and-playable consensus like DPoS (Delegated Proof of Stake) - Proof of Share Authority, DPOS is EOS (Fastest), PoET (Proof of Elapsed Time) is used in permissioned Blockchain networks, PBFT (Practical Byzantine Fault Tolerance) and Hashgraph based on gossip protocol.

Can come up with the integration of more than one consensus: PoET and PoB (Proof of Burn) in such a way as burn the coins to reduce waiting time to add new block (can also reduce waiting time based on importance), DPoS and PoI (Proof of Importance) in such a way as selecting forger based optimal ratio between both importance and amount of stake or PoS and PBFT in such a way first to achieve consensus by communicating (gossiping) within the group of forgers got selected based on stake (can also make a group based on importance.

We also can use the CAPTCHA system as a difficulty for mining to prevent ex- cessive inflation (i.e., difficulty creating different longest branches of fake trans- actions or manipulating the existing chain).

Further study and research on Blockchain, Hashgraph, Directed Acyclic Graphs (DAG), and Holochain.

This research can also further work to explain the concepts of creating smart contracts or Non-Fungible/Fungible tokens of pre-trained AI Models for Image processing or any other healthcare-related AI applications and for Intrusion Detection/prevention models that can be added to the network as a mined block. Future technological improvements like Digital twins can also be integrated within the network for medical training and used to simulate by creating a virtual replica of an individual to verify the authenticity of commodities and gather data streams from IoT devices.

Using PPML (Privacy-Preserving in Machine Learning), Homomorphic Encryption, and Differential Privacy can validate the block's content to check its feasi- bility and for different ML models to help doctors analyze patients' test reports and treatment purposes while preserving data privacy.

Advanced cryptography based on AES (Advanced Encryption Standard / Rijndael) with QKD (Quantum key distribution) using BB84/BB92 (QKD E91). Further, DNA-based encoding and decoding will be quantum-safe (like Lattice, Hash, Code or Isogeny based) and include compression.

Explore ensuring integrity (recovery), building method inspired from 2D parity check and improving it for multiple error detection and correction.

An efficient Search algorithm in a linked-list (unsorted) structure based on Nikola Tesla's 369 code math. If possible, use Grover's search algorithm (N complexity).

REFERENCES

Alese, B. K., Philemon, E. D., & Falaki, S. O. (2012). Comparative analysis of public-key encryption schemes. *IACSIT International Journal of Engineering and Technology*, 2(9), 1552–1568.

Bach, L. M., Mihaljevic, B., & Zagar, M. Comparative analysis of blockchain consensus algorithms, in *41st International Convention on Information and Communication Technology, Electronics and Microelectronics (MIPRO)*, pp. 1545-1550, 2018. DOI: 10.23919/MIPRO.2018.8400278

Benet, J. *IPFS–content addressed, versioned, P2P file system*, 2014, arXiv:1407.3561. [Online]. Available: http://arxiv.org/abs/1407.3561

.J.Bos, M. Kaihara, T. Kleinjung, A. K. Lenstra, and P. L. Montgomery, *On the Se- curity of 1024-bit RSA and 160-bit Elliptic Curve Cryptography*, Technical Report, 2009.

Chalaemwongwan, N., & Kurutach, W. State of the art and challenges facing consensus protocols on blockchain, in *International Conference on Information Networking (ICOIN)*, pp. 957-962, 2018. DOI: 10.1109/ICOIN.2018.8343266

Christidis, K., & Devetsikiotis, M. (2016). Blockchains and smart contracts for the Internet of Things. *IEEE Access : Practical Innovations, Open Solutions*, 4, 2292–2303. DOI: 10.1109/ACCESS.2016.2566339

Conoscenti, M., Vetro, A., & De Martin, J. C. (2016, November). Blockchain for the Internet of Things: A systematic literature review. In 2016 IEEE/ACS 13th International Conference of Computer Systems and Applications (AICCSA) (pp. 1-6). IEEE.

Crosby, M., Nachiappan, P., Pattanayak, P., & Verma, S. (2016). Blockchain technology: Beyond Bitcoin. *Applied Innovation*, 2(6-10), 71.

Engelhardt, M. A. (2017). Intelligent energy: A blockchain-powered model for renewable energy marketplaces. *Energy Policy*, 108, 77–86.

Greenspan, G. (2015). Is blockchain the most important IT invention of our age? *New World (New Orleans, La.)*, 32(9), 3.

Gura, N., Patel, A., Wander, A., Eberle, H., & Shantz, S. C. *Comparing elliptic curve cryptography and RSA on 8-bit CPU*, in *CHES*, vol. 4, pp. 119–132, 2004.

Haferkorn, M., & Quintana Diaz, F. D. (2015). The cryptocurrency market landscape. *Business & Information Systems Engineering*, 57(5), 339–348.

Huang, H., Lin, J., Zheng, B., Zheng, Z., & Bian, J. (2020, March 10). When Blockchain Meets Distributed File Systems: An Overview, Challenges, and Open Issues. *IEEE Access : Practical Innovations, Open Solutions*, 8, 43822–43838. DOI: 10.1109/ACCESS.2020.2979881

Hyvarinen, A., Juustila, A., & Seppanen, M. (2017). Blockchain-Enabled Supply Chain Services. *Procedia CIRP*, 64, 639–644.

IBM. *Leading the pack in blockchain banking: Trailblazers set the pace*, 2017. Available: https://www.hyperledger.org/wp-content/uploads/2016/10/Leading-the - pack-in-blockchain-banking-1.pdf

Jansma, N., & Arrendondo, B. (2004). Performance comparison of elliptic curve and rsa digital signatures. nicj. net/files.

Kemp, J. M. (2023). *Enabling Security Analysis and Education of the Ethereum Platform: A Network Traffic Dissection Tool*. James Madison University.

Kim, H., & Laskowski, M. (2018). The impact of blockchain technology on copyright protection. *International Journal of Law and Information Technology*, 26(3), 234–256.

Kiviat, T. (2015). A public blockchain case study. *Ledger*, 1, 35–39.

Krishnamurthi, R., & Shree, T. (January 2021). A Brief Analysis of Blockchain Algorithms and Its Challenges. In *Research Anthology on Blockchain Technology in Business, Health- care* (pp. 23–39). Education, and Government., DOI: 10.4018/978-1-7998-5351-0.ch002

Kumar, A., Saxena, D., & Singh, A. K. (2021, February). A Cryptography and Machine Learning Based Authentication for Secure Data-Sharing in Federated Cloud Services Envi- ronment. *Journal of Applied Security Research*, 17(7), 385–412. Advance online publication. DOI: 10.1080/19361610.2020.1870404

Kute, V. B., Paradhi, P. R., & Bamnote, G. R. (2009). A software comparison of RSA and ECC. *International Journal Computer Science Applications*, 2(1), 43–59.

LibP2P. Accessed: Jan. 2020. [Online]. Available: https://github.com/libp2p

Mahto, D., Khan, D. A., & Yadav, D. K. (2016, June). Security analysis of elliptic curve cryptography and RSA. In *Proceedings of the world congress on engineering* (Vol. 1, pp. 419-422).

Mahto, D., & Yadav, D. K. (2013). Network security using ECC with Biometric. In Quality, Reliability, Security and Robustness in Heterogeneous Networks: 9th International Conference, QShine 2013, Greader Noida, India, January 11-12, 2013, Revised Selected Papers 9 (pp. 842-853). Springer Berlin Heidelberg.

Mahto, D., & Yadav, D. K. (2015, February). Enhancing security of one-time password using elliptic curve cryptography with biometrics for e-commerce applications. In Proceedings of the 2015 third international conference on computer, communication, control and information technology (C3it) (pp. 1-6). IEEE.

Mahto, D., & Yadav, D. K. (2016). Security improvement of one-time password using crypto-biometric model. In Proceedings of 3rd International Conference on Advanced Computing, Networking and Informatics: ICACNI 2015, Volume 2 (pp. 347-353). Springer India.

Mahto, D., & Yadav, D. K. (2017). One-time password communication security improve- ment using elliptic curve cryptography with iris biometric. *International Journal of Applied Engineering Research: IJAER*, 12(18), 7105–7114.

Mahto, D., & Yadav, D. K. (2017). RSA and ECC: A comparative analysis. *International Journal of Applied Engineering Research: IJAER*, 12(19), 9053–9061.

Mahto, D., & Yadav, D. K. (2017). Secure online medical consultations using elliptic curve cryptography with iris biometric. *International Journal of Control Theory and Applications*, 10(13), 169–179.

Mingxiao, D., Xiaofeng, M., Zhe, Z., Xiangwei, W., & Qijun, C. (2017, October). A review on consensus algorithm of blockchain. In 2017 IEEE international conference on systems, man, and cybernetics (SMC) (pp. 2567-2572). IEEE.

Nakamoto, S. (2008). *Bitcoin: A peer-to-peer electronic cash system*. Satoshi Nakamoto.

Nelson, M., & Watson, C. (2022). *The State of the Merge: An Update on Ethereum's Merge to Proof of Stake in 2022*. ConsenSys.

."Networking Layer — Ethereum.org," Ethereum.org, (2023) [Online]. Available: ethereum.org/en/developers/docs/networking-layer/

."Nodes and Clients — Ethereum.org," Ethereum.org, (2020) [Online]. Available: ethereum.org/en/developers/docs/nodes-and-clients.

O'Dair, M., Beaven, Z., Neilson, D., Osborne, R., & Pacifico, P. (2016). Music on the Blockchain. Middlesex University, July.

Paech, P. (2017). Governance in Blockchain Technologies & Social Contract Theories. *Ledger*, 2, 49–78.

Rivest, R. L., Shamir, A., & Adleman, L. (1978). A method for obtaining digital signa- tures and public-key cryptosystems. *Communications of the ACM*, 21(2), 120–126. DOI: 10.1145/359340.359342

Savelyev, A. Blockchain in the monitoring of markets, in *Proceedings of the 2018 International Conference on Advances in Information Technology*, pp. 258-264, 2018.

Sedlmeir, J., Buhl, H. U., Fridgen, G., & Keller, R. (2020). The energy consumption of blockchain technology: Beyond myth. *Business & Information Systems Engineering*, 62(6), 599–608.

Singh, S. K., Azzaoui, A., Choo, K. K. R., Yang, L. T., & Park, J. H. (2023). Articles A Comprehensive Survey on Blockchain for Secure IoT-enabled Smart City beyond 5G: Approaches, Processes, Challenges, and Opportunities. Hum.-. *Centric Comput. Inf. Sci*, 13, 51.

Singh, S. K., Kumar, M., Tanwar, S., & Park, J. H. (2024). GRU-based digital twin framework for data allocation and storage in IoT-enabled smart home networks. *Future Generation Computer Systems*, 153, 391–402. DOI: 10.1016/j.future.2023.12.009

Singh, S. K., Pan, Y., & Park, J. H. (2022). Blockchain-enabled secure framework for energy-efficient smart parking in sustainable city environment. *Sustainable Cities and Society*, 76, 103364. DOI: 10.1016/j.scs.2021.103364

Singhal, S., Betgeri, S., & Singh, S. K. (2024). Strategies for Mitigating Security Concerns in IoT-Enabled Smart Cities. In Secure and Intelligent IoT-Enabled Smart Cities (pp. 239-273). IGI Global. -------

Swanson, T. (2015). Consensus-as-a-service: a brief report on the emergence of permissioned, distributed ledger systems. Report, available online, 28.

Szabo, N. (1996). Smart contracts: building blocks for digital markets. EXTROPY: The Journal of Transhumanist Thought,(16), 18(2), 28.

Tasatanattakool, P., & Techapanupreeda, C. (2018, January). Blockchain: Challenges and applications. In 2018 international conference on information networking (ICOIN) (pp. 473-475). IEEE.

Tschorsch, F., & Scheuermann, B. (2016). Bitcoin and Beyond: A technical survey on de- centralized digital currencies. *IEEE Communications Surveys and Tutorials*, 18(3), 2084–2123. DOI: 10.1109/COMST.2016.2535718

Walport, M. (2016). *Distributed ledger technology: Beyond blockchain.* UK Government Office for Science.

Wang, Y., Cai, S., Lin, C., Chen, Z., Wang, T., Gao, Z., & Zhou, C. (2019). Study of Blockchains's Consensus Mechanism Based on Credit, IEEE Access: Practical Innovations. *Open Solutions*, 7, 10224–10231. DOI: 10.1109/AC- CESS.2019.2891065

Zhao, Y., Zhang, X., & Zhang, Y. (2016). Overview of business innovations and research opportunities in blockchain and introduction to the special issue. *Financial Innovation*, 2(1), 1–10. DOI: 10.1186/s40854-016-0049-2

Chapter 16
SEBAKE-6G Secure Batch Authentication and Key Exchange for 6G-Enabled ITS

Praneetha Surapaneni
https://orcid.org/0000-0003-3822-7270
SRM University, India

Sailaja Chigurupati
https://orcid.org/0009-0009-5253-5799
KL University, India

Sriramulu Bojjagani
https://orcid.org/0000-0002-8801-4292
SRM University, India

ABSTRACT

As the cyber theft is increases, information safety and confidentiality are the major issues in wireless communications. 6G technology overcomes these difficulties to build a secured intelligent transportation system (ITS). Conventional transportation system faces high computation cost when road side unit (RSU) process each authentication vehicle request. In this chapter, to address this issue we introduced batch authentication and key exchange to secure user privacy and prevent attacks. To ensure message integrity, this system provides location-based information safely from RSU to vehicle without any changes. This system reduces the communication and computational costs. Simulation is performed using simulation of urban mobility (SUMO) simulator.

DOI: 10.4018/979-8-3693-8029-1.ch016

INTRODUCTION

VANETs are expected to be a fortunate technological advancement that will enhance the driving effectiveness and safety of roadway transportation systems as intelligent transportation systems advance (Al-Heety et al., 2020). Since all vehicles in VANETs have an on-board unit (OBU) which permits them to lialise with dispersed RSUs and other intelligent vehicles, all vehicles are regarded as intelligent vehicles (Tan and Chung., 2021).

The 6G era leverages widely available mobile broadband to improve network capacity in order to enable infotainment services and deliver high-quality OBU communications. Intelligent vehicles have the ability to broadcast information about traffic conditions and road conditions, such as accidents and congestion, to surrounding vehicles (Guerrero-Ibanez et al., 2018). This way, any receiver car that is nearby may become more aware of the driving conditions and adjust their route as needed. Likewise, upon entering their coverage territory, the RSUs disseminated location-based alerts to all VANET users (Tan and Chung., 2021). It is required for all VANET consumers and RSUs to enrol with the trusted authority (TA) using their authentic login credentials. The information shared via the VANET should be protected from different security threats by the suggested security services since V2V and V2R connections are conducted wirelessly (Vasudev et al., 2020). Because vehicles in VANETs move at the fastest possible speeds, 6G supports a mobility rate of 1000 km/h, while 5G only supports 500 km/h (Jiang et al., 2021).

As VANETs have grown, other new risks, such as privacy and security issues, have also emerged. Before using value-added services on VANETs, safe communication with regard to authentication, integrity, and secrecy must essentially be ensured. Furthermore, protecting user privacy with regard to location and identification is crucial (Zhang et al., 2022). Even though a number of authentication-based solutions have been created to deal with these problems, alot of them are limited to area-based services and do not apply to value-added services. It's obvious that appealing infotainment services have a big impact on users' capacity to engage in active VANET participation. Furthermore, it seems like there is not much time required for V2V and V2I communications given that the speed range of vehicles in VANET is 60 - 160 kilometres/hour (Guerrero-Ibanez et al., 2013). According to the DSRC standard, a vehicle sends location-based signals to the RSU and other adjacent vehicles every 150–300 ms, this means that if there are 200 or more vehicles in the RSU's coverage area, an RSU must confirm around 650 location-based messages (Ansari., 2021). The anticipated 6G data throughput is 1Gbps, which is very compatible with infotainment services on high-mobility 5G networks (Imoize et al., 2021). Consequently, a high-level computational load on RSUs should result from the individual verification of location-based signals. Once more, in the event of traffic congestion, this computational load may grow on RSUs, resulting in a bottleneck scenario (Singh et al., 2021). Notably, location-based communications make it challenging to create an anonymous authentication mechanism that is both computationally efficient and well-organized for infotainment services (Asuquo et al., 2018).

In order to create a safe interaction environment for VANET communications, an efficient anonymous batch authentication technique is devised in this paper together with anonymous key management schemes. The RSUs authenticate each vehicle user separately in the majority of the previous schemes, but in this system's architecture, an RSU can able to verify a batch of vehicle owners in its regional zone at once. As a result, the suggested batch authentication approach may greatly reduce the overall authentication overhead and increase the RSUs' computing efficiency in VANETs. The suggested solution does not require a certificate for anonymous protocols of authentication since it is built on fictitious identities. The previous batch authentication techniques have strong security strength, but they are unable to handle the issue of computing overhead in situations where the overall number of vehicles being used is quite big. Therefore, only the authorized vehicle users engage in improper behavior where the specific users will be identified and their true identities will be revealed to every other entity inside the network.

Thus, one of the ideal specifications for VANETs is conditional privacy protection. However, when an RSU wants to distribute concerning safety information to a subset of dynamic vehicles within its regional area, it must create a batch protocol for communication that requires little processing power (Surapaneni and Bojjagani., 2024). It makes sense that receiving safety-related alerts would help drivers drive more skilfully. Because of the very dynamic topology of VANETs, batch communication is likewise seen as a difficult issue. Because of its little communication and computing cost, the suggested is very helpful for vehicular applications that can withstand delays.

No vehicle user wants to provide sensitive information, such as their driving path or identity, across VANETs. Hence, in order to comply with the communication protocol, a vehicle must interact with other vehicles or RSUs using fake representations rather than true identities. Furthermore, it is imperative to build anonymous, low-cost batch and mutual authentication techniques in order to prevent some potential VANET attacks, such as impersonation and masquerading assaults.

This chapter's innovation is the creation of an efficient anonymous batch authentication technique created especially for VANETs. In contrast to conventional techniques, which validate vehicles one at a time, our suggested approach allows RSUs to concurrently validate several vehicle users inside their coverage region. This improves the computational efficiency of RSUs and drastically lowers the overhead associated with authentication, particularly in high-density vehicle networks. The chapter also presents an innovative method of conditional privacy protection with fake identities that does away with certificates in anonymous authentication methods.

The following is a comprehensive summary of this planned work's accomplishments:

1. A batch authentication methodology is suggested that reduces the authentication overhead of RSU.
2. An anonymous authentication system with little computational complexity is suggested.
3. To publish the location data collected by an RSU to the car with no incurring changes while exchange, an integrity protection protocol is offered.
4. Comparison of SEBAKE-6G security features with the existing schemes is done.
5. Simulation is performed using SUMO simulator.

The subsequent sections of this document have been created as follows.

The relevant work and network model are described in Sections II and III, respectively. Section IV represents the design objectives of the proposed scheme. Section V provides a full explanation of the proposed work's operations, while Section VI addresses potential security flaws in the suggested protocol. Section VII and Section VIII provides a performance analysis and simulation of the suggested approach. The conclusion of the study is found in section IX.

Related Work

The message distribution procedure should be carried out using a pseudonym in order to achieve anonymity (Didouh et al., 2022). As a result, attackers can intentionally send out a lot of false signals, worrying drivers and perhaps even causing accidents. Before being processed further, communications need to be validated in order to avoid being misinterpreted by attackers. Additionally, in an environment with high traffic density, an RSU may occasionally receive between 1000 and 2000 messages per second for verification within its communication range (Zhang et al., 2008). V2V verification technique is not well suited for VANETs because of this circumstance. Numerous batch authentication systems were put out to address this crucial problem and enhance automotive networks' security and computational efficiency.

(Abbade et al., 2020) identified the problems and difficulties in creating and deploying 6G networks. The authors (Yang et al., 20219) of then provided a succinct summary on possible 6G approaches. (Zhu et al., 2013) suggested a combined shared and batch authentication technique to increase the system's overall computing efficiency. However, because this approach requires more bilinear matching operations for the verification of digital signatures, the verification latency is higher. (Tzeng et al., 2015) updated the Identity-based batch verification technique. It requires ECC point multiplication and bilinear pairing operations, independent of the entire number of messages acquired per second. The approach also has a lower message drop percentage and communication time. (Jiang et al., 2016) created a hash function-based batch verification technique that is computationally effective. (Ferng et al., 2019) created a novel technique to determine the precise number of authenticated messages within a batch of communications. To increase the efficacy of message verification on the RSU side, this technique dynamically adjusts the amount of communications to be reviewed in a group of messages to a predetermined number.

Despite the fact that the aforementioned suggested approaches reduce communication and processing cost to some degree, in a high-density, large-scale VANET network, several VANET entities receive the same protected message. Accordingly, when many entities authenticate the same conveyed message, it not only wastes the processing capacity of every device in the vehicular environment but also causes the RSUs' message verification time to increase inadvertently. The fact that future secure messages are being held up while awaiting entity verification is regarded as a grave concern. (Horng et al., 2013) created a centralized level message authentication technique for TA in where the RSU verifies the message sent by the vehicle user in order to address the aforementioned problem (Zhang et al., 2008). Because each message is only verified once in the vehicle networks, the message authentication delay of the RSU is significantly reduced once the authentication of the message is completed. Authentication details for every verified message are provided consistently. However, the RSU is solely accountable for the authentication of communication messages inside its coverage zone due to this central level authentication. Consequently, the limited computational capacity of RSU causes a significant rise in processing load in high-traffic regions, which nonetheless causes message latency in the VANET system. (Wu et al., 2020) created a coordinated authentication system with cloud assistance to lower the computation overhead on RSUs. In order to increase the efficiency of message verification, (Lin et al., 2013) and (Liu et al., 2014) suggested cooperative batch verification systems. In order to effectively manage the processing power of the network's end nodes, (Zhou et al., 2019) proposed the idea of edge computing to social vehicular networks (Wazid et al., 2019).

Using both vehicle-to-vehicle and batch authentication with RSUs to secure communication, the BBAS-IoV scheme (Bagga et al., 2021) presents a novel batch authentication mechanism for IoV-based smart cities. The plan uses blockchain technology where blocks are mined using the PBFT consensus algorithm, especially through fog and cloud servers, to guarantee data authenticity and dependability.

By establishing a privacy-preserving message authentication system based on bilinear groups, the P2BA protocol (Feng et al., 2021) tackles the issues of efficiency and privacy in VANETs. For low-latency message validation, the technique leverages a zero-knowledge proof protocol, requiring only a single end-to-end wireless communication between the vehicle and RSU.

The problems in VANETs are addressed by (Xie et al., 2023) anonymous V2I and V2V authentication protocol, which uses ECC for safe and effective communication. By using batch verification to accomplish both V2I and V2V authentication, the protocol allows for smooth session key negotiation and eliminates the need for repeated authentication across many RSU domains. It presents a dynamic pseudo-identity feature embedding technique to track hostile vehicles and fend off desynchronization threats. Table 1 compares the advantages and disadvantages of the previous authentication methods.

Table 1. Comparative analysis of authentication methods in terms of merits and demerits

Author	Approach	Merits	Demerits
(Didouh et al., 2022)	Message distribution using pseudonym	Anonymity	Vulnerable to attacks that could send out false signals and result in mishaps.
(Zhang et al., 2008)	Batch authentication	Low communication cost	Increased RSU message authentication delay.
(Abbade et al., 2020)	Study of the difficulties in implementing 6G networks.	Highlights possible 6G technology approaches.	Unresolved authentication problem.
(Zhu et al., 2013)	Batch authentication	Computing efficiency	High latency for verification.
(Tzeng et al., 2015)	Identity-based batch verification	Low communication cost	Intricate cryptography processes.
(Jiang et al., 2016)	Batch verification	Computing efficiency	Less reliable compared to elliptical curve.
(Ferng et al., 2019)	Batch verification	Message verification	Authentication delay
(Horng et al., 2013)	TA-based authentication	Reduced message authentication	Limited processing power
(Wu et al., 2020)	Cloud-based authentication	Computing efficiency	Latency
(Lin et al., 2013)	Batch verification	Enhances the verification process	Delay in heavy traffic places.
(Zhou et al., 2019)	Batch verification	Fast message verification	Intricacy of the network architecture

continued on following page

Table 1. Continued

Author	Approach	Merits	Demerits
(Bagga et al., 2021)	Blockchain-based PBFT consensus BBAS-IoV scheme	Lowers processing cost	Network synchronization issues
(Feng et al., 2021)	P2BA protocol	Privacy preserving	High computation cost
(Xie et al., 2023)	Anonymous V2I and V2V authentication	Secure session key	Scalability

Network Model

Three key elements make up the vehicular networks system model: the vehicles, RSUs, and the TA. The TA has the authority to register RSUs and vehicle users in the VANET system. When it comes to processing, storage, security, and communication, the TA is generally more efficient. The RSUs use wireless communication with the vehicles and cable communication with the TA. Only vehicles within its communication range can communicate with an RSU. When authorized vehicles reach an RSU's geographic area, the RSUs are in charge of broadly broadcasting location-based signals to them. Only other vehicles and RSUs within their DSRC range can be connected to by the vehicles. It is necessary for every vehicle or RSU to pre-authenticate other entities in VANET before communicating with them. The below Figure 1 illustrates the proposed architecture.

Figure 1. Proposed architecture

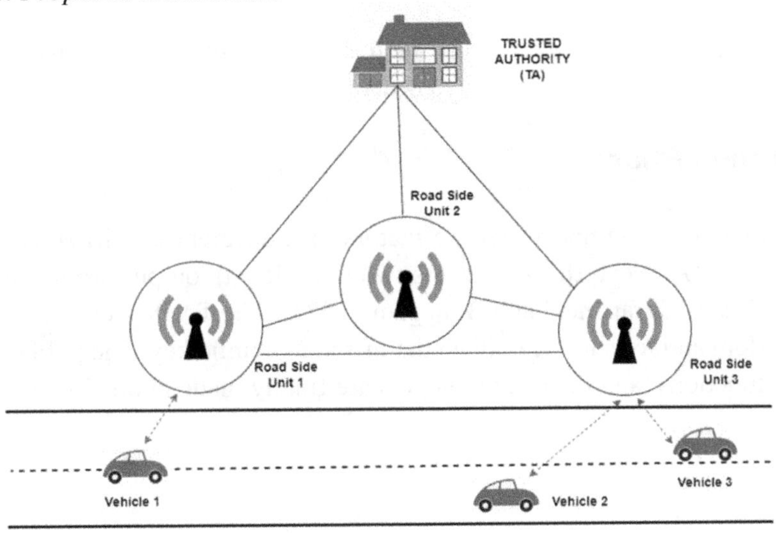

Design Objectives

The four security measures listed below must be met by a protected system in order to provide secure communications in vehicle networks.

- Preserving vehicle users' privacy: During the message communication process, vehicle users' private identities should be hidden from other vehicle users and attackers to protect their actual information.
- Mutual authentication: To protect the VANET system against impersonation attacks, the RSUs and VANET cars should authenticate one another. When communicating safety-related signals, mutual authentication between RSUs and vehicle users is crucial (Surapaneni and Bojjagani., 2023).
- Anonymous session-specific key interchange: Infotainment and safety-related messages in vehicle networks require anonymous key exchange in order to verify data confidentiality. The RSU can establish a secure communication environment for upcoming conversations with the use of short life session keys.
- Minimal complexity of computation and message delay: The suggested approach should focus on computational efficiency and message latency during communication due to the limited time availability in vehicle networks. The quantity of message verifications completed in a constrained amount of time grows with decreasing computing complexity and message latency.

PROPOSED SYSTEM

With the aid of the bilinear pairing methodology, an effective, mutual and batch authentication mechanism is presented in detail in this portion of the proposed work.

Initialization Phase

First, two prime numbers that are factors of a different specified number are chosen by the TA. Next, the TA selects two fixed-length output-producing secure hash algorithms (Surapaneni and Bojjagani., 2024). The TA then chooses a private key at random and uses it to calculate the matching public key. The public key, the two hash functions, and the prime integers are finally made public by the TA.

Vehicle Registration

- The owner of the vehicle provides the TA with their personal information, including name, phone number, and contact address, either in person or by a secure offline means. The TA then confirms that these credentials are genuine.
- For each vehicle owner, the TA chooses a private key at random, which is then used to calculate the matching public key. Only the owner of the car has access to this public key.
- After that, the TA creates a digital signature on behalf of the car owner. The significance of this digital signature lies in its ability to safeguard the integrity of any location-based messages that the car might transmit.
- For the vehicle's owner, the TA additionally generates a batch authentication key. In a batch procedure, this key will be utilized to authenticate the vehicle, enabling more effective communication.
- The TA assigns a false identity in order to preserve the anonymity of the vehicle's owner. This false identity is used for anonymous mutual authentication between RSUs and other vehicles. When speaking with other people, the car doesn't have to disclose its true identity; if needed, the TA is the only one who can connect the false identity to the genuine one.
- To further protect communications, the TA provides the vehicle owner with a re-encryption key.
- Lastly, a set of credentials, comprising the public key, digital signature, phony identity, batch authentication key, private key, and re-encryption key, are provided to the car owner by the TA. To maintain security, the owner of the vehicle must keep their secret key extremely private.

RSU Registration

- The TA chooses an RSU private key at random when the RSU is deployed. With this private key, the TA then computes the equivalent public key for the RSU.
- The RSU receives a batch code from the TA that is used for authentication.
- Lastly, the public key, batch code, and fictitious identity are given to the RSU by the TA together with a set of credentials. To guarantee that the RSU may function in an anonymous manner, the TA creates the false identity. The RSU protects its security by keeping the private key secret.

Mutual Authentication

Before communicating with other vehicle users or RSUs, a mutual authentication must be performed by both parties in order to guarantee secure connection.

- A vehicle user must first complete mutual authentication with an RSU in order to use location-based services from the RSU. The vehicle user first computes a unique value, which they then transmit to the RSU together with their public key and a false identity.
- The RSU verifies that the details provided satisfy a certain requirement after obtaining the information. The vehicle user is verified and approved if the need is met. The request is cancelled if it isn't.
- After calculating its own unique value, the RSU returns the value to the vehicle user along with its public key and fictitious identity.
- The driver of the vehicle verifies that the data obtained from the RSU satisfies the necessary requirements. In that case, the RSU is verified and approved. The procedure is terminated if not.

Key Exchange

The RSU and the vehicle user create and exchange a session key for safe future interactions once they have successfully completed mutual authentication.

- With the use of their personal data and the Trusted Authority's (TA) public key, the vehicle user initially determines a few essential components. Further computations are made by the user using various criteria and the RSU's fictitious identity. The vehicle user then sends the obtained data and a timestamp back to the RSU after completing these computations.
- After obtaining the data, the RSU runs its own computations to confirm that the information is legitimate. The RSU determines if a particular requirement is satisfied. It then verifies the integrity of the session key creation if the condition is met. The RSU produces the session key and sends it back to the vehicle user along with some other data after making sure everything has been confirmed successfully.
- After receiving the session key and associated data, the vehicle user verifies the timestamp to make sure the communication is current and authentic. After that, the vehicle user verifies another condition to make sure the session key is correct. The vehicle user accepts the session key for secure connection if all tests are successful. The key exchange procedure is stopped if it isn't.

Batch Authentication

A RSU's authentication workload may rise when numerous vehicle users seek location-based services at the same time. The RSU employs a batch authentication protocol to manage this effectively, enabling it to authenticate every user simultaneously rather than one at a time.

- All n vehicle users provide specific information to the RSU, including batch authentication keys and re-encryption keys.
- The RSU then uses the information gathered to verify a particular condition. If this requirement is met, it validates the legitimacy of every driver in the batch. By using this procedure, the RSU may authenticate every user simultaneously, lessening its effort and guaranteeing anonymous user authentication.

Preservation of Integrity

A digital signature is calculated by the sender in order to guarantee the message's integrity. In order to verify that the message hasn't been altered during transmission, this signature is used (Surapaneni et al., 2024).

- Based on some secret information and the substance of the message, the sender vehicle creates a digital signature. The message's integrity is confirmed by its signature, which is specific to it.
- The message is sent to the recipient by the sender vehicle once the digital signature has been generated. Included in the sent data are: the message, the false identity of the sender, the digital signature, in order to stop replay attacks, a timestamp an extra value associated with the confidential information of the sender.
- The recipient vehicle receives the message and uses a specific formula to determine whether the digital signature is legitimate. The recipient can be certain that the message is genuine and hasn't been tampered with if the computed result agrees with what it should be. The communication is regarded as authentic if all the checks are complete.

Analysis of Security Attacks

This section analyses a few potential security breaches against the suggested SEBAKE-6G system.

Man-in-the-Middle (MitM) Attacks

These involve an attacker trying to change or intercept a conversation between two people without the other person knowing. An attacker may attempt to intercept a vehicle's authentication message. Usually, this communication contains the public key of the vehicle, a fictitious identity, and an extra value pertaining to the vehicle's confidential data. Any attempt by the attacker to alter the public key or the false identity in this message that has been collected would be promptly detected by the receiving RSU. The message is verified by the RSU based on particular criteria. The verification is unsuccessful if the RSU determines that this requirement is not satisfied, i.e., the message has been changed. The authentication request is instantly denied by the RSU when it uses its verification mechanism to verify the message's integrity. If it doesn't match what is expected. To maintain secure connection, the RSU automatically ends the current authentication process and initiates a new one if tampering is detected. An attacker's ability to carry out a MitM attack covertly is practically non-existent because to this feature.

Guessing Password Attack

Sensitive information about the vehicle users or the RSUs is not included in the authentication message that is exchanged during the anonymous authentication process. This architecture guarantees that no personal information will be revealed, even in the unlikely event that the message is intercepted. Each vehicle is given a phony identity, and these identities are built in such a way that it is very difficult for an attacker to figure out the user's private key from just these identities. It's a difficult effort to guess the other secret parameters in the authentication procedure, even if an attacker is able to extract the private key from the fictitious identity. This is due to the fact that the security of these parameters is predicated on the ECDLP, a well-known challenging cryptography problem.

Replay Attack

In order to obtain illegal access, an adversary would attempt to intercept a legitimate session key, which consists of the session key itself, a timestamp, and a hashed value, and send it to the vehicle user again. If the timestamp is not out-dated, the car user will not accept the session key. The session key will be refused right away if the timestamp is out-dated. The attacker cannot change the associated hash parameter, which is exclusive to the session key and timestamp, not even if they succeed in creating a new timestamp. The vehicle user will reject the session key if this hash is incorrect. This guarantees that replay attacks are successfully repelled.

Impersonation Attack

An attacker tries to impersonate a legitimate vehicle user or RSU in an impersonation attack by constructing a legitimate false identity and public key for that entity. Secret parameters that are only known by the TA are used to generate the false identity and public key. An opponent can hardly extract the TA's secret keys from the false identity or public key because of the difficulty of the discrete logarithm problem. This significantly prevents impersonation attacks by making it exceedingly impossible to imitate an authorized user or RSU.

Performance Evaluation

This section discusses the computational cost and communication cost effectiveness of the suggested SEBAKE-6G systems.

Communication Cost

The overall communication overhead for key exchange and mutual authentication is computed in the SEBAKE-6G system. Thus, 3114 bits are required for the full communication cost. Table 2 lists the various schemes' communication costs. Figure 2 makes it abundantly evident that SEBAKE-6G communication costs are lower than those of the equivalent current schemes.

Table 2. Comparison of communication costs

Scheme	Communication Cost (Bits)
Gayathri et al., 2018	6048
Cui et al., 2019	5048
Wu et al., 2019	5440
Qi and Gao., 2020	4980
Feng et al., 2021	6144
Xie et al., 2023	3136
SEBAKE-6G	3114

Figure 2. Comparison of communication cost

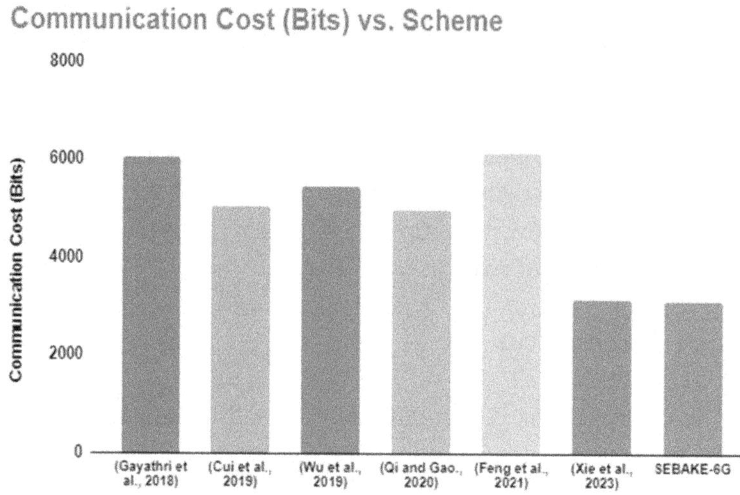

Computation Cost

This section's prior schemes and our devised method's thorough computational cost analysis are related. Computational cost is the amount of time needed to confirm the user count in anonymous mutual or batch authentication procedures. Numerous related authentication techniques are related to the computational cost analysis of the proposed mutual and batch authentication schemes. The computational cost of our suggested technique with different existing systems for batch and mutual authentication is displayed in Table 2. It can be seen from Table 3 that our suggested technique requires less computing power to carry out batch and mutual authentication for n users.

Table 3. Comparison of computation costs

Scheme	Computation Cost (seconds)
Gayathri et al., 2018	203.36
Cui et al., 2019	2.45
Wu et al., 2019	6.116
Qi and Gao., 2020	8.966
Feng et al., 2021	11.14
Xie et al., 2023	26.271
SEBAKE-6G	4.7

Figure 3. Comparison of computation cost

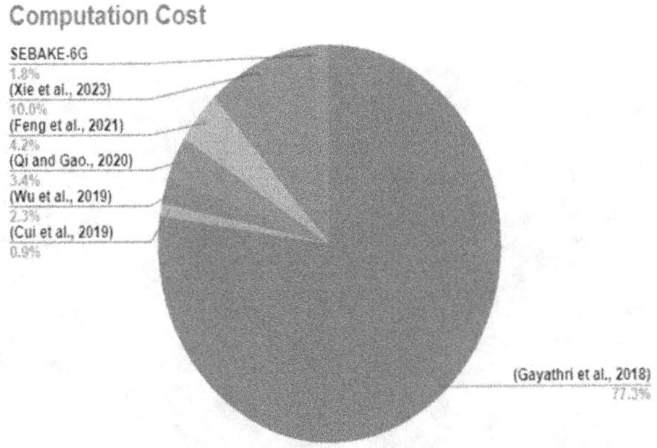

Simulation

Large road networks can be handled with the open-source, incredibly portable, tiny, and continuous road traffic simulation program known as SUMO (Simulation of Urban MObility). SUMO provides in-depth insights into traffic dynamics by modeling every vehicle separately and taking into account its interactions, motions, and behavior. By facilitating communication between vehicles and infrastructure, SUMO enables researchers to simulate and study how IoV-based traffic management systems might optimize traffic flow, lessen congestion, and increase safety (Surapaneni et al., 2024). The SEBAKE-6G scheme's SUMO simulation is shown in Figure 4 below.

Figure 4. SUMO simulation

CONCLUSION

The 6G era's difficulties with privacy, authentication, and computational overhead in vehicular ad hoc networks (VANETs) were addressed by SEBAKE-6G, a powerful and effective security framework that was described in this chapter. The suggested solution greatly lessens the computational load on RSUs while ensuring user privacy and secure communication through the use of batch authentication and key exchange procedures. The SEBAKE-6G technology offers a comprehensive solution to secure vehicle-to-vehicle (V2V) and vehicle-to-RSU (V2R) communications against a variety of security concerns, including man-in-the-middle attacks, through the use of mutual authentication, anonymous key exchange, and integrity preservation protocols. Batch authentication is a viable solution for high-density, large-scale VANET environments since it reduces the processing burden on RSUs and improves system efficiency overall. The SUMO simulator's simulation findings confirm that SEBAKE-6G is an efficient way to save communication and computational expenses without sacrificing strong security characteristics. Adopting cutting-edge technologies like 6G and putting secure communication protocols in place will be essential to guaranteeing the security, privacy, and dependability of future vehicular networks as demand for intelligent transportation systems grows. In order to accomplish these goals, SEBAKE-6G offers a scalable and secure solution for the upcoming generation of vehicular communications, which is a major step forward.

REFERENCES

Abbade, L. R., Ribeiro, F. M., da Silva, M. H., Morais, A. F., de Morais, E. S., Lopes, E. M., & Rodrigues, J. J. (2020). Blockchain applied to vehicular odometers. *IEEE Network*, 34(1), 62–68. DOI: 10.1109/MNET.001.1900162

Al-Heety, O. S., Zakaria, Z., Ismail, M., Shakir, M. M., Alani, S., & Alsariera, H. (2020). A comprehensive survey: Benefits, services, recent works, challenges, security, and use cases for sdn-vanet. *IEEE Access : Practical Innovations, Open Solutions*, 8, 91028–91047. DOI: 10.1109/ACCESS.2020.2992580

Ansari, K. (2021). Joint use of DSRC and C-V2X for V2X communications in the 5.9 GHz ITS band. *IET Intelligent Transport Systems*, 15(2), 213–224. DOI: 10.1049/itr2.12015

Asuquo, P., Cruickshank, H., Morley, J., Ogah, C. P. A., Lei, A., Hathal, W., Bao, S., & Sun, Z. (2018). Security and privacy in location-based services for vehicular and mobile communications: An overview, challenges, and countermeasures. *IEEE Internet of Things Journal*, 5(6), 4778–4802. DOI: 10.1109/JIOT.2018.2820039

Bagga, P., Sutrala, A. K., Das, A. K., & Vijayakumar, P. (2021). Blockchain-based batch authentication protocol for Internet of Vehicles. *Journal of Systems Architecture*, 113, 101877. DOI: 10.1016/j.sysarc.2020.101877

Cui, J., Wu, D., Zhang, J., Xu, Y., & Zhong, H. (2019). An efficient authentication scheme based on semi-trusted authority in VANETs. *IEEE Transactions on Vehicular Technology*, 68(3), 2972–2986. DOI: 10.1109/TVT.2019.2896018

Didouh, A., El Hillali, Y., Rivenq, A., & Labiod, H. (2022). Novel centralized pseudonym changing scheme for location privacy in V2X communication. *Energies*, 15(3), 692. DOI: 10.3390/en15030692

Feng, X., Shi, Q., Xie, Q., & Wang, L. (2021). P2BA: A privacy-preserving protocol with batch authentication against semi-trusted RSUs in vehicular ad hoc networks. *IEEE Transactions on Information Forensics and Security*, 16, 3888–3899. DOI: 10.1109/TIFS.2021.3098971

Ferng, H. W., Chen, J. Y., Lotfolahi, A., Tseng, Y. T., & Zhang, S. Y. (2019). Messages classification and dynamic batch verification scheme for VANETs. *IEEE Transactions on Mobile Computing*, 20(3), 1156–1172. DOI: 10.1109/TMC.2019.2952105

Gayathri, N. B., Thumbur, G., Reddy, P. V., & Rahman, M. Z. U. (2018). Efficient pairing-free certificateless authentication scheme with batch verification for vehicular ad-hoc networks. *IEEE Access : Practical Innovations, Open Solutions*, 6, 31808–31819. DOI: 10.1109/ACCESS.2018.2845464

Guerrero-Ibáñez, J., Zeadally, S., & Contreras-Castillo, J. (2018). Sensor technologies for intelligent transportation systems. *Sensors (Basel)*, 18(4), 1212. DOI: 10.3390/s18041212 PMID: 29659524

Guerrero-Ibáñez, J. A., Flores-Cortés, C., & Zeadally, S. (2013). Vehicular ad-hoc networks (vanets): architecture, protocols and applications. In *Next-Generation Wireless Technologies: 4G and Beyond* (pp. 49–70). Springer London. DOI: 10.1007/978-1-4471-5164-7_5

Horng, S. J., Tzeng, S. F., Pan, Y., Fan, P., Wang, X., Li, T., & Khan, M. K. (2013). b-SPECS+: Batch verification for secure pseudonymous authentication in VANET. *IEEE Transactions on Information Forensics and Security*, 8(11), 1860–1875. DOI: 10.1109/TIFS.2013.2277471

Imoize, A. L., Adedeji, O., Tandiya, N., & Shetty, S. (2021). 6G enabled smart infrastructure for sustainable society: Opportunities, challenges, and research roadmap. *Sensors (Basel)*, 21(5), 1709. DOI: 10.3390/s21051709 PMID: 33801302

Jiang, S., Zhu, X., & Wang, L. (2016). An efficient anonymous batch authentication scheme based on HMAC for VANETs. *IEEE Transactions on Intelligent Transportation Systems*, 17(8), 2193–2204. DOI: 10.1109/TITS.2016.2517603

Jiang, W., Han, B., Habibi, M. A., & Schotten, H. D. (2021). The road towards 6G: A comprehensive survey. *IEEE Open Journal of the Communications Society*, 2, 334–366. DOI: 10.1109/OJCOMS.2021.3057679

Lin, X., & Li, X. (2013). Achieving efficient cooperative message authentication in vehicular ad hoc networks. *IEEE Transactions on Vehicular Technology*, 62(7), 3339–3348. DOI: 10.1109/TVT.2013.2257188

Liu, Y., Wang, L., & Chen, H. H. (2014). Message authentication using proxy vehicles in vehicular ad hoc networks. *IEEE Transactions on Vehicular Technology*, 64(8), 3697–3710. DOI: 10.1109/TVT.2014.2358633

Qi, J., & Gao, T. (2020). A privacy-preserving authentication and pseudonym revocation scheme for VANETs. *IEEE Access : Practical Innovations, Open Solutions*, 8, 177693–177707. DOI: 10.1109/ACCESS.2020.3027718

Singh, S. K., Park, J. H., Sharma, P. K., & Pan, Y. (2021). BIIoVT: Blockchain-based secure storage architecture for intelligent internet of vehicular things. *IEEE Consumer Electronics Magazine*, 11(6), 75–82. DOI: 10.1109/MCE.2021.3089992

Surapaneni, P., & Bojjagani, S. (2023, December). SAKM-ITS: Secure Authentication and Key Management Protocol Concerning Intelligent Transportation Systems. In International Conference on Applied Soft Computing and Communication Networks (pp. 249-264). Singapore: Springer Nature Singapore.

Surapaneni, P., & Bojjagani, S. (2024). SAFE-Connect Secure Authentication and Fog Services in Vehicular Ad Hoc Networks for IoV. In Blockchain-Based Solutions for Accessibility in Smart Cities (pp. 335-358). IGI Global.

Surapaneni, P., & Bojjagani, S. (2024). Forging Digital Trust: The Collaborative Role of Cryptography and Blockchain in Data Security. In Ensuring Security and End-to-End Visibility Through Blockchain and Digital Twins (pp. 224-250). IGI Global.

Surapaneni, P., Bojjagani, S., Bharathi, V. C., Morampudi, M. K., Maurya, A. K., & Khan, M. K. (2024). A Systematic Review on Blockchain-enabled Internet of Vehicles (BIoV): Challenges, Defences and Future Research Directions. IEEE Access.

Surapaneni, P., Bojjagani, S., & Khan, M. K. (2024). VESecure: Verifiable authentication and efficient key exchange for secure intelligent transport systems deployment. *Vehicular Communications*, 49, 100822. DOI: 10.1016/j.vehcom.2024.100822

Tan, H., & Chung, I. (2021). Rsu-aided remote v2v message dissemination employing secure group association for uav-assisted vanets. *Electronics (Basel)*, 10(5), 548. DOI: 10.3390/electronics10050548

Tan, H., & Chung, I. (2021). Rsu-aided remote v2v message dissemination employing secure group association for uav-assisted vanets. *Electronics (Basel)*, 10(5), 548. DOI: 10.3390/electronics10050548

Tzeng, S. F., Horng, S. J., Li, T., Wang, X., Huang, P. H., & Khan, M. K. (2015). Enhancing security and privacy for identity-based batch verification scheme in VANETs. *IEEE Transactions on Vehicular Technology*, 66(4), 3235–3248. DOI: 10.1109/TVT.2015.2406877

Vasudev, H., Deshpande, V., Das, D., & Das, S. K. (2020). A lightweight mutual authentication protocol for V2V communication in internet of vehicles. *IEEE Transactions on Vehicular Technology*, 69(6), 6709–6717. DOI: 10.1109/TVT.2020.2986585

Wazid, M., Bagga, P., Das, A. K., Shetty, S., Rodrigues, J. J., & Park, Y. (2019). AKM-IoV: Authenticated key management protocol in fog computing-based Internet of vehicles deployment. *IEEE Internet of Things Journal*, 6(5), 8804–8817. DOI: 10.1109/JIOT.2019.2923611

Wu, F., Chen, Y., Chen, X., Fan, W., & Liu, Y. A. (2020). An adaptive dual prediction scheme based on edge intelligence. *IEEE Internet of Things Journal*, 7(10), 9481–9493. DOI: 10.1109/JIOT.2020.2997795

Wu, L., Sun, Q., Wang, X., Wang, J., Yu, S., Zou, Y., Liu, B., & Zhu, Z. (2019). An efficient privacy-preserving mutual authentication scheme for secure V2V communication in vehicular ad hoc network. *IEEE Access : Practical Innovations, Open Solutions*, 7, 55050–55063. DOI: 10.1109/ACCESS.2019.2911924

Xie, Q., Ding, Z., & Zheng, P. (2023). Provably secure and anonymous V2I and V2V authentication protocol for VANETs. *IEEE Transactions on Intelligent Transportation Systems*, 24(7), 7318–7327. DOI: 10.1109/TITS.2023.3253710

Yang, P., Xiao, Y., Xiao, M., & Li, S. (2019). 6G wireless communications: Vision and potential techniques. *IEEE Network*, 33(4), 70–75. DOI: 10.1109/MNET.2019.1800418

Zhang, C., Lin, X., Lu, R., Ho, P. H., & Shen, X. (2008). An efficient message authentication scheme for vehicular communications. *IEEE Transactions on Vehicular Technology*, 57(6), 3357–3368. DOI: 10.1109/TVT.2008.928581

Zhang, C., Lin, X., Lu, R., Ho, P. H., & Shen, X. (2008). An efficient message authentication scheme for vehicular communications. *IEEE Transactions on Vehicular Technology*, 57(6), 3357–3368. DOI: 10.1109/TVT.2008.928581

Zhang, S., Li, M., Liang, W., Sandor, V. K. A., & Li, X. (2022). A survey of dummy-based location privacy protection techniques for location-based services. *Sensors (Basel)*, 22(16), 6141. DOI: 10.3390/s22166141 PMID: 36015901

Zhou, Z., Chen, X., Li, E., Zeng, L., Luo, K., & Zhang, J. (2019). Edge intelligence: Paving the last mile of artificial intelligence with edge computing. *Proceedings of the IEEE*, 107(8), 1738–1762. DOI: 10.1109/JPROC.2019.2918951

Zhu, X., Jiang, S., Wang, L., & Li, H. (2013). Efficient privacy-preserving authentication for vehicular ad hoc networks. *IEEE Transactions on Vehicular Technology*, 63(2), 907–919. DOI: 10.1109/TVT.2013.2294032

Chapter 17
Integrating Blockchain IoT and 6G Technologies for Secure Efficient and Sustainable Smart City Applications Enhancing Urban Living Through Innovation

S. Cloudin
KCG College of Technology, India

M. Robinson Joel
https://orcid.org/0000-0002-3030-8431
KCG College of Technology, India

G. Manikandan
https://orcid.org/0000-0002-4323-8233
RMK Engineering College, India

I. Milcah Blessy
Kings Engineering College, India

ABSTRACT

Smart cities are revolutionised by integrating Blockchain, IoT, and 6G technologies, which improve sustainability, efficiency, and security. IoT permits real-time data

DOI: 10.4018/979-8-3693-8029-1.ch017

gathering and analysis from a variety of urban sensors, while blockchain guarantees data integrity and secure transactions. With 6G's lightning-fast connection, devices can communicate with one other with ease, facilitating better public services, energy optimisation, and intelligent traffic control. By fostering inventive solutions to urban problems and promoting environmental sustainability via resource efficiency, this synergy enhances the quality of life of inhabitants by fostering smarter, more responsive urban settings. When combined, these technologies change cities into intelligent, networked ecosystems that open up new possibilities for urban existence.

1. INTRODUCTION

Global urbanization is accelerating, and this is putting increasing pressure on cities' infrastructure, resource management, and general quality of life. As a result, innovative technologies are being used by smart city projects to make cities more habitable, sustainable, and efficient. Blockchain technology, the Internet of Things (IoT),(Madakkam et al., 2015) and 6G networks are key components of this revolution. The integration of these technologies promises to change urban living by improving security, efficiency, and sustainability. Each technology brings special skills to the table. Blockchain technology guarantees security, trust, and transparency in digital transactions by providing a decentralized and unchangeable ledger system. Blockchain technology (Yli-Huumo et al., 2016) can protect and simplify a number of applications in the context of smart cities, such as public transportation, energy management, healthcare, and public services. This is because it removes the need for central intermediaries and lowers the danger of fraud and data breaches. The Internet of Things (IoT) links physical objects with software and sensors to allow for the interchange and collecting of data in real time. Cities can more efficiently monitor and manage public services, environmental conditions, and infrastructure thanks to this connectivity. However, blockchain can offer strong security and effective data management solutions, which are necessary given the massive amount of data created by IoT devices.

The next generation of wireless networks, known as 6G networks, offer previously unheard-of speed, capacity, and ultra-low latency. These features are essential for enabling the enormous data flows and real-time processing that Internet of Things applications demand. 6G will enable smooth communication between billions of linked devices, enabling cutting-edge applications like real-time holographic communication, autonomous vehicles, and immersive augmented reality experiences. Data rates are predicted to reach up to 1 terabit per second. Smart cities may achieve higher efficiency and sustainability, better security and privacy, and better quality of life for their citizens by combining Blockchain, IoT, and 6G technology.(Nawaz,

F et al., 2020) This technological convergence opens the door to creative and interconnected urban living by offering a strong framework for tackling the intricate problems of contemporary urbanization.

1.2. Blockchain Technology

Although blockchain technology is most commonly associated with cryptocurrency, it has much more potential applications outside of virtual currencies. Blockchain provides a decentralized, immutable ledger system that can greatly improve the efficiency, security, and transparency of a range of urban applications in the context of smart cities. To tackle some of the most important urban issues, blockchain technology can be incorporated into smart city initiatives in the following ways. The decentralized and unchangeable ledger system of blockchain technology provides a strong foundation for improving the security, efficiency, and transparency of smart city applications. Blockchain technology can guarantee the integrity of information in a variety of industries, including energy management, transportation, healthcare, and public services, as well as secure digital transactions and sensitive data(Cheng, Q et al., 2024) protection in urban settings. Due to its decentralized design, which distributes data among numerous nodes to make it tamper-proof and dependable, it lowers the danger of fraud and data breaches. Additionally, smart contracts self-executing contracts that are directly programmed into the blockchain can be used to automate and streamline procedures like property transactions, utility billing, and maintenance services, which lowers administrative overhead and boosts operational effectiveness.

1.2.1 Enhanced Security and Trust

Blockchain's decentralized and immutable ledger architecture(Milcah Blessy et al., 2023) greatly improves security and trust in applications related to smart cities. Because of its decentralized nature, data is more resilient to manipulation and hacks since it is dispersed among numerous nodes. A safe and unchangeable chain of records is created by each transaction on the blockchain being encrypted and connected to its predecessor. For critical applications like digital identity management, financial transactions, and public administration, this ensures data integrity and reliability. Furthermore, residents can have secure digital identities via blockchain, protecting private data and simplifying access to local services. Blockchain increases confidence between individuals, companies, and governmental organizations by removing central points of failure and facilitating transparent, verifiable transactions.

Blockchain technology's as shown in Figure 1, it decentralized and unchangeable ledger system greatly improves security and trust in applications related to smart cities. By distributing data among several nodes, this architecture makes data extremely resistant to manipulation and cyberattacks. (Mantere, M. 2013, September) Data integrity and reliability are ensured by the encryption and chaining of records created between each transaction, which makes the records safe and unchangeable. Here are some more details about how blockchain technology improves security and trust.

Figure 1. Blockchain technology

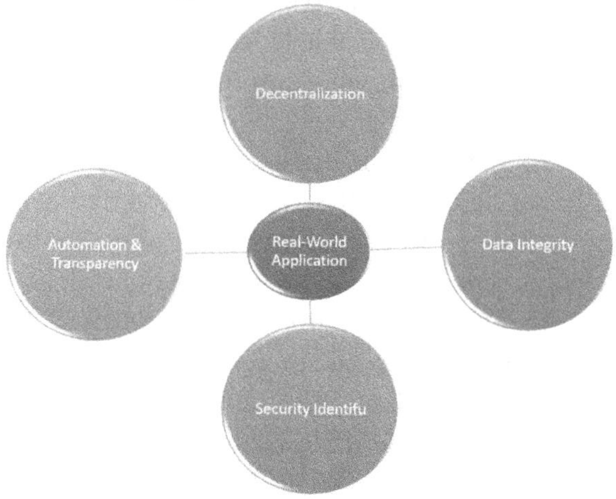

1.2.2. Real-World Application

By tackling important issues and improving urban living, the combination of blockchain, IoT,(Athinarayanan et al., 2023) and 6G technologies is set to transform smart cities in practical applications. Imagine a metropolis where blockchain protects the security and integrity of data transferred between Internet of Things (IoT) devices positioned all throughout the city(Joel et al., 2023). These sensor-equipped gadgets continuously collect and provide data about energy use, traffic movement, air quality, and other topics. This data can be transferred at lightning speeds with very little latency using 6G networks, allowing for real-time analysis and decision-making.(Coito, T et al., 2021)

For example, traffic signals adapt to the flow of traffic, minimizing pollution and maximizing congestion. Waste management systems reduce fuel consumption and increase efficiency by autonomously rerouting collection vehicles depending on current fill levels. By ensuring that transactions within these systems—like paying for energy use or public services are safe and transparent, blockchain helps to build confidence among people, service providers, and local government officials. Furthermore, agreements and transactions are automated using blockchain-powered smart contracts, which streamline operations and cut down on administrative overhead. Overall, by lowering resource waste and environmental impact, this integration not only increases the operational effectiveness of critical services but also fosters sustainability.

1.2.3 Automation and Transparency

The convergence of blockchain, IoT, and 6G technologies is transforming urban environments through automation and transparency. Practically speaking, real-time monitoring and administration of vital infrastructure, including waste management systems, electricity grids, and transportation networks, is made possible by automation powered by Internet of Things sensors.(Chui, M et al., 2010) For example, intelligent traffic control systems employ Internet of Things data to dynamically modify traffic signals, enhancing traffic movement and decreasing gridlock without the need for human involvement.

Blockchain technology guarantees transparency at the same time by generating an unchangeable, safe record of all transactions and data exchanges. Accountability is improved by this transparency in a number of areas, including supply chain management and governance. Blockchain makes it easier to track public spending in smart cities transparently,(Brauneis, R., & Goodman, E. P. 2018) ensuring that money is spent wisely and removing the possibility of fraud or poor management. Smart cities may operate at previously unheard-of levels(Fulci et al.,2017) of dependability, efficiency, and credibility by combining various technologies. Automation makes the best use of resources and delivers services more efficiently, but blockchain makes sure these processes are transparent, safe, and responsible. In the end, this combination makes cities safer, more sustainable, and more receptive to the demands of their citizens, all of which improve the quality of urban life.

1.2.4 Security Identify Management

In smart cities, where there are many connected IoT devices and digital services, security identity management is essential for protecting digital systems and networks. It includes authentication, in which devices and users confirm their identities using a variety of techniques such digital certificates, biometrics, and passwords. Authorization, which ensures the least privilege principle is respected, determines, after authentication, what resources or functionalities each entity can access based on preset policies and permissions. Furthermore, strong secure identity management incorporates accountability systems like real-time monitoring and audit logs that track access activity and quickly identify anomalies or unauthorized access attempts. By being proactive, we can reduce security risks and make sure that possible threats are addressed quickly.

Ensuring the security and dependability of vital infrastructure, such as electricity grids, public services, and transportation systems, is crucial in smart cities. Proper identity management not only safeguards confidential information but also boosts overall operational resilience. Cities may progress toward a safer and more sustainable urban future by integrating cutting-edge technologies and strict regulations to maintain a secure environment that fosters confidence among citizens, companies, and governing bodies.

1.2.5. Decentralization and Data Integrity

The fundamental ideas of decentralization and data integrity specify the dependability and security of blockchain technology. Fundamentally, blockchain maintains data integrity by arranging data into a network of linked blocks, each of which has a distinct cryptographic hash(Windarta et al., 2022) of the block before it. Because of this layout, any modification to one block would require changing all following blocks, which is computationally difficult and readily observable. This forms a chain that is resistant to tampering. This capability is essential for applications like financial transactions, supply chain management, and medical records where keeping an unchangeable record is essential.

Blockchain decentralization differs from typical centralized systems in that it distributes data storage and verification throughout a network of nodes instead of depending on a single entity. Every node in the network keeps a copy of the whole blockchain and uses a consensus method to take part in the validation process. Through the removal of middlemen and transparent transaction verification, this decentralized method not only increases system resilience against malicious assaults and failures but also cultivates participant confidence.

1.3. Internet of Things (IoT)

With the use of connectivity, the Internet of Things (IoT) as shown in Figure 2 is using common things to become intelligent, interconnected systems, thereby redefining how devices interact and exchange data. IoT devices automatically gather and communicate data. They range from wearable technology and domestic appliances to industrial sensors and smart city infrastructure. Real-time monitoring, analysis, and control made possible by this data boost productivity in a number of industries, including manufacturing, transportation, healthcare, and agriculture.(Chhipa, H. 2017) IoT facilitates innovation in consumer and industrial applications, improves decision-making processes, allows predictive maintenance, and manages resources better by combining sensors and connections.

IoT adoption is becoming more and more common, but there are drawbacks as well, such as security flaws, privacy issues with data, and the difficulty of managing many IoT ecosystems. To optimize the advantages of IoT while reducing haza(Thibaud, M et al., 2018) strong cybersecurity safeguards, interoperability standards, and moral data management procedures are crucial. IoT will have a greater and more significant impact on corporate operations, urban development, and individual lifestyles as it develops, creating a world that is more connected and productive.

Figure 2. Internet of Things (IoT)

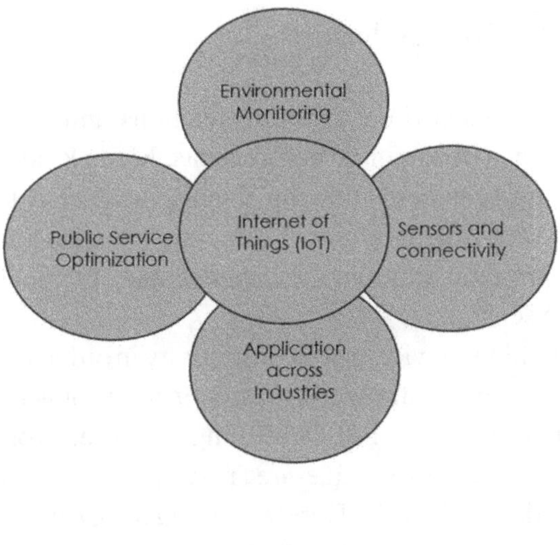

1.3.1 Environmental Monitoring

The use of IoT technology for environmental monitoring has completely changed how we monitor and control environmental conditions in a variety of ecosystems. Data on temperature, humidity, air quality, water quality, and other environmental characteristics can be gathered in real-time and sent to centralized systems for analysis by deploying Internet of Things (IoT) devices with sensors. This capacity makes it possible to monitor biodiversity, detect pollution in its early stages, and evaluate the effects of climate change. IoT-enabled sensors,(Gomes, J et al., 2019) for instance, are used in metropolitan areas to continually monitor greenhouse gas emissions and air pollutants. This data is used by policymakers to implement tailored mitigation methods. IoT devices are used in agriculture to optimize irrigation and fertilization techniques, save water, and increase crop yields(Chowdary et al., 2022) in a sustainable manner. These devices track soil moisture levels and nutrient content.

In a similar vein, IoT sensors monitor wildlife migrations and habitat conditions in natural settings, supporting conservation initiatives and protecting biodiversity. Incorporating IoT into environmental monitoring not only improves data gathering speed and accuracy, but it also makes proactive decision-making for environmental stewardship and sustainable resource management easier. The use of IoT technology in environmental monitoring has great potential to address global issues like climate change and leave a healthier and more resilient planet for coming generations.

1.3.2 Sensors and Connectivity

The Internet of Things (IoT) ecosystem functions and is effective because of sensors and connection, two essential components. Many kinds of sensors are built into Internet of Things devices, allowing them to collect data from the devices themselves or from their surroundings. Numerous characteristics, including temperature, humidity, pressure, motion, light, sound, and chemical compositions, can be detected by these sensors.

These Internet of Things devices need connectivity in order to send the data they've gathered to cloud platforms, centralized systems, or other connected devices for additional processing, analysis, and action. Depending on the needs of the application, IoT devices usually employ low-power wide-area networks (LPWAN),(Chaudhari et al., 2020) cellular networks (such 4G LTE and emerging 5G), Bluetooth, Zigbee, Wi-Fi, and low-power wide-area networks (LPWAN). IoT solutions encourage innovation in both consumer and industrial contexts, optimize resource management, increase operational efficiencies, and promote smarter decision-making by utilizing sensors to gather precise and timely data and connection to transfer this data effectively.

1.3.3 Public Service Optimization

The Internet of Things (IoT) has made it possible for public services to be delivered more effectively and responsively across a range of industries, greatly improving public service optimization. IoT technologies are used in urban settings to monitor and control vital infrastructure, including waste management, public utilities, and transportation networks. IoT sensors integrated into the infrastructure of smart cities gather data in real-time on waste levels, energy usage, traffic movement, and air quality, among other topics.

With the use of this information, city officials are able to make data-driven choices on things like waste collection routes that are dynamically scheduled based on fill levels, energy usage adjustments based on demand patterns, and traffic signal optimization to minimize congestion. Public services can function more pro-actively and effectively by deploying IoT-enabled technologies, improving service delivery while lowering costs and environmental effect. Urban dwellers' quality of life is eventually improved by this integration of IoT, which creates a more responsive and linked public service ecosystem in addition to increasing operational efficiency.

1.4. 6G Networks

The next step forward in wireless communication technology is represented by 6G networks, which have the potential to redefine connectivity standards and outperform the current 5G networks. With ultra-high speeds(Sun, X et al., 2022) predicted to reach terabits per second, 6G is likely to be deployed in the next ten years. This will allow for lightning-fast data transmission rates that will support cutting-edge applications like augmented reality, virtual reality, and real-time holographic communications.

Furthermore as shown in Figure 3, 6G promises to drastically cut latency to microseconds, improving responsiveness that is essential for uses like industrial automation, remote medical procedures, and driverless cars. 6G networks will increase the capacity to link an unprecedented number of devices simultaneously with a focus on large connectivity, making it easier to deploy Internet of Things (IoT) devices and smart city infrastructure widely. 6G also promises to use artificial intelligence to improve network management and resource allocation as research and development continue. All things considered, 6G networks are poised to bring in a new era of innovation, connection, and game-changing technologies that will influence the direction of the digital world in the future.

Figure 3. 6G network

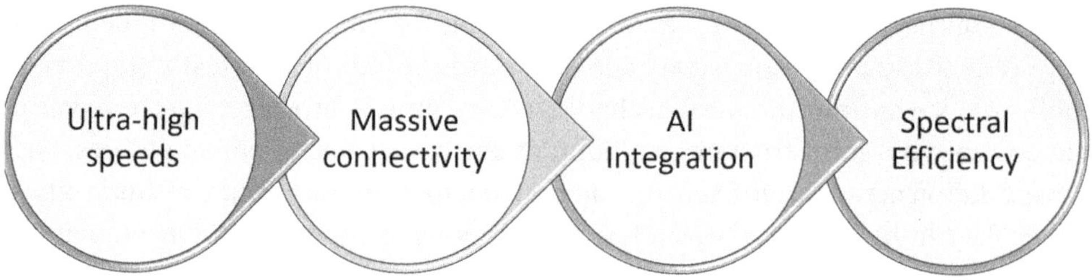

1.3.1 Ultra-High Speeds

It is expected that 6G networks would reach previously unheard-of ultra-high speeds, possibly outperforming the existing 5G networks by multiple orders of magnitude. With predicted throughput of terabits per second (Tbps),(Kiasaraei et al., 2023) 6G promises to completely transform the way that data is handled, processed, and used in a wide range of applications. Not only will these lightning-fast speeds allow for the instantaneous download of enormous files and high-definition material, but they will also provide unmatched clarity and responsiveness for new technologies like augmented reality (AR), virtual reality (VR),(Holly et al., 2021) and holographic communications.

Immersive entertainment experiences, like as virtual concerts and interactive games, have the potential to completely revolutionize user engagement. By utilizing 6G's high-speed capabilities, content can now be delivered in previously unthinkable ways. The development of 6G technology is anticipated to have a significant impact on technological innovation and worldwide connection, paving the way for a future in which connectivity will be more widespread, dependable, and rapid than in the past.

1.4.2 Massive Connectivity

One of the main features of 6G networks is massive connectivity, which is intended to accommodate an unprecedented number of devices that are seamlessly integrated at once. Expanding upon the capabilities of 5G, 6G seeks to facilitate a hyper-connected world in which billions of devices ranging from wearables and smartphones to sensors and self-driving cars can engage and communicate instantly, free from latency or congestion. For the Internet of Things (IoT) to function on a large scale and support smart city infrastructures, industrial automation, and customized digital experiences, this degree of connectivity is essential. For instance, in urban settings, 6G's capacity to manage enormous volumes of data from numerous IoT devices would improve city management systems, improving real-time public service, energy usage, and traffic flow optimization. Similar to this, 6G's strong connectivity will enable sophisticated automation processes in industrial settings, allowing for effective supply chain management, real-time machinery monitoring, and predictive maintenance.

6G networks promise to open up new possibilities in connection, altering industries, boosting productivity, and enriching daily life experiences with dependable and smooth digital interactions on a global scale by increasing the capacity to link a wide range of devices simultaneously.

1.4.3 AI Integration

With the potential to completely change how 6G networks function and engage with users and devices, AI integration is set to be a game-changer. (Plastino, E., & Purdy, M. 2018) 6G, the next phase beyond 5G, seeks to use artificial intelligence (AI) to improve network performance, optimize resource distribution, and allow for real-time intelligent decision-making. Network optimization and management is one of the main uses of AI in 6G networks. In order to guarantee peak performance, artificial intelligence (AI) algorithms can forecast demand variations(Manikandan et al., 2023), continuously examine network traffic patterns, and dynamically distribute resources like bandwidth and processing power. This proactive management strategy lowers operating costs, increases energy economy, and improves network stability. AI integration in 6G networks will facilitate personalized services and user experiences in addition to improving network operations.

AI systems are able to provide personalized information, services, and suggestions in real-time by analyzing user behavior, preferences, and environmental data. For applications where responsiveness and personalization are critical, such as augmented reality (AR), virtual reality (VR), and immersive gaming, this functionality is essential. All things considered, the incorporation of AI into 6G networks has the potential to build more intelligent, effective, and flexible communication systems that will spur industry-wide innovation, raise service standards, and open the door to new applications that will improve our quality of life, work, and social interactions in the digital age.

1.4.4 Spectral Efficiency

A key component of 6G networks is spectral efficiency, which focuses on making the most of the radio frequency spectrum that is available to satisfy the expanding need for high-speed data transmission and communication. 6G, which replaces 5G, seeks to improve spectral efficiency by utilizing cutting-edge methods and cutting-edge technologies. Higher spectral efficiency is anticipated from 6G networks through the use of sophisticated modulation techniques, astute antenna designs, and enhanced signal processing algorithms. Through these advancements, the restricted radio spectrum can be used more effectively, resulting in higher data throughput and network capacity without the need for extra spectrum allocation.

These methods enable the dynamic sharing of spectrum resources among various users and applications according to demand, location, and quality of service needs. 6G networks are able to effectively manage network resources in real-time and adjust to changing traffic patterns by dynamically distributing spectrum resources. Improving spectral efficiency in 6G networks is essential to enable the growth of Internet of Things (IoT) applications, connected devices, and new technologies like smart cities and driverless cars. 6G networks will make it possible to access higher data rates, lower latency, and more dependable connectivity by optimizing the use of spectrum.

1.4.5 Support for Advanced Applications

It is anticipated that 6G networks would offer strong support for a broad range of cutting-edge applications that demand never-before-seen levels of responsiveness, speed, and dependability. By providing ultra-high data transfer rates, extremely low latency, and huge connection to enable disruptive use cases across multiple industries, these networks seek to dramatically surpass the capabilities of current 5G technology. Supporting immersive and interactive apps like augmented reality (AR), virtual reality (VR), and mixed reality (MR) (Hagmann et al., 2010) is one of the main areas where 6G will shine. Whether for gaming, remote collaboration, or virtual tourism, these applications require ultra-low latency and ultra-high-speed data transfer to create smooth and lifelike user experiences.

With 6G networks, telemedicine and robotic surgery might be performed remotely with unprecedented accuracy and dependability because to fast data transfer and dependable connectivity. Similar to this, 6G's huge connectivity and AI integration support will improve industrial automation by improving production processes and facilitating effective supply chain management,(Jahid, A et al., 2023) real-time monitoring, and predictive maintenance. All things considered, 6G networks are positioned to open up fresh doors for economic expansion and innovation by enabling cutting-edge applications that will transform entire industries, raise global standards of living, and increase productivity. With further research and development, 6G has the ability to propel technological progress and establish new digital ecosystems, paving the way for a time when connectivity will be quicker, smarter, and more revolutionary than in the past.

1.5. Integrating Blockchain, IoT, and 6G for Smart Cities

Smart cities can experience a revolution in terms of operational efficiency, security, and sustainability through the integration of Blockchain, IoT, and 6G technology. The decentralized ledger of blockchain technology guarantees the transparency and integrity of data exchanges and transactions in smart city infrastructures. Managing a variety of IoT devices that gather and exchange real-time data on public services, energy consumption, urban transportation, and environmental factors requires this capability. In addition, 6G networks offer the incredibly fast speeds, extremely low latency, and extensive connectivity required to sustain the enormous IoT device ecosystem found in smart cities. This facilitates speedy decision-making and improves responsiveness in administering city services by enabling rapid data transmission and smooth connection across devices.

Table 1. Related work

Study Title	Author(s)	Focus	Key Findings
The Convergence of Blockchain, IoT, and 6G: Potential, Opportunities, Challenges and Research Roadmap	Researchers from arXiv 2021	Discusses the integration of Blockchain, IoT, and 6G, focusing on security, network scalability, and business models for sustainable smart cities	Outlines key roles of blockchain in 6G networks, addressing scalability and data privacy concerns in industrial IoT
Leveraging AI-enabled 6G-driven IoT for Sustainable Smart Cities	Gera, R. et al. 2023	Examines AI in 6G for enhancing IoT in smart cities	Emphasizes AI and blockchain-enabled smart grids and energy management within 6G networks
Artificial Intelligence Applications and Self-Learning 6G Networks for Smart Cities Digital Ecosystems	Ismail, L. & Buyya, R. 2022	Explores AI and blockchain applications in 6G for smart cities, focusing on distributed, self-learning networks	Proposes a taxonomy of AI, IoT, and blockchain applications in smart cities, identifying smart energy and traffic solutions
Blockchain-Enabled IoT Architecture for 6G Smart City Applications	Ali, R. & Shen, J. 2022	Analyzes blockchain's role in IoT systems for urban infrastructure	Demonstrates blockchain's potential in securing smart city IoT data and supporting real-time decisions in 6G

Smart cities can achieve increased resilience, sustainability, and public participation through the integration of Blockchain, IoT, and 6G technology.(Wu, L et al., 2016) This convergence not only improves urban living conditions but also creates the conditions for future innovations in urban development and administration, leading to smarter, more interconnected cities. The safe and transparent management of data and transactions is being completely transformed by the incorporation of blockchain technology into a wide range of industries and applications. Blockchain is essentially a decentralized ledger that records transactions over a network of computers. It is frequently connected to cryptocurrencies like Bitcoin. Every transaction is safely encrypted and connected to other transactions, creating a chain of blocks that are organized chronologically and impenetrable to manipulation. Blockchain is proven to be extremely useful in industries outside of banking since it can improve security, traceability, and transparency. Blockchain, for example, may follow the path of items from manufacture to delivery in supply chain management, guaranteeing authenticity and lowering the risk of fraud or counterfeit goods.

6G technology, with its unmatched connectivity, speed, and responsiveness, is the next step towards improving smart cities as shown in Figure 4. 6G networks are anticipated to enable ultra-high-speed data transfer rates, possibly approaching terabits per second, with extremely low latency in the range of microseconds, building on the foundations set by 5G. (Shafi, M., et al., 2017) These developments are critical to the maintenance of a large-scale Internet of Things (IoT) network and to the provision of real-time interactions required for applications in smart cities. Moreover, the exponential expansion of IoT devices and sensors positioned throughout smart cities will be facilitated by 6G's huge communication capabilities. For the integration of several technologies all of which depend on dependable, high-bandwidth communication networks such as smart grids, environmental monitoring systems, and healthcare solutions, this scalability is crucial.

Figure 4. Overview of smart city

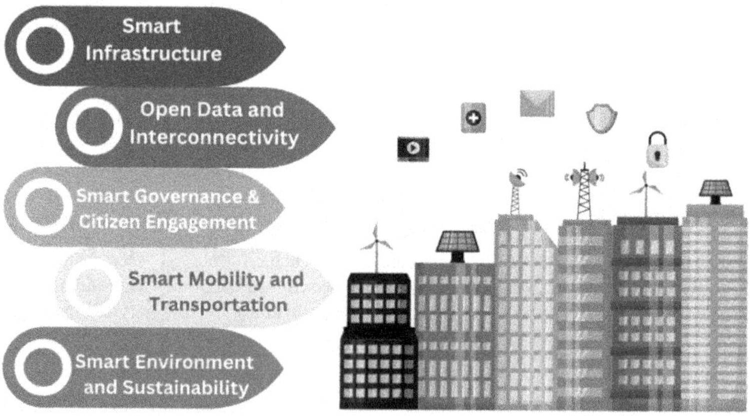

1.5.1 Efficiency

First of all, the decentralized and secure nature of Blockchain technology guarantees efficiency.(Muzylyov, D., & Shramenko, N. 2019) It improves confidence and transparency in all aspects of smart city infrastructure transactions, from supply chain management to the automation of administrative procedures like property transfers and permit applications. Blockchain simplifies processes, lowers costs, and speeds up transaction times by doing away with middlemen and lowering the possibility of mistakes or fraud. This effectiveness is especially useful in industries like healthcare, where high standards of data integrity and auditability are necessary. Blockchain technology can safely manage patient records and guarantee privacy compliance.

1.5.2 Sustainability

One of the main advantages of incorporating Blockchain, IoT, and 6G technology into applications for smart cities is sustainability, which encourages eco-friendly (Mallett, R. K. 2012) behavior and effective resource management. Sensor-equipped and networked via 6G, Internet of Things (IoT) devices constantly track and analyze resource utilization, energy consumption, and environmental conditions. Cities may minimize their environmental impact by optimizing energy distribution, cutting waste, and improving resource management with the use of this real-time data.

Blockchain technology provides safe and transparent record-keeping for processes and transactions, which further improves sustainability. For instance, blockchain can make it easier to trade renewable energy credits in the energy management industry and guarantee that data about energy use is reliable and unchangeable. In addition to promoting the use of renewable energy sources, this aids in monitoring and lowering carbon emissions. The development of smart grids, where energy consumption can be balanced and maximized based on real-time supply and demand data, is made possible by the integration of various technologies.

Water resources can be preserved by using smart water management systems, which can identify leaks and optimize irrigation. Additionally, by streamlining collection routes and recycling procedures, intelligent waste management systems can lower trash and raise recycling rates. By implementing more sustainable practices, increasing resource efficiency, and lowering their environmental effect, smart cities enabled by blockchain, IoT, and 6G can contribute to a more sustainable and healthy urban future.

1.5.3 Improved Quality of Life

Urban residents' quality of life is greatly improved by integrating Blockchain, IoT, and 6G technology into smart city applications, which provide more sustainable, efficient, and responsive urban settings. Connected via lightning-fast 6G networks, Internet of Things (IoT) devices allow for real-time control and monitoring of city services including public safety, healthcare, and transportation. As a result, there is less traffic, commute times are shortened, and car emissions are reduced, which improves air quality and traffic management. Data security and integrity are guaranteed by blockchain technology, which is essential for sensitive data-related applications like identity management and healthcare. Blockchain enables citizens to have better access to healthcare services, ensuring fast and accurate treatment, by enabling safe and transparent access to health records. (Jayabalan, M., & O'Daniel, T. 2017)

Additionally, Blockchain's capacity to enable safe transactions and automate procedures via smart contracts improves the dependability and efficiency of public services, including social and utility management, by cutting down on red tape and enhancing service delivery. Advanced applications like augmented reality, (Craig, A. B. 2013) remote healthcare, and smart home technologies are supported by 6G networks' high-speed connectivity, which makes daily living more connected and convenient. Improved connectivity makes it possible for smart gadgets to integrate seamlessly, giving inhabitants easy access to services, control over their homes, and health monitoring. Furthermore, city planners may make well-informed judgments on infrastructure development with the support of real-time data analytics powered by IoT and 6G, guaranteeing that urban growth(Gera, B et al., 2023) is sustainable and satisfies population needs.

1.5.4 Security and Privacy

Smart city apps that incorporate Blockchain, IoT, and 6G technologies greatly improve security and privacy, resolving some of the most important issues with urban technology implementation. The decentralized and unchangeable ledger of blockchain technology(Pilkington, M. 2016) guarantees the security and transparency of data transfers. Applications needing high standards of data integrity and trust, like supply chain management, financial transactions, and identity verification, will especially benefit from this. Blockchain improves the security of vital infrastructure and sensitive data by thwarting manipulation and unwanted access.

Massive volumes of data are collected and sent in real time by IoT devices when they are connected to 6G networks. 6G's high-speed, low-latency capabilities guarantee fast, secure data transmission while lowering the possibility of interception or delays that could jeopardize security. Data is further protected during transmission between devices and central systems by sophisticated authentication and encryption procedures. Furthermore, real-time threat detection and response are made possible by the integration of AI with 6G networks, detecting and averting possible security breaches before they have a chance to inflict damage. By using these technologies, privacy is also greatly enhanced. Because blockchain is decentralized and uses smart contracts to restrict access and usage rights, people can have more control over their personal data.

1.5.5 Operational Optimization

One major advantage of incorporating blockchain technology into smart city applications is operational optimization. Through the use of smart contracts self-executing contracts that have the terms of the agreement explicitly put into code Blockchain can expedite transactions and automate procedures. Because of this automation, there is less need for manual intervention, which minimizes the possibility of human error and reduces administrative overhead. Because smart contracts record transactions on an immutable ledger that is available to all relevant parties, they guarantee transparency and dependability.

Transparency fosters confidence among stakeholders and improves the effectiveness of operations in a number of areas, such as financial transactions, public services, and supply chain management. For example, blockchain can be used in a smart city to automate utility billing and payment procedures, guarantee the safe and effective transfer of property titles, and enable the open distribution of public resources. Blockchain's capacity to streamline these processes not only increases transaction dependability but also frees up city officials to work on more strategic projects, which makes the urban environment more responsive and efficient overall.

1.5.6 Data Management

IoT device and 6G network integration greatly improves data management in smart cities. Urban surroundings are filled with Internet of Things (IoT) sensors that are used to collect data in real time on a variety of parameters, such as energy use, traffic patterns, and air quality. With this data, city administrators can keep an eye on things and react appropriately to changing circumstances since it gives them a complete and current view of how the city is run. The introduction of 6G networks offers low-latency communication and ultra-high-speed data transfer, both of which are essential for managing the enormous volumes of data produced by IoT devices. (Rathore, M. et al., 2016) These networks make it possible for data to be transferred quickly from sensors to central systems, which speeds up decision-making and improves responsiveness in the administration of city services.

For example, energy management systems can more effectively balance supply and demand, cutting waste and fostering sustainability, while traffic management systems can use real-time data to modify traffic lights and lessen congestion. Additionally, IoT and 6G work better together to improve predictive analytics, which can identify possible problems before they become serious ones. For the purpose of managing resources, keeping the public safe, and sustaining infrastructure, this predictive skill is vital. City managers can improve the overall efficiency and quality of urban living by using proactive measures with faster data processing and real-time information.

1.5.7. Resource Allocation

The integration of real-time data insights from IoT devices and the fast transmission capabilities of 6G networks significantly improves resource allocation in smart city infrastructures. Cities can more cost-effectively and sustainably distribute vital resources like energy, water, and transportation services thanks to these technology. IoT-enabled smart grids,(Goudarzi, A et al., 2022) for instance, have the ability to track patterns in energy usage in real-time, allowing for accurate modifications to energy distribution and a decrease in waste. A balanced and effective energy supply can be ensured by directing energy during peak usage periods to where it is most needed and storing or redistributing excess energy. In a similar vein, real-time data-driven irrigation schedule optimization,(Zhao, H et al., 2023) leak detection, and use monitoring are all possible features of smart water management systems that help save money and conserve water.

Real-time data from IoT sensors integrated into cars, highways, and public transportation systems can enhance traffic flow, lessen congestion, and boost the effectiveness of public transportation. Transportation services can be made both efficient and responsive to the demands of the city's citizens by modifying public transit timetables to match demand and dynamically adjusting traffic lights based on traffic patterns. Smart cities can increase operational efficiency and sustainability by making well-informed decisions about resource allocation by utilizing the capabilities of IoT and 6G technology(Guo, F et al., 2021) This ensures that vital services are reliably and effectively handled, which raises inhabitants' quality of life in addition to resulting in significant cost savings.

1.6 Advantage

By combining Blockchain, IoT, and 6G technologies, smart city applications may be developed in a secure, effective, and sustainable manner, improving urban living through innovation and connectivity. Blockchain ensures data integrity, lowers the possibility of fraud and tampering, and offers a transparent and safe platform for managing transactions and data. Applications like financial transactions, identification verification, and public records management depend on this. IoT devices that are fitted with a variety of sensors collect data in real time on urban metrics such as energy use, traffic patterns, and air quality. When transferred via 6G networks that are fast and have low latency, this data enables quick decision-making(Provost, F., & Fawcett, T. 2013) and real-time responsiveness in the management of city services.

Figure 5. Advantages of 6G and IoT in Smart Cities

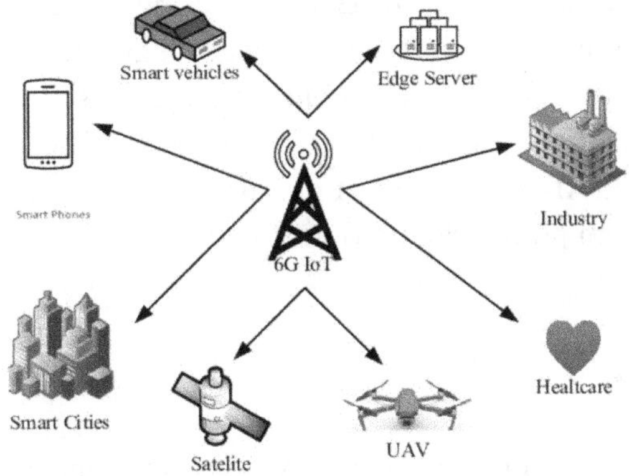

When these technologies are combined, operational optimization results from blockchain's capacity to automate procedures through smart contracts, which lowers administrative overhead and improves reliability. The integration of IoT and 6G networks enhances data administration and resource distribution, facilitating more effective utilization of energy, water, and transportation services through real-time insights. This improves cost-effectiveness while also advancing sustainability through waste reduction and resource conservation. Furthermore, 6G networks' improved connectivity and data analytics powers enable cutting-edge(Zhuang, K et al., 2021) applications like smart grids, driverless cars, and infrastructure maintenance that anticipates needs before they arise. Urban environments that are safer, more effective, and resilient are enhanced by these advancements.

1.7 Disadvantage

Although incorporating Blockchain, IoT, and 6G technology into smart city applications has many benefits, there are a number of drawbacks and difficulties that must be taken into consideration. The high expense of deploying and maintaining these cutting-edge technologies is one major disadvantage. The costly infrastructure needed for blockchain systems, IoT devices, and 6G networks may prevent their widespread adoption in cities due to financial constraints. Furthermore, the intricacy of combining these technologies may provide difficulties for their implementation, necessitating a high level of coordination amongst multiple parties and specialized knowledge. The widespread usage of IoT devices and the massive amounts of data they produce also give rise to privacy and security issues. Although blockchain offers improved security and transparency, concerns around data privacy and potential misuse are brought up by the vast amount of data that IoT devices collect.

Although it might be difficult to handle on a big scale, ensuring strong data protection procedures and compliance with privacy legislation is crucial. Moreover, the dependence on fast 6G networks creates security and dependability risks for the network. The operation of smart city apps can be significantly impacted by any outage or cyberattack(Al-Mohannadi et al., 2016) on the network infrastructure, affecting anything from public safety to traffic control.

2. CONCLUSION

In summary, the incorporation of Blockchain, IoT, and 6G technologies into smart city applications presents a revolutionary strategy for augmenting urban life via safe, effective, and environmentally friendly advancements. IoT devices enable real-time monitoring and administration of urban resources, 6G networks offer the high-speed connectivity needed to support these technologies, and blockchain offers a transparent and safe framework for managing data and transactions. When combined, they maximize operational effectiveness, enhance resource allocation, and promote sustainable behaviors, greatly enhancing the standard of living for city dwellers. To fully reap the rewards of these cutting-edge technologies, it is necessary to handle the related difficulties, which include expensive implementation costs, privacy issues, security risks, and interoperability problems. By solving these challenges, cities can open the door to an increasingly intelligent, connected, and resilient urban future where technological breakthroughs will inevitably improve the quality of life for all residents.

Furthermore, the amalgamation of these technologies facilitates the advancement of sophisticated applications like self-driving cars, intelligent energy systems, and anticipatory maintenance, so augmenting the security, effectiveness, and adaptability of metropolitan settings. By enabling city planners to make well-informed decisions, improved connectivity and data analytics skills guarantee that infrastructure development is sustainable and fulfills the demands of the expanding urban population. To fully reap the rewards of these cutting-edge technology, it is imperative to overcome the corresponding difficulties. Widespread adoption may be hampered by high implementation costs, necessitating creative funding sources and public-private partnerships. Careful management of privacy and security issues is necessary to safeguard sensitive data and guarantee adherence to rules.

REFERENCES

Al-Mohannadi, H., Mirza, Q., Namanya, A., Awan, I., Cullen, A., & Disso, J. (2016, August). Cyber-attack modeling analysis techniques: An overview. In *2016 IEEE 4th international conference on future internet of things and cloud workshops (FiCloudW)* (pp. 69-76). IEEE.

Ali, R., & Shen, J. (2022). Blockchain-enabled IoT architecture for 6G smart city applications. *IEEE Communications Magazine*.

Athinarayanan, S., Selvi, R., Rajakumari, K., Arunadevi, R., & Joel, M. R. (2023, December). An Advanced Strategy for Efficient Agricultural Production using Machine Learning. In *2023 2nd International Conference on Automation, Computing and Renewable Systems (ICACRS)* (pp. 680-686). IEEE. DOI: 10.1109/ICACRS58579.2023.10405182

Blessy, I. M., Manikandan, G., & Joel, M. R. (2023, December). Blockchain Technology's Role in an Electronic Voting System for Developing Countries to Produce Better Results. In *2023 3rd International Conference on Innovative Mechanisms for Industry Applications (ICIMIA)* (pp. 283-287). IEEE.

Brauneis, R., & Goodman, E. P. (2018). Algorithmic transparency for the smart city. *Yale JL & Tech.*, 20, 103.

Chaudhari, B. S., Zennaro, M., & Borkar, S. (2020). LPWAN technologies: Emerging application characteristics, requirements, and design considerations. *Future Internet*, 12(3), 46. DOI: 10.3390/fi12030046

Cheng, Q., Gong, Y., Qin, Y., Ao, X., & Li, Z. (2024). Secure Digital Asset Transactions: Integrating Distributed Ledger Technology with Safe AI Mechanisms. *Academic Journal of Science and Technology*, 9(3), 156–161. DOI: 10.54097/2qhab557

Chhipa, H. (2017). Nanofertilizers and nanopesticides for agriculture. *Environmental Chemistry Letters*, 15(1), 15–22. DOI: 10.1007/s10311-016-0600-4

Chowdary, V. T., Joel, M. R., Ebenezer, V., Edwin, B., Thanka, R., & Jeyaraj, A. (2022, March). A Novel Approach for Effective Crop Production using Machine Learning. In *2022 International Conference on Electronics and Renewable Systems (ICEARS)* (pp. 1143-1147). IEEE. DOI: 10.1109/ICEARS53579.2022.9751798

Chui, M., Loffler, M., & Roberts, R. (2010). *The internet of things*. McKinsey Global Institute.

Coito, T., Firme, B., Martins, M. S., Vieira, S. M., Figueiredo, J., & Sousa, J. M. (2021). Intelligent sensors for real-Time decision-making. *Automation*, 2(2), 62–82. DOI: 10.3390/automation2020004

Convergence of Blockchain, IoT, and 6G: Potential, Opportunities, Challenges, and Research Roadmap. (2021). arXiv.

Craig, A. B. (2013). Understanding augmented reality: Concepts and applications.

Fulci, C., Rotili, D., De Luca, A., Stella, L., Morozzo della Rocca, B., Forgione, M., Di Paolo, V., Mai, A., Falconi, M., Quintieri, L., & Caccuri, A. M. (2017). A new nitrobenzoxadiazole-based GSTP1-1 inhibitor with a previously unheard of mechanism of action and high stability. *Journal of Enzyme Inhibition and Medicinal Chemistry*, 32(1), 240–247. DOI: 10.1080/14756366.2016.1247059 PMID: 28097896

Gera, B., Raghuvanshi, Y. S., Rawlley, O., Gupta, S., Dua, A., & Sharma, P. (2023). Leveraging AI-enabled 6G-driven IoT for sustainable smart cities. *International Journal of Communication Systems*, 36(16), e5588. DOI: 10.1002/dac.5588

Gera, R., et al. (2023). Leveraging AI-enabled 6G-driven IoT for sustainable smart cities. *International Journal of Distributed and Connected Systems*.

Gomes, J. B., Rodrigues, J. J., Rabêlo, R. A., Kumar, N., & Kozlov, S. (2019). IoT-enabled gas sensors: Technologies, applications, and opportunities. *Journal of Sensor and Actuator Networks*, 8(4), 57. DOI: 10.3390/jsan8040057

Goudarzi, A., Ghayoor, F., Waseem, M., Fahad, S., & Traore, I. (2022). A survey on IoT-enabled smart grids: Emerging, applications, challenges, and outlook. *Energies*, 15(19), 6984. DOI: 10.3390/en15196984

Guo, F., Yu, F. R., Zhang, H., Li, X., Ji, H., & Leung, V. C. (2021). Enabling massive IoT toward 6G: A comprehensive survey. *IEEE Internet of Things Journal*, 8(15), 11891–11915. DOI: 10.1109/JIOT.2021.3063686

Hagmann, P., Cammoun, L., Gigandet, X., Gerhard, S., Grant, P. E., Wedeen, V., & Sporns, O. (2010). MR connectomics: Principles and challenges. *Journal of Neuroscience Methods*, 194(1), 34–45. DOI: 10.1016/j.jneumeth.2010.01.014 PMID: 20096730

Holly, M., Pirker, J., Resch, S., Brettschuh, S., & Gütl, C. (2021). Designing VR experiences–expectations for teaching and learning in VR. *Journal of Educational Technology & Society*, 24(2), 107–119.

Ismail, L., & Buyya, R. (2022). Artificial Intelligence Applications and Self-Learning 6G Networks for Smart Cities Digital Ecosystems. *Sensors (Basel)*, 22(15), 5750. DOI: 10.3390/s22155750 PMID: 35957307

Jahid, A., Alsharif, M. H., & Hall, T. J. (2023). The convergence of Blockchain, IoT and 6G: Potential, opportunities, challenges and research roadmap. *Journal of Network and Computer Applications*, 217, 103677. DOI: 10.1016/j.jnca.2023.103677

Jayabalan, M., & O'Daniel, T. (2017, November). Continuous and transparent access control framework for electronic health records: A preliminary study. In *2017 2nd International conferences on Information Technology, Information Systems and Electrical Engineering (ICITISEE)* (pp. 165-170). IEEE. DOI: 10.1109/ICITISEE.2017.8285487

Joel, M. R., Manikandan, G., & Bhuvaneswari, G. (2023, March). An Analysis of Security Challenges in Internet of Things (IoT) based Smart Homes. In *2023 Second International Conference on Electronics and Renewable Systems (ICEARS)* (pp. 490-497). IEEE. DOI: 10.1109/ICEARS56392.2023.10085106

Kiasaraei, M. M., Nikitopoulos, K., & Tafazolli, R. (2023). Towards Ultra-Power-Efficient, Tbps Wireless Systems via Analogue Processing: Existing Approaches, Challenges and Way Forward. *IEEE Communications Surveys and Tutorials.*

Madakam, S., Ramaswamy, R., & Tripathi, S. (2015). Internet of Things (IoT): A literature review. *Journal of Computer and Communications*, 3(5), 164–173. DOI: 10.4236/jcc.2015.35021

Mallett, R. K. (2012). Eco-guilt motivates eco-friendly behavior. *Ecopsychology*, 4(3), 223–231. DOI: 10.1089/eco.2012.0031

Manikandan, G., Bhuvaneswari, G., & Joel, M. R. (2023, August). Artificial Intelligence to the Assessment, Monitoring, and Forecasting of Drought in Developing Countries. In *2023 International Conference on Circuit Power and Computing Technologies (ICCPCT)* (pp. 886-892). IEEE. DOI: 10.1109/ICCPCT58313.2023.10245072

Mantere, M. (2013, September). Stock market manipulation using cyberattacks together with misinformation disseminated through social media. In *2013 International Conference on Social Computing* (pp. 950-954). IEEE. DOI: 10.1109/SocialCom.2013.149

Muzylyov, D., & Shramenko, N. (2019, September). Blockchain technology in transportation as a part of the efficiency in industry 4.0 strategy. In *Grabchenko's International Conference on Advanced Manufacturing Processes* (pp. 216-225). Cham: Springer International Publishing.

Nawaz, F., Ibrahim, J., Muhammad, A. A., Junaid, M., Kousar, S., & Parveen, T. (2020). A review of vision and challenges of 6G technology. *International Journal of Advanced Computer Science and Applications*, 11(2). Advance online publication. DOI: 10.14569/IJACSA.2020.0110281

Pilkington, M. (2016). Blockchain technology: principles and applications. In *Research handbook on digital transformations* (pp. 225–253). Edward Elgar Publishing. DOI: 10.4337/9781784717766.00019

Plastino, E., & Purdy, M. (2018). Game changing value from Artificial Intelligence: Eight strategies. *Strategy and Leadership*, 46(1), 16–22. DOI: 10.1108/SL-11-2017-0106

Provost, F., & Fawcett, T. (2013). Data science and its relationship to big data and data-driven decision making. *Big Data*, 1(1), 51–59. DOI: 10.1089/big.2013.1508 PMID: 27447038

Rathore, M. M., Ahmad, A., & Paul, A. (2016). Real time intrusion detection system for ultra-high-speed big data environments. *The Journal of Supercomputing*, 72(9), 3489–3510. DOI: 10.1007/s11227-015-1615-5

Shafi, M., Molisch, A. F., Smith, P. J., Haustein, T., Zhu, P., De Silva, P., Tufvesson, F., Benjebbour, A., & Wunder, G. (2017). 5G: A tutorial overview of standards, trials, challenges, deployment, and practice. *IEEE Journal on Selected Areas in Communications*, 35(6), 1201–1221. DOI: 10.1109/JSAC.2017.2692307

Sun, X., Yao, P., Qu, S., Yu, S., Zhang, X., Wang, W., Huang, C., & Chu, D. (2022). Material properties and machining characteristics under high strain rate in ultra-precision and ultra-high-speed machining process: A review. *International Journal of Advanced Manufacturing Technology*, 120(11), 7011–7042. DOI: 10.1007/s00170-022-09111-5

Thibaud, M., Chi, H., Zhou, W., & Piramuthu, S. (2018). Internet of Things (IoT) in high-risk Environment, Health and Safety (EHS) industries: A comprehensive review. *Decision Support Systems*, 108, 79–95. DOI: 10.1016/j.dss.2018.02.005

Windarta, S., Suryadi, S., Ramli, K., Pranggono, B., & Gunawan, T. S. (2022). Lightweight cryptographic hash functions: Design trends, comparative study, and future directions. *IEEE Access : Practical Innovations, Open Solutions*, 10, 82272–82294. DOI: 10.1109/ACCESS.2022.3195572

Wu, L., Yue, X., Jin, A., & Yen, D. C. (2016). Smart supply chain management: A review and implications for future research. *International Journal of Logistics Management*, 27(2), 395–417. DOI: 10.1108/IJLM-02-2014-0035

Yli-Huumo, J., Ko, D., Choi, S., Park, S., & Smolander, K. (2016). Where is current research on blockchain technology?—A systematic review. *PLoS One*, 11(10), e0163477. DOI: 10.1371/journal.pone.0163477 PMID: 27695049

Zhao, H., Di, L., Guo, L., Zhang, C., & Lin, L. (2023). An Automated Data-Driven Irrigation Scheduling Approach Using Model Simulated Soil Moisture and Evapotranspiration. *Sustainability (Basel)*, 15(17), 12908. DOI: 10.3390/su151712908

Zhuang, K., Fu, C., Weng, J., & Hu, C. (2021). Cutting edge microgeometries in metal cutting: A review. *International Journal of Advanced Manufacturing Technology*, 116(7), 2045–2092. DOI: 10.1007/s00170-021-07558-6

Compilation of References

Abbade, L. R., Ribeiro, F. M., da Silva, M. H., Morais, A. F., de Morais, E. S., Lopes, E. M., & Rodrigues, J. J. (2020). Blockchain applied to vehicular odometers. *IEEE Network*, 34(1), 62–68. DOI: 10.1109/MNET.001.1900162

Abbate, J. (2000). *Inventing the Internet*. MIT Press., DOI: 10.7551/mitpress/3866.001.0001

Abd Elaziz, M., Al-qaness, M. A. A., Dahou, A., Ibrahim, R. A., & El-Latif, A. A. A. (2023). Intrusion detection approach for cloud and IoT environments using deep learning and Capuchin Search Algorithm. *Advances in Engineering Software*, 176, 103402. Advance online publication. DOI: 10.1016/j.advengsoft.2022.103402

Abdel Hakeem, S. A., Hussein, H. H., & Kim, H. (2022). Security requirements and challenges of 6G technologies and applications. *Sensors (Basel)*, 22(5), 1969. DOI: 10.3390/s22051969 PMID: 35271113

Abdulhakeem, S. A., & Hu, Q. (2021). Powered by Blockchain Technology, DeFi (Decentralized Finance) Strives to Increase Financial Inclusion of the Unbanked by Reshaping the World Financial System. *Modern Economy*, 12(01), 1–16. DOI: 10.4236/me.2021.121001

Abubakari, M. S., & Kalinaki, K. (2024). Digital Competence in Islamic Education for Lifelong Learning: Preliminary Analysis Using DigComp 2.1 Framework. In *Embracing Technological Advancements for Lifelong Learning* (pp. 1-31). IGI Global. https://doi.org/DOI: 10.4018/979-8-3693-1410-4.ch001

Adem, N., Benfaid, A., Harib, R., & Alarabi, A. (2021). How Crucial Is It for 6G Networks to Be Autonomous? *ArXiv (Cornell University)*. https://doi.org//arxiv.2106.06949DOI: 10.48550

Aggarwal, S., Kumar, N., & Tanwar, S. (2020). Blockchain-envisioned UAV communication using 6G networks: Open issues, use cases, and future directions. *IEEE Internet of Things Journal*, 8(7), 5416–5441. DOI: 10.1109/JIOT.2020.3020819

Agiwal, M., Roy, A., Saxena, N., & Patra, N. (2023). Security and privacy issues in 6G networks. *Journal of Communications and Networks (Seoul)*, 22(1), 1–12. DOI: 10.1016/j.ijinfomgt.2022.102655

Aguiar-Castillo, L., Guerra, V., Rufo, J., Rabadan, J., & Perez-Jimenez, R. (2021). Survey on optical wireless communications-based services applied to the tourism industry: Potentials and challenges. *Sensors (Basel)*, 21(18), 6282. DOI: 10.3390/s21186282 PMID: 34577489

Ahad, A., Jiangbina, Z., Tahir, M., Shayea, I., Sheikh, M. A., & Rasheed, F. (2024). 6G and Intelligent Healthcare: Taxonomy, technologies, open issues and future research directions. *Internet of Things : Engineering Cyber Physical Human Systems*, 25, 101068. DOI: 10.1016/j.iot.2024.101068

Ahad, A., Tahir, M., & Yau, K.-L. A. (2020). 5G-based smart healthcare network: Architecture, taxonomy, challenges and future research directions. *IEEE Access : Practical Innovations, Open Solutions*, 8, 153947–153979. DOI: 10.1109/ACCESS.2020.3017859

Ahmad, I., Ashar, S. W., Khalid, U., Irfan, A., & Khalil, W. (2021). Blockchain for Sustainable Smart Cities. *Digital Cities Roadmap*, 127–161. DOI: 10.1002/9781119792079.ch4

Ahmad, H. F., Rafique, W., Rasool, R. U., Alhumam, A., Anwar, Z., & Qadir, J. (2023). Leveraging 6G, extended reality, and IoT big data analytics for healthcare: A review. *Computer Science Review*, 48, 100558. DOI: 10.1016/j.cosrev.2023.100558

Ahmadi-Assalemi, G., Al-Khateeb, H., Epiphaniou, G., & Aggoun, A. (2022). Super Learner Ensemble for Anomaly Detection and Cyber-Risk Quantification in Industrial Control Systems. *IEEE Internet of Things Journal*, 9(15), 13279–13297. Advance online publication. DOI: 10.1109/JIOT.2022.3144127

Ahmed, S. F., Alam, M. S. B., Afrin, S., Rafa, S. J., Taher, S. B., Kabir, M., Muyeen, S. M., & Gandomi, A. H. (2024). Toward a Secure 5G-Enabled Internet of Things: A Survey on Requirements, Privacy, Security, Challenges, and Opportunities. *IEEE Access : Practical Innovations, Open Solutions*, 12, 13125–13145. DOI: 10.1109/ACCESS.2024.3352508

Ahokangas, P., Matinmikko-Blue, M., Basaure, A., & Yrjölä, S. (2024). Use cases for local 6G networks. *2024 Joint European Conference on Networks and Communications & 6G Summit (EuCNC/6G Summit)*, 1127-1132. https://doi.org/ DOI: 10.1109/EuCNC/6GSummit60053.2024.10597019

Akbari, E., Wu, Q., Zhao, W., Arabnia, H. R., & Yang, M. Q. (2017, December 1). *From Blockchain to Internet-Based Voting*. IEEE Xplore. DOI: 10.1109/CSCI.2017.34

Akgul, O. U., Ericson, M., Burguera, P. G., Arar, B., Khorsandi, B. M., Querio, R., Varvara, A., Harkous, H., Wänstedt, S., Groshev, M., De la Oliva, A., Pieczerak, J., Kukliński, S., Nande, S. S., Bassoli, R., & Fitzek, F. H. (2024). Discussion on 6G architecture evolution: Challenges and emerging technology trends. *2024 Joint European Conference on Networks and Communications & 6G Summit (EuCNC/6G Summit)*, 664-669. https://doi.org/DOI: 10.1109/EuCNC/6GSummit60053.2024.10597056

Akhtar, M. W., Hassan, S. A., Ghaffar, R., Jung, H., Garg, S., & Hossain, M. S. (2020). The shift to 6G communications: Vision and requirements. *Human-centric Computing and Information Sciences*, 10(1), 1–27. DOI: 10.1186/s13673-020-00258-2

Akyildiz, I. F., Kak, A., & Nie, S. (2020). 6G and beyond: The future of wireless communications systems. *IEEE Access : Practical Innovations, Open Solutions*, 8, 133995–134030. DOI: 10.1109/ACCESS.2020.3010896

Al Amin, A., Hong, J., Bui, V. H., & Su, W. (2023). Emerging 6G/B6G wireless communication for the power infrastructure in smart cities: Innovations, challenges, and future perspectives. *Algorithms*, 16(10), 474. DOI: 10.3390/a16100474

Al Amin, M.. (2023). Convergence of AI and Mobile Edge Computing for Autonomous IoT Service Provisioning in Beyond 5G Networks. *Sensors (Basel)*, 24(13), 4254. https://www.mdpi.com/1424-8220/24/13/4254

Alaali, A. M., Alateeq, A., & Elmedany, W. (2022). Cybersecurity Threats and Solutions of IoT Network Layer. 2022 International Conference on Innovation and Intelligence for Informatics, Computing, and Technologies, 3ICT 2022. https://doi.org/DOI: 10.1109/3ICT56508.2022.9990734

Alagic, G., Alperin-Sheriff, J., Apon, D., Cooper, D., Dang, Q., Kelsey, J., ... & Zhao, Y. (2020). Status report on the second round of the NIST post-quantum cryptography standardization process. NIST Interagency/Internal Report (NISTIR), 8309. DOI: 10.6028/NIST.IR.8309

Alavi, A. H., Jiao, P., Buttlar, W. G., & Lajnef, N. (2018). Internet of Things-enabled smart cities: State-of-the-art and future trends. *Measurement*, 129, 589–606. DOI: 10.1016/j.measurement.2018.07.067

Al-Edrus, S. M., Khan, M. A., & Shah, S. M. (2024). Challenges and Solutions in Security and Privacy for 6G Networks. *IEEE Access*. https://ieeexplore.ieee.org/stamp/stamp.jsp?arnumber=9426946

Alese, B. K., Philemon, E. D., & Falaki, S. O. (2012). Comparative analysis of public-key encryption schemes. *IACSIT International Journal of Engineering and Technology*, 2(9), 1552–1568.

Al-Fuqaha, A., Guizani, M., Mohammadi, M., Aledhari, M., & Ayyash, M. (2020). Internet of Things: A survey on enabling technologies, protocols, and applications. *IEEE Communications Surveys and Tutorials*, 17(4), 2347–2376. DOI: 10.1109/COMST.2015.2444095

Alghamedy, F. H., El-Haggar, N., Alsumayt, A., Alfawaer, Z., Alshammari, M., Amouri, L., Aljameel, S. S., & Albassam, S. (2024a). Unlocking a Promising Future: Integrating Blockchain Technology and FL-IoT in the Journey to 6G. *IEEE Access : Practical Innovations, Open Solutions*, 1, 115411–115447. Advance online publication. DOI: 10.1109/ACCESS.2024.3435968

Alhammadi, A., Shayea, I., El-Saleh, A. A., Azmi, M. H., Ismail, Z. H., Kouhalvandi, L., & Saad, S. A. (2024). Artificial Intelligence in 6G Wireless Networks: Opportunities, Applications, and Challenges. *International Journal of Intelligent Systems*, 2024(1), 8845070. DOI: 10.1155/2024/8845070

Alharbi, S., Attiah, A., & Alghazzawi, D. (2022). Integrating Blockchain with Artificial Intelligence to Secure IoT Networks: Future Trends. *Sustainability (Basel)*, 14(23), 16002. Advance online publication. DOI: 10.3390/su142316002

Alhazmi, H. E., Eassa, F. E., & Sandokji, S. M. (2022). Towards big data security framework by leveraging fragmentation and blockchain technology. *IEEE Access : Practical Innovations, Open Solutions*, 10, 10768–10782. DOI: 10.1109/ACCESS.2022.3144632

Al-Heety, O. S., Zakaria, Z., Ismail, M., Shakir, M. M., Alani, S., & Alsariera, H. (2020). A comprehensive survey: Benefits, services, recent works, challenges, security, and use cases for sdn-vanet. *IEEE Access : Practical Innovations, Open Solutions*, 8, 91028–91047. DOI: 10.1109/ACCESS.2020.2992580

Ali, H., Elzeki, O. M., & Elmougy, S. (2022). Smart Attacks Learning Machine Advisor System for Protecting Smart Cities from Smart Threats. *Applied Sciences (Basel, Switzerland)*, 12(13), 6473. Advance online publication. DOI: 10.3390/app12136473

Ali, M. Z., Abohmra, A., Usman, M., Zahid, A., Heidari, H., Imran, M. A., & Abbasi, Q. H. (2023). Quantum for 6G communication: A perspective. *IET Quantum Communication*, 4(3), 112–124. DOI: 10.1049/qtc2.12060

Ali, R., & Shen, J. (2022). Blockchain-enabled IoT architecture for 6G smart city applications. *IEEE Communications Magazine*.

Aljumah, A., & Ahanger, T. A. (2023). Blockchain-Based Information Sharing Security for the Internet of Things. *Mathematics*, 11(9), 2157. DOI: 10.3390/math11092157

Alladi, T., Chamola, V., Sikdar, B., & Choo, K. K. R. (2020). Consumer IoT: Security vulnerability case studies and solutions. *IEEE Consumer Electronics Magazine*, 9(2), 17–25. DOI: 10.1109/MCE.2019.2953740

Allam, Z. (2019). The emergence of anti-privacy and control at the nexus between the concepts of safe city and smart city. *Smart Cities*, 2(1), 96–105. DOI: 10.3390/smartcities2010007

Allam, Z., & Jones, D. S. (2021). Future (post-COVID) digital, smart and sustainable cities in the wake of 6G: Digital twins, immersive realities and new urban economies. *Land Use Policy*, 101, 105201. DOI: 10.1016/j.landusepol.2020.105201

Allam, Z., & Newman, P. (2023a). Smart Cities and Sustainability: How Smart City Helps with Sustainability. In *Revising Smart Cities with Regenerative Design* (pp. 21–34). Springer International Publishing. DOI: 10.1007/978-3-031-28028-3_2

Almadani, Y., Plets, D., Bastiaens, S., Joseph, W., Ijaz, M., Ghassemlooy, Z., & Rajbhandari, S. (2020). Visible light communications for industrial applications—Challenges and potentials. *Electronics (Basel)*, 9(12), 2157. DOI: 10.3390/electronics9122157

Al-Mohannadi, H., Mirza, Q., Namanya, A., Awan, I., Cullen, A., & Disso, J. (2016, August). Cyber-attack modeling analysis techniques: An overview. In *2016 IEEE 4th international conference on future internet of things and cloud workshops (FiCloudW)* (pp. 69-76). IEEE.

Alotaibi, A., & Barnawi, A. (2023). Securing massive IoT in 6G: Recent solutions, architecture, and future directions. In Internet of Things (Netherlands) (Vol. 22). https://doi.org/DOI: 10.1016/j.iot.2023.100715

Alrehaili, A., Namoun, A., & Tufail, A. (2021). A Comparative Analysis of Scalability Issues within Blockchain-based Solutions in the Internet of Things. *International Journal of Advanced Computer Science and Applications*, 12(9). Advance online publication. DOI: 10.14569/IJACSA.2021.0120955

Alsharif, M. H., Jahid, A., Kannadasan, R., & Kim, M. K. (2024). Unleashing the potential of sixth generation (6G) wireless networks in smart energy grid management: A comprehensive review. *Energy Reports*, 11, 1376–1398. DOI: 10.1016/j.egyr.2024.01.011

Alzoubi, Y. I., Al-Ahmad, A., Kahtan, H., & Jaradat, A. (2022). Internet of things and blockchain integration: Security, privacy, technical, and design challenges. *Future Internet*, 14(7), 216. DOI: 10.3390/fi14070216

Andrade, R. O., Yoo, S. G., Tello-Oquendo, L., & Ortiz-Garces, I. (2020). *A Comprehensive Study of the IoT Cybersecurity in Smart Cities*. IEEE., DOI: 10.1109/ACCESS.2020.3046442

Anedda, M., & Giusto, D. D. (2020, October). Urban mobility services based on user virtualization and social IoT. In *2020 IEEE International Symposium on Broadband Multimedia Systems and Broadcasting (BMSB)* (pp. 1-4). IEEE. DOI: 10.1109/BMSB49480.2020.9379791

Anedda, M., Muntean, G. M., & Murroni, M. (2016, June). Adaptive real-time multi-user access network selection algorithm for load-balancing over heterogeneous wireless networks. In *2016 IEEE International Symposium on Broadband Multimedia Systems and Broadcasting (BMSB)* (pp. 1-4). IEEE. DOI: 10.1109/BMSB.2016.7521907

Anedda, M., Murroni, M., & Muntean, G. M. (2017, June). E-ARMANS: Energy-aware device-oriented video delivery in heterogeneous wireless networks. In *2017 IEEE International Symposium on Broadband Multimedia Systems and Broadcasting (BMSB)* (pp. 1-6). IEEE. DOI: 10.1109/BMSB.2017.7986147

Angel, S., Parent, J., Civco, D. L., Blei, A., & Potere, D. (2011). The dimensions of global urban expansion: Estimates and projections for all countries, 2000–2050. *Progress in Planning*, 75(2), 53–107. DOI: 10.1016/j.progress.2011.04.001

Ansari, K. (2021). Joint use of DSRC and C-V2X for V2X communications in the 5.9 GHz ITS band. *IET Intelligent Transport Systems*, 15(2), 213–224. DOI: 10.1049/itr2.12015

Antón-Haro, C., Trichias, K., De Majo, C., Kaloxylos, A., & Beriere, J. (2024). 6G smart networks and services: Global strategies, main work directions & Future outlook. *2024 Joint European Conference on Networks and Communications & 6G Summit (EuCNC/6G Summit)*, 1115-1120. https://doi.org/DOI: 10.1109/EuCNC/6GSummit60053.2024.10597046

Aslam, M. M., Ahmed, Z., Du, L., Hassan, M. Z., Ali, S., & Nasir, M. (2022). An Overview of Recent Advances of Resilient Consensus for Multiagent Systems under Attacks. *Computational Intelligence and Neuroscience*, 2022(1), 6732343. DOI: 10.1155/2022/6732343 PMID: 39411550

Aslam, M. M., Du, L., Zhang, X., Chen, Y., Ahmed, Z., & Qureshi, B. (2021). Sixth generation (6G) cognitive radio network (CRN) application, requirements, security issues, and key challenges. *Wireless Communications and Mobile Computing*, 2021(1), 1331428. DOI: 10.1155/2021/1331428

Asuquo, P., Cruickshank, H., Morley, J., Ogah, C. P. A., Lei, A., Hathal, W., Bao, S., & Sun, Z. (2018). Security and privacy in location-based services for vehicular and mobile communications: An overview, challenges, and countermeasures. *IEEE Internet of Things Journal*, 5(6), 4778–4802. DOI: 10.1109/JIOT.2018.2820039

Ateya, A. A., Muthanna, A., Vybornova, A., Algarni, A. D., Abuarqoub, A., Koucheryavy, Y., & Koucheryavy, A. (2021). Smart core network for 6G technology. *IEEE Access : Practical Innovations, Open Solutions*, 9, 44795–44813. DOI: 10.1109/ACCESS.2021.3065525

Athinarayanan, S., Selvi, R., Rajakumari, K., Arunadevi, R., & Joel, M. R. (2023, December). An Advanced Strategy for Efficient Agricultural Production using Machine Learning. In *2023 2nd International Conference on Automation, Computing and Renewable Systems (ICACRS)* (pp. 680-686). IEEE. DOI: 10.1109/ICACRS58579.2023.10405182

Azzaoui, A. E., Singh, S. K., Pan, Y., & Park, J. H. (2020). Block5GIntell: Blockchain for AI-Enabled 5G Networks. *IEEE Access : Practical Innovations, Open Solutions*, 8, 145918–145935. DOI: 10.1109/ACCESS.2020.3014356

Bach, L. M., Mihaljevic, B., & Zagar, M. Comparative analysis of blockchain consensus algorithms, in *41st International Convention on Information and Communication Technology, Electronics and Microelectronics (MIPRO)*, pp. 1545-1550, 2018. DOI: 10.23919/MIPRO.2018.8400278

Bagga, P., Sutrala, A. K., Das, A. K., & Vijayakumar, P. (2021). Blockchain-based batch authentication protocol for Internet of Vehicles. *Journal of Systems Architecture*, 113, 101877. DOI: 10.1016/j.sysarc.2020.101877

Bagloee, S. A., Heshmati, M., Dia, H., Ghaderi, H., Pettit, C., & Asadi, M. (2021). Blockchain: The operating system of smart cities. *Cities (London, England)*, 112, 103104. DOI: 10.1016/j.cities.2021.103104

Bakare, B. I., & Bassey, E. E. (2021). A comparative study of the evolution of wireless communication technologies from the first generation (1G) to the fourth generation (4G). *Int J Elect Commun Comp Eng*, 12(3), 2249–071X.

Baker, T., Asim, M., MacDermott, Á., & Abbasi, A. (2021). Security and privacy in 6G networks: Research opportunities and challenges. *IEEE Access : Practical Innovations, Open Solutions*, 9, 37895–37909. DOI: 10.1109/ACCESS.2021.3056203

Banafaa, M., Shayea, I., Din, J., Azmi, M. H., Alashbi, A., Daradkeh, Y. I., & Alhammadi, A. (2023). 6G mobile communication technology: Requirements, targets, applications, challenges, advantages, and opportunities. *Alexandria Engineering Journal*, 64, 245–274. DOI: 10.1016/j.aej.2022.08.017

Bansal, D., & Bhattacharya, N. (2024). Artificial Intelligence and Metaverse Applications in the Healthcare Sector. In *Multi-Sector Analysis of the Digital Healthcare Industry* (pp. 110–132). IGI Global. DOI: 10.4018/979-8-3693-0928-5.ch004

Basar, E., Di Renzo, M., De Rosny, J., Debbah, M., Alouini, M. S., & Zhang, R. (2019). Wireless communications through reconfigurable intelligent surfaces. *IEEE Access : Practical Innovations, Open Solutions*, 7, 116753–116773. DOI: 10.1109/ACCESS.2019.2935192

Batista, E., Lopez-Aguilar, P., & Solanas, A. (2023). Smart health in the 6G era: Bringing security to future smart health services. *IEEE Communications Magazine*.

Beaumont, C. D., Berry, D., & Ricketts, J. (2022). Technology has empowered the consumer, but marketing communications need to catch-up: An approach to fast-forward the future. *Businesses*, 2(2), 246–272. DOI: 10.3390/businesses2020017

Bekkali, A. E., Essaaidi, M., & Boulmalf, M. (2023). A Blockchain-Based Architecture and Framework for Cybersecure Smart Cities. *IEEE Access : Practical Innovations, Open Solutions*, 11, 76359–76370. DOI: 10.1109/ACCESS.2023.3296482

Belchior, R., Vasconcelos, A., Guerreiro, S., & Correia, M. (2021). A survey on blockchain interoperability: Past, present, and future trends. *ACM Computing Surveys*, 54(8), 1–41. DOI: 10.1145/3471140

Benchoufi, M., & Ravaud, P. (2017). Blockchain technology for improving clinical research quality. *Trials*, 18(1), 335. DOI: 10.1186/s13063-017-2035-z PMID: 28724395

Benet, J. *IPFS–content addressed, versioned, P2Pfile system*, 2014, arXiv:1407.3561. [Online]. Available: http://arxiv.org/abs/1407.3561

Benzaid, C., & Taleb, T. (2020). AI for Beyond 5G Networks: A Cyber-Security Defense or Offense Enabler? *IEEE Network*, 34(6), 1–8. DOI: 10.1109/MNET.011.2000088

Bera, S., Misra, S., & Vasilakos, A. V. (2021). Software-defined networking for Internet of Things: A survey. *IEEE Internet of Things Journal*, 4(6), 1994–2008. DOI: 10.1109/JIOT.2017.2746186

Berners-Lee, T., & Fischetti, M. (2021). *Weaving the Web: The original design and ultimate destiny of the World Wide Web by its inventor*. HarperCollins.

Bertolusso, M., Spanu, M., Anedda, M., Fadda, M., & Giusto, D. D. (2021, June). Vehicular and pedestrian traffic monitoring system in smart city scenarios. In 2021 IEEE 7th World Forum on Internet of Things (WF-IoT) (pp. 60-64). IEEE. DOI: 10.1109/WF-IoT51360.2021.9595188

Bhardwaj, A., Kumar, M., Stephan, T., Shankar, A., Ghalib, M. R., & Abujar, S. (2022). IAF: IoT Attack Framework and Unique Taxonomy. *Journal of Circuits, Systems, and Computers*, 31(2), 2250029. Advance online publication. DOI: 10.1142/S0218126622500293

Bhattacharya, N., & Kishore, S. Metaverse in Healthcare: A Review. *SARALA BIRLA UNIVERSITY*, 13.

Bhattacharya, N., & Kumar, P. (2024). Integrating Healthcare Analytics to Improve Diabetes Management and Prevent Heart Attacks: A Data-Driven Approach. https://doi.org/DOI: 10.21203/rs.3.rs-4310669/v1

Bhowmik, T., Bhadwaj, A., Kumar, A., & Bhushan, B. (2022). *Machine Learning and Deep Learning Models for Privacy Management and Data Analysis in Smart Cites* (Vol. 215). In Intelligent Systems Reference Library., DOI: 10.1007/978-3-030-90119-6_13

Bhushan, N., & Mogensen, P. (2019). 6G wireless systems: Vision, requirements, challenges, insights, and opportunities. arXiv preprint arXiv:1909.11738.

Bhushan, B., Khamparia, A., Sagayam, K. M., Sharma, S. K., Ahad, M. A., & Debnath, N. C. (2020). Blockchain for smart cities: A review of architectures, integration trends and future research directions. *Sustainable Cities and Society*, 61, 102360. DOI: 10.1016/j.scs.2020.102360

Bilali, V. G., Kosyvas, D., Theodoropoulos, T., Ouzounoglou, E., Karagiannidis, L., & Amditis, A. (2022). IRIS Advanced Threat Intelligence Orchestrator- A Way to Manage Cybersecurity Challenges of IoT Ecosystems in Smart Cities. Lecture Notes in Computer Science (Including Subseries Lecture Notes in Artificial Intelligence and Lecture Notes in Bioinformatics), 13533 LNCS. https://doi.org/DOI: 10.1007/978-3-031-20936-9_25

Blessy, I. M., Manikandan, G., & Joel, M. R. (2023, December). Blockchain Technology's Role in an Electronic Voting System for Developing Countries to Produce Better Results. In *2023 3rd International Conference on Innovative Mechanisms for Industry Applications (ICIMIA)* (pp. 283-287). IEEE.

Borgianni, L., Adami, D., & Giordano, S. (2023). Optimizing network performance and reliability with an integrated SD-WAN and satellite 6G architecture. *2023 2nd International Conference on 6G Networking (6GNet), 21*, 1-4. https://doi.org/DOI: 10.1109/6GNet58894.2023.10317704

Bouzidi, M., Amro, A., Dalveren, Y., Alaya Cheikh, F., & Derawi, M. (2023). LPWAN Cyber Security Risk Analysis: Building a Secure IQRF Solution. *Sensors (Basel)*, 23(4), 2078. Advance online publication. DOI: 10.3390/s23042078 PMID: 36850676

Brauneis, R., & Goodman, E. P. (2018). Algorithmic transparency for the smart city. *Yale JL & Tech.*, 20, 103.

Bregni, S., Sari, H., Letaief, K., Ben Othman, J., Dobre, O., Sripimanwat, K., & Korai, U. (2023). 2nd IEEE International Mediterranean Conference on Communications and Networking (IEEE MeditCom 2022) 5-8 September 2022, Athens, Greece. *IEEE COMMUNICATIONS MAGAZINE, 61*(2), 17-21.

Brewer, J. N., & Dimitoglou, G. (2019, December 1). *Evaluation of Attack Vectors and Risks in Automobiles and Road Infrastructure*. IEEE Xplore. DOI: 10.1109/CSCI49370.2019.00021

Cao, Y., Zhao, Y., Yu, Y., Wu, J., Yang, X., & Zhang, J. (2019). Integration of software-defined networking and quantum key distribution: A survey. *Quantum Engineering*, 1(3), e26. DOI: 10.1002/que2.26

Caragliu, A., & Del Bo, C. (2020). Do smart city policies work? *Digital transformation of the design, construction and management processes of the built environment*, 149-159.

Case, J. A. (2022). Deep Learning and Artificial Intelligence: What Does the Cardiologist Really Need to Know? In Circulation: Cardiovascular Imaging (Vol. 15, Issue 9). https://doi.org/DOI: 10.1161/CIRCIMAGING.122.014744

Casillo, M., Colace, F., Lorusso, A., Marongiu, F., & Santaniello, D. (2022). An IoT-based system for expert user supporting to monitor, manage and protect cultural heritage buildings. In *Robotics and AI for Cybersecurity and Critical Infrastructure in Smart Cities* (pp. 143–154). Springer International Publishing. DOI: 10.1007/978-3-030-96737-6_8

Cha, J., Singh, S. K., Kim, T. W., & Park, J. H. (2021). Blockchain-empowered cloud architecture based on secret sharing for smart city. *Journal of Information Security and Applications*, 57, 102686. DOI: 10.1016/j.jisa.2020.102686

Cha, J., Singh, S. K., Pan, Y., & Park, J. H. (2020). Blockchain-Based Cyber Threat Intelligence System Architecture for Sustainable Computing. *Sustainability (Basel)*, 12(16), 6401. DOI: 10.3390/su12166401

Chalaemwongwan, N., & Kurutach, W. State of the art and challenges facing consensus protocols on blockchain, in *International Conference on Information Networking (ICOIN)*, pp. 957-962, 2018. DOI: 10.1109/ICOIN.2018.8343266

Chamola, V., Jolfaei, A., Chanana, V., Parashari, P., & Hassija, V. (2021). Information security in the post quantum era for 5G and beyond networks: Threats to existing cryptography, and post-quantum cryptography. *Computer Communications*, 176, 99–118. DOI: 10.1016/j.comcom.2021.05.019

Charu, M., Kumar, M. A., Upadhyay, M. A., & Chauhan, M. P. A 6G Network: Future of Nations? Challenges in 6G Communications. Tuijin Jishu/Journal of Propulsion Technology, 44(04), 2023.

Chataut, R., Nankya, M., & Akl, R. (2024). 6G Networks and the AI Revolution—Exploring Technologies, Applications, and Emerging Challenges. *Sensors (Basel)*, 24(6), 1888. DOI: 10.3390/s24061888 PMID: 38544151

Chaudhari, B. S., Zennaro, M., & Borkar, S. (2020). LPWAN technologies: Emerging application characteristics, requirements, and design considerations. *Future Internet*, 12(3), 46. DOI: 10.3390/fi12030046

Che, X., Gao, W., & Zhang, Q. (2024). Energy efficiency and sustainability in 6G networks: Challenges and solutions. *Journal of Network and Computer Applications*. https://www.sciencedirect.com/science/article/pii/S1084804524000113

Cheikhrouhou, O. Ichrak Amdouni, Khaleel Mershad, Meryem Ammi, & Nguyen, T. V. (2022). Blockchain for the Cybersecurity of Smart City Applications. *INDIGO (University of Illinois at Chicago)*. DOI: 10.36227/techrxiv.19990367

Chemisto, M., Kalinaki, K., Oloya, I. T., Tar, J. L., Percival, E. G. A. U., KIRYA, F., ... & KISITU, R. (2024, May). ICT for Improved Maternal Healthcare in Uganda: A Systematic Literature Review. *In 2024 IST-Africa Conference (IST-Africa)* (pp. 1-11). IEEE. https://doi.org/DOI: 10.23919/IST-Africa63983.2024.10569857

Chen, X., Li, H., & Zhang, Y. (2024). Terahertz and millimetre-wave communication challenges in 6G networks. *IEEE Transactions on Wireless Communications.* https://ieeexplore.ieee.org/document/9397776

Cheng, Q., Gong, Y., Qin, Y., Ao, X., & Li, Z. (2024). Secure Digital Asset Transactions: Integrating Distributed Ledger Technology with Safe AI Mechanisms. *Academic Journal of Science and Technology*, 9(3), 156–161. DOI: 10.54097/2qhab557

Chen, J., Li, J., & Zhang, Q. (2021). Privacy-preserving data aggregation for smart cities: A comprehensive survey. *IEEE Internet of Things Journal*, 7(10), 10199–10212. DOI: 10.1109/JIOT.2021.2969210

Chentouf, F. Z., & Bouchkaren, S. (2023). Security and privacy in smart city: A secure e-voting system based on blockchain. *Iranian Journal of Electrical and Computer Engineering*, 13(2), 1848. Advance online publication. DOI: 10.11591/ijece.v13i2.pp1848-1857

Chen, X., Deng, Y., Ding, H., Qu, G., Zhang, H., Li, P., & Fang, Y. (2024). Vehicle as a Service (VaaS): Leverage Vehicles to Build Service Networks and Capabilities for Smart Cities. *IEEE Communications Surveys and Tutorials. IEEE Communications Surveys and Tutorials*, 26(3), 1–1. DOI: 10.1109/COMST.2024.3370169

Cheon, J. H., Kim, D., Kim, D., & Song, Y. (2021). Toward Post-Quantum Security for IoT: Performance Analysis of Lattice-Based Cryptography on a Low-Cost IoT Platform. *IEEE Internet of Things Journal*, 8(11), 9095–9106. DOI: 10.1109/JIOT.2020.3041313

Chhabra, S., Aiden, M. K., Sabharwal, S. M., & Al-Asadi, M. (2023). 5G and 6G technologies for Smart City. In *Enabling Technologies for Effective Planning and Management in Sustainable Smart Cities* (pp. 335–365). Springer International Publishing. DOI: 10.1007/978-3-031-22922-0_14

Chhipa, H. (2017). Nanofertilizers and nanopesticides for agriculture. *Environmental Chemistry Letters*, 15(1), 15–22. DOI: 10.1007/s10311-016-0600-4

Chillotti, I., Gama, N., Georgieva, M., & Izabachène, M. (2020). TFHE: Fast fully homomorphic encryption over the torus. *Journal of Cryptology*, 33(1), 34–91. DOI: 10.1007/s00145-019-09319-x

Cho, J. H., Sharma, D. P., Alavizadeh, H., Yoon, S., Ben-Asher, N., Moore, T. J., & Lim, H. (2020). Toward Proactive, Adaptive Defense: A Survey on Moving Target Defense. *IEEE Communications Surveys and Tutorials*, 22(1), 709–745. DOI: 10.1109/COMST.2019.2963791

Chourabi, I., & Donato, P. (2015). Homogenization and correctors of a class of elliptic problems in perforated domains. *Asymptotic Analysis*, 92(1-2), 1–43. DOI: 10.3233/ASY-151288

Chowdary, V. T., Joel, M. R., Ebenezer, V., Edwin, B., Thanka, R., & Jeyaraj, A. (2022, March). A Novel Approach for Effective Crop Production using Machine Learning. In *2022 International Conference on Electronics and Renewable Systems (ICEARS)* (pp. 1143-1147). IEEE. DOI: 10.1109/ICEARS53579.2022.9751798

Chowdhury, M. Z., Shahjalal, M., Ahmed, S., & Jang, Y. M. (2021). 6G wireless communication systems: Applications, requirements, technologies, challenges, and research directions. *IEEE Open Journal of the Communications Society*, 1, 957–975. DOI: 10.1109/OJCOMS.2020.3010270

Christidis, K., & Devetsikiotis, M. (2016). Blockchains and smart contracts for the Internet of Things. *IEEE Access : Practical Innovations, Open Solutions*, 4, 2292–2303. DOI: 10.1109/ACCESS.2016.2566339

Chui, M., Loffler, M., & Roberts, R. (2010). *The internet of things*. McKinsey Global Institute.

Cigno, R. L., Nitti, M., & Toninelli, A. (2022). Integrating CSI sensing in wireless networks: Challenges to privacy and countermeasures. *IEEE Communications Magazine*, 60(4), 44–49. https://ieeexplore.ieee.org/stamp/stamp.jsp?arnumber=9919737

Cioara, T., Pop, C., Zanc, R., Anghel, I., Antal, M., & Salomie, I. (2020). Smart Grid Management Using Blockchain: Future Scenarios and Challenges. *2020 19th RoEduNet Conference: Networking in Education and Research (RoEduNet)*. DOI: 10.1109/RoEduNet51892.2020.9324874

Coito, T., Firme, B., Martins, M. S., Vieira, S. M., Figueiredo, J., & Sousa, J. M. (2021). Intelligent sensors for real-Time decision-making. *Automation*, 2(2), 62–82. DOI: 10.3390/automation2020004

Conoscenti, M., Vetro, A., & De Martin, J. C. (2016, November). Blockchain for the Internet of Things: A systematic literature review. In 2016 IEEE/ACS 13th International Conference of Computer Systems and Applications (AICCSA) (pp. 1-6). IEEE.

Convergence of Blockchain, IoT, and 6G: Potential, Opportunities, Challenges, and Research Roadmap. (2021). arXiv.

Cordova Morales, D. A., Nguyen, T., & Pujolle, G. (2023). Towards a blockgraph-based trustless authentication scheme for future 6G technology. *2023 2nd International Conference on 6G Networking (6GNet)*. https://doi.org/DOI: 10.1109/6GNet58894.2023.10317665

Craig, A. B. (2013). Understanding augmented reality: Concepts and applications.

Crosby, M., Nachiappan, P., Pattanayak, P., & Verma, S. (2016). Blockchain technology: Beyond Bitcoin. *Applied Innovation*, 2(6-10), 71.

Cui, J., Wu, D., Zhang, J., Xu, Y., & Zhong, H. (2019). An efficient authentication scheme based on semi-trusted authority in VANETs. *IEEE Transactions on Vehicular Technology*, 68(3), 2972–2986. DOI: 10.1109/TVT.2019.2896018

Dadkhah, S., Mahdikhani, H., Danso, P. K., Zohourian, A., Truong, K. A., & Ghorbani, A. A. (2022). Towards the Development of a Realistic Multidimensional IoT Profiling Dataset. 2022 19th Annual International Conference on Privacy, Security and Trust, PST 2022. https://doi.org/DOI: 10.1109/PST55820.2022.9851966

Dahlman, E., Parkvall, S., & Skold, J. (2018). *5G NR: The next generation wireless access technology*. Academic Press., DOI: 10.1016/C2017-0-01347-2

Dang, S., Amin, O., Shihada, B., & Alouini, M. S. (2020). What should 6G be? *Nature Electronics*, 3(1), 20–29. DOI: 10.1038/s41928-019-0355-6

Darwish, A., & Hassanien, A. E. (2022). IoHCT: Internet of cultural heritage things digital twins for conservation and health monitoring of cultural in the age of digital transformation. In *Digital Twins for Digital Transformation: Innovation in Industry* (pp. 1–21). Springer International Publishing. DOI: 10.1007/978-3-030-96802-1_1

Das, S., & Mitra, A. (2024). Advancing lightweight digital trust architectures in the internet of medical things: A multi-dimensional analysis. In *Lightweight Digital Trust Architectures in the Internet of Medical Things (IoMT)* (pp. 1-14). DOI: 10.4018/979-8-3693-2109-6.ch001

Dasika, S. R. C. M., Kakulapati, V., & Saligrama, S. (2024). Network Security and Data Privacy in 6G Environment: Impacts and Challenges.

David, K., & Berndt, H. (2018). 6G vision and requirements: Is there any need for beyond 5G? *IEEE Vehicular Technology Magazine*, 13(3), 72–80. DOI: 10.1109/MVT.2018.2848498

De Alwis, C., Kalla, A., Pham, Q. V., Kumar, P., Dev, K., Hwang, W. J., & Liyanage, M. (2021). Survey on 6G frontiers: Trends, applications, requirements, technologies and future research. *IEEE Open Journal of the Communications Society*, 2, 836–886. DOI: 10.1109/OJCOMS.2021.3071496

Desai, B., Patil, K., Mehta, I., & Patil, A. (2024). A Secure Communication Framework for Smart City Infrastructure Leveraging Encryption, Intrusion Detection, and Blockchain Technology. Advances in Computer Sciences, 7(1)

Desogus, C., Anedda, M., & Murroni, M. (2017, June). Real-time load optimization for multimedia delivery content over heterogeneuos wireless network using a MEW approach. In *2017 IEEE International Symposium on Broadband Multimedia Systems and Broadcasting (BMSB)* (pp. 1-4). IEEE. DOI: 10.1109/BMSB.2017.7986194

Desogus, C., Anedda, M., Murroni, M., & Muntean, G. M. (2019). A traffic type-based differentiated reputation algorithm for radio resource allocation during multi-service content delivery in 5G heterogeneous scenarios. *IEEE Access : Practical Innovations, Open Solutions*, 7, 27720–27735. DOI: 10.1109/ACCESS.2019.2902190

Dhanaraj, R. K., Rajasekar, V., Hafizul Islam, S. K., Balusamy, B., & Hsu, C. H. (2022). Quantum blockchain: An emerging cryptographic paradigm. In Quantum Blockchain: An Emerging Cryptographic Paradigm. https://doi.org/DOI: 10.1002/9781119836728

Didouh, A., El Hillali, Y., Rivenq, A., & Labiod, H. (2022). Novel centralized pseudonym changing scheme for location privacy in V2X communication. *Energies*, 15(3), 692. DOI: 10.3390/en15030692

Dong, L. E. (4). Commonly-Used Smart City Technologies. Earth. org. URL: https:// earth. org/smart-city-technologies

Dunnewijk, T., & Hultén, S. (2007). A brief history of mobile communication in Europe. *Telematics and Informatics*, 24(3), 164–179. DOI: 10.1016/j.tele.2007.01.013

El Houda, Z. A., Brik, B., & Khoukhi, L. (2022). "Why Should I Trust Your IDS?": An Explainable Deep Learning Framework for Intrusion Detection Systems in Internet of Things Networks. *IEEE Open Journal of the Communications Society*, 3, 1164–1176. Advance online publication. DOI: 10.1109/OJCOMS.2022.3188750

Elbamby, M. S., Perfecto, C., Bennis, M., & Doppler, K. (2019). Toward low-latency and ultra-reliable virtual reality. *IEEE Network*, 33(2), 78–84. DOI: 10.1109/MNET.2018.1700268

Engelhardt, M. A. (2017). Intelligent energy: A blockchain-powered model for renewable energy marketplaces. *Energy Policy*, 108, 77–86.

Estrela, V. V., Deshpande, A., Stutz, D., de Assis, J. T., Laghari, A. A., Shi, F., & Lin, Y. D. (2023). 6G in Healthcare–Anticipating Needs and Requirements. In *Intelligent Healthcare Systems* (pp. 159–181). CRC Press. DOI: 10.1201/9781003196822-9

Fadhil, A. M. (2023). Next-Generation Urban Intelligence: Integrating 6G Communication and Blockchain Technology for Smart City Advancements.

Fadhil, A. (2023). Integration of 6G Communication and Blockchain Technology for Smart City Advancements. *Sensors (Basel)*, 24(13), 4254. https://www.mdpi.com/1424-8220/24/13/4254

Farahani, B., Firouzi, F., Chang, V., Badaroglu, M., Constant, N., & Mankodiya, K. (2018). Towards fog-driven IoT eHealth: Promises and challenges of IoT in medicine and healthcare. *Future Generation Computer Systems*, 78, 659–676. DOI: 10.1016/j.future.2017.04.036

Faria, T. H., Shamim Kaiser, M., Hossian, C. A., Mahmud, M., Al Mamun, S., & Chakraborty, C. (2021). Smart city technologies for next generation healthcare. In *Data-Driven Mining, Learning and Analytics for Secured Smart Cities: Trends and Advances* (pp. 253–274). Springer International Publishing. DOI: 10.1007/978-3-030-72139-8_12

Farooq, M. S., Nadir, R. M., Rustam, F., Hur, S., Park, Y., & Ashraf, I. (2022). Nested Bee Hive: A conceptual multilayer architecture for 6G in futuristic sustainable smart cities. *Sensors (Basel)*, 22(16), 5950. DOI: 10.3390/s22165950 PMID: 36015707

Faye, S., Camelo, M., Sottet, J., Sommer, C., Franke, M., Baudouin, J., Castellanos, G., Decorme, R., Fanti, M. P., Fuladi, R., Kesik, G., Mendes, B., Murphy, C., Parker, S., Pryor, S., Senouci, S. M., & Turcanu, I. (2024). Integrating network digital twinning into future AI-based 6G systems: The 6G-TWIN vision. *2024 Joint European Conference on Networks and Communications & 6G Summit (EuCNC/6G Summit)*, 883-888. https://doi.org/DOI: 10.1109/EuCNC/6GSummit60053.2024.10597058

Feng, X., Shi, Q., Xie, Q., & Wang, L. (2021). P2BA: A privacy-preserving protocol with batch authentication against semi-trusted RSUs in vehicular ad hoc networks. *IEEE Transactions on Information Forensics and Security*, 16, 3888–3899. DOI: 10.1109/TIFS.2021.3098971

Feng, Y., Huang, S., Chen, Q. A., Liu, H. X., & Mao, Z. M. (2018). Vulnerability of Traffic Control System Under Cyberattacks with Falsified Data. *Transportation Research Record: Journal of the Transportation Research Board*, 2672(1), 1–11. DOI: 10.1177/0361198118756885

Ferng, H. W., Chen, J. Y., Lotfolahi, A., Tseng, Y. T., & Zhang, S. Y. (2019). Messages classification and dynamic batch verification scheme for VANETs. *IEEE Transactions on Mobile Computing*, 20(3), 1156–1172. DOI: 10.1109/TMC.2019.2952105

Fiore, M., & Mongiello, M. (2023). *Blockchain for Smart Cities Improvement: an Architecture Proposal. ArXiv*. Cornell University., DOI: 10.1109/ICCSM60247.2023.00009

Flagship, G. (2019). Key drivers and research challenges for 6G ubiquitous wireless intelligence. 6G Research Visions, 1, 1-36.

Fulci, C., Rotili, D., De Luca, A., Stella, L., Morozzo della Rocca, B., Forgione, M., Di Paolo, V., Mai, A., Falconi, M., Quintieri, L., & Caccuri, A. M. (2017). A new nitrobenzoxadiazole-based GSTP1-1 inhibitor with a previously unheard of mechanism of action and high stability. *Journal of Enzyme Inhibition and Medicinal Chemistry*, 32(1), 240–247. DOI: 10.1080/14756366.2016.1247059 PMID: 28097896

Fuqaha, A., Khamayseh, Y., & Al-Majali, A. (2021). *6G security challenges and potential solutions*. IEEE Xplore Digital Library., DOI: 10.1109/ACCESS.2021.9482609

Gabriel, A., & Cruz, F. (2022). Open source IoT-based collection bin applied to local plastic recycling. *HardwareX*, X, e00389. DOI: 10.1016/j.ohx.2022.e00389 PMID: 36619212

Galego, N. M. C., & Pascoal, R. M. (2022). Cybersecurity in Smart Cities: Technology and Data Security in Intelligent Transport Systems. Smart Innovation. *Systems and Technologies*, 256. Advance online publication. DOI: 10.1007/978-981-16-5063-5-2

Gao, W., Chen, Z., & Liu, Y. (2024). Energy consumption and optimization techniques in 6G networks. *IEEE Access*. https://ieeexplore.ieee.org/document/9505512

Garach, J., Singh, S. K., Ravikumar, R. N., Reddy, A. P. C., & Khan, H. (2024). A Comprehensive Review on Artificial Intelligence in Digital Forensics With Taxonomies, Issues, and Solutions: AI in Digital Forensics. Strategies for E-Commerce Data Security: Cloud, Blockchain, AI, and Machine Learning, 1-28.

Garg, S., Kaur, K., Aujla, G. S., Kaddoum, G., Garigipati, P., & Guizani, M. (2023). Trusted explainable AI for 6G-Enabled edge cloud ecosystem. *IEEE Wireless Communications*, 30(3), 163–170. DOI: 10.1109/MWC.016.220047

Gayathri, N. B., Thumbur, G., Reddy, P. V., & Rahman, M. Z. U. (2018). Efficient pairing-free certificateless authentication scheme with batch verification for vehicular ad-hoc networks. *IEEE Access : Practical Innovations, Open Solutions*, 6, 31808–31819. DOI: 10.1109/ACCESS.2018.2845464

Gera, R., et al. (2023). Leveraging AI-enabled 6G-driven IoT for sustainable smart cities. *International Journal of Distributed and Connected Systems.*

Gera, B., Raghuvanshi, Y. S., Rawlley, O., Gupta, S., Dua, A., & Sharma, P. (2023). Leveraging AI-enabled 6G-driven IoT for sustainable smart cities. *International Journal of Communication Systems*, 36(16), e5588. DOI: 10.1002/dac.5588

Gharaibeh, A., Salahuddin, M. A., Hussini, S. J., Khreishah, A., Khalil, I., Guizani, M., & Al-Fuqaha, A. (2017). Smart Cities: A Survey on Data Management, Security, and Enabling Technologies. *IEEE Communications Surveys and Tutorials*, 19(4), 2456–2501. DOI: 10.1109/COMST.2017.2736886

Ghor, H. E., & Nakhal, B. (2023). A Blockchain-Enabled Approach for Secure Data Sharing in 6G-based Internet of Things Networks. In Advanced sciences and technologies for security applications (pp. 227–246). DOI: 10.1007/978-3-031-33631-7_8

Giordani, M., Polese, M., Mezzavilla, M., Rangan, S., & Zorzi, M. (2020). Toward 6G Networks: Use Cases and Technologies. *IEEE Communications Magazine*, 58(3), 55–61. DOI: 10.1109/MCOM.001.1900411

Global, T. W. I. (2023). What is a smart city? https://www.twi-global.com/technical-knowledge/faqs/what-is-a-smart-city

Gomes, J. B., Rodrigues, J. J., Rabêlo, R. A., Kumar, N., & Kozlov, S. (2019). IoT-enabled gas sensors: Technologies, applications, and opportunities. *Journal of Sensor and Actuator Networks*, 8(4), 57. DOI: 10.3390/jsan8040057

Goudarzi, A., Ghayoor, F., Waseem, M., Fahad, S., & Traore, I. (2022). A Survey on IoT-Enabled Smart Grids: Emerging, Applications, Challenges, and Outlook. In Energy (Vol. 15, Issue 19). https://doi.org/DOI: 10.3390/en15196984

Greenspan, G. (2015). Is blockchain the most important IT invention of our age? *New World (New Orleans, La.)*, 32(9), 3.

Guerrero-Ibáñez, J. A., Flores-Cortés, C., & Zeadally, S. (2013). Vehicular ad-hoc networks (vanets): architecture, protocols and applications. In *Next-Generation Wireless Technologies: 4G and Beyond* (pp. 49–70). Springer London. DOI: 10.1007/978-1-4471-5164-7_5

Guerrero-Ibáñez, J., Zeadally, S., & Contreras-Castillo, J. (2018). Sensor technologies for intelligent transportation systems. *Sensors (Basel)*, 18(4), 1212. DOI: 10.3390/s18041212 PMID: 29659524

Gui, G., Liu, M., Tang, F., Kato, N., & Adachi, F. (2020). 6G: Opening New Horizons for Integration of Comfort, Security and Intelligence. *IEEE Wireless Communications*, 27(5), 1–7. DOI: 10.1109/MWC.001.1900516

Gul, H., Al-Obeidat, F., Majdalawieh, M., Amin, A., & Moreira, F. (2024a). Features Extraction and Structure Similarities Measurement of Complex Networks. In Rocha, A., Adeli, H., Dzemyda, G., Moreira, F., & Colla, V. (Eds.), *Information Systems and Technologies. WorldCIST 2023. Lecture Notes in Networks and Systems* (Vol. 799). Springer., DOI: 10.1007/978-3-031-45642-8_4

Gul, H., Al-Obeidat, F., Wasim, M., Amin, A., & Moreira, F. (2024b). Advancing Fake News Detection with Graph Neural Network and Deep Learning. *Journal of Physics. Complexity*. Advance online publication. DOI: 10.1088/2632-072X/ad744d

Guo, F., Yu, F. R., Zhang, H., Li, X., Ji, H., & Leung, V. C. (2021). Enabling massive IoT toward 6G: A comprehensive survey. *IEEE Internet of Things Journal*, 8(15), 11891–11915. DOI: 10.1109/JIOT.2021.3063686

Gupta, A., & Jha, R. K. (2020). A survey of 5G network: Architecture and emerging technologies. *IEEE Access : Practical Innovations, Open Solutions*, 3, 1206–1232. DOI: 10.1109/ACCESS.2015.2461602

Gupta, M., Ved, C., & Kumari, M. (2022). Emergence of Blockchain Applications with the 6G-Enabled IoT-Based Smart City. In *Blockchain for 6G-Enabled Network-Based Applications* (pp. 213–235). CRC Press. DOI: 10.1201/9781003264392-9

Gupta, N., & Jha, S. (2023). Exploring cybersecurity frameworks for the next-gen 6G networks. *Telecommunication Systems*, 79(2), 211–228. DOI: 10.1007/s11235-023-01045-7 PMID: 36531286

Gura, N., Patel, A., Wander, A., Eberle, H., & Shantz, S. C. *Comparing elliptic curve cryptography and RSA on 8-bit CPU*, in *CHES*, vol. 4, pp. 119–132, 2004.

Gu, S., Wang, L., Han, R., Liu, X., Wang, Y., Chen, T., & Zheng, Z. (2023). Detection of sarcopenia using a deep learning-based artificial intelligence body part measure system (AIBMS). *Frontiers in Physiology*, 14, 1092352. Advance online publication. DOI: 10.3389/fphys.2023.1092352 PMID: 36776966

Gu, Y., Zha, X., & Li, J. (2020). Surgical robotics and navigation for minimally invasive surgery: A review of the state-of-the-art and future perspectives. *IEEE Access : Practical Innovations, Open Solutions*, 8, 136959–136979. DOI: 10.1109/ACCESS.2020.3012497

Habib, A., Alsmadi, D., & Prybutok, V. R. (2023). Factors that determine residents' acceptance of smart city technologies. In *Smart Cities at Play: Technology and Emerging Forms of Playfulness* (pp. 4-17). CRC Press.

Habib, M. Y., Qureshi, H. A., Khan, S. A., Mansoor, Z., & Chishti, A. R. (2023). Cybersecurity and Smart Cities: Current Status and Future. 2023 IEEE International Conference on Emerging Trends in Engineering, Sciences and Technology (ICES&T), 1–7. https://doi.org/DOI: 10.1109/ICEST56843.2023.10138843

Haferkorn, M., & Quintana Diaz, F. D. (2015). The cryptocurrency market landscape. *Business & Information Systems Engineering*, 57(5), 339–348.

Hagmann, P., Cammoun, L., Gigandet, X., Gerhard, S., Grant, P. E., Wedeen, V., & Sporns, O. (2010). MR connectomics: Principles and challenges. *Journal of Neuroscience Methods*, 194(1), 34–45. DOI: 10.1016/j.jneumeth.2010.01.014 PMID: 20096730

Hall, S. T. (2003). Fountain of Cities: An Examination of Urban Growth and Growth Management with a Regional Proposal for Greater Kansas City. *Kan. JL & Pub. Pol'y*, 13, 619.

Han, H., Zhai, W., & Zhao, J. (2021). Smart city enabled by 5G/6G networks: An intelligent hybrid random access scheme. *arXiv preprint arXiv:2101.06421.*

Haq, I., & Muselemu, O. (2021). Blockchain technology in pharmaceutical industry to prevent counterfeit drugs. *International Journal of Computer Applications*, 174(3), 14–17. DOI: 10.5120/ijca2021920834

Hasan, M., Islam, T., & Bhuiyan, T. (2021). Blockchain and AI in smart cities: A review of recent applications and future trends. *Journal of Information Security and Applications*, 58, 102620. DOI: 10.1016/j.jisa.2021.102620

Hashem, I. A. T., Usmani, R. S. A., Almutairi, M. S., Ibrahim, A. O., Zakari, A., Alotaibi, F., Alhashmi, S. M., & Chiroma, H. (2023). Urban Computing for Sustainable Smart Cities: Recent Advances, Taxonomy, and Open Research Challenges. In Sustainability (Switzerland) (Vol. 15, Issue 5). https://doi.org/DOI: 10.3390/su15053916

Hathaliya, J. J., & Tanwar, S. (2020). An exhaustive survey on security and privacy issues in Healthcare 4.0. *Computer Communications*, 153, 311–335. DOI: 10.1016/j.comcom.2020.02.018

Henrique, P. S. R., & Prasad, R. (2022). *6G: the road to the future wireless technologies 2030*. River Publishers.

Hilmes, M. (2020). *Radio's Second Century: Past, Present, and Future Perspectives*. Rutgers University Press., DOI: 10.36019/9780813598505

Hirschberg, J., & Manning, C. D. (2015). Advances in natural language processing. *Science*, 349(6245), 261–266. DOI: 10.1126/science.aaa8685 PMID: 26185244

Holly, M., Pirker, J., Resch, S., Brettschuh, S., & Gütl, C. (2021). Designing VR experiences–expectations for teaching and learning in VR. *Journal of Educational Technology & Society*, 24(2), 107–119.

Horng, S. J., Tzeng, S. F., Pan, Y., Fan, P., Wang, X., Li, T., & Khan, M. K. (2013). b-SPECS+: Batch verification for secure pseudonymous authentication in VANET. *IEEE Transactions on Information Forensics and Security*, 8(11), 1860–1875. DOI: 10.1109/TIFS.2013.2277471

Hossain, M. S., Muhammad, G., & Alamri, A. (2019). Smart healthcare monitoring: A voice pathology detection paradigm for smart cities. *Multimedia Systems*, 25(5), 565–575. DOI: 10.1007/s00530-017-0561-x

Huang, H., Lin, J., Zheng, B., Zheng, Z., & Bian, J. (2020, March 10). When Blockchain Meets Distributed File Systems: An Overview, Challenges, and Open Issues. *IEEE Access : Practical Innovations, Open Solutions*, 8, 43822–43838. DOI: 10.1109/ACCESS.2020.2979881

Huang, T., Yang, W., Wu, J., Ma, J., Zhang, X., & Zhang, D. (2019). A Survey on Green 6G Network: Architecture and Technologies. *IEEE Access : Practical Innovations, Open Solutions*, 7, 175758–175768. DOI: 10.1109/ACCESS.2019.2957648

Hui, C. X., Dan, G., Alamri, S., & Toghraie, D. (2023). Greening smart cities: An investigation of the integration of urban natural resources and smart city technologies for promoting environmental sustainability. *Sustainable Cities and Society*, 99, 104985. DOI: 10.1016/j.scs.2023.104985

Hussain, A. A., & Al-Turjman, F. (2021). Artificial intelligence and blockchain: A review. *Transactions on Emerging Telecommunications Technologies*, 32(9), e4268. Advance online publication. DOI: 10.1002/ett.4268

Huynh, L. N., & Huh, E. (2021). Envisioning edge computing in future 6G wireless networks. *2021 Fifth World Conference on Smart Trends in Systems Security and Sustainability (WorldS4)*, 307-311. https://doi.org/DOI: 10.1109/WorldS451998.2021.9514026

Hyvarinen, A., Juustila, A., & Seppanen, M. (2017). Blockchain-Enabled Supply Chain Services. *Procedia CIRP*, 64, 639–644.

IBM. (2023). What is a smart city? https://www.ibm.com/topics/smart-city

IBM. *Leading the pack in blockchain banking: Trailblazers set the pace*, 2017. Available: https://www.hyperledger.org/wp-content/uploads/2016/10/Leading-the - pack-in-blockchain-banking-1.pdf

IJERT. (2021). How 6G Has an Influence on Smart Cities: An Overview. *International Journal of Engineering Research & Technology (Ahmedabad)*, 10(5). https://www.ijert.org/research/how-6g-has-an-influence-on-smart-cities-an-overview -IJERTV10IS050447.pdf

Imoize, A. L., Adedeji, O., Tandiya, N., & Shetty, S. (2021). 6G Enabled Smart Infrastructure for Sustainable Society: Opportunities, Challenges, and Research Roadmap. *Sensors (Basel)*, 21(5), 1709. DOI: 10.3390/s21051709 PMID: 33801302

In Compliance Magazine. (2023). The 6G Future: How 6G Will Transform Our Lives. https://incompliancemag.com/the-6g-future-how-6g-will-transform-our-lives/

Inomata, M., Yamada, W., Kuno, N., Sasaki, M., Kitao, K., Nakamura, M., Ishikawa, H., & Oda, Y. (2021). Terahertz propagation characteristics for 6G mobile communication systems. *2021 15th European Conference on Antennas and Propagation (EuCAP)*. https://doi.org/DOI: 10.23919/EuCAP51087.2021.9411143

Interactive, N. X. T. (2023). Augmented reality in Singapore: Navigating the landscape of innovation. Retrieved from: https://www.nxtinteractive.sg/blog/augmented -reality-in-singapore-navigating-the-landscape-of-innovation

Islam, S., Atallah, Z. A., Budati, A. K., Hasan, M. K., Kolandaisamy, R., & Nurhizam, S. (2024). *Mobile Networks Toward 5G/6G: Network Architecture, Opportunities and Challenges in Smart City*. IEEE Open Journal of the Communications Society.

Ismail, L., & Buyya, R. (2022). Artificial intelligence applications and self-learning 6G networks for smart cities digital ecosystems: Taxonomy, challenges, and future directions. *Sensors (Basel)*, 22(15), 5750. DOI: 10.3390/s22155750 PMID: 35957307

ITU. (2021). Focus Group on Technologies for Network 2030. International Telecommunication Union. https://www.itu.int/en/ITU-T/focusgroups/net2030/

ITU. (2022, July). ITU-Recommendation SM.2352-0. Technology Trends of Active Services in the Frequency Range 275–3000 GHz.. Available online: https://www .itu.int/dms_pub/itu-r/opb/rep/R-REP-SM.2352-1-2022-PDF-E

ITU. IMT towards 2030 and Beyond. (2023a). Available online: https://www.itu.int/ en/ITU-R/study-groups/rsg5/rwp5d/imt-2030/Pages/default.aspx

ITU. IMT towards 2030 and Beyond. (2023b). Available online: https://www.itu.int/en/ITU-R/study-groups/rsg5/rwp5d/imt-2030/Pages/default.aspx

Jacob, S., Alagirisamy, M., Xi, C., Balasubramanian, V., Srinivasan, R., Parvathi, R., & Islam, S. M. (2021). AI and IoT-enabled smart exoskeleton system for rehabilitation of paralyzed people in connected communities. *IEEE Access : Practical Innovations, Open Solutions*, 9, 80340–80350. DOI: 10.1109/ACCESS.2021.3083093

Jahid, A., Alsharif, M. H., & Hall, T. J. (2023). The convergence of Blockchain, IoT and 6G: Potential, opportunities, challenges and research roadmap. *Journal of Network and Computer Applications*, 217, 103677. DOI: 10.1016/j.jnca.2023.103677

Jain, V., & Mitra, A. (2024). Case studies and practical implementation of biomimicry in bio-inspired optimization. In *Bio-Inspired Intelligence for Smart Decision-Making* (pp. 85-100). DOI: 10.4018/979-8-3693-5276-2.ch005

Jamil, S. U., Khan, M. A., & ur Rehman, S. (2020). Intelligent task off-loading and resource allocation for 6G smart city environment. In *2020 IEEE 45th Conference on Local Computer Networks (LCN)* (pp. 441-444). IEEE.

Janjua, M. B., Duranay, A. E., & Arslan, H. (2020). Role of wireless communication in healthcare system to cater disaster situations under 6G vision. *Frontiers in Communications and Networks*, 1, 610879. DOI: 10.3389/frcmn.2020.610879

Jansma, N., & Arrendondo, B. (2004). Performance comparison of elliptic curve and rsa digital signatures. nicj. net/files.

Javed, A. R., Shahzad, F., Rehman, S., Zikria, Y. B., Razzak, I., Jalil, Z., & Xu, G. (2022). Future smart cities: Requirements, emerging technologies, applications, challenges, and future aspects. *Cities (London, England)*, 129, 103794. DOI: 10.1016/j.cities.2022.103794

Jayabalan, M., & O'Daniel, T. (2017, November). Continuous and transparent access control framework for electronic health records: A preliminary study. In *2017 2nd International conferences on Information Technology, Information Systems and Electrical Engineering (ICITISEE)* (pp. 165-170). IEEE. DOI: 10.1109/ICITISEE.2017.8285487

Jeremiah, S. R., Ha, J., Singh, S. K., & Park, J. H. (2024) ArticlesPrivacyGuard: Collaborative Edge-Cloud Computing Architecture for Attribute-Preserving Face Anonymization in CCTV Networks.

Jiang, S., Zhu, X., & Wang, L. (2016). An efficient anonymous batch authentication scheme based on HMAC for VANETs. *IEEE Transactions on Intelligent Transportation Systems*, 17(8), 2193–2204. DOI: 10.1109/TITS.2016.2517603

Jiang, W., Han, B., Habibi, M. A., & Schotten, H. D. (2021). The Road Towards 6G: A Comprehensive Survey. *IEEE Open Journal of the Communications Society*, 2, 334–366. DOI: 10.1109/OJCOMS.2021.3057679

Jiang, X., Yuan, Z., Li, Y., & Wu, W. (2021). AI-based security and privacy issues in smart city networks: A survey. *IEEE Internet of Things Journal*, 8(8), 5866–5876. DOI: 10.1109/JIOT.2021.3061005

Ji, B., Wang, Y., Song, K., Li, C., Wen, H., Menon, V. G., & Mumtaz, S. (2021). A survey of computational intelligence for 6G: Key technologies, applications and trends. *IEEE Transactions on Industrial Informatics*, 17(10), 7145–7154. DOI: 10.1109/TII.2021.3052531

Joel, M. R., Manikandan, G., & Bhuvaneswari, G. (2023, March). An Analysis of Security Challenges in Internet of Things (IoT) based Smart Homes. In *2023 Second International Conference on Electronics and Renewable Systems (ICEARS)* (pp. 490-497). IEEE. DOI: 10.1109/ICEARS56392.2023.10085106

Jo, W., Kim, S. J., Kim, H., Shin, Y., & Shon, T. (2022). Automatic whitelist generation system for Ethernet based in-vehicle network. *Computers in Industry*, 142, 103735. Advance online publication. DOI: 10.1016/j.compind.2022.103735

Jun, Y., Craig, A., Shafik, W., & Sharif, L. (2021; Vol. 2021). Artificial Intelligence Application in Cybersecurity and Cyberdefense. In Wireless Communications and Mobile Computing., DOI: 10.1155/2021/3329581

Kalinaki, K. (2024). IoT and Blockchain Integration for Enhanced AI-Driven Business Intelligence. In *Intersection of AI and Business Intelligence in Data-Driven Decision-Making* (pp. 21–52). IGI Global., DOI: 10.4018/979-8-3693-5288-5.ch002

Kamruzzaman, M. M. (2022). Key technologies, applications and trends of internet of things for energy-efficient 6G wireless communication in smart cities. *Energies*, 15(15), 5608. DOI: 10.3390/en15155608

Kamruzzaman, M. M., Hossin, M. A., Alruwaili, O., Alanazi, S., Alruwaili, M., Alshammari, N., Alaerjan, A., & Zaman, R. (2022). IoT-Oriented 6G Wireless Network System for Smart Cities. *Computational Intelligence and Neuroscience*, 2022(1), 1874436. DOI: 10.1155/2022/1874436 PMID: 35990150

Karthikeyan, H., & Usha, G. (2023). A secured IoT-based intelligent transport system (IoT-ITS) framework based on cognitive science. *Soft Computing*, •••, 1–11. DOI: 10.1007/s00500-023-08410-7 PMID: 37362258

Kasinathan, P., Pugazhendhi, R., Elavarasan, R. M., Ramachandaramurthy, V. K., Ramanathan, V., Subramanian, S., Kumar, S., Nandhagopal, K., Raghavan, R. R. V., Rangasamy, S., Devendiran, R., & Alsharif, M. H. (2022). Realization of sustainable development goals with disruptive technologies by integrating industry 5.0, society 5.0, smart cities and villages. *Sustainability (Basel)*, 14(22), 15258. DOI: 10.3390/su142215258

Kathole, A. B., Katti, J., Dhabliya, D., Deshpande, V., Rajawat, A. S., Goyal, S. B., Raboaca, M. S., Mihaltan, T. C., Verma, C., & Suciu, G. (2022). Energy-Aware UAV Based on Blockchain Model Using IoE Application in 6G Network-Driven Cybertwin. *Energies*, 15(21), 8304. DOI: 10.3390/en15218304

Kaur, J., & Khan, M. A. (2022). Sixth generation (6G) wireless technology: An overview, vision, challenges and use cases. In *2022 IEEE region 10 symposium (TENSYMP)* (pp. 1-6). IEEE.

Kavitha, A. R. (2022). 6G with Smart Healthcare Systems. In Handbook of Research on Design, Deployment, Automation, and Testing Strategies for 6G Mobile Core Network (pp. 284-302). IGI Global.

Kemp, J. M. (2023). *Enabling Security Analysis and Education of the Ethereum Platform: A Network Traffic Dissection Tool.* James Madison University.

Khadidos, A. O., Shitharth, S., Manoharan, H., Yafoz, A., Khadidos, A. O., & Alyoubi, K. H. (2022). An Intelligent Security Framework Based on Collaborative Mutual Authentication Model for Smart City Networks. *IEEE Access : Practical Innovations, Open Solutions*, 10, 85289–85304. DOI: 10.1109/ACCESS.2022.3197672

Khalil, U., Malik, O. A., Uddin, M., & Chen, C. (2022). A Comparative Analysis on Blockchain versus Centralized Authentication Architectures for IoT-Enabled Smart Devices in Smart Cities: A Comprehensive Review, Recent Advances, and Future Research Directions. *Sensors (Basel)*, 22(14), 5168. DOI: 10.3390/s22145168 PMID: 35890848

Khalil, U., Mueen-Uddin, , Malik, O. A., & Hussain, S. (2022). A Blockchain Footprint for Authentication of IoT-Enabled Smart Devices in Smart Cities: State-of-the-Art Advancements, Challenges and Future Research Directions. *IEEE Access : Practical Innovations, Open Solutions*, 10, 76805–76823. DOI: 10.1109/ACCESS.2022.3189998

Khan, A., Jameel, M., & Loo, J. (2021). AI-driven predictive analytics for smart cities: A comprehensive review. *Sensors (Basel)*, 21(6), 2029. DOI: 10.3390/s21062029 PMID: 33809368

Khan, I. A., Pi, D., Abbas, M. Z., Zia, U., Hussain, Y., & Soliman, H. (2022). Federated-SRUs: A Federated Simple Recurrent Units-based IDS for Accurate Detection of Cyber Attacks Against IoT-augmented Industrial Control Systems. *IEEE Internet of Things Journal*. Advance online publication. DOI: 10.1109/JIOT.2022.3200048

Khan, L. U., Saad, W., Han, Z., Hossain, E., & Hong, C. S. (2021). Artificial intelligence-enabled wireless networks for the 6G era. *IEEE Network*, 35(6), 200–209. DOI: 10.1109/MNET.011.2100019

Khan, M. A., Shafiq, M., Ullah, I., & Khattak, A. M. (2020). Security and privacy issues in the key areas of the 6G network. *Journal of Network and Computer Applications*, 169, 102656. DOI: 10.1016/j.jnca.2020.102656

Khan, M. J. (2023). Zero trust architecture: Redefining network security paradigms in the digital age. *World Journal of Advanced Research and Reviews*, 19(3), 105–116. DOI: 10.30574/wjarr.2023.19.3.1785

Khan, P. W., Byun, Y.-C., & Park, N. (2020). A Data Verification System for CCTV Surveillance Cameras Using Blockchain Technology in Smart Cities. *Electronics (Basel)*, 9(3), 484. DOI: 10.3390/electronics9030484

Kharche, A., Badholia, S., & Upadhyay, R. K. (2024). Implementation of blockchain technology in integrated IoT networks for constructing scalable ITS systems in India. *Blockchain Research and Applications*, 5(2), 100188. DOI: 10.1016/j.bcra.2024.100188

Khattak, S. B. A., Nasralla, M. M., & Rehman, I. U. (2022, September). The role of 6g networks in enabling future smart health services and applications. In 2022 IEEE International Smart Cities Conference (ISC2) (pp. 1-7). IEEE.

Khattak, S. B. A., Nasralla, M. M., & Rehman, I. U. (2022). The role of 6g networks in enabling future smart health services and applications. In *2022 IEEE International Smart Cities Conference (ISC2)* (pp. 1-7). IEEE.

Khrais, L. T. (2020). IoT and Blockchain in the Development of Smart Cities. *International Journal of Advanced Computer Science and Applications*, 11(2). Advance online publication. DOI: 10.14569/IJACSA.2020.0110220

Kiasaraei, M. M., Nikitopoulos, K., & Tafazolli, R. (2023). Towards Ultra-Power-Efficient, Tbps Wireless Systems via Analogue Processing: Existing Approaches, Challenges and Way Forward. *IEEE Communications Surveys and Tutorials*.

Kim, H., & Laskowski, M. (2018). The impact of blockchain technology on copyright protection. *International Journal of Law and Information Technology*, 26(3), 234–256.

Kim, J., & Lee, H. (2020). The smart city: A case study of Songdo City. *International Journal of Urban Sciences*, 24(3), 298–315. DOI: 10.1080/12265934.2020.1763297

Kiviat, T. (2015). A public blockchain case study. *Ledger*, 1, 35–39.

Konhäuser, W. (2021). Digitalization in Buildings and Smart Cities on the Way to 6G. *Wireless Personal Communications*, 121(2), 1289–1302. DOI: 10.1007/s11277-021-09069-9

Krishnamurthi, R., & Shree, T. (January 2021). A Brief Analysis of Blockchain Algorithms and Its Challenges. In *Research Anthology on Blockchain Technology in Business, Health- care* (pp. 23–39). Education, and Government., DOI: 10.4018/978-1-7998-5351-0.ch002

Kulkarni, R., & Kulkarni, S. (2021). How 6G has an influence on smart cities: An overview. *International Journal of Engineering Research & Technology (Ahmedabad)*, 10(5), 258–275.

Kumar Singh, S., Pan, Y., & Hyuk Park, J. (2021). OTS scheme based secure architecture for energy-efficient IoT in edge infrastructure. *Computers, Materials & Continua*, 66(3), 2905–2922. DOI: 10.32604/cmc.2021.014151

Kumar, A., Jain, R., Gupta, M., & Islam, S. M. (Eds.). (2023). *6G-enabled IoT and AI for smart healthcare: Challenges, impact, and analysis*. CRC Press. DOI: 10.1201/9781003321668

Kumar, A., Saxena, D., & Singh, A. K. (2021, February). A Cryptography and Machine Learning Based Authentication for Secure Data-Sharing in Federated Cloud Services Envi- ronment. *Journal of Applied Security Research*, 17(7), 385–412. Advance online publication. DOI: 10.1080/19361610.2020.1870404

Kumari, A., Gupta, R., & Tanwar, S. (2021). Amalgamation of blockchain and IoT for smart cities underlying 6G communication: A comprehensive review. *Computer Communications*, 172, 102–118. DOI: 10.1016/j.comcom.2021.03.005

Kumar, M., Singh, S. K., & Kim, S. (2024). Predictive Analytics for Mortality: FSRNCA-FLANN Modeling Using Public Health Inventory Records. *IEEE Access : Practical Innovations, Open Solutions*, 12, 81252–81264. DOI: 10.1109/ACCESS.2024.3411162

Kumar, R., Jain, V., Yie, L. W., & Teyarachakul, S. (2023). *Convergence of IoT, Blockchain, and Computational Intelligence in Smart Cities*. CRC Press. DOI: 10.1201/9781003353034

Kunwar, F. B., Singh, H. S., & Yadav, R. K. Y. (2024). Role of blockchain-enabled Secure Supply Chain management using IIoT for Anomaly detection in 6G. *Research Square(Research Square)*. DOI: 10.21203/rs.3.rs-3882212/v1

Kuru, K., & Ansell, D. (2020). TCitySmartF: A comprehensive systematic framework for transforming cities into smart cities. *IEEE Access : Practical Innovations, Open Solutions*, 8, 18615–18644. DOI: 10.1109/ACCESS.2020.2967777

Kute, V. B., Paradhi, P. R., & Bamnote, G. R. (2009). A software comparison of RSA and ECC. *International Journal Computer Science Applications*, 2(1), 43–59.

Latif, S., Qadir, J., Farooq, S., & Imran, M. A. (2017). How 5G wireless (and concomitant technologies) will revolutionize healthcare? *Future Internet*, 9(4), 93. DOI: 10.3390/fi9040093

Latif, S., Zafar, N. A., Qadir, J., & Gawande, A. (2021). Security in 6G: Key enablers and challenges. *IEEE Access : Practical Innovations, Open Solutions*, 9, 167074–167092. DOI: 10.1109/ACCESS.2021.3121239

Lee, H., Lee, B., Yang, H., Kim, J., Kim, S., Shin, W., Shim, B., & H. Vincent Poor. (2023). *Towards 6G hyper-connectivity: Vision, challenges, and key enabling technologies*. 1–11. DOI: 10.23919/JCN.2023.000006

Lei, S., & Liu, H. (2022). Deep Learning Dual Neural Networks in the Construction of Learning Models for Online Courses in Piano Education. *Computational Intelligence and Neuroscience*, 2022, 1–8. Advance online publication. DOI: 10.1155/2022/4408288 PMID: 35875728

Letaief, K. B., Chen, W., Shi, Y., Zhang, J., & Zhang, Y. J. A. (2019). The Roadmap to 6G: AI Empowered Wireless Networks. *IEEE Communications Magazine*, 57(8), 84–90. DOI: 10.1109/MCOM.2019.1900271

Li, J., Wang, H., & Zhang, L. (2024). Advances in THz and mmWave communications for 6G systems. *IEEE Communications Magazine*. https://ieeexplore.ieee.org/document/9505514

Li, W., Zhang, X., & Liu, C. (2022). Privacy taxonomy in B5G/6G networks: Challenges and solutions. *arXiv preprint*. https://arxiv.org/pdf/2203.04264

Liao, S. K., Cai, W. Q., Handsteiner, J., Liu, B., Yin, J., Zhang, L., Rauch, D., Fink, M., Ren, J.-G., Liu, W.-Y., Li, Y., Shen, Q., Cao, Y., Li, F.-Z., Wang, J.-F., Huang, Y.-M., Deng, L., Xi, T., Ma, L., & Pan, J. W. (2018). Satellite-relayed intercontinental quantum network. *Physical Review Letters*, 120(3), 030501. DOI: 10.1103/PhysRevLett.120.030501 PMID: 29400544

LibP2P. Accessed: Jan. 2020. [Online]. Available: https://github.com/libp2p

Ling, R. (2021). *Mobile communication: The story of a technology that changed society*. John Wiley & Sons.

Ling, R., & Lai, C. H. (2016). Mobile communication: Digital media and society series. *Polity*.

LinkedIn. (2023). Impact of 6G Technology: Anticipating the Next Generation of Wireless Communication. https://www.linkedin.com/pulse/impact-6g-technology-anticipating-next-generation-wireless-qlnnc/

Lin, X., & Li, X. (2013). Achieving efficient cooperative message authentication in vehicular ad hoc networks. *IEEE Transactions on Vehicular Technology*, 62(7), 3339–3348. DOI: 10.1109/TVT.2013.2257188

Liu, H., Zhang, Y., & Wang, J. (2023). Intelligent network management and orchestration for 6G smart cities. *IEEE Transactions on Network and Service Management*. https://ieeexplore.ieee.org/document/9473125

Liu, H., Zong, J., Wang, Q., Liu, Y., & Yang, F. (2022). Cloud native based intelligent RAN architecture towards 6G programmable networking. *2022 7th International Conference on Computer and Communication Systems (ICCCS)*. https://doi.org/ DOI: 10.1109/ICCCS55155.2022.9846266

Liu, Y., Peng, S., Zhang, M., Shi, S., & Fu, J. (2024). Towards secure and efficient integration of blockchain and 6G networks. *PLoS One*, 19(4), e0302052. DOI: 10.1371/journal.pone.0302052 PMID: 38603725

Liu, Y., Wang, L., & Chen, H. H. (2014). Message authentication using proxy vehicles in vehicular ad hoc networks. *IEEE Transactions on Vehicular Technology*, 64(8), 3697–3710. DOI: 10.1109/TVT.2014.2358633

Li, W., Su, Z., Li, R., Zhang, K., & Wang, Y. (2020). Blockchain-Based Data Security for Artificial Intelligence Applications in 6G Networks. *IEEE Network*, 34(6), 31–37. DOI: 10.1109/MNET.021.1900629

Liwen, Z., Qamar, F., Liaqat, M., Hindia, M. N., & Ariffin, K. Z. (2024). Towards Efficient 6G IoT Networks: A Perspective on Resource Optimization Strategies, Challenges, and Future Directions. *IEEE Access : Practical Innovations, Open Solutions*, 12, 76606–76633. DOI: 10.1109/ACCESS.2024.3405487

Li, X., Li, T., & Wu, Y. (2020). Possible capabilities of 6G in comparison with 5G. *Dianzi Yu Xinxi Xuebao*, 42(4), 1000–1007. https://www.researchgate.net/figure/Possible-capabilities-of-6G-in-comparison-with-5G_tbl1_339370534

Li, Y., & Chan, K. H. (2021). Smart cities in China: AI and digital governance in urban development. *Journal of Urban Affairs*, 43(5), 739–752. DOI: 10.1080/07352166.2020.1806346

Li, Y., Liu, C., Qian, Y., & Wang, X. (2021). Secure AI frameworks for smart city systems. *IEEE Network*, 35(4), 36–41. DOI: 10.1109/MNET.2021.3135925

Li, Y., Xiao, Y., Liang, W., Cai, J., Zhang, R., Li, K. C., & Khan, M. K. (2024). The security and privacy challenges toward cybersecurity of 6G networks: A comprehensive review. *Computer Science and Information Systems*, 21(00), 16–16. DOI: 10.2298/CSIS230804016L

Lopez-Martin, M., Carro, B., Sanchez-Esguevillas, A., & Lloret, J. (2017). Network traffic classifier with convolutional and recurrent neural networks for Internet of Things. *IEEE Access : Practical Innovations, Open Solutions*, 5, 18042–18050. DOI: 10.1109/ACCESS.2017.2747560

Losavio, M., Sun, J., Kerrick, S., Elmaghraby, A., Purdy, C., & Johnson, C. (2022). Integrating Democratic Cybersecurity. *International Conference on Cyber Warfare and Security*, 17(1). https://doi.org/DOI: 10.34190/iccws.17.1.37

Lupton, B., Zappe, M., Thom, J., Sengupta, S., & Feil-Seifer, D. (2022). Analysis and Prevention of Security Vulnerabilities in a Smart City. 2022 IEEE 12th Annual Computing and Communication Workshop and Conference, CCWC 2022. https://doi.org/DOI: 10.1109/CCWC54503.2022.9720824

Luther, W., Baloian, N., Biella, D., & Sacher, D. (2023). Digital twins and enabling technologies in museums and cultural heritage: An overview. *Sensors (Basel)*, 23(3), 1583. DOI: 10.3390/s23031583 PMID: 36772623

Lu, Y., & Ning, X. (2020). A vision of 6G–5G's successor. *Journal of Management Analytics*, 7(3), 301–320. DOI: 10.1080/23270012.2020.1802622

Lu, Y., & Zheng, X. (2020). 6G: A survey on technologies, scenarios, challenges, and the related issues. *Journal of Industrial Information Integration*, 19, 100158. DOI: 10.1016/j.jii.2020.100158

Ma, G., Khalili, M., Parthiban, R., & Katz, M. (2023). A low-complexity handover scheme using unsupervised learning techniques for 6G multi-networking. *2023 2nd International Conference on 6G Networking (6GNet), 101*, 1-5. https://doi.org/DOI: 10.1109/6GNet58894.2023.10317655

Ma, C. (2021a). Smart city and cyber-security; technologies used, leading challenges, and future recommendations. *Energy Reports*, 7, 7999–8012. DOI: 10.1016/j.egyr.2021.08.124

Madakam, S., Ramaswamy, R., & Tripathi, S. (2015). Internet of Things (IoT): A literature review. *Journal of Computer and Communications*, 3(5), 164–173. DOI: 10.4236/jcc.2015.35021

Mahmood, N. H., Alves, H., Lopez, O. A., Shehab, M., Osorio, D. P., & Latva-Aho, M. (2020). Six key features of machine type communication in 6G. *2020 2nd 6G Wireless Summit (6G SUMMIT)*. https://doi.org/DOI: 10.1109/6GSUMMIT49458.2020.9083794

Mahto, D., & Yadav, D. K. (2013). Network security using ECC with Biometric. In Quality, Reliability, Security and Robustness in Heterogeneous Networks: 9th International Conference, QShine 2013, Greader Noida, India, January 11-12, 2013, Revised Selected Papers 9 (pp. 842-853). Springer Berlin Heidelberg.

Mahto, D., & Yadav, D. K. (2015, February). Enhancing security of one-time password using elliptic curve cryptography with biometrics for e-commerce applications. In Proceedings of the 2015 third international conference on computer, communication, control and information technology (C3it) (pp. 1-6). IEEE.

Mahto, D., & Yadav, D. K. (2016). Security improvement of one-time password using crypto-biometric model. In Proceedings of 3rd International Conference on Advanced Computing, Networking and Informatics: ICACNI 2015, Volume 2 (pp. 347-353). Springer India.

Mahto, D., Khan, D. A., & Yadav, D. K. (2016, June). Security analysis of elliptic curve cryptography and RSA. In *Proceedings of the world congress on engineering* (Vol. 1, pp. 419-422).

Mahto, D., & Yadav, D. K. (2017). One-time password communication security improve- ment using elliptic curve cryptography with iris biometric. *International Journal of Applied Engineering Research: IJAER*, 12(18), 7105–7114.

Mahto, D., & Yadav, D. K. (2017). RSA and ECC: A comparative analysis. *International Journal of Applied Engineering Research: IJAER*, 12(19), 9053–9061.

Mahto, D., & Yadav, D. K. (2017). Secure online medical consultations using elliptic curve cryptography with iris biometric. *International Journal of Control Theory and Applications*, 10(13), 169–179.

Maier, M., Ebrahimzadeh, A., Beniiche, A., & Rostami, S. (2022). The Art of 6G (TAO 6G): How to wire Society 5.0. *Journal of Optical Communications and Networking*, 14(2), A101–A112. DOI: 10.1364/JOCN.438522

Mallett, R. K. (2012). Eco-guilt motivates eco-friendly behavior. *Ecopsychology*, 4(3), 223–231. DOI: 10.1089/eco.2012.0031

Manikandan, G., Bhuvaneswari, G., & Joel, M. R. (2023, August). Artificial Intelligence to the Assessment, Monitoring, and Forecasting of Drought in Developing Countries. In *2023 International Conference on Circuit Power and Computing Technologies (ICCPCT)* (pp. 886-892). IEEE. DOI: 10.1109/ICCPCT58313.2023.10245072

Mansoor, A., Nasir, A., & Rehman, M. H. (2023). Taxonomy for the Threat Model in 6G Mobile Networks. *Symmetry*, 15(6), 1147. DOI: 10.3390/sym15061147

Mantere, M. (2013, September). Stock market manipulation using cyberattacks together with misinformation disseminated through social media. In *2013 International Conference on Social Computing* (pp. 950-954). IEEE. DOI: 10.1109/SocialCom.2013.149

Manville, C., Hinrichs, S., Parks, S., Kamenetzky, A., Gunashekar, S., Wilkinson, B., & Grant, J. (2015). *Characteristics of high-performing research units*. Prepared for the Higher Education Funding Council for England.

Mavroeidis, V., Vishi, K., Zych, M. D., & Jøsang, A. (2018). The impact of quantum computing on present cryptography. *International Journal of Advanced Computer Science and Applications*, 9(3), 405–414. DOI: 10.14569/IJACSA.2018.090354

McGraw, G., Migues, S., & West, J. (2018). *Building security in maturity model (BSIMM9)*. Synopsys Software Integrity Group.

Mingxiao, D., Xiaofeng, M., Zhe, Z., Xiangwei, W., & Qijun, C. (2017, October). A review on consensus algorithm of blockchain. In 2017 IEEE international conference on systems, man, and cybernetics (SMC) (pp. 2567-2572). IEEE.

Mishra, P., & Singh, G. (2023). 6G-IoT framework for sustainable smart city: Vision and challenges. In *Sustainable Smart Cities: Enabling Technologies, Energy Trends and Potential Applications* (pp. 97–117). Springer International Publishing. DOI: 10.1007/978-3-031-33354-5_5

Mitra, A., & Lohochoudhury, B. (2019). Identifying anthropogenic factors of groundwater pollution through student's opinion in rural West Bengal. *Anthropogenic Pollution*, 3(2), 49–59.

Mohammadi Makrani, H., He, Z., Rafatirad, S., & Sayadi, H. (2022). Accelerated Machine Learning for On-Device Hardware-Assisted Cybersecurity in Edge Platforms. Proceedings - International Symposium on Quality Electronic Design, ISQED, 2022-April. https://doi.org/DOI: 10.1109/ISQED54688.2022.9806150

Mohammad, N. (2019). A Multi-Tiered Defense Model for the Security Analysis of Critical Facilities in Smart Cities. *IEEE Access : Practical Innovations, Open Solutions*, 7, 152585–152598. DOI: 10.1109/ACCESS.2019.2947638

Mohapatra, H., & Dalai, A. K. (2022). IoT based V2I framework for accident prevention. *2022 2nd International Conference on Artificial Intelligence and Signal Processing (AISP), 0*, 1-4. https://doi.org/DOI: 10.1109/AISP53593.2022.9760623

Mohapatra, H., Mohanta, B. K., Nikoo, M. R., Daneshmand, M., & Gandomi, A. H. (2023). MCDM-based routing for IoT-enabled smart water distribution network. *IEEE Internet of Things Journal*, 10(5), 4271–4280. DOI: 10.1109/JIOT.2022.3216402

Mora, H., Mendoza-Tello, J. C., Varela-Guzmán, E. G., & Szymanski, J. (2021). Blockchain technologies to address smart city and society challenges. *Computers in Human Behavior*, 122, 106854. DOI: 10.1016/j.chb.2021.106854

Moudoud, H., Cherkaoui, S., & Khoukhi, L. (2021). *An Overview of Blockchain and 5G Networks. Computational Intelligence in Recent Communication Networks. EAI/Springer Innovations in Communication and Computing*. Springer., DOI: 10.1007/978-3-030-77185-0_1

Mucchi, L., Jayousi, S., Caputo, S., Paoletti, E., Zoppi, P., Geli, S., & Dioniso, P. (2020). How 6G Technology Can Change the Future Wireless Healthcare. *2020 2nd 6G Wireless Summit (6G SUMMIT)*. DOI: 10.1109/6GSUMMIT49458.2020.9083916

Mukherjee, A., Maiti, D., & Acharya, D. (2021). Smart cities: AI-driven urban development. *IEEE Internet of Things Journal*, 8(10), 7923–7935. DOI: 10.1109/JIOT.2021.3063267

Mukherjee, M. (2022). Quantum computing—An emerging computing paradigm. In *Emerging computing: From devices to systems: Looking beyond Moore and Von Neumann* (pp. 145–167). Springer Nature Singapore.

Murroni, M., Anedda, M., Fadda, M., Ruiu, P., Popescu, V., Zaharia, C., & Giusto, D. (2023). 6G—Enabling the New Smart City: A Survey. *Sensors (Basel)*, 23(17), 7528. DOI: 10.3390/s23177528 PMID: 37687986

Muzylyov, D., & Shramenko, N. (2019, September). Blockchain technology in transportation as a part of the efficiency in industry 4.0 strategy. In *Grabchenko's International Conference on Advanced Manufacturing Processes* (pp. 216-225). Cham: Springer International Publishing.

Mylrea, M., & Gourisetti, S. N. G. (2017). *Blockchain for smart grid resilience: Exchanging distributed energy at speed, scale and security. 2017 Resilience Week*. RWS., DOI: 10.1109/RWEEK.2017.8088642

Nag, A., & Mishra, S. (2023). Stakeholders' perception and competitiveness of heritage towns: A systematic literature review. *Tourism Management Perspectives*, 48, 101156. DOI: 10.1016/j.tmp.2023.101156

Nakamoto, S. (2008). *Bitcoin: A peer-to-peer electronic cash system.* Satoshi Nakamoto.

Nasralla, M. M., Khattak, S. B. A., Ur Rehman, I., & Iqbal, M. (2023). Exploring the role of 6G technology in enhancing quality of experience for m-health multimedia applications: A comprehensive survey. *Sensors (Basel)*, 23(13), 5882. DOI: 10.3390/s23135882 PMID: 37447735

Nassereddine, M., & Khang, A. (2024). Applications of Internet of Things (IoT) in smart cities. In *Advanced IoT technologies and applications in the industry 4.0 digital economy* (pp. 109–136). CRC Press. DOI: 10.1201/9781003434269-6

Nawaz, F., Ibrahim, J., Muhammad, A. A., Junaid, M., Kousar, S., & Parveen, T. (2020). A review of vision and challenges of 6G technology. *International Journal of Advanced Computer Science and Applications*, 11(2). Advance online publication. DOI: 10.14569/IJACSA.2020.0110281

Nawaz, S. J., Sharma, S. K., Wyne, S., Patwary, M. N., & Asaduzzaman, M. (2019). Quantum Machine Learning for 6G Communication Networks: State-of-the-Art and Vision for the Future. *IEEE Access : Practical Innovations, Open Solutions*, 7, 46317–46350. DOI: 10.1109/ACCESS.2019.2909490

Nayak, S., & Patgiri, R. (2021). 6G communication technology: A vision on intelligent healthcare. *Health informatics: A computational perspective in healthcare*, 1-18.

Nayak, S., & Patgiri, R. (2021). 6G communication technology: A vision on intelligent healthcare. In *Health informatics: A computational perspective in healthcare* (pp. 1–18). Springer., DOI: 10.1007/978-981-15-5909-2_1

Nelson, M., & Watson, C. (2022). *The State of the Merge: An Update on Ethereum's Merge to Proof of Stake in 2022.* ConsenSys.

Nguyen, T. Q., Ngoc Quyen Tran, Lovén, L., Juha Partala, Tahar Kechadi, & Pirttikangas, S. (2020). *Privacy-Aware Blockchain Innovation for 6G: Challenges and Opportunities.* .DOI: 10.1109/6GSUMMIT49458.2020.9083832

Nguyen, D. C., Ding, M., Pathirana, P. N., Seneviratne, A., Li, J., Niyato, D., Dobre, O., & Poor, H. V. (2021). 6G Internet of Things: A comprehensive survey. *IEEE Internet of Things Journal*, 9(1), 359–383. DOI: 10.1109/JIOT.2021.3103320

Nguyen, D. C., Pathirana, P. N., Ding, M., & Seneviratne, A. (2022). Blockchain for 6G: Challenges, opportunities, and future directions. *IEEE Internet of Things Journal*, 9(11), 8551–8564. DOI: 10.1109/JIOT.2021.3114320

Nguyen, G. T., & Kim, K. (2018). A survey about consensus algorithms used in blockchain. *Journal of Information Processing Systems*, 14(1).

Noman, H. M. F., Hanafi, E., Noordin, K. A., Dimyati, K., Hindia, M. N., Abdrabou, A., & Qamar, F. (2023). Machine Learning Empowered Emerging [Recent Advancements, Challenges & Future Trends. IEEE Access.]. *Wireless Networks*, •••, 6G.

Noori, N., Hoppe, T., & de Jong, M. (2020). Classifying pathways for smart city development: Comparing design, governance and implementation in Amsterdam, Barcelona, Dubai, and Abu Dhabi. *Sustainability (Basel)*, 12(10), 4030. DOI: 10.3390/su12104030

Norp, T., Sachdeva, P., Anton, C., Trichias, K., & Mohnani, P. (2024). 6G research & Innovation activities in Europe: An overview of EU & Nationally funded programmes. *2024 Joint European Conference on Networks and Communications & 6G Summit (EuCNC/6G Summit)*, 1109-1114. https://doi.org/DOI: 10.1109/EuCNC/6GSummit60053.2024.10597076

Nova, S. N., Rahman, M. S., & Chakraborty, C. (2021). Patients' health surveillance model using IoT and 6G technology. Green Technological Innovation for Sustainable Smart Societies: Post Pandemic Era, 191-209.

O'Dair, M., Beaven, Z., Neilson, D., Osborne, R., & Pacifico, P. (2016). Music on the Blockchain. Middlesex University, July.

Osama, M., Ateya, A. A., Ahmed Elsaid, S., & Muthanna, A. (2022). Ultra-reliable low-latency communications: Unmanned aerial vehicles assisted systems. *Information (Basel)*, 13(9), 430. DOI: 10.3390/info13090430

Osorio, D. P. M., Ahmad, I., Sánchez, J. D. V., Gurtov, A., Scholliers, J., Kutila, M., & Porambage, P. (2022). Towards 6G-enabled internet of vehicles: Security and privacy. *IEEE Open Journal of the Communications Society*, 3, 82–105. DOI: 10.1109/OJCOMS.2022.3143098

Ounza, J. E. (2023). A taxonomical survey of 5G and 6G security and privacy issues. *Global Journal of Engineering and Technology Advances, 14*(3), 042-060.

Overby, H., & Audestad, J. A. (2020). Standards, Regulations, and Net Neutrality in the Digital Economy. *Regulations, and Net Neutrality in the Digital Economy.*

Ożadowicz, A., & Grela, J. (2017). Energy saving in the street lighting control system—A new approach based on the EN-15232 standard. *Energy Efficiency*, 10(3), 563–576. DOI: 10.1007/s12053-016-9476-1

Özarpa, C., Avci, İ., & Kinaci, B. F. (2023). Cyberattack Measures in Smart Cities and Grids. In EAI/Springer Innovations in Communication and Computing. https://doi.org/DOI: 10.1007/978-3-031-09729-4-7

Padmal, M., Marasinghe, D., Isuru, V., Jayaweera, N., Ali, S., & Rajatheva, N. (2022, June). Elevated lidar based sensing for 6g-3d maps with cm level accuracy. In 2022 IEEE 95th Vehicular Technology Conference:(VTC2022-Spring) (pp. 1-5). IEEE.

Paech, P. (2017). Governance in Blockchain Technologies & Social Contract Theories. *Ledger*, 2, 49–78.

Pagliari, C. (2020). The ethics and value of contact tracing apps: International insights and implications for Scotland's COVID-19 response. *Journal of Global Health*, 10(2), 020103. Advance online publication. DOI: 10.7189/jogh.10.020103 PMID: 33110502

Pajooh, H. H., Demidenko, S., Aslam, S., & Harris, M. (2022). Harris. M. Blockchain and 6G-Enabled IoT. *Inventions (Basel, Switzerland)*, 2022(7), 109. DOI: 10.3390/inventions7040109

Palaniappan, D., Davda, Y., & Premavathi, T. (2023). Digital Marketing Based on Machine Learning. In *Advances in logistics, operations, and management science book series* (pp. 143–170). DOI: 10.4018/978-1-6684-9062-4.ch009

Pamungkas, B. (2022). The Future of Cities in the Metaverse Era: Are Indonesian Cities Ready. *Megafury Apriandhini, SH, MH Chair of 4th OSC, 401*.

Panwar, N., Sharma, S., & Singh, A. (2022). The road ahead to 6G: Technology advances and challenges. *IEEE Communications Standards Magazine*, 6(2), 24–32. DOI: 10.1109/MCOMSTD.2022.9751483

Pardini, K., Rodrigues, J. J. P. C., Diallo, O., Das, A. K., de Albuquerque, V. H. C., & Kozlov, S. A. (2020). A Smart Waste Management Solution Geared Towards Citizens. *Sensors (Basel)*, 20(8), 2380. DOI: 10.3390/s20082380 PMID: 32331464

Parra-Ullauri, J. M., Zhang, X., Bravalheri, A., Moazzeni, S., Wu, Y., Nejabati, R., & Simeonidou, D. (2024). Federated Analytics for 6G Networks: Applications, Challenges, and Opportunities. *IEEE Network*.

Pilkington, M. (2016). Blockchain technology: principles and applications. In *Research handbook on digital transformations* (pp. 225–253). Edward Elgar Publishing. DOI: 10.4337/9781784717766.00019

Pilosu, L., Mossucca, L., Scionti, A., Giordanengo, G., Renga, F., Ruiu, P., . . . Vecchi, G. (2017). Low power computing and communication system for critical environments. In Advances on P2P, Parallel, Grid, Cloud and Internet Computing: Proceedings of the 11th International Conference on P2P, Parallel, Grid, Cloud and Internet Computing (3PGCIC–2016) November 5–7, 2016, Soonchunhyang University, Asan, Korea (pp. 221-232). Springer International Publishing. DOI: 10.1007/978-3-319-49109-7_21

Pirandola, S., Andersen, U. L., Banchi, L., Berta, M., Bunandar, D., Colbeck, R., Englund, D., Gehring, T., Lupo, C., Ottaviani, C., Pereira, J. L., Razavi, M., Shamsul Shaari, J., Tomamichel, M., Usenko, V. C., Vallone, G., Villoresi, P., & Wallden, P. (2020). Advances in quantum cryptography. *Advances in Optics and Photonics*, 12(4), 1012–1236. DOI: 10.1364/AOP.361502

Pires, R., Blue, H., Malinen, J., De Angelis, M., Giardina, P. G., Landi, G., Laukkanen, M., Ahola, K., & Porambage, P. (2024). Closed-loop automation in 6G for minimum downtime task continuity in surveillance Cobots. *2024 Joint European Conference on Networks and Communications & 6G Summit (EuCNC/6G Summit)*, 860-865. https://doi.org/DOI: 10.1109/EuCNC/6GSummit60053.2024.10597048

Plastino, E., & Purdy, M. (2018). Game changing value from Artificial Intelligence: Eight strategies. *Strategy and Leadership*, 46(1), 16–22. DOI: 10.1108/SL-11-2017-0106

Porambage, P., Gur, G., Moya Osorio, D. P., Livanage, M., & Ylianttila, M. (2021). 6G security challenges and potential solutions. *2021 Joint European Conference on Networks and Communications & 6G Summit (EuCNC/6G Summit)*. https://doi.org/DOI: 10.1109/EuCNC/6GSummit51104.2021.9482609

Porambage, P., Gür, G., Osorio, D. P. M., Liyanage, M., Gurtov, A., & Ylianttila, M. (2021). The roadmap to 6G security and privacy. *IEEE Open Journal of the Communications Society*, 2, 1094–1122. DOI: 10.1109/OJCOMS.2021.3078081

Porambage, P., Okwuibe, J., Liyanage, M., Ylianttila, M., & Taleb, T. (2021). Survey on multi-access edge computing for internet of things realization. *IEEE Communications Surveys and Tutorials*, 23(2), 1119–1148. DOI: 10.1109/COMST.2021.3070940

Prazeres, N., Costa, R. L. de C., Santos, L., & Rabadão, C. (2023). Engineering application of machine learning in IDS based on IoT traffic flow. *Intelligent Systems with Applications*, 17, 200189. Advance online publication. DOI: 10.1016/j.iswa.2023.200189

Premavathi, T., Shekhar, A., Raj, A., Agrawal, S., & Palaniappan, D. (2024). Crafting the Future. In *Advances in logistics, operations, and management science book series* (pp. 199–217). DOI: 10.4018/979-8-3693-1198-1.ch009

Provost, F., & Fawcett, T. (2013). Data science and its relationship to big data and data-driven decision making. *Big Data*, 1(1), 51–59. DOI: 10.1089/big.2013.1508 PMID: 27447038

Puspitasari, S.. (2023). Emerging Technologies for 6G Communication Networks. *Sensors (Basel)*, 24(13), 4254. https://www.mdpi.com/1424-8220/24/13/4254 PMID: 37765765

Qadir, Z., Le, K. N., Saeed, N., & Munawar, H. S. (2023). Towards 6G Internet of Things: Recent advances, use cases, and open challenges. *ICT express, 9*(3), 296-312.

Qi, J., & Gao, T. (2020). A privacy-preserving authentication and pseudonym revocation scheme for VANETs. *IEEE Access : Practical Innovations, Open Solutions*, 8, 177693–177707. DOI: 10.1109/ACCESS.2020.3027718

Qi, J., Yang, P., Waraich, A., Deng, Z., Zhao, Y., & Yang, Y. (2018). Examining sensor-based physical activity recognition and monitoring for healthcare using Internet of Things: A systematic review. *Journal of Biomedical Informatics*, 87, 138–153. DOI: 10.1016/j.jbi.2018.09.002 PMID: 30267895

Raddo, T. R., Rommel, S., Cimoli, B., Vagionas, C., Perez-Galacho, D., Pikasis, E., Grivas, E., Ntontin, K., Katsikis, M., Kritharidis, D., Ruggeri, E., Spaleniak, I., Dubov, M., Klonidis, D., Kalfas, G., Sales, S., Pleros, N., & Tafur Monroy, I. (2021). Transition technologies towards 6G networks. *EURASIP Journal on Wireless Communications and Networking, 2021*(1). DOI: 10.1186/s13638-021-01973-9

Raja Santhi, A., & Muthuswamy, P. (2023). Industry 5.0 or industry 4.0 S? Introduction to industry 4.0 and a peek into the prospective industry 5.0 technologies. *International Journal on Interactive Design and Manufacturing*, 17(2), 947–979. DOI: 10.1007/s12008-023-01217-8

Rajasekar, V., Premalatha, J., & Saracevic, M. (2022). Cybersecurity in 5G and IoT Networks. In EAI/Springer Innovations in Communication and Computing. https://doi.org/DOI: 10.1007/978-3-030-79766-9-3

Rajatheva, N., Atzeni, I., Bjornson, E., Bourdoux, A., Buzzi, S., Dore, J.-B., Erkucuk, S., Fuentes, M., Guan, K., Hu, Y., Huang, X., Hulkkonen, J., Jornet, J. M., Katz, M., Nilsson, R., Panayirci, E., Rabie, K. M., Rajapaksha, N., Salehi, M., . . . Zetterman, T. (2020). White paper on broadband connectivity in 6G. arXiv preprint arXiv:2004.14247.

Ramudu, K., Bansal, S. K., Shahnazeer, C. K., Yaseen, S. M., Alimovna, P. Z., & Arumugam, M. (2024). 6G Cyber Physical System Based Smart Healthcare Modelling by Mobile Edge Network and Artificial Intelligence. *Wireless Personal Communications*, •••, 1–16. DOI: 10.1007/s11277-024-11137-9

Rangelov, D., Lämmel, P., Brunzel, L., Borgert, S., Darius, P., Tcholtchev, N., & Boerger, M. (2023). Towards an Integrated Methodology and Toolchain for Machine Learning-Based Intrusion Detection in Urban IoT Networks and Platforms. *Future Internet*, 15(3), 98. Advance online publication. DOI: 10.3390/fi15030098

Rappaport, T. S., Xing, Y., Kanhere, O., Ju, S., Madanayake, A., Mandal, S., Alkhateeb, A., & Trichopoulos, G. C. (2019). Wireless Communications and Applications Above 100 GHz: Opportunities and Challenges for 6G and Beyond. *IEEE Access : Practical Innovations, Open Solutions*, 7, 78729–78757. DOI: 10.1109/ACCESS.2019.2921522

Rathod, T., Jadav, N., Tanwar, S., Sharma, R., Tolba, A., Raboaca, M., Marina, V., & Said, W. (2023). Blockchain-Driven Intelligent Scheme for IoT-Based Public Safety System beyond 5G Networks. *Sensors (Basel)*, 23(2), 969. DOI: 10.3390/s23020969 PMID: 36679767

Rathore, M. M., Ahmad, A., & Paul, A. (2016). Real time intrusion detection system for ultra-high-speed big data environments. *The Journal of Supercomputing*, 72(9), 3489–3510. DOI: 10.1007/s11227-015-1615-5

Ravikumar, S. S., Betgeri, S., & Singh, S. K. (2024). Strategies for mitigating security concerns in IoT-enabled smart cities. *Advances in Computational Intelligence and Robotics*, 239-273. https://doi.org/DOI: 10.4018/979-8-3693-2373-1.ch012

Razmjoo, A., Gandomi, A., Mahlooji, M., Astiaso Garcia, D., Mirjalili, S., Rezvani, A., Ahmadzadeh, S., & Memon, S. (2022). An investigation of the policies and crucial sectors of smart cities based on IoT application. *Applied Sciences (Basel, Switzerland)*, 12(5), 2672. DOI: 10.3390/app12052672

Rejeb, A., Rejeb, K., Appolloni, A., Jagtap, S., Iranmanesh, M., Alghamdi, S., Alhasawi, Y., & Kayikci, Y. (2024). Unleashing the power of internet of things and blockchain: A comprehensive analysis and future directions. *Internet of Things and Cyber-Physical Systems*, 4, 1–18. DOI: 10.1016/j.iotcps.2023.06.003

Riordan, M., Hoddeson, L., & Herring, C. (2019). The invention of the transistor. *Reviews of Modern Physics*, 71(2), S336–S345. DOI: 10.1103/RevModPhys.71.S336

Rivest, R. L., Shamir, A., & Adleman, L. (1978). A method for obtaining digital signa- tures and public-key cryptosystems. *Communications of the ACM*, 21(2), 120–126. DOI: 10.1145/359340.359342

Robinson, T., & Ji, M. (2022). Smart City Seoul: Solving the Urban Puzzle. In *Sustainable, Smart and Solidary Seoul: Transforming an Asian Megacity* (pp. 99–134). Springer International Publishing. DOI: 10.1007/978-3-031-13595-8_5

Rodríguez, E., Otero, B., & Canal, R. (2023). A Survey of Machine and Deep Learning Methods for Privacy Protection in the Internet of Things. In Sensors (Vol. 23, Issue 3). https://doi.org/DOI: 10.3390/s23031252

Rojas, E., Carrascal, D., Lopez-Pajares, D., Alvarez-Horcajo, J., Carral, J. A., Arco, J. M., & Martinez-Yelmo, I. (2024). A Survey on AI-Empowered Softwarized Industrial IoT Networks. *Electronics (Basel)*, 13(10), 1979. DOI: 10.3390/electronics13101979

Rojek, I., Jasiulewicz-Kaczmarek, M., Piszcz, A., Galas, K., & Mikołajewski, D. (2024a). Review of the 6G-Based Supply Chain Management within Industry 4.0/5.0 Paradigm. *Electronics (Basel)*, 13(13), 2624. DOI: 10.3390/electronics13132624

Roupé, M., Johansson, M., Maftei, L., Lundstedt, R., & Viklund-Tallgren, M. (2020). Virtual collaborative design environment: Supporting seamless integration of multitouch table and immersive VR. *Journal of Construction Engineering and Management*, 146(12), 04020132. DOI: 10.1061/(ASCE)CO.1943-7862.0001935

Rugkhapan, N. T., & Murray, M. J. (2019). Songdo IBD (International Business District): Experimental prototype for the city of tomorrow? *International Planning Studies*, 24(3-4), 272–292. DOI: 10.1080/13563475.2019.1650725

Saad, W., Bennis, M., & Chen, M. (2020). A Vision of 6G Wireless Systems: Applications, Trends, Technologies, and Open Research Problems. *IEEE Network*, 34(3), 134–142. DOI: 10.1109/MNET.001.1900287

Saha, T., Aaraj, N., Ajjarapu, N., & Jha, N. K. (2022). SHARKS: Smart Hacking Approaches for RisK Scanning in Internet-of-Things and Cyber-Physical Systems Based on Machine Learning. *IEEE Transactions on Emerging Topics in Computing*, 10(2), 1. Advance online publication. DOI: 10.1109/TETC.2021.3050733

Saini, H. K., & Jain, K. L. (2023, April). A New Way of Improving Network by Smart IoE with UAV. In *2023 International Conference on Computational Intelligence, Communication Technology and Networking (CICTN)* (pp. 485-489). IEEE. DOI: 10.1109/CICTN57981.2023.10140227

Salam, M. A., Rayun, S. N., Islam, W., Hasan, R., Firmansyah, E. A., & Kalinaki, K. (2024). Consumer Engagement: Exploring Deepfake Applications in Consumer Marketing Communication. In *Navigating the World of Deepfake Technology* (pp. 397-421). IGI Global. https://doi.org/DOI: 10.4018/979-8-3693-5298-4.ch020

Salameh, A. I., & El Tarhuni, M. (2022). From 5G to 6G—Challenges, technologies, and applications. *Future Internet*, 14(4), 117. DOI: 10.3390/fi14040117

Salih, A. A., Zeebaree, S. R., Abdulraheem, A. S., Zebari, R. R., Sadeeq, M. A., & Ahmed, O. M. (2020). Evolution of mobile wireless communication to 5G revolution. *Technology Reports of Kansai University*, 62(5), 2139–2151.

Salles, R. S., & Ribeiro, P. F. (2022). Smart Cities, Connected World, and Internet of Things. In Internet of Things. https://doi.org/DOI: 10.1007/978-3-030-89328-6-2

Samanta, S., Sarkar, A., & Bulo, Y. (2022). Secure 6G Communication in Smart City Using Blockchain. In Lecture notes in networks and systems (pp. 487–496). DOI: 10.1007/978-981-19-4193-1_48

Samardzic, N., Feldmann, A., Krastev, A., Saniee, N., Li, N., Geisse, D., & Sanchez, C. (2021). F1: A Fast and Programmable Accelerator for Fully Homomorphic Encryption. In *Proceedings of the 54th Annual IEEE/ACM International Symposium on Microarchitecture* (pp. 238-252). DOI: 10.1145/3466752.3480070

Sarker, I. H. (2022). Smart City Data Science: Towards data-driven smart cities with open research issues. In Internet of Things (Netherlands) (Vol. 19). DOI: 10.1016/j.iot.2022.100528

Sarker, I. H., Khan, A. I., Abushark, Y. B., & Alsolami, F. (2022). Internet of Things (IoT) Security Intelligence: A Comprehensive Overview, Machine Learning Solutions and Research Directions. *Mobile Networks and Applications*. Advance online publication. DOI: 10.1007/s11036-022-01937-3

Savelyev, A. Blockchain in the monitoring of markets, in *Proceedings of the 2018 International Conference on Advances in Information Technology*, pp. 258-264, 2018.

Scalise, P., Boeding, M., Hempel, M., Sharif, H., Delloiacovo, J., & Reed, J. (2024). A Systematic Survey on 5G and 6G Security Considerations, Challenges, Trends, and Research Areas. *Future Internet*, 16(3), 67. DOI: 10.3390/fi16030067

Security foundation. (n.d.). Smart Cities – The Emergence of the Cyber Safe Building. Https://Iotsecurityfoundation.Org/Smart_cities_the_emergence_of_the_cyber_safe_building/

Sedlmeir, J., Buhl, H. U., Fridgen, G., & Keller, R. (2020). The energy consumption of blockchain technology: Beyond myth. *Business & Information Systems Engineering*, 62(6), 599–608.

Seoul: A City Based on Data. Available online: https://earth.org/top-7-smart-cities-in-the-world/

Series, M. (2015). IMT Vision–Framework and overall objectives of the future development of IMT for 2020 and beyond. *Recommendation ITU*, 2083(0), 1–21.

Serodio, C., Cunha, J., Candela, G., Rodriguez, S., Sousa, X. R., & Branco, F. (2023). The 6G ecosystem as support for IoE and private networks: Vision, requirements, and challenges. *Future Internet*, 15(11), 348. DOI: 10.3390/fi15110348

Shafik, W. (2023). A Comprehensive Cybersecurity Framework for Present and Future Global Information Organization. In Effective Cybersecurity Operations for Enterprise-Wide System, 56-79. https://doi.org/DOI: 10.4018/978-1-6684-9018-1.ch002

Shafik, W. (2024a). Incorporating Artificial Intelligence for Urban and Smart Cities' Sustainability. In *Maintaining a Sustainable World in the Nexus of Environmental Science and AI* (pp. 23-58). IGI Global. https://doi.org/DOI: 10.4018/979-8-3693-6336-2.ch002

Shafik, W. (2024b). Ethical Use of Machine Learning Techniques in Smart Cities. In Ethical Artificial Intelligence in Power Electronics (pp. 21-47). CRC Press. https://doi.org/DOI: 10.1201/9781032648323-3

Shafi, M., Molisch, A. F., Smith, P. J., Haustein, T., Zhu, P., De Silva, P., Tufvesson, F., Benjebbour, A., & Wunder, G. (2017). 5G: A tutorial overview of standards, trials, challenges, deployment, and practice. *IEEE Journal on Selected Areas in Communications*, 35(6), 1201–1221. DOI: 10.1109/JSAC.2017.2692307

Shafique, K., Tataria, H., Molisch, A. F., & Tufvesson, F. (2020). Evolution toward 6G: Technology advancements and challenges. *IEEE Journal of Selected Topics in Signal Processing*, 14(3), 509–523. DOI: 10.1109/JSTSP.2020.2984601

Shahidinejad, A., & Abawajy, J. (2024). An All-Inclusive Taxonomy and Critical Review of Blockchain-Assisted Authentication and Session Key Generation Protocols for IoT. *ACM Computing Surveys*, 56(7), 1–38. DOI: 10.1145/3645087

Shahzadi, S., Iqbal, M., & Chaudhry, N. R. (2021). 6G vision: Toward future collaborative cognitive communication (3C) systems. *IEEE Communications Standards Magazine*, 5(2), 60–67. DOI: 10.1109/MCOMSTD.001.2000044

Sharma, V., & Kumar, S. (2023, May). Role of Artificial Intelligence (AI) to Enhance the Security and Privacy of Data in Smart Cities. In 2023 3rd International Conference on Advance Computing and Innovative Technologies in Engineering (ICACITE) (pp. 596-599). IEEE.

Sharma, A., & Aulakh, R. S. (2023). Sustainable Development Goals2030 and Management of Heritage: Indian and Global Contexts. *Engineering Proceedings*, 56(1), 290.

Sharma, S., Popli, R., Singh, S., Chhabra, G., Saini, G. S., Singh, M., Sandhu, A., Sharma, A., & Kumar, R. (2024). The Role of 6G Technologies in Advancing Smart City Applications: Opportunities and Challenges. *Sustainability (Basel)*, 16(16), 7039. DOI: 10.3390/su16167039

Sharma, V., Vashishth, T. K., Kumar, B., Sharma, K. K., Vidyant, S., & Chaudhary, S. (2023, December). Health Interpretation of Covid-19 Patients using Artificial Intelligence. In *2023 International Conference on Artificial Intelligence for Innovations in Healthcare Industries (ICAIIHI)* (Vol. 1, pp. 1-5). IEEE Computer Society. DOI: 10.1109/ICAIIHI57871.2023.10488924

Shayea, I., Azmi, M. H., Ergen, M., El-Saleh, A. A., Han, C. T., Arsad, A., Rahman, T. A., Alhammadi, A., Daradkeh, Y. I., & Nandi, D. (2021). Performance analysis of mobile broadband networks with 5g trends and beyond: Urban areas scope in malaysia. *IEEE Access : Practical Innovations, Open Solutions*, 9, 90767–90794. DOI: 10.1109/ACCESS.2021.3085782

Shehab, M., Khattab, T., Kucukvar, M., & Trinchero, D. (2022). The role of 5G/6G networks in building sustainable and energy-efficient smart cities. In *2022 IEEE 7th International Energy Conference (ENERGYCON)* (pp. 1-7). IEEE.

Sheraz, M., Chuah, T. C., Lee, Y. L., Alam, M. M., Al-Habashna, A., & Han, Z. (2024). A Comprehensive Survey on Revolutionizing Connectivity Through Artificial Intelligence-Enabled Digital Twin Network in 6G. *IEEE Access : Practical Innovations, Open Solutions*, 1, 1. Advance online publication. DOI: 10.1109/ACCESS.2024.3384272

Shi, J., Qi, L., Li, K., & Lin, Y. (2021). Signal modulation recognition method based on differential privacy federated learning. *Wireless Communications and Mobile Computing*, 2021(1), 2537546. DOI: 10.1155/2021/2537546

Singh, S. K., Park, L., & Park, J. H. (2022). Blockchain-based Federated Approach for Privacy-Preserved IoT-enabled Smart Vehicular Networks. 2022 13th International Conference on Information and Communication Technology Convergence (ICTC), 11, 1995–1999. DOI: 10.1109/ICTC55196.2022.9952835

Singhal, S., Betgeri, S., & Singh, S. K. (2024). Strategies for Mitigating Security Concerns in IoT-Enabled Smart Cities. In Secure and Intelligent IoT-Enabled Smart Cities (pp. 239-273). IGI Global. -------

Singhal, S., Betgeri, S., & Singh, S. K. (2024). Strategies for Mitigating Security Concerns in IoT-Enabled Smart Cities. In *Secure and Intelligent IoT-Enabled Smart Cities* (pp. 239–273). IGI Global. DOI: 10.4018/979-8-3693-2373-1

Singh, P. R., Singh, V. K., Yadav, R., & Chaurasia, S. N. (2023). 6G networks for artificial intelligence-enabled smart cities applications: A scoping review. *Telematics and Informatics Reports*, 9, 100044. DOI: 10.1016/j.teler.2023.100044

Singh, S. K., Azzaoui, A. E., Choo, K. K. R., Yang, L. T., & Park, J. H. (2023). Articles A Comprehensive Survey on Blockchain for Secure IoT-enabled Smart City beyond 5G: Approaches, Processes, Challenges, and Opportunities. Hum.-. *Centric Comput. Inf. Sci*, 13, 51.

Singh, S. K., Azzaoui, A., Choo, K. K. R., Yang, L. T., & Park, J. H. (2023). A comprehensive survey on blockchain for secure IoT-enabled smart city beyond 5G: Approaches, processes, challenges, and opportunities. *Human-Centric Computing and Information Sciences*, 13, 51.

Singh, S. K., Azzaoui, A., Choo, K. K. R., Yang, L. T., & Park, J. H. (2023). Articles A Comprehensive Survey on Blockchain for Secure IoT-enabled Smart City beyond 5G: Approaches, Processes, Challenges, and Opportunities. *Hum.-.Centric Comput. Inf. Sci*, 13, 51.

Singh, S. K., Jeong, Y. S., & Park, J. H. (2020). A deep learning-based IoT-oriented infrastructure for secure smart city. *Sustainable Cities and Society*, 60, 102252. DOI: 10.1016/j.scs.2020.102252

Singh, S. K., Kumar, M., Tanwar, S., & Park, J. H. (2024). GRU-based digital twin framework for data allocation and storage in IoT-enabled smart home networks. *Future Generation Computer Systems*, 153, 391–402. DOI: 10.1016/j.future.2023.12.009

Singh, S. K., Lee, C., & Park, J. H. (2022). CoVAC: A P2P smart contract-based intelligent smart city architecture for vaccine manufacturing. *Computers & Industrial Engineering*, 166, 107967. DOI: 10.1016/j.cie.2022.107967 PMID: 35136280

Singh, S. K., Pan, Y., & Park, J. H. (2022). Blockchain-enabled Secure Framework for Energy-Efficient Smart Parking in Sustainable City Environment. *Sustainable Cities and Society*, 76, 103364. DOI: 10.1016/j.scs.2021.103364

Singh, S. K., & Park, J. H. (2022). TaLWaR: Blockchain-Based Trust Management Scheme for Smart Enterprises With Augmented Intelligence. *IEEE Transactions on Industrial Informatics*, 19(1), 626–634. DOI: 10.1109/TII.2022.3204692

Singh, S. K., Park, J. H., Sharma, P. K., & Pan, Y. (2021). BIIoVT: Blockchain-Based Secure Storage Architecture for Intelligent Internet of Vehicular Things. *IEEE Consumer Electronics Magazine*, 11(6), 75–82. DOI: 10.1109/MCE.2021.3089992

Singh, S. K., Rathore, S., & Park, J. H. (2019). BlockIoTIntelligence: A Blockchain-enabled Intelligent IoT Architecture with Artificial Intelligence. *Future Generation Computer Systems*, 110, 721–743. DOI: 10.1016/j.future.2019.09.002

Singh, S. K., Yang, L. T., & Park, J. H. (2023). FusionFedBlock: Fusion of blockchain and federated learning to preserve privacy in industry 5.0. *Information Fusion*, 90, 233–240. DOI: 10.1016/j.inffus.2022.09.027

Sinha, D. (2021).Metropolis Spotlight: Nota Is Transforming Traffic Management Systems With AI. Retrieved from: https://developer.nvidia.com/blog/metropolis-spotlight-nota-is-transforming-traffic-management-systems-with-ai/

Siriwardhana, Y., Porambage, P., Liyanage, M., & Ylianttila, M. (2021). AI and 6G security: Opportunities and challenges. *2021 Joint European Conference on Networks and Communications & 6G Summit (EuCNC/6G Summit)*. https://doi.org/ DOI: 10.1109/EuCNC/6GSummit51104.2021.9482503

Slimani, K., Khoulji, S., & Kerkeb, M. L. (2023). Advancements and challenges in energy-efficient 6G mobile communication network. In *E3S Web of Conferences* (Vol. 412, p. 01036). EDP Sciences. DOI: 10.1051/e3sconf/202341201036

Soare, S. R.Senior, Analyst, A., & Burton, J. (n.d.). *Smart Cities*. Cyber Warfare and Social Disorder.

Sohag, M. U., & Podder, A. K. (2020). Smart garbage management system for a sustainable urban life: An IoT based application. *Internet of Things : Engineering Cyber Physical Human Systems*, 11, 100255. DOI: 10.1016/j.iot.2020.100255

Srinivasu, P. N., Ijaz, M. F., Shafi, J., Woźniak, M., & Sujatha, R. (2022). 6G driven fast computational networking framework for healthcare applications. *IEEE Access : Practical Innovations, Open Solutions*, 10, 94235–94248. DOI: 10.1109/ACCESS.2022.3203061

Stojanovska, S., Madzova, V., & Matlievska, M. (2018). The impact of human capital on sustainable growth - The case of Republic of Macedonia. *Knowledge based sustainable economic development*, 884. https://doi.org/DOI: 10.31410/eraz.2018.884

Strinati, E. C., Di Lorenzo, P., Sciancalepore, V., Aijaz, A., Kountouris, M., Gündüz, D., Popovski, P., Sana, M., Stavrou, P. A., Soret, B., Cordeschi, N., Scardapane, S., Merluzzi, M., Zanzi, L., Renato, M. B., Quek, T., Pietro, N. D., Forceville, O., Costanzo, F., & Li, P. (2024). Goal-oriented and semantic communication in 6G AI-native networks: The 6G-GOALS approach. *2024 Joint European Conference on Networks and Communications & 6G Summit (EuCNC/6G Summit), 5*, 1-6. https://doi.org/DOI: 10.1109/EuCNC/6GSummit60053.2024.10597087

Suartika, G. A. M., & Cuthbert, A. (2020). The sustainable imperative—Smart cities, technology and development. *Sustainability (Basel)*, 12(21), 8892. DOI: 10.3390/su12218892

Subashini, B., & Hemavathi, D. (2023). Scalable Blockchain Technology for Tracking the Provenance of the Agri-Food. *Computers, Materials & Continua*, 75(2), 3339–3358. DOI: 10.32604/cmc.2023.035074

Sullivan, S., Brighente, A., Kumar, S. A., & Conti, M. (2021). 5G security challenges and solutions: A review by OSI layers. *IEEE Access : Practical Innovations, Open Solutions*, 9, 116294–116314. DOI: 10.1109/ACCESS.2021.3105396

Sundqvist, P., Ekman, L., & Hansson, E. (2020). AI for smart cities: Opportunities and challenges. *IEEE Access : Practical Innovations, Open Solutions*, 8, 33344–33362. DOI: 10.1109/ACCESS.2020.2975925

Sun, X., Yao, P., Qu, S., Yu, S., Zhang, X., Wang, W., Huang, C., & Chu, D. (2022). Material properties and machining characteristics under high strain rate in ultra-precision and ultra-high-speed machining process: A review. *International Journal of Advanced Manufacturing Technology*, 120(11), 7011–7042. DOI: 10.1007/s00170-022-09111-5

Surapaneni, P., & Bojjagani, S. (2023, December). SAKM-ITS: Secure Authentication and Key Management Protocol Concerning Intelligent Transportation Systems. In International Conference on Applied Soft Computing and Communication Networks (pp. 249-264). Singapore: Springer Nature Singapore.

Surapaneni, P., & Bojjagani, S. (2024). Forging Digital Trust: The Collaborative Role of Cryptography and Blockchain in Data Security. In Ensuring Security and End-to-End Visibility Through Blockchain and Digital Twins (pp. 224-250). IGI Global.

Surapaneni, P., & Bojjagani, S. (2024). SAFE-Connect Secure Authentication and Fog Services in Vehicular Ad Hoc Networks for IoV. In Blockchain-Based Solutions for Accessibility in Smart Cities (pp. 335-358). IGI Global.

Surapaneni, P., Bojjagani, S., Bharathi, V. C., Morampudi, M. K., Maurya, A. K., & Khan, M. K. (2024). A Systematic Review on Blockchain-enabled Internet of Vehicles (BIoV): Challenges, Defences and Future Research Directions. IEEE Access.

Surapaneni, P., Bojjagani, S., & Khan, M. K. (2024). VESecure: Verifiable authentication and efficient key exchange for secure intelligent transport systems deployment. *Vehicular Communications*, 49, 100822. DOI: 10.1016/j.vehcom.2024.100822

Suyama, S., Okuyama, T., Nonaka, N., & Asai, T. (2022). Recent studies on massive MIMO technologies for 5G evolution and 6G. *2022 IEEE Radio and Wireless Symposium (RWS)*. https://doi.org/DOI: 10.1109/RWS53089.2022.9719949

Swanson, T. (2015). Consensus-as-a-service: a brief report on the emergence of permissioned, distributed ledger systems. Report, available online, 28.

Szabo, N. (1996). Smart contracts: building blocks for digital markets. EXTROPY: The Journal of Transhumanist Thought,(16), 18(2), 28.

Szymanski, T. H. (2022). The "Cyber Security via Determinism" Paradigm for a Quantum Safe Zero Trust Deterministic Internet of Things (IoT). *IEEE Access : Practical Innovations, Open Solutions*, 10, 45893–45930. Advance online publication. DOI: 10.1109/ACCESS.2022.3169137

Taha, H. M., Mohammed, M. A., Jghef, Y. S., Sulaiman, S. K., & Mustafa, T. S. (2024). The integration of blockchain technology in 5G-enabled IoT. *ITM Web of Conferences, 64*, 01001. DOI: 10.1051/itmconf/20246401001

Talreja, V., Ferrett, T., Valenti, M. C., & Ross, A. (2020). Biometrics-as-a-service: A framework to promote innovative biometric recognition in the cloud. In *2020 IEEE International Conference on Consumer Electronics (ICCE)* (pp. 1-6). IEEE. DOI: 10.1109/ICCE46568.2020.9043068

Tang, F., Kawamoto, Y., Kato, N., & Liu, J. (2020). Future intelligent and secure vehicular network toward 6G: Machine-learning approaches. *Proceedings of the IEEE*, 108(2), 292–307. DOI: 10.1109/JPROC.2019.2954595

Tan, H., & Chung, I. (2021). Rsu-aided remote v2v message dissemination employing secure group association for uav-assisted vanets. *Electronics (Basel)*, 10(5), 548. DOI: 10.3390/electronics10050548

Tariq, F., Khandaker, M. R. A., Wong, K. K., Imran, M. A., Bennis, M., & Debbah, M. (2020). A speculative study on 6G. *IEEE Wireless Communications*, 27(4), 118–125. DOI: 10.1109/MWC.001.1900488

Tasatanattakool, P., & Techapanupreeda, C. (2018, January). Blockchain: Challenges and applications. In 2018 international conference on information networking (ICOIN) (pp. 473-475). IEEE.

Techopedia. (2023). 6G Networks: What You Need to Know. https://www.techopedia.com/6g-networks-what-you-need-to-know

Tekale, S., Rajagopal, R., & Bhoopathy, V. (2022). 6G: Transformation of Smart Cities With Blockchain and AI. In *Challenges and Risks Involved in Deploying 6G and NextGen Networks* (pp. 220–228). IGI Global. DOI: 10.4018/978-1-6684-3804-6.ch014

Thakur, S. S., Bandyopadhyay, S., & Datta, D. (2023). The Metaverse as a Virtual Form of Smart Cities: Opportunities and Challenges. *International Journal of Computer Applications*, 975(17), 8887. DOI: 10.5120/ijca2023922892

Thanganadar, H., Yaseen, S. M., Shukla, S. K., Bist, A. S., Shavkatovich, S. N., & Vijayakumar, P. (2024). 6G Wireless Communication Cyber Physical System Based Smart Healthcare Using Quantum Optimization with Machine Learning. *Wireless Personal Communications*, •••, 1–20. DOI: 10.1007/s11277-024-11189-x

Thibaud, M., Chi, H., Zhou, W., & Piramuthu, S. (2018). Internet of Things (IoT) in high-risk Environment, Health and Safety (EHS) industries: A comprehensive review. *Decision Support Systems*, 108, 79–95. DOI: 10.1016/j.dss.2018.02.005

Thilakarathne, N. N., & Madhuka Priyashan, W. D. (2022). An Overview of Security and Privacy in Smart Cities. In EAI/Springer Innovations in Communication and Computing. https://doi.org/DOI: 10.1007/978-3-030-82715-1_2

Thuemmler, C., & Bai, C. (Eds.). (2017). *Health 4.0: How virtualization and big data are revolutionizing healthcare*. Springer International Publishing., DOI: 10.1007/978-3-319-47617-9

Toma, C., Boja, C., Popa, M., Doinea, M., & Ciurea, C. (2022). Viruses, Exploits, Malware and Security Issues on IoT Devices. Lecture Notes in Computer Science (Including Subseries Lecture Notes in Artificial Intelligence and Lecture Notes in Bioinformatics), 13195 LNCS. https://doi.org/DOI: 10.1007/978-3-031-17510-7_22

Top 10 Leading Global Smart Cities. Available online: https://mobile-magazine.com/articles/top-10-leading-global-smart-cities

Toumi, N., & Dimitrovski, T. (2024). AI-native architecture for 6G networks and services with model dependencies. *2024 Joint European Conference on Networks and Communications & 6G Summit (EuCNC/6G Summit)*, 901-906. https://doi.org/DOI: 10.1109/EuCNC/6GSummit60053.2024.10597080

Tran, D. A., & Krishnamachari, B. (2022). *Blockchain in a Nutshell. Handbook on Blockchain. Springer Optimization and Its Applications* (Vol. 194). Springer., DOI: 10.1007/978-3-031-07535-3_1

Treiblmaier, H., Rejeb, A., & Strebinger, A. (2020). Blockchain as a Driver for Smart City Development: Application Fields and a Comprehensive Research Agenda. *Smart Cities*, 3(3), 853–872. DOI: 10.3390/smartcities3030044

Trichias, K., Kaloxylos, A., & Willcock, C. (2024). 6G global landscape: A comparative analysis of 6G targets and technological trends. *2024 Joint European Conference on Networks and Communications & 6G Summit (EuCNC/6G Summit)*, 1-6. https://doi.org/DOI: 10.1109/EuCNC/6GSummit60053.2024.10597064

Tripathi, N. G., & Goel, M. (2022). Citizen-Centric Smart Planning: Case Study San Diego, California. In *Smart Master Planning for Cities: Case Studies on Domain Innovations* (pp. 271–300). Springer Nature Singapore. DOI: 10.1007/978-981-19-2386-9_8

Tripi, G., Iacobelli, A., Rinieri, L., & Prandini, M. (2024). Security and Trust in the 6G Era: Risks and Mitigations. *Electronics (Basel)*, 13(11), 2162. DOI: 10.3390/electronics13112162

Tschorsch, F., & Scheuermann, B. (2016). Bitcoin and Beyond: A technical survey on de- centralized digital currencies. *IEEE Communications Surveys and Tutorials*, 18(3), 2084–2123. DOI: 10.1109/COMST.2016.2535718

Tu, Z., Zhou, H., Li, K., Song, H., & Quan, W. (2023). Blockchain-based differentiated authentication mechanism for 6G heterogeneous networks. *Peer-to-Peer Networking and Applications*, 16(2), 727–748. Advance online publication. DOI: 10.1007/s12083-022-01437-x

Tzeng, S. F., Horng, S. J., Li, T., Wang, X., Huang, P. H., & Khan, M. K. (2015). Enhancing security and privacy for identity-based batch verification scheme in VANETs. *IEEE Transactions on Vehicular Technology*, 66(4), 3235–3248. DOI: 10.1109/TVT.2015.2406877

Ullah, H., Nair, N. G., Moore, A., Nugent, C., Muschamp, P., & Cuevas, M. (2019). 5G communication: An overview of vehicle-to-everything, drones, and healthcare use-cases. *IEEE Access : Practical Innovations, Open Solutions*, 7, 37251–37268. DOI: 10.1109/ACCESS.2019.2905347

UN. The Sustainable Development Goals Report. (2023). Available online: https://unstats.un.org/sdgs/report/2023/The-Sustainable-Development-Goals-Report-2023.pdf

Uusitalo, M. A., Rugeland, P., Boldi, M. R., Strinati, E. C., Demestichas, P., Ericson, M., Fettweis, G. P., Filippou, M. C., Gati, A., Hamon, M.-H., Hoffmann, M., Latva-Aho, M., Parssinen, A., Richerzhagen, B., Schotten, H., Svensson, T., Wikstrom, G., Wymeersch, H., Ziegler, V., & Zou, Y. (2021). 6G vision, value, use cases and technologies from European 6G flagship project Hexa-X. *IEEE Access : Practical Innovations, Open Solutions*, 9, 160004–160020. DOI: 10.1109/ACCESS.2021.3130030

Vaghani, A., Sood, K., & Yu, S. (2022). Security and QoS issues in blockchain enabled next-generation smart logistic networks: A tutorial. *Blockchain: Research and Applications*, 3(3), 100082.

Vashishth, T. K., Sharma, V., Kumar, B., Panwar, R., Sharma, K. K., & Chaudhary, S. (2024). AI-Integrated IoT in Healthcare Ecosystem: Opportunities, Challenges, and Future Directions. AI and IoT Technology and Applications for Smart Healthcare Systems, 37-54.

Vashishth, T. K., Sharma, V., Sharma, K. K., Kumar, B., Chaudhary, S., & Panwar, R. (2023). Virtual Reality (VR) and Augmented Reality (AR) Transforming Medical Applications. In A. Khang (Ed.), AI and IoT-Based Technologies for Precision Medicine (pp. 324-348). IGI Global.

Vashishth, T. K., Sharma, V., Sharma, K. K., Kumar, B., Chaudhary, S., & Panwar, R. (2024). IoMT in Smart Cities Scaling Challenges, Smart Healthcare Applications, Data Integrity. In Lightweight Digital Trust Architectures in the Internet of Medical Things (IoMT) (pp. 281-309). IGI Global.

Vashishth, T. K., Sharma, V., Sharma, K. K., Kumar, B., Chaudhary, S., & Panwar, R. (2024). Revolutionizing cloud computing security with the power of artificial intelligence: Advancements, challenges, and opportunities. Smart Electric and Hybrid Vehicles, 163-177.

Vashishth, T. K., Sharma, V., Sharma, K. K., Kumar, B., Chaudhary, S., & Panwar, R. (2024). Waste-to-Energy Solutions Harnessing IoT and ML for Sustainable Power Generation in Smart Cities. In Methodologies, Frameworks, and Applications of Machine Learning (pp. 125-146). IGI Global. DOI: 10.4018/979-8-3693-1062-5.ch007

Vashishth, T. K., Sharma, V., Sharma, K. K., Kumar, B., Chaudhary, S., & Panwar, R. (2024). Environmental sustainability and carbon footprint reduction through artificial intelligence-enabled energy management in electric vehicles. In *Artificial Intelligence-Empowered Modern Electric Vehicles in Smart Grid Systems* (pp. 477–502). Elsevier. DOI: 10.1016/B978-0-443-23814-7.00017-1

Vasudev, H., Deshpande, V., Das, D., & Das, S. K. (2020). A lightweight mutual authentication protocol for V2V communication in internet of vehicles. *IEEE Transactions on Vehicular Technology*, 69(6), 6709–6717. DOI: 10.1109/TVT.2020.2986585

Verma, P., Sharma, R., & Mistry, M. (2022). A Paradigm Shift in IoT Cyber-Security: A Systematic Review. *International Journal for Research in Applied Science and Engineering Technology*, 10(10), 1024–1034. Advance online publication. DOI: 10.22214/ijraset.2022.47129

Vishnu, S., Ramson, S. R. J., Senith, S., Anagnostopoulos, T., Abu-Mahfouz, A. M., Fan, X., Srinivasan, S., & Kirubaraj, A. A. (2021). IoT-Enabled Solid Waste Management in Smart Cities. *Smart Cities*, 4(3), 1004–1017. DOI: 10.3390/smartcities4030053

Walport, M. (2016). *Distributed ledger technology: Beyond blockchain*. UK Government Office for Science.

Wang Yue Dong, M., & Yortsos, Y. (2022). Application of Machine Learning Technologies for Transport layer Congestion Control. Journal of Computing and Natural Science. https://doi.org/.DOI: 10.53759/181X/JCNS202202010

Wang, D., Wang, P., He, D., & Tian, Y. (2020). Birthday, name and bifacial-security: Understanding passwords of Chinese web users. In 29th USENIX Security Symposium (USENIX Security 20) (pp. 1537-1554). https://doi.org/DOI: 10.5555/3489212.3489404

Wang, C., You, X., Gao, X., Zhu, X., Li, Z., Zhang, C., Wang, H., Huang, Y., Chen, Y., Haas, H., Thompson, J. S., Larsson, E. G., Renzo, M. D., Tong, W., Zhu, P., Shen, X., Poor, H. V., & Hanzo, L. (2023). On the road to 6G: Visions, requirements, key technologies, and Testbeds. *IEEE Communications Surveys and Tutorials*, 25(2), 905–974. DOI: 10.1109/COMST.2023.3249835

Wang, D., Wang, P., Wang, C., & Ren, K. (2020). A new hope for IoT security: Physically unclonable function. *IEEE Security and Privacy*, 18(3), 12–19. DOI: 10.1109/MSEC.2020.2975730

Wang, J., Ling, X., Le, Y., Huang, Y., & You, X. (2021). Blockchain-enabled wireless communications: A new paradigm towards 6G. *National Science Review*, 8(9), nwab069. Advance online publication. DOI: 10.1093/nsr/nwab069 PMID: 34691739

Wang, Q., Liu, Y., Wang, Y., Xing, Y., Zong, J., & Liu, H. (2023). Deep edge node enables AI native toward 6G*. *2023 IEEE International Symposium on Broadband Multimedia Systems and Broadcasting (BMSB)*, 1-6. https://doi.org/DOI: 10.1109/BMSB58369.2023.10211613

Wang, X., Shankar, A., Li, K., Parameshachari, B., & Lv, J. (2024). Blockchain-Enabled Decentralized Edge Intelligence for Trustworthy 6G Consumer Electronics. *IEEE Transactions on Consumer Electronics*, 1(1), 1214–1225. Advance online publication. DOI: 10.1109/TCE.2024.3371501

Wang, Y., Cai, S., Lin, C., Chen, Z., Wang, T., Gao, Z., & Zhou, C. (2019). Study of Blockchains's Consensus Mechanism Based on Credit, IEEE Access: Practical Innovations. *Open Solutions*, 7, 10224–10231. DOI: 10.1109/AC- CESS.2019.2891065

Wang, Y., Kang, X., Li, T., Wang, H., Chu, C.-K., & Lei, Z. (2023). SIX-Trust for 6G: Towards a Secure and Trustworthy Future Network. *IEEE Access : Practical Innovations, Open Solutions*, 11, 107657–107668. DOI: 10.1109/ACCESS.2023.3321114

Wazid, M., Bagga, P., Das, A. K., Shetty, S., Rodrigues, J. J., & Park, Y. (2019). AKM-IoV: Authenticated key management protocol in fog computing-based Internet of vehicles deployment. *IEEE Internet of Things Journal*, 6(5), 8804–8817. DOI: 10.1109/JIOT.2019.2923611

Wei, X., Yang, H., & Huang, W. (2023). Low-delay routing scheme for UAV communications in smart cities. *IEEE Internet of Things Journal*, 10(21), 18837–18843. DOI: 10.1109/JIOT.2023.3267131

Wikström, G., Peisa, J., Rugeland, P., Johansson, N., Parkvall, S., Girnyk, M., & Da Silva, I. L. (2020). *Challenges and technologies for 6G. In 2020 2nd 6G wireless summit (6G SUMMIT)*. IEEE.

William, M., Sharif, S., & Ejaz, W. (2023, August). Enabling communication and networking technologies for 6G in healthcare sector. In *2023 Second International Conference On Smart Technologies For Smart Nation (SmartTechCon)* (pp. 699-704). IEEE. DOI: 10.1109/SmartTechCon57526.2023.10391790

Windarta, S., Suryadi, S., Ramli, K., Pranggono, B., & Gunawan, T. S. (2022). Lightweight cryptographic hash functions: Design trends, comparative study, and future directions. *IEEE Access : Practical Innovations, Open Solutions*, 10, 82272–82294. DOI: 10.1109/ACCESS.2022.3195572

Wong, P. F., Chia, F. C., Kiu, M. S., & Lou, E. C. W. (2020). The potential of integrating blockchain technology into smart sustainable city development. *IOP Conference Series. Earth and Environmental Science*, 463(1), 012020. DOI: 10.1088/1755-1315/463/1/012020

Wu, F., Chen, Y., Chen, X., Fan, W., & Liu, Y. A. (2020). An adaptive dual prediction scheme based on edge intelligence. *IEEE Internet of Things Journal*, 7(10), 9481–9493. DOI: 10.1109/JIOT.2020.2997795

Wu, L., Sun, Q., Wang, X., Wang, J., Yu, S., Zou, Y., Liu, B., & Zhu, Z. (2019). An efficient privacy-preserving mutual authentication scheme for secure V2V communication in vehicular ad hoc network. *IEEE Access : Practical Innovations, Open Solutions*, 7, 55050–55063. DOI: 10.1109/ACCESS.2019.2911924

Wu, L., Yue, X., Jin, A., & Yen, D. C. (2016). Smart supply chain management: A review and implications for future research. *International Journal of Logistics Management*, 27(2), 395–417. DOI: 10.1108/IJLM-02-2014-0035

Xie, Q., Ding, Z., & Zheng, P. (2023). Provably secure and anonymous V2I and V2V authentication protocol for VANETs. *IEEE Transactions on Intelligent Transportation Systems*, 24(7), 7318–7327. DOI: 10.1109/TITS.2023.3253710

Yadav, R., Prathapa Reddy, S. L., Upmanyu, A., Sanapala, R. K., Malathy, V., & Gohatre, U. B. (2024). Fast Computing Network Infrastructure for Healthcare Systems Based on 6G Future Perspective. Human Cancer Diagnosis and Detection Using Exascale Computing, 153-170.

Yang, F., Hua, Y., Li, X., Yang, Z., Yu, X., & Fei, T. (2022). A survey on multi-source heterogeneous urban sensor access and data management technologies. In *Measurement* (Vol. 19). Sensors., DOI: 10.1016/j.measen.2021.100061

Yang, G., Lv, H., Zhang, Z., Yang, L., Deng, J., You, S., Du, J., & Yang, H. (2019). Keep healthcare workers safe: Application of teleoperated robot in isolation ward for COVID-19 prevention and control. *Chinese Journal of Mechanical Engineering*, 33(1), 47. DOI: 10.1186/s10033-020-00464-0

Yang, J., & Sun, L. (2022). A Comprehensive Survey of Security Issues of Smart Home System: "Spear" and "Shields," Theory and Practice. *IEEE Access : Practical Innovations, Open Solutions*, 10, 124167–124192. DOI: 10.1109/ACCESS.2022.3224806

Yang, P., Xiao, Y., Xiao, M., & Li, S. (2019). 6G wireless communications: Vision and potential techniques. *IEEE Network*, 33(4), 70–75. DOI: 10.1109/MNET.2019.1800418

Yang, Z., Jianjun, L., Faqiri, H., Shafik, W., Talal Abdulrahman, A., Yusuf, M., & Sharawy, A. M. (2021). Green Internet of Things and Big Data Application in Smart Cities Development. *Complexity*, 2021(1), 4922697. Advance online publication. DOI: 10.1155/2021/4922697

Yaqoob, I., Ahmed, E., Rehman, M. H. U., Ahmed, A. I. A., Al-garadi, M. A., Imran, M., & Guizani, M. (2017). The rise of ransomware and emerging security challenges in the Internet of Things. *Computer Networks*, 129, 444–458. DOI: 10.1016/j.comnet.2017.09.003

Yigitcanlar, T., Kankanamge, N., & Vella, K. (2021). How are smart city concepts and technologies perceived and utilized? A systematic geo-Twitter analysis of smart cities in Australia. *Journal of Urban Technology*, 28(1-2), 135–154. DOI: 10.1080/10630732.2020.1753483

Yildirim, O., & Çakici, A. C. (2022). Cultural heritage and digitalization in city branding. In *Handbook of research on digital communications, Internet of things, and the future of cultural tourism* (pp. 467–483). IGI Global. DOI: 10.4018/978-1-7998-8528-3.ch025

Yli-Huumo, J., Ko, D., Choi, S., Park, S., & Smolander, K. (2016). Where is current research on blockchain technology?—A systematic review. *PLoS One*, 11(10), e0163477. DOI: 10.1371/journal.pone.0163477 PMID: 27695049

Yrjölä, S., Matinmikko-Blue, M., & Ahokangas, P. (2023). Developing 6G visions with stakeholder analysis of 6G ecosystem. *2023 Joint European Conference on Networks and Communications & 6G Summit (EuCNC/6G Summit)*. https://doi.org/ DOI: 10.1109/EuCNC/6GSummit58263.2023.10188379

Yuvaraj, N., Praghash, K., Raja, R. A., & Karthikeyan, T. (2022). An Investigation of Garbage Disposal Electric Vehicles (GDEVs) Integrated with Deep Neural Networking (DNN) and Intelligent Transportation System (ITS) in Smart City Management System (SCMS). *Wireless Personal Communications*, 123(2), 1733–1752. Advance online publication. DOI: 10.1007/s11277-021-09210-8

Zhang, C., Lin, X., Lu, R., Ho, P. H., & Shen, X. (2008). An efficient message authentication scheme for vehicular communications. *IEEE Transactions on Vehicular Technology*, 57(6), 3357–3368. DOI: 10.1109/TVT.2008.928581

Zhang, S., Li, M., Liang, W., Sandor, V. K. A., & Li, X. (2022). A survey of dummy-based location privacy protection techniques for location-based services. *Sensors (Basel)*, 22(16), 6141. DOI: 10.3390/s22166141 PMID: 36015901

Zhang, X., Yu, F. R., & He, Z. (2021). AI-based network security management in 6G wireless networks: Challenges and opportunities. *IEEE Network*, 35(6), 35–41. DOI: 10.1109/MNET.2021.3108755

Zhang, Y. (2022). *Mobile edge computing*. Springer Nature. DOI: 10.1007/978-3-030-83944-4

Zhao, H., Di, L., Guo, L., Zhang, C., & Lin, L. (2023). An Automated Data-Driven Irrigation Scheduling Approach Using Model Simulated Soil Moisture and Evapotranspiration. *Sustainability (Basel)*, 15(17), 12908. DOI: 10.3390/su151712908

Zhao, Q., Feng, Q., Lu, H., Li, Y., Wang, A., Tian, Q., Zhan, Q., Lu, Y., Zhang, L., Huang, T., Wang, Y., Fan, D., Zhao, Y., Wang, Z., Zhou, C., Chen, J., Zhu, C., Li, W., Weng, Q., & Huang, X. (2018). Pan-genome analysis highlights the extent of genomic variation in cultivated and wild rice. *Nature Genetics*, 50(2), 278–284. DOI: 10.1038/s41588-018-0041-z PMID: 29335547

Zhao, S. (2022). Creating Futuristic Heritage Experiences: An Exploratory Co-Design Study through Design Fiction. *Sustainability (Basel)*, 14(19), 12027. DOI: 10.3390/su141912027

Zhao, Y., Yu, G., & Xu, H. (2021). 6G mobile communication networks: Vision, challenges, and key technologies. *Science China. Information Sciences*, 64(4), 1–26. DOI: 10.1007/s11432-020-3057-3

Zhao, Y., Zhang, X., & Zhang, Y. (2016). Overview of business innovations and research opportunities in blockchain and introduction to the special issue. *Financial Innovation*, 2(1), 1–10. DOI: 10.1186/s40854-016-0049-2

Zheng, X., Mukkamala, R. R., Vatrapu, R., & Ordieres-Mere, J. (2021). Blockchain-based personal health data sharing system using cloud storage. In 2018 IEEE 20th International Conference on e-Health Networking, Applications and Services (Healthcom) (pp. 1-6). IEEE. https://doi.org/DOI: 10.1109/HealthCom.2018.8531125

Zhou, Z., Chen, X., Li, E., Zeng, L., Luo, K., & Zhang, J. (2019). Edge intelligence: Paving the last mile of artificial intelligence with edge computing. *Proceedings of the IEEE*, 107(8), 1738–1762. DOI: 10.1109/JPROC.2019.2918951

Zhou, Z., Wang, J., Xu, Y., & Li, H. (2020). AI-driven security framework for smart cities. *IEEE Communications Magazine*, 58(3), 60–66. DOI: 10.1109/MCOM.2020.2903257

Zhuang, K., Fu, C., Weng, J., & Hu, C. (2021). Cutting edge microgeometries in metal cutting: A review. *International Journal of Advanced Manufacturing Technology*, 116(7), 2045–2092. DOI: 10.1007/s00170-021-07558-6

Zhu, X., Jiang, S., Wang, L., & Li, H. (2013). Efficient privacy-preserving authentication for vehicular ad hoc networks. *IEEE Transactions on Vehicular Technology*, 63(2), 907–919. DOI: 10.1109/TVT.2013.2294032

Zhu, Y., Mao, B., & Kato, N. (2022). Intelligent reflecting surface in 6G vehicular communications: A survey. *IEEE Open Journal of Vehicular Technology*, 3, 266–277. DOI: 10.1109/OJVT.2022.3177253

Zong, J., Liu, Y., Liu, H., Wang, Q., & Chen, P. (2022). 6G cell-free network architecture. *2022 IEEE 2nd International Conference on Electronic Technology, Communication and Information (ICETCI)*. https://doi.org/DOI: 10.1109/ICETCI55101.2022.9832308

About the Contributors

Sushil Kumar Singh (Member, IEEE) is an Associate Professor in the Department of Computer Engineering at Marwadi University, Rajkot, Gujarat, India. He is pursuing PostDoc at London Metropolitan University, London, United Kingdom, under the supervision of Professor Bal Virdee. He received Ph.D. degree from Seoul National University of Science and Technology, Seoul, South Korea under the supervision of Professor Jong Hyuk Park. He received M.Tech. Degree in Computer Science and Engineering from Uttarakhand Technical University, Dehradun, India. He also received an M.E. degree in Information Technology from Karnataka State University, Mysore, India. He has also been the lab leader of the UCS Lab at the Department of Computer Science Engineering, Seoul National University of Science and Technology, Seoul, South Korea. He has received the Best Lab Leadership Award from UCS Lab for 2019-2021. He is selected in Top 2% Scientist for the (2022-2023, 2023-2024) year as per the list compiled by Stanford University and published by Elsevier. He has more than 13 years of experience teaching in the field of computer science. He has published Five Books: Computer C Programming, Cyber Security, Big Data Analytics, Mobile Computing, and Secure and Intelligent IoT-Enabled Smart Cities. He has also published many high-quality papers (Q1, Top 10% JCR Rank) in international journals and conferences. He has already delivered international lectures in many countries. His research interests include Blockchain, Artificial Intelligence, Big Data, Internet of Things, Smart City Security, and Cyber-Physical Systems. He is an Associate/ Guest Editor in the Human-centric Computation and Information Sciences (HCIS) Journal, IEEE Journal of Biomedical and Health Informatics (IEEE JBHI) Journal, IGI Global Publication, and Wiley Scrivener Publication. He is a reviewer of the IEEE Wireless Communication Magazine, IEEE SYSTEMS, IEEE Internet of Things, FGCS, TETT, EXSY, JISA, Computer Network, MDPI, CIE, HCIS, JIPS, Computing (COMP), Multimedia Tools & Applications, and SCIS Journal. He also organizes the Research Activities Club, which promotes quality research activities among young researchers at Marwadi University, Rajkot, Gujarat, India.

Bal S. Virdee (Senior Member, IEEE) received the B.Sc. and M.Phil. degrees in communications engineering from the University of Leeds, U.K., and the Ph.D. degree in electronic engineering from the University of London, U.K. He has worked in industry for various companies, including Philips, U.K., as a Research and Development Engineer and Teledyne Defence and Space as a Future Products Developer in RF/microwave communications. He has taught at several academic institutions before joining London Metropolitan University, where he is currently a Senior Professor in communications technology with the School of Computing and Digital Media, where he is also the Head the Communications Technology Research Center. His research, in collaboration with industry and academia, is in wireless communications encompassing mobile-phones to satellite-technology. He has chaired technical sessions at IEEE international conferences and published numerous research papers. He is an Executive Member of IET's Technical and Professional Network Committee on RF/Microwave-Technology. He is a fellow of IET.

Rajendrasinh B. Jadeja (Senior Member, IEEE) is working as a Dean at the Faculty of Engineering, Marwadi University - Gujarat, India. He completed his B.E. in Electrical Engineering from L. D. College of Engineering (Gujarat University) in 1998, M. Tech. in Electrical Engineering from Nirma University and a Ph.D. from the M S University, Baroda respectively in the year of 2005 and 2010. He has been awarded the title "ING.PAED.IGIP" in 2020.He is a Senior Member of IEEE. He has worked as a Treasurer of IEEE Region-10 during the year 2021. He is currently working as a Chair, Membership Development Committee of IEEE Region-10. He has worked as a Treasurer of IEEE India Council and worked as a Chair of IEEE Gujarat Section during the Year 2017. The areas of Research and Interest include control of power electronic converters, AC drives, Pulse Width Modulated power electronic converters and Power Quality Issues and its mitigation techniques. Various projects have been undertaken and have completed a project funded by GUJCOST (Gujarat Council on Science & Technology) and he is working on a project making "Deep Learning and AI skills" mainstream in India to fulfil trilateral needs of entrepreneurship, Industry-academia partnership and application-inspired Engineering Research. He actively participates and initiates ERASMUS+ for staff mobility and has also completed such a program for teaching between partner countries. A recipient of young Professional Award for travel grant to attend IEEE Section Congress held on 22- 24 August 2014, Amsterdam, Netherlands. He has been working as a member of Board of Studies of Electrical Engineering of the

Gujarat state's largest public Technical University Gujarat Technological University and also a BoS member at PDPU, Gandhinagar.

Sudeep Tanwar (Senior Member, IEEE) is working as a professor at the Nirma University, India. He is also a Visiting Professor with WSG University, Bydgoszczy, Poland, Jan Wyzykowski University, Poland, WSG University, Bydgoszcz, and the University of Pitesti, Romania. He is senior member of IEEE and also Vice Chair of IEEE Computer Society Gujarat Section. He received B.Tech in 2002 from Kurukshetra University, India, M.Tech (Honor's) in 2009 from Guru Gobind Singh Indraprastha University, Delhi, India and Ph.D. in 2016 with specialization in Wireless Sensor Network. He has authored 05 books and edited 25 books, more than 400 technical articles, including top cited journals and conferences, such as IEEE TNSE, IEEE TVT, IEEE TII, IEEE TGCN, IEEE TCSC, IEEE IoTJ, IEEE NETWORKS, IEEE WCM, ICC, IWCMC, GLOBECOM, CITS, and INFOCOM. He initiated the research field of blockchain technology adoption in various verticals in the year 2017. His H-index as per Google Scholar and Scopus is 71 and 57, respectively. His research interests include blockchain technology, D2D communication, Deep Learning/ machine Learning, wireless sensor networks, fog computing, smart grid, and the IoT. He is a member of the Technical Committee on Tactile Internet of IEEE Communication Society. Recently, He has been awarded cash prize of Rs, 50,000 for publishing papers with 5+ Impact factor and publication of books with Springer, IET & CRC under the scheme of "Faculty Awards and Incentives" of Nirma University for the year 2019-2020. He has been awarded the Best Research Paper Awards from IEEE SCIoT 2022, IEEE IWCMC-2021, IEEE ICCCA-2021, IEEE GLOBECOM 2018, IEEE ICC 2019, and Springer ICRIC-2019. He has won Dr KW Wong Annual Best Paper Prize (with 750 USD) for 2021 sponsored by Elsevier (publishers of JISA). He has served many international conferences as a member of the Organizing Committee, such as the Publication Chair for FTNCT-2020, ICCIC 2020, and WiMob2019, and a General Chair for IC4S 2019, 2020, 2021, 2022, ICCSDF 2020, FTNCT 2021. He is also serving the editorial boards of COMCOM-Elsevier, IJCS-Wiley, Cyber Security and Applications-Elsevier, Frontiers of blockchain, SPY, Wiley, IJMIS journal of Inderscience, JCCE, and JSSS. He is also leading the ST Research Laboratory, where group members are working on the latest cutting-edge technologies.

Ashish Khanna [IEEE Member'2019, Senior Member'2020, MACM] has expertise in Teaching, Entrepreneurship, and Research and development with a specialization in Computer Science Engineering Subjects. He is part of the world's leading 2% research community list from STANFORD UNIVERSITY, USA. He is also part of the top research community, including the AD research community and research.com group. He has done a postdoc at INATEL BRAZIL and the University of Valladolid, Spain, Europe. He received his Ph.D. degree from the National Institute of Technology, Kurukshetra, in March 2017. He completed his M. Tech. in 2009 and B. Tech. from GGSIPU, Delhi, in 2004. He has around 200 accepted and published research papers and book chapters in reputed SCI, Scopus journals, conferences, and reputed book series, including 98 papers accepted and published in TOP SCI-indexed Journals. He also has ten published Patents and 1 granted German Patent to his credit. Additionally, He has co-authored, edited, and edited around 50 books. He has also served as a keynote speaker resource person and given several invitations. He was a resource person speaker and delivered a lecture at the ATAL program at JNU in 2020. He has worked as a Guest Editor in several reputed journals. He is also serving as a Series Editor in publishing houses like De Gruyter (Germany) of the "Intelligent Biomedical Data Analysis" series, Elsevier of "Intelligent Biomedical Data Analysis" and CRC Press of "Intelligent Techniques in Distributed Systems: Principles and Applications.

***

B. Subashini received the bachelor's degree in information technology from PSG Tech Coimbatore and the master's degree in information technology and computer science from Anna University and SRM University.She received her PhD from SRMIST. She is an Assistant Professor with the Data Science and Business Systems Department, SRM Institute of Science and Technology, Chengalpattu, India. She possesses more than ten years of teaching experience. Her research incorporates blockchain technology to address traceability concerns in the agro-food supply chain. Her areas of interests include database management systems, supply chain management, the IoT, web technology, information security, network security, cryptography, 6G Technology and blockchain technology.

Divya Bansal, Associate Professor cum Deputy Director at Amity University Online, Noida has more than 19 years of experience in teaching Business Management students at UG and PG level. She has published more than thirty research articles in various reputed journals and presented many papers in National and International conferences. Her research interests lie in the diverse areas of marketing, Universal Banking, customer satisfaction, Environmental Sciences, Artificial Intelligence, Big Data and entrepreneurship. She has keen interest in learning new packages and analytical tools in Statistics and has organised various guest lectures, conferences and workshops.

Naboshree Bhattacharya is an assistant professor with a specialization in healthcare economics and a broader research focus on development economics. With a rich academic background, she holds alumni status from prestigious institutions including St. Xavier's College, Ranchi University, and Jadavpur University. Over the course of her career spanning 12 years, Naboshree has garnered extensive experience in both academic and industrial settings. Currently serving as an Assistant Professor at Amity University Jharkhand, she brings a wealth of knowledge and expertise to her role. Naboshree's contributions to the field extend beyond the classroom. She is a prolific author, having penned six books on various topics within economics, collaborating with both national and international authors. Additionally, her research output includes numerous papers and book chapters published in esteemed journals and publications, both domestically and internationally.

Sriramulu Bojjagani received the Ph.D. degree from the School of Com- puter and Information Sciences, University of Hy- derabad (UoH) and the Institute for Development and Research in Banking Technology, established by the Reserve Bank of India (RBI), in 2019, with a focus on Design, Testing and Formal Verification of Secure Mobile Payment Protocols. He is cur- rently working as an Assistant Professor with the Department of Computer Science and Engineering, SRM University AP, Amaravathi, India. He has published many SCI/SCIE-indexed journals with good impact factors and many conference papers of international repute. In addition, he is an inventor of several patents. His research interests include vulnerability analysis and penetration testing, cybersecurity, digital authentication, and the IoV security.

Sailaja Chigurupati is pursuing her B. Tech in the department of Computer Science and Engineering at KL University-AP. Her area of interests are network security, internet of things, cryptography and artificial intelligence.

G.Manikandan received the B.E degree in Computer Science & Engineering from Madras University, M.E degree in Computer Science & Engineering from Sathyabama University, Post Graduate Diploma in Geo Spatial Information Technology from Periyar Maniammai University, the M.B.A degree in HR from Tamil Nadu Open University, Ph.D degree in Computer Science & Engineering at Sathyabama University. He is having more than 24 years of Valuable in depth and extensive experience in Academics, Research & Development and Administration. He is Currently working as a Professor in the department of Artificial Intelligence and Data Science Department at R.M.K Engineering College. He completed the Post-doctoral Research in the topic of "Enhanced AI Based machine learning model for an accurate segmentation and classification method", under the guidance of Dr. Bui Thanh Hung, Artificial Intelligence Laboratory, Faculty of Information Technology,

Industrial University of Ho Chi Minh City VIETNAM. He is having more than seven pattern and one Copyright on different topics. He has published more than 36 Research papers in Scopus / SCI / WoS Journals and more than 32 Research papers presented in different National and International level Conferences. His area of interests includes Data mining, Spatial Databases, Geographic information System and intelligent Transportation Systems, Artificial Intelligence and Machine Learning.

Krupali Gosai is an Assistant Professor, Department of Computer Engineering, Marwadi University, Rajkot-Gujarat, India She has 5+ years of teaching experience in Computer Engineering. Her research domain areas are Cyber Security, Machine Learning and Deep Learning.

Rituraj Jain is currently working in the Department of Electrical and Computer Engineering, Wollega University, Nekemte - Ethiopia. He has published many papers in International Journals and Conferences. He has published 4 books. He is an Oracle Database SQL Certified Expert. He is also associated with professional bodies like the Indian Society of Technical Education (ISTE), Computer Science Teachers Association (CSTA), Academy & Industry Research Collaboration Center (AIRCC), International Association of Computer Science and Information Technology (IACSIT), International Association of Engineers (IAENG). His research interests include Cloud Computing, Machine Learning, Deep Learning, Fuzzy Logic, IoT, Genetic Algorithms, Big Data and Software Engineering.

Vishal Jain is presently working as a Professor at the Department of Computer Science and Engineering, School of Engineering and Technology, Sharda University, Greater Noida, India. Before that, he worked for several years as an Associate Professor at Bharati Vidyapeeths Institute of Computer Applications and Management (BVICAM), New Delhi. He has more than 18 years of experience in the academics. He has earned degrees: Ph.D (CSE), M.Tech (CSE), MBA (HR), MCA, MCP, and CCNA. He has more than 1900 research citations with Google Scholar (h-index score 21 and i-10 index 49) and has authored more than 150 research papers in professional journals and conferences. He has authored and edited more than 60 books (most of them are indexed at the Scopus) with various reputed publishers, including Elsevier, Springer, IET, Apple Academic Press, CRC, Taylor and Francis Group, Scrivener, Wiley, Emerald, NOVA Science, River Publishers, IGI-Global and Bentham Science. He has more than 160 Scopus publications. He is the book series editor of 10 book series with the reputed international publishers. His research areas include machine learning, information retrieval, semantic web, ontology engineering, data mining, ad hoc networks, sensor networks and network security. He received a Young Active Member Award for the year 2012–13 from the Computer Society of India, and Best Faculty Award for the year 2017 and Best Researcher Award for the year 2019 from BVICAM, New Delhi.

M. Robinson Joel received the Doctorate Ph.D degree in Computer and Information Technology from the Manonmaniam Sundaranar University, Tirunelveli in March 2019. He completed his M.Tech and MCA from the same university year 2008 and 2002 respectively. He is currently working as an Associate Professor in the Department of Computer Science and Engineering at KCG College of Technology, Chennai. He has 16 years of teaching experience.

Habib Khan (Member, IEEE) is an AI Researcher and Coordinator of the CIP research network at Gachon University, South Korea. His research interests focus under the umbrella of Machine Learning and Deep Learning with a specific focus on Visual Intelligence in Surveillance, Healthcare Informatics, Video Analytics, Fire Detection, Segmentation, Cybersecurity, Underwater robotics, and Energy Analytics (Energy Consumption and Generation Prediction). He holds two MS degrees from Sejong University, Seoul, South Korea, and a BS Degree in Computer Science from Islamia College University Peshawar. He has contributed many scientific articles to prestigious international journals and prestigious conferences, and some of his articles are accepted in the pipeline of the Q1, top ten, A* venues. He is actively involved as a reviewer in the Engineering Applications of Artificial Intelligence, JKSUCI, IoTJ, ESWA, IEEE Transaction on Consumer Electronics, Nanotechnology Reviews, IEEE Systems Man and Cybernetics Magazine, Supercomputing journals, and prestigious conferences including INFOCOM, AIAI 2022, ICANN 2023, EAAI 2024, IWCMC 2024 (Edge Intelligence) and AIAI 2024

Archan Mitra is an Assistant Professor at School of Media Studies (SOMS) at Presidency University, Bangalore. He is the author of two book "Cases for Classroom Media and Entertainment Business" and "Multiverse and Media", he also has other several edited books to his credit. He has done his doctorate from Visva-Bharati Santiniketan, West Bengal in the field of "environmental informatics and communication for sustainability". In addition to that he is a certified Science Communicator and Journalism from Indian Science Communication Society (ISCOS), certified Corporate Trainer with Amity Institute of Training and Development, Certified Social Media Network Analyst. He has a strong interest in environmental communication. He was awarded certificate of merit by PRSI, Kolkata Chapter and Medal of Honor by Journalistic Club of Kolkata. He was working as a research assistant with the World Bank's "Environmental Capacity Building in Southeast Asia" project at IIM Kashipur. He was instrumental in launching the World Bank's Green MBA MOOC, he has also assisted in the research project on

Uttarakhand disaster mitigation by ICSSR, the leading research on Uttarakhand disaster.

Hitesh Mohapatra received the B.E. degree in Information Technology from Biju Patnaik University of Technology (BPUT), Odisha in 2006, and the MTech. Degree in CSE from Odisha University of Technology and Research (OUTR) University, Odisha in 2009. He received his Ph.D. in Computer Science & Engineering in 2021 from Veer Surendra Sai University of Technology (VSSUT), Burla, India. He has contributed 30 SCI and Scopus indexed research papers, 21 international/national conferences and books on Software Engineering and C Programming respectively. He has 15 years of teaching experience both in industry and academia. He has served the research community with various capacities like session chair, technical chair, keynote speaker etc. His research interests include wireless sensor network, smart city, smart grid and smart water. Currently he is working as Associate professor at School of Computer Engineering, KIIT DU, Bhubaneswar, and Odisha.

Aditi Nag is an Architect and Urban Planner, currently serving as an Assistant Professor in the Faculty of Design at Manipal University Jaipur. She is pursuing a Ph.D. in the Department of Architecture and Planning at Birla Institute of Technology, Mesra, Ranchi, India. Her research focuses on urban and rural planning, and she has several publications to her credit. Notably, she is the first recipient of the DST Inspire Fellowship in Architecture and Planning, awarded by the Ministry of Science and Technology, Government of India.

Damodharan Palaniappan works as an Associate Professor & Head in the Department of Information Technology, Marwadi University, Rajkot, Gujarat. He completed his Ph.D. at Anna University, Chennai, M.E. in Computer Science and Engineering at C.I.E.T, Coimbatore and B.E. in Computer Science and Engineering at CSI College of Engineering, Ketty, Nilgiri. He has 19 years' experience of teaching and research. Currently, he guides 6 Ph.D. research scholars. He has authored 8 book chapters, and he has published research papers in reputed journals. His interested areas of research are Data Mining, Image Processing, Software, Machine Learning and Deep Learning.

Anurag Singh Rathore is a student of Tourism Studies, pursuing a degree course from IGNOU, New Delhi in the Department of Tourism. He has a fascination in the field of modern tourism trends and traditional branding techniques.

Wasswa Shafik (Member, IEEE) received a Bachelor of Science degree in information technology (BIT) from Ndejje University, Kampala, Uganda, a

Master of Engineering degree in information technology engineering (Computer and communication networks) from Yazd University, Iran, and a Ph.D. degree in computer science with the School of Digital Science, Universiti Brunei Darussalam, Brunei Darussalam. He is also the Founder and a Principal Investigator of the Dig Connectivity Research Laboratory (DCRLab) after serving as a Research Associate at Network Interconnectivity Research Laboratory, Yazd University. Prior to this, he worked as a Community Data Analyst at Population Services International (PSI-Uganda), Community Data Officer at Programme for Accessible Health Communication (PACE-Uganda), Research Assistant at the Socio-Economic Data Centre (SEDC-Uganda), Prime Minister's Office, Kampala, Uganda, an Assistant Data Officer at TechnoServe, Kampala, IT Support at Thurayya Islam Media, Uganda, and Asmaah Charity Organization. He has hundreds of publications in renowned journals and conferences. His research interests include AI, smart agriculture, health computing and ecological informatics.

Mukesh Kumar Sharma is a Professor and Head in Mathematics Department in Chaudhary Charan Singh University, Meerut, U.P, India. He has published several book chapters and research papers of national and international reputed journals.

Rajeev Sharma is the Assistant professor in IIMT Engineering College, Meerut. He has more than 15 years of teaching as well as administrative experience. He has a conference Proceeding on Modified CPU Scheduling Process to his Credit published by Springer Nature. He has published five research papers and reputed journals. He has attended many conferences, workshops, FDP's and symposium and presented research papers. His research area is fuzzy logic, Neural Networks and CPU scheduling.

Vikas Sharma completed his Graduation and Post Graduation from Chaudhary Charan Singh University, Meerut, U.P. Currently Pursuing his Ph.D. in Computer Science and Engineering from Govt. Recognized University. Presently, he is working as an Assistant Professor in the Department of Computer Science and Applications, IIMT University, Meerut, U.P. He has been awarded as Excellence in teaching award 2019. He is the reviewer member of some reputed journals. He has published several book chapters and research papers of national and international reputed journals.

Praneetha Surapaneni has BTech and MTech degrees in Computer Science from VRSEC – Velagapudi Ramakrishna Siddhartha Engineering, Acharya Nagarjuna University, Vijayawada, in 2008 and 2011, respectively. She is working toward a PhD at SRM University-AP, Amaravati, AP. She has ten years of teaching experience. Her research includes the secu- rity in Intelligent Vehicles, BlockChain Technology and Machine Learning.

Premavathi T is a working as Assistant Professor in the Department of Computer Engineering – Artificial Intelligence, Marwadi University, Rajkot, Gujarat. She did B.E in Computer Science and Engineering at Dhanalakshmi Srinivasan Engineering College, Perambalur, TamilNadu. She did her M.E in Software Engineering with Distinction in Anna University. She is pursuing her Ph.D. at the Marwadi University. She is having 14 years experiences in teaching. She authored 3 book chapters and she published 3 research papers in national and international seminars and conferences. Her interested areas of academics are Object Oriented Programming, Software Engineering, Database Management Systems, Design and Analysis of Algorithms, Python Programming, Machine Learning and Deep Learning.

Muhammad Talha Usman received a B.S. in Software Engineering from the University of Engineering and Technology Taxila (UET), Pakistan. His research interests focus on Computer Vision and Pattern Recognition, Image Processing, Generative Adversarial Networks (GANs), and Graph Neural Networks (GNNs).

Tarun Kumar Vashishth is an active academician and researcher in the field of computer science with 22 years of experience. He earned Ph.D. Mathematics degree specialized in Operations Research; served several academic positions such as HoD, Dy. Director, Academic Coordinator, Member Secretary of Department Research Committee, Assistant Center superintendent and Head Examiner in university examinations. He is involved in academic development and scholarly activities. He is member of International Association of Engineers, The Society of Digital Information and Wireless Communications, Global Professors Welfare Association, International Association of Academic plus Corporate (IAAC), Computer Science Teachers Association and Internet Society. His research interest includes Cloud Computing, Artificial Intelligence, Machine Learning and Operations Research; published more than 45 research articles with 2 books and 40 book chapters in edited books. He is contributing as member of editorial and reviewers boards in conferences and various computer journals published by CRC Press, Taylor and Francis, Springer, IGI global and other universities.

Index

Symbols

A

B

C

D

E

www.ingramcontent.com/pod-product-compliance
Lightning Source LLC
LaVergne TN
LVHW080615300926
849162LV00005B/1169